CHILDES/BIB

An annotated bibliography of child language and language disorders

1997 Supplement

Roy Higginson
Center for Research in Language
University of California
San Diego

Brian MacWhinney
Carnegie Mellon University

LEA LAWRENCE ERLBAUM ASSOCIATES, PUBLISHERS
1997 Mahwah, New Jersey

Lawrence Erlbaum Associates, Inc., Publishers
10 Industrial Avenue
Mahwah, New Jersey 07430

ISBN 0-8058-2411-1

Books published by Lawrence Erlbaum Associates are printed on acid-free paper, and their bindings are chosen for strength and durability.

Printed in the United States of America

10 9 8 7 6 5 4 3 2 1

Dedicated to the memory of

Allen Gilbert

ACKNOWLEDGMENTS

The compilers wish to acknowledge their gratitude to Eve Clark who sent us the bibliography from her book, *The Lexicon in Acquisition,* and to Gabrielle Konopcyznski for permission to include references from her book, *Prosodie du Langage Enfantin: Une Bibliographie Thématic*, in the present work. We are also grateful to Oralia Rodríguez and Maria Paz Berruecos for their permission to include references from their book, *La Adquisición del Español como Lengua Materna: Bibliogafia Descriptiva*, herein. We are indebted to Jose Angel Alvarez who undertook the reading and annotation with *CHILDES/BIB* keywords of *La Adquisición del Español como Lengua Materna* entries.

Thanks are also due to Adele Abrahamsen, Barbara Gelbart, Dan Slobin and Ragnhild Söderbergh for their generous contributions to the previous two volumes which helped to make *CHILDES/BIB* so comprehensive. We would also like to repeat our previous acknowledgment of Werner Leopold's bibliographic work.

As with the previous volumes, the present volume has been enhanced by the donation of personal bibliographies by numerous scholars from around the world, and we would like to extend our thanks to them also. Again, we apologize to them for this public collective acknowledgment as their numbers prevent us from acknowledging each of them individually at this time.

Endnote2-Plus is used in the construction and maintenance of this bibliography, and is the platform for the electronic database of the work. We gratefully acknowledge Niles and Associates for extending to us a license to distribute a version of their program with the *CHILDES/BIB* database.

Funding for the hardware and software needs of the project was provided by *CHILDES* at Carnegie Mellon University. The Regents of the University of California, through the Center for Research in Language (CRL) at the University of California at San Diego, extended professional support, and e-mail access to the project. Thanks are due to Elizabeth Bates, CRL director, for her continued support of the project, and to Jeffrey Elman for his previous support of the project.

Finally, the compilers wish to acknowledge the American Psychological Association for its permission to reproduce materials from the *PsycLIT* database in the present work.

PREFACE

The present supplement of approximately 2,700 references extends the previous volumes, *CHILDES/BIB - 1991*, and the *CHILDES/BIB - 1994 Supplement*, to a total of over 13,000 references. 25% of the new entries come from Gabrielle Konopczynski's 1988 bibliography* on prosody, 6% are drawn from Oralia Rodríguez and Maria Paz Berruecos's 1993 bibliography† on Spanish acquisition, and 23% are from *PsycLIT*‡. The remaining entries include works from all around the world. All of the entries have keyword annotations, and many of them include lengthier abstracts.

This supplement is structured the same way as the 1994 supplement. The references are arranged alphabetically by the name of the first author, and the subject index provides access to the references using the *CHILDES/BIB* keywords. At the back of the book, the present volume includes a categorical listing of the complete set of keywords used in the *CHILDES/BIB* system. The printed version includes the keywords used in the electronic version, and indicates the language the text is written in if the text language is not English. The keywords appear at the end of each citation, prior to the abstract (if one is available). The text language appears after the ":" symbol in the keyword listing. The absence of any notation for English texts is neither meant to bestow any special status upon English, nor to convey any lack of respect for other languages; it merely reflects the fact that this is an English language publication.

The majority of works in this supplement were published after 1990, but there are also many works included from earlier years that have not previously been listed in *CHILDES/BIB*. The new inclusions are drawn from the worldwide community. Of the total 2,680 references, 1,344 are from 1993 and later, and an additional 242 were published between 1990 and 1993. 380 were published between 1981 and 1989, and 526 between 1970 and 1980. 180 of the references predate 1970.

We believe that this addition to the *CHILDES/BIB* series continues to maintain it as the most comprehensive access to the literature currently available to researchers in acquisition related fields, and that the three volumes betoken the state of child language and language disorders research worldwide.

*Konopczynski, Gabrielle. (1988). *Prosodie du Langage Enfantin: Une Bibliographie Thématic*. Hamburg, Germany: Buske.

†Rodríguez, Oralia, & Berruecos, Maria Paz. (1993). *La Adquisición del Español como Lengua Materna: Bibliogafia Descriptiva*. Pedregal de Santa Teresa, Mexico: El Colegio de Mexico.

‡*PsycLIT* published by the American Psychological Association

CONTENTS

A

Abaurre, Maria Bernadete M. (1988). The interplay between spontaneous writing and underlying linguistic representations. *European Journal of Psychology of Education*, 3(4), 415-430. LITERACY WRITTEN LANGUAGE : FRENCH

Special Issue: Early literacy. Discusses the importance of incorporating naturalistic data from spontaneous written texts in language acquisition research in general and in writing acquisition studies in particular. It is argued that spontaneous data can be revealing of the nature of local, epilinguistic procedures which, in their turn, are seen as indexes of underlying system construction. Data are analyzed from 1st graders' spontaneous writing in Portuguese that bear on the problem of the underlying representation of phonological nasality in the language. It is argued that the data are best accounted for by a constructivist model that attributes a constitutive status to social interaction and to children's history of contact with particular words and structures within the context of specific discourse events. (French abstract) From - PsycLIT.

Abbeduto, Leonard, Benson, Glenis, Short, Katherine, & Dolish, Joanna. (1995). Effects of sampling context on the expressive language of children and adolescents with mental retardation. *Mental Retardation*, 33(5), 279-288. RETARDED CHILDREN ASSESSMENT PROCEDURES:

Examined whether conversational samples of language should be supplemented with samples obtained in narrative, or storytelling, contexts when evaluating the expressive language skills of individuals with mental retardation (MR). Samples were elicited in both conversational and narrative contexts from 16 school-age Ss (aged 9-20 yrs) with MR and 16 typically developing children (aged 5-9 yrs) matched to them on mental age. Analysis of the samples demonstrated that both groups produced more syntactically complex language in narration than in conversation, whereas they were more talkative in conversation than in narration. Results suggest that conversational and narrative contexts should be used together when evaluating the expressive language performance of individuals with MR. Summary of standardized features of conversational procedures explanation and instructions to participants in the narrative context are appended.

Abbott, Valerie, Black, John B., & Smith, Edward E. (1985). The representation of scripts in memory. *Journal of Memory and Language*, 24, 179-199. LEXICAL DEVELOPMENT EVENTS/SCRIPTS:

Abbs, M., & Minifie, Fred D. (1969). Effects of acoustic cues in fricatives on perceptual confusions in preschool children. *Journal of the Acoustical Society of America*, 44, 1535-1542. FRICATIVES SPEECH PERCEPTION ACOUSTIC PHONETICS:

From Konopczynski.

Abecassis, Janine, & Tardy, Michel. (1977). Intonation et communication. Recherches prosodiques sur les premiers mots d'une enfant de 10 mois. [Intonation and communication. Prosodic research on the first words of a 10 month old infant.]. *Bulletin de Psychologie,* 31(335), 572-580. PROSODY FIRST WORDS INTONATION: FRENCH

From Konopczynski.

Abecassis, Janine. (1986). Importance du geste dans la communication verbale chez l'enfant. [The importance of gesture in verbal communication with children.]. *Bulletin d'Audiophonologie*, N.S.1(5-6), 657-674. GESTURE INTERSUBJECTIVITY: FRENCH

From Konopczynski.

Acuña, María L., & Menegotto, Andrea C. (1992). Dativo sin `a' y verbos pronominales sin `se': rasgos dialectales del español de zona mapuche. *Revista Argentina de Lingüística*, (Marzo), MORPHOSYNTACTIC DEVELOPMENT SPANISH MAPUCHE INTERFERENCE DATIVES MAPUCHE-SPANISH PRONOUNS: SPANISH

From Spanish Bibliographies.

Acuña, María L., & Menegotto, Andrea C. (1994). Plural nominal en la zona de influencia mapuche de las provincias del Neuquén y de Río Negro. In *Primeras Jornadas de Etnolingüística* (vol. II,). Departamento de Etnolingüística de la Facultad de Humanidades y Artes de la Universidad Nacional de Rosario: MORPHOSYNTACTIC DEVELOPMENT BILINGUALISM SPANISH - MAPUCHE INTERFERENCE MAPUCHE-SPANISH NOUNS: SPANISH

From Spanish Bibliographies.

Acuña, María L., & Menegotto, Andrea C. (1994). Observaciones sobre clíticos en el español de área mapuche. *Actas de las Segundas Jornadas de Lingüística Aborigen*,, MORPHOSYNTACTIC DEVELOPMENT BILINGUALISM SPANISH - MAPUCHE INTERFERENCE CLITICS: SPANISH

From Spanish Bibliographies.

Acuña, María L., & Menegotto, Andrea C. (1995). El contacto lingüístico español-mapuche en la Argentina. *Signo & Seña*, (-), -. SPANISH-MAPUCHE MAPUCHE-SPANISH: SPANISH

From Spanish Bibliographies.

Acuña, María L., & Menegotto, Andrea C. (1996). Dialecto y sistema pronominal del área mapuche. In *Primer Simposio Binacional sobre lingüística y literatura indígena*. Temuco, Chile: SPANISH MAPUCHE MORPHOSYNTACTIC DEVELOPMENT PRONOUNS NONSTANDARD DIALECTS: SPANISH

From Spanish Bibliographies.

Adams, Valerie . (1973). *An introduction to Modern English word-formation*. London, UK: Longman. LEXICAL DEVELOPMENT :

Adamson, Lauren B., & McArthur, D. (1995). Joint attention, affect, and culture. In C. Moore, & P. J. Dunham (Eds.), *Joint Attention: Its Origin and Role in Development*. Mahwah, NJ: Lawrence Erlbaum Associates. JOINT REFERENCE ATTENTION LANGUAGE AND AFFECT:

Adamson, Lauren B., Romski, Mary A., Deffebach, Kim P., & Sevcik, Rose A. (1992). Symbol vocabulary and the focus of conversations: Augmenting language development for youth with mental retardation. *Journal of*

Speech and Hearing Research, 35(6), 1333-1343. RETARDED CHILDREN INTERVENTION PROGRAMS VOCABULARY DEVELOPMENT LANGUAGE AND SOCIAL TRANSMISSION:

Communication devices designed to augment the language development of individuals with severe cognitive disabilities and little or no functional speech typically contain primarily nouns because they seem easiest to acquire and evaluate. In this study, the effect of a more diverse vocabulary was assessed. Systematic observations of the use of computerized speech-output devices by 12 youth (mean age 12 yrs 4 mo) with moderate or severe mental retardation and severe spoken language disability and by their partners were made over a 2-yr period. Social-regulative symbols (e.g., "please," "I'm finished") were used as soon as they were introduced, and their availability expanded the focus of conversations both at home and at school. From - PsycLIT.

Adamzik, K., & Schmitter, P. (1983). *Spracherwerbforschung I: Auswahlbibliographie der Literatur bis 1977. [Language acquisition I: Select bibliography of the literature since 1977.]*. Munich, Germany: Studium Sprachwissenschaft. BIBLIOGRAPHY: GERMAN

From Konopczynski.

Adone, Danny. (1995). *The Acquisition of Mauritian Creole*. Philadelphia, PA: John Benjamins. PIDGINS/CREOLES:

This is the first major study of the development of child grammar in a Creole context.

Affolter, F. (1980). Perceptual prerequisites for language development. *Folia Phoniatrica*, 32(3), 158. ABSTRACT PERCEPTION LANGUAGE PRECURSORS:

From Konopczynski.

Aimard, Paule. (1974). *L'enfant et son langage. [The child and his language.]*. Villeurbanne: Simép Editions. LEXICAL DEVELOPMENT :

Aimard, Paule. (1975). *Les jeux de mots de l'enfant. [Children's word games.]*. Villeurbanne: Simép Editions. LEXICAL DEVELOPMENT LANGUAGE GAMES:

Aimard, Paule. (1977). L'enfant et le verbe ou l'insaisissable premier mot. [The child and the word or the imperceptible first word.]. *Bulletin d'Audiophonologie*, 8(2), 37-50. LEXICAL DEVELOPMENT: FRENCH

From Konopczynski.

Aimard, Paule. (1979). A propos des batteries de tests de langage: un essai de synthése. [About language test batteries: a synthetic essay.]. *Bulletin d'Audiophonologie,* 9(3), 57-66. LANGUAGE TESTING ASSESSMENT PROCEDURES: FRENCH

From Konopczynski.

Aksu-Koç, Ayhan A. (1994). Development of linguistic forms: Turkish. In R. A. Berman, & D. I. Slobin (Eds.), *Relating Events in Narrative: A crosslinguistic developmental study*. Mahwah, NJ: Lawrence Erlbaum Associates. TURKISH NARRATIVES:

Aksu-Koç, Ayhan A., & von Stutterheim, C. (1994). Temporal relations in narrative: Simultaneity. In R. A. Berman, & D. I. Slobin (Eds.), *Relating Events in Narrative: A crosslinguistic developmental study*. Mahwah, NJ: Lawrence Erlbaum Associates. NARRATIVES TEMPORAL TERMS:

Alarcos-Llorach, Emilio. (1976). La adquisición del lenguaje por el niño. In A. Martinet (Ed.), *Tratado de lenguaje*. Buenos Aires: Nueva Visión. SPANISH ACQUISITION THEORIES PHONOLOGICAL DEVELOPMENT SYNTACTIC DEVELOPMENT LEXICAL DEVELOPMENT SEMANTIC DEVELOPMENT: SPANISH

From Spanish Bibliographies.

Alarcos-Llorach, Emilio. (1968). L'acquisition du langage par l'enfant. [Children's language acquisition.]. In A. Martinet (Ed.), *Encyclopédie de la Pléiade*. Paris, France: Gallimard. OVERVIEW-GENERAL: FRENCH

From Konopczynski.

Albano de Vázquez, Hilda. (1986-1988). Uso de la forma pronominal de primera persona singular en niños de 4 y 5 años. *Letras*, XVII-XVIII, SPANISH PRONOUNS-PERSONAL SYNTACTIC DEVELOPMENT: SPANISH

From Spanish Bibliographies.

Albano de Vázquez, Hilda. (1991). La expresión lingüística de la condicionalidad. *Lenguas Modernas*, 18, SPANISH SEMANTICS AND SYNTAX CONDITIONALS CONNECTIVES SYNTACTIC DEVELOPMENT: SPANISH

From Spanish Bibliographies.

Albano de Vázquez, Hilda. (1992). La expresión de la contrafactualidad en el habla de niños bonaerenses y madrileños. In *Actas del III Congreso Nacional de Hispanistas*. Buenos Aires, Argentina: SPANISH SEMANTICS AND SYNTAX: SPANISH

From Spanish Bibliographies.

Albert, Martin L., Sparks, R. W., & Helm, Nancy A. (1973). Melodic intonation therapy for aphasia. *Archives of Neurology*, 29, 130-131. APHASIAS INTONATION INTERVENTION PROGRAMS:

From Konopczynski.

Aldridge, Michelle, Borsley, Robert D., & Clack, Susan. (1995). The acquisition of Welsh clause structure. In D. MacLaughlin, & S. McEwan (Eds.), *Proceedings of the 19th annual Boston University Conference on Language Development, Vol. 1*. Somerville, MA: Cascadilla Press. WELSH SYNTACTIC STRUCTURES:

Alegria, Jesus (1995). On the origins of phonological representations in deaf people. In M. Carreiras, J. E. Garcia-Albea, & N. Sebastian-Galles (Eds.), *Language processing in Spanish*. Mahwah, NJ: Lawrence Erlbaum Associates. DEAF CHILDREN REPRESENTATIONS-PHONOLOGICAL:

Allen, T. W., Walker, K., Symonds, L., & Marcell, M. (1977). Intrasensory and intersensory perception of temporal sequences during infancy. *Developmental Psychology*, 13, 225-229. RHYTHM PROSODY:

From Konopczynski.

Allen, George D., & Hawkins, Sarah. (1978). The development of phonological rhythm. In A. Bell, & J. B. Hopper (Eds.), *Syllables and*

Segments. Amsterdam, The Netherlands: North-Holland. RHYTHM PROSODY:

From Konopczynski.

Allen, George D., & Hawkins, Sarah. (1979). Trochaic rhythm in children's speech. In H. Hollien, & P. Hollien (Eds.), *Current Issues in the Phonetic Sciences, Vol. 2*. Amsterdam, The Netherlands: John Benjamins. RHYTHM PROSODY:

From Konopczynski.

Allen, George D., Hawkins, Sarah, & Morris, Margaret R. (1979). Development of "nuclear accent" marking in children's phrases. In H. Hollien, & P. Hollien (Eds.), *Current Issues in the Phonetic Sciences, Vol. 2*. Amsterdam, The Netheralnds: John Benjamins. RHYTHM PROSODY STRESS:

From Konopczynski.

Allen, George D. (1980). Early rhythmic development in children's speech: Cross-language comparison. *Folia Phoniatrica,* 32(3), 158-159. RHYTHM CROSSLINGUISTIC STUDY-PHONOLOGY PROSODY:

From Konopczynski.

Allen, George D. (1981). Development of prosodic phonology in children's speech. Further evidence from the TAKI task . *Phonologica,* 36, 9-14. RHYTHM CROSSLINGUISTIC STUDY-PHONOLOGY PROSODY:

From Konopczynski.

Allen, Joe. (1995). Tense doubling in early grammars. In D. MacLaughlin, & S. McEwan (Eds.), *Proceedings of the 19th annual Boston University Conference on Language Development, Vol. 1.* Somerville, MA: Cascadilla Press. TENSE EARLY SYNTACTIC DEVELOPMENT:

Allen, Marybeth S., Kertoy, Marilyn K., Sherblom, John C., & Pettit, John M. (1994). Children's narrative productions: A comparison of personal event and fictional stories. *Applied Psycholinguistics,* 15(2), 149-176. NARRATIVES GENRE:

Compared personal event narratives (PENs) and fictional stories (FSs) across 2 language-ability groups (LAGs) using episodic analysis. 36 normal children (aged 4-8 yrs) were divided into high and low LAGs using Developmental Sentence Scoring. Narrative genre differences significantly influenced narrative structure for both LAGs and narrative length for the high LAG. PENs had more reactive sequences and complete episodes than did FSs, whereas FSs had more action sequences and multiple-episode structures. Results suggest that narrative structures for PENs and FSs may follow different developmental paths. Differences in productive language abilities contributed to the distinctions in narrative structure between FSs and PENs. The high LAG produced more complete and multiple episodes, and their FSs were longer than their PENs. From - PsycLIT.

Allen, Shanley (1995). Acquisition of causatives in Inuktikut. In E. V. Clark (Ed.), *The Proceedings of the 27th annual Child Language Research Forum.* New York, NY: Cambridge University Press. CAUSALITY INUKTIKUT

Allen, Shanley, & Crago, Martha B. (1993). Early acquisition of passive morphology in Inuktikut. In E. V. Clark (Ed.), *The Proceedings of the*

24th annual Child Language Research Forum. New York, NY: Cambridge University Press. INUKTIKUT PASSIVES MORPHOLOGICAL DEVELOPMENT MORPHOSYNTACTIC DEVELOPMENT

Allport, D. Alan. (1984). Speech production and comprehension: One lexicon or two? In W. Prinz, & A. F. Sanders (Eds.), *Cognition and motor processes*. New York, NY: Springer-Verlag. LEXICAL DEVELOPMENT LEXICAL ACCESS LANGUAGE AND MEMORY PRODUCTION/COMPREHENSION LEXICON

Allport, D. Alan, & Funnell, Elaine. (1981). Components of the mental lexicon. *Philosophical Transactions of the Royal Society [London]*, B295, 397-410. LEXICAL DEVELOPMENT LANGUAGE AND MEMORY LEXICON:

Altman, Gerry T. M., & Shillcock, Richard (Eds.). (1994). *Cognitive Models of Speech Processing, vol.* Mahwah, NJ: Lawrence Erlbaum Associates. REPRESENTATIONS-LEXICAL PHONOLOGICAL DEVELOPMENT CONNECTIONISM LANGUAGE PROCESSING:

This volume provides a comprehensive overview of speech and language processing. Topics covered include: phonological development and language specificity, lexical and prelexical representations in infants, the role of morphology and syntax in the lexicon. The editors also look at the role of connectionism in language processing.

Altoma, Salih J. (1974). Language education in Arab countries and the role of Academies. In J. A. Fishman (Ed.), *Advances in language planning*. The Hague, The Netherlands: Mouton. LEXICAL DEVELOPMENT LANGUAGE AND EDUCATION ARABIC:

Amon, Patricia, Beck, Birgit, Castell, Rolf, Mall, Werner, et al. (1993). Umschriebene Sprachentwicklungsruckstande bei Sonderschulern. [Specific deficits in the language development of special education students.]. *Praxis der Kinderpsychologie und Kinderpsychiatrie*, 42(5), 150-156. LANGUAGE AND EDUCATION LANGUAGE AND COGNITIVE DEVELOPMENT LANGUAGE AND MEMORY AUDITORY DISCRIMINATION: GERMAN

Studied specific deficits in the language development of 1st-grade special education students. Ss were 152 male and female West German school-age children (mean age 7 yrs) (special education students). Ss were evaluated with the Multiaxial Classification for Child Psychiatric Disorders (M. Rutter et al) and with a series of tests assessing articulation and expressive and receptive language abilities. The incidence of specific deficits was determined and analyzed in relation to auditory short-term memory performances. Tests used: Several German-language instruments, including the German version of the Wechsler Intelligence Scale for Children (WISC). From - PsycLIT.

Amon, Patricia, Beck, Birgit, Castell, Rolf, Teicher, Christina, et al. (1995). Intelligenz und sprachliche Leistungen bei Sonderschulkindern mit 7 und 9 Jahren. [Intelligence and language performances of special education students at the ages of 7 and 9 years.]. *Praxis der Kinderpsychologie und Kinderpsychiatrie*, 44(6), 196-203. GERMAN ASSESSMENT PROCEDURES RETARDED CHILDREN LANGUAGE AND COGNTIIVE DEVELOPMENT HANDICAPPED CHILDREN: GERMAN

Studied the development of intelligence and language abilities in children with learning disabilities (LDs). Human Ss: 71 male and female German school-age children (mean age at baseline 7 yrs) (LDs) (special education students from Erlangen). 49 male and female German school-age children (mean age at baseline 7 yrs) (LDs) (special education students from Munich). Ss' intelligence test performances and language development were evaluated at baseline and again 1.5-2 yrs later. Changes in these parameters were analyzed. Tests used: Several instruments, including the Speech Therapy Language Comprehension Test (P. Wettstein, 1987), the Psycholinguistic Development Test (M. Angermaier, 1974), the Adaptive Intelligence Test (K. Kubinger and E. Wurst, 1988) and a German version of the %WISC-R%. From - PsycLIT.

Andersen, Elaine S., Dunlea, Anne, & Kekelis, Linda. (1993). The impact of input: Language acquisition in the visually impaired. *First Language*, 13(37/1), 23-49. BLIND CHILDREN ATYPICAL DEVELOPMENT INPUT FACTORS:

Special Issue: Language development in special populations. Examines the argument that variation in language development between blind and sighted children may result from a diminution of experience or differences in linguistic input or it may be a product of other factors. Data and findings are reviewed from studies of blind children's language, and the possible impact of input, both environmental and linguistic, is examined. Variation is shown to not be uniquely attributed to either environmental or linguistic input, but evidence is presented that experiential input may influence some areas while linguistic input more strongly affects others.

Independent adaptive strategies by the children are found, and a plasticity in the acquisition process is highlighted. From - PsycLIT.

Andersen, E., Brizuela, M., DuPuy, B., & Gonnerman, J. (1995). The acquisition of discourse markers as sociolinguistic variables: A crosslinguistic comparison. In E. V. Clark (Ed.), *The Proceedings of the 27th annual Child Language Research Forum*. New York, NY: Cambridge University Press. CROSSLINGUISTIC STUDY-DISCOURSE:

Anderson, Barbara, Vietze, Peter, & Dokecki, Paul R. (1977). Reciprocity in vocal interactions of mother-infants. *Child Development*, 48(4), 1676-1681. INTERSUBJECTIVITY ADULT-CHILD INTERACTION:

From Konopczynski.

Andreae, John H., & Ryan, Shaun W. (1994). Associative learning and task complexity. *Behavioral and Brain Sciences*, 17(2), 357-365. PHYLOGENETIC ORIGINS NEUROLINGUISTICS-NEURAL SUBSTRATES LANGUAGE AND OTHER PRIMATES LANGUAGE AND ACTION:

Presents comments by J. H. Andreae and S. W. Ryan, I. M. Pepperberg, and G. C. Westergaard on the discussion on the ontogeny and phylogeny of hierarchically organized sequential behavior by P. M. Greenfield (1992/93). Each author describes a comparative behavioral approach beyond Greenfield's article, extending to monkeys (Westergaard), birds (Pepperberg), and robots (Andreae and Ryan). Greenfield and D. Pinon respond that the best change for homology with the human cortical substrate and behavioral capacities for basic tool use lies with the monkeys. The bird capacities are more likely to be analogs than homologs to human counterparts, and computer simulations, no matter how sophisticated, cannot compete with the study of the human brain to produce knowledge of the neural foundations of language and tools. From - PsycLIT.

Andriessen, Jerry, de Smedt, Koenraad, & Zock, Michael. (1996). Discourse planning: Empirical research and computer models. In T. Dijkstra, & K. d. Smedt (Eds.), *Computational Psycholinguistyics: AI and Connectionist Models of Human Language Processing* . London, UK: Taylor & Francis. SPEECH PRODUCTION COMPUTER SIMULATIONS DISCOURSE REPRESENTATION:

Angelilli, Mary-Lu, Fischer, Howard, Delaney-Black, Virginia, Rubinstein, Michelle, et al. (1994). History of in utero cocaine exposure in language-delayed children. *Clinical Pediatrics*, 33(9), 514-516. AT-RISK CHILDREN LANGUAGE DELAY PRENATAL INFLUENCES:

Determined if children with language delays were more likely to have been exposed to cocaine in utero than those with normal language development. 29 children (aged 24-48 mo) identified as language-delayed were compared with an approximate 2:1 match of children without language delay who had been seen at the same primary care clinic on the same days and who were of similar age. There was more reported maternal cocaine use during pregnancy among language-delayed Ss. Discriminant analysis revealed that both cocaine and nicotine exposure were associated with delayed language development, with an unexpected negative interactive effect. From - PsycLIT.

Anglin, Jeremy M. (1993). Knowing versus learning words. *Monographs of the Society for Research in Child Development*, 58(10)(238), 176-186. METHODOLOGY-ANALYSIS VOCABULARY DEVELOPMENT MORPHOLOGICAL DEVELOPMENT:

Replies to comments by G. A. Miller and P. C. Wakefield concerning the article by J. M. Anglin, which morphologically analyzed the vocabulary development of children. It is contended that adopting Miller and Wakefield's definition of a word would strengthen, rather than undermine, Anglin's conclusions. From - PsycLIT.

Anglin, Jeremy M. (1993). Vocabulary development: A morphological analysis. *Monographs of the Society for Research in Child Development*, 58(10)(238), 1-165. METHODOLOGY-ANALYSIS VOCABULARY DEVELOPMENT MORPHOLOGICAL DEVELOPMENT:

Examined the contribution made by different morphologically defined word types and by knowledge of morphology and word formation to the total recognition vocabulary (TRV) of 96 children in Grades 1, 3, and 5. Results indicate that comprehension of derived words in particular improved dramatically between Grades 1 and 5, contributing relatively little to TRV in Grade 1, but contributing more to TRV than any other morphologically defined type of word by Grade 5. Multimorphemic words were also associated with particular growth, being not well known in Grade 1 but being relatively much better known by Grade 5. Data indicate the importance of making the distinction between knowing words because they have been previously learned and knowing words by means of morphological analysis and composition. From - PsycLIT.

Anglin, Jeremy M. (1995). Classifying the world through language: Functional relevance, cultural significance, and category name learning. *International Journal of Intercultural Relations*, 19(2), 161-181. SAPIR-WHORF HYPOTHESIS LANGUAGE AND COGNITION LANGUAGE AND CULTURE: FRENCH SPANISH

Special Issue: Language, culture, and world view. Asserts that language learning is accomplished through a process of cultural transmission in which parents and other members of the society in which the children are growing up interact and converse with them, enabling them to learn how to talk and to understand speech. Research suggests that children learn early to name objects that are functionally relevant and experientially salient for them; furthermore, because of the way in which their parents name these objects for them, they often initially learn terms that classify things in maximally useful ways. Cross-culture research on children learning different languages indicates that when a domain of experience is particularly culturally significant in a given society, children growing up in it acquire more specific terminology to classify that domain earlier than do children being reared in other societies in which that domain of experience is less culturally significant. (French & Spanish abstracts) From - PsycLIT.

Antelmi, D. (1996). Complex sentence acquisition in Italian: A case study. In C. E. Johnson, & J. H. V. Gilbert (Eds.), *Children's Language, Vol. 9*. Mahwah, NJ: Lawrence Erlbaum Associates.
METHODOLOGY/DIARY/CASE STUDY ITALIAN COMPLEX SENTENCES:

Antilla, Raimo. (1976). Child language, abduction, and the acquisition of linguistic theory by linguists. In W. v. Raffler-Engel, & Y. Lebrun (Eds.), *Baby talk and infant speech*. New York, NY: Humanities Press.
ACQUISITION AND LINGUISTIC THEORY:

From Konopczynski.

Appleton, T., Clifton, Rachel K., & Goldberg, S. (1975). Behavioral competence in infancy. In F. D. Horowitz (Eds.), *Review of Child Development Research, vol.5* . Chicago, IL: University of Chicago Press.
OVERVIEW-GENERAL:

From Konopczynski.

Arbelle, Shoshana, Sigman, Marian D., & Kasari, Connie. (1994). Compliance with parental prohibition in autistic children. *Journal of Autism and Developmental Disorders*, 24(6), 693-702. AUTISM DEVELOPMENTAL DISORDERS GAZE:

Examined responses to a parental prohibition in 28 autistic children (mean age 43 mo), 29 developmentally delayed children (mean age 41 mo), and 28 normal children (mean age 19 mo) who were matched for mental age. Ss' behavioral response, affect, and gaze patterns were observed when Ss were offered a candy that a parent had prohibited them from eating. Autistic Ss exhibited significantly less compliant behavior than control Ss. Autistic Ss who did comply showed less positive affect when compared to others. Behavior correlated with chronological age, not with mental age or language development. Affect and gaze patterns of the autistic Ss were different from the controls; they looked less at their parents. This shows that autistic Ss regulated the situation differently from other Ss. From - PsycLIT.

Arcaini, Enrico. (1983). "Definizione" lessicale e procedimenti esplicativi nei bambini. . In M. Dardano, W. U. Dressler, & G. Held (Eds.), *Parallela*. Tübingen, Germany: Gunter Narr. LEXICAL DEVELOPMENT : ITALIAN

Archibald, John (Ed.). (1994). *Phonological Acquisition and Phonological Theory, vol.* Hillsdale, NJ: Lawrence Erlbaum Associates. PHONOLOGICAL DEVELOPMENT ACQUISITION AND LINGUISTIC THEORY ACQUISITION THEORIES-PHONOLOGY LEARNABILITY UNDERSPECIFICATION-PHONOLOGY:

This collection examines phonological development in the light of learnability and Universal Grammar. It applies phonological theory to development and looks beyond phonetic development. Topics covered include segmental considerations, underspecification and negative constraints, stress and tone, disordered acquisition, and some problems associated with learning the phonology of a second language.

Archibald, John. (1994). Phonological competence. In J. Archibald (Ed.), *Phonological acquisition and phonological theory*. Hillsdale, NJ: Lawrence Erlbaum Associates. PHONOLOGICAL DEVELOPMENT ACQUISITION AND LINGUISTIC THEORY:

Archibald, John. (1994). The acquisition of stress. In J. Archibald (Ed.), *Phonological acquisition and phonological theory*. Hillsdale, NJ: Lawrence Erlbaum Associates. ACQUISITIN AND LINGUISTIC THEORY PHONOLOGICAL DEVELOPMENT STRESS SUPRASEGMENTALS:

Ardila, Alfredo, & Rosselli, Monica. (1994). Development of language, memory, and visuospatial abilities in 5- to 12-year-old children using a neuropsychological battery. *Developmental Neuropsychology*, 10(2), 97-120. ASSESSMENT PROCEDURES SEX DIFFERENCES SOCIOLINGUISTIC FACTORS LANGUAGE AND MEMORY:

A neuropsychological battery was given to 233 children in Colombia balanced according to age, socioeconomic level (high or low), and sex. Language was assessed via the Boston Naming Test, Token Test-shortened version, and verbal fluency, both semantic and phonologic. Memory was assessed via the Wechsler Memory Scale (WMS) and a sequential verbal memory test. Visuospatial abilities were assessed by Rey-Osterrieth Complex Figure copy and immediate reproduction and by recognition of superimposed Poppelreuter-type figures. Sex of S was a significant variable in 3 of the tests, and socioeconomic level was significant in 7 of them. Three factors were found in a factor analysis of the WMS in which delayed recall for Logical Memory, Visual Reproduction, and Associative Learning subtests was included. From - PsycLIT.

Arends, Jacques (Ed.). (1996). *The Early Stages of Creolization, vol.* Philadelphia, PA: John Benjamins. PIDGINS/CREOLES:

A collection of studies dealing with the early stages of creolization. Topics covered include: reconstruction of creolization as a historical linguistic process based on recently discoverd written samples of Neger-hollands, Bajan, and Sranan, sociolinguistic aspects of creolization, is creolizationa first or second language phenomenon, and how does creol development differ from first langauge development.

Aristow-Journoud, M. (1965). *Le geste et le rythme : Rondes et jeux dansés. [Gesture and rhythm: Rounds and dance-games.]*. Paris, France: A. Colin. RHYTHM PROSODY GESTURE: FRENCH

From Konopczynski.

Arleo, Andy, & Flament, Bernard. (1986). De quelques caractéristiques rythmiques et mélodiques de la comptine une poule sur un mur. [About the characteristic rhythms and melodies of "A chicken on a wall."]. *Actes des XV J.E.P./GALF* (pp. 83-86). RHYTHM PROSODY FRENCH: FRENCH

From Konopczynski.

Armon-Lotem, Sharon. (1995). Locating parameters: Evidence from early word order. In E. V. Clark (Ed.), *The Proceedings of the 27th annual Child Language Research Forum*. New York, NY: Cambridge University Press. PARAMETER SETTING WORD ORDER:

Arnold, David H., Lonigan, Christopher J., Whitehurst, Grover J., & Epstein, Jeffery N. (1994). Accelerating language development through picture book reading: Replication and extension to a videotape training format. *Journal of Educational Psychology*, 86(2), 235-243. DIALOGIC READING INTERVENTION PROGRAMS FOR PARENTS ADULT-CHILD INTERACTION:

G. J. Whitehurst et al taught mothers specific interactive techniques to use when reading picture books with their preschool-age children. This intervention program, called "dialogic reading", produced substantial effects on preschool children's language development. However, the costs of one-on-one training limit the widespread use of dialogic reading techniques. In this study the authors aimed to replicate and extend the results of the original study of dialogic reading by developing and evaluating an inexpensive videotape training package for teaching dialogic reading techniques. Mothers were randomly assigned to receive no training, traditional direct training, or videotape training. Results supported the conclusions of Whitehurst et al: Dialogic reading had powerful effects on children's language skills and indicated that videotape training provided a cost-effective, standardized means of implementing the program. From - PsycLIT.

Aronson, Eric, & Tronick, Edward. (1971). Perceptual capacities in early infancy. In J. Eliot (Ed.), *Human Development and Cognitive Processes*. New York, NY: Holt, Rinehart, & Winston. INFANT PERCEPTION:

From Konopczynski.

Ashton, Elizabeth. (1994). Metaphor in context: An examination of the significance of metaphor for reflection and communication. *Educational*

Studies, 20(3), 357-366. FIGURATIVE LANGUAGE LANGUAGE AND EDUCATION:

Discusses how children's early facility to engage in wordplay forms a basis for future development of language skills, helping them move on from familiar contexts that are understood intuitively by transferring their skills in order to interpret metaphorical language empirically in unfamiliar contexts. Theories concerning "dead" and "living" metaphors are explored, and attention is drawn to the need to teach children how to rediscover the original meaning of Biblical metaphors, many of which have become so embedded in language and culture that they have lost their metaphorical significance. The interpretation and use of metaphor are shown to extend the capacity to reason and

think reflectively, and the importance of education in developing this potential is discussed. From - PsycLIT.

Aslin, Richard N., Woodward, J., Lamendola, N., & Bever, Thomas G. (1995). Models of word segmentation in fluent speech to infants. In J. L. Morgan, & K. Demuth (Eds.), *Signal to Syntax: Bootstrapping from speech to grammar in early acquisition*. Mahwah, NJ: Lawrence Erlbaum Associates. WORD BOUNDARIES INPUT FACTORS SEGMENTATION BOOTSTRAPPING:

Assink, Egbert, & Kattenberg, Goran. (1993). Computerized assessment of verbal skill. *Journal of Psycholinguistic Research*, 22(4), 427-444. DUTCH LITERACY ASSESMENT PROCEDURES:

Describes a computerized diagnostic test for the assessment of basic literacy skills in Dutch. Central in this test is a skill labeled word image, referring to the S's implicit knowledge of orthographic structure. Test norms were obtained in a group of reference Ss (N = 97). The most notable trend found in the standardization study was that the development of word image performance showed a nonlinear, U-shaped trend. Two case studies are reported. A supplementary validation study, based on test data collected from standard reference groups of normal (n = 52) and poor (n = 54) readers, demonstrated that word image performance is significantly related to between-group differences. From - PsycLIT.

Atkinson-King, Kay, MacWhinney, Brian, & Stoel, Caroline M. (1970). An experiment in the recognition of babbling. *Papers and Reports on Child Language Development*, 1, 71-76. BABBLING:

Atkinson-King, Kay. (1973). Children's acquisition of phonological stress contrasts . *UCLA Working Papers in Phonetics*, 25, RHYTHM PROSODY STRESS CONTRAST-STRESS:

From Konopczynski.

Atkinson-King, Kay. (1976). On the recognition of babbling. In W. v. Raffler-Engel, & Y. Lebrun (Eds.), *Baby Talk and Infant Speech*. New York, NY: Humanities Press. BABBLING:

From Konopczynski.

Au, Terry K.-F., & Markman, Ellen M. (1987). Acquiring new words via linguistic contrast. *Cognitive Development*, 2, 217-236. LEXICAL DEVELOPMENT CONTRAST-SEMANTIC MUTUAL EXCLUSIVITY:

Au, Terry Kit-fong, Dapretto, Mirella, & Song, You-Kyung. (1994). Input vs constraints: Early word acquisition in Korean and English. *Journal of Memory and Language*, 33(5), 567-582. KOREAN NOUNS LEXICAL DEVELOPMENT CONSTRAINTS-SEMANTIC CROSSLINGUISTIC STUDY-LEXICAL DEVELOPMENT INPUT FACTORS VERBS MUTUAL EXCLUSIVITY:

A. Gopnik and S. Choi have argued that the prevalence of object names among children's early words in languages such as English could be accounted for by the prevalence and salience of nouns in the input. The present studies compared linguistic input and early vocabularies in Korean and English. In Study 1, far more verbs than nouns appeared in salient positions in 3 female Korean adults' speech to 3 Korean infants (aged 12-17 mo), whereas the opposite was true for English (2 female adults, 2 infants aged 11-18 mo). Nonetheless, both Korean- and English-speaking infants (7 Ss aged 15-25 mo and 4 Ss aged 17-21 mo, respectively) acquired nouns (mostly object names) much faster than verbs (Studies 2a, 2b, and 2c). Results suggest that constraints on word meanings, more so than natural variations in input, are important for explaining basic patterns of semantic development across languages. From - PsycLIT.

Auerbach, Elsa, Barahona, Byron, Midy, Julio, Vaquerano, Felipe, Zambrano, Ana, & Arnaud, Joanne. (1996). *Adult ESL/Literacy from the Community to the Community: A Guidebook for Particpating Literacy Teachers.* Mahwah, NJ: Lawrence Erlbaum Associates. L2 READING PROFICIENCY L2 EDUCATION:

Augst, Gerhard, Bauer, Andrea, & Stein, Anette. (1977). *Grundwortschatz und Ideolekt: Empirische Untersuchung zur semantischen und lexicalischen Struktur des kindlichen Wortschatzes. [The basic lexicon and ideolect: An empirical study of the semantic and lexical structure of children's lexica.].* Tübingen, Germany: Max Niemeyer. LEXICAL DEVELOPMENT LEXICON SEMANTIC MAPPING CONTRAST-SEMANTIC:

Augst, Gerhard (Ed.). (1984). *Kinderwort: Der aktive Kinderwortschatz. Theorie und Vermittlung der Sprache 1. [Children's words: The active children's lexicon.], vol.* Frankfurt am Main, Germany: Verlag Peter Lang. LEXICAL DEVELOPMENT LEXICON: GERMAN

Aureli, Tiziana, & Procacci, Mario A. (1992). Day-care experience and children's social development. *Early Child Development and Care*, 83, 45-54. LANGUAGE AND EDUCATION LANGUAGE SOCIALIZATION LANGUAGE AND PLAY:

Compared the interactional and linguistic skills of 20 children who had attended day care centers (DCCs) for at least 2 yrs with that of 20 children who had not attended DCCs. Ss were 38-42 mo old. The Ss were observed over a period of weeks during free-play sessions in their 1st yr in nursery school and were rated for social participation and language. The Ss who had attended DCCs showed greater positive orientation toward their peers, engaged in more cooperative play, and showed greater capacity to direct linguistic initiative toward their peers than did Ss who had not attended DCCs. Ss who had not attended DCCs preferred to play alone or in parallel, and produced less linguistic initiatives. From - PsycLIT.

Aureli, Tiziana. (1994). L'influenza sociale nella prima infanzia: Le ricerche piu recenti sull'attivita condivisa madre-bambino. Rassegna. [Social influence in early childhood.]. *Eta evolutiva*, 49, 102-113. ADULT-CHILD INTERACTION JOINT REFERENCE INPUT FACTORS PARENTAL INPUT SOCIAL INTERACTION: ITALIAN

Reviews recent research on social influence in early childhood with respect to the role of mother-infant joint activity (JA) in the development of communicative and linguistic abilities in children. Emphasis is on social factors that influence the realization of mother-infant JA. The role of mother-infant JA on early cognitive development is also considered. From - PsycLIT.

Austerlitz, Robert. (1956). Gilyak nursery words. *Word*, 12, 260-279. GILYAK PARENTAL SPEECH-VOCABULARY RHYTHM :

From Konopczynski.

Avila, Raúl, & al., et. (1972). *Léxico infantil de México. Recopilación preliminar*. México: El Colegio de México. SPANISH SEMANTIC DEVELOPMENT LEXICAL DEVELOPMENT: SPANISH

From Spanish Bibliographies.

Avila, Raúl. (1978). La investigación del léxico infantil y la enseñanza. In *Lingüística y Educación, Actas del VI Congreso Internacional de la Asociación de Lingüística y Filología de América Latina (ALFAL)*. Universidad Nacional Mayor de San Marcos, Lima: SPANISH SEMANTIC DEVELOPMENT LEXICAL DEVELOPMENT METHODOLOGY: SPANISH

From Spanish Bibliographies.

Avrutin, S., & Wexler, Kenneth. (1992). Development of Principle B in Russian. *Language Acquisition: A Journal of Developmental Linguistics*, 2(4), -. RUSSIAN BINDING:

A special edition on the development of binding.

Axia, Giovanna, Ramponi, Raffaella, & Fumagalli, Monica. (1994). Il Test del Primo Linguaggio: Studio di validazione. [The First Language Test: A validation study.]. *Bollettino di Psicologia Applicata*, 212, 49-57. ITALIAN ASSESSMENT PROCEDURES: ITALIAN

Studied the validity of a test designed to measure the 1st language abilities in infants and young children. Human Ss: 104 normal male and female Italian infants and preschool children (aged 12-36 mo) (nursery school students). Information on sociodemographic variables and 1st language abilities was obtained by questionnaire and observation. The results were evaluated according to age, sex, SES, city of residence, pragmatic language comprehension and production, vocabulary comprehension and production, and syntax production. Factorial structure and reliability were determined. Test used: The First Language Test (G. Axia). An ANOVA and other statistical tests were used. From - PsycLIT.

B

Baayen, R. Harald, & Schreuder, Robert. (1996). Modelling the processing of morphologically complex words. In T. Dijkstra, & K. d. Smedt (Eds.), *Computational Psycholinguistyics: AI and Connectionist Models of Human Language Processing* . London, UK: Taylor & Francis. COMPUTER SIMULATIONS MORPHOLOGICAL PROCESSES COMPREHENSION:

Bacchini, Sylvia, Kuiken, Folkert, & Schoonen, Rob. (1995). Generalizability of spontaneous speech data: The effect of occasion and place on the speech production of children. *First Language*, 15(44/2), 131-150. DUTCH METHODOLOGY-COMPUTERS MORPHOSYNTACTIC DEVELOPMENT GENERALIZATION:

Evaluated the effect of occasion and place on the generalizability of spontaneous speech data. Language samples were obtained from 4 normally developing children (aged 3 yrs 8 mo or 3 yrs 9 mo) from Dutch-speaking professional homes. Four samples of 100 utterances were gathered from each S, 2 samples at home and 2 in a clinical setting. All samples were recorded under unstructured conversational conditions. GRAMAT, a computer program for grammatical analysis of child language disorders was used for analysis at 3 levels: clause, phrase, and morphological level. Data were analyzed using loglinear model fitting. Results reveal a lack of generalizability at all 3 levels of morphosyntactic analysis. From - PsycLIT.

Bacri, Nicole. (1984). L'intelligibilité du langage enfantin: intonation et compréhension de la parole. [The intelligibility of children's language: intonation and comprehension.]. In M. Moscato, & G. Pierraut.-Le Bonniec (Eds.), *Construction et Actualisation du Langage*. Rouen, France: Presses Universitaires. INTONATION COMPREHENSION INTELLIGIBILITY : FRENCH
From Konopczynski.

Badry, Fatima. (1982). The centrality of the root in Semitic lexical derivation: Evidence from children's acquisition of Moroccan Arabic. *Papers and Reports on Child Language Development*, 21, 9-15. LEXICAL DEVELOPMENT ARABIC MORPHOLOGICAL DEVELOPMENT:

Bagg, C.E., & Crookes, T.G. (1975). The responses of neonates to noise in relation to the personalities of their parents. *Developmental Medicine and Child Neurology*, 17, 732-735. INFANT PERCEPTION NEONATES INTERSUBJECTIVITY ADULT-CHILD INTERACTION:

From Konopczynski.

Bailyn, J. F. (1992). LF movemment of anaphors and the acquisition of embedded clauses in Russian. *Language Acquisition: A Journal of Developmental Linguistics*, 2(4), -. RUSSIAN EMBEDDING BINDING:

A special edition on the development of binding.

Balaban, Marie T., & Waxman, Sandra R. (1996). An examination of the factors underlying the facilitative effect of word phrases on object categorization in nine-month-old infants. In A. Stringfellow, D. Cahama-Amitay, E. Hughes, & A. Zukowski (Eds.), *Proceedings of the 20th annual Boston University Conference on Language Development, Vol. 1*. Somerville, MA: Cascadilla Press. LEXICAL DEVELOPMENT CATEGORIZATION:

Baldwin, Dare A. (1993). Early referential understanding: Infants' ability to recognize referential acts for what they are. *Developmental Psychology*, 29(5), 832-843. JOINT REFERENCE GAZE PRELINGUISTICS REFERENCE ADULT-CHILD INTERACTION:

Previous research has documented infants' ability to follow adults' line-of-regard and pointing gestures by 9-12 mo of age, but it has not been clear whether infants appreciate that such cues are a priviledged source of information about word reference. Study 1 demonstrated that this is understood by at least 19-20 mo: Infants used referential cues to guide a new word-object mapping even though this required that they ignore competition from temporal contiguity. In Study 2, the effects observed in Study 1 were not obtained with actions that served to enhance the salience of an object nonreferentially (e.g., manipulating without looking), suggesting that infants appreciate that actions that accompany labeling are not necesssarily referential. Taken together, these indicate that language learning is grounded in a relatively rich understanding of cues to reference, at least from late infancy on. From - PsycLIT.

Baldwin, Dare A. (1993). Infants' ability to consult the speaker for clues to word reference. *Journal of Child Language*, 20(2), 395-418. REFERENCE LABELING SEMANTIC MAPPING JOINT REFERENCE:

Examined whether infants actively seek information from a speaker regarding the referent of the speaker's utterance. 48 infants (aged 1 yr 2 mo to 1 yr 7 mo) heard novel labels for novel objects in 2 situations: follow-in labelling vs discrepant labelling. Subsequently, half of the Ss were asked comprehension questions. The other half were asked preference questions to ensure that their comprehension performance was not merely the result of preferential responding. The comprehension results revealed developmental change in the Ss' abilities to establish new word-object mappings and to pinpoint the correct referent during discrepant labelling. From - PsycLIT.

Baldwin, Dare A. (1995). Understanding the link between joint attention and language. In C. Moore, & P. J. Dunham (Eds.), *Joint Attention: Its Origin and Role in Development*. Mahwah, NJ: Lawrence Erlbaum Associates. JOINT REFERENCE ATTENTION PRELINGUISTICS INTERSUBJECTIVITY:

Ball, Eileen W. (1993). Assessing phoneme awareness. *Language, Speech, and Hearing Services in Schools*, 24(3), 130-139. PHONEMIC DEVELOPMENT LITERACY LANGUAGE AND EDUCATION PHONOLOGICAL DEVELOPMENT METALINGUISTICS:

Reviews the importance of phonological awareness (the understanding that words in the speech stream consist of smaller units (phonemes)) within the broader context of language literacy learning. Consideration for a broad continuum of phoneme awareness skills is discussed. Literature is reviewed linking phoneme awareness and reading acquisition. Specific techniques are offered to guide the speech-language pathologist in the assessment of phonological awareness skills. From - PsycLIT.

Baltaxe, Christiane, Simmons, J. Q., & Zee, E. (1983). Intonation patterns in normal, autistic, and aphasic children. In *Proceedings of the Tenth I.C.P.S.* Utrecht/Dordrecht, The Netherlands: Foris Publications. INTONATION PROSODY LANGUAGE DISORDERS PHONOLOGICAL DISORDERS AUTISM APHASIAS: (From Konopczynski.)

(19)

```
                    H*+L
                    |/
Nire   amen       di.ru.a   galdu  dot
my     mother-GEN money     lose   have-1SG
'I have lost my mother's money'
```

If an accented word is phrase-final, then the location of phrasal stress is determined by the location of the word stress; that is, the phrase-level stress when the last word in the phrase is accented falls on the penultimate syllable of the word.

3.3 Tone spreading and tone insertion

So far we have discussed the tonal features of stress in Lekeitio Basque, but we have not discussed the tonal specifications of the unstressed syllables to the left of the stressed syllable in a word. Of these, the initial syllable receives a L tone, and the rest of the syllables, up to the stressed one, surface with a H tone. This is illustrated by the word *liburuenári* 'to the one of the book' and Figure 3 below (cf. Azkue 1923, 1931, 1932 for a first description of the tonal pattern of Lekeitio Basque, and Hualde 1989 for an autosegmental analysis):

(20)

```
L  H  H  H  H*+L
|  |  |  |  |/
li.bu.ru.e.ná.ri
```

If the accented word is bisyllabic, and the first syllable is consequently stressed, the initial syllable receives a H tone and the second syllable receives a L tone, the pitch lowering having already started at the end of the initial syllable. This kind of tone assignment is exemplified by the word *móno* 'monkey' (cf. Figure 4):[14]

(21)

```
H* +L
|   |
mó.no
```

Hualde (1991a) adopts an underspecification theory approach in order to explain this tonal pattern, suggesting that only syllables which are assigned lexical pitch accents by the metrical rules in (10) are tonally specified. All other syllables on which no lexical accent falls are tonally underspecified. He proposes analyzing the tonal implementation on underlyingly underspecified syllables as a process of leftward spreading of the H tone of the accented syllable up to the initial syllable. This syllable receives the L tone by virtue of the phonetic realization of an initial L% boundary tone if the word occurs at the beginning of an intonational phrase (cf. Pierrehumbert 1980, Pierrehumbert and Beckman 1988, on boundary tones). The following representation for the word *liburuenári* (cf. (20)) would serve to illustrate this:

```
(22)    L%             H*+L
        |              |  |
        li.bu.ru.e.ná.ri
```

Although I agree with Hualde's H tone leftward-spreading analysis, there is a call for clarification regarding the proposal on the initial L% boundary tone. We have to account for the two tonal patterns observed for initial syllables of words within an intonational phrase. Words can surface with a L tone or a H tone on their initial syllables, as illustrated by the two examples in (23), which contrast minimally in the number specification of the genitive phrases *lagunen* 'of the friend' and *lagúnen* 'of the friends' (see Figures 5 and 6, respectively):

```
(23) a.  L% H  H    H  H H*+L
         |  |  |    |  | |/
         la.gu.nen  di.ru.a   'the friend's money'

     b.  L% H*+L    L  H H*+L
         |  |  |    |  | |/
         la.gú.nen  di.ru.a   'the friends' money'
```

Hualde tries to account for the initial H tone on *dirua* in (23a) by positing a floating L tone deletion between two H tones. However, he does not explain why initial syllables following a word-final syllable with a L tone surface with a L tone (cf. (23b)). In earlier articles, Hualde (1986, 1989) suggests that the initial syllable of words in Western Basque dialects is extratonal (except for initially-accented bisyllabic words, such as the one in (21) above), and that it receives a default L tone by insertion at the end of the derivation. To make a combined interpretation of Hualde's (1986, 1989, 1991a) analyses, it would be argued that the initial syllable in an unaccented word or a trisyllabic accented word will receive a L or a H tone depending on the context in which it occurs. If the syllable begins an intonational phrase, as in (22), it is assigned a L tone by a rule of default tone insertion (cf. Pulleyblank 1983 for evidence on low tones as default tones). If the syllable is located within an intonational phrase, whether it receives a L or H tone will depend on the tonal nature of the preceding syllable.

With this in mind, we might propose that in Lekeitio Basque there is a process of leftward spreading of the accented H tone in a word, be it accented or unaccented, which leaves the initial syllable intact because of its extratonality. In utterance-initial position, this syllable receives a default L tone, or is associated to an utterance-initial L% boundary tone. Within an utterance, this syllable will surface with a L or a H tone depending on the tonal nature of the preceding syllable, i.e., the last syllable of the preceding word. If the preceding syllable has a L tone, it will surface with a L tone. If the preceding syllable has a H tone, it will surface with a H tone. This pattern could be amenable to an analysis of rightward spreading of the tone of the syllable preceding the initial syllable of a word onto it. We will use the word *laguna* 'the friend' to illustrate this analysis. In (24) *laguna* is uttered in isolation, and is thus the initial word in an utterance (note also the H*+L pitch accent it receives by virtue of being phrase final, much like the phrase-final syllables in (25)). In (25) it appears phrase-internally, and surfaces with the tone corresponding to the immediately preceding syllable, that is, the last syllable of the preceding word: L in (25a), and H in (25b) (in these and subsequent examples, square brackets are used to indicate extratonality):

(24) 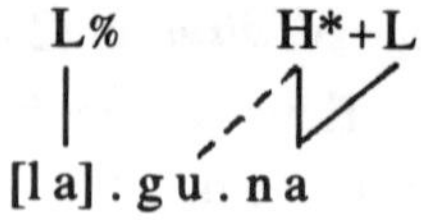

'the friend'

(25) a. 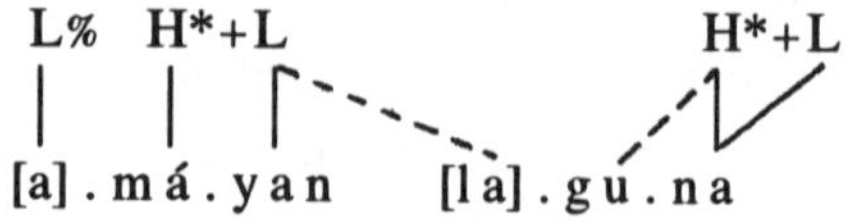

'Amaya's friend'

b. 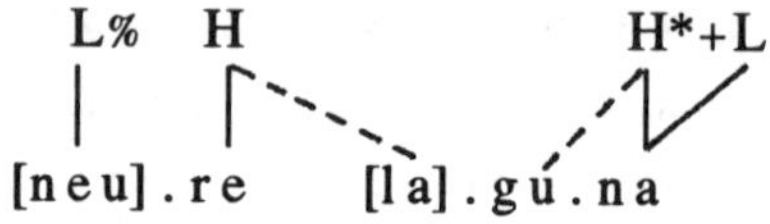

'my friend'

Although this analysis appears to account for the assignment of tones in Western Basque, we have to point out its *ad-hoc* flavor regarding the directionality of tone spreading. On the one hand, we have to posit a process of leftward spreading of the accented H which excludes the extratonal initial syllable, and on the other hand we have to posit a later process of rightward spreading by which the initial syllable acquires the tone of the preceding syllable. Moreover, we have to propose two stages in the derivation: one in which the initial syllable of a word is extratonal, where leftward H tone spreading applies, and a second one in which the initial syllable loses its extratonality, a stage at which rightward tonal spreading takes place. Clearly, an analysis which posits a single direction of spreading and a single stage in the derivation would be simpler, and thus more elegant and appealing. The alternative analysis that I will propose in this paper does not have to make recourse to bidirectionality, and thus it constitutes substantial progress in accounting for the tonal realization of the syllables not associated with lexical pitch accents. The analysis will be based on the organization of tones in Lekeitio Basque.

I want to propose that the distribution and phonological implementation of tones in Lekeitio Basque are not only a property of words, but also of prosodic phrases. The H and L tones of a H*+L lexical pitch accent are a property of the word because of their lexical association to it, aligning with the penultimate syllable. The H and L tones surfacing in other syllables belong to higher intonational phrases and not to the minimal tone-bearing units (i.e., the syllables), although they are realized phonologically on them. With Hualde, I will assume that all syllables except the ones associated to lexical pitch accents H*+L are phonologically underspecified for tone at the word level. We can then identify tones that belong to higher prosodic constituents than the word, i.e., prosodic phrases. I want to suggest that the utterance is divided in several tonal phrases, with pitch accent tones or intermediate phrase tones delimiting their boundaries. This hypothesis is based in great part on the ideas regarding the tone structure of Japanese developed by Beckman and Pierrehumbert (1986) and Pierrehumbert and Beckman (1988), more concretely on the Tokyo dialect, and we will therefore review these in the following section.

4 The tone structure of Tokyo Japanese

In the studies of Japanese intonational structure made by Beckman and Pierrehumbert (1986) and Pierrehumbert and Beckman (1988), several prosodic units or constituents are distinguished, organized hierarchically in an *n*-ary prosodic tree (cf. Nespor and Vogel 1986, Beckman 1986). Each level in the tree corresponds to a particular prosodic unit, such as the mora, the syllable, the word, and higher domains of intonational phrasing, such as the accentual phrase, the intermediate phrase, and the utterance. The main innovation in Pierrehumbert and Beckman's (1988) work is that tones are autosegmentally linked to this structure, not only to minimal tone-bearing units at the bottom of the prosodic tree, such as the mora or the syllable (cf. Goldsmith 1976), but also to any higher-level node. Thus, boundary tones are not considered to be floating tones, but rather tones which are linked or associated with a specific constituent in the prosodic hierarchy or level in the phonological representation above the word level, although they are realized on a mora or syllable of a word.

4.1 The accentual phrase

The lowest level of prosodic phrasing that is well defined by the intonation pattern is the *accentual phrase* (McCawley 1968 used the term *minor phrase*, also used by later researchers such as Poser 1984 and Selkirk and Tateishi 1988, among others). The defining mark of the accentual phrase is the presence of two delimitative tones whose occurrence is determined solely by the prosodic phrase structure of the utterance. One of these delimitative tones is a high tone, the *phrasal H*. The phrasal H is phonologically associated to the second sonorant mora of the accentual phrase unless the first mora is accented or the first syllable is long and contains two sonorant moras. The other delimitative tone is a L% boundary tone that occurs at the beginning of every utterance and at the end of every accentual phrase. By a phonological rule, however, the L% boundary tone is realized on the initial mora of the following accentual phrase. If the first mora is accented, that is, if it carries a lexical H*+L pitch accent, then the L% boundary tone is realized at the periphery of the accentual phrase, giving rise to a *weak* L% boundary tone which is hardly perceptible. This phonological association of the L% boundary tone is what led several researchers to believe that the L% boundary tone belonged to the beginning of an accentual phrase rather than to its end (cf. Poser 1984, among others). The reasons that the L% boundary tone has to be taken as a property of the preceding accentual phrase are discussed in Pierrehumbert and Beckman (1988), and they have to do with local prominence and the application of catathesis (similar to the process called 'downstep' of African tone languages). The L% boundary tone and the phrasal H together produce a rising pitch shape which marks the beginning of every new accentual phrase.

Pitch accents are not necessary to an accentual phrase. Thus, there can be accentual phrases which are composed of unaccented words, but there can be a maximum of only one pitch accent phonetically per accentual phrase. In an accentual phrase which includes two lexically accented words, the second one must be deleted. That is, in Japanese any accent is culminative to its phrase by the deletion of all subsequent accents. Moreover, the accentual H* tone normally has greater tonal prominence than the phrasal H.

Another important observation by Pierrehumbert and Beckman is that the phrasal H and the L% boundary tone are the only tones that exist in the phonological representation of accentual phrases in Tokyo Japanese. The moras not associated to these tones are phonologically underspecified for tone even at the most surface level. The F_0 patterns at places not occupied by these tones are interpreted to arise from the phonetic transitions between the assigned target values for these tones.

4.2 The intermediate phrase

In Japanese, accentual phrases are organized into a larger unit called the *intermediate phrase* (originally called *major phrase* by McCawley 1968, term which Poser 1984 and Selkirk and Tateishi 1988, 1991 also use). The intermediate phrase can have as few as one single accentual phrase, and it seldom contains more than three. Its boundary is often marked by a pause or by glottalization, although in the absence of such signs, phrase-final lengthening and the realization of the L% boundary tone are sufficient indicators of the disjuncture.

The intermediate phrase is also the domain of catathesis, a phonetic rule of tonal implementation that reduces all tones triggered by particular tone sequences on the tone tier. Catathesis has to be distinguished from declination, which is a phonetic process of gradual backdrop or reduction of the pitch range, without regard to the phonological sequences of tones. In Japanese, after the accentual H*+L tone sequence, all subsequent tones in a domain get their mean tonal prominence lowered. That is, those bitonal accents have the property of lowering and compressing the pitch range in the region after them.[15] At an intermediate phrase boundary, the pitch range is reset at a new value and catathesis is blocked or stopped. Thus, catathesis may apply within and across the accentual phrases contained in an intermediate phrase, but the process does not cross intonational phrase boundaries.

4.3 The utterance

The utterance is the topmost constituent in the prosodic hierarchy, and contains all other phrasal units, i.e., intermediate phrases and accentual phrases. In Japanese, and in other languages, it is the domain of declination and of final raising or lowering, triggered by L% and H% final boundary tones. It is also marked by an initial L%.

The following would be the surface prosodic representation for the Japanese sentence *Ane-no akai se'etaa-wa do'ko desu ka?* 'Where is big sister's red sweater?' proposed by Pierrehumbert and Beckman (1988:21) (U = Utterance; IP = Intermediate Phrase; AP = Accentual Phrase; W = Word; S = Syllable; M = Mora; TT = tone tier; PT = Phoneme tier):

(26)

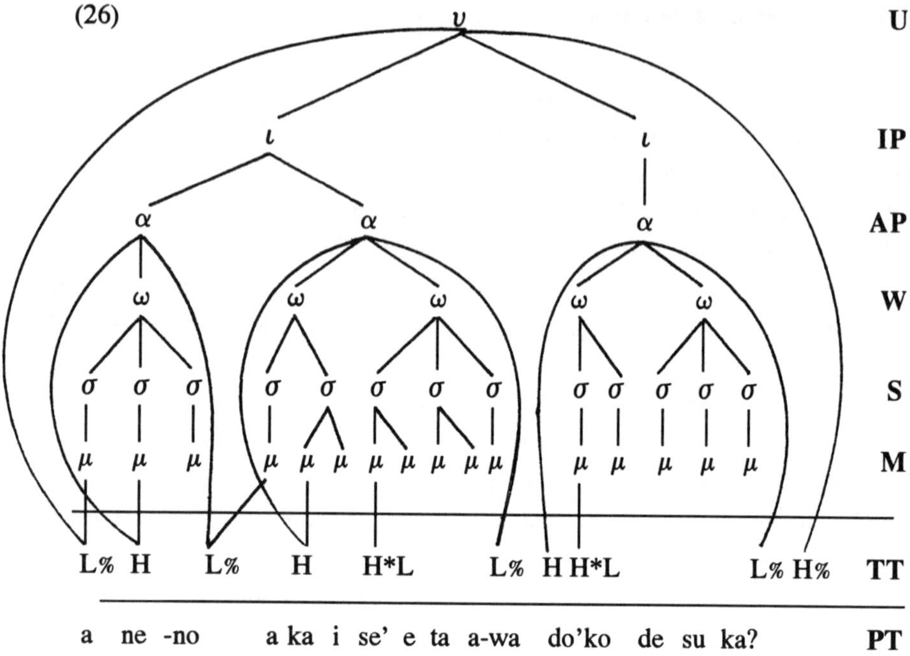

As we see in (26), the tones that are realized on the minimal tone-bearing units (moras in Japanese) can correspond to lexically specified pitch accents (i.e., H*L, which we write as H*+L in this paper), or they can belong to higher levels of phrasing. The initial L% boundary tone, for example, is a property of the utterance, but is phonologically aligned with the first mora in the utterance. The H tone linked to the second mora in the first two words is the phrasal H, associated with an accentual phrase. This phrasal H does not link to the second mora in the word which begins the third accentual phrase because its initial mora is accented (i.e., *do'ko*). Another tone which belongs to a prosodic phrase but is realized on a mora is the final L% boundary tone of the first accentual phrase, which links to the first mora of the following word. The L% boundary tone of the second accentual phrase does not link to a following mora because it is accented (i.e., *do'ko*). The final L% boundary tone of the last accentual phrase and the utterance-final H% are not phonologically aligned with any mora, but are phonetically realized on the last mora of the utterance.

In the following section, I will argue that tones in Lekeitio Basque are also organized in prosodic constituents, as in Tokyo Japanese. Hoping to improve on previous accounts of the facts, I will also provide an analysis for the distribution of tones on syllables underspecified for tone.

5 Lekeitio Basque tone structure

5.1 The accentual phrase

In Lekeitio Basque there is a level of phrasing which could correspond to the lowest prosodic group in Japanese: the accentual phrase. The accentual phrase in Lekeitio Basque may contain one or more words, and is marked by an initial L% boundary tone and a H*+L pitch accent. The L% boundary tone is associated to the first syllable in the phrase, and the pitch accent is realized on the penultimate or the final syllable of the word, depending on whether the word is accented or unacented, respectively. Accentual phrases have at most one pitch accent. Unlike Japanese, the L% boundary tone linked to the first syllable in the accentual phrase belongs to the accentual phrase itself, not to the preceding accentual phrase. That is, it is an initial L% boundary tone, not a final L% boundary tone of the preceding accentual phrase.

With these characteristics of Lekeitio Basque accentual phrases in mind, we are in a position to offer an alternative solution to the distribution of tones on syllables which do not receive a pitch accent.

5.1.1 Leftward H tone spreading and association to L%

Agreeing with Hualde (1991a), I propose that the H tone appearing on syllables not associated with pitch accents comes from a process of leftward spreading of the accentual H* tone occurring on the penultimate syllable of an accented word or on the last syllable of an unaccented phrase located immediately preceding the verb. The domain where we find this H tone spreading is the accentual phrase. This is illustrated by the examples in (27), with the unaccented word *lagunenari* 'to the one of the friend' and the accented word *lagunenári* 'to the ones of the friend' forming single-word accentual phrases (cf. (27a,b), respectively):

(27) a.

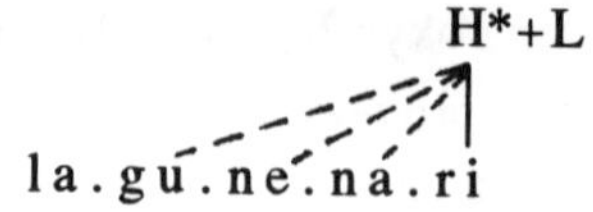

b.

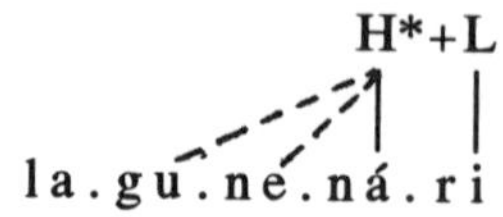

The main empirical evidence in favor of positing such a process of H tone spreading comes from the observation of the H tone plateau that arises from the second syllable in an accentual phrase up to the syllable on which the pitch accent is realized. This is illustrated in Figures 7-8 (cf. also Figures 3-5).

In this respect, Lekeitio Basque differs from Tokyo Japanese. Pierrehumbert and Beckman (1988) reject leftward H tone spreading as a means of providing an interpretation for the realization of pitch in the regions between the phrasal H and the boundary L% that marks the accentual phrase boundary, because the F_0 contour in this region slopes downward and does not show the level high stretch that would be predicted by tone spreading. That is Pierrehumbert and Beckman's main motivation for positing the existence of a phrasal H tone associated to the second mora in an accentual phrase. In Lekeitio Basque the existence of a H tone plateau suggests that a process of tone spreading occurs and thus that there appears to be no need for positing a phrasal H tone on the second syllable of an accentual phrase.[16]

To account for the distribution of the L tone appearing on the initial syllables of certain words, we will posit that the initial L % boundary tone of an accentual phrase is associated to its first syllable. This is illustrated in (28) for the two words in (27):

(28) a.

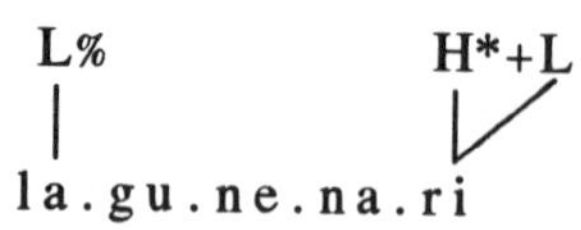

b.

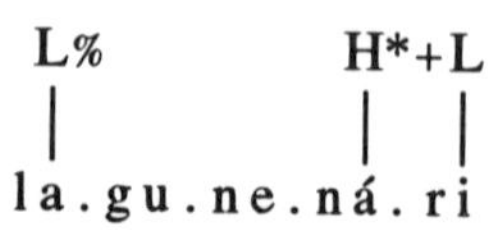

An important point that has to be discussed is the existence of well-formedness constraints on the formation of accentual phrases. We address this issue in the following subsection.

5.1.2 Well-formedness contraints on accentual phrase formation

We mentioned earlier the two tones that minimally distinguish an accentual phrase: the initial L% boundary tone and a pitch accent H*+L. As in Tokyo Japanese, there is a condition limiting the number of pitch accents that can occur in an accentual phrase to one. The difference from Tokyo Japanese is that in Lekeitio Basque the constraint on the number of accented morphemes in an accentual phrase is imposed on the phonological representation, without allowing for the possibility of having two pitch accents in the phrase and deaccenting one of them phonetically. We could formulate this condition as follows:

(29) *Accent Condition on Accentual Phrases*
An accentual phrase may contain at most one accented word[17]

Moreover, an accented word marks the right boundary for an accentual phrase. To put it roughly, an accentual phrase ends at the right edge of an accented word. This is because a L tone is observed on the syllable which begins the following word. If an accentual phrase is signaled by the presence of an initial L% boundary tone linked to its initial syllable, then the occurrence of a L tone on the initial syllable of the word following an accented word is an indication of the existence of a boundary dividing two accentual phrases. This is illustrated by the contrasting pairs of examples in (23) and (25) above, repeated here as (30) and (31), respectively. The initial syllable of the second word in (30b) and (31b) is associated to a L% boundary tone by virtue of beginning an accentual phrase:

```
(30)  a.  L%  H   H      H   H  H*+L
          |   |   |      |   |  |/
          la.gu.nen      di.ru.a       'the friend's money'

      b.  L%  H*+L       L%  H  H*+L
          |   |   |      |   |  |/
          la.gú.nen      di.ru.a       'the friends' money'
```

(31) a.

```
L%  H       H  H  H*+L
|   |       |  |  |/
neu.re      la.gu.na        'my friend'
```

b.

```
L%  H*+L       L%  H   H*+L
|   |   |      |   |   |/
a.má.yan       la.gu.na        'Amaya's friend'
```

We provide F_0 contours for the utterances in (31) in Figures 9-10, showing their tonal pattern (cf. Figures 5-6 for the utterances in (30)).

Thus, the limit of one accented word per accentual phrase stated by the Accent Condition on Accentual Phrases expressed in (29) is a side effect of the principle of formation of accentual phrases, which says that the presence of an accented word automatically forces the termination of an accentual phrase. One advantage of this analysis is that it offers an explanation for the L and H tones appearing on word-initial syllables: L tones appear on the initial syllables of words starting an accentual phrase; H tones surface on the initial syllables of words included within an accentual phrase (cf. (30a), (31a)).[18] We do not have to make recourse to two cycles of tone assignment with two directions of tone spreading: one in which the first syllable is extratonal and a process of H tone leftward spreading takes place, and another in which the tone assigned to the last syllable of the preceding word is spread rightward onto the initial syllable of the following word, which has lost its extratonality.

In fact, it is not only the lexical H*+L pitch accent of an accented word that creates a boundary for an accentual phrase. The H*+L accent introduced on the last element of a phrase (when immediately preceding the verb) also creates a boundary for an accentual phrase. Thus, I want to make the suggestion that any H*+L pitch accent creates a boundary for an accentual phrase in Lekeitio Basque. In the example in (19) above, repeated below as (32) for convenience, the phrase *nire amen dirua* 'my mother's money' constitutes an accentual phrase. It is marked by the pitch accent H*+L, realized on the last syllable of the phrase (cf. Figure 2, repeated below as Figure 11):

(32)

```
                    H*+L
                    |/
Nire  amen        diru.a  galdu  dot
my    mother-GEN  money   lose   have-1SG
'I have lost my mother's money'
```

The L tone appearing on the initial syllable of the verb *galdu* indicates that the sequence formed by the verb and the inflected auxiliary (i.e., *galdu dot*) forms an accentual phrase on it own. That is to say, the L tone on the initial syllable of the verb *galdu* is analyzed as an initial L% boundary tone of an accentual phrase. As we can see in Figure 11, the pitch range of this phrase is radically decreased with respect to the one of previous accentual phrases, thus coming very close to the baseline. In declarative sentences in Lekeitio Basque, this pitch compression is a property of accentual phrases following the most prominent stress in the sentence; this stress is always located in the last element of the accentual phrase immediately preceding the verb.[19] When more material follows the verb, it appears at the same depressed pitch range. See, for example, the contour in Figure 12 for the sentence in (33) (a phrasal pitch accent, i.e., main sentence stress, is indicated with a grave accent mark):

(33)
H* +L
eweldi onà emon dau mariñeruak
weather good give AUX fisherman-ERG

It is worth pointing out, however, that if the verbal sequence or the postverbal material has a lexical pitch accent, it will surface with a very low peak but will nevertheless be perceptible. Thus, we cannot analyze the pitch compression in the region following the main stress in the utterance as deaccenting. For instance, in Figure 13 we see how the pitch accent of the inflected auxiliary *dábe* in (34) surfaces with a peak in the fundamental frequency contour. The pitch accent of the word *mariñerúak* 'fishermen' does not surface with a peak in the F_0 contour, but is still perceptible to the ear of native speakers. The absence of a peak can be argued to be due to a combination of pitch compression and catathesis, triggered by the preceding H*+L pitch accents (cf. next section):

(34)
H* +L H*+L H*+L
eweldi o.nà emon dá . be ma.ri.ñe.rú . ak
weather good give AUX fisherman-ERG
'The fishermen have predicted good weather'

Given the radically low pitch range of the string following the most prominent syllable in the utterance, I will not indicate in this paper any tones associated to the syllables in such strings. This part of the utterance includes at least the verb phrase, although more material may follow, as has been illustrated in (33)-(34).

To summarize, we can claim that the following statement holds for accentual phrase formation in Lekeitio Basque:

(35) A prosodic word on which a pitch accent H*+L is realized marks the right edge boundary on an accentual phrase.

There are certain conditions that have to be met in order for the L% boundary to surface. These are dictated by the accentual properties of the initial word in the phrase, where this tone is realized. If the first word in an accentual phrase is bisyllabic and accented, such as the one exemplified in (21) above, the H*+L pitch accent takes priority and the L% tone will not be realized (cf. (36a) below, which repeats (21)). Unaccented words beginning an accentual phrase could also lack an initial L% boundary tone. That would be the case for monosyllabic unaccented words which received a phrasal H*+L pitch accent, that is, the pitch accent which is assigned to the word immediately preceding the verb and which is identified as the most prominent stress in the sentence (cf. (36b) below, with a grave accent indicating phrasal pitch accent). Unaccented words with two or more syllables initiating an accentual phrase would always surface with a L% boundary tone, regardless of their position with respect to the verb:

(36) a.
```
H* +L
|   |
mó.no
```

b.
```
H* +L
|/
ùtz   ein   dau
miss  do    AUX
```
'(S)he has missed it'

Following Pierrehumbert and Beckman's (1988) similar discussions on the realization of L% boundary tones and phrasal H tones in Japanese, we would argue that the L% boundary tone is present in the phonological representation of the utterance, but the timing available for its phonetic realization is too short. To state it informally, we would say that its potential time for realization is already *occupied* by the pitch accent.

Summarizing, we can say that a L% boundary tone will be associated to the first syllable in an accentual phrase unless this syllable has been assigned a pitch accent at the word level or at the phrasal level. The conclusion that can be drawn from such a restriction is that tones are assigned from the bottom up. That is, the realization of tones belonging to higher levels of phrasing is contingent upon the realization of tones at lower levels. This is another conclusion that our study shares with Pierrehumbert and Beckman (1988).

An interesting observation is that accentual phrases are not isomorphic with syntactic phrases, such as subject/object NPs, Prepositional Phrases, or Adverbial Phrases. Notice that a branching NP can be divided into two or more accentual phrases, depending on the number of lexical pitch accents occurring in the phrase. This was exemplified by (30b) and (31b), with two accentual phrases (cf. Figures 6 and 10). A more dramatic example is provided in (37), where four accentual phrases are distinguished within the same NP. See Figure 14, where we can see the four L tones beginning each accentual phrase:

(37)	L% H*+L	L% H*+L	L% H*+L	L% H*+L
	| | |	| | |	| | |	| |/
	a. má. yen	la. gú. nen	u . mí . en	o . yà
	Amaya-GEN	friends-GEN PL	children-GEN-PL	bed

'The bed of the children of Amaya's friends'

Only in phrases in which no pitch accent occurs will we find an initial L tone followed by a string of H tones, which extends to the end of the phrase. Thus, we have (38) almost as a minimal pair with (37), the difference being that in (38) no accented roots or accented suffixes occur (the genitive suffixes in (38) are singular, opposed to the plural genitives of (37)). We illustrate the F_0 contour for this sentence in Figure 15:

(38)
```
L% H     H  H      H  H  H      H  H H     H  H*+L
|  |     |  |      |  |  |      |  | |     |  |/
ni . re  a. men    la.gu.nen    u.mi. en   o . ya
my       mother-GEN friend-GEN  child-GEN  bed
```
'The bed of the child of my mother's friend'

Another piece of evidence showing the lack of isomorphism between syntactic and intonational constituency comes from the opposite direction, namely from the fact that an accentual phrase may span more than one syntactic phrase. In sentences such as the ones in (39) and (40) there is more than one syntactic maximal projections preceding the verb, as indicated by the brackets. These syntactic phrases contain only unaccented words, and the last word in the last syntactic phrase receives the most prominent stress in the utterance, by virtue of being in a position immediately preceding the verb. The phrasal H*+L pitch accent that is assigned to this phrase marks the right edge of an accentual phrase, and the H tone of this pitch accent spreads onto the syllables to the left, except for the initial syllable of the utterance, which is assigned a L% boundary tone (cf. Figures 16-17):

(39)
```
      L% H  H   H       H   H   H  H*+L
      |  |  |   |       |   |   |  |/
[NP ni . re  a . m a]  [PP I . r u . ñ a . r à] [VP allaga da]
      my mother             Iruña-ALL            arrive AUX
```
'My mother has arrived at Iruña'

(40)
```
     L% H H H          H   H H H        H  H*+L
     |  | | |          |   | | |        |  |/
[NP u.mi. a.ri] [AdvP nor.ma.li. an] [NP u.rà] [VP emoten dotzágu]
     child-DAT          normally         water     give   AUX
```
'Normally, we give water to the child'

This intonational pattern comes as no surprise to generative linguists, given the common assumption about the modularity of grammar, that is, that the different components of grammar (lexicon, syntax, semantics, phonology) are interconnected, but that each of them has its own inner structure and follows different algorithms for building constituency.

5.1.3 Catathesis

The contour shown in Figure 14 is indicative of catathesis having applied. The four peaks descend progressively in tonal value, in a stairway fashion. This progressive descent suggests that catathesis forms chains across accentual phrases in Lekeitio Basque, triggered by a H*+L pitch accent on a subsequent H*+L pitch accent. Note that the pitch accents affected by catathesis do not have to be lexical pitch accents. Catathesis affects phrasal pitch accents as well. Observe for example Figure 18, which represents the contour of the utterance in (41), with a lexical pitch accent being followed by a phrasal pitch accent:

(41) L% H*+L   L% H H*+L
a. má. yen   u . mi .à   allaga   da
Amaya-GEN   child-GEN   arrive   AUX
'Amaya's child has arrived'

An interesting aspect to consider is the domain of catathesis in Lekeitio Basque, that is, whether catathesis creates chains across intonational domains larger than accentual phrases. We will discuss this issue in the following section, in which we argue for the existence of the intermediate phrase as an intonational domain in Lekeitio Basque.

So, to summarize the structure of accentual phrases in Lekeitio Basque: there is an initial L% boundary tone which is associated to the first syllable in the phrase, unless this syllable receives a H*+L pitch accent (i.e., unless this syllable is lexically accented or the only syllable of an unaccented word receiving the main prominence in the sentence). The right edge of an accentual phrase is marked by a H*+L pitch accent, be it lexical or phrasal, and the H tone of the pitch accent spreads onto the syllables to its left.

5.2 The intermediate phrase

In Lekeitio Basque we could identify a prosodic constituent immediately dominating accentual phrases: the intermediate phrase. The major indicator of an intonational phrase break is the blocking of catathesis, as in Japanese. In the sentence illustrated in (42), for instance, there are three accentual phrases, represented by the words *amáyen*, *amumári* and *liburúa*, each of them carrying a lexical pitch accent:

(42)
L% H*+L L%H H*+L L% H H*+L
| | | | | | | | | | |
[$_{NP}$ a . má . yen a.mu.má . ri] [$_{NP}$ li . bu . rú . a] emon dotzo
Amaya-GEN grandmother-DAT book-ABS give AUX
'(S)he has given the book to Amaya's grandmother'

In Figure 19 it can be observed that the second pitch accent, corresponding to the accented syllable in *amumári*, is catathesized with respect to the first pitch accent, but the third pitch accent is not catathesized with respect to the second pitch accent. Contrast this contour with the one in Figure 14, where catathesis has applied across all four accentual phrases. One could argue that the difference lies in the fact that the accentual phrases in (37) form part of the same syntactic constituent, i.e., an NP, and that those in (42) are divided in two syntactic phrases, i.e., two NPs. The first two accentual phrases are part of the dative NP, and the third accentual phrase is part of the direct object NP. Thus, the idea would be that catathesis does not chain across two syntactic maximal projections. This hypothesis, however, encounters the problem posed by the fact that catathesis applies between two accentual phrases belonging to different syntactic phrases. In (43) below there are two accentual phrases, as shown by the two peaks in the intonational contour of the utterance (cf. Figure 20), and each of them corresponds to a different syntactic maximal category:

(43)
L% H H*+L L% H H*+L
| | | | | | | |
[$_{NP}$ a . ma . yá . ri] [$_{NP}$ li . bu . rú . a] emon dotzo
Amaya-DAT book-ABS give AUX
'(S)he has given the book to Amaya'

As Figure 20 shows, catathesis has downstepped the second pitch accent in the presence of a preceding H*+L pitch accent, even though the two accentual phrases are in two separate syntactic maximal projections.

When we consider three maximal projections preceding the verb, each of them containing one accentual phrase, however, an interesting pattern obtains. Catathesis applies to the second pitch accent, triggered by the first H*+L pitch accent, but the third pitch accent is not downstepped. See the example in (44), and its intonational contour illustrated in Figure 21:

(44)

```
       L% H*+L        L% H  H    H H*+L        L% H    H H*+L
        |  |  |        |  |  |    |  |  |        |  |    | |/
[NP  a.má. ya] [PP on.go  e.we.ní . an]  [NP on.da.rre.rà]   žungó-da
     Amaya          thius-OF Thursday-INES    beach-ALL      go-FUT AUX
     'Amaya will go to the beach this Thursday'
```

The intonational contour in Figure 21 looks very similar to the one we presented in Figure 19, where the first two accentual phrases were part of the same maximal projection, and the third one was part of another maximal projection. Our analysis of this pattern is the following: first, we argue that a syntactic maximal projection marks the boundaries of an intermediate phrase; and second, we assume that an intermediate phrase break blocks catathesis, as in Japanese (cf. section 4.2). That is, a syntactic phrase is a barrier for catathesis. This is why catathesis does not apply between the second and third accentual phrases in Figures 19 and 21. Now, to account for the occurrence of catathesis between the two accentual phrases in Figure 20 and the first two accentual phrases in Figure 21, we must assume that an intermediate phrase composed of a single accentual phrase cannot be left stranded on the left edge of the utterance and is restructured as part of the following intermediate phrase. This phenomenon would be similar to the cases of restructuring in phonological phrase formation that Nespor and Vogel (1986) discuss for Italian and English. Notice in this regard that there is a contraint in the directionality of restructuring; an intermediate phrase containing only one accentual phrase may remain on the right edge of the utterance (cf. (42), (44) and Figures 19 and 21).

The paradigm is completed with an example in which there are three accentual phrases, the first one contained in a maximal projection and the other two contained in another maximal projection (cf. (45) below). As expected from our analysis, catathesis applies in a chain formation (cf. Figure 22). The first intermediate phrase, being composed of a single accentual phrase, is incorporated into the following intermediate phrase, and thus the first pitch accent triggers catathesis onto the second pitch accent. The second pitch accent, in turn, triggers catathesis on the following pitch accent, since they are contained in the same intermediate phrase.

```
(45)     L% H  H*+L        L%  H*+L       L% H  H*+L
          |  |  |  |         |   |  |       |  |  |  |
      [NP a.mu.má . ri]  [NP a . má . yen   li . bu . rú . a]  emon dotzat
          grandmother-DAT  Amaya-GEN        book-ABS            give  AUX
      'I have given Amaya's book to the grandmother'
```

5.3 The utterance

The utterance is the largest intonational phrase in Lekeitio Basque, comprising intermediate phrases and accentual phrases within them. This domain is marked by L% and H% boundary tones occurring at its beginning and end. The initial L% boundary tone is a property of declarative sentences, and is associated to the initial syllable in the utterance, provided it does not bear a pitch accent. I will show in section 7 that an initial H% tone is a property of interrogative sentences. An interesting observation is that Basque does not have final rising at the end of interrogative sentences, except in recent innovations among young speakers (cf. sections 7.2.1 and 7.2.2). In sum, these L% and H% boundary tones, together with pitch range, contribute to indicate whether an utterance is declarative or interrogative. The utterance is also the domain of declination.

To summarize this section, let us recapitulate the different intonational units we have distinguished in Lekeitio Basque, as well as their main features:

1) *accentual phrase*:

   - initial L% boundary tone associated to the first syllable in the phrase, provided it has not been assigned a pitch accent;
   - a H*+L pitch accent marks the right edge of an accentual phrase; the H tone spreads onto all the syllables to the left up to the initial syllable;

2) *intermediate phrase*:

   – comprises one or more accentual phrases;

   – every syntactic maximal projection marks the boundary of an intermediate phrase. A syntactic maximal projection occurring on the left edge of an utterance and containing a single accentual phrase cannot constitute an independent intermediate phrase, and is included as an accentual phrase within the following intermediate phrase;

   – the intermediate phrase is the domain of catathesis;

3) *utterance*:

   – initial L% and H% boundary tones, indicative of declarative or interrogative utterances, respectively (the initial L% is assigned to the first syllable in the utterance, provided it has not been assigned a pitch accent);

   – final L% and H% boundary tones (L% is a property of both declarative and interrogative utterances; H% is an alternative marker of interrogatives - cf. section 7);

   – the utterance is the domain of declination.

6 Empirical consequences: prosodic constraints on focalization

At this point, it is important to discuss the prosodic constraints imposed on focalization. As in all other dialects of Basque, the focalized constituent in a sentence in Lekeitio Basque has to occupy a position immediately preceding the verbal complex formed by the lexical verb and the inflected auxiliary. The focalized constituent is the most prominent element in the sentence prosodically; that is, it receives the main sentence stress. However, as already noted in Hualde, Elordieta, and Elordieta (1993) and in Hualde, Elordieta, and Elordieta (1994), certain prosodic restrictions appear to hold in Lekeitio Basque when words are grouped in phrases. Within a phrase formed only by unaccented words, located immediately preceding the verb, as in (46) below, only the rightmost word can be prosodically prominent, by virtue of being in the position immediately preceding the verbal sequence. The semantic interpretation of the utterance is ambiguous: either the whole phrase or any of the elements within it can be be understood as focalized, provided they can be identified as elements in contrastive focus with an earlier element in the discourse. The crucial point is that the only way this sentence can be pronounced is with main stress on the last element of the phrase. The other words in the phrase cannot receive prosodic prominence, even though the speaker may intend to assign semantic focality to a nonphrase-final word. A pronunciation in which any of the nonphrase-final words carried the most prominent stress would be ungrammatical. We mark focus stress with a circumflex accent above the relevant syllable nucleus; the focalized element is shown in capital letters in the English translation:

(46) [sure erriko andra sarrâ] ikusi dot
your town-OF woman old see AUX
'I have seen THE OLD WOMAN FROM YOUR TOWN' / 'I have seen THE OLD WOMAN from your town' / 'I have seen the OLD woman from your town', etc.

(47) a. *[sure erriko andrâ sarra] ikusi dot
b. *[sure errikô andra sarra] ikusi dot
c. *[surê erriko andra sarra] ikusi dot

The same pattern of prosody-semantics (dis)association would apply for a phrase in which the last element were an accented word (e.g., *sure erriko andra altía* 'the tall woman from your town'). The observation we make is that the only way a word can stand out prosodically and be understood unambiguously as the focalized element in the utterance is if it constitutes an accentual phrase on its own. That is, a focalized word will also stand out prosodically when it is uttered in isolation, when it is the only constituent preceding the verb, or when it is the sole word in an accentual phrase. These situations are exemplified in (48)-(50):

(48) diruâ
money
'THE MONEY'

(49) diruâ emon nau
money give AUX
'(S)he has given me THE MONEY'

(50) L% H*+L L% H H*+L
a. má. yen di. ru. â emon nau
Amaya-GEN money give AUX
'(S)he has given me Amaya's MONEY'

The cases in (48)-(49) do not need further explanation. The example in (50) illustrates a contrast with the utterance in (46), in which the unaccented words form part of the same accentual phrase. As we mentioned above, in (46) only the last unaccented word can be the most prominent one prosodically, but this does not necessarily entail an interpretation in which only the last word is semantically focalized. Any of the unaccented words in the accentual phrase could be the semantic focus of the sentence. In (50), however, the unaccented word *dirua* 'the money' can be unambiguously interpreted as the semantic focus of the utterance. That is because this word forms its own accentual phrase; it follows an accented word, hence the initial L% boundary tone, and it immediately precedes the verb, thus receiving a phrasal H*+L pitch accent (cf. Figure 23). The right edge boundary is created by the H*+L pitch accent that the unaccented word receives by virtue of being phrase final. The peak corresponding to this focalized constituent is still lower than that of the preceding accented word, as an effect of declination.

By the same token, the accented word in (50) constitutes its own accentual phrase, and thus it could be the most prominent element in the utterance and also be interpreted as the semantic focus in the utterance. See for example the sentence in (51) and its corresponding illustration in Figure 24.[20]

(51) amâyen diruà emon nau
'(S)he has given me AMAYA'S money'

The same would hold true in sentences with two accented words. Each of them would form their own accentual phrases, and thus if they were the semantic focus of the sentence, they would be able to stand out prosodically. See examples (52)-(53) and their F_0 contours illustrated in Figures 25-26.

```
(52)  L% H*+L     L% H   H*+L
      |   |  |    |   |   |  |
      a. má. yen  li . bu . rû . a   emon  nau
      Amaya-GEN       book           give  AUX
      '(S)he has given me Amaya's BOOK'
```

(53) amâyen liburúa emon nau
'(S)he has given me AMAYA's book'

From the occurrence of these patterns we conclude that the unity of an accentual phrase formed by more than one word cannot be altered. If a word does not constitute an accentual phrase by itself, it cannot be independently focalized. This contrasts with the Japanese dialect of Tokyo studied by Pierrehumbert and Beckman (1988), in which all words, accented and unaccented, can be made prosodically prominent. This contrast is due to the fact that in Lekeitio Basque not all words can be independently stressed. That is, unaccented words will receive independent stress only if they are in phrase-final position and they constitute a single accentual phrase. In Tokyo Japanese all words, unaccented and accented, can be made prosodically prominent.

Another observation we can make about the prosodic focalization patterns seen above is that focalization creates an intermediate phrase boundary. By virtue of this boundary, the second words in (50) and (52) do not undergo the phenomenon of catathesis that we observe in their nonfocalized versions, ilustrated in Figures 27 and 28, respectively (cf. (54) and (55) below). This has also been observed by Pierrehumbert and Beckman (1988) for Japanese.

(54) amáyen diruà emon nau
'(S)he has given me Amaya's money'

(55) amáyen liburúa emon nau
'(S)he has given me Amaya's book'

After having presented the accentual pattern of Lekeitio Basque, we will proceed to analyze the intonation contours of the major types of sentences in this dialect: declaratives (affirmative and negative), yes/no interrogatives, wh-interrogatives, and yes/no and wh-echo questions.

7 Intonation contours of the major types of sentences in Lekeitio Basque

7.1 Declarative sentences

Declarative sentences in Lekeitio Basque present a decreased pitch range up to the level of the baseline (i.e., the bottom of the speaker's range) at the end of the utterance, a pattern which is also shared by declarative sentences in most well-analyzed languages. We will thus posit the existence of a L% boundary tone at the end of declarative sentences in Lekeitio Basque. As we saw in section 5.1, the pitch region is reduced dramatically after the most prominent stress in the sentence. This could lead us to think that this region is deaccented. However, this would imply that all underlying pitch accents following the main stress are erased, until the L% boundary tone is reached. The fact that lexical pitch accents do surface in this region indicates that there is no deaccenting, but compression of the pitch range. That is, pitch accents are not erased, although they are weakened by a radical decrease of pitch range after the nuclear stress in the sentence. See, for instance, Figure 13, where the pitch accent of the verb is perceptible as a peak, although downstepped with respect to the first pitch accent. In this respect, Basque differs from English (cf. Pierrehumbert 1980), and resembles Swedish in its ability to realize pitch accents after the main sentence stress (cf. Pierrehumbert and Beckman 1988: 246-251, fn. 19). It should be noted that, unlike Swedish, pitch accents in Lekeitio Basque surface with very low peaks.

7.2 Interrogative sentences

7.2.1 Yes/no questions

The most common pattern in Lekeitio Basque yes/no questions is for the element about which the inquiry is being made to appear leftmost in the sentence, followed by the sequence formed by the lexical verb and the auxiliary. The object of inquiry receives the most prominent stress in the sentence, after which a sharp drop in pitch is observed. Lekeitio Basque yes/no questions differ from languages such as Spanish and English in that they do not show a final rise (cf. Pierrehumbert 1980, for English; Navarro Tomás 1944, Sosa 1991, on Spanish intonation). In other words, they do not have a final H% boundary tone. Instead, they present a low or deaccented tonal contour after the most prominent tone on the left periphery of the sentence, without raising it. Thus, we posit a L% boundary tone for this kind of sentences, similar to declaratives. The difference between yes/no questions and declaratives lies in the substantially higher pitch range extending over the whole utterance that the former have, as well as the final lengthening of the last syllable in the utterance. We can see these features in the F_0 contour shown in Figure 29, for the sentence in (56) (we mark the most prominent syllable with a circumflex accent):

(56) H*+L L%
ma.ri.bî allaga da e.rri.ra?
Maribi arrive AUX town-ALL
'Has Maribi arrived in town?'

Compare the F_0 contour in Figure 29 to the one in Figure 30, which corresponds to the declarative sentence (57):

(57) H*+L L%
ma.ri.bî allaga da e.rri.ra
'Maribi has arrived in town'

The absolute peak value for the pitch accent in Figure 29 is 184.8 Hz, and in the region after the peak the tonal values are in the 130-140 Hz range, the lowest point being 121.5 Hz. In contrast, the absolute peak value for the pitch accent in Figure 30 is substantially lower, at 160.8 Hz, and the tonal region located after it does not surpass 116.2 Hz. On the basis of these differences, we could posit an initial H% boundary tone for the utterance, which raises the baseline and sets the high pitch level. That is, we do not want to argue that the size of the pitch drop after the most prominent peak in the utterance is smaller in interrogative sentences than in declarative sentences. Indeed, we claim that the size of the pitch drop is the same in both types of utterances. But given the higher initial pitch level of interrogatives, the region which follows the most prominent peak in interrogative sentences will have a higher frequency than in declarative sentences, measured in absolute values.

Final lengthening is another characteristic of interrogative sentences. Note that the final syllable of *errira* is considerably longer in the interrogative sentence (56) than it in the declarative sentence (57). This is shown in Figures 29 and 30, where we measure the duration of the final syllable by positioning a vertical line on the nucleus of the last syllable of the respective utterances. The length of the region of the utterance located after the vertical line serves as a rough indicator of the duration of the final syllable.

Another property that distinguishes yes/no questions from declaratives is accent placement. In declaratives, an unaccented synthetic verb forms a single constituent with the focalized element if it is unaccented, by prosodic cliticization. The stress falls on the last syllable of the synthetic verb. We illustrate this pattern in example (58) below, where we indicate the prosodic unit by hyphenation (see Figure 31):

(58) H*+L

oyan - da . gô
bed-IN is
'(S)he is in bed'

In yes/no questions the inquired or focalized element always constitutes an independent locus of pitch accent, i.e., the synthetic verb does not cliticize onto it. Thus, compare sentence (58) with (59), whose F_0 contour is represented in Figure 32.

(59) H% H*+L L%

o . yân da.go?
'Is (s)he in bed?'

Before we finish this issue, it must be pointed out that younger speakers of Lekeitio Basque have started to use final raising patterns, perhaps influenced by Spanish. Nevertheless, this pattern is very rare, even among these speakers. The following is an example (cf. Figure 33):

(60)
```
H%                      H%
|                       |
allagâ  ra   Maribi  erri.ra?
arrive  AUX  Maribi  town-ALL
'Has Maribi arrived in town?'
```

7.2.2 Wh-questions

Like yes/no questions, wh-questions also present a raised baseline and a high pitch level, and thus we will posit an initial H% boundary tone belonging to the utterance level. Wh-questions are characterized by a sharp drop in pitch after the high peak level of the wh-word, which is always accented. In most natural circumstances, these constructions do not present final raising at the end of the contour, as in the case of yes/no questions. Observe, for example, the F_0 contour in Figure 34 for the sentence in (61):

(61)
```
H% H*+L                  L%
|   |   |                |
no . rê . na  da   ori   umi.a?
whose         is   that  child
'Whose is that child?'
```

These constructions also have the idiosyncratic property of introducing penultimate stress on the compound formed by the lexical verb and the auxiliary. Compare the declarative sentence in (62) with its wh-counterpart in (63) (Figures 35 and 36, respectively):

(62)
```
umiâ   erun  dogu  mendira
child  take  AUX   mountain-ALL
'We have taken the child to the mountain'
```

(63)
```
H% H*+L        H*+L%         L%
  \ | /         |  |         |
   nôr   erun  dó . gu    men.di.ra?
   who   take    AUX      mountain-ALL
'Who have we taken to the mountain?'
```

Finally, like in yes/no questions, we have to point out that a pronunciation of wh-questions with final raising at the end is also possible among younger speakers, although it is very rare. The utterance in (63) could thus have an alternative counterpart in (64) (cf. Figure 37):

```
(64)   H% H*+L                    H%
         \ | /                     |
          nôr  erun  dógu  mendi.ra?
```

7.2.3 Echo questions

7.2.3.1 Yes/no echo questions

By yes/no echo questions I refer to those interrogative sentences which are used to request confirmation on a previous piece of the discourse. In Lekeitio Basque these sentences are characterized by their high pitch range, an effect related to an initial H%. However, this pitch range is higher than that of non-echo interrogatives, such that the pitch drop after a pitch accent is not as perceptible as in other types of utterances. In (65) and (66) we provide examples of yes/no echo questions, whose F_0 contours are represented in Figures 38 and 39:

```
(65)   H%   H*+L                 L%
       |    |/                   |
       u.mi.â  erun  dau  mendi.ra?
       child   take  AUX  mountain-ALL
       '(Are you saying that) (s)he has taken the child to the mountain?'
```

```
(66)   H%   H*+L                       L%
       |     |  |                      |
       li.bu.rû . a  erun  dau  mendi.ra?
       book          take  AUX  mountain
       '(Are you saying that) (s)he has taken the book to the mountain?'
```

As we can see in Figures 38 and 39, the pitch drop which would correspond to the pitch accents in declarative or non-echo interrogative sentences is reduced in yes/no echo questions. In other words, there is no deaccenting of the portion of the utterance which follows the preverbal element (cf. the discussion of sentences (32)-(34) in section 5.1.2). This feature is more salient in yes/no echo questions formed by unaccented words (cf. (65), Figure 38). In these sentences a high pitch plateau is formed after the first H tone in the utterance (i.e., the second syllable in the utterance), and the pitch drop which in other types of sentences would be part of the phrasal pitch accent assigned to the element immediately preceding the verb is almost imperceptible (cf. the shallow dip in the total contour between the last syllable of *umia* and the verb *erun*). The high pitch plateau is maintained until the end of the utterance, where final lowering applies, dropping the pitch level dramatically. It should be pointed out that unlike for non-echo yes/no questions, final lowering is the only possible way to end these sentences. Final raising is excluded as an alternative, even among young speakers. The vertical line placed on the last segment of the utterance serves to indicate final lengthening, typical of interrogatives in Lekeitio Basque. Thus, we posit a final L% boundary tone at the end of the utterance for yes/no echo questions.

In yes/no echo questions with an accented word before the verb, the pitch accent of the accented word is more perceptible than that of an unaccented word, according to the F_0 contour shown in Figure 39. Nevertheless, the pitch drop of the H*+L pitch accent is still very small compared to the one found in the other types of utterances. For a better illustration of this property of echo questions, let us compare the F_0 contours in Figures 38 and 39 with those of their declarative and non-echo counterparts, represented in (67) and (68) (cf. Figures 40-43):

(67) a.

```
    H*+L
    |/
u.mi.â  erun dau mendira
```

'(S)he has taken the child to the mountain'

b.

```
       H*+L
       |  |
li.bu.rû . a  erun dau mendira
```

'(S)he has taken the book to the mountain'

(68) a.
```
      H*+L
      |/
u.mi.â  erun dau mendira?
```
'Has (s)he taken the child to the mountain?'

b.
```
        H*+L
        |  |
li.bu.rû . a  erun dau mendira?
```
'Has (s)he taken the book to the mountain?'

Echo questions have a higher overall pitch level than declaratives and interrogatives in Lekeitio Basque. This does not mean that the most prominent peak in echo utterances always has a higher tonal value than the most prominent peak in other utterances. Rather, what characterizes echo questions is the high frequency of the rest of the utterance. In the utterance in (65), for instance, the tonal contour in the high tone plateau never goes below 150 Hz, and the lowest point is registered at 123.1 Hz, at the end. In the utterance in (66) the frequency after the pitch accent is maintained at 163-165 Hz, lowering at the end until it reaches 126.5 Hz. The corresponding declarative and non-echo counterparts, however, show a lower frequency rate after the main stress in the utterance. For the declarative sentences in (67a,b) we recorded frequency rates of 115-122 Hz and 109-115 Hz, respectively, the lowest points being 112.8Hz and 109 Hz, at the end of the utterances. In the interrogative sentences in (68a,b) the tonal values are 118-125 Hz and 129 Hz, respectively, the lowest points being 109.1 Hz and 113 Hz, at the end of the utterances.

7.2.3.2 Wh-echo questions

Wh-echo questions share with yes/no echo-questions the property of having a high pitch level extending over the whole utterance and having a shallow pitch drop after the most prominent pitch accent. The only difference which wh-echo questions present with respect to yes/no echo questions is the final raising that they present at the end. Indeed, this is a property which also distinguishes wh-echo questions from their non-echo counterparts. As we mentioned in section 7.2.2, non-echo wh-questions present final lowering in natural circumstances, final raising being an alternative only among younger speakers. In wh-echo questions, however, only final raising is possible. We would thus posit a final H% boundary tone, as well as an initial H% boundary tone responsible for the high pitch range of all interrogatives. See the examples in (69)-(70), and their respective F_0 contours in Figures 44 and 45:

(69) H% H*+L H%

nôr erun dau mendi.ra?
who take AUX mountain-ALL
'Who (did you say that) (s)he took to the mountain?'

(70) H% H*+L H%

no . rê . na ra umi.a?
who-GEN AUX child
'Whose (did you say that) the child is?'

There is a pending issue in our treatment of echo questions: how do we account for the high pitch level that echo questions present through the whole utterance? Positing an initial H% boundary tone would not be sufficient to distinguish echo questions from non-echo questions. Echo questions differ from non-echo questions in that they maintain the high pitch level until the end of the utterance, such that the pitch drop after a pitch accent is less perceptible than in non-echo questions. One possibility would be to suggest the existence of a final H^- boundary tone anchored to the right edge of the accentual phrase preceding the verb in echo questions, and that this tone maintains the high pitch level. This H^- tone is the reinterpretation that Beckman and Pierrehumbert (1988) make of Pierrehumbert's (1980) phrasal accent. If our hypothesis is correct, then this would lead us to assume the existence of a L^- boundary tone after the final stress in declaratives and non-echo interrogatives, which would be responsible for the fall in pitch (cf. section 5.1.2). In order to decide on the validity of this proposal, further investigation would be required. At this point, we would limit ourselves to suggesting these plausible alternatives.

8 Summary and conclusions

In this paper I have studied the intonational system of Lekeitio Basque. Based on original ideas by Beckman and Pierrehumbert (1986) and Pierrehumbert and Beckman (1988), I have argued that the best way to capture the different patterns of tones in this language is to assume the existence of several well-defined intonational domains to which these tones belong, hierarchically structured in the phonological representation of an utterance. These intonational units impose their own well-formedness constraints on the shapes of the tones associated to them. Together they create and model the intonational contours of utterances. Specifically, we have shown that this theory allows a more systematic account of the distribution and realization of tones not associated to pitch accents, such as the L tones appearing on the initial syllables of words and the high tones occurring between this initial L tone and a pitch accent located to their right. We suggested that they belong to a prosodic phrase located above the word level, the accentual phrase, which governs their distribution by means of collocational restrictions. The initial L tone is in reality an initial L% boundary tone, which associates to the initial syllable of the phrase, and the H tones result from the spreading of a phrasal H tone associated to the second syllable of the phrase. We also identified a higher prosodic constituent under which accentual phrases are grouped: the intermediate phrase. This unit is independently motivated as the domain within whose boundaries catathesis may apply, but not across them. We have argued that every syntactic maximal projection constitutes an intermediate phrase, except for a maximal projection containing a single accentual phrase on the left edge of the sentence, which is joined into the following intermediate phrase. Finally, the utterance is the level where L% and H% boundary tones are inserted.

Among other interesting properties of Lekeitio Basque intonation, we have seen that a word can only be focalized prosodically if it forms an accentual phrase by itself, and that focalization creates intermediate phrase boundaries by blocking the chain of catathesis effects.

We finished our study by analyzing the intonational contours of the major types of sentences in Lekeitio Basque. The presence of final lowering in interrogative sentences and the differences between echo and non-echo utterances were stressed in the discussion.

Appendix: Index of Figures

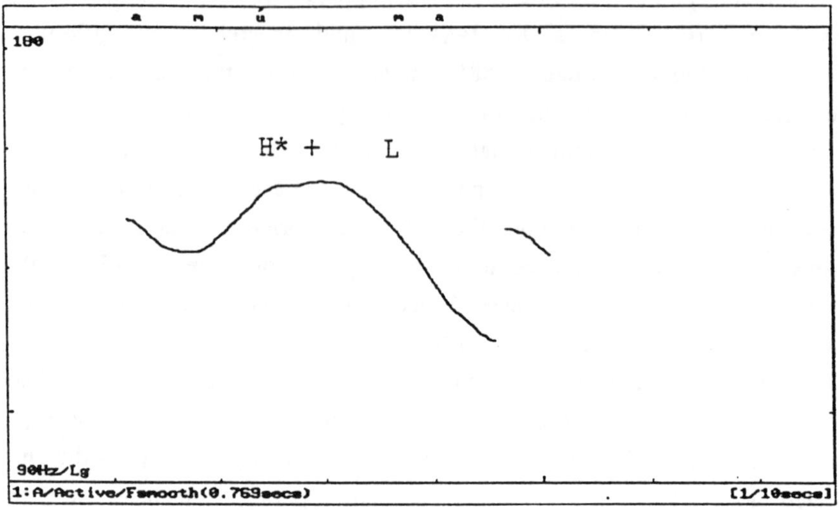

Fig. 1

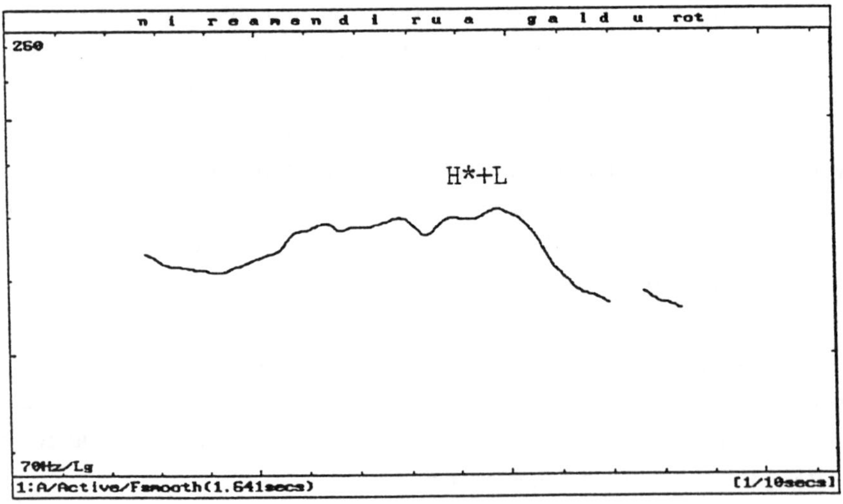

Fig. 2

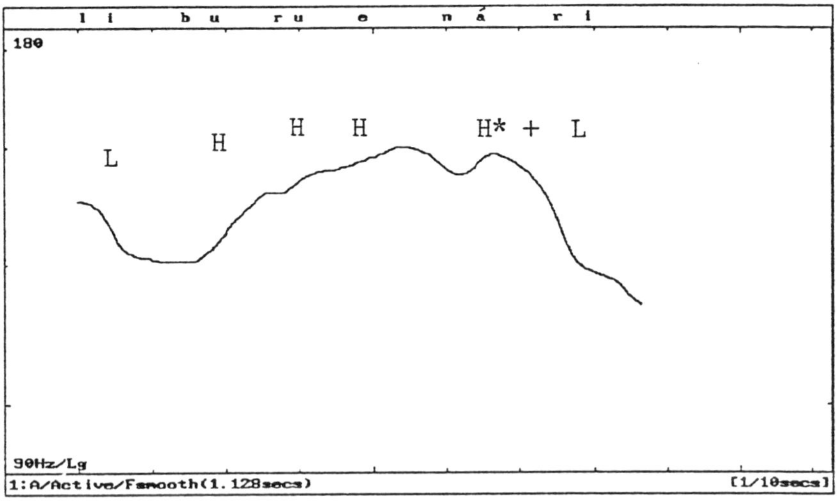
l i b u r u e n á r i
180
L
H
H H
H* + L
90Hz/Lg
1:A/Active/Fsmooth(1.128secs)
[1/10secs]

Fig. 3

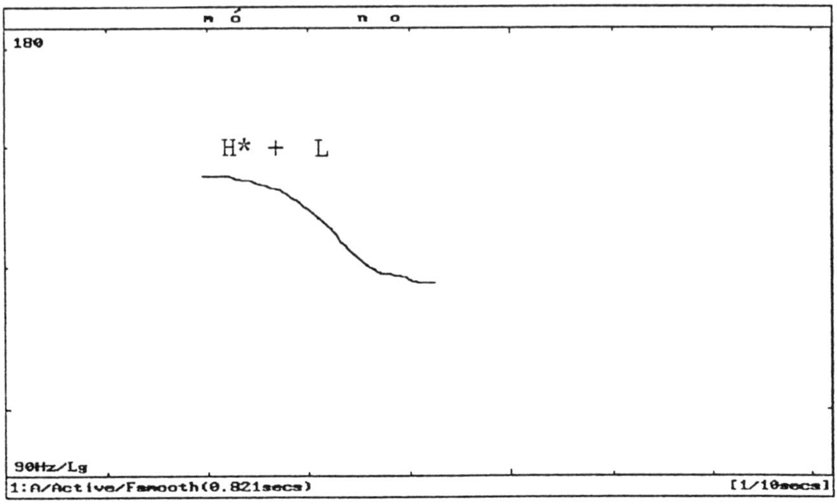
m ó n o
180
H* + L
90Hz/Lg
1:A/Active/Fsmooth(0.821secs)
[1/10secs]

Fig. 4

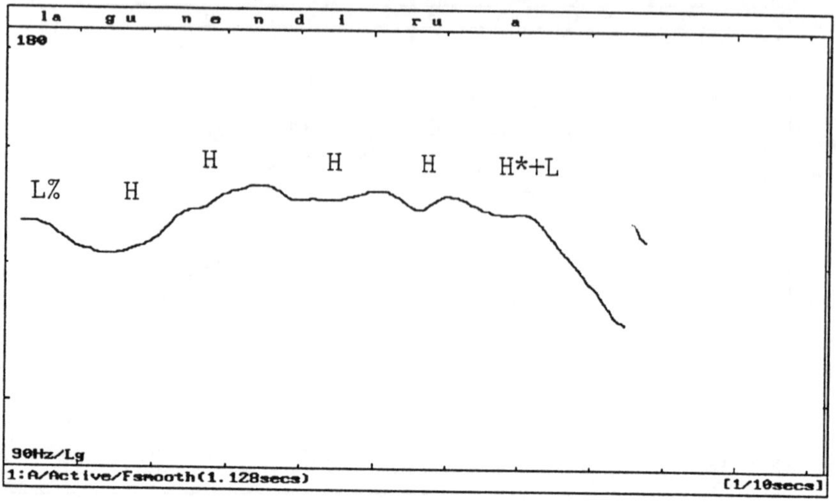
la gu n e n d i r u a
180
L% H H H H H*+L
90Hz/Lg
1:A/Active/Fsmooth(1.128secs)
[1/10secs]

Fig. 5

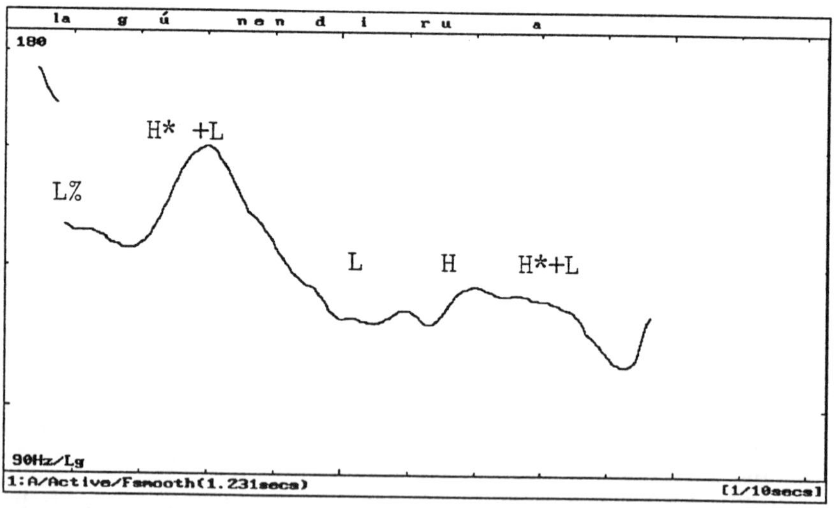
la g ú n e n d i r u a
180
H* +L
L%
L H H*+L
90Hz/Lg
1:A/Active/Fsmooth(1.231secs)
[1/10secs]

Fig. 6

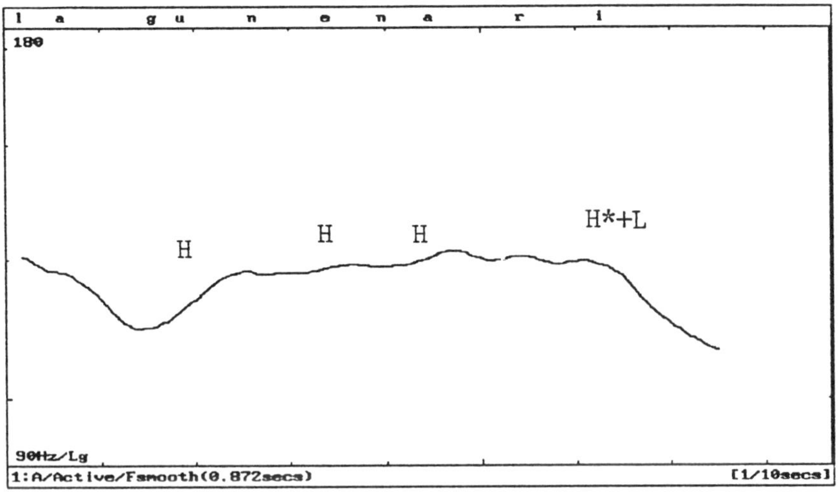
l a g u n e n a r i
180
H
H
H
H*+L
90Hz/Lg
1:A/Active/Fsmooth(0.872secs)
[1/10secs]

Fig. 7

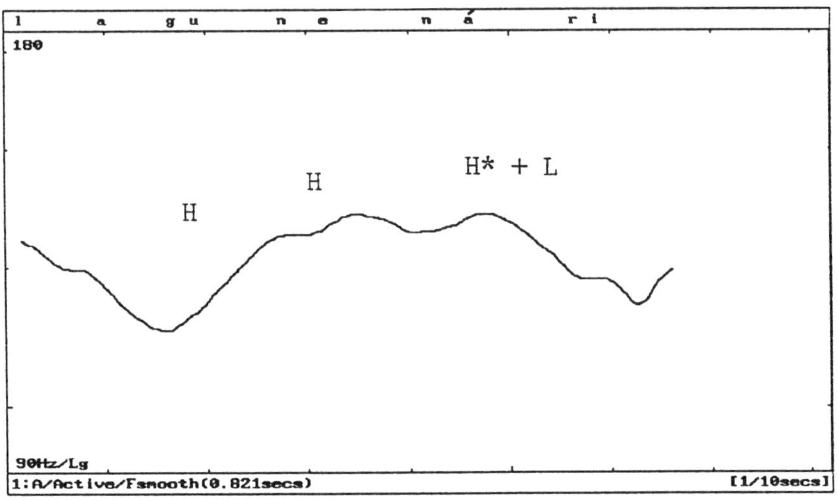
l a g u n e n á r i
180
H
H
H* + L
90Hz/Lg
1:A/Active/Fsmooth(0.821secs)
[1/10secs]

Fig. 8

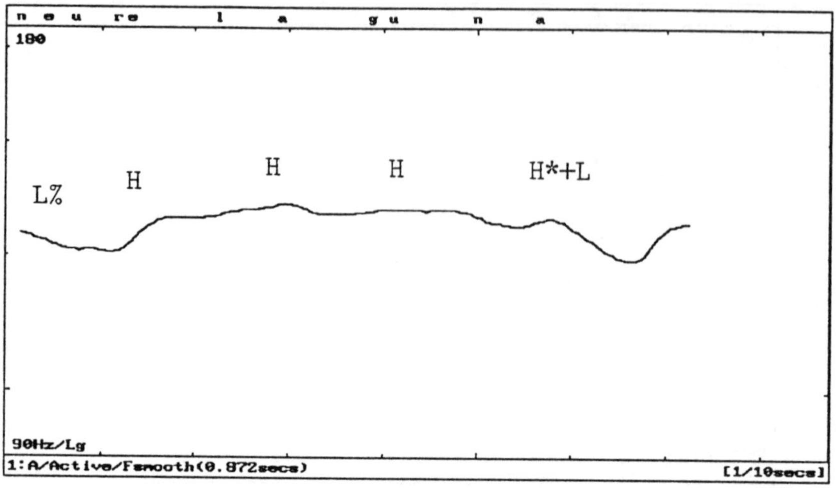
n e u r e l a g u n a
180
L%
H
H
H
H*+L
90Hz/Lg
1:A/Active/Fsmooth(0.872secs)
[1/10secs]

Fig. 9

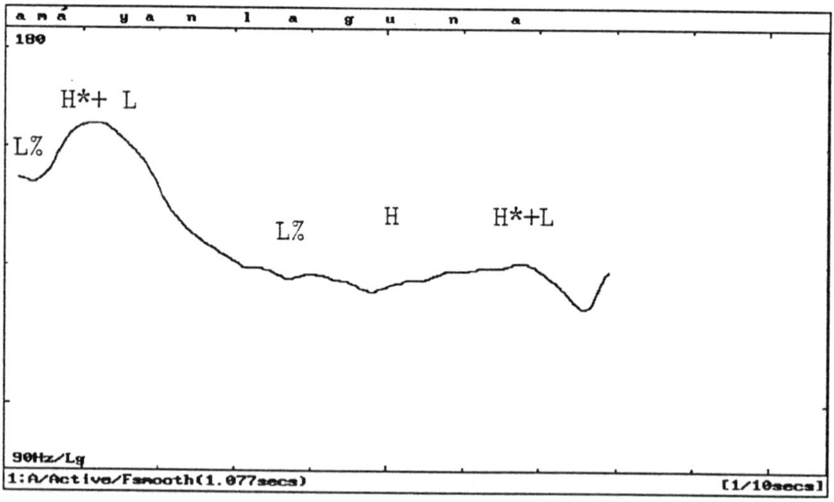
a m á y a n l a g u n a
180
H*+ L
L%
L%
H
H*+L
90Hz/Lg
1:A/Active/Fsmooth(1.077secs)
[1/10secs]

Fig. 10

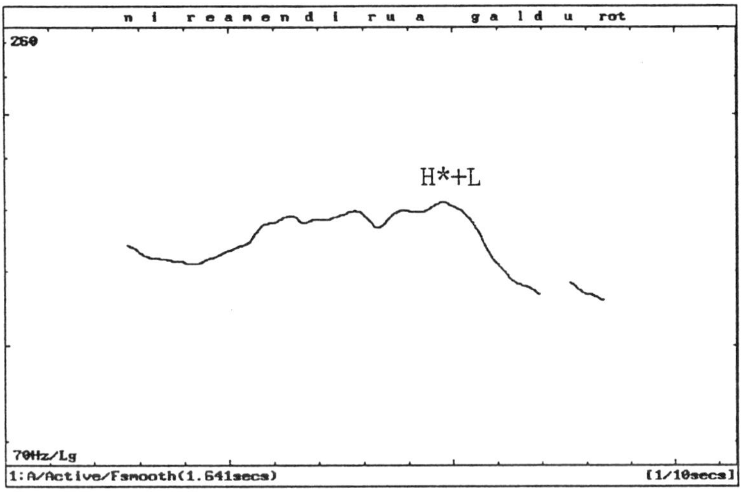
n i r e a m e n d i r u a g a l d u rot
260
H*+L
70Hz/Lg
1:A/Active/Fsmooth(1.641secs)
[1/10secs]

Fig. 11

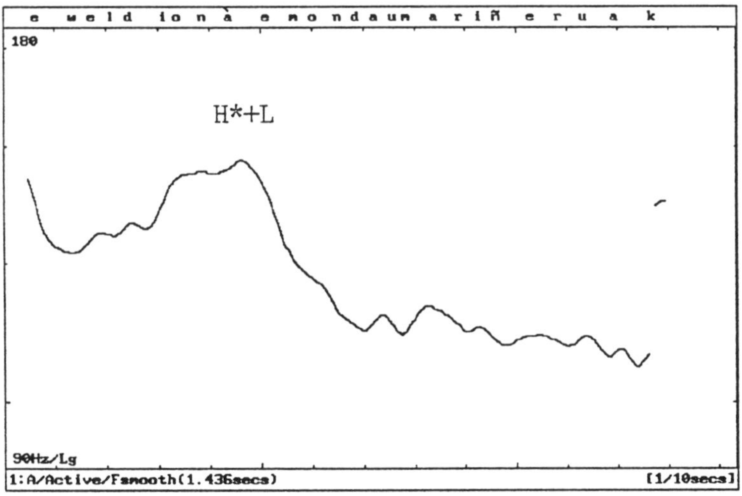
e w e l d i o n à e m o n d a u m a r i ñ e r u a k
180
H*+L
90Hz/Lg
1:A/Active/Fsmooth(1.436secs)
[1/10secs]

Fig. 12

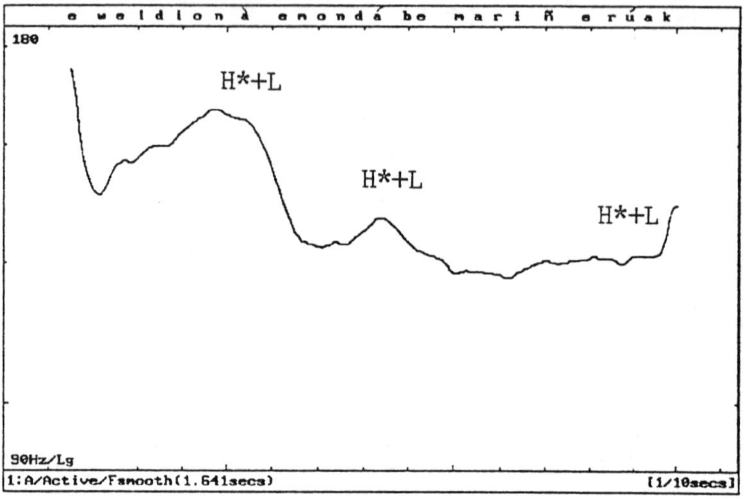
e w e l d i o n à e m o n d á b e m a r i ñ e r ú a k
180
H*+L
H*+L
H*+L
90Hz/Lg
1:A/Active/Fsmooth(1.641secs)
[1/10secs]

Fig. 13

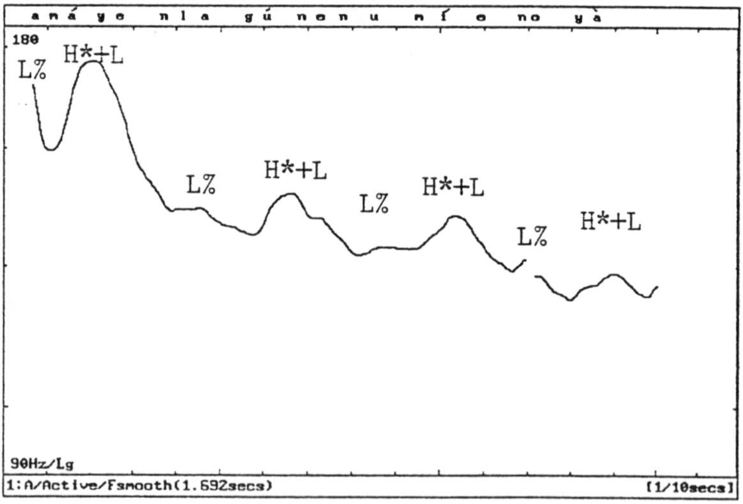
a m á y e n l a g ú n e n u m í e no y à
180
L%
H*+L
L%
H*+L
L%
H*+L
L%
H*+L
90Hz/Lg
1:A/Active/Fsmooth(1.692secs)
[1/10secs]

Fig. 14

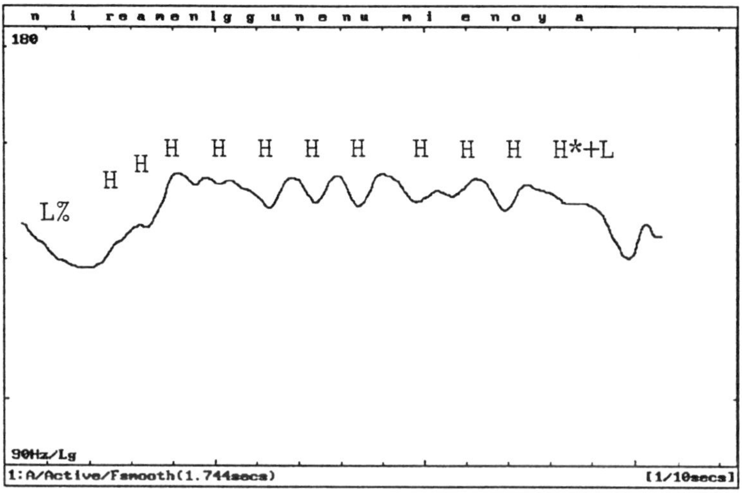
n i reamenlggunenu mi enoya
180
L% H H H H H H H H H H H*+L
90Hz/Lg
1:A/Active/Fsmooth(1.744secs)
[1/10secs]

Fig. 15

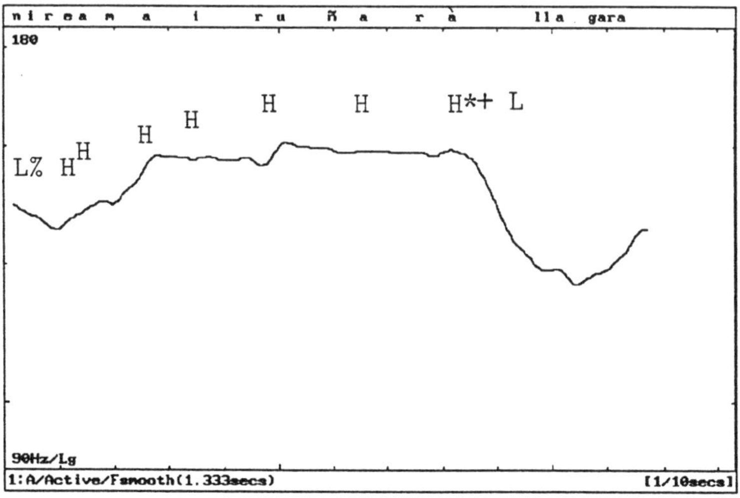
nirea m a i ru ña r à lla gara
180
L% H H H H H H H*+ L
90Hz/Lg
1:A/Active/Fsmooth(1.333secs)
[1/10secs]

Fig. 16

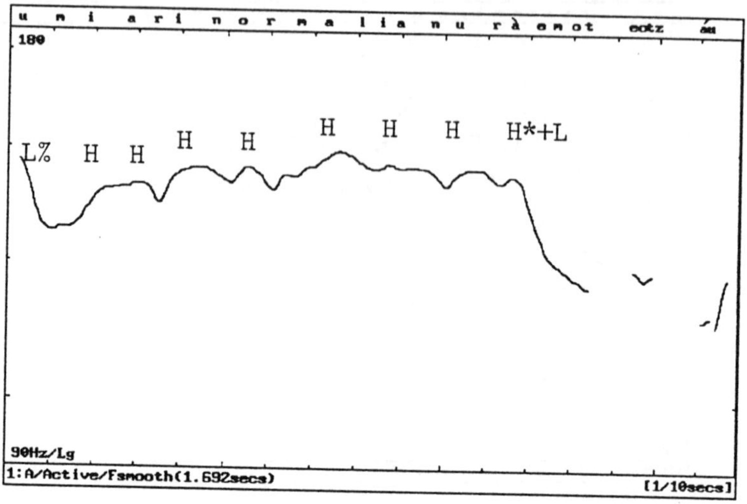
180
L% H H H H H H H H*+L
90Hz/Lg
1:A/Active/Fsmooth(1.692secs)
[1/10secs]

Fig. 17

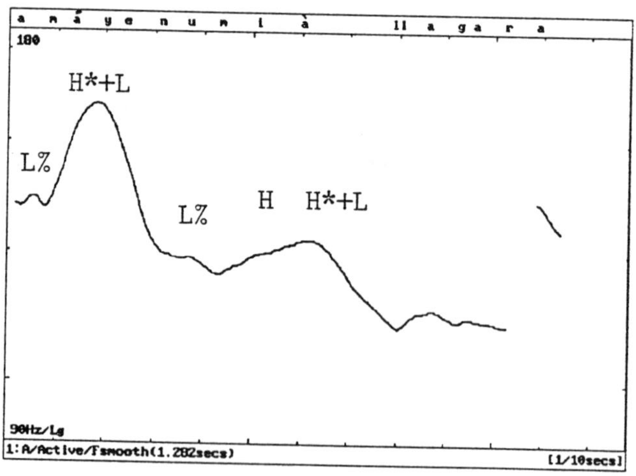
180
H*+L
L%
L% H H*+L
90Hz/Lg
1:A/Active/Fsmooth(1.282secs)
[1/10secs]

Fig. 18

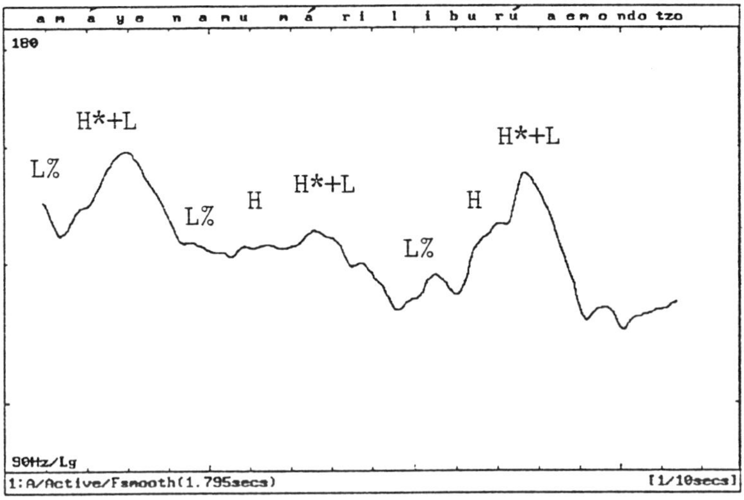
a m á y e n a m u m á r i l i b u r ú a e m o ndo tzo
180
H*+L
L%
L%
H
H*+L
L%
H
H*+L
90Hz/Lg
1:A/Active/Fsmooth(1.795secs)
[1/10secs]

Fig. 19

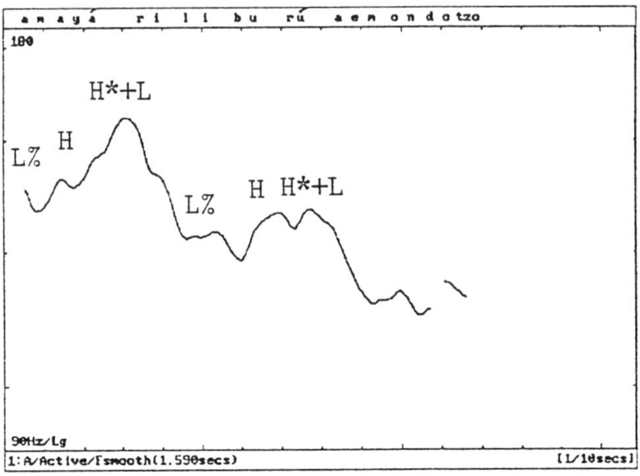
a m a y á r i l i b u rú a e m o n d o tzo
180
H*+L
L%
H
L%
H
H*+L
90Hz/Lg
1:A/Active/Fsmooth(1.590secs)
[1/10secs]

Fig. 20

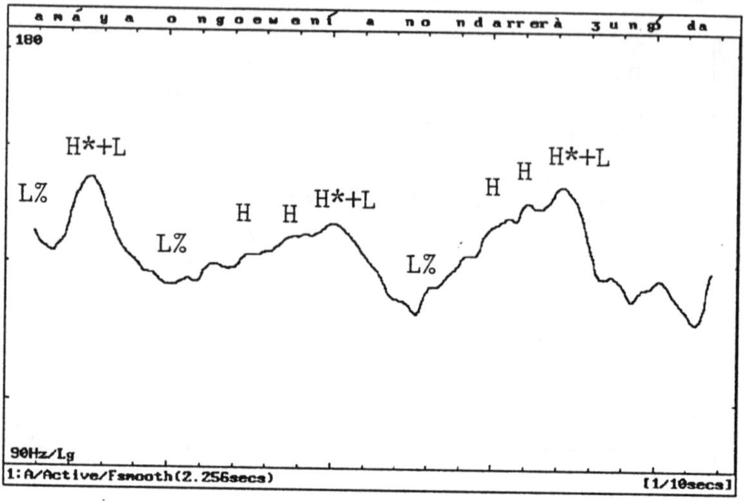
180
H*+L
L%
L%
H H H*+L
L%
H H H*+L
90Hz/Lg
1:A/Active/Fsmooth(2.256secs)
[1/10secs]

Fig. 21

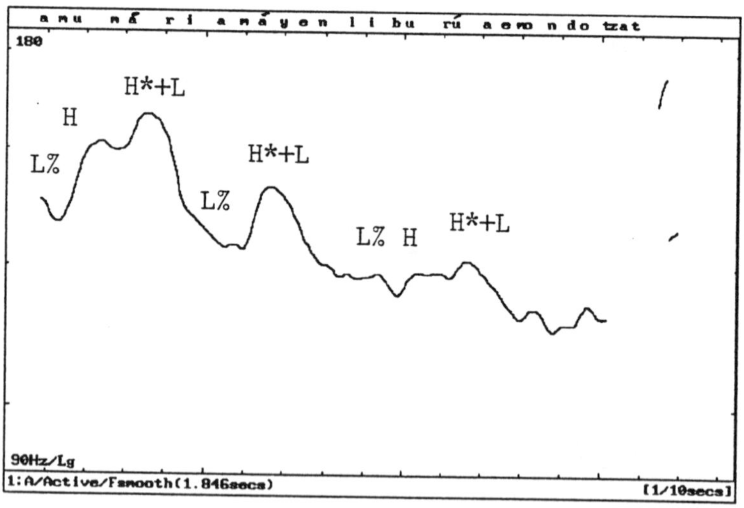
180
H*+L
H
L%
H*+L
L%
L% H H*+L
90Hz/Lg
1:A/Active/Fsmooth(1.846secs)
[1/10secs]

Fig. 22

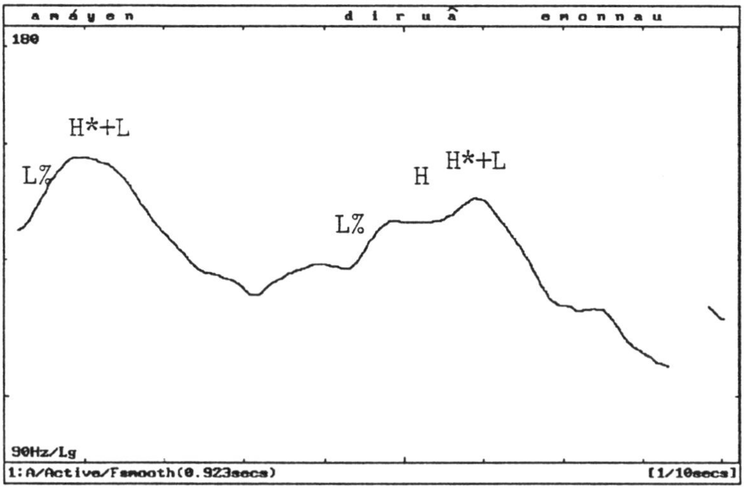
a m á y e n
d i r u â
e m o n n a u
180
H*+L
L%
H
H*+L
L%
90Hz/Lg
1:A/Active/Fsmooth(0.923secs)
[1/10secs]

Fig. 23

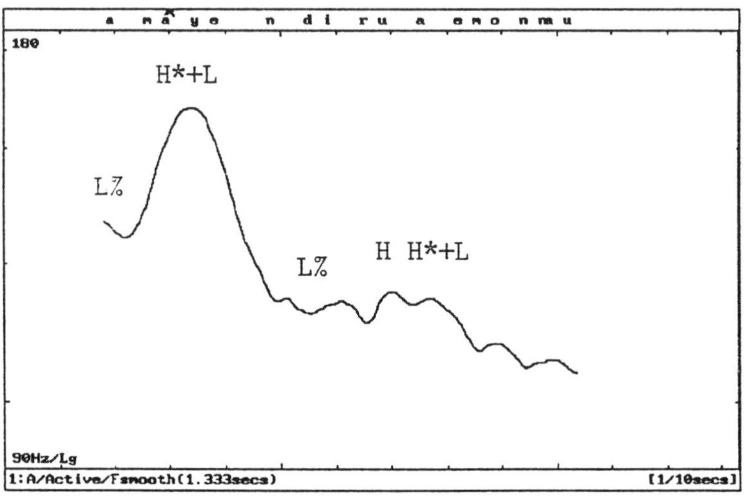
180
H*+L
L%
L%
H H*+L
90Hz/Lg
1:A/Active/Fsmooth(1.333secs)
[1/10secs]

Fig. 24

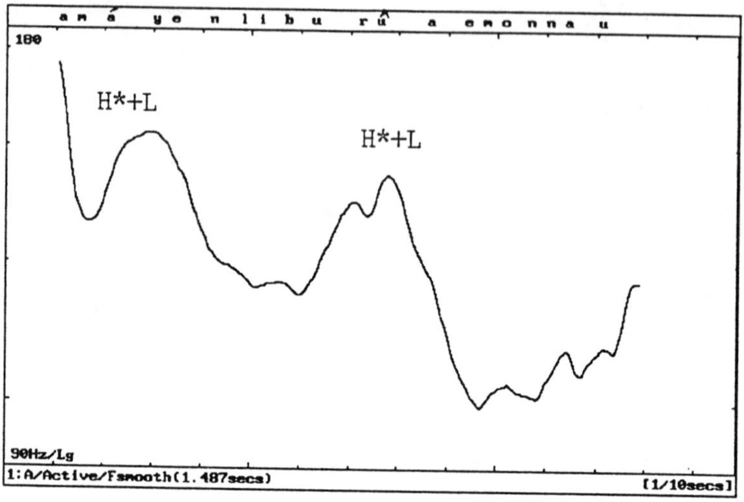
a m á y e n l i b u r ú a e m o n n a u
180
H*+L
H*+L
90Hz/Lg
1:A/Active/Fsmooth(1.487secs)
[1/10secs]

Fig. 25

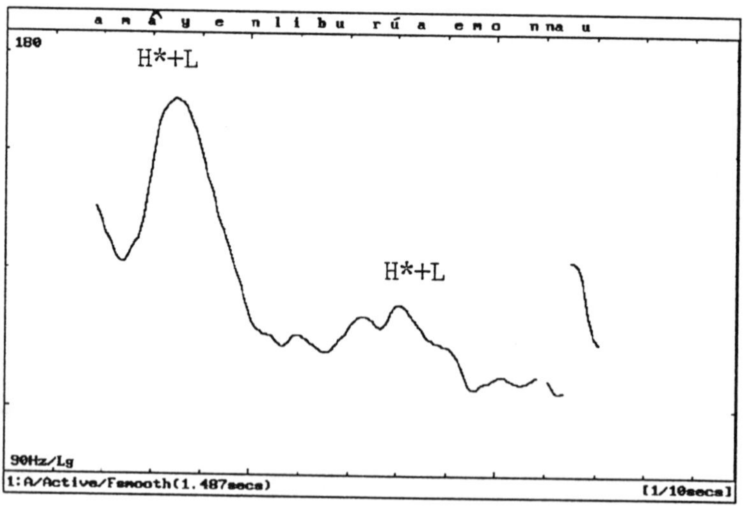
a m á y e n l i b u r ú a e m o n na u
180
H*+L
H*+L
90Hz/Lg
1:A/Active/Fsmooth(1.487secs)
[1/10secs]

Fig. 26

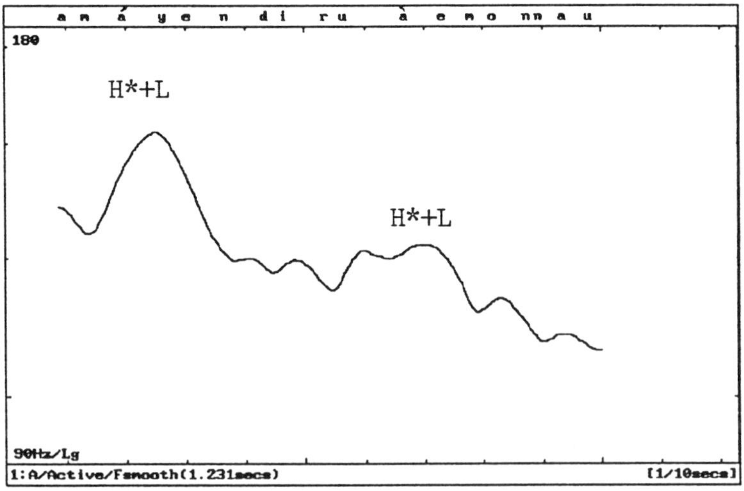

180
H*+L
H*+L
90Hz/Lg
1:A/Active/Fsmooth(1.231secs)
[1/10secs]

Fig. 27

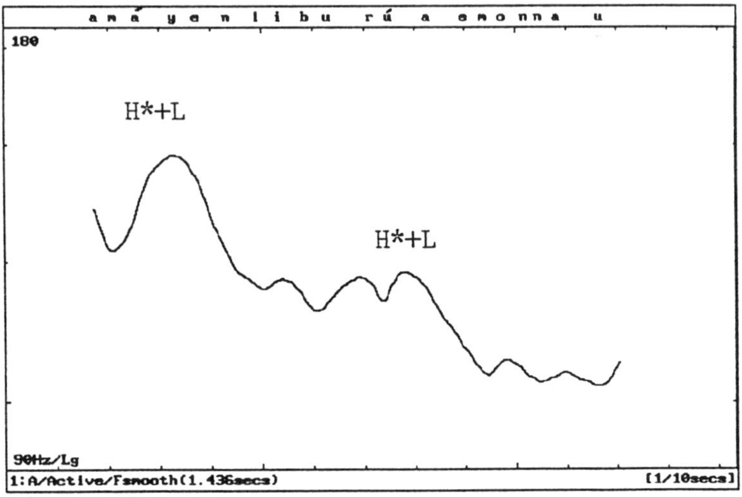

180
H*+L
H*+L
90Hz/Lg
1:A/Active/Fsmooth(1.436secs)
[1/10secs]

Fig. 28

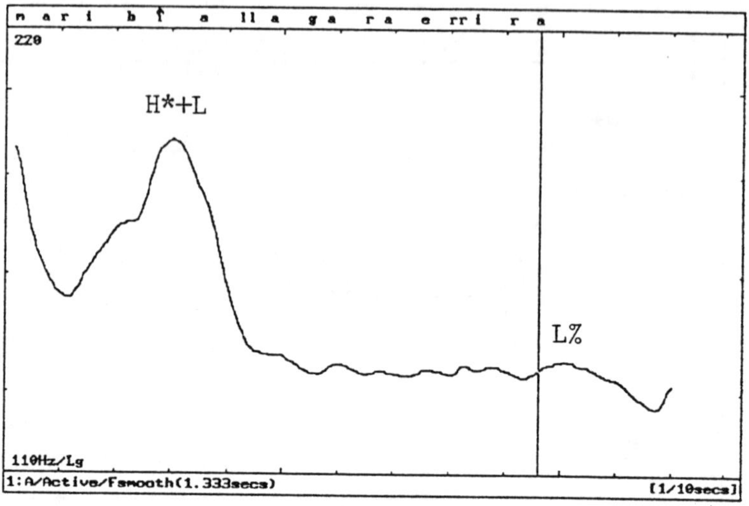
m a r i b a ll a g a r a e rri r a
220
H*+L
L%
110Hz/Lg
1:A/Active/Fsmooth(1.333secs)
[1/10secs]

Fig. 29

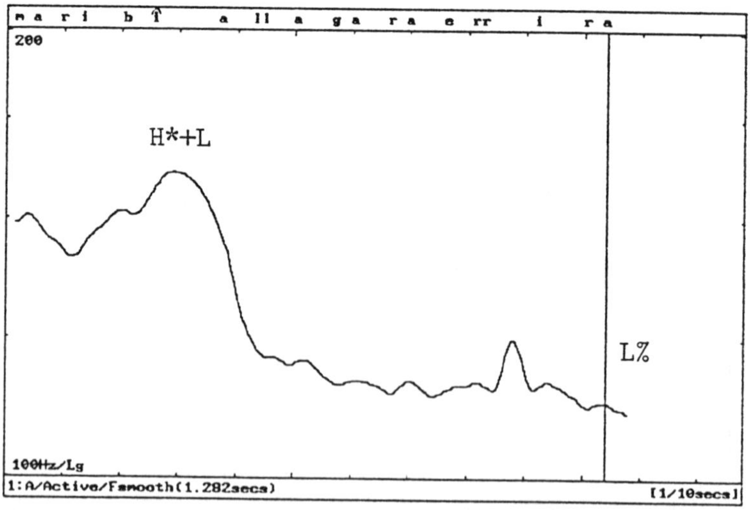
m a r i b a ll a g a r a e rr i r a
200
H*+L
L%
100Hz/Lg
1:A/Active/Fsmooth(1.282secs)
[1/10secs]

Fig. 30

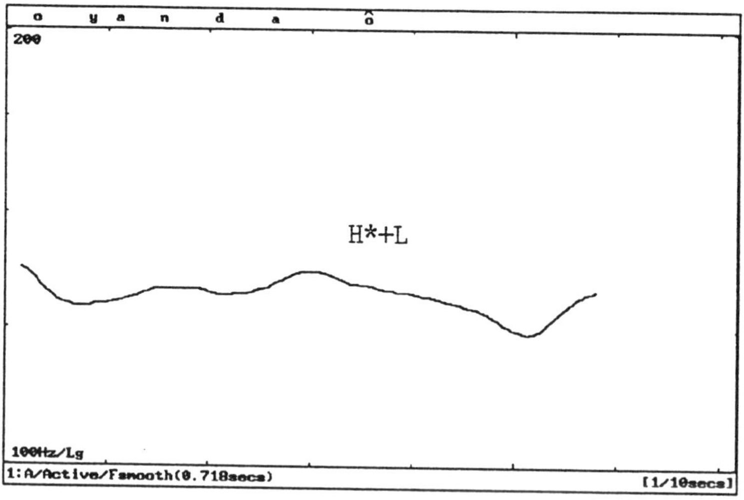
o y a n d a ô
200
H*+L
100Hz/Lg
1:A/Active/Fsmooth(0.718secs)
[1/10secs]

Fig. 31

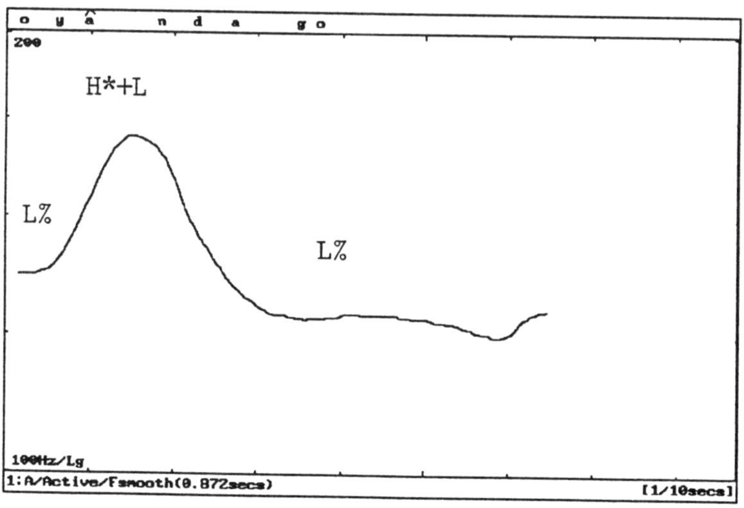
o y â n d a g o
200
H*+L
L%
L%
100Hz/Lg
1:A/Active/Fsmooth(0.872secs)
[1/10secs]

Fig. 32

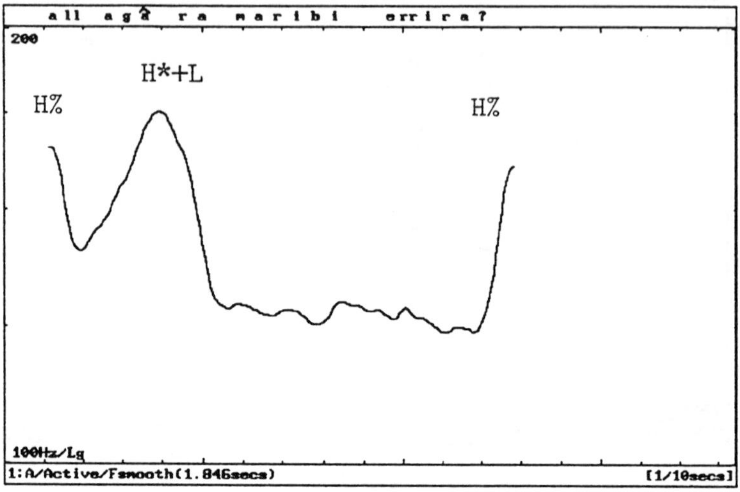
all agâ ra maribi erriira?
200
H*+L
H%
H%
100Hz/Lg
1:A/Active/Fsmooth(1.846secs)
[1/10secs]

Fig. 33

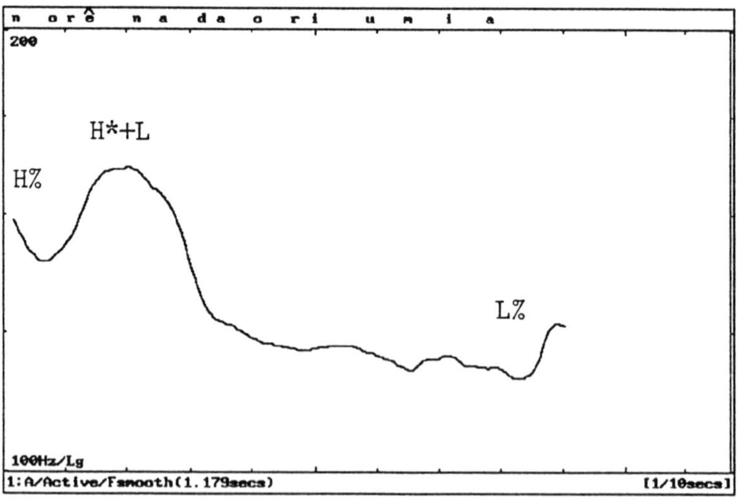
n orê na da o ri u m i a
200
H*+L
H%
L%
100Hz/Lg
1:A/Active/Fsmooth(1.179secs)
[1/10secs]

Fig. 34

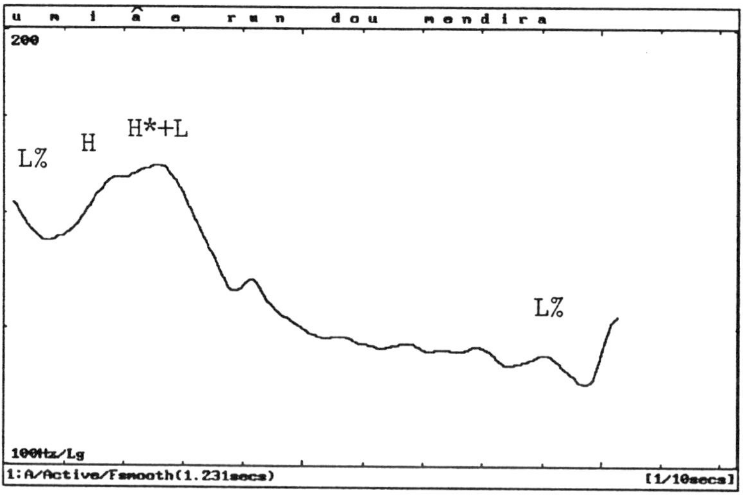
u m i â e r u n d o u m e n d i r a
200
L%
H
H*+L
L%
100Hz/Lg
1:A/Active/Fsmooth(1.231secs)
[1/10secs]

Fig. 35

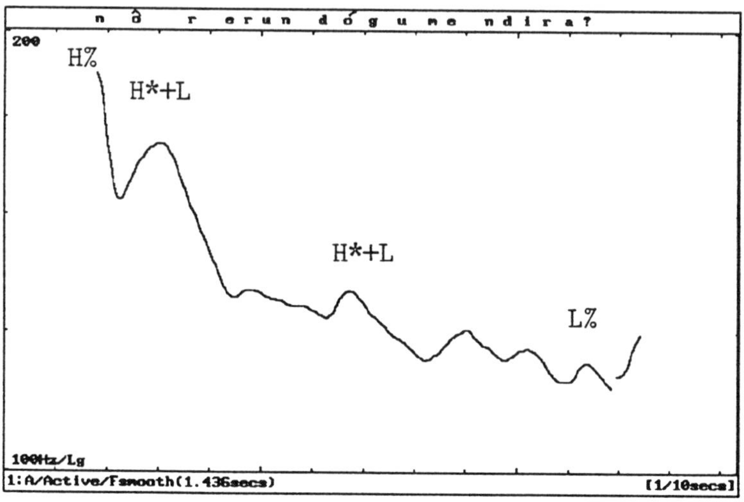
n ə̂ r e r u n d ó g u m e n d i r a ?
200
H%
H*+L
H*+L
L%
100Hz/Lg
1:A/Active/Fsmooth(1.436secs)
[1/10secs]

Fig. 36

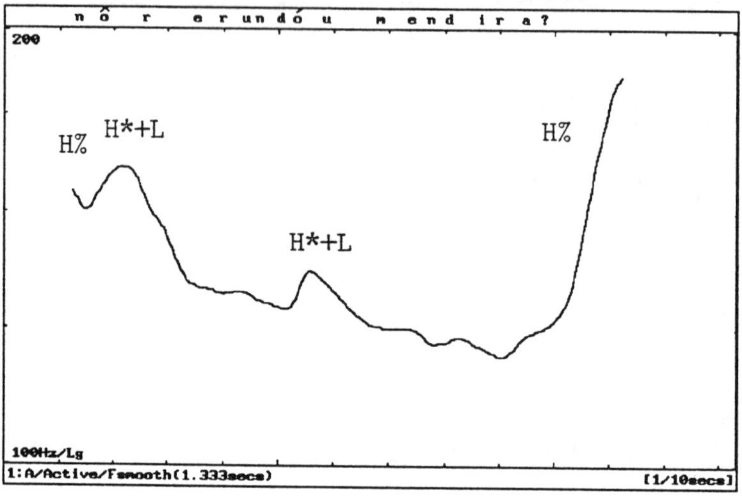
200
H%
H*+L
H*+L
H%
100Hz/Lg
1:A/Active/Fsmooth(1.333secs)
[1/10secs]

Fig. 37

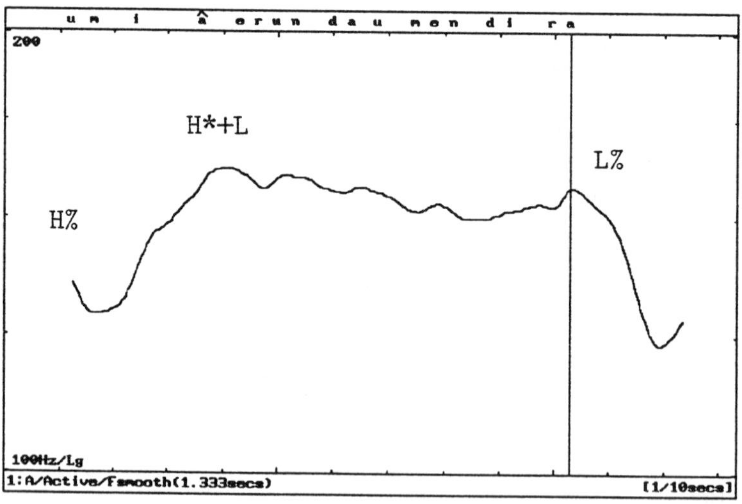
200
H*+L
L%
H%
100Hz/Lg
1:A/Active/Fsmooth(1.333secs)
[1/10secs]

Fig. 38

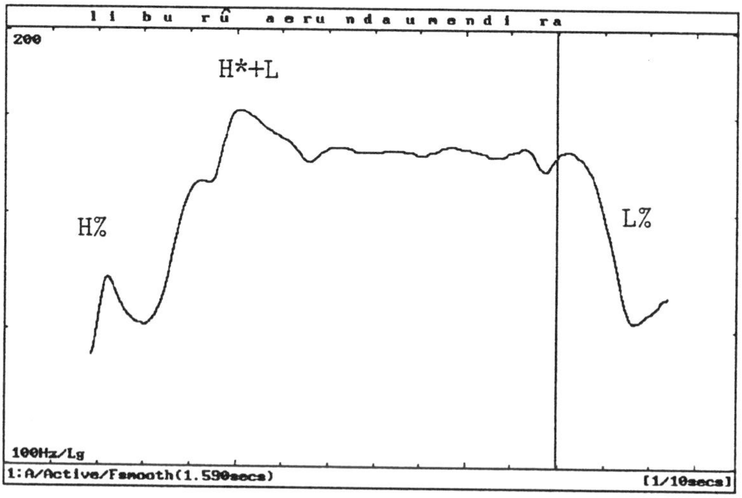
l i b u r û a e r u n d a u m e n d i r a
200
H*+L
H%
L%
100Hz/Lg
1:A/Active/Fsmooth(1.590secs)
[1/10secs]

Fig. 39

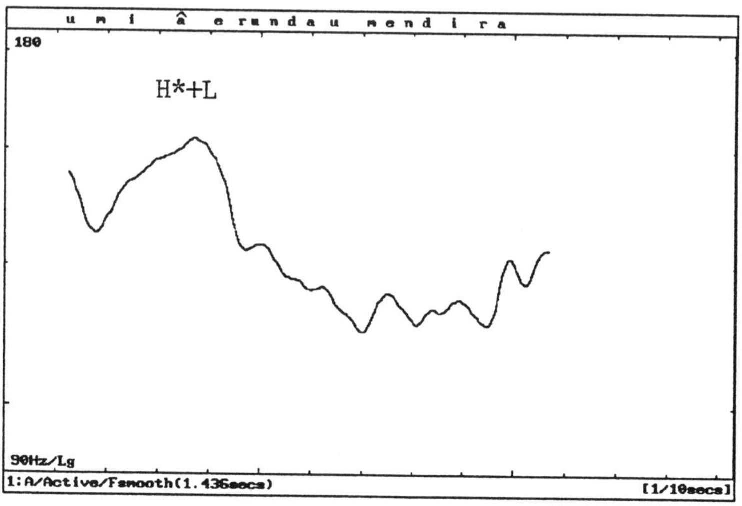
u m i â e r m n d a u m e n d i r a
180
H*+L
90Hz/Lg
1:A/Active/Fsmooth(1.436secs)
[1/10secs]

Fig. 40

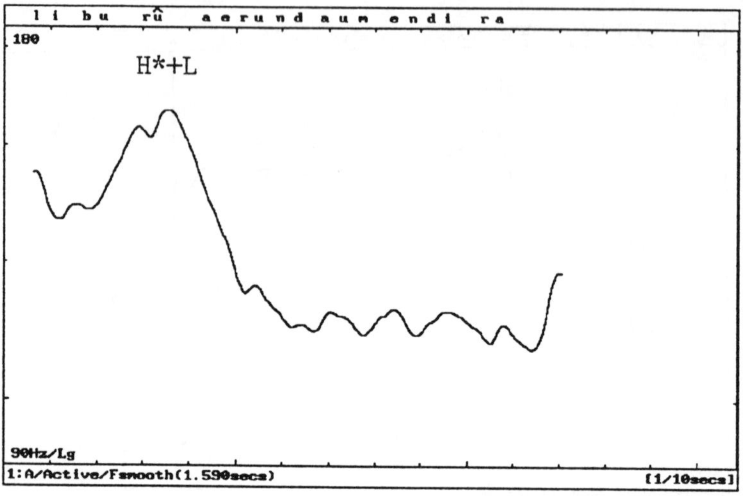
l i b u r û a e r u n d a u m e n d i r a
180
H*+L
90Hz/Lg
1:A/Active/Fsmooth(1.590secs)
[1/10secs]

Fig. 41

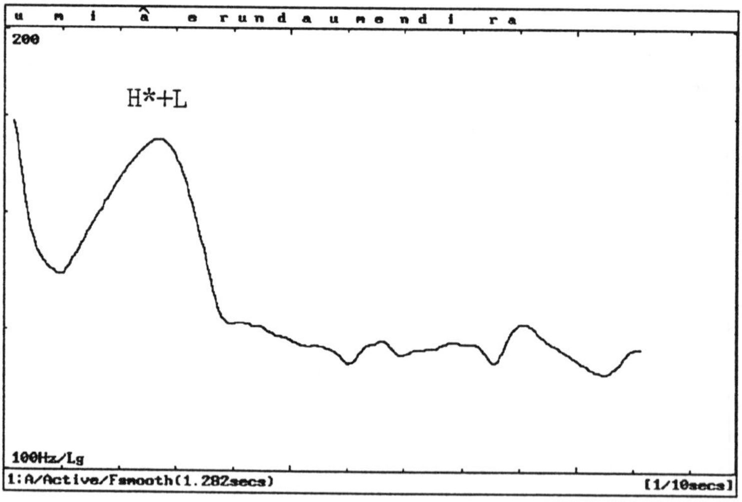
u m i â e r u n d a u m e n d i r a
200
H*+L
100Hz/Lg
1:A/Active/Fsmooth(1.282secs)
[1/10secs]

Fig. 42

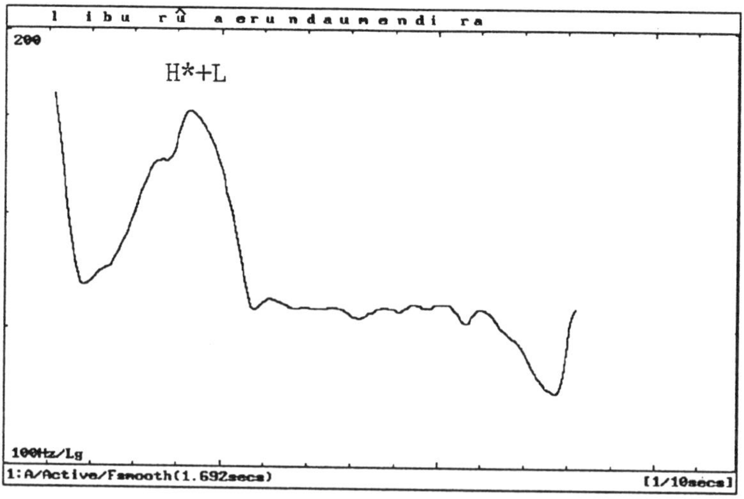
l i b u r ú a e r u n d a u m e n d i r a
200
H*+L
100Hz/Lg
1:A/Active/Fsmooth(1.692secs)
[1/10secs]

Fig. 43

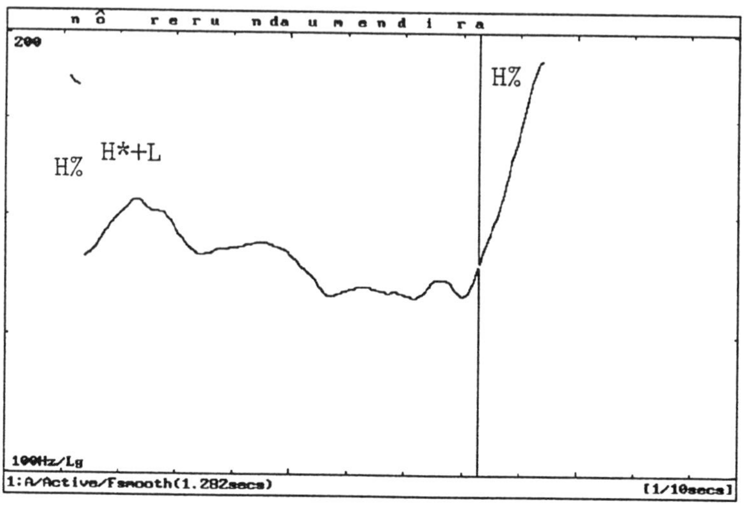
n ó r e r u n da u m e n d i r a
200
H%
H%
H*+L
100Hz/Lg
1:A/Active/Fsmooth(1.282secs)
[1/10secs]

Fig. 44

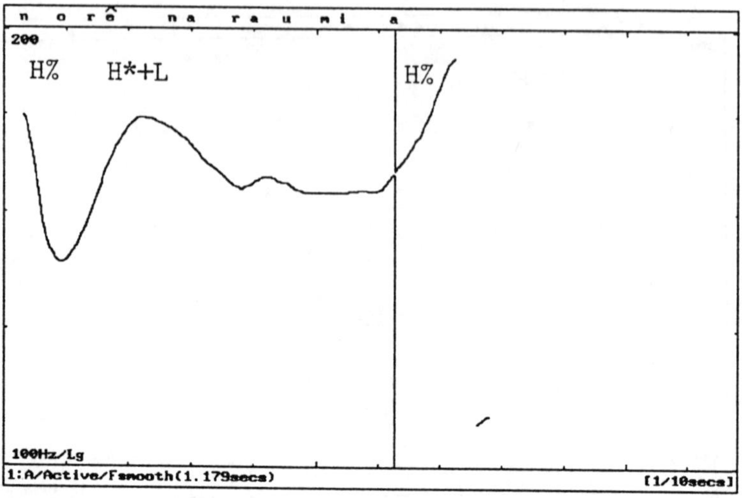
n o r ô na r a u m i a
200
H%
H*+L
H%
100Hz/Lg
1:A/Active/Fsmooth(1.179secs)
[1/10secs]

Fig. 45

Notes

* I wish to thank José Ignacio Hualde for his encouragement to write this article, as well as for his feedback on the first draft of this paper. Pilar Prieto and Paloma García Bellido provided me with detailed comments and suggestions on a pre-final version which ultimately led to a an improved product, I hope. This work also benefited from the questions and comments raised by the audience at the Linguistic Colloquium Series at the University of Deusto, in the Basque Country, where parts of this paper were presented. I also want to thank Fernando Martínez-Gil for his patient editorial help. The usual disclaimer applies. This research was funded by a doctoral fellowship from the Department of Education, Universities, and Research of the Basque Government.

1 Pierrehumbert (1980) also made use of H*+H, but in Beckman and Pierrehumbert (1986) this is reanalyzed as a sequence of two single H* tones.

2 Following Bruce's (1977) analysis of Swedish intonational patterns, Pierrehumbert (1980) identifies another kind of tone occurring at the end of the intonation phrase. This is the *phrase accent*, which is located shortly after the nuclear pitch accent and before the boundary tone. Like boundary tones, phrase accents can be only H and L (H^- and L^- in Pierrehumbert's notation). In Beckman and Pierrehumbert (1986) the phrase accent is reanalyzed as a terminal tone for a prosodic constituent smaller than the intonational phrase, namely the intermediate phrase.

3 I follow the original source in including phrase accents, but I have omitted the hyphen which marks unstarred tones of bitonal pitch accents, to avoid confusion with phrase accent notation, as in Beckman and Pierrehumbert (1986).

4 Pierrehumbert does not specify what the pragmatic meaning associated to the tune represented in (c) could be.

5 Cf. Hualde, Elordieta and Elordieta (1994) for a complete paradigm of accented and unaccented morphemes, as well as a vocabulary listing of all the roots in the lexicon of Lekeitio Basque.

6 I indicate accented morphemes by writing an apostrophe before the morpheme.

7 In (3) and in subsequent examples, dots indicate syllable boundaries. The following abbreviations are used in this article: ABS = absolutive, ERG = ergative, DAT = dative, GEN = genitive, BEN = benefactive, COM/INST = comitative/instrumental, INES = inesive, ALL = allative, ABL = ablative, GEN-LOC = genitive locative.

8 The accentual system of Lekeitio was first described by Azkue (1923, 1931, 1932), although the reader should be warned that the author refers to it as the general Basque accentual system. Naturally, this is far from being true, as the work of several researchers has demonstrated the existence of different accentual types among Basque dialects (Larrasquet 1928, Altube 1934, Lafon 1935, Michelena 1958, 1972, 1976, 1977, Basterrechea 1974, 1975, Jacobsen 1978, Hualde 1989, 1990, 1991abc, 1992, 1993bc, 1994, to appear b, Hualde and Sagarzazu 1991, Jansen 1992, Gaminde and

Hualde, to appear). Cf. also Preface 2 of Hualde, Elordieta and Elordieta (1994), in which some misinterpretations resulting from Azkue's work are discussed.

9 The following abbreviations are used in (7): PLAC = place-adjective forming; COMP = comparative; SUPERL = superlative; EXCESS = excessive; FREQ = frequentative. For a complete list of derivational suffixes along with their accentual properties, see Hualde, Elordieta and Elordieta (1994: 152-162).

10 Cf. Hualde, Elordieta, and Elordieta (1994: 56, and section 3.4) for an extensive list of compound forms in Lekeitio Basque.

11 There is an alternative analysis, proposed by Hualde (1991a), which is to posit a High tone for the accented morpheme in the underlying representation, as well as the insertion of a Low tone on the syllable immediately following (i.e., the last syllable). This analysis is similar to the one Haraguchi (1977) and Poser (1984) suggest for Japanese accentuation, with the difference that the Low tone spreads rightward in Japanese, in cases where there is more than one syllable or mora following the accented mora. In Lekeitio this is impossible, because there is only one syllable after the accented one (or none, in phrase-final unaccented words, as we will see later). We choose the analysis of a H*+L pitch accent over Hualde's for reasons of simplicity: it eliminates the need to refer to two insertion rules, one for H and another one for L.

12 To be precise, Pierrehumbert and Beckman (1988) posit a separate mora tier, which contains the mora to which the lexical tone associates. Given the absence of any role played by the mora in Lekeitio Basque for metrical and tonal purposes, I omit this tier from the representation in (14).

13 The fundamental frequency contours in this paper were obtained using the speech analysis system called *Computerized Extraction of Components of Intonation in Language* (CECIL), version 2.0, developed by the Summer Institute of Linguistics. The recordings correspond to a native speaker of Lekeitio Basque.

14 From now on and for ease of exposition, I will represent the phonetic realization of lexical accents by inserting two association lines, one linking the L tone with the stressed syllable, and another one linking the L tone with the following syllable. The reader should bear in mind, however, that both tones are phonologically associated with the penultimate syllable.

15 We could also analyze this L tone as an initial L% boundary tone of the level of the utterance, and then posit a linking of this L% tone to the initial syllable of the utterance (cf. Pierrehumbert and Beckman 1988 for an analysis of Japanese tone structure along these lines).

16 I am grateful to Paloma García Bellido for helpful discussion of this point.

17 This is similar to the Accent Condition on Minor Phrasing that Selkirk and Tateishi (1988) formulate for Japanese.

18 Unlike Japanese, which limits the number of words in an accentual phrase to three, Lekeitio Basque imposes no restrictions on the number of words that can appear in an accentual phrase. One can find long strings of unaccented words in an accentual phrase, before a pitch accent marking the accentual phrase boundary is reached. This effect is exemplified in (i):

```
(i)   L% H   H    H  H   H  H  H     H  H  H   H    H*+L
      |  |   |    |  |   |  |  |     |  |  |   |    |/
      gu.re  al.bo.ko    erri.ko     a.ba.de   sa.rra
      our    side-GEN-LOC town-GEN-LOC priest  old
      'The old priest from the town next to us'
```

19 Deaccenting of pitch accents after the nuclear stress in an utterance can be observed in Japanese, English, and Spanish, among many other languages, but this is not a universal property. In Swedish, for example, pitch accents can occur non-deaccented after the sentence stress (cf. Pierrehumbert and Beckman 1988: 246-251, as well as the discussion in section 7.1).

20 It is important to remember that the only syntactic elements that can be focalized are those contained in the phrase immediately preceding the verb. Although the two words preceding the verb in (50) and (51) constitute independent accentual phrases, they form part of the object NP preceding the verb:

(i) [$_{NP}$ amáyen diruà] [$_{VP}$ emon nau]
'(S)he has given me Amaya's money'

A word not contained in the phrase adjacent to the verb cannot be focalized, irrespective of whether or not it is accented:

(ii) *[$_{NP}$ lagunâk] [$_{NP}$ amáyen diruà] [$_{VP}$ emon nau]
'The friend has given me Amaya's money'

(iii) *[$_{NP}$ lagûnak] [$_{NP}$ amáyen diruà] [$_{VP}$ emon nábe]
'The friends have given me Amaya's money'

References

Altube, Seber. 1934. *Observaciones al tratado de 'Morfología vasca' de Don R. M. de Azkue*. Bermeo: Gaubeka. [Reprinted in 1969 with vol. 3 of Azkue 1969 (1923)].

Azkue, Resurrección M. 1923. *Morfología vasca*. Bilbao: Academia de la Lengua Vasca. [Reprinted in 1969, 3 volumes. Bilbao: La gran enciclopedia vasca].

Azkue, Resurrección M. 1931. Del acento tónico vasco en algunos de sus dialectos. *Euskera* 4.282-318, part I.

Azkue, Resurrección M. 1932. Del acento tónico vasco en algunos de sus dialectos. *Euskera* 6.3-50, part II.

Basterrechea, José. 1974. Estudios sobre entonación vasca según el habla de Guernica. *Fontes Linguae Vasconum* 18.353-393, part I.

Basterrechea, José. 1975. Estudios sobre entonación vasca según el habla de Guernica. *Fontes Linguae Vasconum* 21.289-338, part II.

Beckman, Mary. 1986. *Stress and Non-Stress Accent*. Dordrecht: Foris.

Beckman, Mary, and Janet Pierrehumbert. 1986. Intonational structure in Japanese and English. *Phonology Yearbook* 3.255-309.

Bruce, Gösta. 1977. Swedish word accents in sentence perspective. *Travaux de l'Institut de Linguistique de Lund* 12. Malmö: CWK Gleerup.

Chomsky, Noam. 1993. A minimalist program for linguistic theory. *The View from Building 20*, ed. Kenneth Hale and Samuel Jay Keyser, 1-52. Cambridge, Mass.: MIT Press.

Chomsky, Noam. 1994. Bare phrase structure. *MIT Occasional Papers in Linguistics* 5. Cambridge, Mass.: MIT Working Papers in Linguistics.

Chomsky, Noam. 1995. *The Minimalist Program*. Cambridge, Mass.: MIT Press.

Chomsky, Noam, and Morris Halle. 1968. *The Sound Pattern of English*. New York: Harper and Row.

Cinque, Guglielmo. 1993. A null theory of phrase and compound stress. *Linguistic Inquiry* 24.239-297.

Elordieta, Gorka. 1994. Answer to qualifying exam question #2. Los Angeles, CA: University of Southern California, ms.

Gaminde, Iñaki, and José Ignacio Hualde. To appear. Euskal azentu-ereduen atlaserako: zenbait isoglosa. *Anuario del Seminario de Filología Vasca Julio de Urquijo*.

Goldsmith, John. 1976. *Autosegmental Phonology*. Doctoral dissertation, MIT. [Published in 1979, New York: Garland].

Halle, Morris, and Jean-Roger Vergnaud. 1987. *An Essay on Stress*. Cambridge, Mass.: MIT Press.

Haraguchi, Shosuke. 1977. *The Tone Pattern of Japanese: An Autosegmental Theory of Tonology*. Tokyo: Kaitakusha.

Hualde, José Ignacio. 1986. Tone and stress in Basque: a preliminary study. *Anuario del Seminario de Filología Vasca Julio de Urquijo* 3.867-896.

Hualde, José Ignacio. 1989. Acentos vizcaínos. *Anuario del Seminario de Filología Vasca Julio de Urquijo* 23.275-325.

Hualde, José Ignacio. 1990. Euskal azentuaren inguruan. *Anuario del Seminario de Filología Vasca Julio de Urquijo* 24.699-720.

Hualde, José Ignacio. 1991a. A metrical analysis of western Basque pitch accent. University of Illinois, ms.

Hualde, José Ignacio. 1991b. *Basque Phonology*. New York: Routledge.

Hualde, José Ignacio. 1991c. Manuel de Larramendi y el acento vasco. *Anuario del Seminario de Filología Vasca Julio de Urquijo* 25.737-749.

Hualde, José Ignacio. 1992. Notas sobre el sistema acentual de Zeberio. *Anuario del Seminario de Filología Vasca Julio de Urquijo* 26.767-776.

Hualde, José Ignacio. 1993a. On the historical origin of Basque accentuation. *Diachronica* 10.13-50.

Hualde, José Ignacio. 1993b. Topics in Souletin phonology. *Generative Studies in Basque Linguistics*, ed. José Ignacio Hualde and Jon Ortiz de Urbina, 289-327. Philadelphia: John Benjamins.

Hualde, José Ignacio. 1993c. Observaciones acerca de los sistemas acentuales de la zona occidental de Gipuzkoa. *Anuario del Seminario de Filología Vasca Julio de Urquijo* 27.241-263.

Hualde, José Ignacio. 1994. Euskal azentuaren sailkapenaz eta historiaz. Euskal dialektologiako kongresua (Donostia, 1991ko irailaren 21-6), ed. Ricardo Gómez and Joseba A. Lakarra, 189-208. *Supplements of Anuario del Seminario de Filología Vasca Julio de Urquijo* 28. Donostia-San Sebastián: Diputación de Gipuzkoa.

Hualde, José Ignacio. To appear a. Reconstructing the old Basque accentual system: hypotheses and evidence. *On the History of the Basque Language: Studies in Basque Historical Linguistics*, ed. José Ignacio Hualde, Joseba A. Lakarra and Robert L. Trask. Philadelphia: John Benjamins.

Hualde, José Ignacio. To appear b. Basque accentuation. *Word-prosodic Systems of the Languages of Europe*, ed. Harry van der Hulst. Berlin: Mouton.

Hualde, José Ignacio, and Xabier Bilbao. 1993. The prosodic system of the Basque dialect of Getxo: A metrical analysis. *Linguistics* 31.59-85.

Hualde, José Ignacio, Gorka Elordieta and Arantzazu Elordieta. 1993. Focalización y prosodia en vascuence vizcaíno. *Anuario del Seminario de Filología Vasca Julio de Urquijo* 27.731-749.

Hualde, José Ignacio, Gorka Elordieta and Arantzazu Elordieta. 1994. *The Basque Dialect of Lekeitio*. Supplements of the *Anuario del Seminario de Filología Vasca Julio de Urquijo*. Bilbao and Donostia-San Sebastián: Editorial Service of the University of the Basque Country and Diputación de Gipuzkoa.

Hualde, José Ignacio, and Txomin Sagarzazu. 1991. Acentos del Bidasoa: Hondarribia. *Anuario del Seminario de Filología Vasca Julio de Urquijo* 25.139-152.

Jacobsen, William. 1975. Historical implications of the Western Basque tonal accent. University of Nevada, Reno, ms.

Jansen, Wim. 1992. Acento y entonación en Elorrio. *Anuario del Seminario de Filología Vasca Julio de Urquijo* 6.67-109.

Kisseberth, Charles. 1984. Digo tonology. *Autosegmental Studies in Bantu Tone*, ed. George N. Clements and John Goldsmith, 105-182. Dordrecht: Foris.

Lafon, René. 1935. Observations sur la place de l'accent dans quelques formes basques des parlers souletins. *Mélanges de littérature, d'histoire et de philologie offerts à Paul Laumonier par ses èlèves et ses amis*, 635-643. Paris: Librairie E. Droz.

Larrasquet, Jean. 1928. *Action de l'accent dans l'évolution des consonnes étudiée dans le basque souletin*. Paris: Vrin.

Liberman, Mark. 1975. *The Intonation System of English*. Doctoral dissertation, MIT. (Reproduced in 1978 by Indiana University Linguistics Club).

Liberman, Mark, and Janet Pierrehumbert. 1984. Intonational invariance under changes in pitch range and length. *Language Sound Structure*, ed. Mark Aronoff and Richard Oehrle, 157-233. Cambridge, Mass.: MIT Press.

McCawley, James D. 1968. *The Phonological Component of a Grammar of Japanese*. The Hague: Mouton.

Michelena, Luis. 1958. À propos de l'accent Basque. *Bulletin de la Societé de Linguistique* 53.204-233.

Michelena, Luis. 1972. A note on Old Labourdin accentuation. *Anuario del Seminario de Filología Vasca Julio de Urquijo* 6.110-120.

Michelena, Luis. 1976. Acentuación alto-navarra. *Fontes Linguae Vasconum* 23.147-162.

Michelena, Luis. 1977. *Fonética histórica vasca* (2nd ed). Donostia-San Sebastián: Diputación de Gipuzkoa.

Navarro Tomás, Tomás. 1944. *Manual de entonación española*. New York: Hispanic Institute in the United States.

Nespor, Marina, and Irene Vogel. 1986. *Prosodic Phonology*. Dordrecht: Foris.

Pierrehumbert, Janet. 1980. *The Phonetics and Phonology of English Intonation*. Doctoral dissertation, MIT. (Reproduced in 1987 by Indiana University Linguistics Club).

Pierrehumbert, Janet, and Mary Beckman. 1988. *Japanese Tone Structure*. Cambridge, Mass.: MIT Press.

Poser, William J. 1984. *The Phonetics and Phonology of Tone and Intonation in Japanese*. Doctoral dissertation, MIT.

Pulleyblank, Douglas. 1983. *Tone in Lexical Phonology*. Doctoral dissertation, MIT.

Selkirk, Elisabeth, and Koichi Tateishi. 1988. Constraints on minor phrase formation in Japanese. *Chicago Linguistic Society* 24.316-336.

Selkirk, Elisabeth, and Koichi Tateishi. 1991. Syntax and downstep in Japanese. *Interdisciplinary Approaches to Language: Essays in Honor of S.-Y. Kuroda*, ed. Carol Georgopoulos and Roberta Ishihara, 519-544. Dordrecht: Kluwer.

Sosa, Juan Manuel. 1991. *Fonética y fonología de la entonación del español hispanoamericano*. Doctoral dissertation, University of Massachusetts at Amherst.

2

Rules vs. constraints: Palatalization in Biscayan Basque and related phenomena

JOSÉ IGNACIO HUALDE

1 Introduction*

Perhaps the most important development in phonological theory in recent years has been a shift from rules and derivations to declarative models based on constraints. Proposals along this line include work such as Bird (1990), Scobbie (1991a, 1991b), Paradis (1988), Calabrese (1988, 1991), and the papers in Goldsmith (1993a), among others. However without a doubt the most influential model, if we judge by the amount of work that is being produced within this framework, is Optimality Theory (henceforth OT, cf. McCarthy and Prince 1993a, 1993b, Prince and Smolensky 1993, and a rapidly growing bibliography).

The reanalysis of some set of phonological data using a constraint-based or nonderivational approach may be motivated by the author's basic assumptions about the nature of the phonological component of languages. For anyone who holds the view that phonological derivations with ordered rules are cognitively implausible, the demonstration that facts that had been analyzed as requiring rule ordering can also be analyzed without ordered rules may be enough of a reason to justify presenting a reanalysis. The reanalysis need not be simpler or superior in any manner; simply showing that it is possible may be sufficient. But, of course, anyone who does this cannot expect other researchers with different views about what is cognitively plausible or implausible to immediately accept the reanalysis as improving on previous work. Some work that is being produced within OT falls into this category. In such cases, the goal of the author is to show that some phenomena that had been previously analyzed using certain derivational devices can also be accounted for in the OT framework. This type of work is necessary in any transition. However, the more interesting results are those which show us that we can obtain a deeper understanding of the facts by viewing them in a certain way rather than in another; in this case, why it is preferable to interpret phonology as being based on constraints rather than on ordered rules. This is what I intend to do in this paper. What I will try to demonstrate is that there are cases where a constraint-based approach provides a better analysis in terms of simplicity and insightfulness than is possible in a rule-based approach.

This paper discusses a set of facts in Basque which, in a rule-based analysis, appears to require a complex order of rules, with one rule applying both before and after another rule. That is, when the facts are analyzed in terms of rules, one must postulate that a rule A is sandwiched between two distinct and separate applications of another rule B, producing an order BAB. What I want to show in this paper is that if we instead adopt a constraint-based approach, the complexity of the analysis disappears. I will argue that an analysis in terms of constraints is not only simpler than a rule-based analysis but also more satisfactory in that it allows us to gain a better understanding of the phenomenon. The facts that I will be concerned with involve the interaction between the processes of Nasal Assimilation and Palatalization in some Biscayan Basque varieties. These facts were analyzed as involving a complex interaction of lexical and postlexical applications of rules in Hualde (1991a).

2 Palatalization and Nasal Assimilation in Lekeitio Basque: A rule-based analysis

Certain Basque varieties have a process whereby coronal consonants are palatalized after a front high vocoid. As the examples in (1) show, in Lekeitio /n/, /l/, and /t/ are palatalized after nuclear or non-nuclear /i/:[1]

(1)	/bi-na/	bi[ɲ]a	'two for each'
	/ʒakin/	ʒaki[ɲ]	'to know'
	/min-a/	mi[ɲ]a	'the pain'
	/mutil-a/	muti[λ]a	'the boy'
	/abil/	abi[λ]	'skillful'
	/amai-tu/	amai[c]u	'to finish'
	/mendi-tik/	mendí[c]ik	'from the mountain'

The consonant /d/ shows more complex behavior. This consonant is palatalized when a lateral or a nasal intervenes between the trigger /i/ and /d/, as in (2a) (a context in which /t/ also undergoes Palatalization), but not when it is directly preceded by /i/, as shown in (2b):

(2) a.	/ein dau/	ei[ɲɟ]au	‘s/he has done it’
	/il da/	i[ʎɟ]a	‘s/he has died’
	/indar/	i[ɲɟ]ar	‘strength’
	/martin da/	Marti[ɲɟ]a	‘it is Martin’
	/pinta/	pi[ɲc]a	‘paint’
b.	/bide/	bi[ð]e, bi[ɾ]e,*bi[ɟ]e,	‘path’
	/idi/	i[ð]i, i[ɾ]i, *i[ɟ]i,	‘ox’

The lack of palatalization in the case where /d/ is found directly after /i/ clearly has to do with the fact that in this intervocalic context it is realized as a continuant segment [ð] or [ɾ]. To explain the palatalization of /d/ and /t/ in the sequences /int/, /ind/, /ild/, /ilt/, in Hualde (1991a) I proposed that the rule of Palatalization applies to the output of a rule of Nasal and Lateral Assimilation, which produces homorganic clusters sharing a single point of articulation node. The single coronal node shared by the two consonants receives a dorsal specification from a preceding high front vocoid producing the apparent result of iterative palatalization. This is illustrated in (3):

(3) *Palatalization in homorganic clusters*

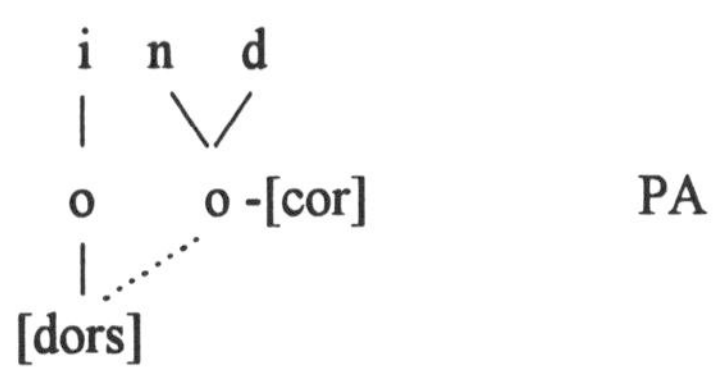

The rule of Nasal (and Lateral) Assimilation which creates the complex structures upon which Palatalization applies is a general, obligatory rule in the language, as can be seen in the examples in (4):

(4)	*Nasal Assimilation*	
	egu[m] bat	‘one day’
	egu[n̪] dának	‘all days’
	egu[ŋ] gorri	‘red day’

Before pause or a vowel, word-final nasals (and laterals) are also neutralized, being realized as alveolar, unless they are preceded by a high front vocoid, in which case they surface as palatal:

(5) *Nasal Neutralization*

esa[n]	'to say'
emo[n]	'to give'
artu[n]	'to take'
ʒaki[ɲ]	'to know'
*-m	

The process of Nasal (and Lateral) Assimilation also conditions the realization of /d/ (and the other voiced obstruents) as noncontinuant. As in standard Spanish, in Basque, voiced obstruents are realized as stops precisely in those contexts where homorganic clusters are created: after a nasal and, in the case of /d/, also after a lateral. We thus must postulate an ordering of rules as in (6):

(6) *Rule ordering*

1. Nasal Neutralization and Assimilation
2. Palatalization

However, the ordering of the rules postulated in (6) raises some serious problems. To begin with, whereas Nasal Assimilation applies freely across word boundaries, as the examples above in (4) show, Palatalization is a lexical rule, restricted to certain morphological environments. As shown in (7), Palatalization does not take place across word boundaries:

(7) *Palatalization is a lexical rule*

saldi [n]ekatu , *[ɲ]	'tired horse'
amabi [n]eska, *[ɲ]	'twelve girls'

The only case where Palatalization applies across syntactic word boundaries is in cases of cliticization. Thus Palatalization (optionally) applies with the copula *da* 'is', which behaves like a clitic, (8a); but not when the copula carries a complementizer (8b), in which case it is an independent phonological word. Nor does the rule of Palatalization apply with other finite verbal forms, (8c):

(8) a. /martin da/ Marti[ɲɟ]a 'it is Martin'
b. /martin da-la/ Marti[n̪d]ala 'that it is Martin'
c. /martin dator/ Marti[n̪d]ator 'Martin is coming'

Clitic groups (in the sense given to this term in Nespor and Vogel 1986; that is, sequences of morphological word + clitic) constitute single word domains for the application of phonological rules (i.e., phonological words), independently of their syntactic status. We can thus maintain the generalization that Palatalization is restricted to the word-internal domain, where by word we must understand a phonological word, including clitic groups.

As mentioned, Nasal Assimilation, on the other hand, is a postlexical rule, which applies across the board. Under the standard assumption that lexical rules precede postlexical rules in their application, the lexical and postlexical status of Palatalization and Nasal Assimilation, respectively, is at odds with the ordering that we have established above in (6).

(9) *1st problem for ordering in (6)*:
- Palatalization is a lexical rule, cf. (7), (8)
- Nasal Assimilation is a postlexical rule , cf. (4)

Another problem is that, when both rules of Palatalization and Nasal Assimilation could apply in a given example producing different outputs, the process that takes precedence is Nasal Assimilation, as shown in (10c). It therefore appears that Nasal Assimilation can override the effects of Palatalization:

(10) *2nd problem for ordering in (6): Nasal Assimilation overrides Palatalization*:
a. Marti[ɲ]
b. Marti[ɲ] etorri da 'Martin has come'
c. Marti[m] bakarrik 'only Martin'

From the considerations in (9) and (10) we arrive at the order in (11):

(11) *Rule ordering required from the facts in (9) and (10)*
1. Palatalization
2. Nasal Assimilation

The ordering in (11) is, of course, the opposite of that assumed above in (6) as being necessary for the correct analysis of Palatalization in consonant clusters. Now, within the Theory of Lexical Phonology, this situation is not as contradictory as it may seem. The Lexical Phonology model allows the application of the same rule in several components, which may produce situations in which a given phonological rule applies both before and after some other rule. In Hualde (1991a), where this theoretical model is assumed, it is thus proposed that, whereas Palatalization is a purely lexical rule, Nasal Assimilation applies both lexically and postlexically. Within the lexicon, Nasal Assimilation is ordered before Palatalization, as indicated in (12):

(12) *Rule ordering* (final)

Lexical:	Nasal Assimilation
	Palatalization
Postlexical:	Nasal Assimilation

Given the order in (12), we can account for all the facts that have been mentioned. Some sample derivations are given in (13):

(13)	kanpo 'outside'	bina 'two by two'	indar 'strength'	min danak 'all pains'	egun bat 'one day'
Lexical					
N Assim	kampo	--	in̪dar	--	--
Pal	--	biɲa	iɲɟar	miɲ	--
Postlexical					
N Assim				min̪ danak	egum bat
	ka[m]po	bi[ɲ]a	i[ɲɟ]ar	mi[n̪] danak	egu[m] bat

In this derivation, the postlexical application of Nasal Assimilation can undo the effects of Palatalization, as the following examples make clear:

(14)	martin	martin bakarrik	'only M'
<u>Lexical</u>			
N Assim	--	--	
Pal	martiɲ	martiɲ	
<u>Postlexical</u>			
N Assim	--	marti[m] bakarrik	
	Marti[ɲ]	Marti[m] bakarrik	

In the derivation in the right column of (14), a word-final nasal which becomes palatal lexically loses this point of articulation postlexically adopting the bilabial point of the following consonant. Let us now considered the examples in (15). The contrast between the palatalization of the sequence /nd/ in *Marti*[ɲɟ]*a* 'it is Martin' and the absence of palatalization in *Marti*[n̪d]*ator* 'M is coming' is explained by the fact that the /ind/ sequence is present lexically in the first example, which constitutes a single phonological word (a clitic group), but not in the second example. In /martin-da/, Nasal Assimilation in its lexical application creates a homorganic dental cluster which serves as a target for the rule of Palatalization. In /martin dator/, on the other hand, the nasal undergoes Palatalization in the sequence /in/ at the lexical level, where the following /d/ is not yet visible; however the palatalization is erased at the postlexical level, by the application of Nasal Assimilation at this level:

(15)	Marti[ɲɟ]a 'it is M'	Marti[n̪d]ator 'Martin is coming'
	martin-da	martin dator
<u>Lexical</u>		
N Assim	martin̪ da	--
Pal	martiɲɟa	martiɲ
<u>Postlexical</u>		
N Assim	--	marti[n̪] dator

This analysis, which I defended in Hualde (1991a), works in the sense that it produces the correct mappings between inputs and outputs. Nevertheless, quite obviously this is a very complicated analysis by any standards. My view, now, is that the complexity is not in the facts, but rather it is forced onto the analysis by the theoretical model within which it is cast. Furthermore, the complexity all but disappears once we replace the rule-based approach that has been employed by a constraint-based one.

3 A constraint-based analysis

In Lekeitio Basque, nasals in a rhyme (which are always phonologically neutralized, cf. (5)) are subject to two potentially conflicting output constraints. On the one hand, they must be realized as palatal after a front high vocoid (within word domains). On the other, they must agree in point of articulation with a following consonant. Well-formed outputs in the language must obey these constraints. Thus the examples in (16a) are well-formed, but those in (16b) are not:

(16) a. ka[m]po 'outside', a[ŋ]go 'of there', Marti[ɲ]
b. *ka[n]po, *ka[ŋ]po, *a[m]go, *a[ɲ]go, *Marti[m], *Marti[n], *Marti[ŋ]

Now, there are cases where these two constraints are in conflict. This is the case when the nasal is both preceded by /i/ and followed by a consonant, as in the examples in (17a). It is clearly impossible for the syllable-final nasal to obey both constraints simultaneously. In this kind of situation, which work in OT has shown is not at all uncommon, the language must solve the conflict by giving priority to one of the incompatible constraints over the other. The fact that, in our case, the correct outputs are as in (17b) shows that in Lekeitio Basque Nasal Assimilation dominates Palatalization:

(17)	a.	ai/n/ka 'leg'	Marti/n/ bakárrik	'only Martin'
	b.	ai[ŋ]ka	Marti[m] bakárrik	

The constraints that we are dealing with and their ranking are thus as in (18):

(18) *Constraints*:

PAL: In word domains (including clitic groups), noncontinuant coronals are palatal after /i/ (shared [dorsal] node)

N-ASSIM: A nasal shares a PA node with an immediately following consonant.

Ranking:

N-ASSIM dominates PAL

In case of conflict, the preferred input is the one that obeys Nasal Assimilation, as shown in (19):

(19)

	N-ASSIM	PAL
☞ ai[ŋ]ka		*
ai[ɲ]ka	*!	
ai[n]ka	*!	*

Let us consider now the case of a phonological-word-internal /ind/ sequence, as in (20a) /indar/ 'strength' or /martin-da/ 'it is Martin'. Unlike in the examples in (17) above, in this case, it is possible for the output to satisfy both constraints. This is because the consonant following the nasal is a palatalizable one and the relevant sequence is included within a single word domain. It is thus possible for the nasal to surface as palatal after /i/ and simultaneously as homorganic with a following consonant. And this is what the surface forms show, (20b):

(20) a. i/nd/ar 'strength' Marti/nd/a 'it is Martin'
b. i[ɲɟ]ar Marti[ɲɟ]a

In (21), the first form given satisfies Nasal Assimilation but not Palatalization, which is the solution for the example in (19) above. In this case, however, there is a better solution: namely, the third form that is given, which satisfies both constraints. This form is thus preferred:

(21)

	N-ASSIM	PAL
Marti[n̪] da		*!
Marti[ɲ] da	*!	
☞ Marti[ɲɟ]a		

So far, we have considered the treatment of sequences arising within phonological word domains, including clitic groups. As mentioned above, the PAL constraint is not relevant outside of this domain. Within an OT analysis, the irrelevance of a constraint is obtained by ranking this constraint below another constraint. In our particular case, we can interpret the facts as indicating that it is more important to keep a word-initial consonant unaltered across contexts than to palatalized this consonant. The higher ranking constraint would thus be a member of the family of constraints known collectively as Faithfulness (FAITH). This is a universal constraint which requires inputs and outputs to be identical. This general constraint can be expanded into a family of constraints requiring identity in specific positions or specific features. In our case, we are concerned with the invariability of word-initial consonants. The specific instantiation of the FAITH constraint that we must rank above PAL can be defined as follows:

(22) FAITH-WIC:
A word-initial consonant in a given lexical item has an invariable feature composition.

The ranking of FAITH-WIC above PAL determines that the initial consonant of *neska* 'girl' should remain an alveolar nasal in *bi* [n]*eska* 'two girls' where it is preceded by a palatalizing segment in a different word:

(23)

	FAITH-WIC	PAL
☞ bi [n]eska		*
bi [ɲ]eska	*!	

In a word-internal example such as /bi-na/ 'two by two', on the other hand, PAL is undominated by any other relevant constraints and *bi*[ɲ]*a* is selected as the best output.

It was pointed out before that /inC/ sequences are treated identically word-internally and across word boundaries in some cases but not in all cases. When the consonant following the nasal is not a palatalizable one (a noncoronal), the results are the same in both contexts: the nasal takes the point of articulation of the following consonant, as shown above in (17). When the word-initial consonant is a coronal, on the other hand, the output is different in phonological word-internal environments (including clitic groups) and across word boundaries, as was also mentioned above (cf. (8)). In lexical domains *i*[ɲɟ]*ar* 'strength' is preferred over **i*[n̪d]*ar* and with cliticization of the copula we obtain *Marti*[ɲɟ]*a* 'it is Martin'. Across phonological word boundaries, in contrast, we have realizations such as *Marti*[n̪d]*ator* and not **Marti*[ɲɟ]*a tor* 'Martin is coming'. The palatalization of the /d/ is prevented when this is a word-initial consonant. This is a consequence of FAITH-WIC being ranked above PAL. The relative ranking of the constraints is responsible for these results. In (24) FAITH-WIC and N-ASSIM are unranked, since they do not conflict with each other. They are both ranked above PAL:

(24)

	FAITH-WIC	N-ASSIM	PAL
☞ i[ɲɟ]ar			
i[n̪d]ar			*!
i[md]ar		*!	*

	FAITH-WIC	N-ASSIM	PAL
☞ Marti[n̪d]ator			*
Marti[ɲɟ]a tor	*!		
Marti[nd]ator		*!	*

None of the candidates in the first set of examples in (24) incurs in a violation of FAITH-WIC. Since there is no word-initial consonant, all of them satisfy this requirement vacuously. As in (21), the candidate that satisfies the remaining two constraints is chosen. The candidates in the second set in (24) contain two phonological words. The presence of a word-initial consonant makes FAITH-WIC relevant for this example. The preferred candidate is the one which does not violate either of the two top-ranked constraints, FAITH-WIC and N-ASSIM.

This analysis in terms of constraints eliminates the need for a complex order of operations which is required in a rule-based approach. However, the advantage of this analysis is not only one of simplicity. The analysis is also more insightful in that it allows us a deeper understanding of the facts of the language than is possible within the rule-based analysis given above in section 2. In a case like this I believe we can speak of true progress in the analysis of phonological facts.

4 Interdialectal variation

It has often been emphasized in the OT literature that analyses in terms of ranked and violable constraints offer a more appropriate means for accounting for cross-linguistic variation than rule-based approaches. As was shown in Hualde (1991a), the palatalization phenomenon in Basque is subject to some degree of interdialectal variation. At least certain aspects of this variation are more insightfully characterized in terms of constraint interaction. Let us consider the following examples in the dialects of Lekeitio and Getxo, in (25):

(25)	Lekeitio	Getxo	
	mi[ɲ]	mi[n]	'pain'
	mi[ɲ]a	min[ɲ]e	'the pain'
	mi[ɲ] andi	mi[ɲ] andi	'great pain'
	muti[λ]	muti[l]	'boy'
	muti[λ]a	muti[λ]e	'the boy'
	muti[λ] andi	muti[λ] andi	'big boy'

As shown, Getxo differs from Lekeitio in that a word-final /l/ or /n/ is not palatalized unless the following word starts with a vowel (cf. Hualde and Bilbao 1992:22-26). The same situation is obtained in the dialect of Donostia-San Sebastián studied in Iverson and Oñederra (1985) and Hualde (1991a:120-121). In Hualde (1991a) this interdialectal variation is captured by proposing somewhat different rules for each of the two dialects. In Getxo, the rule of Palatalization would make reference to syllable structure, applying only when the target segment is in onset position. In Lekeitio, the position of the segment in the syllable would not be included in the description of the environment for the rule of Palatalization. If we consider the facts in terms of constraints, however, what seems to happen is that the two dialects differ in the way they solve a conflict between Palatalization and a Place Neutralization constraint (P-NEUT) that requires coda sonorants to be coronal, cf. (5) above (an instantiation of the Coda Condition of Prince and Smolensky 1993, McCarthy and Prince 1993a, 1993b):

(26) P-NEUT:
sonorants in a coda are coronal.

In Getxo P-NEUT is ranked higher than PAL. In Lekeitio, the opposite ranking prevails:

(27) *Ranking of P-NEUT and PAL*

a. *Getxo*: P-NEUT » PAL

	P-NEUT	PAL
☞ mi[n]		*
mi[ɲ]	*!	

b. *Lekeitio*: PAL » P-NEUT

	PAL	P-NEUT
mi[n]	*!	
☞ mi[ɲ]		*

In both dialects, P-NEUT is dominated by N-ASSIM, since a nasal in a coda will assimilate in place to a following consonant.

5 Interaction with syllabification

We may now ask why, in Getxo, the word-final nasal palatalizes in the example *mi*[ɲ] *andi* 'great pain' (third example in (22), and similarly for the word-final lateral). The answer obviously has to do with the fact that, in this case, the word-final consonant syllabifies in an onset with the following word-initial vowel. But why do we find syllabification across word boundaries? To answer this question we need to examine syllabification in Basque in some detail. A first approach might be to assume that phonological phrases of the relevant type constitute single domains for syllabification. But this position would not explain the fact that we find some differences in the syllabification of certain sequences of segments depending on whether they are word-internal or occur across word boundaries. The facts are the same in all Basque dialects and are also identical in all relevant respects to the Spanish facts (which have received a considerable amount of attention):

(28) a. *Basque*

le.ku			'place'
a.zu.kre			'sugar'
amak esan	→	a.ma.ke.san	'mother said'
amak lotu	→	a.mak.lo.tu	'mother tied'
		*a.ma.klo.tu	

b. *Spanish*

so.fá			'sofa'
chi.fla, *chif.la			'it maddens'
chef alto	→	che.fal.to	'tall chef'
chef loco	→	chef.lo.co	'crazy chef'
		*che.flo.co	

As the examples in (28) show, a consonant is always syllabified with a following vowel, both word-internally and across word boundaries. On the other hand, onsets are maximized word-internally, but not across word boundaries. That is, a sequence of consonants that can constitute a well-formed onset cluster (which both in Basque and Spanish can only be a group of oral stop or /f/ plus liquid) is syllabified as an onset cluster word-internally, but the same sequence is heterosyllabic when a word-boundary intervenes between both consonants.

In a rule-based approach to syllabification, such as that of Levin (1985), onset maximization is obtained by ordering all onset-building operations before all rules that incorporate segments to the coda. The Spanish facts in (28b) are analyzed in Harris (1983, 1989) and Hualde (1991b) within such a rule-based framework. In particular, in Hualde (1991b) it is postulated that at the lexical level both a CV-rule that adjoins a coda to a following nucleus as onset and an Onset Cluster rule that incorporates a second consonant to the onset if the result is a well-formed onset group apply before any adjunctions in coda position. This ensures the correct syllabification of *so.fá* and *chi.fla*. Consonants that cannot be added to the onset are incorporated into the coda as in the case of both nasals in *can.tan* 'they sing' or the final consonant in *chef*. Postlexically, however, a word-final consonant is moved from the coda to the onset of the following syllable if it is followed by a vowel. This is done by a second, postlexical, application of the CV-rule. On the other hand, the Onset Cluster rule must not reapply postlexically, since onset clusters are not maximized across word boundaries. That is, the order in (29) is proposed:

(29) *Lexical level:*
Nucleus projection
CV-rule
Onset Cluster rule
Coda rules

Postlexical level:
CV-rule

This order of operations gives us derivations like those in (30), where, to save space, syllabified segments are enclosed within parentheses, instead of using the Levin-style N-bar trees employed in Harris (1989) and Hualde (1991b):

(30) a. *Spanish*

	sofa	chifla	chef# alto	chef# loco
LEXICAL				
Nucleus proj	s(o)f(a)	ch(i)fl(a)	ch(e)f (a)lt(o)	ch(e)f l(o)c(o)
CV-rule	(so)(fa)	(chi)f(la)	(che)f (a)l(to)	(che)f (lo)(co)
Onset Cluster		(chi)(fla)		
Coda rule			(chef)	(chef)
lexical output:	(so)(fa)	(chi)(fla)	(chef) (al)(to)	(chef) (lo)(co)
POSTLEXICAL				
CV-rule			(che)(fal)(to)	

b. *Basque*

	azukre	amak# esan	amak# lotu
LEXICAL			
Nucleus proj	(a)z(u)kr(e)	(a)m(a)k (e)s(a)n	(a)m(a)k l(o)t(u)
CV-rule	(a)(zu)k(re)	(a)(ma)k (e)(sa)n	(a)(ma)k (lo)(tu)
Onset Cluster	(a)(zu)(kre)		
Coda rule		(a)(mak) (e)(san)	(a)(mak)
lexical output:	(a)(zu)(kre)	(a)(mak) (e)(san)	(a)(mak) (lo)(tu)
POSTLEXICAL			
CV-rule		(a)(ma)(ke)(san)	

In this account of syllabification in Spanish and Basque, we again find a situation in which a complex order of operations is required in a rule-based approach. Rules must apply in a specific order and one of the rules applies twice, both lexically and postlexically, that is, it applies both before and after some other rules. Again, even though the analysis can account for the facts, it can hardly be said that it gives us a profound understanding of the reasons why the facts are as they are. The analysis does not reveal the universal principles and tendencies that motivate this particular array of syllabification facts. However, it is widely recognized that syllabification obeys universal principles.

To begin with, the CV-rule which forces a VCV sequence to be syllabified as V.CV is a manifestation of a universal principle of avoidance of onsetless syllables (Itô's 1986 Onset Principle (ONSET)). This principle appears as undominated in languages such as Arabic and Farsi where onsetless word-initial syllables are given an epenthetic onset, namely a glottal stop. In Basque and Spanish, the Onset Principle is violated when the only way to satisfy it would be to insert or delete (unparse) a segment. Thus these principles against inserting or unparsing material (collectively known as Faithfulness (FAITH) in the Optimality literature) have a higher status in Basque and Spanish than ONSET:

(31) *Constraints*:

ONSET: every syllable must have an onset.
FAITH: do not insert or unparse phonological material.
Ranking:
FAITH » ONSET

(32)

/ama/	FAITH	ONSET
ʔa.ma	*!	
☞ a.ma		*
am.a		**!

The second and third candidates in (32) incur in, at least, one violation of ONSET, since the word starts with a vowel. The candidate with the fewest number of violations of constraints is chosen.

ONSET is a strong enough constraint in these languages to force the syllabification as a single syllable of CV sequences across word boundaries. This syllabification is in violation of another universal principle, Alignment (ALIGN), which demands that the boundaries of morphological domains and syllables must coincide (McCarthy and Prince 1993b):[2]

(33)

/zuk esan/	FAITH	ONSET	ALIGN
zuk. e.san		*!	
zuk. ʔe.san	*!		
☞ zu.k e.san			*

In languages without syllabification across word boundaries, ALIGN is ranked higher that ONSET.

Now we can understand why syllabification across word boundaries takes place in examples such as *zuk esan* 'you say' but not in *zuk lotu* 'you tie'. In the first of these two examples this syllabification is needed in order not to violate ONSET. In the second, this principle is already satisfied, and maximization of the onset would result in a violation of Alignment. Onset maximization can be considered an effect of NO-CODA, a principle that states that codas must be avoided. This principle is ranked lower than ALIGN in Basque and Spanish:[3]

(34)

	FAITH	ONSET	ALIGN	NO-CODA
a.zuk.re[4]		*		*!
☞ a.zu.kre		*		
☞ zuk.lo.tu				*
zu.klo.tu			*!	

Now we can go back to our palatalization example in Getxo Basque. In *min andi* 'great pain', ONSET requires syllabification across the word boundary and PAL requires the word-final nasal to be palatal. Given the particular hierarchy of constraints in this dialect, *mi.*[ɲ] *an.di* is the best output, since it satisfies both ONSET and PAL. P-NEUT is vacuously satisfied since the word-final consonant is not syllabified in the coda:

(35)

	ONSET	P-NEUT	PAL
☞ mi.[ɲ]an.di			
mi.[n]an. di			*!
mi[ɲ].an.di	*!	*	
mi[n].an.di	*!		*

6 Universal principles and language-specific constraints

A final issue that we should address is that of the nature of the phonological constraints or principles that we have used in our analysis. The strongest hypothesis within OT is that all constraints are universal and that individual grammars can differ only in their ranking. I consider this only as a desideratum. That is, in the analysis of phonological facts one should have the identification of universal principles as a final goal. It is, however, my view that,t together with universal principles, one must also recognize the existence of language-particular constraints. Nevertheless, one should also strive to identify the universal aspects of language-specific constraints (cf. McCarthy 1993). In our analysis of syllable structure in Spanish and Basque, all constraints that have been put to use are of a universal character. Certain aspects of phonological structure such as syllabification and stress are undoubtedly guided by universal principles to a very large extent, as has long been recognized. Long-distance assimilatory phenomena (harmonies) also fall into this category (cf. Cole and Kisseberth 1994). In the realm of purely segmental alternations, on the other hand, we find much more cross-linguistic variation, which I very much doubt could be reduced to different rankings of a set of universal constraints. Nevertheless, as mentioned, the universal principles involved in particular alternations should still be identified.

In this paper, we have dealt primarily with two segmental phonological phenomena in Basque: Nasal Assimilation and Palatalization. Nasal Assimilation is a phenomenon whose frequency in human languages warrants a universal characterization. Indeed, the amount of cross-linguistic variation that Nasal Assimilation presents appears to be reducible to a limited amount of parametrization (or differences in the hierarchies among constraints that are established, in OT terms), as Padgett (1994) shows. As for Palatalization, although in the particular form that it presents in Basque, is a much more peculiar process, we were able to reduce some variation between dialects to a different interaction between constraints. The way Palatalization works in Basque is certainly specific to this language. It is more common, for instance, to have palatalization of consonants triggered by a following vocoid, rather than a preceding one (Iverson and Oñederra 1985); the palatalizing segments may be the velars intead of the coronals, etc. But it is also true that there are certain universal constraints limiting the variation that is possible among palatalization processes. For instance, there appears to be a hierarchy of triggers [j] » [i] » [e], such that if vocalic [i] triggers palatalization, nonvocalic [j] does too, and if [e] triggers this process so do [i] and [j]. To the extent that they are universal, these constraints should be recognized as such. In any event, I hope to have shown that, for the cases that we have examined, even language-particular processes are better understood as wellformedness constraints than as rules. That is, (some) phonological phenomena may be analyzed more insightfully in terms of constraints that in terms of rules even if those constraints are not universal.

Notes

* For comments, I want to thank Eulàlia Bonet, Jennifer Cole, Gorka Elordieta and Jorge Guitart. I am also thankful to audiences at USC and at the January 1994 LSA Meeting, where oral versions of parts of this paper where presented.

1 Younger speakers produce prepalatal affricates [tʃ], [dʒ] instead of the palatal stops [c], [ɟ]. /s/ also palatalizes under similar (but not identical) conditions. The phonology of Lekeitio Basque is discussed in detail in Hualde, Elordieta and Elordieta (1994).

2 ALIGN is, more precisely, a family of constraints.

3 This is essentially the analysis proposed in Hualde (1994, 1995) and, independently, in Colina (1995). A somewhat similar analysis which employs language-particular constraints is found in Morales-Front (1994).

4 Both candidates contain one violation of ONSET since the first syllable of the word is vowel initial.

References

Bird, Steven. 1990. *Constraint-based Phonology*. Doctoral dissertation, Univ. of Edinburgh.

Calabrese, Andrea. 1988. *Towards a Theory of Phonological Alphabets*. Doctoral dissertation, MIT.

Calabrese, Andrea. 1991. *The notion of phonological complexity in phonological theory: a new approach to markedness theory*. Harvard University, ms.

Cole, Jennifer and Charles Kisseberth. 1994. An optimal domains theory of harmony. *Proceedings of FLSM 5*. Studies in the Linguistic Sciences 24.

Cole, Jennifer and John Coleman. 1992. No need for cyclicity in generative grammar. *Chicago Linguistic Society* 28.36-50.

Colina, Sonia. 1995. *A Constraint-based Approach to Syllabification in Spanish, Catalan, and Galician*. Doctoral dissertation, Univ. of Illinois, Urbana.

Goldsmith, John. 1993a. *The Last Phonological Rule: Reflections on Constraints and Derivations*. Chicago and London: Univ. of Chicago.

Goldsmith, John. 1993b. Harmonic phonology. In Goldsmith 1993a, 21-60.

Harris, James. 1983. *Syllable Structure and Stress in Spanish: A Nonlinear Analysis*. Cambridge, Mass.: MIT Press.

Harris, James. 1989. Our present understanding of Spanish syllable structure. *American Spanish Pronunciation: Theoretical and Applied Perspectives*, ed. Peter Bjarkman and Robert Hammond, 151-169. Washington, DC: Georgetown Univ. Press.

Hualde, José I. 1991a. *Basque Phonology*. London and New York: Routledge.

Hualde, José I. 1991b. On Spanish Syllabification. *Current Studies in Spanish Linguistics*, ed. Héctor Campos and Fernando Martínez-Gil, 475-493. Washington, DC: Georgetown Univ. Press.

Hualde, José I. 1991c. Aspiration and resyllabification in Chinato Spanish. *Probus* 3.55-76.

Hualde, José I. 1994. *La silabificación en español*. Univ. of Illinois, ms.

Hualde, José I. 1995. *Rules vs. constraints in Spanish syllabification*. Paper presented at GURT 1995, 2nd Pre-session on Spanish Linguistics, Georgetown Univ.

Hualde, José I. and Xabier Bilbao. 1992. *A Phonological Study of the Basque Dialect of Getxo*. Supplements of *Anuario del Seminario de Filología Vasca 'Julio de Urquijo'* 29. Donostia-San Sebastián: Diputación de Gipuzkoa.

Hualde, José I., Gorka Elordieta and Arantzazu Elordieta. 1994. *The Basque Dialect of Lekeitio*. Bilbao and Donostia-San Sebastián: Univ. of the Basque Country Press and Supplements of *Anuario del Seminario de Filología Vasca 'Julio de Urquijo'*.

Itô, Junko. 1986. *Syllable Theory in Prosodic Phonology*. Doctoral dissertation. Univ. of Massachusetts at Amherst.

Iverson, Gregory and Miren L. Oñederra. 1995. On Basque palatalization. *Folia Linguistica* 19.51-61.

Lakoff, George. 1993. Cognitive phonology. In Goldsmith 1993a, 117-145.

Levin, Juliette. 1985. *A Metrical Theory of Syllabicity*. Doctoral dissertation, MIT.

McCarthy, John and Alan Prince. 1993a. *Prosodic morphology I: Constraint interaction and satisfaction*. University of Massachusetts, Amherst and Rutgers University ms.

McCarthy, John and Alan Prince. 1993b. *Generalized alignment*. University of Massachusetts, Amherst and Rutgers University, ms.

McCarthy, John. 1993. A case of surface constraint violation. *Canadian Journal of Linguistics* 38.

Morales-Front, Alfonso. 1994. *A Constraint-based Approach to Spanish Phonology. Doctoral dissertation*, Univ. of Illinois, Urbana.

Nespor, Marina and Irene Vogel. 1986. *Prosodic Phonology*. Dordrecht: Foris.

Padgett, Jaye. 1994. Stricture and Nasal Place Assimilation. *Natural Language and Linguistic Theory* 12.465-513.

Paradis, Carole. 1988. On constraints and repair strategies. *The Linguistic Review* 6.71-97.

Prince, Alan and Paul Smolensky. 1993. *Optimality Theory: Constraint interaction in Generative Grammar*. Rutgers University and University of Colorado, Boulder, ms.

Scobbie, James. 1991a. *Attribute-value Phonology*. Doctoral dissertation, University of Edinburgh.

Scobbie, James. 1991b. Towards declarative phonology. *Edinburgh Working Papers in Cognitive Science* 7.1-26.

II Catalan

3

On the representation of contrasting rhotics*

EULÀLIA BONET AND JOAN MASCARÓ

0. Introduction

It is well known that the phonetic realization of rhotics varies considerably from language to language, even from dialect to dialect. Rhotics can be realized as flaps, taps, trills (uvular, coronal or bilabial), or as assibilated or fricative variants. They can alternate with a lateral liquid, with glides, and in some cases, a flap can occur as the phonetic realization of a coronal stop in specific environments.

The aspect that has drawn most attention with respect to rhotics, however, is that often, different realizations of rhotics can contrast in a given language; in some environments their distribution is complementary, while in other cases rhotic variants contrast. In this paper we will concentrate on the problem posed by Iberian Romance languages (i.e. Catalan, Portuguese, and Spanish), and will leave aside the case of not so-well-studied languages (Somali, Ngizim, Lak, etc.), which have a somewhat different pattern, but which should be taken into consideration within a more comprehensive account of the phonology of rhotics. The main goal of this article is to draw attention to facts that have not been taken into account previously and to point to an approach of the problems posed by rhotics at a descriptive level. Implementation in a particular theoretical framework is left for further research.

1. The distribution of rhotics

The main concern in the analysis of rhotics in the Iberian Romance languages has been the fact that they appear in complementary distribution in all contexts but one.[1] In Catalan, Portuguese, and Spanish there is a contrast in intervocalic position between the flap and the trill (1). In all other environments, the appearance of a flap or a trill is entirely predictable.[2] In word initial position (2a), and in onset position after a consonant (2b), the trill occurs; the flap appears in the second position of an onset (2c), while in syllable final position (3) the realization of rhotics shows a lot of variation across languages and dialects, and within a dialect it also varies depending on speech rate and other factors. The examples in (1) and (2) are from Catalan; in (3) the last column shows the phonetic value of the rhotic in the intervocalic contrast position:

(1) Contrast cases: Intervocalic position:

	Catalan	*Portuguese*	*Spanish*	
a. **trill**:	[mírə]	[mírə]	[míra]	'myrrh'
b. **flap**:	[míɾə]	[míɾə]	[míɾa]	'(s/he) looks at'

(2) Predictable fixed cases: Non-intervocalic, Onset:

	Catalan	*Portuguese*	*Spanish*	
a. Word initial: **trill**:	[rísk]	[ríʃku]	[rjézɣo]	'risk'
b. 1st in onset, /C__: **trill**	[unrát]	[unráðu]	[onráðo]	'honest'
c. 2nd in onset: **flap**	[fɾέt]	[fɾíu]	[fɾío]	'cold'

(3) Predictable variable cases: Non-intervocalic, Coda: Intervocalic contrast

ma[ɾ] 'sea'	*Catalan (Valencian)*	ɾ / r
ma[ɾ]	*Spanish (Castilian)*	ɾ / r
ma[r], [ɾ]	*Spanish (Mexican)*	ɾ / r
ma[ɾ]	*European Portuguese*	ɾ / R, r
ma[r]	*Catalan (Central)*	ɾ / r
ma[r]	*Spanish (Nicaragua, El Salvador)*	ɾ / r
ma[x]	*Brazilian Portuguese*	ɾ / x

The term intervocalic should be understood as including contexts with a preceding or following surface glide, as in Catalan aura [áwɾə] 'air' glòria [glɔ́rjə] 'glory' (the same results are obtained with the corresponding words in Spanish and Portuguese). In the rest of the paper we will continue to refer to this *intervocoidal* context as *intervocalic*, and *after V*, *before V* has to be interpreted as V = vowel, glide.

2. Previous accounts of Iberian rhotics

In the traditional literature on rhotics, one of the main issues has been how to account for the contrast that appears, as already said, only in intervocalic position. We may distinguish two periods: a) works based on an SPE formalism, or earlier studies, and b) studies that introduce syllable structure. Câmara (1953) posits a single rhotic phoneme /ɾ/ and uses the geminate/nongeminate /ɾɾ/ - /ɾ/ contrast to account for intervocalic [r] - [ɾ].[3] Within generative phonology, all authors[4], starting with Harris (1969), also postulate an underlying geminate flap for the surface intervocalic trill. In Harris (1969) the geminate flap /ɾɾ/ becomes a trill through a specific rule. Wheeler (1979) derives the trill through an independent rule that interprets phonological geminates (i.e. /ll/. /nn/, /ʎʎ/) as [+tense, +long]. In Mascaró (1976) /ɾɾ/ → [r] is arrived at through independently motivated processes. The use of syllable structure introduces some simplifications in the set of rules accounting for the distribution of rhotics. The analysis changes partially when syllable structure is taken into account. In Harris (1983) /ɾɾ/ → [r] is now the result of processes that apply independently. All trills are obtained from underlying flaps through rules. Syllabic structure is incorporated for two environments: onset position after a consonant, and coda position (in emphatic speech), the contexts in (2b) and (3) above. Below, (4a) reproduces Harris' (3.45), and (4b) his (3.49) (we adapt the notation to the IPA).

(4) a. ɾ → r / [+cons] ___ or ɾ → r / [+cons] $_{\sigma}$[___
                |
                R

b. ɾ → r (in emphatic speech)
   |
   R

In the case of underlying geminates (i.e., surface intervocalic trills, context (1) above), the rule in (4a) turns the second flap into a trill: /ɾ ɾ/ → [ɾ r]. This rule precedes another rule that deletes a syllable final flap when followed by a trill, given that on the surface only a single trill occurs: [ɾ r] → [Ø r]. This rule is needed independently to account for cases like the one illustrated in (5a), where a word final flap (or some kind of trill) occurs next to a word initial trill. The rule responsible for this effect is given in (5b), and corresponds to Harris' (3.44):

(5) a. *salir rápido*: *sal*[ír]*ápido* 'to leave rapidly'
b. ɾ → ø / ___r

Word initial trills, context (2a) above, are accounted for by a rule different from the ones mentioned so far. This rule is given in (6) and corresponds to his (3.46):

(6) ɾ → r / $_X$[___

3. Syllable structure and sonority

In our opinion, the effects of syllable structure on the distribution of rhotics have not been explored enough. As a result, some generalizations have been lost. Moreover, some important questions have not been addressed or have not received a satisfactory answer, namely: 1) why is there a contrast only in intervocalic position, and not in other environments in all Iberian Romance languages? 2) why do all these languages show the same distribution in syllable initial position (after a consonant), where only the trill occurs, and in second position in an onset, where only the flap occurs? Why can't we find the opposite distribution? The systematicity in the distribution of flaps and trills in these environments contrasts with the variation in syllable final position (across languages, dialects, and speech rates). In what follows we will try to give a more complete account of the distribution of flaps and trills by addressing these questions directly.

The distribution of flaps and trills in the predictable fixed environments in (2), repeated below as (7), is completely determined by syllable structure.

(7) Predictable fixed cases: Non-intervocalic, onset:

a. word initial position: **trill**:	[rísk] 'risk'
b. onset position, after a consonant: **trill**	[unrát] 'honest'
c. second position of onset: **flap**	[fɾɛ́t] 'cold'

In fact, these environments are reducible to two: syllable initial position and noninitial position in the onset. In the first case, (7a) the context is word initial position, not a syllabic concept in itself; but, since the rule is a lexical rule, word initial position is also syllable initial position in these cases. The other context that makes reference to syllable initial position is the context C]$_\sigma$ [$_\sigma$__ (7b); in both cases we find a surface trill [r]. Given these facts, a natural step is to assume that the trill occurs in σ-initial position, without further specifications. Of course, this assumption raises a problem for the cases in (1): given that a consonant that appears after a vowel is also in onset position ([míɾə] = (1b)), why can flaps occur intervocalically?

It is important to note that, given our generalized syllabic analysis for the non-contrast environments, the prediction is that in the contrast context V__V a trill should occur. This line of reasoning takes us to the conclusion that, in the context V__V, the unmarked case corresponds to the trill ([mírə] = (1a)), and that the exceptional case is the occurrence of the flap ([míɾə] = (1b)). As mentioned earlier, in previous analyses of rhotics it has always been assumed that the converse is true, i.e. that the exceptional case is the intervocalic trill. Under these analyses, flaps are the reflex of an underlying /ɾ/, and intervocalic trills derive from an underlying geminate flap /ɾɾ/. Our claim is that the exceptional case is precisely the intervocalic flap. The intervocalic trill is simply the regular outcome of a rhotic in syllable initial position; as such it has the normal surface properties product of all other syllable initial rhotics, those exemplified in (7a,b).

Before addressing the problem of the exceptional case, the intervocalic flap (1b), let us analyze the non-contrasting cases, namely onset cases (2) = (7) and coda cases (3), in more detail. The coda cases should be treated separately from the rest (including contrasting cases) for a clear reason. While rhotics in the onset always show up with the same characteristic flap or trill phonetic properties (or flap vs. [x], etc.), the realization of coda rhotics shows a lot of variation across languages and dialects, as mentioned above. Some Iberian dialects have a clear flap, and others (not many) have a clear trill; in other cases, however, the result is something like a very short trill, which can vary in length and tension, etc., depending on speech rate and other factors (see, for Catalan, Recasens 1991: 326-328). For all these cases we will assume that, at the output of the lexical phonology, all dialects have a flap; tensing and similar phenomena are the product of late postlexical rules that apply across-the-board. Tensing must be clearly postlexical since resyllabification bleeds it, as shown in (8) (syllable boundaries (.) are supplied):

(8) a. *Catalan (Central)*

ma[r.]	'sea'
ma[.ɾ u]bert *ma[.r u]bert	'open sea'
ma[r. t]ranquil	'quiet sea'

b. *Brazilian Portuguese (Rio)*

ma[χ.]	'sea'
ma[.ɾ a]zul *ma[.χ a]zul	'blue sea'
ma[χ. t]ranqüilo	'quiet sea'

c. *Spanish (Nicaragua)*

ma[r.]	'sea'
ma[.ɾ a]zul *ma[.r a]zul	'blue sea'
ma[r. t]ranquilo	'quiet sea'

In the onset, the choice of the rhotic depends on its onset internal position. The trill (never the flap) occurs in syllable initial position, when it is the only element of an onset. On the other hand, the flap (never the trill) occurs in second position of an onset. The fact that the opposite distribution is never found is understandable if one can relate the trill and the flap to different positions in the sonority scale. If the flap, like glides, is more sonorous than the trill, which could be considered close to obstruents in sonority, it is natural that the trill occurs as the only element of an onset, while the flap appears, like glides (or laterals), as the second element of an onset.[5] For Catalan we propose the implementation of the sonority scale in (9a). (9b) gives the restriction on onset complexity:

(9) a. Sonority scale

0	1	2	3	4
obstruents -	nasals -	laterals -	glides-	vowels[6]
trill			**flap**	

b. $[_\sigma [_O (C(C))]...]$ Catalan has maximally two consonants in the onset.

In the application of the sonority scale to syllabic wellformedness we follow Clements (1990), with some extensions to be discussed below.

Clements (1990) proposes that syllabification is based on two principles: *Core Syllabification*, reproduced in (10), ensures that syllables conform to a rising-falling sonority curve; *Dispersion*, reproduced in (11), ensures that the first demisyllable (onset + nucleus) shows maximal rise and uniform dispersion of sonority distances among segments, and that the contrary obtains for the second demisyllable (nucleus + coda):

(10) (=(27)) Core Syllabification Principle, revised (CSP):

a. Associate each [+syllabic] segment to a syllabic node.

b. Given P (an unsyllabified segment) adjacent to Q (a syllabified segment), if P is lower in sonority rank than Q, adjoin it to the syllable containing Q (iterative).

(11) (=(19)) Dispersion Principle

a. The preferred initial demisyllable minimizes *D*.

b. The preferred final demisyllable maximizes *D*.

(=(16))

c. $D = \sum_{i=1}^{m} 1/d_i^2$ [given a sequence of segments $s_1, s_2, \ldots, s_m$, d is the sonority distance between any two different segments s_i-s_j. EB-JM]

To illustrate (11), consider the sequence *lalpap.* For the demisyllables *pa* and *la*, given the sonority scale in (9), we get sonority transitions 0-4 and 2-4, respectively. The sonority distance is hence d=4 for *pa* and d=2 for *la*. Applying (11c), we get D=1/16 = 0.625 for *pa* and D=1/4= 0.250 for *la*. Hence *pa* is a better initial demisyllable than *la*, and *al* is a better final demisyllable than *ap*. This illustrates the relation of dispersion to maximal/minimal rise. Consider now cases in which several sonority distances have to be added, i.e. cases with more than one segment in the onset or in the coda. Let us compare *pna* and *pla*, *anp* and *alp*, where *pna* and *anp* show a lesser uniform dispersion in sonority, since the sonority of *n* is close to that of *p* and far from that of *a*. For *pna* and *anp* the sonority values are 0-1-4, and 4-1-0, respectively. Sonority distances are, for both cases, 1 (=1–0), 4 (=4–0), 3 (=4–1). The sum of the inverse squares of the distances is 1/1 + 1/16 + 1/3 =1,396. In the case of the more evenly distributed cases *pla* and *alp* we get 0-2-4, 4-2-0, respectively, and D=1/4+1/16+1/4 = 0,5625. Hence *pla* is a better initial demisyllable than *pna*, and *anp* is a better final demisyllable than *alp*. Instead of using directly the values of D, Clements (1990) ranks possible demisyllables, of different dispersion such that, e.g., *pa* > *na* > *la* > *ja,* and assigns accordingly complexity values to each of them as initial or final demisyllables. We reproduce in (12) his table 17.1 (*D* = dispersion; *C* = complexity value; V = vowel; G = glide; L = liquid; N = nasal; O = obstruent):

(12) (= Table 17.1) *Complexity rankings for demisyllables of two and three members based on the sonority scale O < N < L < G < V*

	D	*C*
a. Two-member demisyllables:		
i. initial:		
OV	0.06	1
NV	0.11	2
LV	0.25	3
GV	1.00	4
ii. final:		
VO	0.06	4
VN	0.11	3
VL	0.25	2
VG	1.00	1
b. Three-member demisyllables:		
i. initial:		
OLV	0.56	1
ONV, OGV	1.17	2
NLV, NGV	1.36	3
LGV	2.25	4
ii. final:		
VLO	0.56	4
VGO, VNO	1.17	3
VLN, VGN	1.36	2
VGL	2.25	1

Consider now how this approach applies to the five different contexts in which rhotics appear (1-3). In (13), below, we repeat examples with a possible *ɾ* in the left column and a possible *r* in the right column for all contexts. Application of *Core Syllabification* only has the effect of not syllabifying the first consonant in the complex onset *[frɛ́t], since *f* has a sonority which is not lower than the sonority of the adjacent segment *r*; *ɾ* is preferred in this context, as shown in (13d). Hence we assume that the choice of the rhotics *r* and *ɾ* is governed by their best satisfaction of syllabic structure; more specifically, we choose the one which is preferable, given the Dispersion Principle and the complexity values it provides. The sequence rV (13a-c) has a complexity value 1, while ɾV has a complexity value 4; in a syllable beginning with a rhotic, then, rV is preferred over ɾV because it has a lower complexity value. The sequence Vr (13e), on the other hand, has a complexity value 4 and therefore ranks worse than the sequence Vɾ, with a complexity value 1. In the second demisyllable, then, Vɾ is preferred over Vr. An asterisk before a form marks the unacceptable option, a check mark after a form marks the syllabically less complex one:

(13) *Onset:*	*flap*		*trill*	
a. Intervocalic position	[mí.ɾə]	4	[mí.rə] √	1
b. Word initial position	* [ɾísk]	4	[rísk] √	1
c. Onset initial, after a C	* [un.ɾát]	4	[un.rát] √	1
d. 2nd position in onset	[fɾɛ́t]	2	* [(f)rɛ́t] (unsyllab. by CSP)	
e. *Coda*:	ma[ɾ] √	1	* ma[r]	4

The principle of the Sonority Cycle favors the observed distribution of flaps and trills. As a result, we find the trill in syllable initial position, since, compared to the flap, it will cause a sharper rise. We find only the flap in second position in the onset, given the fact that a trill would violate the minimal distance in the sonority scale. And finally we find the flap in coda position since it constitutes a more gradual fall in sonority than the trill.[7] This distribution is shown in (14):

(14) $[_\sigma$ r V...]
$[_\sigma$ C ɾ V...]
$[_\sigma$ ...V ɾ...]

In the literature on rhotics it is not very clear what feature distinguishes flaps from trills. Harris (1969) and Wheeler (1979) assume that the trill is [+tense] while the flap is [–tense]. Mascaró (1976) claims that the trill is [+continuant] and the flap is [–continuant], while Bonet (1988) assumes exactly the opposite.[8] We will not discuss this issue here because we think that a broader study on rhotics and laterals which takes other languages into account is called for. For the sake of the argument we will assume that there is a feature [f] (suggesting *flap*), such that flaps are [+f], while trills are [–f]. Since in all cases but one the value of [f] is predictable, we can assume that the value of this feature is generally not present underlyingly. The value of [f] will be inserted when syllabification takes place. The value that will be inserted (or the one that will get a better evaluation, in Optimality Theory terms, cf. Prince and Smolensky 1993) will be the one that better conforms to the Principle of the Sonority Cycle. (15) illustrates all the predictable cases (including [mírə], the normal, unmarked value for the contrasting environment). The underlying rhotic, not originally specified for [f] is represented by R. C, V stand for consonant and vowel, and syllable boundaries are indicated by dots (.):

(15)

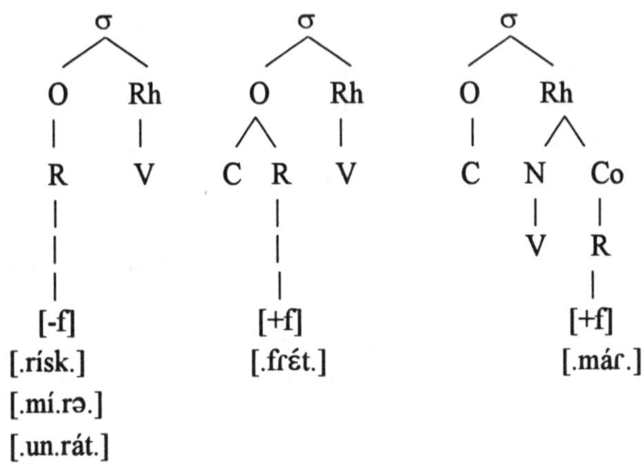

Rhotics in word initial position ([.rísk.] 'risk'), in syllable initial position before a consonant ([.un.rát.] 'honest'), and in intervocalic position for the cases with a trill ([.mí.rə.] 'myrrh') all constitute cases of a syllable initial rhotic. The trill will be preferred over the flap because the rise in sonority will be more abrupt.

When the rhotic appears in second position in the onset ([.frɛ́t.]), the feature [+f] will be inserted because the flap is more sonorous than the trill. In syllabic structures like C_1C_2V..., C_1 must be a stop or the fricative *f* if C_2 is a rhotic. Given the sonority hierarchy, *Stop-trill-V* will cause a violation of the uniformity of the sonority rise.

In syllable final position, within a word or at the end of it ([.pɔ́ɾ.tə.], [.maɾ.]) the flap will be preferred since it will cause a minimal fall in sonority. This specification of rhotics for [f] is a word-level phenomenon. The fact that in phrasal phonology all word final rhotics followed by a vowel initial word are realized as a flap is a consequence of the fact that at the word level these rhotics were in coda position and, as such, they were specified as [+f], that is, as flaps.

As mentioned above ((8) and corresponding discussion), in some varieties there is a postlexical process of tensing which applies to these coda [ɾ]s.

In (16) the word *reprorrogar-(se)* 'to get an extension (for oneself)' and *honrat* 'honest' show the derivation of all the predictable cases:

(16)

(2a) (2c) (1a) (3) (2b)
R e p R o R o g a R - s e h o n R a t

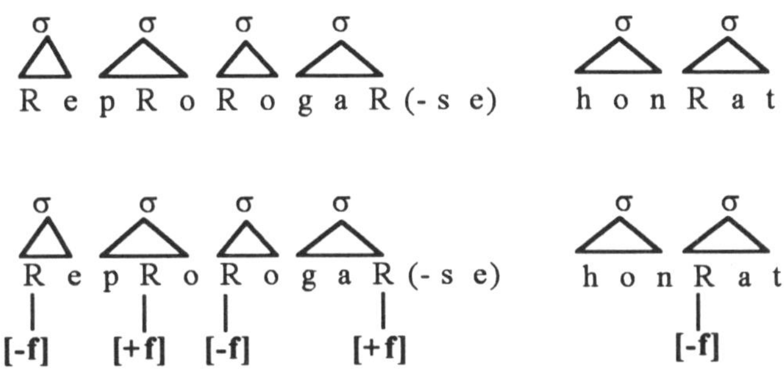

The approach sketched above has two advantages. First, it answers the question posed earlier about the regular behavior of the distribution of flaps and trills across dialects and languages in fixed (2a,b) and variable (2c) non-contrasting environments. Second, it fully incorporates the crucial role played by syllabic structure, which makes it possible to collapse the three different environments proposed in earlier accounts into a single one: onset position.

4. Intervocalic flaps

One case that remains to be accounted for is the occurrence of intervocalic flaps (1b), which contrast with trills in this position. An intervocalic flap, e.g. [míɾə], occurs, like the trill, e.g. [mírə], in syllable initial position, but it does not surface as a trill, as would be expected under the analysis presented so far. As in other proposals, we assume that the contrast between flaps and trills in intervocalic position is the product of a representational difference, an underlying property that distinguishes surface [ɾ] from surface [r]. Contrary to those proposals, the exceptional, marked property is attributed to the flap, not to the trill. Our claim is that the difference between intervocalic flaps and all other occurrences of rhotics is due to the fact that only intervocalic flaps are underlyingly marked with a property, [+f]. This is the only active value with respect to other rhotics: [–f] can never appear in an underlying representation. The underlying difference between the minimal pair [mírə] 'myrrh' and [míɾə] '(s/he) looks at' is illustrated in (17):

```
(17)      m í r a          m í ɾ a
                               |
                             [+f]
```

Consider again the complexity values derived from dispersion that were assigned to syllables containing rhotics; we add to (18) the intervocalic *r*/*ɾ* distinction:

(18) *Onset:*	*flap*		*trill*	
a. Intervocalic **[r]**	* [mí.ɾə]	4	[mí.rə]	√ 1
b. Intervocalic **[ɾ]**	[mí.ɾə]	4	* [mí.rə]	√ 1
c. Word initial position	* [ɾísk]	4	[rísk]	√ 1
d. 1st in onset, /C__:	* [un.ɾát]	4	[un.rát]	√ 1
e. 2nd position in onset	[fɾɛ́t]	2	* [(f)rɛ́t] (unsyllab. by CSP)	
f. *Coda*:	ma[ɾ]	√ 1	* ma[r]	4

In the unmarked case, an underlying syllable initial rhotic /R/ is interpreted as a trill. This is the case in (18a,c,d). In (18e) and in (18f) the insertion of the unmarked value for /R/ [-f] would give either an unsyllabifiable segment, and a considerably more complex final demisyllable, respectively. Therefore /R/ is supplied, for syllable structure reasons, with the marked value [+f], and /R/ is interpreted as [ɾ] ([fɾɛ́t], ma[ɾ]). (18b) is the problematic case, since the actual form contains the more complex demisyllable ([ɾi] = 4).

Let us compare previous proposals to ours schematically:

```
(19)  Example    Harris (1983), etc.    Present proposal
(1a)  [mírə]          / ɾ ɾ /               / R /
(1b)  [míɾə]          / ɾ /                 / R /  (= /ɾ/)
                                              |
                                            [+f]
```

(2a)	[rísk]	/ ɾ /	/ R /
(2b)	[unrát]	/ ɾ /	/ R /
(2c)	[fɾɛ́t]	/ ɾ /	/ R /
(3)	ma[ɾ] / ma[r]	/ ɾ /	/ R /

One might ask why the positive value of [f] appears underlyingly only in intervocalic position. At first sight this should be a problem because there does not seem to be a way of preventing this value to appear, for instance, in word initial position. The fact is, however, that there are no words starting with a flap in any of the languages considered. Under approaches such as Harris (1983), this specific problem does not arise: intervocalic flaps are subject to no rule (they are not considered to be an exceptional case), while intervocalic trills are assumed to be underlying geminate flaps. To obtain a geminate/nongeminate contrast in any other position would be impossible because a geminate flap would presumably not be allowed in any of the four non-contrasting contexts; hence, under his approach, the impossibility of initial, adconsonantal, or final geminates is due to general language-particular constraints on possible clusters[9]:

(20) a.	b.	c.	d.
*/ɾɾ ísk/	*/un ɾɾ át/	*/f ɾɾ ɛ́t/*/ma ɾɾ /	

Under the present proposal such a straightforward solution is not possible. But if this proposal is on the right track, some additional factor must be responsible for the fact that syllable initial flaps are only possible in intervocalic position. (21) contains all the environments in which one might potentially find an underlying specification [+f], the only source for a surface contrast:

(21) a.	b.	c.	d.	e.
/míRə/	*/R ísk/	*/un R át/	/f R Ét/	/ma R /
|	|	|	|	|
[+f]	[+f]	[+f]	[+f]	[+f]

(21d,e) do not pose a problem because, independently of whether or not [+f] is present underlyingly, they will surface with [+f] anyway because the relevant segment is either in second position in the onset, in (21d), or in coda position, in (21e). In these two cases, then, a surface contrast would be impossible. In the rest of the cases (21a,b,c) an underlyingly specified rhotic appears in onset position, but the result is ungrammatical whenever the rhotic is preceded by another consonant or when it is word initial. It seems, then, that an underlying flap is only possible in syllable initial position when it is preceded by a vowel. This brings us to the conclusion that a syllable initial [ɾ] is licensed by a preceding V because they make a good syllable contact (21a), but not by a preceding C because they do not make a good syllable contact (21c).

The descriptive generalization that a flap *ɾ* is licensed in syllable initial position only by a preceding V because it makes a good syllable contact with this vowel can be incorporated into the general framework of Clements (1990). He proposes two separate measures of complexity: the complexity of a given demisyllable, and the complexity of the contact between two syllables. The latter is derived from the former and it equals the sum of the complexities of the two demisyllables in contact. This gives a ranking of syllable contacts, from best to worse, between 1 and 9. In (22) (= (30) in Clements 1990) the rows correspond to the end of the first demisyllable making contact, and the columns to the beginning of the second demisyllable making contact:

(22) *Contact complexity* (= (30), Clements 1990)

	V	G	L	N	O
V	5	4	3	2	1
G	6	5	4	3	2
L	7	6	5	4	3
N	8	7	6	5	4
O	9	8	7	6	5

We will assume that there is, in addition, a measure of the *total complexity* of a demisyllable, which depends on its own complexity, as measured in table (12), and on the complexity of the syllable contact it makes, if any. More specifically, we propose that a bad (complex) syllable contact increases the total complexity of a demisyllable, and that a good contact decreases it. One of the important consequences of this approach to demisyllable complexity is that an asymmetry between peripheral and internal demisyllables is derived. Initial or final demisyllables (in a word, for instance) do not add or reduce complexity since they do not make any syllable contact.

In (23), below, we give a modified version of the *contact complexity* table given by Clements. In order to derive the measure of total complexity, we assume the following: a) V.V, G.G, L.L, N.N and O.O (the contacts with complexity value 5, according to Clements 1990) are contacts that do not add nor reduce complexity; b) contacts with values greater than 5 add complexity, and contacts with values smaller than 5 reduce complexity. Therefore, in our terms, the values to be added to the inherent complexity of a demisyllable are those in (22) minus 5:

(23) *Contact complexity* (modified)

	V	G	L	N	O
V	0	–1	–2	–3	–4
G	1	0	–1	–2	–3
L	2	1	0	–1	–2
N	3	2	1	0	–1
O	4	3	2	1	0

The total complexity of a demisyllable, then, equals its inherent complexity, which was given in the table in (12), plus the values in (23). The total complexity values are given below for the first demisyllable, (23a), and for the second demisyllable, (23b), both in boldface:

(23) a. *Total complexity* (first demisyllable)

	V	G	L	N	O
V	0	–1	–2	–3	–4
G	2	1	0	–1	–2
L	4	3	2	1	0
N	6	5	4	3	2
O	8	7	6	5	4

b. *Total complexity* (second demisyllable)

	V	**G**	**L**	**N**	**O**
V	5	3	1	–1	–3
G	6	4	2	0	–2
L	7	5	3	1	–1
N	8	6	4	2	0
O	9	7	5	3	1

To give an example, consider a demisyllable ending in a liquid, VL in VL.NV; according to (23a), VL has *total complexity* 1 when it is followed by a demisyllable starting with a nasal. Similarly, according to (23b), a demisyllable beginning with a glide, like GV in V.GV has a *total complexity* 3 when it follows a demisyllable ending in a V.

We can now return to the problematic cases in (21). Consider the predicted total complexity values for a demisyllable RV in word initial position and, word-internally, after a vowel and after a non-obstruent consonant (after an obstruent, a rhotic is syllabified in second position in the onset):

(24)	a.	#ɾV	4	*[ɾísk]
	b.	V.ɾV	3	[míɾə]
	c.	L.ɾV	5	*[fulɾá]
	d.	N.ɾV	6	*[unɾát]
	e.	Maximal complexity of a demisyllable CV=3.		

We must conclude that in the languages examined a demisyllable CV cannot have total complexity values greater than 3, (24e). Therefore, underlying or derived structures #ɾV, with total complexity 4, L.ɾV, with total complexity 5, and N.ɾV, with total complexity 6 are ill-formed.[10]

Notice that if this approach is correct, there should be two environments where a contrast between flaps and trills would be *a priori* possible: syllable initial position before a vowel, where a contrast *does* occur, and also coda position after a vowel. In the latter case, the underlying flap (i.e., the rhotic with an underlying [+f] specification) in the coda could be licensed by a preceding V. However, a surface contrast cannot be found in this environment because coda rhotics will get the value [+f] anyway, precisely because of their position in the syllable (the Principle of the Sonority Cycle will prefer a minimal fall, therefore a flap).

In the next section we give evidence supporting the claim that only intervocalic flaps are underlyingly specified for the feature [+f] and that this feature can only be licensed, when it belongs to the only segment of an onset, by a preceding V. As will be shown, other approaches cannot give a satisfactory account for the data discussed in the next section.

5. Additional Evidence

Catalan furnishes additional evidence in favor of the approach based on the view that the underlying [+f] specification can only be licensed by a preceding V. The evidence comes from three sources, apheresis, hypochoristics, and future and conditional verbal affixation. Let us consider them in turn.

In many dialects of Catalan apheresis is very common: a word initial unstressed schwa can delete, as shown in (25a). Whenever a word initial impossible onset arises, like *ps or *dʒ in (25b), apheresis cannot take place. In the case of rhotics, there are two possibilities: if [r] appears after the initial schwa ([ərV...]) in the nondeleted form, apheresis is also possible (25c); but apheresis is impossible when the initial schwa is followed by an (intervocalic) flap in the nondeleted form ([əɾV...], (25d)):

(25)

a.	[ə]nar	→	nar	'to go'
	[ə]gafar	→	gafar	'to take'
	[ə]gulla	→	gulla	'needle'
b.	[əps]urd	→	*[ps]urd	'absurd'
	[ədʒ]udicar	→	*[dʒ]udicar	'assign'
c.	[ər]ibar	→	[r]ibar	'to arrive'
	[ər]onsar	→	[r]onsar	'to shrink'
	[ər]acada	→	[r]acada	'earring'
d.	[əɾ]omatitzar	→	*[ɾ]omatitzar or *[r]omatitzar	'to flavor'
	[əɾ]engada	→	*[ɾ]engada or *[r]engada	'herring'
	[əɾ]anya	→	*[ɾ]anya or *[r]anya	'spider'

The account of the contrast between (25c) and (25d) is fairly straightforward under the present proposal. The forms in (25c) do not have any underlying specification for [f] and they will get a value for this feature depending on their position in the syllable. Both in the form without apheresis and in the form with apheresis the rhotic is syllable initial and, therefore, it will get the value [–f] (a surface trill). In (25d), however, the underlying [+f] specification can only be licensed by a preceding V, the only way of getting an allowed syllable contact. If this vowel is deleted the licensor disappears, and the output is ruled out. Of course one could ask why the flap does not become a trill. Under our proposal this possibility can easily be rejected, since it would imply getting rid of an underlying specification. The only process needed is specification of unspecified /R/; in other words, there is no rule like "delete [f]."[11]

In standard accounts (e.g. Mascaró 1976, Wheeler 1979) this sort of data is difficult to account for. Surface intervocalic flaps are not the product of any rules; they are underlying flaps /ɾ/, and they surface with their underlying form unchanged. One could then ask what would prevent apheresis to apply and be followed by the rule given in (6), which turns word initial flaps into trills. If one were to pursue this derivation, the ungrammatical form *[Ør]*omatitzar* would be obtained. The only possibility of preventing this output would be to invert the ordering between the two processes: the tensing rule (6) would then precede the apheresis rule. However, in such a case we would not be able to rule out the other form in (17d), *[Øɾ]*omatitzar*, given that there is no additional constraint specifically banning word initial flaps.

The other piece of evidence that favors our proposal comes from hypochoristic formation in Catalan, studied in detail in Cabré (1993) (see also Cabré and Kenstowicz 1995). In Catalan, hypochoristics are formed by isolating a trochee starting at the right edge of the word. (26a) contains some examples of this process. In (26b), hypochoristic formation results in a word starting with a trill. Hypochoristic formation is blocked, however, when the truncated form would start with a flap:

(26) a. Josefina → Fina
Francisco → Cisco
Joaquim → Quim

b. Montse[r]at → [r]at

c. Au[ɾ]ora → *[ɾ]ora or *[r]ora

The argument in this case is identical to the argument given above based on apheresis. Under the present proposal, (26b) is well-formed because intervocalic trills are not specified as such underlyingly. In onset position they will become [−f], and this will be the case both in the full form and in the truncated form. The underlying flap (i.e., the underlying [+f] value) of the full form in (26c), however, is licensed by the preceding V. If truncation takes place, the preceding V disappears and the underlying flap cannot be licensed. Therefore truncation is blocked in (26c). Again, in an approach in the line of Harris (1983), cases like these are very difficult to account for, unless some ad hoc stipulation is added to prevent *any* syllable initial flap to occur. It is also interesting to note that in a similar language but with no ɾ/r contrast, like Italian, there is no problem constructing truncated hypochoristic forms like Margherita → Rita, Caterina → Rina, Lorenzo → Renzo (Thornton 1996).

Another case that supports our analysis of intervocalic [ɾ] regards future and conditional verbal affixation in Catalan and Spanish. These tenses have a tense/person morpheme sequence beginning in an underlying flap. The flap normally follows the thematic vowel, but in some cases it follows a stem ending in a consonant. Some Catalan examples of these suffixes appear in (27). In (27a), the suffix follows a vowel; in (27b), it follows a stem ending in a consonant. The suffix always appears in boldface:

(27)	a.	Catalan Spanish		
		balla+**[ɾ]à**	baila+**[ɾ]á**	'(s/he) will dance'
		dormi+**[ɾ]ia**	dormi+**[ɾ]ia**	'(s/he) would sleep'
	b.	vin+[d**ɾ**]**à**	ven+[d**ɾ**]**á**	'(s/he) will come'

In the first two cases, the flap initial suffix is preceded by a vowel, the thematic vowel, and nothing happens. In (27b), however, the suffix is preceded by a bare root ending in the consonant /n/. In this case an epenthetic consonant [d] is inserted. Under the present proposal, the reason for this epenthesis is clear: the rhotic from the suffix is not /R/, but the marked /R, +f/, underlyingly specified as [+f]. This feature cannot be licensed as the only element in onset position unless it is preceded by a vowel; when the epenthetic consonant is inserted, the rhotic becomes the second element of an onset, whose first element is the epenthetic [d]; in this position the expected value is [+f], the one the rhotic already has underlyingly. Under the standard proposal, the suffix begins with /ɾ/, which, being in syllable initial position after a consonant, should be tensed to [r] by rule (4a). This is not the case for all Spanish varieties and for almost all Catalan varieties. If there is a rule tensing /ɾ/ in this context we should not expect d-insertion as the general solution[12].

6. Concluding Remarks

Our proposal makes extensive use of syllabic information by assigning the flap and the trill to different points in the sonority scale and by claiming that in all cases but one the feature that distinguishes flaps and trills receives one value or the other depending on which one best satisfies Clements' principle of the Sonority Cycle. With respect to the contrast that we find in intervocalic position, our claim is that, contrary to previous proposals, the exceptional case is the flap, since the trill is what we generally expect in syllable initial position. Surface intervocalic flaps correspond to underlying flaps, that is rhotics with an additional underlying property, the specification [+f].

One of the arguments that has been advanced in the traditional literature on rhotics supporting the view that intervocalic trills are underlyingly geminate flaps is stress. The argument is based on the fact that there does not seem to be any words (in Spanish, Catalan, or Portuguese) with antepenult stress and with a trill after the vowel following the stressed vowel. Harris (1983) gives examples like the following, from Spanish:

(28)	señó[ɾ]a	cáma[ɾ]a
	camó[r]a	*cáma[r]a

If the intervocalic trill is an underlyingly geminate flap, antepenultimate stress is impossible in cases like the last one in (28) because the penultimate syllable is heavy i.e. /ká.maɾ.ɾa/, and heavy syllables attract stress. In our account, it is not possible to relate stress attraction in these cases to syllable heaviness since for us the intervocalic trill is not a geminate; it is a single segment.

As a matter of fact, it is not at all clear why trills, which seem to attract stress, should be related to weight in this sense. If this were the case, we should also have to posit a similar type of structure for /ʎ/, /x/, and /ɲ/, for instance, given that these segments also "attract stress." Notice that, in the context of this discussion, "attract stress" is a predicate meaning that no proparoxytones can be found within the existing lexicon with any of these consonants joining the penultimate and the final syllable. There are no alternations showing stress attraction, and informant intuitions reported are inconclusive. Historically, it is easy to account for the fact that these segments, i.e. /ʎ/, /x/, /ɲ/, and /r/, attracted stress: etymologically, they all come from sequences of segments (/ll/, /jl/, /jn/,

/nj/ /ɾɾ/, etc.), and as such they did attract stress in Latin and, presumably, in Vulgar Latin and for some time afterwards (see Roca 1990). Synchronically, an account that covers all these segments, not just one of them, becomes necessary (in case the stress attraction effect is actually still active).

Another argument adduced for /ɾɾ/ is that in Catalan an underlying geminate flap causes final epenthesis in words like the ones in (29a), versus the ones in (29b) (Wheeler 1979: 193, Mascaró 1976: 49-50). For the word final rhotic, we have transcribed a flap, even though, as mentioned earlier, syllable final rhotics show a lot of variation:

(29)	a.	esque[rə]	'left'	esque[rá]	'left-handed'
		co[rə]	'(s/he) runs'	co[ríə]	'(s/he) used to run'
	b.	ca[ɾ]	'expensive'	ca[ɾ]ot	'expensive' (augment.)
		líde[ɾ]	'leader'	lide[ɾ]atge	'leadership'

If the words in the first column in (29a) were to have an underlying geminate final flap, an epenthetic vowel would be needed to properly syllabify the second half of the geminate (even though one could think of simplification as an alternative option). However, as it turns out, there are only two words (plus derivates) of this type in Catalan, (i.e. (29a)). This constitutes fewer words than the ones that end in a flap plus a schwa (not related to feminine gender). Therefore, there is hardly any reason to think that the final schwa in the words in (29a) is an epenthetic vowel at all.

Finally, in spite of the fact that underlying geminate flaps have been rejected, a process of [ɾ] deletion, similar to the one proposed by Harris (1983: 63, 70) (=(5b) above), or Mascaró (1976: 49-51) is needed. According to that rule, a rhotic is deleted when a trill follows. This postlexical deletion is an unquestionable process in our opinion, but it will affect only word final rhotics followed by a word initial rhotic.

Notes

* This paper was partially supported by grants 1995SGR 00486 (Generalitat de Catalunya) and PB93-0893-CO4.

1 Rhotics have been analyzed, among others, in Harris (1969, 1983), for Spanish, and Mascaró (1976) and Wheeler (1979), for Catalan.

2 In some dialects, instead of a trill there is some sort of alveolar fricative ([z̆]), Canfield

1981; see also the description in Harris 1969: 46-56. In Portuguese the "strong" *r* is realized as an alveolar or uvular trill, or as as a uvular fricative. We ignore here all these distinctions for simplification; see Angenot and Vandresen 1979, Barbosa 1962.

3 The same proposal appears in Bowen, Stockwell, and Silva-Fuenzalida (1956).

4 Like Wheeler (1979: 191-194), Mascaró (1978: 47-51), Mateus (1975).

5 The idea that the distribution of flaps and trills should be related to sonority appears in Bonet (1988). It is interesting to notice that many varieties of the languages studied here present variants that show more clearly the sonority differences: [ɾ] presents often an *approximant* realization [ɾ̞], [ɹ], and [r] a *fricative* realization [r̝], [z˞], [s˞] (see Navarro Tomás 1971 117-119, 122-123, Canfield (1981), Recasens (1991: 324-328 Angenot and Vandresen (1979).

6 We have included glides and the flap in the same point of the sonority hierarchy for simplicity, but it might be the case that glides have no place in the sonority hierarchy (they might be considered non-nuclear vowels). We leave this issue for further research.

7 Given the account argued for here, the distribution of flaps constitutes a counterexample to Prince and Smolensky's (1992) Onset/Coda Licensing Asymmetry (their (258)): "There are languages in which some possible onsets are not possible codas, but no languages in which some possible codas are not possible onsets." In the Iberian Romance languages, the flap can occur in coda position, but it cannot be an onset.

8 Chomsky and Halle (1968:318) suggest that [r] is [+cont] and that it is [+heightened subglottal pressure]. Kean (1975) uses [±flap], [±trill], flaps being less marked.

9 Although Harris' approach works, one might wonder why languages that hardly have any surface geminates do have underlying geminate flaps, which never surface as geminates, while other languages, like Italian, which do have surface geminates, do not show a contrast between rhotics. Catalan has only some (residual) cases of geminates (mainly *m, n, l,* and *ʎ*). Spanish has no geminates. In general, in these two languages geminates arise only through assimilation processes.

10 The only C.C contact with a value greater than 3 that might appear problematic at first sight is the sequence N.L. Within a word this combination is unattested in the native vocabulary of languages like Catalan. Moreover, in loans or acronyms, like *Chandler*, *Bentley* or *INLE* (Instituto Nacional del Libro Español), the nasal becomes a (nasalized) lateral: [tʃal̃lər], [bɛl̃li], [il̃le]. Therefore, in this case the resulting total complexity is not 4 but 3.

11 In Optimality Theory terms this would mean that Rec-F (underlying features cannot be suppressed) is ranked higher than the constraint that allows for the deletion of the initial schwa.

12 Forms like *venrà, molrà* are restricted to some places in the Northern dialects.

References

Angenot, Jean-Pierre and Paulino Vandresen. 1979. The Portuguese [R]'s revisited. Manuscript. 23 p.

Barbosa, Jorge Morais. 1962. Sur le /R/ portugais. *Estructuralismo e Historia.* Miscelánea homenaje a André Martinet, ed. Diego Catalán, vol. III, 211-226. La Laguna: Universidad de La Laguna.

Bonet, Eulàlia. 1988. Trills and flaps in Catalan and Spanish. MIT, ms.

Bowen, J. Donald, Robert Stockwell and Ismael Silva-Fuenzalida. 1956. Spanish juncture and intonation. *Language* 32. 641-665.

Cabré i Monné, Teresa. 1993. *Estructura Gramatical i Lexicó: el Mot Mínim Català.* Doctoral dissertation, Universitat Autònoma de Barcelona.

Cabré, Teresa, and Michael Kenstowicz. 1995. Prosodic trapping in Catalan, *Linguistic Inquiry* 26.4. 694-705.

Câmara Jr., Joaquim Mattoso. 1953. *Para o Estudo da Fonémica Portuguesa.* Rio de Janeiro: Organização Simões.

Canfield, D. Lincoln. 1981. *Spanish Pronunciation in the Americas.* Chicago: The University of Chicago Press.

Chomsky, Noam, and Morris Halle. 1968. *The Sound Pattern of English.* New York: Harper and Row.

Clements, George N. 1990. The role of the sonority cycle in core syllabification. *Papers in Laboratory Phonology I. Between the Grammar and Physics of Speech*, ed. by John Kingston and Mary E. Beckman, 283-333. Cambridge: Cambridge University Press.

Harris, James W. 1969. *Spanish Phonology.* Cambridge, Mass.: MIT Press.

Harris, James W. 1983. *Syllable Structure and Stress and Spanish.* Cambridge, Mass: MIT Press.

Kean, Mary-Louise. 1975 *The Theory of Markedness in Generative Grammar.* Doctoral dissertation, MIT.

Mascaró, Joan. 1976. *Catalan Phonology and the Phonological Cycle.* Doctoral dissertation, MIT. [Bloomington: Indiana University Linguistic Club, 1978].

Mateus, Maria Helena Mira. 1975. *Aspectos da Fonologia Portuguesa.* Lisboa: INIC, Centro de Linguística da Universidade de Lisboa. 2nd ed. 1984.

Navarro Tomás, Tomás. 1971. *Manual de Pronunciación Española.* Madrid: Consejo Superior de Investigaciones Científicas. 16th edition.

Prince, Alan and Paul Smolensky. 1992. *Optimality Theory: Constraint interaction in generative grammar.* Rutgers University and University of Colorado at Boulder, ms.

Recasens, Daniel. 1991. *Fonètica Descriptiva del Català.* Barcelona: Institut d'Estudis Catalans.

Roca, Iggy. 1990. Diachrony and synchrony in Spanish stress. *JL* 26, 133-164.

Thornton, Anna M. 1996. On some phenomena of prosodic morphology in Italian: accorciamenti, hypochoristics and prosodic delimitation. *Probus* 8. 81-112.

Wheeler, Max. 1979. *Phonology of Catalan*. Oxford: Basil Blackwell.

4

Sonorant Dissimilation in the Iberian Languages

MARIA-ROSA LLORET

1. Introduction

The original Feature Geometry models of Clements (1985) and Sagey (1986) have been continuously revised in order to improve different aspects of the internal structure of sounds. Significantly enough, the representation of certain segments have been treated recurrently in the literature, presumably because the phenomena they involve remain poorly understood, failing to capture their inherent similarities. The representation of sonorants is one of these controversial issues. Current proposals contrast two different models, which directly establish (Rice and Avery 1989, 1991; Yip 1990; Piggott 1991, 1992; Rice 1993), indirectly establish (McCarthy 1988, 1989; Clements 1989; Halle 1992, 1995; Kenstowicz 1994; Clements and Hume 1995), or do not establish (Clements 1985, Sagey 1986, Levin 1988, Archangeli and Pulleyblank 1994) some kind of dependency relation between the features and/or nodes which refer to sonorancy. Argumentation for the previous models is based for the most part on assimilatory processes which involve spreading of the set of nodes and features defining the segment tree. One cannot ignore, however, that sonorant dissimilation is also commonly found in natural languages and thus a definitive model of feature geometry must represent it with the same simplicity. Few works of the current literature have addressed the issue of dissimilation and these few instances are almost exclusively devoted to regular phenomena (Odden 1987, McCarthy 1988, Yip 1988, Cohn 1992, Archangeli and Pulleyblank 1994, Steriade 1995). Sonorant dissimilation is not rare in natural languages, but in many cases it tends to occur sporadically and produces variable surface effects.[1] Because of this lack of systematicity, these data have been usually ignored in the discussion of the internal representation of sounds. Sonorant dissimilation has been frequently attributed to perceptual reasons, i.e., it has been attributed to the fact that both the original consonants and the resulting dissimilated consonant show similar acoustic characteristics.[2]

The purpose of this paper is to show that sonorant dissimilation is not as marginal as it may appear since it is frequently found in the history of the Iberian languages (1a), among others, and still synchronically occurs in many substandard forms (1b), where substandard is to be understood as colloquial and dialectal forms.[3]

(1)

a.*Diachr.*: PEREGRINUS>pelegrí (Catalan), pellegrino (Italian) 'wandering'
ROBURE>roble 'oak' (Portuguese, Spanish)
ANIMA>alma (Port., Sp); (*alima>) arima[4] (Basque)'soul'
Cf. marbre (French)>marble (English)

b.*Synchr.*: només>domés 'only', faldilla>fandilla 'skirt' (coll. Catalan)
peregrino>pelegrino 'wandering', glándula>grándula 'gland' (coll. Spanish)
nenhum>denhum 'no one', nomear>lomear 'to name' (coll. Portuguese)

Another goal of this paper will be to prove that these irregular data show a limited range of variability. Consequently, current phonological theory will have to take these irregular data into account if the inherent similarities of sonorants are to be captured. If what counts as the same category must receive a simple formal expression, the study of sonorant dissimilatory effects will turn out to be a crucial source of evidence bearing on feature organization.

The paper is organized as follows. To begin, I will briefly describe the current view of dissimilation. I will then show that some regularity exists within marginal sonorant dissimilation. Next, I will contrast previous models of sonorant representation in order to highlight the model supported by the data presented in this work, which are analyzed in the next section. Finally, I will summarize the results of this analysis.

2 Dissimilation and current theory

Although it is a useful descriptive term, dissimilation is considered a derivative surface effect in non-linear phonology. There is no such operation as dissimilation, rather it falls into more general processes and derives from the interaction of a small set of operations or formal parameters. In general, languages disfavor neighboring segments which are too alike. Phonological theories face the problem of stipulating a formal explanation for observations such as "too adjacent" and "too alike" elements. A first explanation was provided through the Obligatory Contour Principle (OCP), which prohibits adjacent identical segments (McCarthy 1986). The OCP was later expanded to operate on individual tiers (McCarthy 1988, Yip 1988). However, recent studies by Pierrehumbert (1992) and Buckley (1993) have shown the insufficiency of this model to account for actual instances of cooccurrence restrictions. Pierrehumbert (1992) proposes the Similarity Model according to which the perceived similarity of the consonants being constrained is a function of both their featural identity and their proximity. Sonorant dissimilation clearly favors the Similarity Model. The OCP standard approach cannot account for the marginal effects of dissimilation because it does not consider the fact that restrictions may show a gradient effect. For instance, these restrictions may not be absolute or they may show some preferences and subregularities. Instead, the Similarity Model accounts for the gradient effect based on relative adjacency and relative similarity between elements.

In order to avoid adjacent elements that are too similar, languages may turn to three different strategies. Either (i) a sound deletes, (ii) a new sound is inserted or (iii) one of the sounds changes its properties. These strategies are interpreted as follows: (i) a delinking process resulting in total erasure of one of the elements, (ii) insertion of an epenthetic element, and (iii) loss of some properties and/or insertion of some new properties in order to create a different sound. This paper will not deal with the first two cases. The first strategy is a plain deletion process which takes place in order to completely avoid the other like-segment (e.g., *ARATRU* > arc. *aradro* > *arado* in Spanish; *arada* in Catalan, *arato* in Italian 'plough'; cf. the dissimilated-by-change forms *aladre* in Western Catalan and *aladro* in Asturian). The second strategy does only affect strictly adjacent elements and sonorant dissimilation is not limited to strict locality. Case (iii), however, becomes a real challenge for non-linear approaches because, contrary to standard linear models, no operation can change features. Instead, the change has to be explained as the delinking of some properties (in order to destroy the original similitude) and/or the insertion of others (in order to create a different sound). Accordingly, our attention is drawn to these changing effects.

3 Sonorant dissimilation and regularity

As already noted, data from sonorant dissimilation in the Iberian languages are usually disregarded in the literature because they are viewed as irregular phonetic changes. An inter- and intra-linguistic study shows, however, that this phenomenon is very widespread since it appears diachronically, as well as synchronically, in standard, colloquial, and dialectal forms. Additionally, sonorant dissimilation occurs in accordance with two general principles. First, similar conditions have to be met for dissimilation to occur. Second, the changes involved are not random, but they follow some general tendencies. (This is exemplified in (2)-(6)).

As the examples in (2) show, the change affects a coronal sonorant, that may dissimilate as the effect of another non-homorganic sonorant (2b). Other conditions can also determine which sonorant dissimilates, i.e., their position in the syllable or their position with respect to stress. Since it is not clear how all these parameters interact, I leave this issue to further research and focus on the changing effects.[5]

(2) a. bona nit>bora nit 'good night' (coll. Cat.)
cerebro>celebro 'brain' (arc. and coll. Sp.)
FILICULA>f(a)rigola 'thyme' (Cat.)
LOCALE>lugar (Sp.), logar (Port.) 'place'

b. només>domés 'only', faldilla>fandilla 'skirt' (coll. Cat.)
nenhum>denhum 'no one', Jerónimo>Jerolmo 'Jerome' (coll. Port.)
MEMORARE>arc. nembrar>lembrar 'to remember' (Port.)
ANIMA>arima (Basque), alma (Sp., Port.) 'soul'
HOMINE>omne>hombre 'man' (Sp.)

The observed regularities in the changing effect are as follows: nasals and laterals normally change into a rhotic (3a), while rhotics change into a lateral (3b); a nasal less frequently changes into a lateral (4); a sonorant sporadically loses its sonorant character and becomes an obstruent (5); a lateral rarely becomes a nasal (6); and a rhotic is scarcely replaced by a nasal (7). Sometimes, sonorant dissimilation also takes place between distinct liquids in benefit of nasals (8).

(3) a. bona nit>bora nit 'good night', juliol>juriol 'July' (coll. Cat.)
glàndula>gràndula (coll. Cat.), glándula>grándula (coll. Sp.) 'gland'
*NONANTA>noranta 'ninety' (Cat.)
*LUSCINIOLU > rossinyol 'nightingale' (Cat.)
ANIMALIA>arc. alimalia>alimária 'vermin' (Port.)
LILIU>lliri (Cat.), lirio (Sp.), lírio (Port.) 'lily'
SEMENO>arc. Semero>Semeroyz (Basque patronymic)

b. armari>almari 'wardrobe', frare>flare 'friar' (coll. Cat.)
cerebro>celebro 'brain' (arc. and coll. Sp.)
arc. miércores>miércoles 'Wednesday' (Sp.)
ROBURE>roble 'oak' (Port., Sp.)
ARMARIU>almário 'wardrobe' (Port.)
ARATRUM>aladre (Western Cat.), aladro (Asturian) 'plough'
ARBITRIARE>albirar (Cat.), alvidrar (Port.) 'conjecture'
arc. erur>el(h)ur 'snow' (Basque)

(4) monument>moliment 'monument' (Southern Cat.)
nomear>lomear 'to name' (arc. and coll. Port.)
ninho>linho 'nest' (coll. Port.)
BARCINONE>Barcelona (Cat., Sp.)
DE-IN-ANTE>delante 'in front' (Sp.)
UNICORNE>licorne 'unicorn' (Port.)
MEMORARE>arc. nembrar>lembrar 'remember' (Port.)

(5) només>domés 'only', ningú>dingú 'no one' (coll. Cat.)
arc. berar>bedar 'grass' (W. Basque) (cf. E. Basque bel(h)ar)
arc. erur>e(d)ur 'snow' (W. Basque) (cf. E. Basque el(h)ur)
carrereta>carredeta (coll. Cat.) 'kind of mushroom'
nenhum>denhum 'no one' (coll. Port.)
ULULARE>udolar 'howl' (Cat.)

(6) faldilla>fandilla 'skirt', qualsevol>consevol 'any one' (coll. Cat.)

(7) ROSMARINU>romaní 'rosemary' (Cat.)

(8) farigola>fanigola 'thyme' (coll. Cat.)
galeria>galenia 'gallery' (coll. Cat, coll. Sp.)

In light of the previous observations and in view of the non-linear account of dissimilation, I will show that these data favor a feature geometry model which displays a minimal hierarchical organization between features that refer to sonorant consonants.

4 The feature organization of sonorants

I consider here some competing models of sonorant representation in order to examine what type of hierarchical organization can capture sonorant dissimilation better. For the purpose of this discussion, I will focus only on aspects directly related to the representation of sonorants. The defining aspect of current models is to consider whether or not the features which refer to sonorancy, laterality, and nasality (and rhoticity?) are organized within the same unit. The first model to take this aspect into account is a view—reminiscent of proposals by Clements (1985) and Sagey (1986)—in which [sonorant], [lateral], and [nasal] are not hierarchically organized but are represented as independent and/or sister features.

(9) (a) *reminiscent of Sagey (1986):*[6] (b) *reminiscent of Clements (1985):* [7]

The crucial weakness of this view, which does not directly relate sonorancy to the particular characteristics of the sonorant consonants (i.e., [lat] and [nas]), is that any possible connection between sonorant consonants—such as the one induced by sonorant dissimilation—cannot be captured straightforwardly.

Though [lateral] is often considered a manner feature, many recent works have been devoted to determining whether laterality should be regarded as a place feature. Levin (1988), following Steriade (1986), argues that [lateral] is a terminal feature of the Coronal node:

(10) *Levin (1988)*:

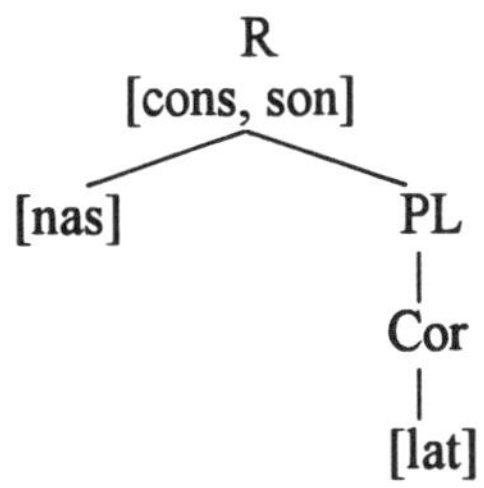

This model claims to capture the fact that lateral consonants always have a coronal place of articulation, as well as the observation that laterality behaves like a place of articulation with respect to place assimilation. It has been reported, though, that not only do velar laterals exist (in the New Guinea languages Melpa, Kanite, and Mid-Waghi; cf. Ladefoged, Cochran and Disner 1977), but also place assimilation does not necessarily entail lateral assimilation (e.g., Chukchee ŋ-assimilation; cf. Kenstowicz 1986, 1994).[8] Both facts are problematic for the view of [lateral] under Coronal.[9]

Halle (1992, 1995), following McCarthy (1988), proposes that [consonantal] and [sonorant] are root features that distinguish the three major classes (obstruents, sonorant consonants, and vocoids), which for the most part determine the (sonority-driven) syllabification process. In this model, [lateral] and [nasal] are not directly related since the former is considered a stricture feature not bound to a particular articulator (i.e., it directly links to the Root), while the latter is considered to be bound to the articulator Soft Palate, which together with the (Oral) Place articulators constitute the Supralaryngeal (SL) node.

(11) *Halle (1992, 1995):*

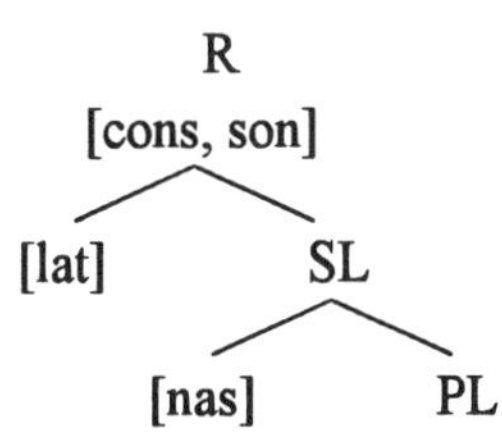

It is claimed that this organization explains why [consonantal] and [sonorant] do not usually spread unless complete assimilation is accomplished. Kaisse

(1992), on the other hand, presents several cases where [consonantal] spreads and dissimilates quite independently of any other feature. However, she recognizes that she has not found good examples where [sonorant] acts independently. She ends up proposing a partially modified version of McCarthy (1988) and Halle's (1992) model according to which [sonorant] remains on the Root node while [consonantal] hangs from the Root. Sonorant dissimilation, though, challenges the observation that [sonorant] does not participate in phonological processes as a phonologically active feature, since one of its changing effects is precisely the loss of sonorancy (e.g., *nenhum* > *denhum* 'no one' in coll. Port., *només* > *domés* 'only' in coll. Cat., *ULULARE* > *udolar* 'howl' in Catalan, *berar* > *bedar* 'grass' in Western Basque, *carrerita* > *carredita* 'small run' in coll. Sp.). Alternations between sonorants and voiced obstruents should also be captured through the feature tree.

Contrary to the previous models, Rice and Avery (1989, 1991) propose a hierarchy, subsequently adopted by Piggott (1991, 1992) and Rice (1993), which directly relates sonorancy with laterality, nasality, and rhoticity. They incorporate a Spontaneous Voicing (or Sonorant Voice) node (SV henceforth) as an organizing node to represent sonorant properties. SV may also be present in the underlying (lexical) representation of voiced obstruents in some languages.[10]

(12) *Rice and Avery (1989, 1991), Rice (1993):*

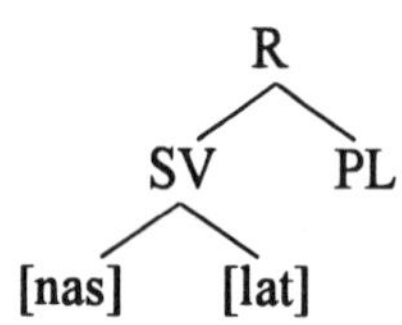

One of the strengths of this model is that it directly captures the fact that sonorant consonants may behave as a class in assimilatory processes. This model also provides a natural account of how sonorant consonants pattern with voiced obstruents in some languages: they both may display the SV node underlyingly. Both claims are further supported by the analysis of sonorant dissimilation presented below.[11]

Rice (1993) posits that nasals are the unmarked sonorants because they often serve as targets for assimilation, but not usually as triggers. Although this is arguable in the languages she refers to, which do not phonemically contrast [l] and [r], this assumption does not clearly hold for the Iberian languages, which contrast /l/ and /r/.[12] In these languages, /r/ behaves like the unmarked segment and thus is more likely to be underspecified.[13] Very few works address the issue of rhotic representation, and hence little attention is paid to their behavior. Rice and Avery (1989) suggest that SV may dominate another feature, which they provisionally name [r-features] (13a). However, they generally posit the representation in (13b), where /r/ is solely defined through SV and continuancy. Yet Yip (1990) suggests that in languages with a sole rhotic phoneme, place of articulation is not distinctive and thus it is underlyingly absent (cf. Mester and Itô 1989). She does not consider [+cont] to be present either, rather /r/ is represented by a bare SV node (14).

(13) *Rice and Avery (1989):*

a. 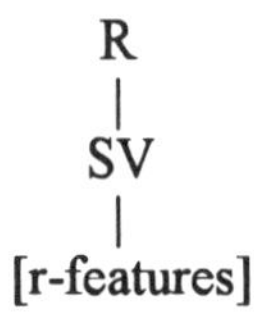

b. 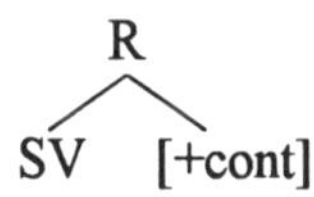

(14) *Yip (1990):* 

Sonorant dissimilation supports Yip's (1990) idea that rhotics are the unmarked sonorants because the most common change triggered by nasals and laterals is to become /r/ (as in *bona nit* > *bora nit* 'good night', *juliol* > *juriol* 'July', in coll. Cat.; *SEMENO>arc. Semero>Semeroyz*, a Basque patronymic; *LILIU* > *lliri* in Cat., *lirio* in Sp., and *lírio* in Port.). However, the fact that sonorant dissimilation sometimes takes place between distinct liquids (*farigola* > *fanigola* 'thyme', *galeria* > *galenia* 'gallery', in coll. Cat.)[14] raises the classic issue on the binary use of features. This natural grouping of liquids is present in most traditional descriptive works and has also been pointed out by many linguists with respect to different processes. For instance, Mester and Itô (1989) refer to "Liquid Placelessness" in some assimilatory processes; Pierrehumbert (1992) refers to a subdivision of /l/ and /r/ against /n/ in her analysis of the cooccurrence restrictions in Arabic verbal roots; and Steriade (1995) also mentions this not-well captured patterning with respect to blocking of liquid dissimilation in Latin and other languages. Perhaps the best well-known example of liquids phonologically acting as a class is the /l/-dissimilation rule of Latin. In Latin, the suffix *-alis* (*nav-alis*) becomes dissimilated in *-aris* when the stem already contains a lateral (*line-aris*), but dissimilation is blocked by an intervening /r/ (*flor-alis*). It is generally claimed that this subdivision is captured by the binary (and contrastive) use of [lateral]. In other words, laterals are assumed to be [+lateral] while rhotics are assumed to be [-lateral].[15] In this sense, Latin /l/-dissimilation applies to the [lateral] tier and any intervening /r/, which is [-lateral], blocks the process. Along the same lines, the marginal cases of liquid dissimilation found in the Iberian languages also support the claim that, in these cases, dissimilation applies on the [lateral] tier, regardless of the specific value of the feature. The representation of sonorant consonants assumed in this work is shown in (15). The feature [-lat] is absent from the underlying representation of the rhotic, because it can be directly inferred from SV. (Redundant features are given in parentheses.)[16]

(15)

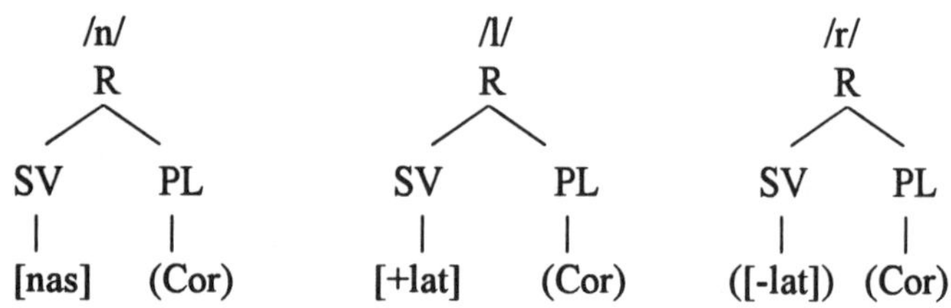

Following Rice and Avery (1989) and Rice (1993), I further assume that, in the Iberian languages, SV is also underlyingly present in voiced obstruents (16) because they pattern with sonorants in some phonological processes. Notice for instance that in the Iberian languages voice assimilation applies both to a following sonorant consonant and to a following voiced obstruent (17a), while in languages such as Dutch or Korean voice assimilation only applies to a following voiced obstruent (17b). Under this approach, while voice assimilation is interpreted as the spreading of SV in the former languages, it is interpreted as the spreading of the laryngeal feature [voice] in the latter languages.

(16)

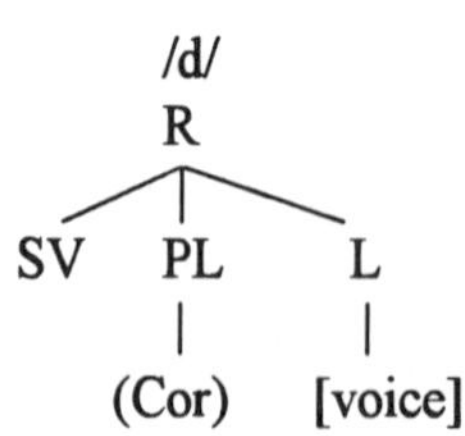

(17)

a. *Catalan:*

do[s] 'two', do[s] pares 'two fathers', do[z] bancs 'two banks'
do[z] mars 'two seas', do[z] reis 'two kings', do[z] lemes 'two mottos'

b. *Dutch:*

hui[s] 'house', hui[s] kamer 'living room' hui[z] baas 'landlord'
hui[s] nummer 'house number', hui[s] raad 'household goods'

5 The analysis of sonorant dissimilation

In general, it can be assumed that marginal sonorant dissimilation allows a certain degree of variability with respect to the items it affects and its possible effects. It can also be assumed that the surface effect of dissimilation encodes two operations, namely, delinking and default fill-in (Odden 1987, McCarthy 1988, Yip 1988, Cohn 1992). First, some features delink in order that one of the original elements loses the primitive similitude. Then, a fill-in operation inserts other feature specifications in order to properly yield the resulting dissimilated consonant. The former operation raises the question of which properties are lost. One possibility is that the target sonorant only loses the relevant sonorant characteristic (i.e., nasality, laterality, or rhoticity) and becomes another sonorant. Another possibility, though, is that the sonorant becomes an obstruent. The fill-in operation is assumed to be a default fill-in through redundancy rules; however, I show below that under the compulsion of more urgent dissimilarity other strategies can exceptionally be appealed. Unmarked features are underlyingly absent, but they may fill in at the point of phonetic implementation. At this stage, a limited range of variation is possible.

Consider first the most common case, where /n/ and /l/ become [r] (18). This effect is the simple result of delinking the relevant sonorant feature (i.e., [nasal] or [+lateral]) in order to destroy the original similitude (19). In each case, the minimal structure left behind resembles that of a rhotic (see previous (15)), and thus feature fill-in rules provide an [r] output.

(18) n>r: bona nit>bora nit 'good night' (coll. Cat.)
*NONANTA>noranta 'ninety' (Cat.)
SEMENO>arc. Semero>Semeroyz (Basque patronymic)
MINIMARE>mermar 'reduce' (Sp.)

l>r: juliol>juriol 'July' (coll. Cat.)
glàndula>gràndula 'gland' (coll. Cat., coll. Sp.)
LILIU>lliri (Cat.), lirio (Sp.), lírio (Port.) 'lily'
LOCALE>lugar (Sp.), logar (Port.) 'place'

(19) n>r: Delinking of [nas]: l>r: Delinking of [+lat]:

As shown in (20), the change of a nasal or a lateral into a voiced obstruent can be explained through delinking of the sonorant properties after the redundancy rule, which fills in [voice] on sonorants, has applied. This process is indicated by a dotted line in the diagrams in (21). The resulting structure, which displays SV and [voice], is then interpreted as an obstruent (see (16)).

(20) n>d: ningú>dingú 'no one' (coll. Cat., Majorcan Cat.)
nenhum>denhum 'no one' (coll. Port.)

l>d: ULULARE>udolar 'howl' (Cat.)
lentilla>dentilla 'lens' (Alacant and Ribagorça Cat.)

(21) n>d: Delinking of [nas]: l>d: Delinking of [+lat]:

The fact that [voice], which is underlyingly absent in sonorants, is already present when the specific sonorant property delinks does not cause any problem to our analysis because sonorant dissimilation is assumed to take place postlexically, and thus unmarked features may be filled in at different stages. The Portuguese example in (22) shows that place of articulation may also be retained.[17]

(22) m>b: morna>borna 'tepid (fem.)' (coll. Port.)

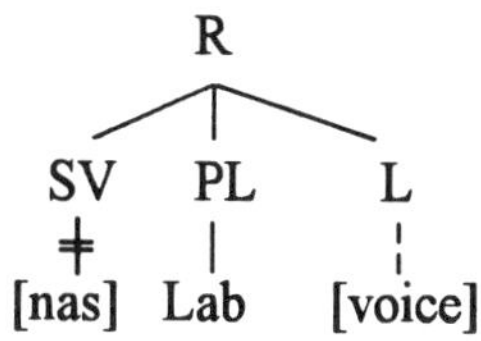

An apparent challenge to our analysis is the switch of a lateral into a nasal (23). The feature [+lateral] delinks (24a). The question, however, is whether the changing effect is due to the insertion of the feature [nasal] or the insertion of the feature [-cont]. It is crucial to note here that, within the Iberian languages, and also within the other Romance languages, the l-to-n change is only found in Catalan and in coda position. My claim is that [-cont] is acquired by position because, as Mascaró (1984,1987a) has argued, in Catalan [-cont] is favored in coda position.[18] Once [-cont] is inserted (24b), [nasal] is inserted in order to fulfill the structure left behind (24c).[19]

(23) l>n: faldilla>fandilla 'skirt', qualsevol>consevol 'anyone' (coll. Cat.)
baldufell>bandufell 'kind of bolt' (coll. Cat.)
Cf. baldufa>*bandufa 'spinning top' (Cat.)

(24)

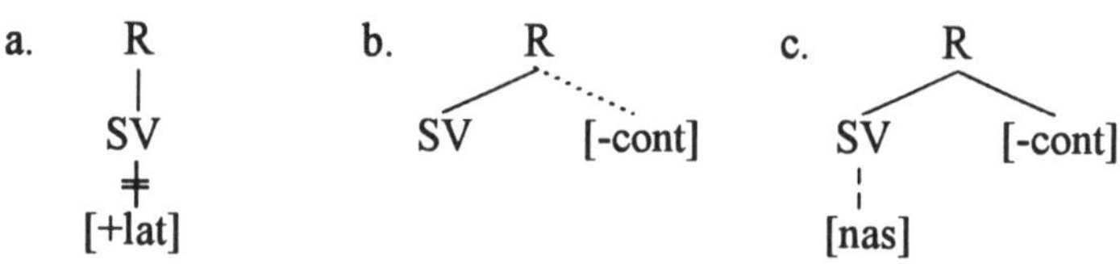

A further point to be taken into account is whether one can justify or not that the original lateral consonant is not marked as [+cont] when [-cont] is inserted. This assumption can indeed be supported with independent data because the contrast between the approximant in *a*[lβ]*a* 'dawn' and in *a*[lɣ]*a* 'algue' and the stop in *sa*[l̪d]*o* 'balance' provides evidence for the fact that laterals receive [+cont] late in the derivation.

The change of a nasal into a lateral (25) does not have a straightforward motivation either. The feature [nasal] delinks in order to undo the original similitude (26a). However, instead of resulting in the plain unmarked sonorant [r], [+lateral] is inserted and becomes [l] (26b).

(25) n>l: monument>moliment 'monument' (Southern Catalan)
nomear>lomear 'to name' (arc. and coll. Port.)
MEMORARE>arc. nembrar>lembrar 'to remember' (Port.)
BARCINONE>Barcelona (Cat., Sp.)
DE-IN-ANTE> delante 'in front' (Sp.)

(26) a. R | SV ǂ [nas] b. R | SV ¦ [+lat]

One possible explanation is that some kind of articulatory strengthening is involved. That is, originally the nasal changes into the rhotic, as expected, but then strengthens, i.e., it dissimilates a further degree and becomes lateral. Significantly enough, there are also some cases in the history of these languages where an intermediate /r/-stage is posited between initial /n/ and final /l/, as in *CONDOMINIA* > arc. *conomina* > *coromina* (Northern Cat.) > *colomina* (Northeastern Cat.) 'countryside' (cf. Coromines 1981)

We may now tentatively recapitulate the argumentation that has been provided for the unmarked status of /r/. First, sonorant dissimilation does not provide evidence in favor of an underlying rhotic feature. Assimilatory processes due to SV spreading do not support this claim either. In Catalan, for instance, the nasal and the lateral show regressive sonorant assimilation to a coronal stop (*set nois* [sɛn nɔ́js] 'seven boys', *set línies* [sɛl líniəs] 'seven lines'). The rhotic, on the other hand, only entails voice and further secondary place assimilation (*set rams* [sɛɖ r̄áms] 'seven bouquets'), exactly like palatal fricatives do, as in (*set jocs* [sɛdʲ ʒɔ́ks] 'seven games'). Second, there is no reason to posit that [+cont] is underlyingly present.[20] In contrast, I have argued that [+cont] is the unmarked value for sonorants after [-cont] has been inserted for nasals. Finally, since rhotics do not underlyingly show place contrasts in the languages discussed in this work, there is no reason to posit that /r/ has a (Coronal) place underlyingly specified.[21] As a matter of fact, assimilatory processes seem to sustain the claim that only the trill acquires extra phonetically relevant place features. Evidence provided by several Catalan and Spanish dialects shows that only the varieties that realize a flap in coda position may assimilate the rhotic to a following sonorant (27a) while varieties with a trilled realization in coda position never show assimilation (27b).

(27)

a.	*Sp. dial. of Murcia:*	reto[rn]o > retonno	'return'
		canta[rl]as > canta[ll]as	'to sing them'
	Cat. dial. of Majorca:	vore[rm]e > vore[mm]e	'to see me'
		vore[rl]o > vore[ll]o	'to see it'
b.	*Sp. dial. of Salamanca:*	reto[r̄n]o, *reto[nn]o	'return'
		canta[r̄l]as, *canta[ll]as	'to sing them'
	Cat. dial. of Barcelona:	canta[r̄m]e, *canta[mm]e	'to sing me'
		canta[r̄l]es, *canta[ll]es	'to sing to them'

With this analysis of the behavior of /r/ outlined, I can now analyze rhotic dissimilation. As mentioned above, the most regular change is the switch of /r/ into a lateral:

(28) r>l:

armari>almari 'wardrobe', frare>flare 'friar' (coll. Cat.)
peregrino>pelegrino 'wanderer', cerebro>celebro 'brain' (arc. and coll. Sp.)
ARATRU>aladre (Western Cat.), aladro (Asturian) 'plough'
ROBURE>roble 'oak' (Sp, Port), ARMARIU>almário (Port) 'wardrobe'
PEREGRINU>pelegrí (Cat.), pellegrino (It.) 'wanderer'
arc. erur> el(h)ur 'snow', arc. berar>bel(h)ar 'grass' (Basque)

As in the case of nasal and lateral dissimilation, the simplest way to dissimilate is to break sonorant identity (the rhoticity in this case) by becoming the next less marked sonorant. Note that since /r/ is the unmarked sonorant consonant, no feature underlyingly depends on the SV node (29a). In this case, dissimilation applies once the redundant features have been introduced. That is, when feature fill-in rules complete the representation and [-lat] (and [+cont]) is assigned (29b), [-lat] delinks (29c). [+lat] is then inserted because the lateral is the only other sonorant consonant that is also [+cont] (29d).

(29)

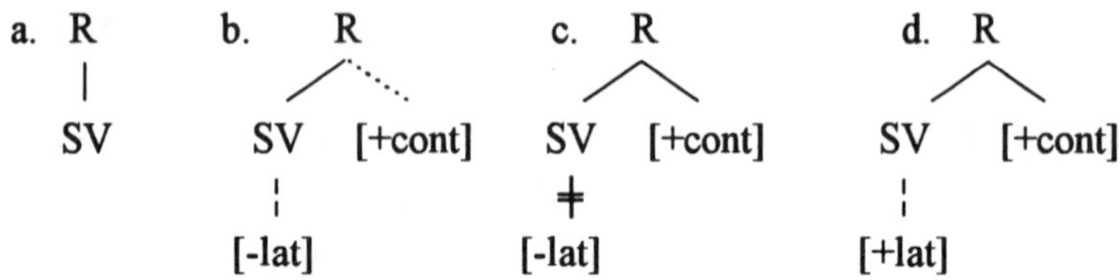

As already noted with the other sonorants, another possibility of dissimilation is to avoid all sonorant properties (30). In this case, delinking from the SV node (31c) takes place after the redundant feature [voice] has been inserted (31b). Feature fill-in rules yield a voiced obstruent. Significantly enough, all r-to-d cases occur intervocalically, where the [+cont] allophone of /d/, [ð], occurs. Therefore, there is no need to justify whether [+cont] has or has not been inserted when [voice] is inserted. (In (31b), I represent [+cont] in parentheses to indicate that its occurrence is not relevant to explain the r-to-d dissimilation.)

(30) r>d: carrereta>carredeta (coll. Cat.) 'kind of mushroom'
arc. berar>bedar 'grass' (W. Basque) (Cf. E. Basque 'bel(h)ar')

(31) r>d: Delinking of [-lat]:

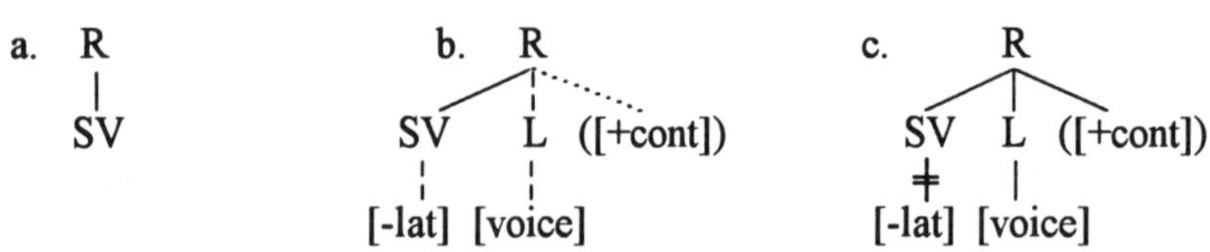

Only one instance of /r/ becoming a nasal has been found, i.e., *ROSMARINU>romaní* 'rosemary' (Cat.). Due to its marginal character, I assume that in this specific case the original /r/ becomes a nasal through assimilation to the other neighboring nasals.[22]

6 Summary

In this paper, I have examined the formal properties of sonorant dissimilation in the Iberian languages in some detail. Although it is postlexical and displays a certain degree of variability, I have argued that sonorant dissimilation shows enough subregularity to be taken into account if we are to capture the inherent similarities of sounds. Within current theory, the Similarity Model (Pierrehumbert 1992) seems to capture the gradient effect that induces dissimilation better than the OCP standard approach. The conditions under which one sonorant is dissimilated instead of the other follow from the ranking of several different conditions, which mainly affect their position in the syllable with respect to stress. These two issues, though, have been left to further investigation.[23] I have instead focused on the analysis of the resulting changing effect. The analysis proposed in this paper clearly favors a model where sonorant features are hierarchically organized. In this sense, I have favored Rice and Avery's (1989) model according to which there is an SV node dominating [nasal] and [lateral]. On the basis of assimilatory processes, Rice and Avery (1989) also argue that in languages such as the Iberian ones, SV is also underlyingly present in voiced obstruents. Dissimilated forms where sonorants become obstruents reinforces this claim too. I have also given support to Yip's (1990) proposal according to which the rhotic is the unmarked sonorant, at least in languages where /l/ and /r/ phonemically contrast. Finally, I have interpreted [lateral] as a binary feature in order to capture the fact that liquids act as a distinct class in sonorant dissimilation (cf. Steriade 1987, 1995).

Notes

* This work was sponsored by a DGICYT grant PB93-0893-C04-04 from the Spanish Government. Earlier insights about this topic were presented at the III Colloquium on Generative Grammar organized by the Universidad Complutense de Madrid (San Lorenzo de El Escorial, 1993), the Workshop on Phonology organized by the Associação Portuguesa de Linguística (Coimbra, 1993), and the X Col.loqui Internacional de Llengua i Literatura Catalanes (Frankfurt, 1994). I am grateful to all these audiences for their valuable suggestions. Special thanks go to J. I. Hualde for his comments on the Basque examples and to the editors of this volume, F. Martinez and A. Morales, for helping me with the English version of this paper. Errors and flaws are my responsibility.

1 Current phonological work only mentions regular cases of liquid dissimilation, cf. Steriade (1987, 1995) for Latin, Cohn (1992) for Sundanese, Crowhurst and Hewitt (1993) for Yidiny, cit. in Steriade (1995).

2 Traditional historical linguists have paid special attention to this phenomenon though recognizing that, contrary to assimilation, the importance of dissimilation is due to its complexity and variable causes and effects. They claim that dissimilation tells us more than assimilation does about the composition and natural groupings of sounds, because in most cases it partially applies to some articulatory elements of the sound, and thus decomposes the phonetic characteristics of sounds. Traditional works always distinguish between the effects of dissimilation, which are easier to understand and justify, and, its causes, which are more variable and difficult to predict. They further relate this peculiarity to the fact that the effects are mainly due to the mechanical phonetic characteristics of sounds while the causes are mainly related to psychological facts such as the speaker's knowledge of the etymological origin of the word or the speaker's familiarity with the word (cf. Grammont 1895).

3 All the data referred to in this paper are well documented forms mentioned in Alcover and Moll (1926-1968), Moll (1952), Badia i Margarit (1981), Coromines (1981), Veny (1983), and Recasens (1991) for Catalan; Menéndez Pidal (1985) and Navarro Tomás (1985) for Spanish; Nunes (1951), García de Diego (1984), and Huber (1986) for Portuguese; Michelena (1985) for Basque.

4 Although it is clear that nasal dissimilation took place in the evolution of *ANIMA* to *arima* 'soul', Michelena (1985) mentions a possible intermediate /l/-stage, i.e., **alima*. In that case, the change from **alima* to *arima* would be related to the fact that, in intervocalic position, *l* usually becomes *r* in Basque (cf. *tselu > zeru 'sky', Alava > Arava 'place-name').

5 Menéndez Pidal (1985) briefly addresses the issue of what determines which consonant is the trigger and which one is the target. The trigger consonant: (i) begins the syllable, especially if the sonorant is preceded by another consonant (as in Catalan, *ROSMARI(NU)* > *romaní* 'rosemary'); (ii) occurs in stressed position (as in Spanish arc., *miércores* > *miércoles* 'Wednesday'); and (iii) is in the second position if both occur between vowels (as in Catalan *ULULARE* > *udolar* 'howl') because most phonological processes are regressive rather than progressive in the Iberian languages.

6 Strictly speaking, Sagey (1986) suggests that [lateral] should be represented as high up as the Place node and as low down as the Root node. Shaw (1989, 1991) argues that [lateral] is immediately dominated by the Root node.

7 Strictly speaking, Clements (1985) proposes a Manner node dominating [sonorant], [lateral], and [nasal] as well as [continuant], [strident], and [consonantal]. The Manner node is a sister of the Place node and both are dominated by Supralaryngeal. Archangeli and Pulleyblank (1994), among others, assume the representation in (9b).

8 In Chukchee, which underlyingly displays /n, m, ŋ/, /ŋ/ assimilates in place to a following consonant (e.g., *wiŋər* 'hoe, absolutive singular', *winri-te* 'hoe, ergative'). When /ŋ/ occurs before a lateral, the nasal assimilates in place, i.e. coronality, but not in laterality (e.g., *ceŋəl* 'box, absolutive singular', *cenle-te* 'box, ergative').

9 Hegarty (1989) presents additional arguments for not treating [lateral] under Coronal.

10 In SPE (Chomsky and Halle 1968), *Spontaneous Voicing* was already considered a phonetic trait of sonorants. It was defined as "a vocal tract configuration in which the vocal cords vibrate in response to the normal, unimpeded air flow".

11 Yip (1990) incorporates Levin's (1988) as well as Rice and Avery's (1989) insights and proposes that [lateral] simultaneously depends on both SV and Coronal. She considers, though, the possibility that the feature [lateral] is underlyingly a sole dependent of the SV node, at least in languages such as Javanese and Cambodjan where Coronal is underlyingly absent. Given that we have previously presented several problems for the view of [lateral] under Coronal, I adopt the simplest representation: [lateral] as a dependent of SV only.

12 Note that as far as languages displaying a flap and a trill (like Catalan and Spanish) are concerned, I assume, following Harris (1969) and Mascaró (1976, 1987b), that the contrast between the flap [r] and the trill [r̄] is not phonemic. Their superficial contrast in intervocalic position is assumed to be an underlying contrast in length, which is later interpreted as a trill. Except between vowels, all other occurrences of [r] and [r̄] are derived from its position in the syllable: [r] occurs in second position of an onset; [r̄] occurs word initially and in onset position after a consonant; in coda position, either the flap or the trill occurs depending on the dialect.

13 Rice and Avery (1989) argue that if voiced obstruents and sonorants display an SV node in a language, [nasal] can be underlyingly present. More generally, though, they argue that [nasal] is the unmarked dependent of SV, and unmarked features are the only features that can be absent in underlying representations (cf. Rice 1993 also).

14 Although in this work I concentrate on the issue of dissimilation, it is worth to note here that this natural grouping of liquids is also found in other sporadic changes such as metathesis, e.g., *MIRACULU>miracle*, in Catalan, but *milagro* in Spanish.

15. Pierrehumbert (1992) points out two other ways of capturing this subdivision. One possibility is to adjust the featural characterizations of the phonemes by incorporating the feature [approximant]. Another possibility is to find some formal means of capturing the fact that some features are more important, across the board, than others (in this sense, for instance, [nasal] will be weighted more than [lateral]). While the latter proposal remains fully open to further research, the use of [approximant] has been argued for by several authors. Clements (1988) (and subsequently adopted by McCarthy 1989 and Clements and Hume 1995) incorporates [approximant] as a feature making up the root

together with [sonorant] and [vocoid], along the same lines of McCarthy (1988) and Halle's (1992, 1995) use of [sonorant] and [consonantal]. On the other hand, Piggott (1991, 1992) (and subsequently adopted by Brown 1993) proposes the use of [approximant] as a dependent feature of SV. One general problem raised by the use of [approximant] to distinguish liquids is that, strictly speaking, in the Iberian languages /r/ is not a true approximant, but instead it displays a true approximant allophone [ɹ] (e.g., *seis ramos* [sejɹ̄rámos], *sis rams* [siɹ̄ráms] 'six bouquets', in Spanish and Catatalan, respectively).

16 Halle (1995), based on Calabrese's (1995) alternative to underspecification through filters and repair strategies, provides an explanation on the use of contrastive features which does not entail that all the set of feature values are visible to phonological processes. According to Halle (1995), /l/-dissimilation of Latin provides evidence for the fact that in this language both [+lateral] and [-lateral] are visible to phonological processes, and thus these feature values are represented at each stage of the derivation. This statement has no bearing on other features.

17 This is the only example that I have found where the target consonant is not coronal. In all other cases where dissimilation takes place between non-homorganic sonorants, the target is always the coronal (cf. *només* > *domés* 'only', *faldilla* > *fandilla* 'skirt', in coll. Cat.; arc. *nembrar* > *lembrar* 'to remember', in Port.; *ANIMA* > *arima* 'soul', in Basque; arc. *omne* > *hombre* 'man' in Sp.)

18 This coda obstruent formation is significantly related to the "Stop Formation" that applies in coda position in Catalan (*a[bd]icar* 'abdicate'), which, in turn, is related to the "Geminate Formation" of voiced stops in coda-stem position (*regl-a* [régglə] 'rule', *pobl-e* [pɔ́bblə] 'village'). It is further related to the tense realization of /r/, i.e., the trill [r̄], in coda position (*ca[r̄]ta* 'letter'). (For discussion, see Mascaró 1984, 1987a.)

19 Although the change of a lateral into a nasal occurs predominantly in coda position, there are also a few cases where this change is brought about by direct assimilation to a nasal (cf. *MELANCHOLIA* > *melanconia*, in Portuguese, *malenconia*, in Catalan, 'melancholy'; *lentilla* > *nentilla* 'lens' in coll. Cat., but *dentilla* in the Catalan dialect of Alacant and Ribagorça). In some cases, more than one factor must have brought about the change, as in Catalan *multiplicar* > *muntiplicar* 'to multiply', where the dissimilated consonant occurs in coda position and is preceded by a nasal. The other few cases where this change is reported in non-coda position are presumably due to partial assimilation to a preceding stop, which is also [-cont] (cf. in coll. Catalan *pel.lícula* > *película* > *penícula* 'film', *poliol* > *poniol* 'polium'; arc. *pelagal* > *penagal* 'a teleost fish').

20 Hall (1993) argues for the German uvular /R/ that [+cont] is underlyingly present.

21 Underlying placelessness of rhotics has been also defended by Hall (1993) for German, Akinlabi (1993) for Yoruba, and Mester and Itô (1989) for several other languages.

22 See note 19.

23 Evaluation of the interaction of these conditions would probably be better interpreted in terms of Optimality Theory through the ranking of these parameters. I leave this issue to further research.

References

Akinlabi, Akinbiyi. 1993. Underspecification and the Phonology of Yoruba /r/. *LI* 24. 139-160.

Alcover, Antoni M., and Francesc de B. Moll. 1926-1968. *Diccionari Català-Valencià-Balear*, 10 vols. Palma de Mallorca: Moll.

Archangeli, Diana, and Douglas Pulleyblank. 1994. *Grounded Phonology*. Cambridge, Mass.: The MIT Press.

Badia i Margarit, Antoni M. 1981. *Gramàtica Històrica Catalana*. València: Tres i Quatre.

Brown, Cindy. 1993. The Feature Geometry of Lateral Approximants and Lateral Fricatives. McGill University, ms.

Buckley, Eugene. 1993. Tigrinya Root Consonants and the OCP. Paper presented at the 24th ACAL, Ohio State University.

Calabrese, Andrea. 1995. A Constraint-Based Theory of Phonological Markedness and Simplification Procedures. *LI* 26.373-463.

Chomsky, Noam and Morris Halle. 1968. *The Sound Pattern of English*. New York: Harper and Row.

Clements, G. N. 1985. The Geometry of Phonological Features. *Phonology Yearbook* 2.223-250.

Clements, G. N. 1988. Toward a Substantive Theory of Feature Specification. *Proceedings of NELS* 18, ed. James Blevins and Juli Carter, 79-93. University of Massachusetts, Amherst.

Clements, G. N. and Elizabeth V. Hume. 1995. The Internal Organization of Speech Sounds. *The Handbook of Phonological Theory*, ed. John Goldsmith, 245-306. Cambridge, Mass. and Oxford: Basil Blackwell.

Cohn, Abigail. C. 1992. The Consequences of Dissimilation in Sundanese. *Phonology* 9. 199-220.

Coromines, Joan. 1981. *Diccionari Etimològic i Complementari de la Llengua Catalana*, vol. II. Barcelona: Curial.

García de Diego, V. 1984. *Elementos de Gramática Histórica Gallega* (Fonética-Morfología) 1909. Verba, Anuario Galego de Filoloxia. Anexo 23. Universidade de Santiago de Compostela.

Grammont, M. 1895. *La Dissimilation Consonantique dans les Langues Indo-Européennes et Dans les Langues Romanes*. Dijon.

Hall, Tracy A. 1993. The Phonology of German /R/. *Phonology* 10.83-106.

Halle, Morris. 1992. Phonological Features. International Encyclopedia of Linguistics, ed. William Bright, 207-212. Oxford: Oxford University Press.

Halle, Morris, 1995. Feature Geometry and Feature Spreading. *LI* 26.1-46.

Hegarty, Michael. 1989. An Investigation of Laterals and Continuancy. MIT, ms.

Huber, Joseph. 1986. *Gramática do Português Antigo*. Lisboa: Fundação Calouste Gulbenkian.

Kaisse, Ellen. 1992. Can [consonantal] spread? *Language* 68:313-332.

Kenstowicz, Michael. 1986. The Phonology of the Chukchee Consonants. *Studies in the Linguistic Sciences* 16.79-96

Kenstowicz, Michael. 1994. *Phonology in Generative Grammar*. Oxford: Blackwell.

Harris, James. W. 1969. *Spanish Phonology*. Cambridge, Mass.: MIT Press.

Ladefoged, P., A. Cochran, and S. Disner. 1977. Laterals and Trills. *Journal of the International Phonetic Association* 7.46-54.

Levin, Juliette. 1988. A Place for Lateral in Feature Geometry. University of Texas, ms.

McCarthy, John J. 1986. OCP Effects: Gemination and Antigemination. *LI* 17. 207-263.

McCarthy, John J. 1988. Feature Geometry and Dependency: a Review. *Phonetica* 83.44-108.

McCarthy, John J. 1989. Guttural Phonology. University of Massachusetts, Amherst, ms.

Mascaró, Joan. 1976. *Catalan Phonology and the Phonological Cycle*. Doctoral dissertation, MIT (Distributed by Indiana University Linguistics Club).

Mascaró, Joan. 1984. Continuant Spreading in Basque, Catalan, and Spanish. *Language Sound Structure*, ed. M. Aronoff and R. T. Oehrle. 287-298. Cambridge, Mass: MIT Press.

Mascaró, Joan. 1987a. A Reduction and Spreading Theory of Voicing and Other Sound Effects. Universitat Autònoma de Barcelona, ms.

Mascaró, Joan. 1987b. Syllable-Final Processes in Catalan. *Studies in Romance Languages*, ed. C.A. Neidle and R. Núñez Cedeño, 163-180. Dordrecht: Foris.

Menéndez Pidal, Ramón. 1985. *Manual de Gramática Histórica Española*. 18th edition. Madrid: Espasa-Calpe.

Mester, R. Armin, and Junko Itô. 1989. Feature Predictability and Underspecification: Palatal Prosody in Japanese Mimetics. *Lg.* 65. 258-293.

Michelena, Luis. 1977. *Fonética Histórica Vasca.* 2nd edition. Donostia: Gipuzkoako Foru Aldundia.

Moll, Francesc de Borja. 1952. *Gramática Histórica Catalana.* Madrid: Gredos.

Navarro Tomás, Tomás. 1985. *Manual de Pronunciación Española.* Madrid: C.S.I.C.

Nunes, José Joaquim. 1951. *Compêndio de Gramática Histórica Portuguesa.* Lisboa: Livraria Clássica Editora.

Odden, David. 1987. Dissimilation as Deletion in Chukchi. *ESCOL'* 87. 235-246.

Pierrehumbert, Jeanette. 1992. Dissimilarity in the Arabic Verbal Roots. Paper presented at *NELS* 23, Ottawa.

Piggott, Glyne L. 1991. The Geometry of Sonorant Features. McGill University, ms.

Piggott, Glyne L. 1992. Variability in Feature Dependency: The Case of Nasality. *NLLT* 10.33-77.

Recasens, Daniel. 1991. *Fonètica Descriptiva del Català.* Barcelona: Institut d'Estudis Catalans.

Rice, Keren. 1993. A Reexamination of the Feature [sonorant]: The Status of 'Sonorant Obstruents'. *Lg* 69. 308-344.

Rice, Keren, and Peter Avery. 1989. On the Interaction between Sonorancy and Voicing. *Toronto Working Papers in Linguistics* 10.65-82.

Rice, Keren, and Peter Avery. 1991. On the Relationship between Laterality and Coronality. *Phonetics and Phonology: The Special Status of Coronals: Internal and External Evidence*, vol. 2, ed. Carole Paradis and Jean François Prunet, 101-124. Orlando: Academic Press.

Sagey, Elizabeth. 1986. The Representation of Features and Relations in Nonlinear Phonology. Doctoral dissertation, MIT. Published by Garland Publications, New York, 1990.

Shaw, Patricia A. 1989. On the Phonological Representation of Laterals and Affricates. University of British Columbia, ms.

Shaw, Patricia A. 1991. Consonant Harmony Systems: The Special Status Of Coronal Harmony. *Phonetics and Phonology: The Special Status of Coronals: Internal and External Evidence*, vol. 2, ed. by Carole Paradis and Jean François Prunet, 125-157. Orlando: Academic Press.

Steriade, Donca. 1986. A Note on Coronal. MIT, ms.

Steriade, Donca. 1987. Redundant Values. *Papers from the Twenty-third Regional Meeting of the Chicago Linguistic Society*, vol. 2, ed. A. Bosch and E. Schiller, 339-362. University of Chicago.

Steriade, Donca. 1995. Underspecification and Markedness. *The Handbook of Phonological Theory*, ed. John Goldsmith. Cambridge, Mass. and Oxford: Basil Blackwell.

Veny, Joan. 1983. *Els Parlars Catalans*. 4th edition. Palma de Mallorca: Moll.

Yip, Moira. 1988. The OCP and Phonological Rules: a Loss of Identity. *LI* 19. 65-100.

Yip, Moira. 1990. Two Cases of Double-Dependency in Feature Geometry. Brandeis University ms.

5

Continuant Spreading and Feature Organization*

BLANCA PALMADA

1. Introduction

Feature patterns are the basic source for the investigation of feature organization. The research of the segment's internal structure requires the reanalysis of classical processes in order to describe them more precisely. This is the only way to proceed since the credibility of our model of grouping and dependency crucially relies on the accuracy of the rethinking of every process. In this paper, I will re-examine the description of a group of Spirantization processes in order to decide if they should be interpreted as phonological operations spreading Continuant. First of all, it is necessary to determine whether the processes I am dealing with are phonological in nature or are only phonetic effects. It is a fact that the validity of Spirantization processes as a descriptive basis for Continuant investigation has not been entirely agreed upon. The following paragraph, from McCarthy (1988), condenses this common view.

> "The postvocalic spirantization rules of Spanish, Tigrinya, and Biblical Hebrew (in which *pbtdkg* —> ɸ*βθdxγ*) are possible examples of this process, although they are open to an alternative interpretation. A better example may be the English dialectal rule changing *z* to noncontinuant *d* before noncontinuant *n*: business —> [bɪdnɪs]."

The main part of this paper is dedicated to showing how difficult an alternative interpretation would be, and how convenient a phonological one is. In the remainder of the paper, the phonological interpretation is used to build a small area of the feature tree. In Section 1, I will present the Spirantization processes dealt with in this paper, and a tentative analysis of them as Continuant Spreading. A detailed study will provide evidence that will become crucial for the choice between a phonetic or phonological status. The existence of well-attested phonological processes applied after Spirantization leads us to the conclusion that Spirantization itself has to be described as a phonological operation. In Section 2, I will proceed immediately to test this conclusion. More precisely, I will test its capacity to explain the descriptive details which are related to the situations demonstrating a lack of spreading, called *blocking effects*. Finally, in Section 3, I will examine the implications of the existence of phonological Continuant Spreading for the hierarchical organization of features. I will consider feature geometry in the light of Continuant Spreading.

2. A double task is assigned to this section. First, there is a demonstration of the descriptive adequacy of the phonological view. Second, there is a report of the problems that an alternative phonetic account would have to face, mainly the application of phonological processes after Spirantization. The empirical data that will be considered correspond to the contextual Spirantization of the voiced obstruents [b], [d], and [g] that occurs in essentially the same way in Catalan, Basque, Portuguese, and Spanish. I follow standard assumptions in considering the stop version as the unmarked one (see, however, Hualde (1991)). The main motivation for this assumption is that Stops are found after pauses, and more generally, when no specific feature value is provided via spreading from a preceding segment.

(1)

Catalan		*Basque*	
gát	'cat'	gori	'red'
bɔ́	'good'	beri	'new'
dulén	'bad'	dore	'tower'
Portuguese		*Spanish*	
gɛ́rʌ	'war'	gáto	'cat'
bɛ́lu	'beautiful'	bóta	'boot'
dizɛ́ɾ	'to say'	dóθe	'twelve'[1]

On the other hand, the approximant allomorphs appear after continuant segments—either vocalic (2a) or consonantal (2b). In (2b), I present examples with a voiced alveolar fricative. However, a similar distribution is found after any segments which can be defined as Continuants (other fricatives, affricates, approximants or liquids).

(2) a.

Catalan		*Basque*	
səɣú	'sure'	laɣun	'friend'
kəβέʎs	'hair'	aβeɾe	'cattle'
kəðíɾə	'chair'	aðar	'horn'
Portuguese		*Spanish*	
páɣu	'payment'	eɣoísta	'egoist'
áβʌ	'leaf'	aβéxa	'bee'
fáðʌ	'fairy'	maðéɾa	'wood'

b.

Catalan		*Basque*	
dəzɣɾát	'displeasure'	dezɣoɣo	'reluctance'
bízβə	'bishop'	dezβerðin	'uneven'
dəzðí	'to retract'	ezðujn	'unworthy'
Portuguese		*Spanish*	
esgotado	'exhausted'	dezɣáste	'wear'
esboço	'sketch'	ezβóθo	'outline'
desdén	'disdain'	dézðe	'from'

From what has been shown up to this point, a fairly neutral description of the basic process of Spirantization can be established. The parameters of a tentative rule are summarized in (3). According to this rule, the alternation of voiced obstruents is attributed to an autosegmental operation that spreads the Continuant specification rightward. No restrictions are imposed on the trigger, the segment that spreads the relevant feature. In contrast, the target class able to undergo the process is restricted to the group of voiced obstruents.

(3) *Spirantization*

Operation:	Spreading
Argument:	Continuant
Direction:	to the right
Trigger:	unrestricted
Target:	voiced obstruents

The obvious alternative to Spirantization as Continuant Spreading is what we can call the *phonetic view*, whose central idea is that the stop-fricative alternation is entirely due to phonetic factors. No complete phonetic analysis has been made, although occasional references to the possibility of a fully phonetic explanation appear throughout the literature. The most concrete argument that we can discuss corresponds to Mascaró (1984, 1991). He accounts for the lack of Spirantization in [l̪d] sequences by referring to the articulatory properties of the lateral. Mascaró argues that the dental obstruent is realized as a stop when preceded by [l] because there is no airflow in the dental region during the pronunciation of the lateral. Below, I will present more instances of blocking effects, parallel to the [l̪d] example, which cannot be explained in a manner similar to the one provided by Mascaró for [l̪d]. Unexpectedly, the absence of more concrete arguments in the phonetic view does not make counterarguments useless. The implications of the existence of Continuant Spreading for the investigation of feature dependencies are important. I will therefore present a detailed description of Spirantization, stressing the properties that represent clear problems for any phonetic analysis.[2]

First, however, one particular detail of the Spirantization process as it occurs in Catalan merits attention. In this language, syllable boundaries play a role in allowing or preventing Continuant Spreading, which can be defined as *syllabic control* of the process. The operation of spreading the Continuant value occurs only across syllable boundaries (i.e. from a segment in the rhyme to a segment in the onset of the following syllable). In the examples in (4a), where dots mark syllable boundaries, a syllable initial voiced obstruent acquires its Continuant value from the vowel in the immediately preceding syllable. In contrast, the examples in (4b) show how the absence of a syllable boundary between the potential trigger and the voiced obstruent disallows the spreading rule to apply.

(4) *Catalan*

a.	su. βlím	'sublime'	b.	sub.li.mi.nál	'subliminal'
	su.βúɾ.βi	'suburb'		sub.sɔ́l	'subsoil'
	bí.βli.ə	'Bible'		kəb.dí	'chief'
	rɛ́b.lə	'receive her'			

There is no such syllabic control in Basque, Spanish, and Portuguese. The examples in (5) show free assimilation of continuancy regardless of where the syllable boundaries are placed.

(5) *Basque* (Hualde & Bilbao, ms.)

bað βákarik	'only one'
suɣ ðústi	'you-erg. everything'

Spanish

aβ.ði.káɾ	'to abdicate'
að.βeɾ.tíɾ	'to warn'

Portuguese

ʌβðɔ́mɛn	'abdomen'
suβɣlutál	'subglottal'

The additional condition imposed by Catalan on the Spreading process must be incorporated into the basic description. (6) accomplishes this, and we observe slightly different processes. The one that applies to Catalan is subject to syllable control, whereas the more general and less constrained one, in (3), deals appropriately with the distribution of facts observed in Basque, Spanish, and Portuguese.

(6) *Spirantization* (Catalan)

Operation:	Spreading
Argument:	Continuant
Direction:	to the right
Trigger:	unrestricted
Target:	voiced obstruents
Condition:	through syllable boundaries

It may be useful to look at a concrete example in order to examine the differences in the application of the two processes: restricted and general. 'To abdicate' has a similar phonetic form in both Catalan and Spanish. Comparing the two forms can help show how Spirantization works in groups of two voiced obstruents. Spreading does not take place in Catalan [əb.di.ká] because the additional condition requiring a syllable boundary between the trigger and the potential target is not satisfied: [ə] and [b] are in the same syllable. In Spanish [aβ.ði.káɾ] Spirantization applies regardless of syllable structure, and thus the Continuant value freely spreads to both target obstruents.

The relevance of syllabic domains in the description of Catalan Spirantization is indicative of a phonological nature, and closer inspection of Catalan syllabification provides further evidence in favor of phonological treatment, making a phonetic explanation more unlikely. When syllable boundaries are revised via resyllabification, the distribution of stop versus approximant observes the initial divisions. This pattern is made evident by the prefix [sub-], when added to a vowel initial radical as in *subàrtic*, *subíndexs* or *subalpí* (see (7)). The labial obstruent is first syllabified as part of a CVC frame and cannot receive its Continuant value from the vowel [u] because both belong to the same syllable. The stop version surfaces as a result of default feature insertion. Since subsequent resyllabification will force the labial stop to act as an onset, [u] and [b] will no longer be in the same syllable. Spirantization does not consider this new position, which would allow [b] to receive Continuant from [u] through the new intervening syllable boundary, thus [b] remains a stop.

(7) *Catalan*

syllabification	resyllabification
sub.áɾ.tik	su.báɾ.tik
sub.íṇ.dəks	su.bíṇ.dəks
sub.əl.pí	su.bəl.pí[3]

The restraint of Spirantization to initial syllabification can be interpreted as a reflection of rule ordering in a model that places Spirantization just between syllabification and resyllabification. This would be the first instance of a general observation reporting that well-attested phonological processes, such as resyllabification, apply after Spirantization. This patterning clearly indicates that Spirantization is a phonological operation.

Following the basic description, two major strategies can be used to account for the systematic presence of stops ([b], [d], [g]) after nasals (see (8)). A 'spreading' analysis requires previous recognition of the existence of the relevant feature (Stop or [-continuant]). In this view, the same formal mechanisms that derive approximants via spreading from a preceding Continuant segment suffice to derive the stop version. The feature spread in this case is [stop] or

[-continuant]. The alternative non-spreading analysis would restrict the object of the spreading process to Continuant (or [+continuant]) and post-nasal [b], [d], [g] would get their stop character by default, reproducing what happens when there is no segment on the left (as in [bɔ́], [dulén] or [gát]).

(8) *Catalan* | | *Basque* |
---|---|---|---
áŋglə | 'angle' | aŋgo | 'of there'
kámbi | 'change' | embor | 'trunk'
kán̪dit | 'candid' | men̪di | 'mountain'
 | | |
Spanish | | *Portuguese* (European) |
áŋgulo | 'angle' | lʌɾĩgutumíʌ | 'laringothomy'
kámbjo | 'change' | 'kwĩbɾʌ | 'Coimbra'
kán̪diðo | 'candid' | kõduzíɾ | 'to drive'

Since a major topic concerning feature inventory is at stake, I will not discuss the two alternatives mentioned. Nevertheless, I will briefly discuss the European Portuguese data of stops after nasalized vowels. The underlying nasal seems to disappear after nasalizing the preceding vowel. The voiced obstruents that follow those nasal vowels remain stops. Phonologically, it can be argued that the stop character of the consonant following the nasal vowel is obtained via spreading from the nasal before its deletion. According to this interpretation, a phonological rule –nasal deletion– would apply after Spirantization and hence constitute new evidence in the argument in favor of the phonological nature of Spirantization.

Hualde's work on Basque phonology provides two more phonological processes which point to the phonological relevance of the stop versus approximant distinction in the phonological component. These two processes are Palatalization and Consonant Epenthesis. In classical terms, we could say that these processes must follow Spirantization. In the examples in (9), Palatalization triggered by the high vowel selectively targets stops (9a), but not approximants (9b). Clearly, Spirantization must be applied before Palatalization and Consonant Epenthesis. The early assignment of Continuant specification by Continuant Spreading crucially intervenes, disallowing the palatalization of voiced obstruents.

(9) *Palatalization in Ondarroa/Gernika Basque* (Hualde, 1991)

a.	/indar/	[iɲɟar]	'strength'
	/egin dau/	[ejɲɟaw]	'he made it'
	/il da/	[iʎɟe]	'he died'
b.	/bide/	[biðe]	'way'
	/idi/	[iði]	'ox'
	/iduri/	[iðuɾi]	'image'

Consonant Epenthesis in Arbizu Basque is the other case that leads us to consider the phonological nature of Spirantization. Postvocalic voiced obstruents surface either as approximants or stops depending on their underlying vs. epenthetic origin. In the examples in (10a), underlying [b] becomes [β], after the application of Continuant Spreading. The examples in (10b) show that epenthetic [b], introduced to provide a CV syllable, keeps its stop character. This distribution can be interpreted as a reflection of the fact that Spirantization precedes Consonant Epenthesis. The segments introduced by this process cannot be affected by Spirantization as they are not present in the representations when Continuant Spreading applies.

(10) *Arbizu Basque* (Hualde, 1991)

a.	[alaβa]	/alaba-a/	'daughter'
	[kuβa]	/kuβa-a/	'Cuba'
b.	[eskuba]	/esku-a/	'the hand'
	[buuba]	/buu-a/	'the head'

Finally, I will examine a case found in Sardinian. The basic process of Spirantization does not differ significantly from the ones that we have seen. What interests us now is the selective pattern that is found in the application of Continuant Spreading across word boundaries, in intervocalic position. As seen in (11), word-initial voiced obstruents do not undergo lenition when an intervocalic context has been created by deletion of the final consonant of a preceding word.

(11) *Sardinian* (Jones, 1988)

a.	kéljɔ ðormíre	'I want to sleep'
b.	kére(t) ddormíre[4]	'(s)he wants to sleep'

Deletion of the final consonant seems to apply after Spirantization has taken place. When the continuant feature is spread, the [d] in (11a) receives its Continuant value from the vowel and becomes [ð]. In (11b), however, the final consonant of [kéret] remains, as do its effects after it is deleted.

A similar situation can be observed in the combination of Spirantization and stop deletion in Basque. Stop deletion simplifies sequences of two stop segments by deleting the first one. The remaining stop is voiceless as a result of previous assimilation from the deleted one: *beinik bein* 'at least' becomes *beinipein* (see Hualde (1991) for a detailed analysis of these processes). Devoicing is optional across word boundaries and it doesn't apply to /g/ in the dialect of Ondarroa. According to Hualde (1987), that refers to Rotaetxe (1979), in the system of Ondarroa Basque a surface post-vocalic velar obstruent is realized as an approximant when it is underlyingly post-vocalic ([eɣon] from /egon/ 'to be, stay', [eɣin] from /egin/ 'to do, make'). In contrast, when the post-vocalic context arises as a result of stop deletion the velar obstruent is realized as a stop: /semat gas/ is pronounced [semagas], and /gisonak gas/ is [gisonagas], with a post-vocalic stop on the surface. The observed distribution of stop and approximants seems to recommend specific rule ordering: Spirantization would apply first and it wouldn't reapply after the application of stop deletion.

Within Optimality Theory, however, the interaction of rules can no longer be expressed as the effect of rule ordering. Constraints on surface representations have replaced rules and, since there is no serial derivation, rule ordering is not available. McCarthy (to appear) is extraordinarily useful in the work of understanding rule ordering in terms of output constraints. Dealing with Tiberian Hebrew post-vocalic Spirantization, McCarthy proposes a NO-V-STOP constraint which asserts that the sequence vowel + stop consonant is prohibited. A constraint of the faithfulness family, IDENT (-cont), looks for the identity of surface and lexical forms, what in rule terms would be the non application of the Spirantization rule. In the derivation of *melex* from /malk/ 'king', disregarding the vowel-quality alternation of the first vowel and the epenthesis of the second, the NO-V-STOP constraint is satisfied and IDENT (-cont) is not, McCarthy's analysis of the surface form *malx* from /malak/ 'kings of' shows how phonological opacity can be handled in Optimality Theory. Since the second vowel in /malak/ is deleted, the optimal output would be *malk*, a form that obeys the IDENT (-cont) constraint. The absence of the vowel in the surface form makes the NO-V-STOP constraint irrelevant and thus unable to guarantee the correct output. As McCarthy points out, we want the NO-V-STOP constraint to be applicable at the underlying level, to /malak/, where it will force Spirantization. At the same time, the output form *melex*, from /malk/, shows that the epenthetic vowel do trigger Spirantization, hence the NO-V-STOP constraint is satisfied at the surface level. Thus, the NO-V-STOP condition obtains at the earlier level in Tiberian Hebrew, the level information that the condition names is 'indifferent'. McCarthy mentions Spirantization of voiced stops in Spanish and claims that the NO-V-STOP condition must be met at the surface level, since all and only surface vowels trigger Spirantization. The analysis of Basque and Sardinian processes just examined provides the third type situation predicted by McCarthy: a system where the NO-V-STOP constraint applies underlyingly but not at the surface level.

Consonant Epenthesis in Arbizu Basque thus confirms the interest of McCarthy's proposal. As he points out, his analysis predicts that stops should not spirantize in a language that imposes the condition underlyingly, a prediction that is satisfied in Basque. The NO-V-STOP constraint is not violated in [eskuba], since the stop is epenthetic and there is no underlying correspondent of the stop preceded by a vowel. In [alaβa] the surface voiced obstruent corresponds to an stop that obeys NO-V-STOP and violates IDENT (-cont) at the underlying level. There is no way to derive this prediction from rule ordering.

Up to this point, I have shown that the interaction between a group of phonological processes and Spirantization forces a phonological analysis of this process. Resyllabification, Nasal Deletion, Palatalization, Consonant Epenthesis, and Final Consonant Deletion interact with Spirantization in a way that can only be accounted for by positing phonological Continuant Spreading.

3. Before entering into a discussion of the consequences of the existence of a continuant-spreading process in the organizational model of phonological features, it is worthwhile to examine several observations which can be grouped as *blocking effects*. In Section 1, I argued in favor of the phonological nature of Spirantization. Now I propose to test this analysis in the descriptive field which has served as the basis for the opposing theory. As we have already seen, the phonetic view has answered basically only the question of why there is blocking of Spirantization in the [l̪d] group. The answer it has provided is purely based on articulatory phonetics, i.e., there is no airflow in the central region during the articulation of the lateral. Therefore, the lateral acts as an occlusive with respect to [d], which is articulated just in this area. In this section, I will show that the phonetic approach cannot be legitimized by blocking effects. In addition, I will point out other questions which must be answered beside the one discussed, and reveal other facts that appear in relation to blocking effects which also require explanation. I will prove the incapacity of the phonetic explanation to answer these questions. Finally, I will propose a phonological solution.

There are two new questions in relation to blocking effects that arise from careful observation of the distribution of approximant and stop variants of voiced obstruents in Catalan. 1) Why is there no Spirantization in the [fb] sequence? 2) Why do we find an asymmetrical pattern in [l̪d] vs. [zð]? In the [fb] sequence, a stop is found after the continuant segment ([f]), even though we expect an approximant. Blocking seems to occur. Focusing now on the [l̪d] sequence, we see that there is blocking of Spirantization, but place features are spread regressively. It may be useful to look at these facts in relation to what happens in the group [zð]. In this sequence the reverse situation is found: Spirantization is allowed, but the Place Assimilation process which would convert the sequence into *[z̪ð] is not accepted.

The first phenomenon examined is the blocking of Spirantization in Catalan [fb] sequences. Systematic blocking effects are commonly described as occurring in homorganic sequences, even though in most cases their observation is restricted to sequences in which an assimilated dental lateral is followed by a voiced dental obstruent. This situation is found systematically in languages having Spirantization.

(12)	*Catalan*		*Basque*	
	əl̪dərúʎ	'disturbance'	tal̪de	'group'
	Spanish		*Portuguese*	
	kál̪do	'broth'	káldu	'broth'

A closer inspection of the data available in Catalan, however, provides other combinations that show blocking of spreading. In (13) we can see two other cases which combine a continuant segment followed by a stop when an approximant would be expected. In (13a) the first segment is a palatal lateral, and the blocking could still be explained by the phonetic means if we accept that [ʎ], as [l], does not allow airflow to pass through the central area. The case exemplified in (13b) is much more challenging. The presence of the stop version after a continuant [f] cannot be accounted for by resorting to the absence of airflow during the production of the labiodental. The systematization of the process allows us to isolate a strategy of the speaker that seems to want to avoid the combination [fβ].

(13) a. [ʎ̪d]

		b. [fb]	
uʎ̪dulén	'bad eye'	buliɣɾəfðulén	'bad pen'
uʎɣɾɔ́k	'yellow eye'	buliɣɾəfɣɾɔ́k	'yellow pen'
uʎβláw	'blue eye'	buliɣɾəfbláw	'blue pen'

Tentatively, we can begin by saying that the system refuses sequences which present the same values with regard to continuity and Place of articulation. This would be sufficient for [l̪d], where the existence of the above mentioned strategy has stopped Spirantization. The same argument holds for [ʎ̪d] if we accept that palatals are complex segments with two articulators, Coronal and Dorsal[5], and we restrict the extent of the problem of cooccurrence to the primary articulator (Coronal in this case). It is quite clear that a general approach to the group of cases is necessary, and that the explanation must link homorganicity and lack of Continuant Spreading ([l̪] and [d] are clearly homorganic and [ʎ̪] and [d] are homorganic with respect to their primary articulators). Along the same lines, I consider the place properties of [f] and [b] equivalent because labiodental does not have a stop version, thus they are as similar as possible.[6]

The second question related to blocking effects is the asymmetrical patterning of [l̪d] and [zð] sequences. There is a clear contrast between these two sequences. They are affected differently by Continuant and Place Spreading. As we have already seen, it does not seem possible to spread both Place and Continuant. This restriction, however, does not affect one of the operations in a systematic way. The sequences that surface are those in (14a). Place Spreading wins in [l̪d] sequences and Continuant Spreading cannot apply. On the other hand, the opposite occurs in [zð] sequences: there is Continuant Spreading and Place Assimilation is blocked. Systematically, none of the other possible combinations considered in (14b) occur, and the precise distribution of facts requires an explanation.

(14) a.

([l̪d], [zð])

b.

*([l̪d], [z̪d])
*([l̪ð], [zð])
*([l̪ð], [z̪d])

Later, I will show how the distribution in (14) can easily be predicted using independent facts relative to the underspecification of phonological units. Before doing this, however, I want to present in more depth what I think could be a phonological analysis of blocking effects. Now I can only say that the solution to the asymmetry in the sequences [l̪d] vs. [zð] is closely related to the volume of information present in the representations below. More concretely, the theory of underspecification can help us understand why Continuant wins in [zð] and not in [l̪d]: [z] is underlyingly marked for Continuant while [l] is not, as Continuant is a redundant value for laterals.

I have added new questions to the problem of blocking effects. For the moment, we have not given a specific phonological answer. It is clear, in any case, that there is no immediate solution apparent in what we have called phonetic view. If the phonetic point of view could claim to have explained the absence of Spirantization in [l̪d], we must conclude that neither the group [fb] nor the asymmetry [l̪d] vs. [zð] can be solved as easily. I shall now make a schematic drawing of what can be a phonological solution to these problems.

4 A first glance at blocking effects has enabled us to see that Continuant and Place properties are strongly related. In Feature Geometry, the node that groups Place and Continuant together is the Oral Cavity node. I will present an analysis of blocking effects that refers specifically to this node. Before doing so, however, I look at another apparently independent process which I attribute to the same combination of principles. I therefore present one instance of a cooccurrence restriction that refers to the Oral Cavity node. Additionally, I will argue that it is triggered by the Obligatory Contour Principle (OCP). Later, I will show that the same principle, also acting on the Oral Cavity node, is responsible for the blocking effects I presented in the preceding section. In (15), I summarize the basic aspects concerning the OCP. I include its definition in (15a), and the class of elements and rules that it can affect in (15b). Finally, the statement in (15c) *Class Node Content* aims to provide a definition of the identity of a class node for the purposes of the OCP. The computation of identity in a class node has to refer to all its dependents according to the basic model of Feature Geometry, which is what I mean by *exhaustive,* in (15c). A consequence of this interpretation is that absent features are not involved in identity based relations.

(15) *Elements of the analysis/working hypothesis*

a. *Obligatory Contour Principle* (OCP) (McCarthy, 1986)
Adjacent identical elements are prohibited.

b. *On OCP activity:*
1. The OCP applies in tiers. The available tiers are the constituents of Feature Geometry, i.e. content nodes and class nodes.
2. The OCP can trigger and block phonological rules, but the introduction of redundant values cannot be affected by this principle.

c. *Class Node Content*
The identity of a class node is exhaustively defined by its dependents, and absent feature values do not participate in identity relations.

I will now consider a descriptive case connected to a restriction on the free cooccurrence of fricatives in Catalan, Basque, Portuguese, and Spanish. I will argue that this restriction is OCP related. Furthermore, I will claim that this principle prohibits sequences of segments with identical specifications for Place and Continuant, i.e., with identical Oral Cavity nodes. The main strategy applied to avoid the OCP is degemination by deletion of the first consonant in the sequence. A more restricted strategy is Dissimilation, observed in Balearic Catalan and, in some specific contexts, in Basque. I will draw my examples from Catalan, although the situation I will describe is also valid for the other three languages.

Turning to the data, the two members of the CC sequences transcribed in (16), have the same Place features. Notice, however, that while the pairs in (16a) can cooccur, the ones in (16b) cannot. Here, one of the members deletes or dissimilates.

(16) a.

ca[p#p]as	ca[pp]as	'no step'
co[m#m]ort	co[mm]ort	'as if dead'
mi[l#l]àmines	mi[ll]àmines	'thousand sheets'
bolígra[f#f]úcsia	bolígra[ff]úcsia	'fuchsia pen'

b.

si[s#s]ots	si[s]ots	'six holes'
si[s#ʃ]ecs	si[ʃ]ecs	'six checks'

b'. *Balearic Catalan*

si[s#s]ots	si[ts]ots	'six holes'
si[s#ʃ]ecs	si[tʃ]ecs	'six checks'

The unifying property of each group of sequences is the absence or presence of an underlying Continuant specification. In (16a), no marked value for continuant is required in stops, nasals, or laterals, since all of them have predictable specifications. In contrast, the segments in the sequences in (16b) are marked as continuants in the initial representations. In (17) a schematic presentation of some of these sequences is given. Under the hypothesis that the OCP checks adjacent Oral Cavity nodes for identity, this principle will not find the sequences in (17a) problematic. The elements in these sequences can cooccur since, although they have the same Place, their continuancy value is underspecified. According to the definition of *Class Node Content* in (15c), both values are required to be present. Since one of them is absent in (17a), no reference can be made to identity at the level of Oral Cavity. It is generally accepted that stops and sonorants lack a marked value for continuant. Additionally, since labiodentals can cooccur as well, I will assume that they also lack a continuant value. Turning now to the sequences in (17b), they have a marked Continuant specification, which means they agree in both Place and continuancy. Here, the OCP applies, disallowing these sequences.

(17) a. [pp], [mm] [ll] [ff]

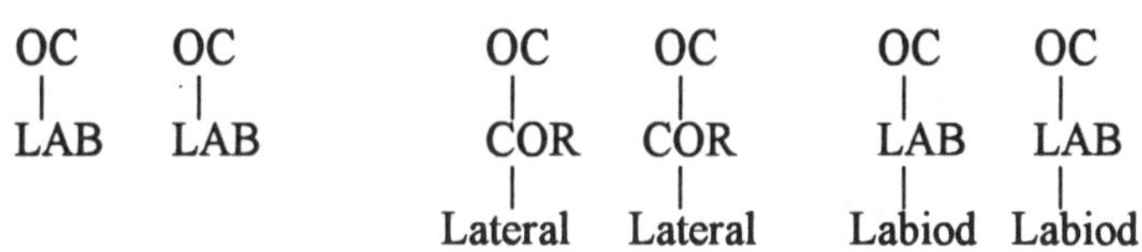

b. *[ss]

*[sʃ]

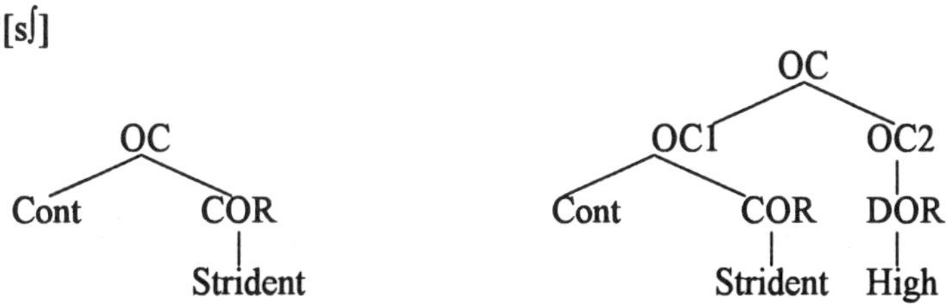

Two rules apply to improve the sequences in (17b); I view them as repair strategies activated by the OCP. Degemination, which occurs in Central Catalan, Basque, Portuguese, and Spanish results from the application of the rule in (18), which delinks the Oral Cavity node of the first element in conflict. Deletion of this node derives from its inability to reattach and from the action of Stray Erasure on floating elements. The empty slot is never realized, rather it deletes before redundancy rules fill in the unmarked values. The other repair strategy, Dissimilation, begins with the application of the same rule in (18). However, in this case, default rules supply the unspecified values to the skeletal position to produce the stop part of the affricate.

(18) *Basic operation for degemination and dissimilation*

Operation:	Delinking
Argument:	Oral Cavity
Direction:	to the right (i.e. delink first)
Trigger:	OCP

To clarify how the mechanism works in the last sequence in (17b), a reference to segments with two articulators must be made. At least for Catalan, there is independent evidence supporting a representation of palatals as complex segments. There is also evidence that no assimilatory process applies before degemination or dissimilation. The representation of the palatal strident in (17b) as a complex segment with two Oral Cavity nodes reflects the fact that different continuant values can be assigned to independent articulators. The absence of continuant specification in the Oral Cavity containing Dorsal qualifies it as secondary, since it is generally assumed that the primary vs. secondary status deals with the presence vs. the absence of a distinctive value for Continuant. According to the definition of *Class Node Content* given in (15c), the adjacent Oral Cavity nodes in (17a) are not identical because they lack a value for continuant, and because absent values do not participate in identity relations. Returning to complex segments, an OCP violation arises in the sequence of a plain strident followed by a palatal strident in (17b). In this example, the identity occurs between the Oral Cavity node of the first segment and, for the palatal strident, the Oral Cavity node appearing in the first place in the representation. Since the two parts of a Complex Segment are unordered, the adjacency requirement mentioned by the OCP would be satisfied anyway. Our prediction is that the Oral Cavity node containing Dorsal will not participate in cooccurrence restrictions as a class node.

The blocking effects found in Continuant Spreading are repeated now in (19) with their corresponding structures. Notice that blocking is derived simply from the same mechanism proposed to account for degemination and dissimilation in homorganic continuants. I want to say now that the OCP blocks the phonological operation of Continuant Spreading when the output would contain a sequence of segments with identical Oral Cavity nodes. Thus what we do find, blocking of spreading in homorganic sequences is just what we expect to find. Blocking arises from the combination of primitives in (15). The OCP blocks those rules leading to adjacent identical Oral Cavity nodes.

(19) l̪d fb

To finish the analysis of blocking effects I want to look at the asymmetry in (20) and try to give an answer in my terms. I derive the asymmetry from the fact that [z], contrary to [l], has a marked Continuant specification underlyingly. There is Continuant Spreading in (20a), and [z] can spread Continuant to [d] while [l] cannot. In (20b), dental assimilation takes place in [l̪d]. It is blocked in the [zð] sequence because of shared Continuant values. Spreading of the dental feature would produce an OCP violation in Oral Cavity. Similarly, in (20c), spreading of Continuant in [l̪d] sequences, would result in an OCP violation, hence it is blocked.

(20) [ld] -> [l̪d] [zd] -> [zð]

a. *Continuant Spreading*

b. *Place Spreading*

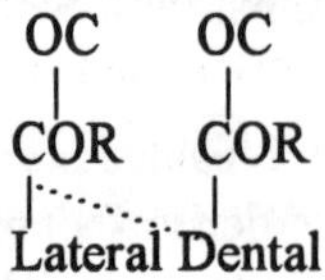

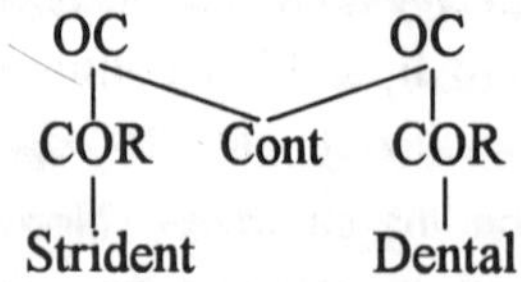

c. *Continuant Spreading*

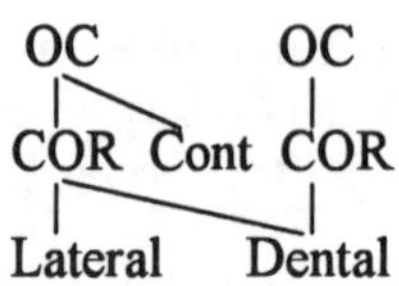

Finally, I present a brief and partial evaluation of the models for Oral Cavity internal organization in light of the Spirantization phenomena discussed. The three basic hypotheses stated regarding the internal structure of the Oral cavity node are summarized in (21).

(21)

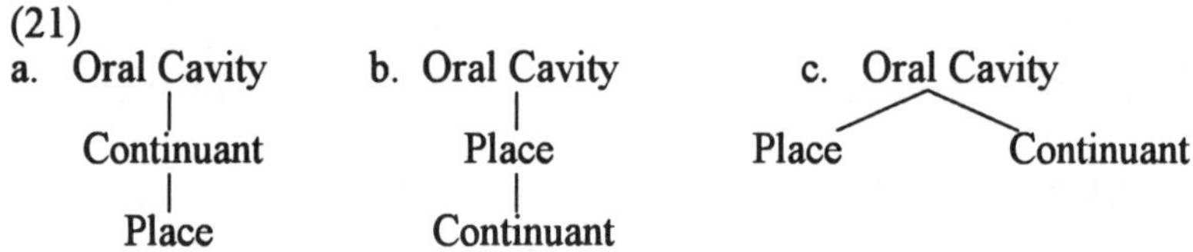

(Selkirk, 1988; Wetzels, 1988) (Padgett, 1991) (Clements, 1987)

If indeed Spirantization is a phonological operation of Continuant Spreading, its sole existence constitutes a counterargument for (21a), which posits the Place node as dependent upon the feature of Continuant. A proposal incorporating this dependency cannot account for Continuant Spreading without Place spreading. The proposals in (21b and 21c) allow free autosegmental spreading of Continuant and thus the basic facts of Spirantization do not constitute a problem.[7]

Notes

* This work was supported by the CIRIT and the DGICYT under the grants CS93-5005 and PB93-0893-C04-03.

1 Data from Catalan correspond to my own native pronunciation. Basque examples are drawn from Hualde (1991). Portuguese examples come from Andrade (1977), there is however a considerable degree of variation among Portuguese dialects in this respect. Spanish examples are not controversial and can be found in any basic description of the language.

2 See Hualde (1991) for a critical evaluation of Mascaró's proposal. I would agree that there is a possible phonetic account for this specific case. However, I do not agree with the phonetic approach in explaining the stop-fricative alternation because it is build up exclusively on one case. The relation between homorganicity and stop/plosive consonants is also reported by Ladefoged (1975:48), who refers to the reverse combination ([dl] instead of [ld]): "A phenomenon similar to nasal plosion takes place when an alveolar stop [t] or [d] occurs after an homorganic lateral [l], as in "little, ladle"(...). The air pressure that is built up during the stop is released lowering the sides of the tongue (...). The contact on the alveolar ridge in the center of the mouth is maintained throughout both the stop and the lateral."

3 These words are often pronounced as [su'paɾtik], [su'pin̪dəks], [supəl'pi] as a result of the application of typically word-final devoicing to the prefix [sub-]. It is significant, however, the forms [su'βaɾtik], [su'βin̪dəks], [suβəl'pi] are never found.

4 The reinforced, apparently geminate, status can be interpreted as a reflection of its failure to undergo lenition, according to Jones (1988).

5 See an argument on this point in Palmada & Serra (1991), and Palmada (1991, 1992 and forthcoming).

6 In earlier works, I have defended the view that bilabials and labiodentals share characterization as labials, and that the differences between these two groups are established by features depending on this articulator. These features define the way Labial must act. See Palmada (1991, 1995).

7 See, however, Palmada (1991, 1995) for an argument against Place-dependent Continuant based on the unmarked status of Continuant in segments with predictable continuant Place properties (labiodentals, interdentals and palatals).

References

Andrade, Ernesto d.' 1977. *Aspects de la Phonologie (Générative) du Portugais*. Lisbon: Instituto Nacional de Investigaçõ Cientifica.

Archangeli, Diana and Douglas Pulleyblank. 1993. *Grounded Phonology*, Cambridge Mass.: MIT Press.

Aronoff, Mark. and Richard T. Oehrle, (eds). *1984. Language Sound Structure.* Cambridge Mass.: MIT Press.

Bibiloni, G. 1983. *La Llengua dels Mallorquins. Anàlisi Sociolingüística.* Doctoral dissertation, Universitat de Barcelona.

Clements, G. Nick. 1985. The geometry of phonological features, *Phonology Yearbook,* 2.225-52

Clements, G. Nick. 1987. Phonological feature representation and the description of intrusive stops, *Chicago Linguistic Society* 23, II. 29-50.

Harris, W. James. 1984a Autosegmental Phonology, Lexical Phonology, and Spanish nasals, in Aronoff and Oehrle (1984).

Harris, W. James. 1984b. La espirantización en castellano y la representación fonológica autosegmental, Estudis Gramaticals 1, *Working Papers in Linguistics* : 149-167. Universitat Autònoma de Barcelona.

Hualde, J. Ignacio. 1987. On Basque affricates, *Proceedings of the WCCFL* 6, 77-89.

Hualde, J. Ignacio. 1991. *Basque Phonology.* London: Routledge.

Hualde, J. Ignacio and Xavier Bilbao. 1993. *A Phonological Study of the Basque Dialect of Getxo*, Supplements of *Anuario del Seminario de Filología Vasca Julio Urquijo.* Donostia-San Sebastián: Diputación de Gipuzkoa.

Mascaró, Joan. 1984. Continuant spreading in Basque, Catalan, and Spanish, in Aronoff and Oehrle (1984).

Mascaró, Joan. 1991. Iberian spirantization and continuant spreading, *Catalan Working Papers in Linguistics*, 1991.167-179.

McCarthy, John. 1986. OCP Effects: Gemination and antigemination, *Linguistic Inquiry,* 17

McCarthy, John. 1988. Feature geometry and dependency: A review, *Phonetica* 43.84-108.

McCarthy, John. (to appear) Remarks on phonological opacity in Optimality Theory, *Proceedings of the Second Colloquium on Afro-Asiatic Linguistics (Sophia Antipolis, June, 1994)*, ed. Jacqueline Lecarme, Jean Lowenstamm and Ur Shlonsky.

Padgett, Jay. 1991. *Stricture in Feature Geometry*, Doctoral Dissertation, University of Massachusetts, Amherst.

Padgett, Jay. 1993. *Stricture and nasal place assimilation*, University of California, Santa Cruz ms.

Palmada, B. 1990. The OCP as a rule blocker and as a rule trigger: some data from two Catalan dialects, Basque and Spanish, paper presented at the 1990 Going Romance, Utrecht.

Palmada, B. 1991. *La Fonologia del Català i els Principis Actius*, Doctoral Dissertation, Universitat Autònoma de Barcelona, published in 1994, *La Fonologia del Català*, Bellaterra: Special Publications of Universitat Autònoma de Barcelona.

Palmada, B. 1992. Gliding processes and complex segments, paper presented at the 7th International Phonology Meeting, Krems, Austria.

Palmada, B. 1993. Constituent structure in the oral cavity, paper presented at the 16th GLOW Colloquium-Phonology Workshop, Lund.

Palmada, B. 1995. From place to continuancy, Leiden in Last, *HIL Phonology Papers I*, ed. by Harry van der Hulst & Jeroen van de Weijer. Leiden.

Palmada, B. 1996. Les palatals del Català, *Caplletra 19*, Universitat de València.

Palmada, B. & P. Serra 1991. On the specification of coronals, *Catalan Working Papers in Linguistics* 1. Bellaterra: Universitat Autònoma de Barcelona.

Recasens, D. 1991. *Fonètica Descriptiva del Català*. Barcelona: Institut Estudis Catalans.

Rotaetxe, K. 1978. *Estudio Estructural del Euskara de Ondarroa*. Durango, Vizcaya: L. Zugaza.

Sagey, E. 1986. *The Representation of Features and Relations in Non-linear Phonology*, Doctoral dissertation, MIT.

Selkirk, E. 1988. A two-root theory of length, paper presented at *NELS*, 19.

Wetzels, L. W. 1988. Contrastive and allophonic properties of Brazilian Portuguese vowels. Paper presented at the *Linguistic Symposium on Romance Languages*.

Yip, M. 1989. Feature Geometry and cooccurrence restrictions. *Phonology*, 6:349-374.

6

Prosodic manifestation of syntactic structure in Catalan*

PILAR PRIETO

1 Introduction

In the last few years experimental research has shown that a variety of small differences in the scaling of F_0 peaks might be attributed to syntactic structure (Ladd & Johnson 1987, Ladd 1988, 1990, 1993, 1994, Kubozono 1989, 1992). For example, Ladd & Johnson (1987) argue that branching structure affects the height of the first peak of phrase initial constituents in English, and Kubozono (1992) reports that right-branching utterances in Japanese exhibit a downtrend pattern which is more distinct from that of left-branching utterances: initial accents of right-branching constituents undergo a process of pitch or metrical *boosting*, allowing listeners to identify syntactic structure through pitch scaling differences.

Recent results on the investigation of such phenomena are affecting the views about the mapping from *syntactic* to *prosodic* structure. In the last decade, a large body of evidence showing that phonological rules do not refer directly to a rich syntactic structure has lead researchers to postulate an intermediate and impoverished *prosodic* structure, which defines the domains to which phonological rules can refer. Even though there are differences between the various syntax-prosody mapping algorithms (Nespor & Vogel 1986, Selkirk 1984), the so-called Strict Layer Hypothesis (SLH) has been widely accepted. In short, SLH defends that prosodic structure is strictly layered, that is, that higher nodes must always contain lower nodes in the hierarchy.

This view has been inherited by what we might call the *standard theory* of intonational phonology (Pierrehumbert 1980, Beckman & Pierrehumbert 1986, Pierrehumbert & Beckman 1988). This framework proposes two levels of phrasing in English: *intermediate phrase* (which consists of one or more pitch accents plus a phrase accent), and *intonational phrase* (which consists of one or more intermediate phrases plus a boundary tone). In accordance with SLH, intonational phrases cannot contain any other prosodic domain except intermediate phrases. Regarding the scaling of peaks, Pierrehumbert and her colleagues state that two possible manipulations of pitch height are predicted by their framework. First, a strictly local downstep, or accent-by-accent compression of the pitch range, whose application is bound to the domains of a given prosodic constituent (generally, intermediate or intonational phrases).[1] And second, pitch reset or a pitch height increase attested at the beginning of a prosodic constituent. This pitch reset is described as a nonphonological manipulation of pitch height, a continuous variable whose changes are attributed to a free choice on the part of the speaker and constrained by the overall pragmatics of the situation.

Ladd (1988, 1990, 1993, 1994) and Kubozono (1992) argue that the Strict Layer Hypothesis is too strict to account for the pitch downtrend differences sensitive to branching structure mentioned before, and that a richer *recursive* prosodic structure is needed. (1) represents two Japanese sentences with left vs. right-branching structures using the recursive prosodic constituency proposed by Kubozono (1992: 385).[2] A *strictly layered* prosodic structure would not be able to account for the pitch scaling differences exemplified by these two sentences, given that upstep or pitch boosting exclusively affects initial accents belonging to a right-branched constituent. Instead, if we allow for a richer recursive prosodic structure, we obtain a mechanism to single out the accents undergoing metrical upstep:

(1) a. Left-branching b. Right-branching

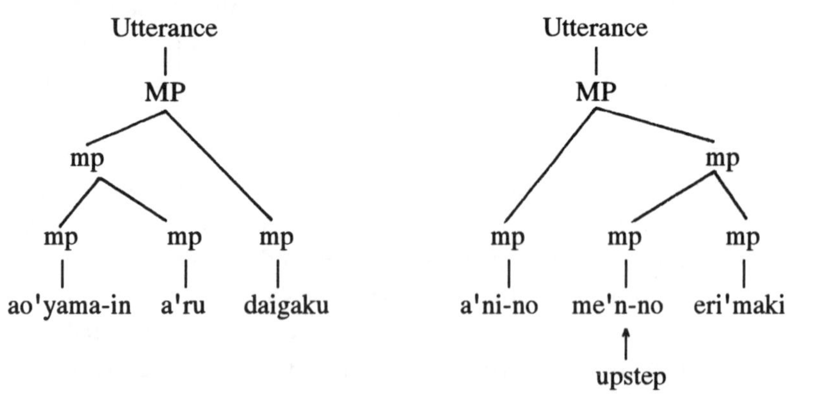

a. Aoyama-in exist university
'a university in Ayoama'

b. brother-GEN cotton-GEN muffler
'(my) brother's cotton muffler'

In light of the present controversy, there is a need to explore the relevance of metrical and syntactic structure in the scaling of F_0 peaks in more depth. In this regard, Catalan seems to be an appropriate case to study. In her description of Central Catalan intonation, Bonet (1984) mentions that the presence of constituent boundaries is signaled through pitch scaling differences, namely, by the presence of a low tone on the constituent-final accented syllable. According to her, the scaling of F_0 peaks (in particular, the pitch level attained by the constituent-final stressed syllable) is crucial to disambiguate right- vs. left-branching utterances like the ones shown in (2). In (2a) the stressed syllable in the word *llança* receives a low tone, and in (2b) it is *vella* that receives the low tone:

(2) a. Left-branching

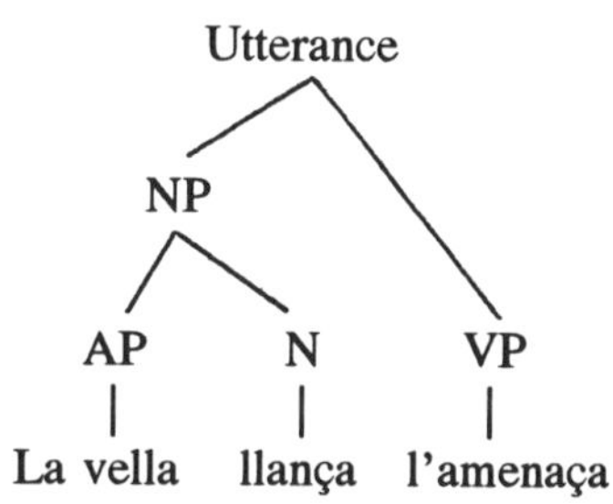

'The old lance threatens him/her'

b. Right-branching

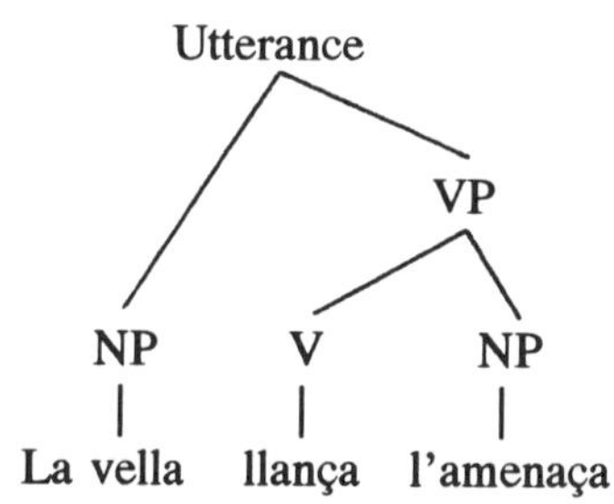

'The old lady threatens him/her'

The aim of this study is twofold. First, to investigate how Catalan speakers disambiguate structurally ambiguous sentences of the type shown above and whether listeners are able to recognize their corresponding meaning. And second, to further explore Bonet's hypothesis about the relationship between F_0 scaling and constituent boundaries in Catalan and, more generally, to seek evidence regarding the influence of syntactic/prosodic structure on pitch downtrend patterns. If pitch scaling were the only cue serving to disambiguate the structures in (2) (with no accompanying phrasing differences), this would indicate the need to revise the Strict Layer Hypothesis and advocate for a recursive type of prosodic structure.

2 Method

2.1 Production test

For many languages, it has been reported that prosodic features such as duration, amplitude and F_0 changes reflect syntactic structure and that speakers and listeners are able to use this prosodic information to disambiguate structurally ambiguous sentences (Klatt 1973, Lehiste 1973, Terken & Collier 1992, Venditti 1994). The main goal of the production part of the experiment is to analyze duration and fundamental frequency differences (concentrating on the scaling of F_0 peaks) between potentially ambiguous sentences in Catalan.

Methodologically, it is important to test the effects of syntactic structure on F_0 and duration patterns of potentially ambiguous sentences, that is, sentences that differ *exclusively* in constituent structure. It is well-known that F_0 and segmental durations are influenced by a variety of factors like the phonetic structure of neighboring segments, degree of stress, within-word position, sentence position, etc. Thus, by using sentences containing the same string of words, we are neutralizing the potential confounding effects of other factors, and more accurate comparisons are possible. (3) lists the four potentially ambiguous utterances used in the experiment, which involve right vs. left-branching structures of the type [NP][[VP][NP]] vs. [[AP][NP]][VP]. The list provides the two possible meanings of the utterances and separates the syntactic subject from the VP by a comma:

(3)

La vella, llança l'amenaça	'The old lady threatens him/her'
La vella llança, l'amenaça	'The old lance threatens him/her'
La vella, escolta la veu	'The old lady LISTENS to the voice'
La vella escolta, la veu	'The old girl scout sees her'
La poderosa, crema la casa	'The powerful lady sets the house on fire'
La poderosa crema, la casa	'The powerful cream helps her get married'
El vell, guarda la porta	'The old man guards the door'
El vell guarda, la porta	'The old guard is wearing it (the scarf)'

Several experimental studies have found that *degree of embedding* or *constituency length* significantly affects the height of the first F_0 peak at the start of each constituent (Ladd and Johnson 1987, Kubozono 1992, Venditti 1994).[3]

The second set of sentences in (4) was designed to analyze the potential effects of degree of embedding on pitch scaling. They were obtained by adding a complement to the utterance-final constituent of each of the sentences in (3). By comparing each of the new sentences in (4) with its corresponding utterance in (3) we can test whether or not the height of the constituent-initial peak is affected by the depth of the constituent:

(4) *La vella, llança l'amenaça terrible*
'The old lady threatens him/her terribly'

La vella llança, l'amenaça terriblement
'The old lance threatens him/her terribly'

La vella, escolta la veu especial
'The old lady listens to the special voice'

La vella escolta, la veu amb encís
'The old girl scout sees her with delight'

La poderosa, crema la casa de Vilamalla
'The powerful lady sets the Vilamalla house on fire'

La poderosa crema, la casa ben casada
'The powerful cream helps her get married for good'

El vell, guarda la porta del carrer
'The old man guards the main door'

El vell guarda, la porta ben content
'The old gard is happily wearing it (the scarf)'

Each utterance in (3) and (4) was placed in a disambiguating paragraph (see Appendix I). Then, three speakers of Central Catalan (PG, JS, and PP)[4] read each paragraph from six to eight times with an effort to differentiate the two meanings of each sentence. In order to obtain two different pronunciations, speakers made a conscious attempt at differenciating between the two possible meanings of each sentence. To avoid the use of pauses to disambiguate the test sentences, subjects were asked to read the paragraphs at a relatively fast tempo.

The final recordings totalled 336 target utterances/paragraphs (16 paragraphs x 7 repetitions x 3 speakers = 336).

After completing the recordings, the target sentences were separated from their paragraphs and prosodically labelled using the TOBI annotation conventions (Pitrelli et al. 1994). The following F_0 and duration measures were taken, using the waveform, spectrogram and corresponding F_0 contour of each file: 1) phrase-initial F_0 value; 2) maximum F_0 peak for each pitch accent (H* or L*); 3) maximum F_0 boundary tone (H^-); 4) phrase-final F_0 value; and 5) duration of each of the syllables in the sentence (only for speaker PP).

2.2 Perceptual test

The second part of the experiment consists of a perceptual test. Its main goal is to investigate whether listeners can easily identify the meaning corresponding to the pronunciations of the left- vs. right-branching utterances. The stimuli consisted of the sentences in (3) read by speakers PP and PG, for a total of 16 sentences.[5] A five-second interval appeared between each stimulus, presented in random order within sentence-types. Eighteen university students and staff having Catalan as a first language participated in the experiment. The stimuli sentences were presented over a portable mini-disc recorder and the listeners were asked to decide on the meaning of each of the sentences (see Appendix 2). In each session, listeners were allowed to pause to make their judgment, but they were not permitted to hear a given sentence twice.

3 Analysis and discussion

3.1 Results of the production experiment

This section describes the intonational and durational differences found between the two productions of each sentence in (3) and (4), focusing on the potential differences in pitch downtrend patterns between right-branching and left-branching structures. In her study of Catalan intonation patterns, Bonet (1984: 15) claims that declarative sentences with more than one syntactic constituent have the following tonal characteristics:[6] 1. All accented syllables belonging to the last constituent in the utterance have a low tone; 2. The last accent in a constituent has a low tone; 3. The rest of the accents have a high tone. According to Bonet, the tonal distribution predicted by the patterns above is crucial to disambiguate the two meanings of ambiguous sentences such as *La vella llança l'amenaça*. When *vella* is the syntactic subject, the phonological constituent ends right after this word and the accent in *ve* is low. In contrast, when *vella llança* is the subject, it is the accent on *llan* that is low. She also notes that an optional high boundary tone can appear at the end of this constituent. The sentences in (5) below show Bonet's intonational transcription of a left-branching utterance (5a) *Una jove veu, l'amenaça* 'a young voice threatens him/her'and a right-branching utterance (5b) *Una jove, veu l'amenaça* 'a young girl sees the threat' (Bonet 1984: 20). The main difference between the two is the pitch level attained by the word *jove*: in (5a), being non-final in the constituent, it is high; instead, in (5b) it is low (constituent-final accent):

(5) a.

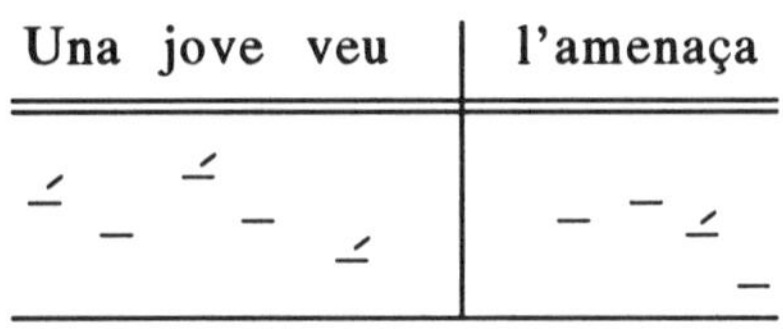

b.

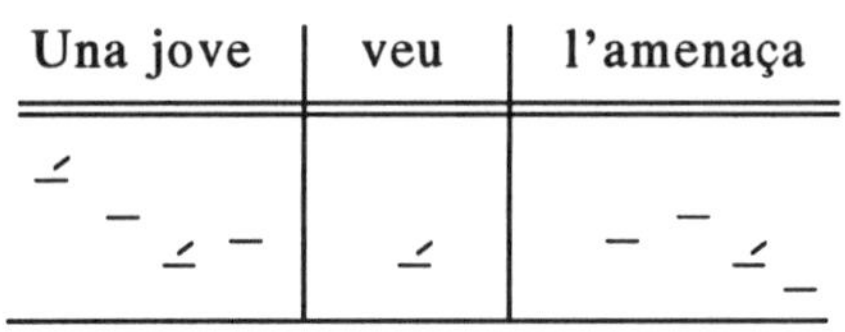

We employed a recent version of Pierrehumbert's accent inventory (Beckman & Hirschberg 1993) to transcribe the examples. This theory of intonational transcription is based on the binary classification of local F_0 minima or maxima located around accented syllables (*pitch accents*) and phrase boundaries (*boundary tones*).[7] The claim is that we can obtain a phonologically adequate tonal transcription by using exclusively H and L tones. The decision between Hs and Ls is based on adjacent tonal values and the speaker's register; for example, L tones are generally manifested as local minima, generally coinciding with the baseline of the speaker. There are two levels of phrasing.

An *intermediate phrase*, which consists of one or more pitch accents plus a phrase accent (or a simple H^- and L^- tone that controls the pitch from the last pitch accent to the end of the phrase). The other is an *intonational phrase*, which consists of one or more intermediate phrases plus a final boundary tone, which may also be high (H%) or low (L%), occurring at the end of the phrase.

(6) shows the intonational transcription of our speaker's pronunciation of right-branching (6a) vs. left-branching utterances (6b).[8] Below each transcription we display the actual F_0 contour of speaker JS producing the right-branching utterance *La vella, llança l'amenaça* in (6a) or the left-branching utterance *La vella llança, l'amenaça* in (6b). Intonational phrasing is the most salient difference between the two realizations of the sentence: an intermediate phrase boundary (phonetically marked by a high phrase accent H^-) is placed in two different positions depending on the constituent structure of the sentence (after the syntactic subject). The presence of a high boundary tone H- is perceptually clear. Also, it is phonetically identified by a steady increase of the pitch level from the pitch accent on *vella* and on *llança* to the phrase boundary. Usually, the three stressed syllables are accented. With the exception of the last accents in the utterance, pitch accents are transcribed as high (H*), as they all attain levels well above the baseline of the particular speaker. Utterance-final pitch accents are transcribed as L*, since F_0 levels at this point generally approach the baseline of each speaker.[9]

(6) Intonational transcription of right vs. left-branching utterances

a. H* H^- H* L* L^-L%
La vella, llança l'amenaça

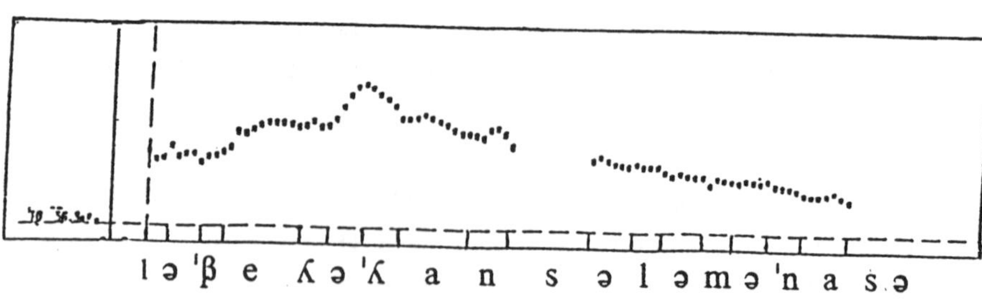

JS contour of *La vella, llança l'amenaça*

b. H* !H* H$^-$ L* L$^-$L%
La vella llança, l'amenaça

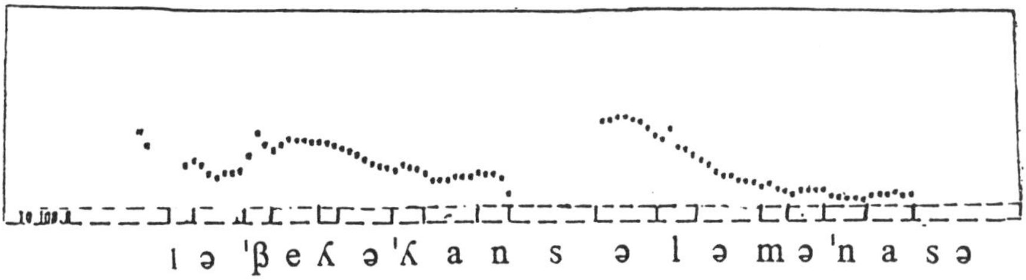

JS contour of *La vella llança, l'amenaça*

The F_0 contours in (6) exhibit different pitch downtrend patterns. The first accent, aligned with the syllable *ve*, attains more or less the same pitch level in both sentences (the phrase accent, H$^-$, is present only in (6b), and aligned with the postonic syllable *lla*). The pitch level of the H* accent on the word *llança* is higher when *llança* starts a new intermediate phrase (after H$^-$) than when it is the last word in the constituent. Thus, the particular pronunciation in (6) shows that F_0resets at the beginning of a new intermediate phrase. To test whether the two types of branching structure exhibit consistent differences in pitch downtrend patterns, we need to analyze the measures of the production test for the three speakers (JS, PP, PG). Table 1 shows the mean F_0 values of four target values corresponding to the following positions in the F_0 contour, for the two types of branching structure: first pitch accent in the sentence (H*), phrase accent (H$^-$), utterance-final accent (L*), and second pitch accent of the sentence (X or Y). The second H* pitch accent is named X or Y depending on its position within the prosodic constituent: X when the accent is at the beginning of a new intermediate phrase, and Y when it is constituent-final. Means were obtained by averaging all of the values of the sentences in (3) (8 sentences x 7 repetitions = 56 examples in each cell). Since the pitch range (or minimum and maximum F_0 values each speaker reaches) is different for each speaker, values in the F_0 contour are comparable only within speakers. The results in Table 1 show that speakers JS and PP exhibit a consistent difference between the pitch level attained by X and Y: when the accent is the last in the constituent (Y), its peak is around 10 Hz lower than when it is constituent-initial (X). Speaker PG, though, does not exhibit a distinct pitch downtrend pattern between the two sentences: the height of the second accent is practically the same in constituent-initial (X) or constituent-final (Y) position. Probably this is an indication that differences in pitch downtrend are not crucial but they can help to disambiguate right-branching and left-branching structures. If that is the case, the perceptual score obtained using PG as stimuli sentences might be lower than using JS or PP sentences.

Table 1. Mean F_0 values (in Hz) of sentences in (3)

Right-branching utterances (La vella, **llança** l'ame**na**ça):

	H*	H^-	X	L*
JS	115	133	107	80
PP	190	213	184	149
PG	147	161	132	105

Left-branching utterances (La **vella llan**ça, l'ame**na**ça):

	H*	Y	H^-	L*
JS	115	98	119	80
PP	195	172	188	154
PG	148	134	148	106

The results in Table 1 also confirm our previous observations. We find that variation in intonational phrasing is a consistent strategy to disambiguate right- vs. left-branching utterances: to distinguish the two meanings of the sentence, Catalan speakers produced an intermediate phrase boundary after the syntactic subject. A consistent and clear phonetic correlate of phrasing is the presence of a H^- boundary tone and, optionally, a short pause at the end of the intermediate phrase. As Table 1 shows, there is a salient distance between the pitch height attained by a Y and a H^-, namely, between 14 and 20 Hz difference between a Y and a following H^-.

In sum, Bonet's hypothesis is partially confirmed. When Catalan speakers try to disambiguate sentences with left- vs. right-branching structures, there is a unanimous tendency to have phrasing differences. Against Bonet's claim, the actual phonetic correlates of phrasing structure are found to be a consistent presence of a H^- boundary tone, and *not* pitch lowering of constituent-final accents. Using Pierrehumbert's framework to interpret the data, we find that the height of the first peak H* (i.e., the one corresponding to the word *vella*) has the same pitch level in both types of branching structure for the three speakers (see Table 1). Again, Table 2 shows the mean F_0 peak (in Hz) of the first H* for right- vs. left-branching structures, as well as utterance-initial and utterance-final F_0 values. The results in Table 2 confirm that the three measures are rather constant in the two pronunciations of the sentence for a given speaker (they also display very low standard deviation values). For each speaker, the differences between the two populations were found to be nonsignificant (at $p < 0.01$).

Table 2. Mean F_0 (in Hz) of different locations in the F_0 contour

Right-branching utterances (La **vella**, **llança** l'**amenaça**):

	Initial	H*	Final
JS	100	115	77
PP	176	190	136
PG	116	147	92

Left-branching utterances (La **vella** **llança**, l'**amenaça**):

	Initial	H*	Final
JS	102	115	79
PP	174	195	134
PG	118	148	98

In general, we conclude that Catalan displays a tendency to *reset* the pitch of a constituent-initial accent, even though it seems that such a reset is *not* an obligatory phonetic cue of phrasing in this language (cf. speaker PG in Table 3). We find an optional pitch reset at the beginning of a new intermediate phrase (after a high boundary tone). The difference in pitch scaling is one of the expected variations in pitch height, and follow from standard assumptions made by Pierrehumbert and her colleagues. Thus, a strictly layered prosodic structure can account for the pitch downtrend differences found in the two types of branching structures, and the Strict Layer Hypothesis is thus not challenged by this data.

With respect to the role of duration, several studies have defended that preboundary lengthening is also a phonetic cue that serves to signal phrasing differences (Klatt 1973, Cooper & Paccia-Cooper 1980). In our data, we expected a significant amount of syllable lengthening before intermediate phrase-boundaries (i.e., syllables with a H^-). Table 3 compares the mean duration (in ms) of the word-final and penultimate syllables of the same word in preboundary and phrase-medial positions for speaker PP. The table shows very inconsistent results: out of the eight cases analyzed, only three have longer syllables in preboundary position. Thus, the duration patterns of the two branching structures reveal no significant differences, suggesting that variations in pitch play a more crucial role in distinguishing the two sentences.

Table 3. Mean syllable duration (in ms) for speaker PP of sentences in (3)

	Pre-boundary		Constituent-medial	
Target word	Penult	Final	Penult	Final
vella	12	15	11	15
vella	8.5	8	7.3	8
poderosa	11	13	11	12
guarda	21	9.3	23	9.4

3.2 Degree of embedding

With the goal of exploring the potential effect of degree of embedding on the height of the constituent-initial peak, we created the new set of sentences shown in (4). We expected that longer constituents would trigger a pitch boost of the constituent-initial accent. For example, assuming that Catalan speakers would read the right-branching utterances in (7) with a phrase break after the syntactic subject *vella*, we expected the peak of the H* in *escolta* to be higher in (7b) than in (7a):[10]

(7) a. *La vella, escolta la veu*
'The old lady listens tothe voice'

b. *La vella, escolta la veu amb encís*
'The old lady listens to the voice with delight'

Yet, the 3 speakers produced unexpected phrase breaks in the case of (7b), which was pronounced as (8). The actual phrase boundary, which was expected to be after the syntactic subject (as in 7a) was moved to the right and located after the verb:

(8) *La vella escolta, la veu amb encís*

The fact that speakers placed intonational boundaries in different locations made it impossible to compare the pitch levels attained by the *constituent-initial* peak in a word like *escolta*, and thus we were unable to test the effects of degree of embedding. Why did speakers consistently change the expected phrasing in sentences like (8)? Clearly, a sentence like *La vella, escolta la veu amb encís*, with a phrase break after the syntactic subject *vella*, is a very marked pronunciation of the sentence. This fact suggests that there is a certain degree of optionality in phrasing decisions and that the choice of prosodic domains is not exclusively dictated by syntax. Other factors, in this case constituency length, seem to play an active role in ruling out a pronunciation like (7b).

3.3 Results of the perceptual test

The goal of the perceptual test is to determine whether the production of the two types of branching structures can be reliably identified by Catalan listeners. To our surprise, the rate of identification was only moderate: each of the 18 listeners correctly classified between 60-80% of the stimuli. In general, the male stimuli (PG) presented more difficulties than the female (PP). This fact might be due to the following factors: 1., the more drastic F_0 movements attested in the female contours might help in the perceptual task; 2., the pitch downtrend differences between the two types of branching structure shown by the female contours might help in identifying phrase boundaries.

The perceptual results reveal an interesting phenomenon regarding the influence of syntactic structure on phrasing decisions. For some reason, a phrasing like *La vella llança, l'amenaça* (with a H^- phrase accent after *llança*) leads to ambiguity, especially when this pronunciation corresponds to the first presentation of the pair of sentences to be disambiguated. Such left-branching utterances reached a mean identification rate of around 40%, indicating that the listener consistently doubted in assigning an interpretation to these sentences. In contrast, the identification rate for right-branching utterances (cf. *La vella, llança l'amenaça*) was 100% for the female speaker and 90% for the male speaker. Thus, we find a sharp contrast between the two phrasing options: while a phrasing such as *La vella, llança l'amenaça* has just one interpretation, *La vella llança, l'amenaça* can be considered ambiguous. Why is this the case? In our opinion, such a contrast can be explained if we interpret phrasing decisions as *partially* constrained by syntax: while a phrase break between *vella* and *llança* immediately rules out an interpretation where *vella llança* is the syntactic subject, the non-presence of such a break leads to ambiguity. Generally, a phrase break cannot separate two words that belong to the same inner constituent; thus, if a phrase break is present between two words this is generally an indication that they belong to different constituents. Instead, if no phrase breaks are present, a structurally ambiguous sentence will probably be left with various grammatical interpretations.

4 Conclusion

We have shown that variation in intonational phrasing is the common strategy Catalan speakers use to disambiguate otherwise ambiguous sentences involving right-branching vs. left-branching structures.[11] Specifically, an utterance like *la vella llança l'amenaça* is generally disambiguated by means of a distinct intonational phrasing: an intermediate phrase break is placed at the end of the first constituent (i.e., the syntactic subject). Phonetically, a constituency break is marked with an obligatory high boundary tone (H^-, in Pierrehumbert's terms) and an optional short pause. Also, pitch downtrend differences between the two types of branching structures seem to be an optional cue: only two of the speakers exhibited a pitch reset in constituent-initial accents.[12]

Thus, the analysis of intonational contours in our production data partially confirm Bonet's observations. Like Bonet, we find that the main difference between the two types of branching structures is phrasing. Yet, our results on the manifestation of such phrasing differences do not support Bonet's claim that pitch lowering of constituent-final accents is crucial. Interpreting the data within Pierrehumbert's framework, pitch lowering is not attested in constituent-final accents, given the equal pitch level attained by the first pitch accent in the two structures. Instead, we attest an optional pitch reset at the beginning of intermediate phrases.[13]

The intonational facts differentiating the two ambiguous sentences can be easily explained by a strictly layered prosodic structure and the standard assumption that pitch tends to be reset at the beginning of a new prosodic domain. The current controversy about the property of SLH, then, is not challenged by our data.

The perceptual results of the test revealed some interesting facts about phrasing differences and their relationship to syntactic structure. We find the following contrast in Catalan listeners' intuitions: a sentence such as *la vella llança, l'amenaça* (pronounced with an intermediate phrase boundary after the *llança*) is considered ambiguous, in contrast with *la vella, llança l'amenaça* (pronounced with an intermediate phrase break after *vella*), which has only one meaning. Our interpretation of this contrast is that phrasing in natural speech is partially guided by syntax, in the sense that certain groupings cannot be separated by phrase breaks. This would explain why *la vella, llança l'amenaça* has only one possible interpretation: the interpretation where noun and adjective together would form the syntactic subject would violate the above-mentioned constraint on phrasing. Instead, *la vella llança, l'amenaça* does not violate any constraint and thus permits two possible interpretations. Thus, we assume that linguistic context is the key disambiguating factor in natural speech, and that phrasing decisions, subject to certain constraints, are highly optional. Still, the status of syntactic constraints and other factors like constituency size and their influence on phrasing decisions deserves further investigation.[14]

We hope to have started the necessary groundwork in the way to predict the F_0 patterns in different prosodic conditions. The description of the effects of syntactic/prosodic structure on downstep patterns and variations in pitch scaling needs to be completed.[15] In order to provide a full description of the patterns of downstep in Catalan it would be important, among other things, to test possible interactions between syntax and downstep and to develop F_0 assignment algorithms as a function of syntactic/prosodic domains.

Appendix I

1: La Maria visita un museu d'armes antigues. És diumenge i el museu és pràcticament buit. En una sala hi ha una llança vella que penja del sostre, amenaçant, amb el filó apuntant cap a terra. La Maria entra en la sala i queda parada. La vella llança l'amenaça. S'espanta i marxa.

2: És un poblet del sud d'Itàlia on ja quasi no hi viu ningú. Uns lladregots estan a punt d'entrar a robar en una de les cases abandonades del poble, i, de sobte, surt una vella del balcó. Va tota vestida de negre i sembla una bruixa. Ells s'espanten. La vella llança l'amenaça. Si tornen diu que els maten.

3. Cada dia la vella Maria escolta la novel·la radiofònica després de dinar: *Camila*. Aquell dia comença a sentir-la i nota una cosa estranya en la veu de la protagonista. La vella escolta la veu. No és la de sempre.

4. Fa vint anys el seu grup d'escoltes va escalar l'Aneto i, amb els anys, van a muntar una pel·lícula. La vella escolta la veu. Ho recorda tot amb nostàlgia.

5. Era una dona no gaire agraciada que es va quedar per vestir sants. Veient-la tan infeliç, una de les seves amigues li regala una crema d'Avon i li diu que es casarà enguany. Després de posar-se la crema va a provar sort a un ball de gent gran organitzat pel casino del poble. Ara que està a punt de casar-se tothom diu: La poderosa crema la casa.

6. Aquesta notícia que he llegit al diari és increïble. Explicava fins on poden arribar els matrimonis amb problemes i peles. En aquest cas, la dona, pubilla que havia heretat fortuna de casa seva, sabia que si es divorciava del seu marit hauria de deixar-li la casa on vivien. Pel títol de l'article endevinareu què va fer abans de demanar el divorci: *La poderosa crema la casa*.

7. Uns amics meus volien llogar un pis al barri vell de Barcelona. El van anar a veure. Mentre esperaven que arribés l'amo, van estar parlant amb un vellet que s'estava a la porta. Quan va arribar, van pujar a dalt. Els va agradar el pis, però la veritat, no el trobaven gaire segur. L'amo els va dir: "No us preocupeu. El vell guarda la porta".

8. Aquella nit no vam poder dormir. Estàvem preocupats per la bufanda vermella!! Segur que me l'havia deixada al museu!! I m'havia costat 100 pessetes al mercat!! De bon matí, vaig tornar al museu. L'encarregat va dir-me: Sé que ve a buscar la bufanda. El vell guarda la porta.

Appendix II

Qüestionari

Sentiràs 8 frases primer llegides per un parlant femení (part I) i després per un parlant masculí. Has d'endevinar el significat de les frases (que podrien ser ambigües si no fos per la pronúncia).

Nom: ______________________________

PART I. Parlant femení

1.	*La vella llança l'amenaça.*	Quin és el verb de la frase?	a. llançar b. amenaçar
2.	*La vella llança l'amenaça.*	Quin és el verb de la frase?	a. llançar b. amenaçar
3.	*La vella escolta la veu.*	Quin és el verb de la frase?	a. escoltar b. veure
4.	*La vella escolta la veu.*	Quin és el verb de la frase?	a. escoltar b. veure
5.	*La poderosa crema la casa.*	Quin és el verb de la frase?	a. cremar b. casar-se
6.	*La poderosa crema la casa.*	Quin és el verb de la frase?	a. cremar b. casar-se

7.	*El vell guarda la porta.*	Quin és el verb de la frase?	a. guardar b. portar
8.	*El vell guarda la porta.*	Quin és el verb de la frase?	a. guardar b. portar

PART II. Parlant masculí

1.	*La vella llança l'amenaça.*	Quin és el verb de la frase?	a. llançar b. amenaçar
2.	*La vella llança l'amenaça.*	Quin és el verb de la frase?	a. llançar b. amenaçar
3.	*La vella escolta la veu.*	Quin és el verb de la frase?	a. escoltar b. veure
4.	*La vella escolta la veu.*	Quin és el verb de la frase?	a. escoltar b. veure
5.	*La poderosa crema la casa.*	Quin és el verb de la frase?	a. cremar b. casar-se
6.	*La poderosa crema la casa.*	Quin és el verb de la frase?	a. cremar b. casar-se
7.	*El vell guarda la porta.*	Quin és el verb de la frase?	a. guardar b. portar
8.	*El vell guarda la porta.*	Quin és el verb de la frase?	a. guardar b. portar

Pregunta: Quina és la característica que creus que t'ha pogut ajudar a desambiguar les frases? ____

____

____

____

Notes

* I am grateful to Eulàlia Bonet, Corinne Cortés, Gorka Elordieta, Sonia Frota, Joan Mascaró, and Jaume Solà, for useful comments and criticism. I would also like to thank my Catalan informants, Joan Salavedra and Pere Gifra, who were always ready to step into the sound booth and start reading. Also, I am grateful to my university colleagues for answering the perceptual test and providing valuable feedback and impressions: Anna Bartra, Eulàlia Bonet, Albert Branchadell, Teresa Cabré, Antonio Chacón, Matilde Delgado, Mariona Ferrer, Mª Teresa Inglés, Teresa Iribarren, Lídia Lluís, Núria Martí, Joan Mascaró, Jaume Mateu, Mª Carme Picallo, Nil Santiáñez, Dolors Sitjà, Jaume Solà, Teresa Vallverdú. I also want to thank Fernando Martínez-Gil for his help in editorial matters. This work was funded by grants awarded by the Comissionat per a Universitats i Recerca de la Generalitat de Catalunya and by the DGICYT from the Ministerio de Educación y Ciencia (research projects 1995-GR00486 and PB-93-0893-C04-04).

1 In some languages, a time-dependent declination function can also lower the peaks in a given utterance.

2 According to Kubozono (1992: 383), MP represents a *major phrase* and is defined as the domain of downstep in Japanese (it corresponds to the intermediate phrase posited by Beckman & Pierrehumbert). mp corresponds to a *minor phrase*.

3 Kubozono (1992: 382), for example, defends that in Japanese "the magnitude of pitch rises in each syntactic boundary can largely be predicted by the depth of right-branching structure."

4 The informants were speakers of Central Catalan, all postdoctoral students in their late twenties: PG (from Barcelona), JS (from Olot) and PP (from Figueres).

5 In order to test the contribution of pitch scaling differences to the meaning identification, the PP and PG productions of the sentences were selected. As we will see, while speaker PG does not exhibit differences in pitch scaling between the two types of branching structures, speaker PP does (shows a consistent pitch reset at the beginning of a new prosodic constituent).

6 Utterances containing only one accent constitute an exception to these rules.

7 The meaningful tonal movements of a sentence have generally been located around accented syllables.

8 Our subjects consistently used the same disambiguating strategy.

9 For more details on the specifics of intonational transcription in Catalan, see Prieto (1996).

10 The effect of degree of embedding cannot be analyzed in the left-branching utterances either (see 2 below). The reason is that the last pitch accent of the sentence in (ia) has a L* in the word *veu* and thus cannot be compared with the H* pitch accent of *veu* in (ib):

(i) a. La vella escolta, la veu
 b. La vella escolta, la veu especial

11 Catalan speakers can also use phrasing variation to indicate differences in PP- or AP-attachment in the same way different types of branching structures are resolved. A sentence like *Un home cansat de París* has two meanings, depending on whether the PP is attached to the NP or the AP: 'a tired man from Paris', and 'a man sick of Paris'. In this case, different phrasing differences inequivocally lead to two different interpretations: *Un home, cansat de París* leads to 'a man sick of Paris', and *Un home cansat, de París* leads to 'a tired man from Paris'. Furthermore, variation in intonational phrasing is a common disambiguation strategy in languages like Spanish, Italian and English (Avesani et al. 1995).

12 Catalan, then, seems to have a smaller reset effect than Japanese. In this language, some phoneticians report a strong pitch reset at the beginning of a constituent: the average difference between peaks in constituent-initial and medial positions is around 40 or 45 Hz (Azuma & Tsukuma 1991, Kubozono 1992: 374).

13 It would be interesting to test the relative importance of acoustic cues like the presence of a H- boundary tone and pauses, differences in the pitch downtrend pattern, etc., in phrase boundary identifications.

14 If speakers did not make a conscious effort to disambiguate the two types of sentences under examination, phrase breaks tended to be the same for both structures.

15 The effect of degree of embedding could not be tested in our data because the informants did not place prosodic boundaries as initially expected; so, it remains to be seen whether lengthy constituents do trigger a stronger pitch reset (Cooper and Paccia-Cooper 1980).

References

Avesani, Cinzia, Julia Hirschberg, and Pilar Prieto. 1995. The Intonational Disambiguation of Potentionally Ambiguous Utterances in English, Italian, and Spanish. *Proceedings of the 13th International Congress of Phonetic Sciences*, vol. 1, 174-177. Stockholm, Sweden.

Azuma, Junichi, and Yoshimasa Tsukuma. 1991. The Role of F_0 and pause in disambiguating syntactically ambiguous sentences in Japanese. *Proceedings of the XIIth International Congress of Phonetic Sciences* 3.274-277. Aix-en-Provence: Université de Provence Service des Publications.

Beckman, Mary, and Janet Pierrehumbert. 1986. Intonational Structure in Japanese and English. *Phonology Yearbook* 3.255-310.

Beckman, Mary, and Julia Hirschberg. 1993. The ToBI annotation conventions. Ohio State University and AT&T Bell Laboratories.

Bolinger, Dwight. 1986. *Intonation and Its Parts: Melody in Spoken English*. Palo Alto: Stanford University Press.

Bonet, Eulàlia. 1984. Aproximació a l'entonació del català. Master's thesis, Universitat Autònoma de Barcelona. (Distributed by UAB-DDL, Dept. de Filologia Catalana, UAB.)

Cooper, William E., and Jeanne Paccia-Cooper. 1980. *Syntax and Speech*. Cambridge, Mass.: Harvard University Press.

Klatt, Denis. 1975. Vowel lengthening is syntactically determined in a connected discourse. *Journal of Phonetics* 3.129-141.

Kubozono, Haruo. 1989. Syntactic and rhythmic effects of downstep in Japanese. *Phonology* 6.39-67.

Kubozono, Haruo. 1992. Modeling syntactic effects on downstep in Japanese. *Papers in Laboratory Phonology II: Segment, Gestures, Tone*, ed. Gerard J. Docherty and D. Robert Ladd, 368-387. New York: Cambridge University Press.

Ladd, Robert, and C. Johnson. 1987. Metrical factors in the scaling of sentence-initial accent peaks. *Phonetica* 44.238-245.

Ladd, Robert. 1988. Declination 'reset' and the hierarchical organization of utterances. *Journal of the Acoustical Society of America* 84. 530-544.

Ladd, Robert. 1990. Metrical representation of pitch register. *Papers in Laboratory Phonology I: Between the Grammar and Physics of Speech*, ed. John Kingston and Mary Beckman, 35-37. Cambridge: Cambridge University Press.

Ladd, Robert. 1993. In defense of a metrical theory of intonational downstep. *The Phonology of Tone: The Representation of Tonal Register*, ed. Harry van der Hulst and K. Snider, 109-132. Berlin, New York: Mouton de Gruyter.

Ladd, Robert. 1994. Constraints on the gradient variability of pitch range, or, pitch level 4 lives! *Phonological Structure and Phonetic Form. Papers in Laboratory Phonology III*, ed. Patricia A. Keating. New York: Cambridge University Press.

Lehiste, Ilse. 1973. Phonetic Disambiguation of Syntactic Ambiguity. *Glossa* 7.107-121.

Nespor, Marina, and Irene Vogel. 1986. *Prosodic Phonology*. Dordrecht: Fopris.

Pierrehumbert, Janet. 1980. *The Phonetics and Phonology of English Intonation*. Doctoral dissertation, MIT.

Pierrehumbert, Janet and Mary Beckman. 1988. *Japanese Tone Structure*. Cambridge, Mass.: MIT Press.

Pitrelli, John, Mary Beckman, and Julia Hirschberg. 1994. Evaluation of prosodic transcription labelling reliability in the TOBI framework. *Proceedings of the Third International Conference on Spoken Language Processing*, vol. 2, 123-126. Yokohama, Japan.

Prieto, Pilar. 1996. Aproximació als contorns tonals del català central. Caplletra, *Revista Internacional de Filologia* 15.161-186.

Selkirk, Elisabeth O. 1984. *Phonology and Syntax. The Relation between Sound and Structure*. Cambridge, Mass.: MIT Press.

Selkirk, Elizabeth O. and Tateishi, K. 1991. Syntax and downstep in Japanese. *Interdisciplinary Approaches to Language: Essays in Honor of S.Y. Kuroda*, ed. C. Georgopoulous and R. Ishihara, 519-543.

Terken, Jacques, and Rene Collier. 1992. Syntactic influences on prosody. *Speech Perception, Production and Linguistic Structure*, ed. Y. Tohkura, El Vatikiotis-Bateson and Y. Sagisaka, 427-438. Tokyo: IOS Press.

Venditti, Jennifer J. 1994. The influence of syntax on prosodic structure in Japanese. *OSU Working Papers in Linguistics 44*.191-223.

7

Prosodic structure and stress in Catalan*

PEP SERRA

0. Introduction

Stress is the manifestation of the metrical structure of language. Anyone who speaks Catalan knows perfectly well where the stress falls, and never doubts whether to say *camí* or *cami* 'path, way', for example. The empirical basis of the research on stress is the shared intuitions of speakers. In theory every word has a stress, but the weak pronouns and some prepositions like *a* or *de* do not carry their own, rather depend on other words in order to form part of discourse. Apart from this small group, every word has a stress associated with the syllable that finally will be interpreted as the most prominent. In the case of monosyllables, the stress has to be placed on the only existing syllable; however, the majority of words are made up of more than one syllable and there seems to be some mechanism to unambiguously determine where stress falls.

Of course, it is possible that this mechanism does not exist, and that speakers learn which syllable bears stress for each particular word. If considered this way, stress would be a lexical property, specific to each word. There are, however, two basic reasons why this does not seem acceptable. The first refers to the fact that we have intuitions about where to place the stress in new or invented words. Even though it can be argued that this is done by analogy with other words, it seems justified to think that there is a reason for the existence of compact groups with regular patterns, and that these homogeneous groups have not been created by chance. The other problem that must be recognized in a strictly lexical view of stress is the complexity involved in the process of learning, and the quantity of information that must be retained.

The basic hypothesis in the study of stress is, then, that a prediction mechanism certainly does exist, that is capable of assigning the stress to the appropriate syllable. In general, only when no results are obtained in the investigation of this mechanism could it be said not to exist. Normally, there are no positive proofs of the absence of mechanisms of regular assignment of stress.

The most important study of the Catalan stress system is the work by Wheeler (1979) (see also Alsina 1989, and Ferrís 1984). The system Wheeler developed is, however, considerably complex and, for that reason, hardly credible. After observing the drawbacks of Wheeler's system, Mascaró (1983) claimed that no better system exists, and that stress in Catalan is a property which is assigned independently to each lexical element. Wheeler (1987) accepts Mascaró's treatment and does not attempt to formulate a process of assignment.

New investigations on stress in Catalan come ten years after the first works. These include studies by Oliva and Serra (1990), Oliva (1991, 1992) and Serra (1992, 1993a). These works take up a line of research begun by Oliva (1977), and have two fundamental characteristics in common: on the one hand, a main interest in the phenomenon of contact between primary stress and the assignment of secondary stress, and on the other, a resort to the metric foot in the analysis of these processes. The assignment of word stress is not, therefore, the subject of these studies which more or less explicitly accept the possibility that Catalan may be a language of unpredictable lexical stress.

In this work, a relatively simple mechanism for the assignment of word stress in Catalan is proposed. The system results from the analysis of the distribution of stress based on knowledge of new general theories formulated in Hayes (1994), Idsardi (1992, 1993), McCarthy and Prince (1990, 1993), and Prince and Smolensky (1993). The explanation is organized in this way. First I present the aspects related to the organization of syllables that intervene in the distribution of stress (section 1). In the next section, I introduce the elements that comprise part of the formal mechanism of stress assignment in natural languages (section 2). I then resume the descriptive generalizations observed in Catalan word stress and identify exceptional lexical groups. Following this is the procedure used in Catalan to determine where stress falls (section 3). Finally, I introduce the theoretical model of Simplified Bracketed Grids (Idsardi 1992, 1993) and Optimality Theory (McCarthy and Prince 1990, 1993, and Prince and Smolensky, 1993) in order to analyze the main stress problems that are raised in the combination of morphemes (section 4). The results obtained are summarized in the concluding section.

1. In some languages the stress assignment system is so simple that it is not necessary to resort to any type of phonological constituent. This is the case of Finnish and Hungarian, for example, which always realize stress on the first vowel of the word, and also of Cambodian or modern Hebrew which assign it to the final vowel. The most common situation, however, is that stress is distributed on the basis of the groups of sounds composing syllables. The mechanisms that assign stress *see* the syllables and often take them into account. Within this great majority of systems which consider the syllable, it is still necessary to distinguish between those which pay attention to the grouping into syllables and those which go even further and also utilize aspects of the internal structure of syllabic constituents. The systems of the first group determine that stress falls on a syllable independently of its internal structure. The systems of the second group, on the other hand, take into consideration the value known as syllabic weight, a concept that refers to the subsyllabic or internal structure of syllables. The stress systems which do not pay attention to weight or syllabic quantity are said to be systems *insensitive* to quantity, and those that take this factor into account are characterized as systems *sensitive* to quantity.

The distinction of weight or syllabic quantity is based on the recognition of two types of syllables: *light*, which are those ending in a vowel (a short vowel in the systems which have a phonological distinction of length), and *heavy*, which are all others. This classification is valid because of the differences observed in the internal structure of the syllables. The segments preceding the nucleus, which is the vowel, form what is known as the *onset,* and do not take part in the calculation of syllabic weight. The relevant elements are, therefore, those that form the *rhyme*; and so, in this way, the *nucleus* and the other segments that are grouped in the *coda*. A *mora* is assigned to each of the segments associated with the rhyme, which is the unit of syllabic weight. It is usually considered that relevant differences regarding weight are based on the existence of one mora (light syllable) or two or more morae (heavy syllable).

(1) *Syllable weight*

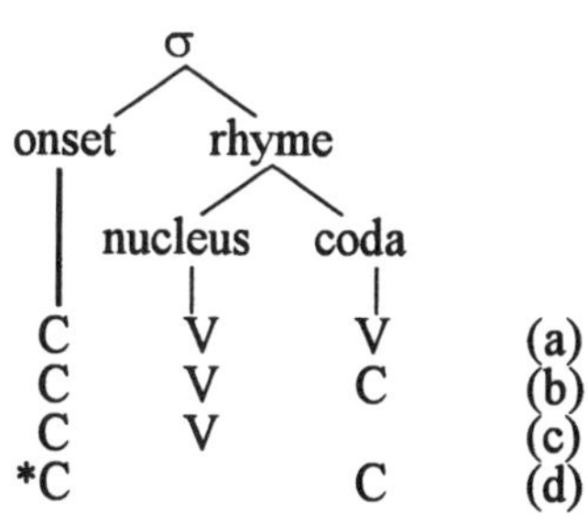

Diagrams (a) and (b) correspond to heavy syllables, and in both cases there are two elements to the rhyme. Diagram (c) is a light syllable, with a single element in the rhyme. When the rhyme contains only one element, this must be the nucleus, because a syllable without nucleus would be ill-formed (diagram (d)).

The recognition of syllabic weight, that materializes in morae, is the main basis in the phenomena related to stress and rhythm. There is also another field, however, within morphology, that exploits distinctions of weight or syllabic quantity. Work by McCarthy and Prince (1986, 1990) have fixed the concept of *minimum word*, determining the minimum length necessary for an element of any language to be a word. This minimum length is two mora. In a good number of languages, this requirement is met without exception (for example, in the Arabic languages). Catalan, in part, differs from this general behavior because it has light monosyllables comprising words, and also words having a syllabic length less than the minimum of two morae, as is the case of *nu* 'nude' or *cru* 'raw'. In order to explain these processes, Kiparsky (1992), and Kager (1993) propose a process called *catalexis*. This consists of filling a prosodic structure empty of segmental content. This operation could be carried out in the languages that admit words of less than two morae and, at the same time, would allow the general explanations to be maintained. It seems, however, that *catalexis* greatly reduces the explanatory value of the theory they want to defend.

In section 4, I will present a more general analysis of monomoraic words. Although Catalan presents an exceptional case, the concept of *minimum word* is also useful to explain certain restrictions affecting the formation of shortened or *hypocoristic* words (see Cabré 1993). Work by McCarthy and Prince (1990, 1993) and Prince and Smolensky (1993) shows, however, that the concept of *minimum word* is derived from the combination of independent restrictions. In section 5, I will show how resorting to the basic restrictions determining the descriptive effect that we know as *minimum word* facilitates a more powerful and profound analysis of apparently unrelated phenomena.

2. Languages assign stress in many different ways according to the superficial results and to the most direct observation of the data. Several comparative studies (see Hayes 1994, McCarthy and Prince 1990, McCarthy 1986, Kager 1995) have shown that behind this great diversity there is quite a simple system and a very limited set of patterns. In order to characterize these basic patterns the concept of the metric foot is used, taken from classical studies of poetic meter. The study of a great number of stress systems has enabled a universal typology to be developed, consisting of a list of metric feet available for the configuration of assignment systems. Despite the great variety of stress systems studied, a very regular behavior is observed regarding basic metrical structures which restricts the number of feet governing the metrical patterns of natural languages.

A metrical foot is a phonological constituent made up of two elements, one of which is more prominent than the other. These elements are syllables in languages with a system insensitive to quantity, and morae in languages that obey syllabic weight. It has been observed that certain systems permit feet of more than two elements. These are called *unbounded* feet. Feet bound to two elements, the most common type, are called *bounded* feet. The possibility of the existence of *degenerate feet*, consisting of a single element, is still being debated (see, however, a new concept of *degenerate feet* in sections 4 and 5).

The linguistic differences between limited feet are basically fixed according to the three following parameters. First, as we have seen, the fact of whether or not the system is sensitive to quantity will determine the nature of the elements that make up the foot (morae or syllables). Second, the direction observed in the application of the algorithm that builds binary feet. The direction is not relevant in an even-numbered sequence. In odd-numbered systems, however, rightward application leaves the last element free, and in leftward application the first element of the sequence is not associated with any foot. The third parameter refers to the position of the prominent element within the foot. The terms used are well known: a left-headed foot is trochaic and a right-headed foot is iambic. In summary, each system must fix its values for the options of sensitivity or insensitivity to syllabic weight, the direction of the construction of feet, and the number of feet (trochaic or iambic). The main hypothesis is that the possible systems of stress are defined by the combinations of these parameters.

I shall not go into an analysis of the different metrical patterns of Catalan. It may be interesting to note, however, that as far as metric feet are concerned, the number of possible forms is reduced to three. There are two kinds of trochaic feet, one quantity-sensitive, called *moraic trochee*, and the other quantity-insensitive, and known as *syllabic trochee*. Iambic feet are always quantity-insensitive. No system has been found that is based on iambic feet and constructed with morae. It is generally accepted that this combination is blocked by perceptual conditions.

In this work I shall only discuss the quantity-sensitive trochee, or moraic trochee. The foot is accepted as fundamental for Latin, and I shall demonstrate that it is also the basic unit used by Catalan to determine stress placement (see Serra 1993a).

It is known that Latin distinguishes light and heavy syllables, and is therefore quantity-sensitive. The stress assignment mechanism in this language fixes on the weight of the penultimate syllable, which if heavy receives stress. If light, the stress falls on the antepenultimate syllable. A predictable exception is the group of disyllabic words that cannot follow this pattern and always carry stress on the first syllable. As it is a language that takes syllable weight into account, the elements forming the metric foot will be morae, and each foot will have two morae. In syllabic terms, it can be made up of two light syllables or one heavy syllable. In order to describe the system further, we must say that, in Latin, the feet are built from right to left, grouping morae in twos. Finally, prominence within the foot is assigned to the element on the left, i.e., trochees are formed. As we have seen, trochees built on morae are called moraic trochees. There is still another mechanism that we must consider as far as Latin is concerned which is also useful in the analysis of Catalan. This concept is extrametricality, which applied to Latin, means that the final syllable falls outside the process and cannot be associated to any metrical structure.

It is observed in Latin that the final syllable is never stressed. In a systematic way this syllable is not affected by the stress assignment process. More generally, we find that there are *invisible* elements to rules and metric principles. The extrametrical concept attempts to explain situations which condition the results of the application of stressed logarithms. Hayes (1982) correctly limits the free application of extrametricality from the study of the stress system in English. He proposes the following group of restrictions on extrametricality: (a) *Constituency*: only constituents (segments, morae, syllables, feet and phonological words) can be marked as extrametrical; (b) *Peripheral situation*: a constituent may be extrametrical only if it occurs at an end, left or right, of its domain; and (c) *Edge marking*: as far as extrametricality is concerned, the unmarked side is the right. According to this idea of extrametricality, we can say that Latin stress never affects the final syllable of words because it is extrametrical. This may be because it is a constituent, a syllable, is peripheral, and is on the right, unmarked side. In order to indicate that a constituent is extrametrical, angular brackets are used. Let us now look at some Latin examples to show how these mechanisms work:

```
(2)  *                      *                 *
     *     *                *            *    *
     (* *) (* *)        *  (* *)        (* *) (* *)
     μ μ   μ μ          μ   μ μ         μ μ   μ μ
     i ni  mí: <cus>    pe  pé r <ci>   co n  fi ci <unt>
```

In the first horizontal line we have words with the stress behavior we wish to explain. The colon means that the preceding vowel is long, and the angular brackets mark the constituents they contain as extrametrical. In the second line, there are the morae that indicate the syllable weight of the line immediately below: a mora for each of the elements in the rhyme. In the next line we attribute a *beat* to each mora. The beats are the units that are used as a basis in the analysis of the accent. Immediately the feet are formed, that group the beats in sets of two beginning from the right. In the next line, prominence is assigned to the element on the left of every foot to form trochees. Finally, we must state that rightmost stress always prevails in Latin. This is formally expressed by adding a beat to the first prominent position beginning from the right in the immediately following level. A condition known as Continuous Column Constraint (Hayes 1994) guarantees that this last operation will be assigned to a column that has a beat at the immediately following level. The syllable containing the mora associated with the column with more asterisks is the one that receives the word's primary accent.

3. On the basis of the mechanisms we have seen, we now focus on the position of stress in Catalan. It is important to see what the distribution of stress is, in terms of syllables, and on which syllable of the word it falls. Following this, it is interesting to see if any relation can be found between where the stress falls and the type of syllables in the word. I have already said that Catalan, like Latin, is quantity-sensitive. We therefore expect the distribution of stress to depend partly on the kind of syllables each word contains. The descriptive generalizations taken from the observation of stress in Catalan are the following:

(3) *Regular patterns*

-if a word ends in a consonant it is an oxytone

-if it ends in a vowel it is a paroxytone

Marked patterns
-there are words that end in a vowel and are oxytones
-there are words that end in a consonant and are paroxytones
-some words are proparoxytones

We see that regular patterns can be defined to cover an important part of the words in the language (see the appendix on marked words in Serra 1993b, and Hualde 1992). The rule is that if a word ends in a consonant it will be an oxytone (*general* 'general', *llençol* 'sheet'...) and will be a paroxytone if it ends in a vowel (*residu* 'residue', *divorci* 'divorce'...). The observation that Catalan is sensitive to syllabic quantity gives us the basis to analyze this behavior. The mechanism that assigns stress in Catalan builds bounded feet of two elements. Since the language is sensitive to syllabic weight, the elements in question will be morae, that is, the segments associated with the rhyme. The procedure applied is the same as what we have seen for Latin, with the only difference being that in Catalan the final syllable is not marked as extrametrical. The following diagrams demonstrate the stages of the process: projection of the morae, construction of binary trochees from right to left, and finally, the assignment of a beat to the rightmost column to mark the prominence of the primary stress.

```
(4)          *                       *                *
        *    *                  *    *                *
       (*  *)(*  *)            (* *) (* *)        * (*  *)
        μ  μ  μ  μ              μ μ   μ μ         μ  μ  μ
       ge  ne ra  l           lle n  ço l        re si du
```

With these diagrams, we see how a mechanism based on the moraic trochee can easily explain regular patterns of primary stress assignment. Secondary stress is usually related to the presence of a beat on the second level. In Catalan, however, the distribution of secondary stress is not lexical. It has a rhythmic basis and depends on the number of syllables. The beat associated with the first syllable of *llençol* must not be taken as secondary stress. These stresses are distributed, as observed by Corominas (1983), to alternate syllables to the left of the primary stress (see also Serra 1993a).

It is necessary to define this with more precision. In applying the system to a word like *Palma*, where the first syllable is heavy and the second is light, we find that the lateral segment is the mora associated with the column with more beats.

It belongs to the rhyme of the first syllable. In diagram (5) it can be seen that the mora of the lateral is the one with more beats. This lateral, however, is not the nucleus of the syllable. As stress is perceptible on the syllable nucleus, we can say that the stress received by the lateral belongs to the whole syllable, and therefore to the nucleus, the vowel *a*.

```
(5)          *
             *
           * (*  *)
           μ  μ  μ
           Pa l  ma
```

We have explained the regular patterns and now we must revise the group characterized as marked patterns. We must see if they are really or only apparently exceptional, and find a way of integrating them into the general system. The first group of the marked patterns is the one formed by oxytone words ending in a vowel, therefore *català* 'catalan' and *camí* belong to the regular pattern for words ending in a consonant. From this observation we find that if it is true that *català* and *camí* have a vowel as a final segment, it is also true that the morphemes of these words end in consonants. Connected with *català* we have *catalana* 'catalan fem.', *catalans* 'catalan plu.' or *catalanisme* 'catalanism', all with an *n* before derivational or inflectional morphemes. In the same way, *camí* makes *caminet* 'small path' or *caminar* 'to walk'. If we look at the words *català* or *camí*, ending in a vowel, their stress as oxytones is marked and exceptional. It would be more correct to state that the mechanisms assigning stress do not take words into account, but rather morphemes, and so the root morphemes *catalan* or *camin* end in consonants and are oxytones. There is nothing exceptional, then, in the patterns of these words, nor in the words *fuster* 'carpenter' or *rentador* 'cleaner'. The only difference is that there is a process that erases the *n* in *català* or the *r* in *fuster* when they are in final position. Valencian, however, maintains the *r* of *fuster* and the stress falls on the same position as in standard Catalan, which erases it. We see, therefore, that the elision of final consonants does not affect the position of stress because it is assigned previously, on the morphemes. It therefore does not take the rules of elision of final consonants into consideration. It is clear, on the other hand, that the elision rule of *n* is applied after stress assignment, because the stress position intervenes in the definition of the context of application of the rule: the final *n* is regularly erased when the preceding vowel is stressed.

We have seen that the situation of oxytones ending in a vowel ceases to be marked if we pay attention to the underlying morphemes ending in a consonant. There is a severely reduced number of words whose roots do not end in a consonant. This is the case of *café* or *sofa,* which have the normal plurals, *cafes* or *sofas*, respectively. However it is usual that the pronunciation *cafens* or *sofans* makes these words fit into the regular pattern. Stress, then, is assigned to the morphemes, and when morphemes are combined to form words, the characteristics of the final morpheme usually prevail because prominence falls to the right. In relation to stress, the morphemes could be classified into three groups: stressed, unstressed and prestressed morphemes. Following is an example that combines prefixes of the first two types. The prestressed suffixes are of the type *-ic*, *-graf* or *-fon*, and they cause stress to fall on the final syllable of the preceding morpheme. In section 5, I present a more detailed analysis of these groups.

The metric structure assigned to a root can change when we perform morphological operations. In the analysis of the word *caseta* 'little house' in (6) there is the root, a diminutive, stressed suffix and an unstressed feminine morpheme. The stress falls on the final suffix *-et,* in the derived word. The process of foot construction is carried out independently in each morpheme and the rightmost predominance prevails.

```
(6)                       *
           *              *
         (* *)          (* *)
          μ μ            μ μ          μ
       [ k a z ]Stem +  [ ɛ  t ]Affix +  [ ə ]Affix
```

I now analyze the second group of marked examples, paroxytones ending in a consonant. An important set of the examples we find are words like *telèfon* 'telephone', *famèlic* 'famished', *fotògraf* 'photographer', *malèvol* 'evil', *hàbil* 'clever', *satèllit* 'satellite'. It should be noted, however, that all these words contain prestressed suffixes of the type already mentioned. This kind of suffix always involves the realization of stress on the last syllable of the preceding morpheme; thus *àtom* 'atom' has the stress on the "o" after the addition of the suffix *-ic* to *àtomic*. Therefore for all of these words there is a regular explanation of their behavior: they are paroxytones because they have prestressed suffixes that are always monosyllabic (see Mascaró 1983, 1984, and 1987 for an analysis of these suffixes and of the change of timbre they cause in the stressed vowel).

There is, however, a group of paroxytones ending in consonants that form part of the root. We cannot apply morphological conditions to this group as we have done with those containing prestressed suffixes. They are words like *àrab*, *àcid*, *àzig*, *llàpis* 'pencil', *bíceps*, *clímax*, *extrínsec*, *adúlter* 'adulterer' and a few others. Although they make up a rather small group we must find a way of explaining their behavior. The device we use will be quite unusual and in keeping with the marked nature of the stress patterns of these words. If we find a way of describing what is shared by these segments, we can explain the regular aspects of this exceptional set. Consonant-final paroxytones can be explained by marking the final mora as extrametrical. We have seen that in Latin extrametricality is regularly applied to the final syllable. Catalan, however, does not use this resource systematically, only for a reduced number of words. The difference is therefore within the scope of extrametricality and also, in this case, the type of constituent affected, i.e., the syllable in Latin and the mora in Catalan.

The examples in (7) demonstrate the stress assignment process in marked paroxytones. The final mora appears between angular brackets to mark it as extrametrical and to exclude it from the construction of feet. Remember that morae construct the metrical grid with the beats following the procedure we have presented. These words are therefore exceptional only because their final mora is extrametrical, but apart from that the stress assignment process is completely regular. We build moraic trochees from right to left and assign prominence to the word on the right.

```
(7)      *             *
        (*  *)        (*  *)
         μ  μ <μ>      μ  μ <μ>
         a  ra  b     lla pi  s
```

There still remains an important group of words which have stress on the antepenultimate syllable, the proparoxytones. A good number of these are feminine, and among these we must distinguish two groups according to whether the root ends in a vowel or a consonant. Words like *família* 'family', *gràcia* 'grace' or *ràdio* 'radius', systematically proparoxitonic in the standard pronunciation, are completely regular. The stress assignment on the root results in a paroxytone pattern, and the addition of the gender morpheme converts the whole word into a proparoxytone. The formation of diphthongs by semivocalization of the final vowel of the root is produced after the flexion process, when stress has already been assigned (see the limits of this process in Recasens 1991:157-58). The stressed syllable remains, even though its relative position changes, i.e., the word changes from proparoxytone to paroxytone because the diphthong makes a syllable on the right disappear.

```
(8)              *
              * (*  *)
              μ   μ  μ
            [ fa  mi  li ]Stem +  a
```

In order to explain feminine proparoxytones derived from roots ending in a consonant, like *pàgina* 'page', *brúixola* 'compass', *màniga* 'sleeve', *fàbrica* 'factory', or *càrrega* 'load', we must pay attention to the root. Oxytone stress of the group of words ending in a vowel already indicated this treatment. We have also seen that the exception represented by paroxytones ending in consonants is explained by marking the final mora as extrametrical. The feminine proparoxytones based on roots ending in a consonant behave analogously to the last group; the final mora of their root is extrametrical. The difference between feminine proparoxytones, like *pàgina* or *brúixola,* and words like *àrab* or *llapis,* is that the former additionally have gender marked by the vowel. The feminine morpheme is represented phonologically by an unstressed vowel. The fact that the morpheme is unstressed does not change stress position, and, as it is a vowel, a syllable is added to the right of the stress.

The exception represented by words with feminine morphemes is, then, represented in the same way as marked paroxytones ending in consonants. The examples in (9) demonstrate the process of stress assignment in this group of proparoxytones.

```
(9)        *                     *
          (*     *)             (*     *)
           μ     μ <μ>           μ     μ <μ>
          [fa   bri  c ] + a    [pa   gi  n ] + a
```

We have marked the final extrametrical morae and have projected the first level of the accentual grid on the basis of morae. Then, we have constructed trochees from right to left. In this way, the marking process of words that do not follow the regular process can be unified, provided the last mora is marked as extrametrical. After this, in all cases, stress has been assigned according to the general model.

We have seen proparoxytones with a feminine morpheme, but there remains another group of proparoxytones which end in consonants comprising part of the root. They are words like *harmònium*, *ínterim*, *Júpiter*, *hipérbaton*, *sífilis*, *isòsceles*, and *hàbitat*. We see that these words behave as exceptions in the reduction of unstressed vowels. They differ from regular phonological behavior and the language treats them differently because they are cultisms, or learned words. To refer to them as learned words is useful because they behave in two different ways. As far as stress assignment is concerned, it is not enough to mark the last mora extrametrical, as this mechanism results in paroxytones, not proparoxytones. In fact, these words are stressed as in Latin. As is customary in Latin, the final syllable is always marked extrametrical. Let us see how the application of this system to *Júpiter* and *ínterim* results in proparoxytones. As in the Latin examples we have seen in (2), the last syllable is excluded from the process and moraic trochees are constructed in order to determine the position of stress.

(10)	*	*
	(* *)	* (* *)
	μ μ	μ μ μ
	ju pi <t e r>	i n te <r i m>

Traditionally, two observations have been made on the stress of Catalan words. The most well-known refers to the fact that there are oxytones, paroxytones and proparoxytones. There are no words stressed on the fourth to last syllable. In studies on stress it is customary to speak of the Three-Syllable Window to describe this situation. The combination of mechanisms intervening in stress assignment in Catalan predict that the leftmost limit for stress is the third to last syllable. If we look at the root of a proparoxytone like *alfàbrega* 'basil', we see that the stress cannot fall any further left than the third syllable. The exceptional nature of this word, which is a proparoxytone and not a paroxytone, is expressed by marking the final mora extrametrical. Immediately after this, the construction of moraic trochees causes stress to fall on the syllable *fa*, and the addition of flexive unstressed morphemes (a vowel when feminine) will add a syllable to the right of the stress. The result is a proparoxytone, and there is no way of causing stress to fall further leftward to coincide with the syllable *al*. The impossibility of deriving patterns which have stress further leftward than the third syllable is positively achieved through this convention, and the system of prediction is restricted, giving information about the real possibilities of Catalan.

Another remarkable observation related to proparoxytones was first formulated by Ferrís (1984), and then used by Wheeler (1987). Expressed in a simple way, the observation requires the penultimate syllable of a proparoxytone to be light. Words like *pàgina*, *dèficit*, *còncava*, or *ínterim* are examples of the possible forms: the penultimate syllable is obligatorily light and imposes no restriction on the others. It is easy to see that words like *dívorci* or *dèfensa*, which are proparoxytones with heavy penultimate syllables, do not exist in Catalan. This generalization regarding proparoxytones is derived directly from the assignment mechanism I have presented. If it is applied to a root like that of *divorci* the result will be a paroxytone word that in no way can be proparoxytone. Even if the final syllable is extrametrical, the presence of the heavy syllable results in two morae that will be the base for the formation of the first foot and bear word stress. It is the same effect that, in Latin, causes the generalization that, if the penultimate syllable is heavy, it bears stress.

In the studies of historical grammar it is usually emphasised that the stressed syllable is maintained in the majority of cases. This coincidence between Latin and Catalan allows two very different interpretations. Diachronic studies tend to see it as a word for word relation. The metaphor that says the stress is the soul of the word suggests that every word has one and that it is maintained apart from any changes. A more realistic approach compares the capacities of the speakers, of Catalan and Latin, in order to decide the stress position. The coincidence is not found in words but rather in the mechanisms, and Catalan conserves many elements of the stress assignment procedure of Latin. The first step in demonstrating that these mechanisms exist is to define them and find a similar assignment procedure. Here, I have talked about the system Latin uses and I have presented one that could be applied to Catalan. These two mechanisms coincide in many ways, the most salient of which is the use of the moraic trochee. The main difference is in the extrametricality: in Latin it is general and is applied to the final syllable, whereas in Catalan it is only applied in exceptional cases and it can affect morae or syllables. This change in the systems of assignment can be related to the loss of final vowels. The disappearance of the vowel and the incorporation of the consonant into the preceding syllable makes the final syllable heavy, and therefore, it receives stress. In special cases, this situation can be avoided by marking as extrametrical the final consonant caused by the loss of the vowel.

The adaptation of words from other languages provides additional evidence of the existence of an assignment mechanism. The English words *football*, *hockey* or *ticket* are originally paroxytone, and in their adaptation into Spanish they have maintained their stress pattern. In Catalan, however, these words become oxytones, following the unmarked pattern. As seen in the examples in (11), regular assignment places stress on the final syllable.

```
(11)        *                   *                  *
         *  *                   *                  *
        (* *)(* *)        *   (* *)          *   (* *)
         μ  μ  μ  μ       μ    μ μ           μ    μ μ
        fu  t bo  l       ti  que t          ho  que  i
```

If we take a word ending in a vowel like *penalty* (penal) or *royalty*, the assignment generates a paroxytone word that contrasts with the proparoxytone pattern that this word has in English.

```
(12)            *               *
             *  *            *  *
           (* *) (* *)     (* *) (* *)
            μ  μ  μ μ       μ μ  μ μ
           pe na  l ty     ro ya l ty
```

Speakers who use these words do not copy English stress placement, instead they reapply the mechanism of stress assignment in Catalan. These changes, then, are an argument in favor of the existence of an autonomous mechanism to decide which syllable is stressed.

4. The use of brackets is shared by very different theories in order to take advantage of the clarity they provide. The theory of the *Simplified Bracket Grids* (*SBG*) first used by Halle and Idsardi (1992) and then Idsardi (1992, 1993) proposes a stronger interpretation of bracketing. The representation with brackets is not a way of expressing a different reality, instead it claims to be the theory directly. Halle (1990) took a clear step in this direction with the introduction of idiosyncratic limits in the analysis of the Arabian of Cairo and the Chugach Alutiiq. In this study, he manipulated brackets to obtain an empirical effect, a usage that goes beyond their usual function as indicators of an operation formulated independently of them.

The descriptive possibilities of the SBG model are largely equivalent to those incorporated in the basic model of Hayes (1994). The projection mechanisms are based on morae or syllables. The construction of feet or the assignment of prominence in the derived word, according to Halle and Idsardi, stems from the combination of a set of parametric rules and conditions. As far as we are concerned in this study, the basic procedures of the SBG can explain without problems all the steps we have seen based on the classical theory. The introduction of the system of SBG is justified in section 5, because of the usefulness of this model in the analysis of exceptional stressed forms in morphemes. Reference to Halle and Idsardi's theory is useful in the treatment of stressed monomoraic morphemes and prestressed morphemes. The convenience of using a homogeneous analysis also forces us to adopt the model of SBG in the neutral cases we have seen so far. I now present the construction parameters of metrical structure applied in the framework of the SBG model.

(13) *Parameters of Metrical Grid Construction*

a. *Grid Mark Projection*
Project syllabic/moraic elements

b. *Boundary Projection*
Project left/right boundaries for certain syllables scanning left/right -ward

c. *Edge Marking*
Insert a left/right boundary to the left/right of the left/right-most element

d. *Iterative Constituent Construction*
Insert left/right boundaries every two elements

e. *Head Marking*
Project the left/right -most element of every constituent

(Idsardi 1993)

The instructions (a) and (e) add beats, and the other three (b, c, and d) add brackets (see Idsardi 1992, 1993 for a detailed justification of these operations). As an example of the application of the SBG model we see the process of assignment of metrical structure to two words with regular patterns.

(14)

	*		*		*	
(e), left	(*	*	(*	*	(*	*
(d), left	(*	*	(*	*	(*	*
(b), left, pesants, (ind.)	*	*	(*	*	*	*
(a), syllabic	*	*	*	*	*	*
	ru	si	ɲol	rə	zi	ðu
	‘nightingale’			‘waste’		

In (14) the steps in the construction of line 0 of the metric grid can be seen. First, the application of (a) projects syllables. There is a bracket to the left of the heavy syllables because Catalan is quantity-sensitive. The possibility of projecting morae by applying (a) and also introducing a bracket in the application of (b) allows a double expression of quantity-sensitivity. Idsardi justifies the need for this combination through analysis of stress patterns in Malayalam, Cairene Arabic, Winnebago, Chugach and Cayuvava (Idsardi 1992: 21-22).

The bracket associated with heavy syllables is a left bracket in Catalan. The other possible parameter here, that of direction of projection, does not seem relevant in Catalan. The same results are obtained whether the heavy syllables are projected starting from the left or right. Idsardi (1992) already warns that the direction in the application of *Boundary Projection* is irrelevant in the majority of cases. He argues, however, that in order to describe Wolof's stress behaviour the application has to be made from left to right.

Instruction (c), the *Edge Marking parameter*, is not necessary to explain assignment in Catalan. In Idsardi's proposal (1992), the function assigned to this operation is linked to the stresses situated at the edge of words in some languages. In a more recent work, Bures (1993) argues in favor of unifying the *Edge Marking Parameter* and instruction (d) the *Iterative Constituent Construction* (ICC) into a single process. In diagram (14) it can be seen how the application of ICC must be made from right to left. In this way the construction of feet on uneven number sequences always leaves the leftmost elements out of the constituents. It is the same effect observed in the direction of foot construction in the former model. Instruction (e) (*Head Marking*) with the "left" option acts on the representations just like the construction of trochees as seen in the classic model.

The most important change in the SBG model is the way the system incorporates syllabic weight. The former model projected a beat for each mora. In the framework of the SBG model, a beat per syllable is projected and quantity is indicated with a bracket to the left of heavy syllables. As a result of this change, the words resolved by marking the extrametrical require another analysis within the SBG system. Extrametricality allowed us to resolve paroxytones ending in consonants and some of the proparoxytones ending in a flective vowel. The SBG model projects only one beat per syllable, and therefore there is no element in line O that can be made to coincide with the morae of the heavy syllables. As this system distinguishes light from heavy syllables with a bracket to the left of syllables with more than one mora, a mora is marked extrametrical, in the SBG, by not projecting its weight. The special characteristics of roots that we have resolved by marking the final mora extrametrical will be specified in the new formulation by the absence of a bracket associated with heavy syllables. In (15), the application of these two mechanisms can be seen. In (15a), the system adopted in earlier sections, with trochees constructed on the morae, allows the same stress pattern to be obtained as the one in (15b), which is derived from the projection of a beat per syllable and application of the *Iterative Constituent Construction*. The exception represented by the word *àrab*, paroxytones ending in consonants, is indicated by marking the last mora extrametrical in (15a), and by not applying *Boundary Projection* in (15b). The diagram (15c) shows that the regular application of these mechanisms, with a bracket to the left of heavy syllables, cannot provide the expected results in the marked cases.

```
(15)  a.   *           b.   *          c.     *
           (*  *)           *  *           * (*
           μ  μ<μ>         (*  *           * (*
           a  ɾə  p         a  ɾə p        a  ɾə p  (*[əɾáp])
```

Words that do not project the quantity of their heavy syllables will have this specific quality expressed as an instruction. The affected elements will be marked, so that the operation of weight-projection will not apply, as indicated (WP) in the diagrams. This system of marking is more suitable than a mark directly on the representation because all implied morphemes share the situation of not applying a part of the regular process: the projection of syllabic weight. The representation does not allow a different expression to treat each lexical element separately, and also, the strategy of non-application also saves backward steps in the derivation.

Contrary to what we have seen in words that do not project weight, reformulation of the treatment of proparoxytones is not necessary in the SBG model. The solution we have adopted of marking the last syllable extrametrical, as in (16a), can also be applied to the new model. In the SBG diagrams, the basic units or beats correspond to syllables, and a right-bracket situated to the left of a beat indicates that this element is outside the constituent, and is extrametrical (see 16b).

```
(16)  a.                          b.
         *                             *
        (*   *)                       (*   * ) *
         μ   μ   <μ>                   *   * ) *
        ʒu   pi  <teɾ >               ʒu   pi ) teɾ
```

The basic formulation does not present any complications, but there are still two basic questions to be resolved in relation to proparoxytones. First, the possibility that the very existence of proparoxytones casts doubt on the credibility of the system of assignment. Second, the formal mechanism to include proparoxitonous words into the system, their incorporation as exceptions in concrete lexical entries.

The presence of proparoxytones of the type *Júpiter* can be used as an argument for abandoning the investigation of a regular assignment mechanism for all lexical entries. The exceptional nature of proparoxytones can be interpreted as an especially clear reflection of a random distribution of stress in words. The usual strategy forces us to reduce the information present in the lexicon as much as possible.

I now begin to introduce some of the postulates of Optimality Theory (Prince and Smolensky 1993, McCarthy and Prince 1993). The central idea of this theory has a direct bearing on the explanation of stress components examined in this work. Of main interest is the possibility of reconciling general principles and the violations of these principles. Explanatory value is maintained because there are very few possible violations. Exceptions are only acceptable when their necessity to satisfy a more important condition can be justified. The relative importance of the conditions can be expressed by means of a hierarchy. The final form of a representation, which the theory can explain, is the one that contains the minimum number of violations. The usefulness of ordering conditions is expounded upon mainly in section 5, in the study of the stress consequences of combining morphemes.

Returning to the treatment of proparoxytones and their integration in the whole, the principle of *Lexicon Optimization* must be mentioned. In the framework of Optimality Theory this principle contains the central idea of the theory of Underspecification (Archangeli 1984).

(17) *Lexicon Optimization.* Suppose that several different inputs I_1, I_2, …, In when parsed by a grammar G lead to corresponding outputs O_1, O_2, …, On, all of which are realized as the same phonetic form Φ – these inputs are all *phonetically equivalent* with respect to G. Now, one of these outputs must be the most harmonic, by virtue of incurring the least significant violation marks: suppose this optimal one is labeled O_k. Then the learner should choose, as the underlying form for Φ, the input I_k.

(Prince and Smolensky, 1993:192)

More informally, Prince and Smolensky (1993:195) also express the *Minimal Redundancy Principle*: "to the maximal extent possible, information should be excluded from the lexicon which is predictable from grammatical constraints." If we pay attention only to proparoxytones, it may be difficult to decide between exceptionally marked stress and the presence of stress already on underlying forms (not assigned in the derivation). However, if we consider all lexical elements, it is clear that the solution proposed by a stress assignment system, including the exceptional treatment of proparoxytones, is favorable over the exceptional treatment of all lexical items. Using this procedure, we can reduce the information in the lexicon as much as possible. If there are no other arguments, the generalization found in the *Lexicon Optimization* and *Minimal Redundancy* principles favors the hypothesis of a regular assignment system with exceptions.

Yet another argument can be proposed in favor of the *integrated* treatment of proparoxytones. Even though they are marked, they show a regularity that can be attributed to phonological principles. The generalization observed is that words with exceptional behavior are always proparoxytones, and there are no preproparoxytones. The restriction known as a *Three-Syllable Window* was explained above as different from of the version claiming the inexistence of preproparoxytones, by using the concept of extrametricality. The fact that the extrametrical elements must be peripheral restricts the power of this mechanism. Formulated in this way, however, the restriction is not enough. In principle, the elements that can be characterized as extrametrical are all the constituents of metrical phonology. Therefore, a foot, composed of two positions/elements, can also be extrametrical. In Catalan, the possibility of a final extrametrical foot and the construction of moraic trochees would produce preproparoxytones if the antepenultimate syllable were not heavy. Extrametricality and the restrictions that accompany it cannot, therefore, account for the inexistence of preproparoxytones. This calls for the partial revision of these mechanisms. In the revision, only constituents smaller than feet, syllables, and morae can be marked as extrametrical. The analysis allowed by Optimality Theory has, therefore, a greater explanatory value. Within this theory the effect of extrametricality results from the interaction of two restrictions, NONFINALITY and EDGEMOST.

(18) NONFINALITY (Prince and Smolensky 1993:43)
The head *foot* of the PrWd must not be final.

(19) EDGEMOST (φ; E; D) (Prince and Smolensky 1993:35)
The item φ is situated at the edge E of domain D.

When NONFINALITY is situated above EDGEMOST in the scale of restrictions a final extrametrical syllable is obtained. The violation of EDGEMOST is accepted by the need to satisfy NONFINALITY. The representation the theory can explain is the one containing the minimum number of violations. A form with two extrametrical syllables will unjustifiably violate the EDGEMOST restriction because NONFINALITY can only justify one extrametrical syllable. The representation with two violations is never as good as the one with two. This observation is summarized in the *Economy Property*.

(20) *Economy Property of Optimality Theory*
Banned options are available only to avoid violations of higher-ranked constraints and can only be used *minimally*.
(Prince and Smolensky, 1993:27)

Finally, another reason for treating proparoxytones as a special class and not as isolated exceptions is based on the special behavior of these words regarding other phonological processes. This list of proparoxytones with final consonants taken from Mascaró-Rafel (1990) shows that this type of words are rare.

(21) rèquiem làudanum làbarum Júpiter
pàncreas hèrcules bòreas cúmulus
càrdias fàcies sìfilis clítoris
àlias magnífcat hipèrbaton isòsceles
acròpolis (and 6 more derivatives with *-polis*)

The words in (21) have final extrametrical syllables. They therefore utilize the same mechanism used systematically by Latin. There are still quite a number of words taken from other languages which still conserve the proparoxytone pattern of origin. Catalan has not revised the stress pattern, and has even accepted proparoxytone patterns in words like *Amsterdam* or *Washington*, which force all the exceptional mechanisms to combine: final syllable extrametricality and non-projection of weight (-WP). Other pronunciations enter to form part of the lexicon in the form adopted by the media. The generalization that can be made from the behavior of these loanwords is that, when alterations are produced in respect to the pattern of origin, these modifications always respond to the unmarked patterns determined by the stress assignment system. Prince and Smolensky (1993:66) see it as "the general sense that colloquial language simplifies prosodic structure, rendering them in closer accord with universal structural constraints, while subordinating *faithfulness*. Where faithfulness is the respect for the specifications present in the representation of each lexical element, the exclusion of the final syllable or the indication *-WP* in the case of proparoxytones.

The second problem mentioned above in connection with proparoxytones ending in consonants is the determination of the formal mechanism for marking these words as exceptions. There are basically two possibilities. The most complex is adopted by Idsardi (1992) in the analysis of lexical stress in Russian. An application of his system to proparoxytones in Catalan would result in the formulation of a specific rule to mark final syllables extrametrical. The roots of proparoxytones would therefore need to contain an indication to force the application of the rule. It seems more reasonable to think that the bracket needed to mark the final syllable extrametrical is already present in the underlying form of the affected morphemes (see also Idsardi 1993). The presence of an indication referring to a specific rule produces the same results and complicates the derivation. It would be convenient to have evidence for the existence of this alternative so that the option of placing the bracket directly in the representations could be abandoned.

5. In this section I study two cases of exceptional behaviour: that of stressed monomoraic morphemes and that of prestressed suffixes. The analysis of their behavior is based on the adoption of SBG theory and Optimality Theory.

Before starting the study of monomoraic morphemes it is necessary to examine the relation between monomoraic character and the absence of stress. This relation is clearly present in morphemes of flexion. These morphemes contain two characteristics: their unstressed nature, and the fact that, when they are represented phonologically, they are formed by only one mora. Morphemes of number, and also those of gender, derived when combined with noun roots (see Mascaró 1987), are represented phonologically by only one element. The masculine morpheme, like the singular morpheme, does not have phonological form in the unmarked case. The feminine morpheme is [ə] in the Oriental dialect and the plural is [z]. As far as the morphemes of gender that are exceptions, Mascaró (1987) recognizes the allomorph [Ø] for the feminine, and [u] and [ə] for the masculine. There are also forms corresponding to more sporadic and doubtful cases like [u] in feminine words (*moto* 'motorcycle'), and elements with *-i* (*bigoti* 'mustache'), and *-s* (*bilis* 'bile'). As to the sequences *-us* and *-is*, which are the only representations of flexion with more than one mora, it seems that they can be considered the result of the combination of *u* plus *s* and *i* plus *s*, respectively. The flexional allomorphs of person in verbal elements are also monomoraic when represented phonologically [z], [m], [w] or [n].

The generalizations noted establish a relation between the absence of stress and monomoraic nature in morphemes of number, gender, and person. In the verbal morphemes of tense, the generalization can also be noticed even though it is not absolute. All morphemes of tense are monomoraic except the conditional and the gerund. Their unstressed nature is also general. The stressed nature of the conditional, and sometimes the gerund, can be related to the fact that they contain two morae. The only case which stands apart from this generalization is the future morpheme, which is monomoraic and stressed. Derivational suffixes are usually stressed, and have more than one mora. Therefore the revision of the non-flexional morphemes allows us to see that the relation between stressed and monomoraic morphemes does not affect the flexional nature of those studied earlier. From this we can say that the unstressed nature of flexional morphemes is a phonological property resulting from another phonological property: their monomoraic nature. As the flexional morphemes are always monomoraic, their unstressed nature may have a morphological explanation. This analysis, however, would not take into consideration the phonological foundation of the generalization and the possibility of successfully extending it to other morphological elements. The observation we have made is summarized in (22).

(22) Monomoraic morphemes are unstressed

However, as we have seen, the generalization of (22) does not satisfy all cases: there are morphemes with only one mora that are stressed. We can admit these *violations* of the generalizations and hope that this one keeps its explanatory value. The Optimality Theory foresees that violations of a condition are produced when the objective is to satisfy a higher-ranked condition. It must be determined, then, which other generalizations force the violation of the generalization in (22), expressed as a condition. These other generalizations, or conditions will rank higher than (22), in the scale that fixes the relative importance of restrictions. We first determine which are the other conditions that intervene, and then we shall see how they combine.

In Catalan, there are lexical elements with only one mora. It is an exceptional situation, but it occurs in some cases. Some examples of monomoraic and stressed words are the adjectives *nu* and *cru*, nouns such as *gnu, nyu* or *fe*, the names of some letters and musical notes (*cu, ce, pi, la, fa, do*...), some verb forms (*du, llu, he, sé, té, ve, ha*..), and the strong pronouns *jo* and *tu*. In these words, the condition we have expressed in (22) is violated, and we have seen how it is maintained systematically in flective morphemes. The basic difference between the two conditions considered is that the morphemes of the words mentioned control the stress of the word. If the word is not a clitic, it must be stressed. Flective morphemes can do without stress, and therefore appear unstressed only when they are monomoraic. The morphemes constituting the only elements with phonological representation in words like *fe* or *cru* must control word stress, and so are stressed, even though they only contain one mora.

The other case of a violation of (22) corresponds to the few existing stressed monomoraic suffixes. The most outstanding cases are that of the stem vowel of the verbal elements and the morpheme of the future. Apart from these, in the list of suffixes from Mascaró (1987) occur *-e* (*piqué, negligé*) and *-i*, as in *porteria* and *miopia*. For this last instance, we could propose an underlying form [i ə]; the systematic elision of the vowel is probable because it is always followed by the feminine morpheme. The general situation is, therefore, that monomoraic elements are unstressed. Words comprised of only one mora, the stem vowel of verbal elements, the future morpheme, and a few derivative suffixes differ clearly from this behavior.

We have to relate these cases which fall outside the generalization with conditions situated higher than the generalization observed in the hierarchy of conditions. It is first necessary to find, however, a formula to break down the generalization into the elements it contains.

To relate stress and the "minimum" number of morae necessary, we must observe that, in the unmarked situation, feet are binary, or, made up of two morae. At the same time, the unmarked manner of receiving stress begins with the construction of at least one foot. If we relate these two unmarked procedures, we can explain the strong relation between monomoraic nature and lack of stress. As this relation is not maintained when the word is represented by only one mora, it can be claimed that the necessity of words to bear stress is more important and explains the exception. The conditions that intervene are FOOT BINARITY and ONE STRESS PER WORD.

(23) FOOT BINARITY
Feet are formed by two elements.

(24) ONE STRESS PER WORD
Each word bears a stress.

The relative importance of these two conditions is indicated by the symbol "»" that indicates that the condition preceding it is ranked higher than the one following it in the hierarchy. The effect of ONE STRESS PER WORD » FOOT BINARITY is thus shown in Diagram (25).

(25)

Candidates	ONE STRESS PER WORD	FOOT BINARITY
☞ kɾú		*
kɾu	*!	

The diagram is explained in the following manner. The symbol * indicates a violation of the condition heading the vertical column of the corresponding derivative in the horizontal column. The presence of an exclamation mark, !, beside the symbol marking a violation indicates that it is fatal in the sense that the derivation loses definitively in favor of another or other derivations that are considered better. In the diagram of (25) the second derivative violates the condition of superior level and therefore loses in favor of the first derivation. The fact that this first derivation violates the lower-ranked condition does not make it worse than or equal to the second because the condition it has violated is less important. The best derivation, according to this system of evaluation, is marked in the diagram by the sign (hand) on the left. The condition ONE STRESS PER WORD is situated above FOOT BINARITY in the hierarchy, and with this order, the expected result is obtained.

In order to establish the relation between the categories of morphology and those of phonology the concept of *prosodic word* (PrWd) (McCarthy and Prince 1986, 1990, 1993) has been proposed. In Prince and Smolensky (1993), the connection between morphology and phonology is expressed by the restriction LX=PR (MCat).

(26) *LX = PR (MCat)*

A member of the morphological category MCat corresponds to a PrWd.

(Prince and Smolensky, 1993:43)

According to the same authors, "the PrWd is composed of feet and syllables; it is the domain in which "main stress" is defined." (Prince and Smolensky 1993:43). The restriction LX = PR (MCat) makes it necessary to analyze phonologically any morphological category whatever. The fact that the condition FOOT BINARITY is ranked high in the hierarchy explains that, in the unmarked case, the smallest possible words are bimoraic, the minimum indispensable elements necessary to construct a foot, and thus assign stress without violating FOOT BINARITY.

We can still ask why we have observed the violations of FOOT BINARITY especially in words made up of only one mora and not in the suffixes. The words we have mentioned have another characteristic in common: they have no affix added. We now see in (27) the derivation of a word with a monomoraic stem, like those we have analyzed, but with a flective morpheme added. We have already seen that it is necessary to treat the morphemes separately in stress assignment.

(27)

Candidates	ONE STRESS PER WORD		FOOT BINARITY	
	root	suffix	root	suffix
☛ [kɾú]+[ə]			*	
[kɾu]+[ə]	*!			
[kɾú]+[ə́]			*	*!
[kɾu]+[ə́]	*!			*

The best representation is the first. It presents only one violation which is necessary and justified: the requirement that the feet are binary to give the word stress. This evaluation notes the fact that a root can be free while suffixes are always linked forms. That is why stems are responsible for the existence of stress in the word, and not suffixes. If we assign stress to a monomoraic suffix we will be unnecessarily violating FOOT BINARITY and in the global valuation a derivation that does not assign this unjustified stress will always be best.

After this observation, it becomes apparent that violations of FOOT BINARITY occur not only in monomoraic words, but also in words like those studied in (27), with more than one mora in the whole but with a monomoraic root. In (28) I give some examples that illustrate this situation.

(28)			
	pua 'plectrum'	rua 'street'	grua 'crane'
	fua 'charge'	cua 'tail'	boa
	pia 'pious fem.'	tia 'aunt'	cia 'hipbone'
	via 'vay'	guia 'guide'	rea 'convict fem.'

In the words in (28) the restriction making it necessary to treat morphemes in isolation could be violated to satisfy FOOT BINARITY. In Optimality Theory, all the restrictions involved must be formulated so that they can enter the hierarchy. There are no absolute conditions to unmistakably determine the wrong formation of the candidates; for each case it must be seen what possible justifications of violations are produced and the alternatives must be evaluated with reference to the scale of restrictions. We have seen that, in Catalan, the stress is assigned first in the domain of the morphemes, and we must express that as a condition that can be formulated in the following manner.

(29) ANALYSIS BY MORPHEMES

Each morpheme is assigned the initial metrical structure in an independent manner.

Formulated now as a condition, the procedure of independent analysis by morphemes is a regular operation, if there is no conflict with a condition situated higher in the hierarchy. We revise the analysis of ['kɾuə] that we have proposed in (27). The new version of (30) incorporates the condition ANALYSIS BY MORPHEMES. We see how the derivation violates this condition to satisfy FOOT BINARITY. It can be argued that the derivations ['kɾu+ə] and ['kɾu]+[ə] have the same final form, and that there is no way of proving the proposed order of the restrictions in conflict: ANALYSIS BY MORPHEMES and FOOT BINARITY. The hypothesis I propose is that the correct order is the one given in (30), that is FOOT BINARITY » ANALYSIS BY MORPHEMES. Later on, in treating prestressed suffixes I will show the results of adopting this analysis in the final surface forms.

(30)

Candidates	ONE STRESS PER WORD		FOOT BINARITY		ANALYSIS BY MORPHEMES	
	root	suffix	root	suffix	root	suffix
[kɾú]+[ə]			*!			
[kɾu]+[ə]	*!					
[kɾú]+[ə́]			*	*!		
[kɾu]+[ə́]	*!			*		
☞ [kɾú + ə]					*	

In the new proposal for the analysis of ['kɾuə], a violation of FOOT BINARITY is avoided by contradicting ANALYSIS BY MORPHEMES. In turn, FOOT BINARITY is violated because the construction of only one position on the root was forced by ONE STRESS PER WORD.

Attending to the plural form of the adjective we have considered, ['kɾuəs], a derivation that builds a foot on the base of the two flective morphemes. This would violate ANALYSIS BY MORPHEMES without justification. Expressed in another way, on principle an affix will never force a violation of ANALYSIS BY MORPHEMES because the violations of this restriction seek to avoid the FOOT BINARITY, which at the same time are caused by the restriction ONE STRESS PER WORD, and only the roots are responsible for this condition. Affixes can always bestow the responsibility of the existence of one stress per word to roots. In the first derivation of Diagram (31), the radical which is responsible for ONE STRESS PER WORD satisfies FOOT BINARITY by a violation of ANALYSIS BY MORPHEMES. In the second derivation, the suffix [ə] violates ANALYSIS BY MORPHEMES without higher-ranked conditions gaining any advantage.

(31)

Candidates	ONE STRESS PER WORD		FOOT BINARITY		ANALYSIS BY MORPHEMES	
	root	suffix	root	suffix	root	suffix
☞ [kɾú + ə] + [z]					*	
[kɾú]+[ə + z]			*!			*

When the stem has more than one mora, the most common situation, it is clear that the unjustified violation of ANALYSIS BY MORPHEMES is fatal. We note that the superficial stress of the second derivation of (32) will be placed on the feminine morpheme after the construction of a trochee with the plural morpheme.

(32)

Candidates	ONE STRESS PER WORD		FOOT BINARITY		ANALYSIS BY MORPHEMES	
	root	suffix	root	suffix	root	suffix
☞ [áɾe]+[ə]+[z]						
[áɾe]+[ə + z]						*!

We say that the violation of FOOT BINARITY can also be given, as an exception, to certain suffixes: the stem vowel, the morpheme of future and, perhaps, -é and -í between the derivationals. They are special morphemes that contradict the generalization of (22) and they have to include this special information in their lexical representation. In this way, the stem vowel or morpheme of future, for example, will have an indication referring to its stressed nature as a lexical characteristic. In the application of SBG theory to Catalan, the stressed nature of these suffixes needs to be marked with a bracket to the left of the segmental representation, as shown in (33).

(33) thematic vowels: (a, (e, (ɛ, (i, (u
morphemes of future: (ɾe, (ɾa, (ɾɛ

The thematic augment [έʃ], appearing in place of the stem vowel [ø] in a subgroup of third conjugation verbs, does not need to be marked as stressed. It is a bimoraic morpheme and, therefore, able to serve as a base for the construction of a foot. I have presented the mechanism that allows syllabic weight to be projected in the metrical representations in SBG theory. (See the application of Boundary Projection in (14) and (15)). The transfer operation of the quantity of syllables to the metric grid can also be seen as a condition combined with the others in the framework of Optimality Theory. We will call it PROJECTION OF WEIGHT, and it will have the following form:

(34) PROJECTION OF WEIGHT
Heavy syllables project a left bracket.

As we have formulated PROJECTION OF WEIGHT as a condition, we can explain violations of FOOT BINARITY when they allow the condition just established to be satisfied. Diagram (35) shows that the appropriate order is PROJECTION OF WEIGHT » FOOT BINARITY.

(35)

Candidates	ONE STRESS PER WORD	PROJECTION OF WEIGHT	FOOT BINARITY
* (* (* (* * (* ☞ rusiɲól			*
* * (* * (* * rusíɲol		*!	

The second derivation of (35) violates PROJECTION OF WEIGHT and provides stress on the penultimate syllable, after the construction of a trochee. The fact that this derivation does not violate FOOT BINARITY does not improve its situation with respect to the first. The derivation resulting in the oxytone pattern is the best, and the violation of FOOT BINARITY avoids the violation of the immediately preceding condition, PROJECTION OF WEIGHT.

The thematic augment [ɛ́ʃ] admits a derivation like the one we have seen in (35): as it is a heavy syllable the condition PROJECTION OF WEIGHT guarantees the construction of a foot in spite of violating FOOT BINARITY. The stem increase therefore receives stress as a result of the combination of conditions, in a regular manner. Now, we must look at the exceptions made up of the stressed monomoraic morphemes of (34). These morphemes cannot be represented in classical theory if the condition that feet are binary is maintained. As we have seen, the formulation of SBG accepts degenerated feet when created by the operation Boundary Projection which transfers the syllabic weight to the metric grid. The stressed monomoraic morphemes of Catalan act as heavy syllables: they force the construction of a foot. It seems justified to give the same treatment, a bracket to the left, to the two cases. The origin of the bracket will be different in each case. The one for heavy syllables will be obtained by applying a regular operation (Boundary Projection or an action linked to PROJECTION OF WEIGHT), and in the stressed monomoraic morphemes the bracket will already be present in the underlying representations. This bracket will remain throughout the derivation. To ensure that it is maintained, we include a new condition in the diagrams to allow evaluation of the derivations. This is the condition of PRESERVATION, formulated as follows.

(36) PRESERVATION

Elements present in the initial representation are maintained.

Diagram (37) shows the best derivation of the verbal form [kəntáβəs], and two more derivations. It must be said that the conditions STRESS PER WORD and PRESERVATION, which appear in this order in the diagram, are not organized in a hierarchical manner as can be seen in the final representations. The condition PROJECTION OF WEIGHT must be situated at a lower position in the scale of conditons (see below). Therefore, ACCENT PER WORD = PRESERVATION » PROJECTION OF WEIGHT.

(37)

Candidates	ONE STRESS PER WORD	PRESER-VATION	PROJECTION OF WEIGHT	FOOT BINARITY	ANALYSIS BY MORPHEMES
* (* (*) (* (* *) * ☞[kənt]+[(a]+[βə]+[z]				*	*
* (*) (* *) * * [kənt]+[(a]+[βə]+[z]		*!			*
* (* (*) (* (*) * * [kənt]+[(a]+[βə]+[z]				**!	

The optimal derivation of (37) must construct a foot on the thematic vowel in order to respect the lexical demands established by this element, and therefore satisfy PRESERVATION. The stem morpheme [kánt] has a heavy syllable, and therefore forces the violation of FOOT BINARITY. The construction of a foot on the stressed vowel would involve a second violation of FOOT BINARITY. This new violation can be avoided because it does not respect ANALYSIS BY MORPHEMES. The second derivation of (37) violates PRESERVATION because it does not take into account the bracket and the initial representation of the thematic vowel. The final derivation presents a fatal violation (marked "*!") because it builds a degenerate foot on the thematic vowel. This is not acceptable because it satisfies a lower-ranked condition (ANALYSIS BY MORPHEMES) at the cost of violating a superior one (FOOT BINARITY). A generalization contained in Optimality Theory is the prediction that violations are always minimal, as the violation of a condition can only be justified by the necessity of satisfying a superior one. Any representation that includes an additional violation will always be worse, and therefore rejected as the optimal representation, in favor of the one containing only one violation, the minimum number.

Monomoraic stressed morphemes, like heavy syllables, only conserve stress in the final representation if no other foot can be built to their right. The reason is that, as we have seen in the framework of the classical analysis, the final prominence in the domain of the word is assigned to the right in Catalan. The particular operation that assures the maintenance of right-most stress could be the projection of the nucleus to the right in the line immediately below. What interests us now is to see how the combination of two stressed monomoraic morphemes results in the disappearance of left-most stress. In the same way, the heavy syllable of the stem project its nucleus to the following line. The violations produced obey the same mechanisms we have seen in diagram (37).

(38)

Candidates	ONE STRESS PER WORD	PRESER-VATION	PROJECTION OF WEIGHT	FOOT BINARITY	ANALYSIS BY MORPHEMES
* (* (* (* (* (* (* *) ☞[kənt]+[(a]+[(ɾa]+[z]				**	*
* (* (*) (* (* *) * [kənt]+[(a]+[(ɾa]+[z]		*!		*	*
* (* (* (*) (* (* (*) * [kənt]+[(a]+[(ɾa]+[z]				***!	

The other group of morphemes with exceptional behavior is prestressed suffixes. The peculiarity of these morphemes must also be present in their lexical representation. They are monosyllabic, but they project the pattern of a trochee. As there are prestressed morphemes formed by a heavy syllable we must mark the representations with the indication *-WP*, in the same way we marked the paroxytones ending in a consonant. If weight is not projected, the single syllable of the suffix will form the weak position of the foot. In the analysis of flexional morphemes, however, we have seen that a monomoraic morpheme which is not a root cannot serve as a base for the construction of a foot. To force the creation of the trochaic pattern we must place a bracket to the right of the prestressed suffixes. The presence of the bracket will have the effect of transferring the stress to the last syllable of the preceding morpheme, because of the combination of the conditions I have presented. Diagram (39) summarizes the situation. The optimal derivation maintains the lexical bracket and respects -*WP*. The cost of this second operation, linked to PRESERVATION, is the violation of PROJECTION OF WEIGHT. The violation of ANALYSIS BY MORPHEMES allows the construction of a binary foot with the weak position in the suffixal syllable and the strong one in the last syllable of the preceding morpheme. The two following derivations violate PRESERVATION; in one case -*WP* is not respected, and in the other the bracket is not maintained. The final derivation of the scheme constructs a degenerate foot on the suffix and unnecessarily violates FOOT BINARITY in order to respect the inferior condition of ANALYSIS BY MORPHEMES. The prestressed morphemes therefore provide evidence for the relation FOOT BINARITY » ANALYSIS BY MORPHEMES.

(39)

Candidates	ONE STRESS PER WORD	PRESER-VATION	PROJECTION OF WEIGHT	FOOT BINARITY	ANALYSIS BY MORPHEMES
* (*) * (* *) ☛ [t ə l ɛ]+[f u n)] [-WP]			*		*
* (* (*) (* * (*) [t ə l ɛ]+[f u n)] [-WP]		*!		*	
* (*) (* *) * [t ə l ɛ]+[f u n)] [-WP]		*!	*		
* (*) *) (* *) *) [t ə l ɛ]+[f u n)] [-WP]			*	*!	

Idsardi (1992) proposes an analysis of prestressed morphemes in Russian based on a rule that introduces a bracket, which is called Doubling, and which has the form in (40).

(40) Ø —> (/ — x (

The solution I have proposed for these suffixes is more restrictive and derived from the combination of conditions justified independently. The resort to rules like (40) allows the existence of very different stress behavior and does not relate the exceptions with ordinary cases.

Conclusions

I have presented a system of stress assignment to words in Catalan, and I have suggested the mechanisms necessary to obtain the desired results in the cases indicated. The incorporation of the basic elements of SBG theory has allowed a homogeneous formulation of unmarked characteristics and special lexical cases. Finally, the use of Optimality Theory has facilitated an explanation of the processes and of the connections they maintain within a coherent framework.

Notes

[*] A Catalan version of this paper will appear in *Caplletra 19*. This work was supported by DGICYT grant PB93-0893-C04-03 and CIRIT grant CS93-5.005. I thank Joan Mascaró, Eulalia Bonet, José Ignacio Hualde, Salvador Oliva, Blanca Palmada and Daniel Recasens for helpful comments.

References

Alsina, À. 1989. *Catalan stress and the autonomy of the CV tier*. ms.

Archangeli, Diana. 1984 *Underspecification in Yawelmani phonology and morphology*. Doctoral dissertation, MIT.

Bures, A. 1993. Avoid A on the grid. Presented at GLOW Colloquium, Lund.

Cabré, Teresa. 1993. *Estructura Gramatical i Lexicó: el Mot Mínim Català*. Doctoral dissertation, Univesitat Autònoma de Barcelona.

Coromines, Joan. 1983. *LLeures i Converses d'un Filòleg*. Barcelona: Club Editor.

Ferrís, V. 1984. Lleis de l'accent en funció de la quantitat. *Miscel.lània Sanchis Guarner I*, p. 117-123. Valencia: Universitat de Valencia.

Halle, Morris. 1990. Respecting metrical structure. *Natural Language and Linguistic Theory* 8.149-176.

Halle, Morris and Jean Roger Vergnaud. 1987. *An Essay on Stress*. Cambridge, Mass: MIT Press.

Hayes, Bruce. 1982. Extrametricality and English stress. *Linguistic Inquiry* 13.227-76.

Hayes, Bruce. 1994. *Metrical Stress Theory: Principles and Case Studies*. Chicago: University of Chicago Press.

Hualde, J. Ignacio. 1992. *Catalan*. London and New York: Routledge.

Idsardi, William. 1992. *The Computation of Prosody*. Doctoral dissertation, MIT.

Idsardi, William. 1993. Some properties of simplified bracketed grids. Presented at GLOW-Workshop, Lund.

Kager, René 1993. Consequences of catalexis. Presented at First HILP Conference in Phonology, Leiden.

Kager, René. 1995. The metrical theory of word stress. *The Handbook of Phonological Theory*, ed. John Goldsmith, 367-403. Cambridge Mass.: Blackwell

Kiparsky, Paul. 1992. Catalexis. Stanford University and Wissenschaftskolleg zu Berlin ms.

Mascaró, Joan. 1983. *La Fonologia Catalana i el Cicle Fonològic*. Doctoral dissertation. Sèrie Lingüística, UAB.

Mascaró, Joan. 1984. Aramon-aramònic: una regla fonològica catalana no descoberta fins ara. *Miscel.lània Aramon i Serra*, vol. VI, p. 123-129. Barcelona: Curial.

Mascaró, Joan. 1987. *Morfologia*. 2nd ed. Barcelona: Biblioteca Universitària, Enciclopèdia Catalana.

Mascaró, Joan. and Joaquim Rafel. 1990. *Diccionari Català Invers amb Informació Morfològica*, Barcelona: Publicacions de l'Abadia de Montserrat.

McCarthy, John and Alan Prince. 1986. Prosodic morphology, University of Massachusetts, Amherst and Brandeis, ms.

McCarthy, John and Alan Prince. 1990. Foot and word in prosodic morphology: the Arabic broken plural. *Natural Language and Linguistic Theory* 8.209-283

McCarthy, John and Alan Prince. 1993. *Prosodic Morphology I: constraint interaction and satisfaction*. University of Massachusetts, Amherst and Rutgers, ms.

Oliva, Salvador. 1977. Dos aspectes del ritme en català modern. *Els Marges* 9.89-96.

Oliva, Salvador. 1991. *La Reestructuració del sintagma fonològic*. Girona University, ms.

Oliva, Salvador. 1992. *La Mètrica i el Ritme de la Prosa*. Barcelona: Quaderns Crema.

Oliva, Salvador and Pep Serra. 1990. Stress resolution at the phonological phrase level: Some examples from Catalan and Spanish, presented at GISELLE 1990, Universitat de Girona.

Prince, Alan. 1983. Relating to the grid. *Linguistic Inquiry* 14.19-100.

Prince, Alan and Paul Smolensky. 1993. *Optimality Theory: constraint interaction in Generative Grammar*. Rutgers University and University of Colorado, Boulder, ms.

Recasens, Daniel. 1986. *Estudis de Fonètica Experimental del Català Oriental Central*. Barcelona: PAM.

Recasens, Daniel. 1991. *Fonètica Descriptiva del Català*. Barcelona: Institut d'Estudis Catalans.

Serra, Pep. 1992. El principi d'economia en les derivacions de la fonologia mètrica. *Actes del VII Congrés de Llenguatges Naturals i Llenguatges Formals*.

Serra, Pep. 1993a. De la representació de l'accent. *Llengua i Literatura* 5 1992- 1993.

Serra, Pep. 1993b. *Estructura Prosòdica i Accent*. Universitat Autònoma de Barcelona, ms.

Wheeler, Max. 1979. *Phonology of Catalan*. Oxford: Blackwell.

Wheeler, Max. 1987. L'estructura fonològica de la síl.laba i del mot en català. *Estudis de Llengua i Literatura Catalanes XIV*.

III Galician

8

Epenthesis and deletion in Galician: an optimality–theoretic approach*

Sonia Colina

1 Introduction

In this article I propose an Optimality Theory (OT) analysis of the processes traditionally known as epenthesis and deletion in Galician. OT analyses of syllabification processes in related languages such as Spanish (Colina 1995, Hualde ms) have been shown to provide more satisfactory accounts than those formulated in other frameworks. Although the dearth of theoretical analyses of Galician syllabification and syllabification–related processes (Hualde and Martínez–Gil 1992, Colina 1993, Colina 1995) hinders comparison, I will show that an OT account is superior to those of other frameworks in a number of ways. For example, it can explain why epenthesis is preferred to deletion or vice versa, and can also predict the epenthesis or deletion site. Furthermore, this analysis provides a unified account of these processes and is able to capture what they have in common.

After a brief introduction to Optimality Theory in section 2, this paper looks at word–initial epenthesis and deletion in section 3: 3.2 deals with glide epenthesis in word initial and word–medial position. Non–initial repair strategies are discussed in section 4: word–final epenthesis is examined in 4.1; sections 4.2 and 4.3 cover particular types of final epenthesis (plural epenthesis and paragogic *–e*, respectively); and section 4.4 looks at deletion word–medially. The article concludes with a summary and review of the advantages of an OT analysis of epenthesis and deletion.

2 Optimality Theory

In recent years phonological theory has attempted to explain the interaction of rules and well–formedness constraints. As a consequence, constraints have assumed a central role in this line of research, as manifested in OT. The present analysis is formalized in the constraint-based framework of OT (Prince and Smolensky 1993, McCarthy and Prince 1993a, 1993b, 1994a, 1994b, 1995). In this section I will review the basic tenets of this theoretical framework.

In generative phonology, phonological rules examine inputs to determine if they meet the Structural Description (SD) of the rule; if the SD is met, the Structural Change (SC) described in the rule applies in order to derive the output. The output of rule 1 can, in turn, become the input for rule 2. The manner of operation is procedural, and input-output relations are governed by rules and transformations. Rule ordering therefore becomes necessary.

In a constraint-based model of phonology, rules are replaced by well-formedness constraints, which may make contradictory claims on the form of the output. However, constraints can be violated, although only minimally. In addition to a set of minimally violable constraints, Universal Grammar (UG) provides a way of resolving the conflict: conflicts arising out of constraint interaction are solved through constraint ranking. A constraint that is more highly ranked will have priority over another one that is lower in the hierarchy. The ranking of the constraints is done on a language particular basis, therefore, linguistic variation is a result of differences in ranking.

In addition to a universal set of constraints and a means to resolve conflicts, UG provides the function *Gen* (for generator) which generates all possible analyses of the input. The role of the grammar is to rate all candidate analyses according to the well-formedness constraints and select the one that best satisfies the set of constraints. Evaluation is carried out by the function *H-eval* (Harmony Evaluator); the optimal candidate, the one which best satisfies the set of constraints, will be the output.

OT abandons operations on the input in favor of evaluation and/or selection of the optimal candidate. Alternate candidates are considered in parallel. Under the OT framework the relation between input and output is fundamentally changed; the output is not the result of an operation on the input, but it is contained in it as an element belonging to the set of all possible analyses of the input. The output is the best candidate analysis of the input. Evaluation, not derivation, is central to the theory.

I will now illustrate the notion of constraint ranking and evaluation. The formalism and basic conventions are taken from McCarthy and Prince (1993a).

Constraint tableaux show the results of the evaluation of various candidates. Left to right order indicates ranking of constraints, from higher to lower. A thick vertical line means that the constraints are ranked, the one to the left of the line dominating the one to its right, and a dotted line indicates that the constraints are not ranked. Violations are marked with an asterisk. Fatal violations, those that make further evaluation of the candidate unnecessary, are marked by *!. Cells are shaded to indicate that they are irrelevant to evaluation because a fatal violation has already occurred. The pointing hand identifies the optimal candidate (output).

Suppose that A and B are two conflicting constraints, /put/ is the input, and c1 and c2 are two candidate analyses of the input produced by *Gen*. *H-eval* would proceed as indicated in tableau (1).

(1) /put/

Candidates	A	B
c_1		*
c_2	*	

C_1 satisfies constraint A, but fails B; c_2 fails A, but satisfies B. If c_1 is the correct output for /put/, constraint A is more highly ranked than B. That is, when A and B conflict, the decision is made by A. Therefore we say that 'A dominates B' (A » B), as in tableau (2). Constraints that are never violated are said to be undominated.

(2) /put/ A » B

Candidates	A	B
☞ c_1		*
c_2	*!	

If c_2 is the correct output, B must dominate A, as in tableau (3).

(3) /put/ B » A

Candidates	B	A
c_1	*!	
☞ c_2		*

In (3), c_1 fails on the more highly ranked constraint B, whereas c_2 satisfies B and fails a lower constraint, A, which at this point is irrelevant, since B is enough to make a decision between the two candidates.

Suppose now that both candidates fail (or both satisfy) B, as in (4).

(4)

Candidates	B	A
c_1	*	*!
☞ c_2	*	

In this particular case, the decision is passed on to constraint A to select the best candidate.

Many constraints admit multiple violations. This is where the concept of minimal violation becomes relevant. The optimal candidate will be the form with fewer violations of the same constraint. Suppose that in a given language the constraint ONSET requires that all syllables have an onset.

(5) /apaka/

Candidates	ONSET
a. ap.ak.a	***!
b. a.pak.a	**!
☞ c. a.pa.ka	*

Given candidate analyses (a), (b), and (c) for the input /apaka/ in (5), the notion of minimal violation determines that (c) will be the winner since it involves only one violation of ONSET, while (b) has two, and (a) three.

In OT, syllable structure is accounted for in the same way as any other part of the grammar; the output syllabic parse of the unsyllabified input is the one that best satisfies the system of constraints.

One recent development within OT is Correspondence Theory (McCarthy and Prince 1994b, 1995, Benua 1995). Correspondence Theory, originally developed to account for a base (S1 in (6)) and a reduplicant (S2 in (6)) in reduplication processes, proposes correspondence as a relation between strings (McCarthy and Prince 1994b).

(6) *Correspondence* (cf. McCarthy and Prince 1994b):
Given two strings S1 and S2, correspondence is a relation R from the elements of S1 to those of S2. Segment α (an element of S1) and β (an element of S2) are referred to as correspondents of one another when $\alpha R \beta$.

Correspondents, however, need not be identical. Identity is regulated by faithfulness constraints such as those given in (7) (where *B* = base, *R* = reduplicant, *I* = input, *O* = output).

(7) (McCarthy and Prince 1994a: 8–9).

a. MAX

Every element of B has a correspondent in R.

Range(f) = B

b. BASE-DEPENDENCE (B-DEP)
Every element of R has a correspondent in B.
Dom(f) = R

c. ANCHORING
Correspondence preserves alignment in the following sense: the left (right) peripheral element of R corresponds to the left (right) peripheral element of B, if R is to the left (right) of B.

d. CONTIGUITY (CONT)
The portion of the base standing in correspondence forms a contiguous string, as does the correspondent portion of the reduplicant.

When the constraints in (7) are dominated by other constraints, the identity of base and reduplicant is sacrificed; if undominated, base and reduplicant will be identical. McCarthy and Prince (1994b) propose that the correspondence relation between base and reduplicant (B–R) is formally equivalent to the relation between input and output (I–O); MAX is formally equivalent to PARSE (no deletion) and BASE-DEPENDENCE corresponds to FILL (no epenthesis); CONTIGUITY-related effects have been observed in the input–output relation (cf. Kentstowicz's 1994 work on Chukchee) in which it is argued that epenthesis can only occur at the edges of morphemes; ANCHORING is related to ALIGN constraints. One important point that must be noted here is that although the B–R and I–O faithfulness constraints are formally equivalent, they cannot be identical. In order to prove that the B–R and I–O faithfulness constraints are formally related but not identical, they must be ranked separately in at least one language. McCarthy and Prince show that this is the case in Axininca Campa, in which PARSE » ONSET » MAX (1994b: 17).

Another important aspect of Correspondence Theory is the reformulation of PARSE and FILL. In Prince and Smolensky (1993), deleted material was present in the output but unparsed; similarly, epenthetic material was present in the input in the form of empty structure, which is filled out later by phonetic implementation principles. Correspondence Theory holds that deleted material is literally absent from the output and epenthetic material is literally inserted, not present, in the input.

Finally, on the basis of the formal correspondence existing between MAX and PARSE and BASE-DEPENDENCE and FILL and of the reformulation of PARSE and FILL, some terminological changes have taken place: PARSE is now MAX-IO and FILL is BASE-DEPENDENCE-IO.

(8)	Base/reduplicant (B-R)	Input/Output (I-O)
	MAX	PARSE = MAX-IO
	BASE DEPENDENCE	FILL = B-DEP-IO

3 Initial epenthesis

3.1 /e/-epenthesis

Galician exhibits a well-known process of initial epenthesis before an unsyllabified word initial /s/. The evidence for the epenthetic nature of this process comes from alternations such as those in (9), and from the adaptation of borrowings with a disallowed consonant cluster word-initially, as in (10).[1]

(9)	*estabilidade*	'stability'	*instabilidade*	'instability'
	espirar	'exhale'	*inspirar*	'inhale'
	eslavo	'Slav'	*yugoslavo*	'Yugoslavian'

(10)	*estrés*	'stress'
	estock	'stock'
	Nguyen [eŋgúɟeŋ]	'Nguyen' (Vietnamese name)

The same process exists in Catalan, Spanish, and Portuguese. To my knowledge, there are no theoretical accounts of this process in Galician. Harris (1983) and Harris (1986) contain standard analyses of initial epenthesis in Spanish, easily transferrable to Galician. Harris (1983: 30) argues for the account in (11), in which syllabification applies to the underlying representation, leaving the initial /s/ unsyllabified. A special rule converts /s/ into a syllabic segment, which triggers the application of another rule in which syllabic consonants branch to the left. This creates an empty V slot, and the presence of this new vowel position prompts the consonant to become [-syllabic] again. Finally, the empty V is filled in with [e] by a default rule.

(11) 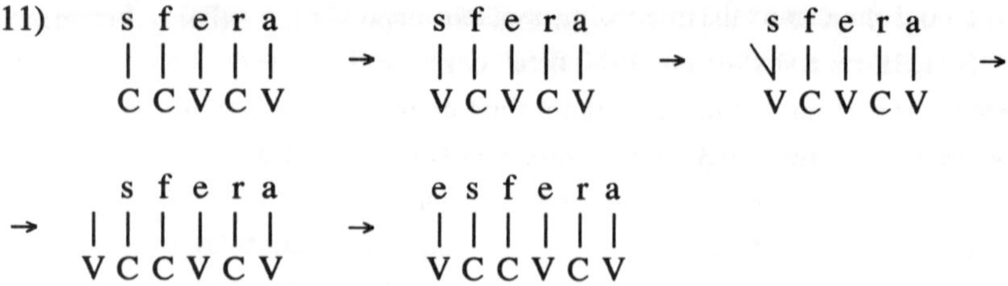

Harris (1986) proposes rules of insertion (12) and default (13). Their application is illustrated in (14).

(12) Insertion: $\emptyset \rightarrow V$ / E[2]

(13) Default: 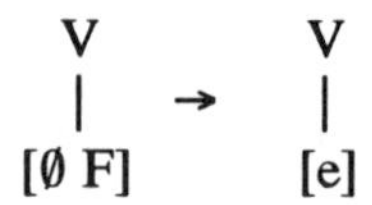

(14) 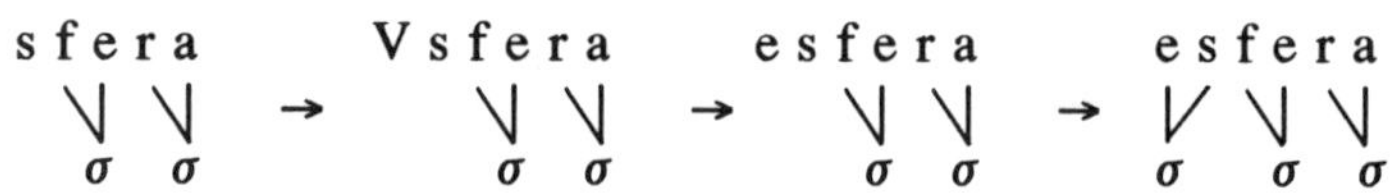

Harris' analysis requires syllabification to apply both before (otherwise insertion would apply before any initial /s/) and after epenthesis (in order to incorporate the vocalic element into syllable structure). Also note that the motivation for epenthesis and for the repair strategy used respond to different principles: while epenthesis takes place because of the need to syllabify an unsyllabified segment, alternative ways of incorporating preconsonantal initial /s/ into syllable structure, i.e., *estabilidade* *[se̲taβiliðáðe], *[taβiliðáðe], are ruled ill-formed on the basis of failing to meet the structural description of a particular rule. Furthermore, in a rule-based approach, the locus of the epenthetic vowel must be stipulated: in (11) the epenthesis site is to the left of /s/ because there is a rule that says that syllabic consonants branch to the left; (12) says that V is inserted in an environment containing an unsyllabified /s/, but it is not clear why insertion is not to the right of /s/, e.g. **se̲fera*. Under generative analyses like Harris', it is also difficult to explain the existence of both epenthesis and deletion word-initially (cf. (9) and (24)). In addition, rules miss the universality of the processes involved in epenthesis and deletion.

In an OT account, the question of ordering in syllabification simply does not arise, given the parallel nature of the model. A non-serial approach needs only one type of motivation for epenthesis, and for the choice of repair strategy –choosing the best possible output given the set of constraints– and it does not have to stipulate the epenthesis site. In what follows, I present an OT analysis of initial epenthesis in Galician.

Galician initial epenthesis results from the need to satisfy ONSET SONORITY (ONS-SON). Forms without epenthesis, e.g. [sta.βi.li.ðá.ðe], violate the highly-ranked constraint ONS-SON, because /st/ is not an acceptable onset cluster.

(15) ONSET SONORITY (Colina 1995):[3]
For two segments to be parsed in the same onset, a certain distance in the sonority scale must be maintained. In Galician it is the maximum distance: the first consonant is the least sonorous in the language, and the second is the most sonorous, an obstruent and a liquid, respectively.

In order to satisfy ONS-SON a violation of the more lowly ranked B-DEP-IO will be incurred. In other words, ONS-SON must dominate B-DEP-IO.

(16) B-DEP-IO:
Do not insert material which is not present in the underlying representation.

Tableau (17) shows candidate evaluation.

(17) Input: /stabilidade/[4] ; Output: [es.ta.βi.li.ðá.ðe]

Candidates	ONS-SON	B-DEP-IO
a. sta.βi.li.ðá.ðe	*!	
☞ b. es.ta.βi.li.ðá.ðe		*

Candidate (17b) is optimal because (17a) violates ONS–SON.

Another relevant constraint is MAX–IO, which bans deletion of underlying material. MAX–IO must dominate B–DEP–IO because epenthesis is preferred to deletion as a way to satisfy ONSET SONORITY.

(18) MAX–IO » B–DEP–IO

(19) Input: /stabilidade/; Output: [es.ta.βi.li.ðá.ðe]

Candidates	ONS–SON	MAX–IO	B–DEP–IO
a. ta.βi.li.ðá.ðe		*!	
☞ b. es.ta.βi.li.ðá.ðe			*

(19b) is chosen as the optimal candidate because (19a) violates the more highly ranked MAX–IO.

Another possible candidate to consider is [se.ta.βi.li.ðá.ðe], with epenthesis after [s]. This candidate is eliminated due to a violation not shown in (19) of a constraint of the MORPHEME–CONTIGUITY (M–CONT) family, also highly ranked, which I state in (20).

(20) M–CONTIGUITY (M–CONT):
No skipping or inserting of phonological material internal to the morpheme.[5]

An obvious consequence of a high ranking of the M–CONT constraint is the preference for either epenthesis or deletion word-initially or word finally, rather than word internally.

As the analysis of glide epenthesis will show (cf. section 3.2), M–CONT must be exploded into two constraints: *INSERT–m–μ, a moraic version of M–CONT which bans insertion of moraic material internal to the morpheme, and M–CONT, the non-moraic counterpart.[6] The relevant constraint for initial epenthesis is *INSERT–m–μ. *INSERT–m–μ dominates ALIGN LEFT because [es.ta.βi.li.ðá.ðe] is preferred to [se.ta.βi.li.ðá.ðe].

(21) ALIGN LEFT/RIGHT (ALIGN-L/R): The left (right) edge of a prosodic word should be aligned with the left (right) edge of the stem. (McCarthy and Prince 1993a: 32).

The prosodic word is represented here by means of a bracket [, and the stem by a vertical line | .

(22) *INSERT-m-μ » ALIGN LEFT

(23) Input: /stabilidade/; Output: [es.ta.βi.li.ðá.ðe]

Candidates	*INSERT-m-μ	ALIGN-L
a. [| se.ta.βi.li.ðá.ðe	*!	
☞ b. [e | s.ta.βi.li.ðá.ðe		*

Although (b) violates ALIGN LEFT due to the misalignment introduced by initial epenthesis, (a) is less optimal because it contains one *INSERT-m-μ violation, incurred by the insertion of a vowel inside the morpheme. Since (a) violates more highly ranked *INSERT-m-μ, (b) is the optimal candidate and the output in tableau (23).

Note that the analysis of initial epenthesis proposed at this point does not account for all initial clusters in Galician. Consider learned or borrowed clusters that violate sonority restrictions in the onset:

(24) *pneumático* [new.má.ti.ko] 'tire'
psicólogo [si.kɔ́.lo.γo] 'psychologist'

It is necessary to explain why the violation of ONS-SON in (24) is avoided through deletion instead of epenthesis. The difference between the clusters in (24) and those in (9-10) is that epenthesis in *[ep.si.kɔ́.lo.γo] would result in one CODA CONDITION (CODA-COND) violation, whereas there is no such violation in *Nguyen* [eŋgúɟeŋ] or *estrés*.

(25) CODA CONDITION (Colina 1995):
Only coronal point of articulation is allowed in a coda position.[7]

Although the ranking MAX–IO » B–DEP–IO predicts insertion, domination of CODA–COND over MAX–IO results in deletion of the initial consonant in [si.kɔ́.lo.γo].

(26) CODA–COND » MAX–IO

(27) Input: /psikɔlogo/[8] ; Output: [si.kɔ́.lo.γo]

Candidates	CODA–COND	MAX–IO	B–DEP–IO
a. ep.si.kɔ́.lo.γo	*!		*
☞ b. si.kɔ́.lo.γo		*	

As shown, (27a) violates CODA–COND (27b). The candidate with initial deletion is the optimal candidate because its highest violation is a violation of MAX–IO, a constraint ranked under CODA–COND. An additional candidate with morpheme internal epenthesis, i.e. *[pe.si.kɔ́.lo.γo], is eliminated due to a violation of *INSERT–m–μ. *[psi.kɔ́.lo.γo] is also eliminated due to a ONS–SON violation.

(28) Summary of constraints

ONS–SON, MAX–IO » B–DEP–IO

*INSERT–m–μ » ALIGN LEFT

CODA–COND » MAX–IO » B–DEP–IO

3.2 Glide epenthesis

In addition to word-initial vocalic epenthesis, some dialects of Galician have glide epenthesis (both word-initial and word-medial, between a verb and a clitic, and between word boundaries).[9] Although not strictly word-initial, glide epenthesis needs to be referred to here because, by showing that M-CONT and *INSERT-m-μ are separately ranked (*INSERT-m-μ » ONSET » M-CONT), it provides support for the explosion of M-CONT into M-CONT and *INSERT-m-μ. The data are provided in (29) (see Carballo Calero 1976: 116–117) through (31).

(29)	*é-a*:	*sé.*[j]*a* '*I am*-SUBJ', *al.dé.*[j]*a* 'small town'
	é-o:	*cé.*[j]o 'sky', *fé.*[j]*o* 'ugly-MASC'
	e-á:	*re.*[j]ál 'royal', *de.*[j]*án* 'dean'
	e-ó:	*pe.*[j]*ór* 'worse'
	ó-o:	*dó.*[j]*o* 'I-give-it-MASC', *só.*[j]*o* 'alone-MASC'
	ó-a:	*só.*[j]*a* 'alone-FEM', *mó.*[j]*a* 'tooth'
	a-é:	*ma.*[j]*és.tro* 'teacher'
	a-ó:	*ka.[j]ó.ba* 'mahogany'

(30)	*alma*	'soul'	*a* [j]*ál.ma*	'the soul'
	época	'time'	*a* [j]*é.po.ca*	'the time'
	ermo	'wasteland'	*o* [j]*ér.mo*	'the wasteland'

(31)	a.	*terá a*	*te.rá.*[j]*a*	'(s)he will have it-FEM'
		terán a	*te.rá.na*	'they will have it-FEM'
		non a terá	*no.na.te.rá*	'(s)he will not have it-FEM'
	b.	*dá os*	*dá.*[j]*os*	'give them-MASC'
		dán os	*dá.nos*	'they give them-MASC'
	c.	*haberá o*	*ha.be.rá.*[j]*o*	'there will be it-MASC'
		haberán os	*ha.be.rá.nos*	'there will be them-MASC'
	d.	*a alma*	*a.*[j]*ál.ma*	'the-FEM soul'
		duas almas	*du.a.sal.mas*	'two-FEM souls'

Instead of [j], some eastern dialects have a back glide, e.g. *chamába*[w]*a* '(s)he called her/it-FEM', (Carballo Calero 1976: 117).

Glide epenthesis results from the need to satisfy ONSET, a constraint that requires that all syllables have onsets.[10] In dialects with glide epenthesis, ONSET must dominate B-DEP-IO, since epenthesis is preferred to an onsetless syllable. It was shown above that MAX-IO dominates B-DEP-IO.

(32) MAX-IO, ONSET » B-DEP-IO

(33) Input: /dá os/; Output: [dá.jos]

Candidates	MAX-IO	ONSET	B-DEP-IO
a. dás	*!		*
b. dá.os		*!	
☞ c. dá.jos			*

(33a) and (33b) violate MAX-IO and ONSET, respectively, and the latter constraints are more highly ranked than B-DEP-IO, the only constraint violated by the optimal candidate (33c).

M-CONT, not *INSERT-m-μ, is the relevant constraint for glide epenthesis because the inserted material surfaces as non-moraic. It must be dominated by ONSET, because insertion takes place inside the stem ([fé.jo]) in order to provide the syllable with an onset. *INSERT-m-μ dominates ONSET as is shown by the initial epenthesis data: [es.ta.βi.li.ðá.ðe] is preferred to [se.ta.βi.li.ðá.ðe]; both [es.ta.βi.li.ðá.ðe] and [se.ta.βi.li.ðá.ðe] satisfy ONS-SON but the first one has one ONSET violation, whereas the latter violates *INSERT-m-μ, suggesting that *INSERT-m-μ dominates ONSET.

A word is necessary here about the realization of the inserted segment. Glide insertion in Galician supports the reformulation of FILL/B-DEP-IO as a constraint against *literal* insertion of segments not present in the underlying representation. Earlier formulations of this constraint in OT claim that FILL violations are incurred by inserting empty structure not present in the underlying representation; the realization of this structure is part of the phonetic component (McCarthy and Prince 1993a, Prince and Smolensky 1993) or is introduced by a phonological rule (McCarthy 1993). McCarthy and Prince (1994a: 31) argue that such conception of epenthetic structure must be inadequate; otherwise, in languages like Makassarese, the fact that the epenthetic consonant position happens to be one of the two types allowed in a coda by the phonology would be accidental. Similarly, in Galician, the fact that the inserted segments are the high melodies--the only ones that can be parsed as onsets-- would also remain unexplained. Both the Makassarese and Galician facts are accounted for under a conception of FILL in which vocoids are literally inserted. The formal account of the Galician data is as follows: an associational constraint *M/I, U[11] ranked under ONSET permits the association of high melodies to onset (margin) positions in order to avoid ONSET violations (cf. Colina 1995 for a demonstration of this ranking). Candidates containing a glide do not violate *INSERT-m-μ (this would be a problem since *INSERT-m-μ » ONSET) because they are non-moraic. In addition, there is no insertion of consonantal segments, which seems to indicate that a constraint against epenthesizing consonants is undominated:[12]

(34) *INSERT Consonant (INSERT-C) (undominated)

No violations of *INSERT-C are incurred because [j, w] are not consonants.[13] Spanish provides further evidence for the above analysis in that it does not allow parsing of high segments in onset position (*O/I, U » ONSET) and, as a result, there is no glide insertion (cf. Colina 1995: 131-ff.).

In sum, epenthesis in Galician cannot take place in the phonetic component because the melody inserted is the only one that can be parsed as an onset. It must consist of literal insertion of a segment and not of empty structure.

4 Non-initial epenthesis/deletion in Galician

4.1 Final epenthesis

The only coda consonants allowed in the native lexical inventory of Galician are /r/, /l/, /s/, /n/, and /θ/.

The data in (35) show that forms with a final consonant other than /r/, /l/, /s/, /n/, /θ/ or with a consonant cluster undergo epenthesis. Unlike words ending in possible consonants, forms with ill-formed final consonantal rhymes must have a terminal element; that is, whereas /a/ and /o/ appear in final position regardless of the preceding consonant or cluster, /e/ appears only after consonants other than /r/, /l/, /s/, /n/, /θ/, and consonant clusters.

(35) /p/: *queipo* 'type of basket', *polpa* 'pulp', *hisope* 'hisop'
/b/: *cibo* 'bait', *cuba* 'barrel', *nube* 'cloud'
/t/: *pito* 'chick', *pita* 'hen', *macete* 'type of mallet'
/d/: *ésodo* 'exodus', *fiada* 'line', *laude* 'lute'
/g/: *logo* 'then', *pega* 'magpie', *segue* '(s)he follows'
/k/: *zoco* 'clog', *caroca* 'deceit', *pique* 'tangy taste'
/m/: *demo* 'devil', *brétema* 'fog', *home* 'man'
/ʃ/: *lixo* 'dust', *lixa* 'type of fish', *hoxe* 'today'
/rt/: *horto* 'garden', *morta* 'dead-FEM', *parte* 'part'
/lf/: *golfo* 'gulf', *golfa* 'slut-FEM', *golfe* 'type of algae'
/st/ : *gasto 'excrement', cesta* 'basket', *hoste* 'army'

(36) /r/: *toro* 'slice of fish', *lora* 'lazy', *mar* 'sea'
/l/: *relo* 'type of mill', *pola* 'hen', *sol* 'sun'
/s/: *naso* 'nose', *presa* 'hurry', *naris* 'nose'
/n/: *pano* 'cloth', *tona* 'peel', *man* 'hand'

The data in (35) show the effects of one more constraint:

(37) *COMPLEX CODA (Colina 1995):
Only one consonant may associate to any coda position.

Since an epenthetic vowel follows a disallowed final consonant or consonant cluster, *COMPLEX CODA and CODA-COND must dominate B-DEP-IO. Epenthesis is preferred to deletion, because B-DEP-IO is ranked lower than MAX-IO. In addition, as shown above (cf. (27)), CODA-COND dominates MAX-IO. *COMPLEX CODA also dominates MAX-IO. Further evidence for this ranking is found in the deletion of word medial consonants (cf. 4.4 below).

(38) CODA-COND, *COMPLEX CODA » B-DEP-IO
MAX-IO » B-DEP-IO

(39) CODA-COND, *COMPLEX CODA » MAX-IO » B-DEP-IO

The adaptation of loanwords provides additional evidence in favor of the epenthetic nature of the final /e/ and the ranking proposed above:

(40) *clube* 'club'
filme 'film'
iogurte 'yogurt'
esnobe 'snob'
buldogue 'bulldog'

Tableaux (41)-(42) and (43)-(44) are provided to show how constraint evaluation chooses the candidates with epenthetic vowels as the output for input forms with non-coronal consonants and with consonant clusters.

(41) Input: /ɔm/; Output: [ɔ́.me]

Candidates	CODA-COND	MAX-IO	B-DEP-IO
a. ɔ́m	*!		
b. ɔ́		*!	
☞ c. ɔ́.me			*

(42) Input: /klub/; Output: [klú.βe]

Candidates	CODA-COND	MAX-IO	B-DEP-IO
a. klúβ	*!		
b. klú		*!	
☞ c. klú.βe			*

In tableaux (41)–(42), candidate (c) is the output, even though it contains a B–DEP–IO violation, given the fact that the competing candidates (a) and (b) violate two more highly ranked constraints: CODA–COND and MAX–IO, respectively.

(43) Input: /gɔlf/; Output [gɔ́l.fe]

Candidates	*COMPLEX CODA	MAX–IO	B–DEP–IO
a. gɔ́lf	*!		
b. gɔ́l		*!	
☞ c. gɔ́l.fe			*

(44) Input: /film/; Output: [fíl.me]

Candidates	*COMPLEX CODA	MAX–IO	B–DEP–IO
a. fílm	*!		
b. fíl		*!	
☞ c. fíl.me			*

Again, in tableaux (43)–(44) candidate (c) is the output because (a) violates *COMPLEX CODA, and (b) violates MAX–IO, both of which are more highly ranked than B–DEP–IO, the constraint violated by (c). As shown in (45), *INSERT–m–μ dominates ALIGN–RIGHT (the right edge of a prosodic word should be aligned with the right edge of the stem; cf. (21) above), and therefore the epenthesis site will be to the right of the cluster.

(45) Input: /gɔlf/; Output [gɔ́l.fe]

Candidates	*INSERT-m-μ	ALIGN-R
a. gɔ́.lef	*!	
☞ b. gɔ́l.fe		*

Form (b) is the optimal candidate in (45) because (a) violates the more highly ranked constraint *INSERT-m-μ.

4.2 Plural epenthesis: a case of final epenthesis[14]

In Galician, plural forms are generally obtained by adding the suffix /s/ to the stem. However, if the stem ends in a consonant other than /n/ or /l/, then the plural marker surfaces as [-es]. And if it ends in /l/, the plural allomorph is [-is] in many varieties, with vocalization of stem-final /l/. I will not deal with plural forms of nouns or adjectives ending in /l/, since they involve segmental changes (i.e. vocalization of /l/) beyond the scope of syllabification, e.g., *anima*[l] vs. *anima*[is].

(46)

león	*leóns*	'lion/s'
man	*mans*	'hand/s'
casa	*casas*	'house/s'
dor	*dores*	'pain/s'
flor	*flores*	'flower/s'
deus	*deuses*	'god/s'
feli[θ]	*feli*[θ]*es*	'happy'
animal	*animáis*	'animal/s'

The cluster /ns/ shows no deletion. One possible explanation that I adopt here is that it somehow satisfies *COMPLEX CODA, something which may be related to nasals lacking an underlying point of articulation. The expression of this possibility within an OT framework is an issue that remains to be investigated. Future developments in underspecification within OT theory may well shed some light on the matter (cf. Itô, Mester, and Padgett 1995). There is an alternative explanation in which /ns/ would not incur a *COMPLEX CODA violation. This can be related to the special status of final /n/, which in some dialects is replaced by nasalization of the previous vowel. Finally, as Martínez–Gil (this volume) points out, /-ns/ could simply be exceptional, since it is only allowed when the final consonant is the plural morpheme.

(47) Input: /man+s/; Output: [máŋs]

Candidates	*COMPLEX CODA	MAX–IO	B–DEP–IO
☞ a. máŋs			
b. más		*!	
c. má.nes			*!

Form (a) in (47) is the optimal candidate and the output because it incurs no violations, while (b) and (c) violate MAX–IO and B–DEP–IO.

The coda sequences /rs/, /ss/, and /θs/ violate *COMPLEX CODA.[15] As I have demonstrated earlier, in Galician, MAX–IO dominates B–DEP–IO and *COMPLEX CODA dominates MAX–IO. The constraint ALIGN–R, requires that the plural suffix be aligned with the right edge of the phonological word, thus inducing vowel epenthesis to the left of the plural morpheme. Thus, constraint ranking accounts for the epenthetic vowel and the epenthesis site. For illustration purposes, consider the evaluation of these candidates in (48).

(48) Input: /flor+s/; Output: [fló.res]

Candidates	*COMPLEX CODA	MAX–IO	B–DEP–IO
a. flórs	*!		
b. flós		*!	
☞ c. fló.res			*

In (48), (a) violates *COMPLEX CODA, (b) violates MAX-IO, and (c) only violates B-DEP-IO, which is more lowly ranked. Therefore, (c) is the optimal candidate. An additional candidate *[flór.se] violates ALIGN-R. Since the violation of ALIGN-R is not required by satisfaction of *INSERT-m-μ (epenthesis takes place at the morpheme boundary, i.e. *flor-e-s*) candidate (a), [flór.se], is less harmonic than (b) in (49).

(49) Input: /flor+s/; Output: [fló.res]

Candidates	*INSERT-m-μ	ALIGN-R
a. flór.se		*!
☞ b. fló.res		

(50) Input: /deus+s/; Output: [déw.ses]

Candidates	*COMPLEX CODA	MAX-IO	B-DEP-IO
a. déwss	*!		
b. déws		*!	
☞ c. déw.ses			*

In (50), (c) is the optimal candidate because all other candidate analyses of the input violate constraints that are more highly ranked than B-DEP-IO.

(51) Input: /deus+s/; Output: [déw.ses]

Candidates	*INSERT-m-μ	ALIGN-R
a. déws.se		*!
☞ b. déw.ses		

In (51), ALIGN-R determines that the epenthesis site is to the left of the plural morpheme. Candidate (a), with insertion to the right of /s/, is less harmonic due to one violation of ALIGN-R.

4.3 Paragogic *-e*

There is one final set of data in Galician related to an epenthetic process (cf. Martínez-Gil, this volume for further data).

(52)	*vai*	[báj] ~ [báji]	'(s)he goes'
	dor	[dór] ~ [dóri]	'pain'
	sofá	[sufá] ~ [sufái]	'sofa'
	amor	[amór] ~ [amóri]	'love'
	muller	[muɟɛ́r] ~ [muɟɛ́ri]	'woman'
	falarei	[falaréj] ~ [falaréji]	'I will speak'

Several dialects of Galician (Hualde and Martínez-Gil 1992, Martínez-Gil this volume) have an optional final /e/ usually realized as [i]. Optional epenthesis applies to words from all lexical categories, regardless of syllable count, final syllable weight or syllable type (i.e., closed or open).[16] Examination of the data reveals that final stress is the necessary condition for paragoge, although some dialects may undergo optional final epenthesis after a word-final consonant regardless of the location of stress (Carballo Calero 1976: 119).

(53) *fácil* [fáθil] ~ [fáθili] 'easy'

Hualde and Martínez-Gil (1992: 4) explain epenthesis as motivated by a tendency to avoid the occurrence of a stressed syllable in phrase-final position. Martínez-Gil (this volume) shows that final epenthesis targets the metrical head of an intonational phrase. As seen in (54b), epenthesis is not possible when an oxytonic form is followed by a complement:

(54) a.	Q: *¿Qué trouxo ela?*	A: *Pan* (~*pan*[i])
	what brought she	bread
	Q: 'What did she bring?	A: (Some) bread'
b.	Q: *¿Qué trouxo ela?*	A: *Pan* (**pan*[i]) *de millo*
	Q: 'What did she bring?	A: (Some) corn bread'

Neither Hualde and Martínez-Gil (1992) nor Martínez-Gil (this volume) provide an account of final *-e* in non-oxytonic forms. The OT analysis presented here will offer an explanation for *e*-epenthesis both in forms with final stress and with non-final stress.

The presence of paragogic *-e* in oxytonic words reveals the high ranking of a constraint against final stress known as NON-FINALITY.

(55) NON-FINALITY:
The final syllable in the IP (Intonational Phrase) is unstressed (cf. McCarthy and Prince 1993a: 150)

(56) NON-FINALITY » B-DEP-IO

In this case NON-FINALITY refers not to the prosodic word, as originally proposed by McCarthy and Prince, but to a higher level of prosodic organization-- the intonational phrase. Words in isolation are one-word IPs.

(57) Input: /pan/; Output: [pá.ŋi]

Candidates	NON-FINALITY	B-DEP-IO
a. páŋ	*!	
☞ b. pá.ŋi		*

(b) is the optimal candidate in (57) because (a) violates NON-FINALITY, whereas (b) only violates the more lowly-ranked B-DEP-IO. When a form is not final in the IP, candidates with epenthesis are eliminated due to a B-DEP-IO violation, as can be seen in (58b):

(58) Input: /pan/ *de millo*; Output: [páŋ] *de millo*

Candidates	NON-FINALITY	B-DEP-IO
☞ a. [páŋ] *de millo*		
b. [pá.ŋi] *de millo*		*!

An alternative candidate in which a NON-FINALITY violation is avoided through stress shift as in (59) is non-optimal because it violates a constraint of the identity family that requires identity of metrical structure between a form and each one of its allomorphs (*lu* → *lú*; *pán* → *pan).*[17] The relevant identity constraint must be ranked higher than B-DEP-IO.

(59) *Ela vai trae-lo pan* (~*pán*[i]) **Ela vai trae* [lú.pan]

Consider now dialects exhibiting *e*-epenthesis in forms with non-final word stress (i.e., non-oxytonic forms; cf. (53) above). NO CODA is often violated in Galician by coronal codas.[18] Therefore, MAX-IO and B-DEP-IO must dominate NO CODA.

(60) MAX-IO, B-DEP-IO » NO CODA

In non-oxitonic forms, epenthetic /e/ follows consonants which are normally allowed in coda position. NO CODA must be ranked above B-DEP-IO in these dialects, because B-DEP-IO is violated in order to avoid a NO CODA violation. The fact that deletion is not possible, and that epenthesis applies only to word-final position is explained through domination of MAX-IO and/or M-CONT over NO CODA and the high ranking of *INSERT-m-μ. ALIGN-L/R must also be dominated by NO CODA, since NO CODA satisfaction is obtained through misalignment.

(61) Constraint ranking in dialects with paragogic *-e* in non-oxytonic forms:

*INSERT-m-μ, MAX-IO, M-CONT » NO CODA » B-DEP-IO

Also possible:

*INSERT-m-μ, M-CONT » NO CODA, MAX-IO » B-DEP-IO

or: *INSERT-m-μ, MAX-IO » NO CODA, M-CONT » B-DEP-IO

When there is no possible violation of *INSERT-m-μ, i.e. in word-final position, the optimal candidate will always have an epenthetic segment because of the domination of MAX-IO over B-DEP-IO. In word-medial position, epenthesis is not an alternative because a candidate with a non-underlying /e/ would also violate the high-ranked *INSERT-m-μ; candidates with unparsed codas are equally ill-formed, which demonstrates that either MAX-IO or M-CONT, or both must dominate NO CODA.

(62) Input: /faθil/; Output: [fá.θi.li]

Candidates	MAX-IO	NO CODA	B-DEP-IO
a. fá.θi	*!		
b. fá.θil		*!	
☞ c. fá.θi.li			*

As (62) shows, the candidate exhibiting final epenthesis, (c), is the optimal candidate because (a) and (b) violate constraints that are more highly ranked than B-DEP-IO.

4.4 Word-medial deletion

With the exception of /θ/, the same set of consonants that are possible in word-final position (/r/, /l/, /s/, /n/, /θ/), are also possible word-medially. All consonant clusters are ill-formed in the latter position.

(63) Word-final: Word-medial:

mel	'honey'	*pil-far*	'to steal'
ben	'well'	*sen-so*	'sense'
flor	'flower'	*for-miga*	'ant'
os	'the' (masc. pl)	*es-ceso*	'excess'
fo[θ]	'mouth of a river'	—	

Illegal codas and all consonant clusters are repaired through deletion.

(64)

distin[g]-ir	'to distinguish'	vs.	distin-to	'distinct'
mo[β]-er	'to move'	vs.	mo-ción	'motion'
esculp-ir	'to sculpt'	vs.	escul-tura	'sculpture'

Coda obstruents and clusters are simplified, as in (65) and (66). They are only pronounced in learned words in very careful, formal styles often under the influence of spelling (67).

(65)

digno	[díɣno] ~ [díno]	'decent'
ignorar	[iɣnɔrár] ~ [inɔrár]	'to ignore'
pugna	[púɣna] ~ [púna]	'fight, battle'

(66)

abstemio	[as.té.mjo]	'teetotaller'
adscribir	[as.kri.bír]	'to adscribe'
e[ks]*periencia*	[es.pe.rjén.θja]	'experience'
transportar	[tras.por.tár]	'to carry'

(67)

ins.pi.rar	'inspire'
ins.ta.bi.li.da.de	'instability'
e[ks]*.pi.rar*	'to expire'

In a previous analysis (Colina 1993, ms.) deletion in Galician is accounted for by means of rules within a rule-based (Levin 1985) model of syllabification. Although it accounted for the data, such approach did not provide an adequate explanation for the fact that deletion is preferred to epenthesis word internally. Furthermore, given the claim that the motivation for deletion is the need to repair ill-formed syllable structure, it is not clear why deletion would be better than epenthesis in certain contexts. The OT account proposed here provides a more direct explanation of these facts.

Satisfaction of CODA-COND and *COMPLEX CODA in word-internal position is not obtained through B-DEP-IO violations (i.e. epenthesis), but by underparsing.[19] The reason for this is the high ranking of the constraint against inserting new phonological material inside a morpheme (*INSERT-m-μ). Although B-DEP-IO is lower in the constraint hierarchy than MAX-IO, vowel insertion violates *INSERT-m-μ, which is more highly ranked than MAX-IO; as a result, a violation of MAX-IO is preferred. M-CONT and MAX-IO are ranked under CODA-COND, *COMPLEX CODA, and *INSERT-m-μ because underparsing and a violation of M-CONT are preferred to *COMPLEX CODA, CODA-COND and *INSERT-m-μ violations. Consider now constraint ranking and evaluation.

(68) CODA-COND, *COMPLEX CODA, *INSERT-m-μ » M-CONT, MAX-IO » B-DEP-IO

(69) Input: /abstemio/; Output: [as.té.mjo]

Candidates	*INSERT-m-μ	*COMPLEX CODA	M-CONT	MAX-IO	B-DEP-IO
a. abs.té.mjo		*!			
b. a.bes.té.mjo	*!				*
☞ c. as.té.mjo			*	*	

In (69), since (a) and (b) violate *COMPLEX CODA and *INSERT-m-μ, and (c) only violates the more lowly ranked M-CONT and MAX-IO, (c) is the optimal candidate. Although not indicated in the tableau, note that *as.té.mio* is preferred to *ab.te.mio* due to a violation of CODA-COND on the part of the latter candidate. The evaluation of candidates for underlying /digno/ in (70) proceeds in a similar fashion.

(70) Input: /digno/; Output: [dí.no]

Candidates	*INSERT-m-μ	*CODA COND	M-CONT	MAX-IO	B-DEP-IO
a. díγ.no		*!			
b. dí.γe.no	*!				*
☞ c. dí.no			*	*	

5 Summary and conclusions

In this paper, I have examined initial, medial, and final epenthesis and deletion in Galician. In word-initial position, epenthesis is the result of ONSET SONORITY being ranked higher than faithfulness constraints and of the ranking MAX-IO » B-DEP-IO. CODA-COND effects are involved in cases of word-initial deletion, i.e. [si.kɔ́.lo.γo]. Word medial deletion is preferred to epenthesis due to the high ranking of the constraint against inserting a mora inside the morpheme. In word-final position, epenthesis is the preferred solution, as a result of the ranking CODA-COND, *COMPLEX CODA » MAX-IO » B-DEP-IO. Our account shows that initial, final, and plural epenthesis and deletion are indeed related.

The analysis proposed here explains why epenthesis is preferred to deletion or vice versa (in the same or different positions), and is able to predict and account for epenthesis and deletion sites. A constraint-based analysis also shows that initial epenthesis and deletion are related to other phonological processes in Galician, such as the need to avoid onsetless syllables and the possibility of association of glides to onset positions.

While rule-based analyses deal with epenthesis and deletion by means of separate rules which view these processes as independent phenomena, the OT analysis proposed offers a unified treatment based on a set of universal constraints and language-specific rankings which stresses what the various types of epenthesis and deletion have in common (producing the optimal analysis of an underlying form). Furthermore, the universal nature of constraints in OT reflects the universality of phonological processes (e.g. the preference for syllables with onsets, the tendency to repair complex codas), a fact which escapes rules due to their language-specific formulation. In rule-based analyses of syllabification, while epenthesis results from the need to syllabify unsyllabified segments, the choice of epenthesis or deletion and the epenthesis site are explained through rules. In an OT account, choice of epenthesis and deletion, their sites, and their motivation are all the result of constraint interaction and candidate evaluation. Prosodic analyses of syllabification also encounter difficulty in trying to account for initial and final epenthesis; initial epenthesis is suggestive of right-to-left syllabification, e.g. estrés, *setrés, while final epenthesis seems to indicate left-to-right directionality, e.g. madre, *mader. In the optimality-theoretic analysis, initial and final epenthesis take place at the word-edges to avoid inserting a mora within the morpheme.

(71) Galician Epenthesis and Deletion: Summary of constraints

a. Word-initially:

ONS-SON, MAX-IO » B-DEP-IO

*INSERT-m-μ » ALIGN-L

CODA-COND » MAX-IO » B-DEP-IO

b. Glide epenthesis:

*INSERT-C, undominated

MAX-IO, ONSET » B-DEP-IO

*INSERT-m-μ » ONSET » M-CONT

ONSET » *M/I, U

c. Word-finally (including plurals):

CODA-COND, *COMPLEX CODA » MAX-IO » B-DEP-IO

*INSERT-m-μ » ALIGN-R

d. Paragogic *-e*:

NON-FINALITY » B-DEP-IO

MAX-IO, B-DEP-IO » NO CODA

Dialects with paragogic /e/ in non-oxytonic forms:

*INSERT-m-μ, MAX-IO, M-CONT» NO CODA » B-DEP-IO

Also possible:

*INSERT-m-μ, M-CONT » NO CODA, MAX-IO » B-DEP-IO

or: *INSERT-m-μ, MAX-IO » NO CODA, M-CONT » B-DEP-IO

e. Word-medially:

CODA-COND, *COMPLEX CODA, *INSERT-m-μ » M-CONT, MAX-IO » B-DEP-IO

Notes

* I would like to thank Fernando Martínez-Gil for very valuable comments and the discussion of issues related to this paper. Thanks also to José Ignacio Hualde for his suggestions. Responsibility for any errors is solely my own.

1 See Martínez-Gil (this volume) for more evidence on initial epenthesis in Spanish.

2 Several environments containing an unsyllabified /s/.

3 For the motivation for the constraints introduced in this analysis readers should refer to the sources quoted.

4 There is strong evidence for the nature of epenthetic [e] (cf. examples (9) and (10), and note 1). Observe, however, that an OT analysis that contains the constraints and the constraint ranking proposed in this paper would predict the same output ([estaβiliðáðe]) for the given input /estabilidade/.

5 This is a modified version of Kenstowicz's (1993) MORPHEME INTEGRITY/ CONTIGUITY, which says: "If /...xyz.../ in input structure then avoid [....x<y>z....] in output"; cf. no skipping of phonemes in template mapping.

6 The justification for such an explosion of the constraint resides in that insertion of a mora internal to the morpheme constitutes a more serious violation than insertion of a non-moraic segment or, in more formal terms, in that *INSERT-m-μ and M-CONT

are distinct constraints because they are separately rankable (cf. *INSERT-m-μ » ONSET » M-CONT).

7 /t/ is not allowed in coda position. This seems to indicate a high ranking, dominating faithfulness, of an associational constraint against parsing /t/ in coda position (*C/t).

8 The presence of an initial /p/ in the underlying form in (27) is not uncontroversial. There is evidence that questions such representation: words such as those in (24) do not participate in alternations. Existing alternations are marginal (*agnosticismo* [aɣnostiθízmo] vs. *gnosticismo* [nostiθízmo]). Although it does not seem possible to formulate a satisfactory solution to the problem at this point, nothing hinges on it. Even under the assumption that /p/ is not present underlyingly, the constraints and the constraint ranking proposed –independently required to account for word-medial deletion– predict the same output. Furthermore, the validity of the analysis proposed in this paper does not depend on the relevance of the data in (24), given that evidence for the constraints and the ranking in (27) can be found in word-medial deletion (cf. section 4.4).

9 I use the term *glide epenthesis* for the sake of convenience. It is not meant as statement on the non-moraic nature of the inserted segment. As we will see below, I claim that the moraic/non-moraic status of the inserted element is the result of candidate evaluation.

10 ONSET satisfaction applies within the morphological (29) and the prosodic word (30)-(31).

11 *M/I,U: Do not associate a high vocoid to a margin position. (Colina 1995: 107). (I and U stand for the high vocoids, i.e. the features of both [j, w] and [i, u] without prosodic information).

12 *INSERT C could not be subsumed under B-DEP-IO because they are ranked separately: while B-DEP-IO has a relatively low ranking, *INSERT C is undominated.

13 The constraints and constraint-ranking determine consonantal status: consonants are segments that can never be associated to Peak positions (*P/C is undominated).

14 See Martínez-Gil (this volume) and Harris (1991) for evidence supporting the epenthetic nature of /e/ in plural forms.

15 In addition, /ss/ and /θs/ contain OCP violations (OCP dominates FILL). /ss/ also violates a constraint against geminate Cs.

16 There is strong internal evidence which shows that this process is the result of epenthesis, not deletion. The arguments have to do with velarization of nasals, the

distribution of the apico-alveolar allophone of /s/, and plural formation (Martínez-Gil, this volume).

17 The constraint referred to is Uniform Exponence (UE). For more on UE and identity constraints see Kenstowicz (1994) and Colina (1996, ms).

18 As discussed earlier, final epenthesis following an illegal consonant or consonant cluster follows from the ranking CODA-COND, *COMPLEX CODA » MAX-IO » B-DEP-IO.

19 In some dialects, we find vocalization of illegal consonants in Castilian loanwords: /kon.θép.to/ [kon.θéw.to], [kon.θéj.to] 'concept'. It involves underparsing of some features instead of the entire segment.

References

Benua, Laura. 1995. Identity effects in morphological truncation. In *Papers in Optimality Theory* (*University of Massachusetts Occasional Papers in Linguistics* 18), ed. J. Beckman, S. Urbanczyk and L. Walsh, 77–136. Amherst, MA: Graduate Linguistic Student Association.

Carballo Calero, Ricardo. 1976. *Gramática elemental del gallego común*. Vigo: Galaxia.

Colina, Sonia. 1993. Syllabification in Galician. Ms., University of Illinois at Urbana-Champaign.

Colina, Sonia. 1995. *A Constraint-Based Analysis of Syllabification in Spanish, Catalan, and Galician*. Doctoral dissertation, University of Illinois at Urbana-Champaign.

Colina, Sonia. 1996. Identity constraints and Spanish resyllabification. Ms., Indiana University, Bloomington.

Harris, James W. 1983. *Syllable Structure and Stress in Spanish: A Nonlinear Analysis*. Cambridge, Mass: MIT Press.

Harris, James W. 1986. Epenthesis processes in Spanish. In *Studies in Romance Languages*, ed. C. Neidle and R. Núñez-Cedeño, 107–22. Dordrecht: Foris.

Hualde, José Ignacio. (No date). La silabificación en español. Ms., University of Illinois at Urbana-Champaign.

Hualde, José Ignacio, and Fernando Martínez-Gil. 1992. Final epenthesis in Galician: A case of reanalysis of a historical change. Ms., University of Illinois at Urbana-Champaign and Georgetown University.

Itô, Junko, Armin Mester, and Jaye Padgett. 1995. Licensing and underspecification in optimality theory. *Linguistic Inquiry* 26.571-613.

Kenstowicz, Michael, 1994. Syllabification in Chukchee: a constraint-based analysis. *Formal Linguistics Society of the Midwest 4.* 160–81.

Levin, Juliette. 1985. *A Metrical Theory of Syllabicity*. Doctoral dissertation, MIT.

Martínez-Gil, Fernando. (This volume). Word-final epenthesis in Galician.

McCarthy, John. 1993. A case of surface constraint violation. *Canadian Journal of Linguistics* 38. 169–95.

McCarthy, John. 1996. Faithfulness in prosodic morphology and phonology: Rotuman revisited. Ms., Univ. of Massachusetts at Amherst. ROA-110.

McCarthy, John, and Alan Prince. 1993a. *Prosodic Morphology I.* Ms., University of Massachusetts at Amherst and Rutgers University.

McCarthy, John, and Alan Prince. 1993b. Generalized alignment. *Yearbook of Morphology* 79–153.

McCarthy, John, and Alan Prince. 1994a. The Emergence of the unmarked. Ms., University of Massachusetts at Amherst and Rutgers University.

McCarthy, John, and Alan Prince. 1994b. An overview of prosodic morphology. Transcript and handout of the talk presented at Prosodic Morphology Workshop, Utrecht, ROA-59.

McCarthy, John, and Alan Prince. 1995. Faithfulness and reduplicative identity. In *Papers in Optimality Theory* (*University of Massachusetts Occasional Papers in Linguistics* 18), ed. J. Beckman, S. Urbanczyk and L. Walsh, 249–384. Amherst, MA: Graduate Linguistic Student Association.

Prince, Alan, and Paul Smolensky. 1993. *Optimality Theory*. Ms., Rutgers University, New Brunswick, and University of Colorado, Boulder.

9

Word-final epenthesis in Galician*

Fernando Martínez-Gil

0 Introduction

A notorious characteristic of early Castilian and neighboring Ibero-Romance dialects is an insecurity in the treatment of final /e/. In part of the Galician territory, the old fluctuation would seem, at first glance, to have been continued up to our days. In particular, the data from present-day Galician dialects would in principle appear to show that apocope is only an optional process, as it seemingly was in early Castilian, since the same Galician speaker may pronounce *coller* or *collere* 'to take, grab', *papel* or *papele* 'paper', etc. However, it can be shown that contrary to what one would expect from historical considerations in present-day Galician, the basic forms in these cases are clearly those ending in a consonant (i.e., *coller*, *papel*) and that the final /e/ is introduced by an epenthesis rule. That is, in cases like these, what historically were the original unapocopated forms, have become the derived forms from the point of the synchronic phonology of modern Galician. I will provide a variety of arguments in favor of this analysis.

This paper investigates the phonological properties and behavior of Galician epenthesis from both a synchronic and a historical point of view. Compelling evidence, both synchronic and historical, will be presented in support of the view that optional word-final [e] is not present in underlying forms; in other words, it is to be considered a case of optional insertion, not optional deletion. Setting this observation with the diachronic dimension, it will be proposed that historically an older (variable) rule of apocope has been reanalyzed in the synchronic grammar of Galician as one of epenthesis, a type of sound change that fits the pattern Vennemann (1972) has dubbed *rule inversion*. Furthermore, it will be shown that Galician exhibits two different types of word-final epenthesis. The first one is optional, it obeys constraints of a purely metrical nature, and it is circumscribed to the postlexical module. The second type is obligatory, it is determined exclusively by syllable structure, and it applies lexically.[1] In particular, it is shown that optional epenthesis is strictly determined by the stress pattern of the word. The primary data illustrating optional epenthesis in this paper are drawn from the variety spoken in the town of Moaña and surrounding areas.[2] In this dialect, for example, epenthesis is blocked whenever the resulting stress contour is not a trochaic one. By providing degenerate (monosyllabic) metrical feet with an additional syllable, epenthesis may be readily interpreted as a strategy to satisfy the requirement that the head of a certain prosodic domain, the intonational phrase, conform to the canonical type of metrical organization: the syllabic trochee (cf. Hayes 1987, 1995). This can be taken to mean that syllabic trochees are afforded the unmarked status in the postlexical phonology of Galician. This assessment is reminiscent of the widespread opinion among grammarians that trochaic rhythm constitutes the normal or default option in Galician (see, among others, Carballo Calero 1979, Alvarez et al. 1986, Costa Casas et al. 1988). In this respect, Galician conforms to a pattern of phrasal rhythmic organization identical to that often attributed to Spanish (Navarro Tomás 1948, 1956, 1966, 1977, Baer 1970, Quilis 1973, Dalbor 1980, Roca 1986).

The organization of this paper is as follows. In section 1, I discuss three major pieces of synchronic evidence in support of the hypothesis that optional word-final [i] in Moañés is inserted by phonological rule, and thus is not present in underlying forms. The phonological constraints that govern optional epenthesis in Moañés Galician will be discussed in section 2. Additional diachronic evidence for a synchronic analysis based on an epenthesis rule will be presented in section 3. Since Old Galician, just as Old Spanish, originally contained a variable rule of word-final apocope, I conclude that at some historical point the language underwent a peculiar type of restructuring, rule inversion (in the sense of Vennemann 1972). It is suggested, then, that at some historical stage the relevant surface forms were derived by a rule of epenthesis, instead of one of apocope. Finally, section 4 contains a brief summary of the major points discussed in this paper, and some concluding remarks.

1 Arguments for optional word-final epenthesis in Galician

In this section I explore the types of internal evidence that can be put forth in favor of an epenthesis-based analysis of the optional word-final vowel in Galician. The data under examination in this section ar drawn from the Moañés dialect, unless otherwise stated.

A number of varieties of Galician exhibit an optional [e] in word-final position (Carballo Calero 1979: 123-124, Alvarez et al. 1986: 23-24).[3] In Moañés, the epenthetic vowel is (predictably) realized as high [i], as a consequence of a general process of vowel reduction in this dialect that raises the underlying mid tense vowels /e, o/ to [i, u], respectively, in unstressed positions.[4] Optional epenthesis may apply to words from all major lexical categories (nouns, adjectives, verbs, and adverbs), as illustrated in (1), where words are arranged according to syllable count.[5]

(1)

a.	*bo*	[bó]~[bó.i]	'good'	*vou*	[bów]~[bó.wi]	'I go'
	fe	[fɛ́]~[fɛ́.i]	'faith'	*pau*	[páw]~[pá.wi]	'stick'
	cu	[kú]~[kú.i]	'buttocks'	*ceu*	[séw]~[sé.wi]	'sky'
	rei	[r̄éj]~[r̄é.ji]	'king'	*mar*	[már]~[má.ri]	'sea'
	pai	[páj]~[pá.ji]	'father'	*dor*	[dór]~[dó.ri]	'pain'
	doi	[dɔ́j]~[dɔ́.ji]	'it hurts'	*sol*	[sól]~[só.li]	'sun'
	viu	[bíw]~[bí.wi]	'(s)he saw'	*mel*	[mɛ́l]~[mɛ́.li]	'honey'

b.	*café*	[ka.fɛ́]~[ka.fɛ́.i]	'coffee'
	papá	[pa.pá]~[pa.pá.i]	'dad'
	bocoi	[bu.kój]~[bu.kó.ji]	'big barrel'
	chorei	[ču.réj]~[ču.ré.ji]	'I cried'
	saíu	[sa.íw]~[sa.í.wi]	'(s)he left'
	xogou	[šu.xów]~[šu.xó.wi]	'(s)he played'
	muller	[mu.ɟ̌ér]~[mu.ɟ̌é.ri]	'woman'
	fuxir	[fu.šír]~[fu.ší.ri]	'to flee'
	papel	[pa.pɛ́l]~[pa.pɛ́.li]	'paper'
	xuncal	[šuŋ.kál]~[šuŋ.ká.li]	'bulrush grove'

c.	*dominó*	[dɔ.mi.nɔ́]~[dɔ.mi.nɔ́.i]	'dominoes'
	falarei	[fa.la.réj]~[fa.la.ré.ji]	'I will speak'
	bocareu	[bu.ka.rɛ́w]~[bu.ka.rɛ́wi]	'anchovy'
	escolleu	[iʂ.ku.ɟéw]~[iʂ.ku.ɟé.wi]	'(s)he chose'
	salgueiral	[sal.xej.rál]~[sal.xej.rá.li]	'willow grove'
	chuchamel	[ču.ča.mɛ́l]~[ču.ča.mɛ́.li]	(type of plant)
	amañecer	[a.ma.ñi.sér]~[a.ma.ñi.sé.ri]	'dawn'
	esquencerei	[iʂ.kiŋ.si.réj]~[iʂ.kiŋ.si.ré.ji]	'I will forget'
	endereitou	[iŋ.di.rej.tów]~[iŋ.di.rej.tó.wi]	'(s)he straightened'
	canaveiral	[ka.na.βej.rál]~[ka.na.βej.rá.li]	'cane thicket'
	esmendrellar	[iʂ.miŋ.dri.ɟár]~[iʂ.miŋ.dri.ɟári]	'to tear to pieces'
	espranzador	[iʂ.praŋ.sa.ðór]~[iʂ.praŋ.sa.ðó.ri]	'hopeful'
	asoballador	[a.su.βa.ɟa.ðór]~[a.su.βa.ɟa.ðó.ri]	'oppressing'

The sample in (1) is representative of the range of lexical items that can be subject to optional epenthesis in Moañés. As is evident in (1), factors such as the number of syllables contained in a given word, or the weight of its final syllable (i.e., whether it is heavy or light), are of no relevance whatsoever for the paragogic vowel. Nor can epenthesis simply be a strategy to eliminate closed syllables, apparently the less preferred syllable type, in favor of open ones, the universal or unmarked option, since it also applies to vowel-final syllables, as seen in items such as *café*, *papá*, etc., (cf. (1b)). The obvious generalization to be drawn from the examples in (1) is that epenthesis may apply *only* to words with final stress.[6] Monosyllabic content words (1a) trivially meet this condition, since the only syllabic vowel must also be the stress-bearer. As for the remainder of items in (1), all the disyllabic (1b) or trisyllabic and longer words (1c) meet the requirement that stress fall on the final syllable. Epenthesis is not permitted in lexical items with a stress pattern other than oxytonic, a constraint to which we will return later.

Most authors who have written on the topic have agreed on the epenthetic nature of this final vowel in Galician dialects, noticing the fact that it may occur in words where it is not etymological (cf. García de Diego 1909, 23-24, 72, Carballo Calero 1979: 119; see also Menéndez Pidal 1962: 60-61, and

Rodríguez Castellano 1954: 108-111 for Leonese dialects), although Alonso (1962: 62) takes the opposite view, one which regards this phenomenon as historically conservative. Azevedo Maia (1986: 525), on the other hand, is of the opinion that, at least when the final vowel appears after a liquid, "[n]ão é fácil saber se se trata da conservação da vogal etimológica ou de um desenvolvimento paragógico posterior."[7]

There is, in fact, internal evidence in the phonology of contemporary Galician dialects such as Moañés which shows that in words presenting the optional alternation, the vowel-final variant is synchronically secondary; that is, the vowel in question is inserted by a rule of final epenthesis. There are three arguments for this hypothesis that have not been previously considered in the literature in this connection, but provide, in my opinion, unassailable proof of the secondary or epenthetic character of the final optional vowel (both diachronically and synchronically) in examples such as those in (1).

The first two arguments are related to a crucial fact of Galician phonology: the final consonants of words with optional final vowel are treated as syllable-final for the purposes of phonological rules, such as the velarization of nasals and apicalization of /s/, even when they are not syllable-final in surface forms due to the presence of the epenthetic vowel.

Consider first words ending in a nasal in their short form. As can be seen from examples such as those in (2), syllable final nasals are subject to a process of velarization, illustrated in (2), that applies both within words (2a), and word-finally (2b).[8] Velarization is a widespread phenomenon in modern Galician dialects (Fernández Rei 1990).

(2)	a.	*lombo*	[lóŋ.bu]	'back (n.)'
		cento	[séŋ.tu]	'a hundred'
		onte	[ɔ́ŋ.ti]	'yesterday'
		penso	[péŋ.su]	'I think'
		cuncha	[kúŋ.ča]	'shell'
		enxebre	[iŋ.šɛ́.βri]	'pure, genuine'
		longo	[lóŋ.gu]	'long'
		cunca	[kúŋ.ka]	'bowl'

b.	*lan*	[láŋ] ~ [lá.ŋi]	'wool'
	din	[díŋ] ~ [dí.ŋi]	'I gave'
	son	[sóŋ] ~ [só.ŋi]	'sound, rhythm'
	cen	[séŋ] ~ [sé.ŋi]	'one hundred'
	irmán	[ir.máŋ] ~ [ir.má.ŋi]	'brother/sister'
	salín	[sa.líŋ] ~ [sa.lí.ŋi]	'I left'
	ninguén	[niŋ.géŋ] ~ [niŋ.gé.ŋi]	'nobody'
	mexilón	[mi.ši.lóŋ] ~ [mi.ši.ló.ŋi]	'mussel'
	lacazán	[la.ka.sáŋ] ~ [la.ka.sá.ŋi]	'lazy'
	corazón	[ku.ra.sóŋ] ~ [ku.ra.só.ŋi]	'heart'
	mangallón	[maŋ.ga.ɟóŋ] ~ [maŋ.ga.ɟó.ŋi]	'big fellow'

The data in (2) suggest that velar is the default point of articulation for nasals in Galician, unlike standard Spanish, for example, in which it is coronal (Harris 1984a, 1984b).[9]

For expository purposes, I will use the syllablic representations of the N-bar theory proposed in Levin (1986), which generates structures such as that illustrated in (3) for the Galician word *mel* 'honey':[10]

(3)

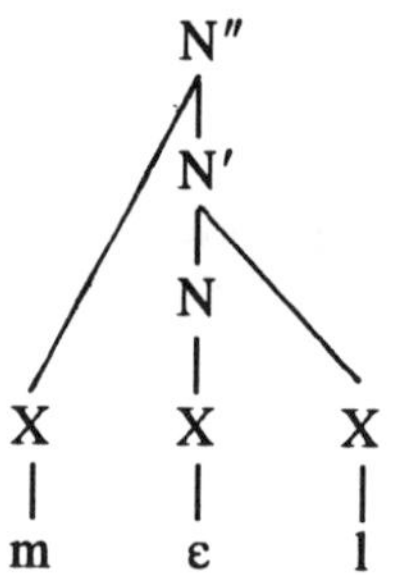

(N″ = Syllable)

(N′ = Rhyme; nucleus + coda)

(N = Nucleus)

I follow closely the analysis of Spanish nasal neutralization proposed in Harris (1984a, 1984b), and assume that nasal velarization in Galician involves two distinct formal operations (see Martínez-Gil 1993). The first consists of a neutralization rule that delinks a nasal's underlying point of articulation (PA) when located in a syllable rhyme, as in (4a). The second step is the redundancy rule (4b), whereby nasals in coda position, once they have been deprived of place features by prior operation of (4a), are assigned the feature [+back] by default. The application of the rules in (4a-b) is illustrated in (4c) for the first example in (2b) *lan* 'wool'.

(4) a. *Nasal neutralization*:

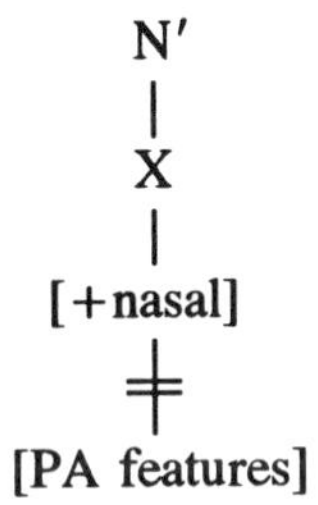

b. *Nasal velarization*:

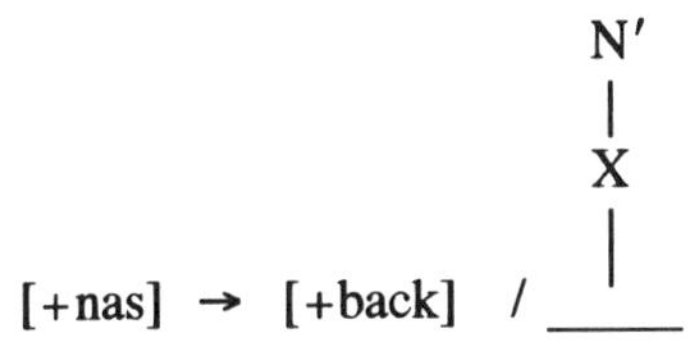

c.

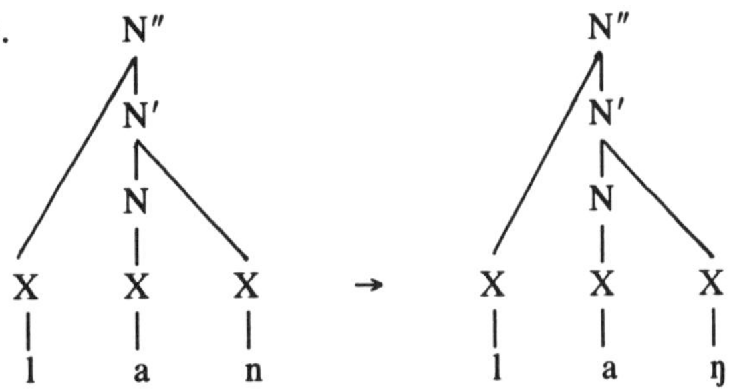

An important observation with regard to the data in (2) concerns the fact that, with the sole exception of cases similar like those in (2b), involving resyllabification of a coda nasal that has undergone velarization, velar nasals do not otherwise occur in onset position in Galician. This is hardly surprising since [ŋ] is not part of the underlying inventory of Galician (cf. note 5). By the principle of Structure Preservation (see Kiparsky 1985 and much later work), the velar nasal would be absent in underlying forms, and therefore it could hardly have been assigned to such syllabic position by core syllabification rules operating in the lexical component.

Consider now the examples in (5). As expected, the velar nasal found in stem-final position in the masculine (5a) is velarized in the short forms, and it also appears resyllabified as such to onset of the syllable containing the epenthetic vowel in their corresponding long ones. On the other hand, a stem-final nasal followed by the feminine gender suffix /-a/ always surfaces as a coronal (5b), never as a velar. This is true of all the instances in which a nasal-final stem is followed by a suffix, whether inflectional or derivational.[11]

(5) a. masculine:

chorón	[ču.róŋ] ~ [ču.ró.ŋi]	'crier-MASC'
Xoán	[šwáŋ] ~ [šwá.ŋi]	'John'
sultán	[šul.táŋ] ~ [šul.tá.ŋi]	'sultan-MASC'
alemán	[a.li.máŋ] ~ [a.li.má.ŋi]	'German-MASC'
cabezón	[ka.βi.sóŋ] ~ [ka.βi.só.ŋi]	'hard-headed-MASC'
parvallón	[par.βa.ɟ̌óŋ] ~ [par.βa.ɟ̌ó.ŋi]	'simpleton-MASC'

b. feminine:

choron-a	[ču.ró.na]	'crier-FEM'
Xoan-a	[šwá.na]	'Joanne'
sultan-a	[sul.tá.na]	'hard-headed-FEM'
aleman-a	[a.li.má.na]	'German-FEM'
cabezon-a	[ka.βi.só.na]	'hard-headed-FEM'
parvallon-a	[par.βa.ɟ̌ó.na]	'simpleton-FEM'

(cf. *[ču.ro.ŋa], *[šwá.ŋa], *[sul.tá.ŋa], etc.)

Again, the velar nasal in the vowel-final variants in (5a) can only be explained if we assume that the underlying coronal nasal is assigned to a syllable rhyme at some point in the derivation, even though on the surface it is intervocalic, and hence in onset position (see Carballo Calero 1979: 124, 127, Alvarez et al. 1986: 33). It can thus be concluded that of the two alternating forms in (5a) and elsewhere, the one without a final vowel is more basic or underlying, and that the final vowel is introduced by an epenthesis rule which applies after the velarization of the word-final nasal. This means that for the representative items *irmán* in (2), *chorón* in (5a) and its feminine *choron-a* in

(5b), we must assume derivations such as that given in (6) (where N represents a neutralized nasal):

(6) *Underlying forms*:	/irman/	/čoron/	/čoron-a/
Core *syllabification*:	ir.man	čo.ron	čo.ro.na
Stress assignment:	ir.mán	čo.rón	čo.ró.na
Neutralization (4a):	ir.maN	čo.róN	—
Velarization (4b):	ir.máŋ	čo.róŋ	—
Epenthesis:	ir.máŋ.e	čo.róŋ.e	—
Resyllabification:	ir.má.ŋe	čo.ró.ŋe	—
Tense mid-vowel raising:	ir.má.ŋi	ču.ró.ŋi	ču.ró.na
Phonetic output:	ir.má.ŋi	ču.ró.ŋi	ču.ró.na

As seen in (6), the word-final nasal in the first two items – *irmán* and *chorón* – is initially assigned to coda position by core syllabification rules. Subsequently, final vowel epenthesis is activated, upon which the nasal is resyllabified to the onset of the newly-created syllable. Both epenthesis and resyllabification must be ordered *after* velarization; indeed if the rules were to apply in the opposite order, resyllabification would remove from the target string the structural condition required by velarization, namely, that the nasal be in coda position. In *chorona*, on the other hand, the final nasal is followed by the feminine desinence /-a/ at the point syllabification rules apply, and so it is incorporated to the onset of the final syllable from the very beginning of the derivation. The conditions of velarization will never be met lexically by such forms.

A second argument in support of the epenthetic nature of the optional final vowel is provided by words ending in the coronal strident /s/ in their short form. As it turns out, the phonetic realization of the phoneme /s/ is variable in Moañés. Thus, we find a predorso-alveolar [s] allophone, and apico-alveolar one [ʂ]. Quite generally, the distribution of these two allophones is entirely predictable on the basis of their location within syllable structure. The predorso-alveolar variant appears in onset position, whether word-initially, as illustrated in (7a), or in a word-medial environment, as in (7b).[12]

(7)	a.	*só*	[sɔ́]	'alone'
		san	[sáŋ]	'healthy-MASC'
		cedo	[sé.ðu]	'early'
		sete	[sɛ́.ti]	'seven'
		saúde	[sa.ú.ði]	'health'
		sardiña	[sar.ðí.ña]	'sardine'
		solteiro	[sul.téj.ru]	'single, bachelor'
	b.	*oso*	[ɔ́.su]	'bone (n.)'
		casa	[ká.sa]	'house'
		cousa	[ków.sa]	'thing'
		facer	[fa.sér]	'to do, make'
		fociño	[fu.sí.ñu]	'snout'
		tesouro	[ti.sów.ru]	'treasure'
		feiticeiro	[fej.ti.séj.ru]	'bewitching'

The apico-alveolar allophone shows up when /s/ is assigned to a rhyme, as can be seen in the examples in (8). When the optional vowel is added word-finally, the apical variant is maintained, in which case it is predictably resyllabified as the onset of the new syllable (cf. (8a)), just as velar nasals.

(8)	a.	*vós*	[bɔ́ş] ~ [bɔ́.şi]	'you-PL'
		dous	[dówş] ~ [dów.şi]	'two-MASC'
		luns	[luŋş] ~ [luŋ.şi]	'Monday'
		arros	[a.r̄ɔ́ş] ~ [ar̄ɔ́.şi]	'rice'
		naris	[na.ríş] ~ [na.rí.şi]	'nose'
		xamais	[ša.májş] ~ [ša.máj.şi]	'never'
		paspallás	[paş.pa.ɟáş] ~ [paş.pa.ɟá.şi]	'partridge'
	b.	*cuspir*	[kuş.pír]	'to spit'
		festa	[fɛ́ş.ta]	'party, celebration'
		esmagar	[iş.ma.xár]	'to crush'
		costume	[kuş.tú.me]	'custom, habit'
		espello	[iş.pé.ɟu]	'mirror'
		desfeito	[diş.féj.tu]	'broken apart, destroyed'
		escoitar	[iş.kúj.tár]	'to listen'

Assuming that /s/-apicalization is to be characterized as an operation that supplies by default the feature [-distributed] to /s/ when found in syllable-final position, the rule can be formulated as in (9a); its application to the item *vos* 'you-PL' in (8a) is illustrated in (9b):

(9) a. /s/-*Apicalization*:

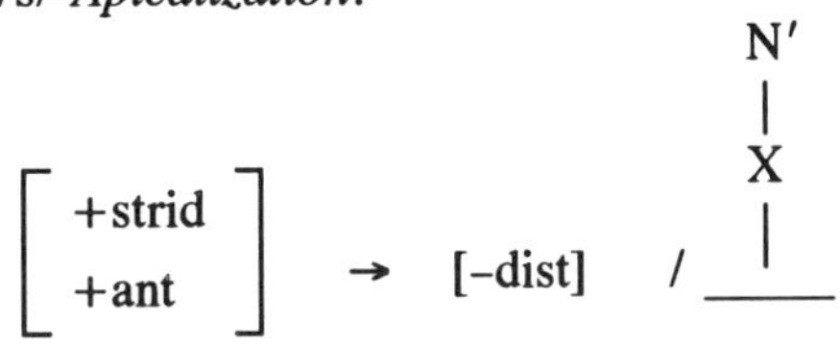

b.

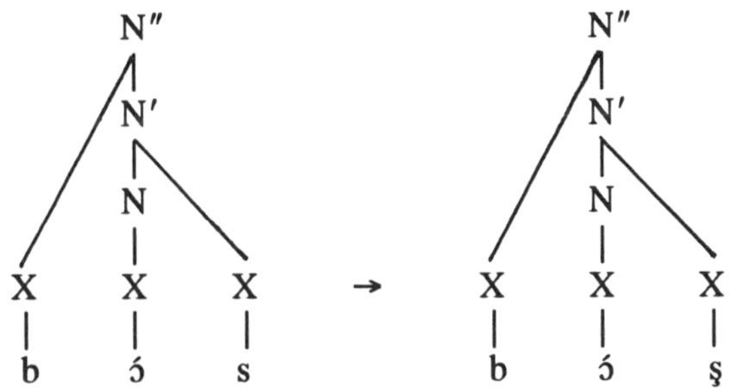

In Galician, the feature [distributed] does not function distinctively among stridents. Pairs such as /s/~/š/ are distinguished by either [anterior] or [high]. Following much recent work in underspecification theory, I assume that redundant features are not to be specified in underlying representations, but rather supplied by redundancy rules in the course of the derivation (cf. Archangeli 1984, 1988, Archangeli and Pulleyblank 1986, 1989, and much subsequent work; see Steriade 1995 for a survey). In this analysis, (9a) is a context-sensitive redundancy rule, since its operation is determined by affiliation to syllable structure.[13]

The intriguing fact about apicalization is that in some instances we do find the apical allophone/ of /s/ in onset position, as observed in (8a) above. Thus, in a fashion formally analogous to that already observed for velar nasals, the occurrence of onset apicals is limited to precisely those cases in which /s/ has undergone resyllabification to a following vowel. In other words, just as nasals,

/s/ is treated as syllable-final for allophony purposes in the forms of words presenting the optional final vowel, as can be seen by the additional examples in (10a). By contrast, when the corresponding stem is followed by an affix in underlying forms, the only possible outcome is the dorsal allophone, as shown by the data in (10b):[14]

(10) a. Apical [ş]:

nos	[nɔ́ş] ~ [nɔ́.şi]	'we, us'
mes	[méş] ~ [mé.şi]	'month'
xuez	[šwɛ́ş] ~ [šwɛ́.şi]	'judge'
dez	[dɛ́ş] ~ [dɛ́.şi]	'ten'
rapaz	[r̄a.páş] ~ [r̄a.pá.şi]	'boy'
arroz	[a.r̄ɔ́ş] ~ [a.r̄ɔ́.şi]	'rice'

b. Dorsal [s]:

nos-o	[nɔ́.su]	'ours-MASC'
mes-es	[mé.siş]	'months'
rapaz-a	[r̄a.pá.sa]	'girl'
xuec-es	[šwɛ́.siş]	'judges'
déc-imo	[dɛ́.si.mu]	'tenth'
arroz-al	[a.r̄ɔ.sál]	'rice field'

(cf. *[nɔ́.şo], *[r̄a.pá.şa], *[šwɛ́.şiş], etc.)

In order to explain the occurrence of the apical variant in onset position in (10a), in contrast with its dorsal counterpart in (10b), we only need to assume that core syllabification rules assign the stem-final /s/ to the onset of the syllable headed by the suffix-initial vowel, and so it fails to satisfy the conditions for apicalization. On the other hand, word-final /s/ in (10a) is first located in rhyme position, where it meets the structural description apicalization, and later it is shifted to the onset of the syllable headed by the optional vowel. In short, we must have derivations as that exemplified in (11), where the considerations on rule ordering adduced earlier to account for the interaction of velarization with epenthesis and resyllabification, can be extended, *mutatis mutandis*, to /s/-apicalization:

(11)			
Underlying forms:	/pas.pa.ǰas/	/nɔs/	/nɔs-o/
Syllabification:	pas.pa.ǰas	nɔs	nɔ.so
Stress assignment:	pas.pa.ǰás	nɔ́s	nɔ́.so
Apicalization:	paş.pa.ǰáş	nɔ́ş	—
Epenthesis:	paş.pa.ǰáş.e	nɔ́ş.e	—
Resyllabification:	paş.pa.ǰá.şe	nɔ́.şe	—
Spirantization:	paş.pa.ɟ̆á.şe	—	—
Tense mid-vowel raising:	paş.pa.ɟ̆á.şi	nɔ́.şi	nɔ́.su
Phonetic output:	paş.pa.ɟ̆á.şi	nɔ́.şi	nɔ́.su

A third and even more compelling argument supporting the epenthetic nature of the final optional vowel in Galician derives from certain facts about plural formation. The plural suffix in Galician has two basic exponents: {*-s*} and {*-es*} (the latter surfaces as [-is] in Moañés, as expected). The distribution of these two allomorphs is as follows: words that end in either a vocoid or /n/ select {*-s*}, as in (12a-b); by contrast, those ending in any consonant other than /n/ select {*-es*}, as in (12c).

(12)				
	a.	singular	plural	
		bo	*bo-s (*bo-*[i]*s*)	'good-MASC'
		cu	*cu-s* (**cu-*[i]*s*)	'buttocks'
		rei	*rei-s* (**rei-*[i]*s*)	'king'
		pau	*pau-s* (**pau-*[i]*s*)	'stick
		café	*café-s* (**cafe-*[i]*s*)	'faith'
		bocoi	*bocoi-s* (**bocoi-*[i]*s*)	'big barrel'
		dominó	*dominó-s* (**dominó-*[i]*s*)	'dominoes'
		bocareu	*bocareu-s* (**bucareu-*[i]*s*)	'anchovie'
	b.	*son*	*son-s* (**son-*[i]*s)*	'sound'
		can	*can-s* (**can-*[i]*s*)	'dog'
		xoven	*xoven-s* (*xoven-[i]*s*)	'young'
		chorón	*chorón-s* (**chorón-*[i]*s*)	'crier-MASC'
		Xoán	*Xoán-s* (**Xoan-*[i]*s*)	'John'
		sultán	*sultán-s* (**sultan-*[i]*s*)	'sultan-MASC'
		alemán	*alemán-s* (**aleman-*[i]*s*)	'German-MASC'

c. singular	plural	
mar	*mar*-[i]*s* (**mar-s*)	'sea'
sol	*sol*-[i]*s* (**sol-s*)	'honey'
mes	*mes*-[i]*s* (**mes-s*)	'month'
papel	*papel*-[i]*s* (**papel-s*)	'paper'
rapaz	*rapac*-[i]*s* (**rapas-s*)	'boy'
muller	*muller*-[i]*s* (**muller-s*)	'woman'
salgueiral	*salgueiral*-[i]*s* (**salgueiral-s*)	'willow grove'
paspallás	*paspallas*-[i]*s* (**paspallás-s*)	'partridge'

Suppose now that on the basis of the {-s} ~ {-Vs} plural allomorphy, one wishes to argue for an optional deletion analysis. In that case, we would posit singular forms whose underlying representations contain a vowel-final stem, and this vowel would, then, be optionally deleted whenever syllable structure conditions permit, that is, whenever vowel deletion would not result in a disallowed consonant cluster in the word-final coda, such as **rs*, **ls, etc.*, (cf. (12c)). We can, then, envisage derivations such as those shown in (13), illustrated with representative examples from (12):

(13)			
Underlying forms:	/boe/	/sone/	/mare/
Syllabification:	bo.e	so.ne	ma.re
Stress assignment:	bó.e	só.ne	má.re
Tense mid-vowel raising:	bó.i	só.ni	má.ri
Optional deletion:	bó	só.n	má.r
Resyllabification:	—	són	már
Nasal velarization:	—	sóŋ	–
Phonetic output:	bó	sóŋ	már

Such an analysis is untenable for several reasons. Perhaps the most conspicuous one is that it entails a contradiction of sorts. That is, optional deletion of the underlying stem-final vowel, which is posited in order to account for the short forms in all the singular forms in (12), would have to apply *obligatorily* in some of the plural counterparts, namely those whose stem-final segment is either a vocoid or /n/ (cf. the starred forms in (12a-b)).

There is a further fact about plural formation and the way in which it interacts with the optional final vowel that argues against an apocope analysis. In Moañés, the final optional vowel may occur in surface structure after the plural suffix /-s/. As we saw in (12b), many dialects of Galician allow the complex coda /ns/ in word-final position, but in such cases the second member is necessarily the plural marker. Bisegmental codas in word-final position are otherwise prohibited. We expect, then, that in words with oxytonic stress whose stem ends in a nasal, both the singular and the plural forms should be legitimate hosts of the final optional vowel, and in fact they are, as seen in (14):

(14)	a.	*pan*	[páŋ] ~ [pá.ŋi]	'bread'
		curmán	[kur.máŋ] ~ [kur.má.ŋi]	'cousin'
		legón	[li.xóŋ] ~ [li.xó.ŋi]	'hoe'
		langrán	[laŋ.gráŋ] ~ [laŋ.grá.ŋi]	'big man'
		almacén	[al.ma.séŋ] ~ [al.ma.sé.ŋi]	'warehouse'
	b.	*pan-s*	[páŋʂ] ~ [páŋ.ʂi]	'breads'
		curmán-s	[kur.máŋʂ] ~ [kur.máŋ.ʂi]	'cousins'
		legóns	[li.xóŋʂ] ~ [li.xóŋ.ʂi]	'hoes'
		langrán-s	[laŋ.gráŋʂ] ~ [laŋ.gráŋ.ʂi]	'big men'
		almacén-s	[al.ma.sɛ́ŋʂ] ~ [al.ma.sɛ́ŋ.ʂi]	'warehouses'

Now, just as in Spanish, it is a systematic and otherwise exceptionless feature in Galician that the plural suffix /-s/ must be the outermost segment on the right edge of the morphological structure of a word. The fact that the final vowel follows the plural suffix in (14b) can only be explained if we assume that it is not present in underlying structure, and thus the putative solution in terms of an apocope rule must be rejected.

In view of the evidence presented in this section, we may safely conclude that the set of Galician dialects of which the Moañés variety is representative possess an optional rule of final-vowel epenthesis which gives rise to the alternations such as those discussed in this section.

2 Constraints on optional epenthesis

So far we have established that the optional word-final vowel in Galician is generated by a process of epenthesis, and provided a description of how this process interacts with other phonological rules in Galician, such as nasal velarization and /s/-apicalization. In the present section, I discuss a number of interesting constraints placed on the occurrence of the optional epenthetic vowel. In addition, it will be established that optional epenthesis belongs to the postlexical component of the grammar. More specifically, its domain of operation is shown to be the intonational phrase. As in section 1, the data discussed in this section is taken primarily from the Moañés dialect.

In order to frame my analysis of the constraints at work in optional epenthesis in a more explicit way, it will be useful to briefly review some relevant theoretical concepts related to the issue at hand.

Broselow (1982) distinguishes three types of vowel epenthesis: (a) syllable-determined epenthesis occurs when some underlying segment cannot be assigned to syllable structure by regular syllabification rules, as in some dialects of Arabic (Kenstowicz 1986, Itô 1989)); (b) metrically-determined epenthesis acts to fulfill some canonical shape in metrical structure (e.g., a disyllabic foot). Thus, in Mohawk [i] is inserted word-initially in words containing only one underlying vowel in order to maintain the general pattern of penultimate stress (Michelson 1981, 1988); and (c) segmentally-determined epenthesis rules are found, for instance, in Logudorese Sardinian and Basque. In both languages, [e] is inserted word-initially before /r̄/, a context in which the trill otherwise does not occur in these languages: (Lug. Sard.) /r̄io/ → [er̄ío] 'river' (Pitau 1986), (Basque) /r̄ueda/ → /er̄uéða/ 'wheel' (Hualde 1991b). As we shall see in section 3, Galician lexical (obligatory) epenthesis belongs to Broselow's type (a). I would like to show next that, by contrast, optional (postlexical) epenthesis is metrically-induced, and so it falls within Broselow's type (b).

Hayes (1985, 1987, 1995) suggests that the foot patterns used in the computation of word-stress crosslinguistically can be restricted to three basic types: the syllabic trochee $(\acute{\sigma}\ \sigma)_F$ (quantity-insensitive, left-headed), as in (15a); the moraic trochee $(\acute{\mu}\ \mu)_F$ (quantity-sensitive, left-headed), as in (15b); and the (generally moraic) iamb $(\mu\ \acute{\sigma})_F$ (quantity-sensitive, right-headed), as in (15c). The notation in (15) is as follows: F = foot; μ = mora; σ = syllable; a vertical line indicate headedness. A notationally equivalent foot structure is also indicated in (15) beneath the syllabic tier: feet are enclosed in parenthesis; the x's signal headedness and the dots represent the weak node of a foot. Both notational variants of foot representation will be used to illustrate my discussion of optional epenthesis in this section.

(15) a. Syllabic trochee b. Moraic trochee c. (Moraic) iamb

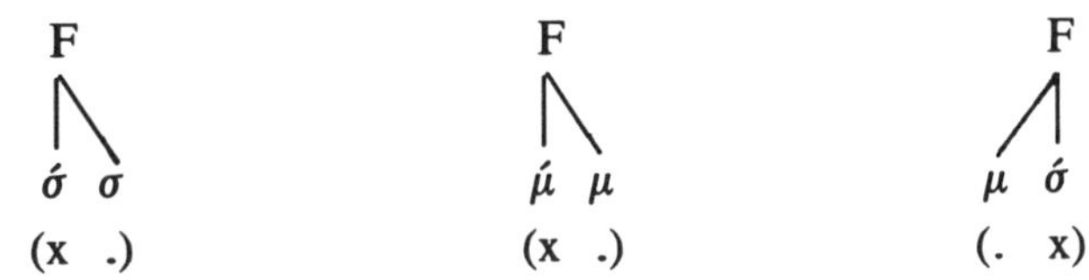

We need not concern ourselves here with the moraic iamb (15c). However, crucial to the analysis of optional epenthesis in Galician proposed here are the two foot types in (15a-b).

It has been frequently observed in recent research that the universally unmarked type of metrical foot is binary; that is, it consists of two constituents. This observation has been incorporated into recent theoretical frameworks, such as Optimality Theory, as the *Foot Binarity Constraint* (McCarthy and Prince 1993, Prince and Smolensky 1993).

The fundamental distinction between the two types of foot in (15a-b) is that foot binarity is computed on distinct units of prosodic representation: syllables in (15a), but moras in (15b). It is important to emphasize that foot binarity in a moraic trochee may encompass either two syllables (the second of which is necessarily light) or a single heavy syllable.

A phonological representation that fails to satisfy foot binarity may be licensed by *catalexis*, the formal opposite of extrametricality (see Giegerich 1985, Kiparsky 1991, Burzio 1994, Nouveau 1994; see also Saltarelli, this volume). Catalexis consists in effectively counting an additional unit at the edge of the relevant prosodic domain, so that foot binarity will be satisfied at the appropriate level of representation.[15] The addition of a catalectic element to degenerate feet in syllabic and moraic trochee systems, respectively, is shown schematically in (16):

(16)

It is not uncommon for a catalectic unit to exhibit an overt phonetic manifestation. In systems that utilize syllabic trochees, such cases typically emerge through epenthesis. In the process, the catalectic syllable in (16a) is given phonetic substance by assignment of default vowel features. An example is the metrically-induced epenthesis rule in Mohawk mentioned earlier (see also Crowhurst 1992b for a similar process in Sierra Miwok). In moraic trochee systems, on the other hand, the catalectic mora in (16b) may link to its preceding counterpart, and thus be realized as lengthening of an underlying short vowel (McCarthy and Prince 1986). Kiparsky (1991) has suggested that degenerate feet should be universally disallowed, and that all feet are strictly binary. In Kiparsky's framework, catalexis thus ensures that potentially degenerate trochaic feet, will become either bisyllabic or bimoraic.

In Optimality Theory (see McCarthy and Prince 1993, 1995, Prince and Smolensky 1993), and specially in the version of this model known as *Correspondence Theory* (McCarthy and Prince 1995), general well-formedness constraints such as foot binarity can be violated if another applicable constraint is ranked higher in the constraint hierarchy. In languages in which the catalectic unit is not realized, a constraint barring the addition of phonological structure not present in underlying forms (*Dependency between Input and Output* or *Dep–IO*) would weigh more heavily than the requirement demanding that feet be binary. Conversely, and all other things being equal, dominance of foot binarity over *Dep–IO* would induce the realization of phonetically overt catalectic elements.

Catalexis can thus be viewed as either a repair strategy (see Paradis 1988a, 1988b, 1993, Paradis and LaCharité 1993), or as the result of a language-particular constraint ranking, as in the Optimality-theoretical framework. Whatever turns out to be the most adequate characterization, I would like to argue here that optional epenthesis in Moañés Galician formally involves the spellout of a catalectic syllable.

The theoretical interest of optional epenthesis stems from the fact that it is subject to two highly specific conditions. Undoubtedly, the first one is of a metrical nature. Consider, some relevant examples, most of them taken from (1) above. Optional epenthesis applies exclusively to forms with final primary stress, whether vowel-final (17a), glide-final (17b), or consonant-final (17c):

(17)	a.	*cú* ~ *cú.*[i]	'buttocks'
		ma.má ~ *ma.má.*[i]	'mummy'
		Pa.na.má ~ *Pa.na.má.*[i]	(country)
	b.	*ré*[j] ~ *ré.*[ji]	'king'
		bo.có[j] ~ *bo.có.*[ji]	'big barrel'
		bo.ca.ré[w] ~ *bo.ca.ré.*[wi]	'anchovy'
	c.	*már* ~ *má.r*[i]	'sea'
		pa.pél ~ *pa.pé.l*[i]	'paper'
		sal.guei.rál ~ *sal.guei.ra.l*[i]	'willow grove'

The data in (17) unequivocally shows that optional epenthesis cannot be simply determined by syllable markedness considerations, such as, for example, the elimination of codas, since the vowel is inserted indistinctly after both open and after closed syllables. In the phonological system of Moañés Galician, epenthesis appears to have merely a prosodic or rhythmic function. As mentioned in section 1, only oxytonic words, such as those in (17), undergo the rule; by contrast, words with a penultimate or an antepenultimate stress pattern disallow optional epenthesis, as illustrated in (18).

(18)	a.	*ró.da* ~ **ró.da.*[i]	'wheel'
		mo.réi.ra ~ **mo.réi.ra.*[i]	'mulberry tree'
	b.	*lá.pis* ~ **lá.pi.s*[i]	'pencil'
		xó.ven ~ **xó.ve.n*[i]	'young'
	c.	*ré.xi.me* ~ **ré.xi.me.*[i]	'regime'
		lós.tre.go ~ *l*ós.tre.go.*[i]	'lightning'
	d.	*Xú.pi.ter* ~ **Xú.pi.te.r*[i]	'Jupiter'
		ca.rá(c).ter ~ **ca.rá(c).te.r*[i]	'character'

The reason for the impossibility of optional epenthesis in (18) appears to be a principled one. As in Spanish, the locus of primary (lexical) stress in Galician is circumscribed to the last three syllables of a word; there are no exceptions to the three-syllable window. The unmarked patterns are: (i) penultimate stress in vowel-final words (cf. (18a)); and (ii) final stress in words that end in a heavy syllable (cf. (17b-c) above). Penultimate stress in consonant-final words (18b), and antepenultimate stress (18c-d), independently of the nature of the final syllable, are marked stress contours. The emerging generalization regarding optional epenthesis appears to be that, since this process creates an additional syllable to the right edge of a word, it is disallowed whenever the result is either a marked or an impermissible stress pattern. The addition of the epenthetic syllable in the starred forms in (18a-b) renders the stress locus proparoxytonic, a clearly marked option in Galician. And in (18c-d), epenthesis produces downright violations of the three-syllable window.

A second constraint on optional epenthesis requires that the target word be the prosodic anchor of sentence stress. As in Spanish (Roca 1986), sentential prominence in Galician falls on the last word bearing primary stress in the phonic group, a domain which descriptive grammars commonly define as the portion of an utterance contained between pauses (see, e.g., Navarro Tomás 1977: 30, Alcina Franch and Blecua 1980: 445, 455-457, Dalbor 1980: 41, Real Academia Española 1982: 10). This domain can be roughly identified as corresponding to the *intonational phrase* in prosodic phonology (cf. Selkirk 1984, 1995, Nespor and Vogel 1986, Ladd 1986, Rice 1987, Inkelas and Zec 1990, 1995, among others). Indeed, according to my personal (impressionistic) observation, although strictly optional, epenthesis is heavily favored in colloquial Moañés whenever a word bears phrasal prominence. Some illustrative instances of intonational phrases corresponding to a variety of syntactic constructions in Galician are given in (19); in all of them, the metrical head is last in its corresponding intonational phrase, and so epenthesis is applicable.

(19) a. Q: *¿Qué trouxo ela?* A: *Pan* (~ *pan*[i])
what brought she — bread
Q: 'What did she bring?' A: (Some) bread'

b. *Ela vai trael-o pan* (~ *pan*[i])
she goes to bring-the bread
'She's going to bring the bread'

c. *O pan (~ pan*[i]), *fixo-no onte*
the bread, made-it yesterday
'(As for) the bread, (s)he made it yesterday'

d. *Dille que traia pan* (~ *pan*[i]), *non viño*
tell-him that bring-SUBJ bread, not wine
'Tell him/her to bring bread, not wine'

Consider now the examples in (20), which are identical in all other respects to those in (19) above, except that now the target word *pan* is followed by a complement within its corresponding intonational phrase. Epenthesis is ruled out in such instances because the noun in question no longer identifies the metrical head of the intonational phrase:

(20) a. Q: *¿Qué trouxo ela?* A: *Pan (*pan*[i]) *de millo*
Q: 'What did she bring?' A: (Some) corn bread'

b. *Ela vai trae-lo pan* (**pan*[i]) que comprou
'She's going to bring the bread that she bought'

c. *O pan (*pan*[i]) *de millo, fixo-no onte*
'(As for) the corn bread, (s)he made it yesterday'

d. *Dille que traia pan* (**pan*[i]) *de millo, non viño*
'Tell him/her to bring corn bread, not wine'

Since, as suggested by the data in (20)-(21), the insertion of the epenthetic vowel is determined at the sentence level, we may conclude the process must take place in the postlexical domain.

The question now arises as to why should optional epenthesis target precisely the metrical head of an intonational phrase *only* when the word in which it is contained is oxytonic. A simple answer to this problem is implicit in the hypothesis suggested earlier that optional epenthesis embodies the phonetic realization of a catalectic syllable. Let us make more explicit the formal basis of this proposal.

It should be recalled that unmarked stress is penultimate in vowel-final words, and final in words that end in a consonant; any other pattern is marked.

As in Spanish, antepenultimate stress is prohibited when either the penultimate or the ultima are heavy.[16] These observations suggest that Galician lexical stress is quantity-sensitive. I will follow closely Dunlap's (1991) analysis of Spanish in assuming that unmarked word stress in Galician is obtained according to the principle in (21):

(21) Place a moraic trochee (cf. (15b) above) at the right edge of a word (lexical level).

Given the algorithm in (21), the derivation of the most common stress patterns of Galician will proceed as in (22). The unmarked contours are shown for the items *papél* 'paper' (22a) and *róda* 'wheel' (22b); the words *lápis* 'pencil' (22c) and *réxime* 'regime' (22d), are representative of the marked patterns. The overwhelming majority of Galician words belong to one of the types illustrated in (22).

(22)

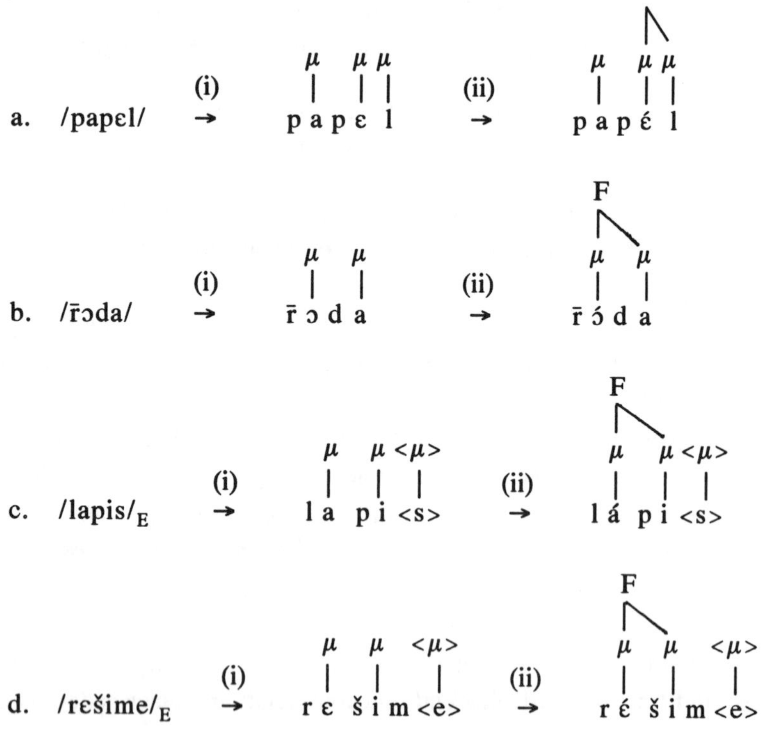

Step (i) in (22) reflects the morification procedure, whereby a mora is assigned to vowels and, in the appropriate cases, also to a following consonant (see McCarthy and Prince 1986, Zec 1988, Hayes 1989, Dunlap 1991, among others, for slightly different approaches to morification). Step (ii) illustrates the operation of foot construction (21) on the output of morification, and concomitant assignment of lexical prominence to the head mora in each case. Following in part Dunlap's (1991) analysis of Spanish lexical stress, I assume that the markedness of items in (22c-d) is expressed via a diacritic that triggers extrametricality of the final mora, indicated with a subscripted *E* in the corresponding underlying representations. The extrametrical unit is the final /s/ in (22c), and the final syllable in (22d). A formal advantage of this analysis is that it accounts for virtually all stress patterns in Galician, both unmarked and marked, by means of the single statement (21).[17]

Whether or not the stress system of Spanish is weight-sensitive has been a matter of dispute for almost a decade (cf. Lipski, this volume, Roca, this volume). It should be emphasized, however, that adherence to the assumption that lexical stress in Galician is sensitive to syllable weight, and thus constructed on moras, not syllables, is not crucial for my account of the issue at hand: the role of optional epenthesis in the post-lexical phonology of Galician.

For consistency with the issues discussed in this section and with the foot typology in (15), I shift now from the X-bar representation of the syllable in (3), repeated here as (23a) to the familiar moraic representation in (23b):

(23) a.

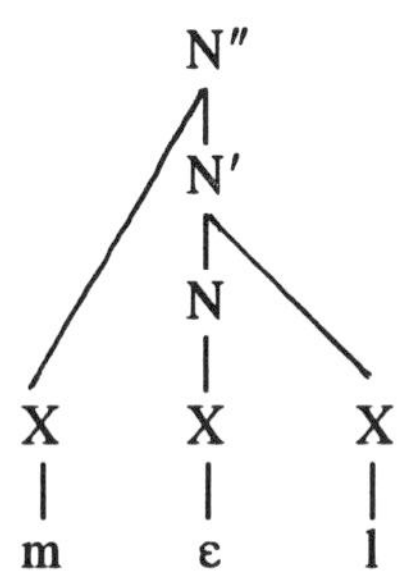

b.

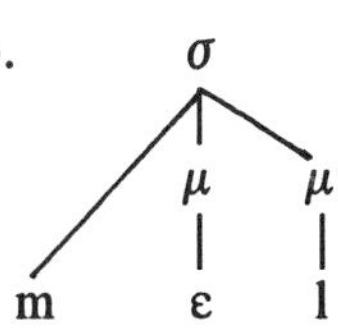

The switch from (23a) to (23b) is merely a matter of descriptive convenience; for the purposes of this paper, no commitment needs to be made to one or the other representational theory in (23).

When phrasal stress is assigned to the last word bearing lexical stress in Galician, the prominence of the other lexically-stressed words in the sentence is automatically lowered by one degree. The facts about phrasal rhythm suggest that the principles in (24) are at work, subject to the condition that syllables bearing lexically-assigned stress may not be demoted to a nonhead position (see Harris 1991a for a discussion of inalterability effects on lexically-assigned prosodic structure in Spanish).

(24) a. Construct syllabic trochees (cf. (15a)) from right to left (post-lexical level).

b. Assign prominence to the rightmost foot in the relevant prosodic domain.

Although (24b) is operative both in post-lexical and lexical representations, it applies vacuously in the latter domain; that is, given the creation of a single metrical foot by (21), word-level prominence can only be assigned to its head by universal convention (see Halle and Vergnaud 1987). In sum, according to the characterization just given, stress in Galician is quantity-sensitive in the lexical phonology, but weight-insensitive in the postlexical level.

The application of (24) can be illustrated with the sentence *Ela vai trae-lo viño* 'she is going to bring the wine', phonetically [è.la. βàj. tra.è.lu. βí.ñu], whose final representation is shown in (25).

(25)

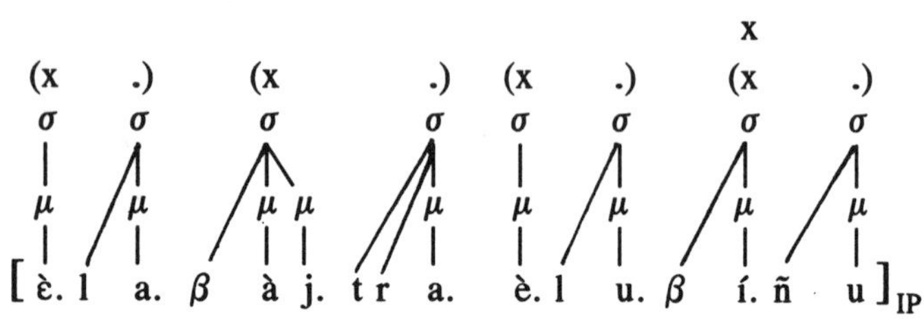

A procedure such as (24a) can be understood in two ways: a) as enforcing binarity of the specified type of foot 'whenever possible' (and degenerate feet in the 'otherwise' case); or b) as enforcing binarity by actually introducing into phonological representations the foot's optimal (disyllabic) prosodic template, which is then mapped onto the appropriate string (see Crowhurst 1991, 1992a,

1992b). It is in the latter sense that I conceive the operation of the metrical construction algorithm in (24a). As the last stressed unit in the intonational phrase, the word *viño* in (25) becomes the host for its metrical head by (24b). This word contains two light syllables (i.e., two moras), and consequently (24a) will construct a disyllabic foot postlexically on the bimoraic foot previously formed at the lexical level. Configurations such as (25), however, are relatively uninteresting for the problem under investigation.

The test-case for our purposes is one in which the lexically-assigned foot is built on a heavy final syllable, because in this particular instance the structural conditions for optional epenthesis are met. A simple illustration of how optional epenthesis proceeds can be provided by merely replacing the paroxytonic final word in (25) *viño* 'wine' by the oxytonic one *pan* 'bread', as in (26) (for visual simplicity only the full prosodic structure of the final foot in the intonational phrase domain is shown):

(26) a.

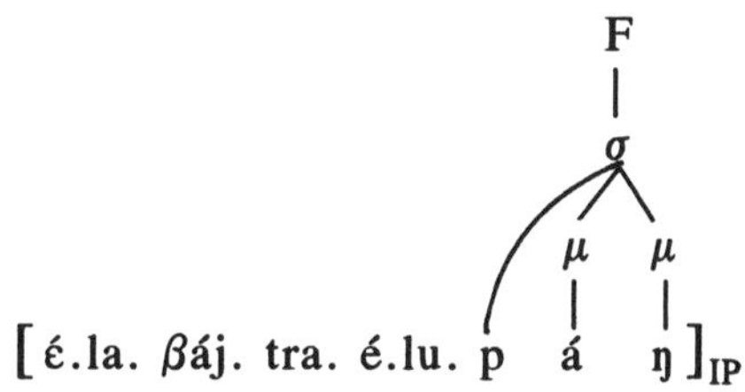

b.

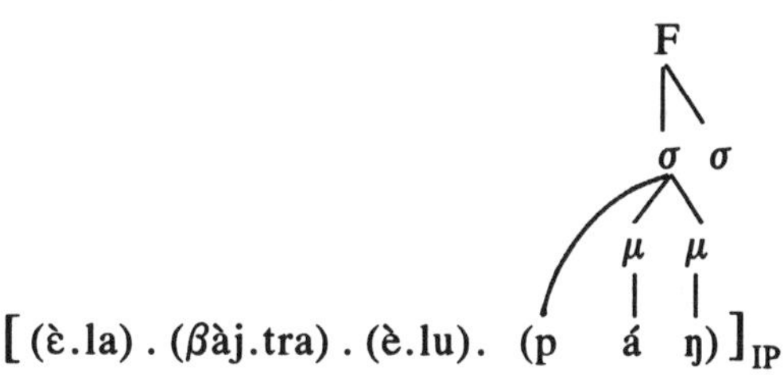

c.

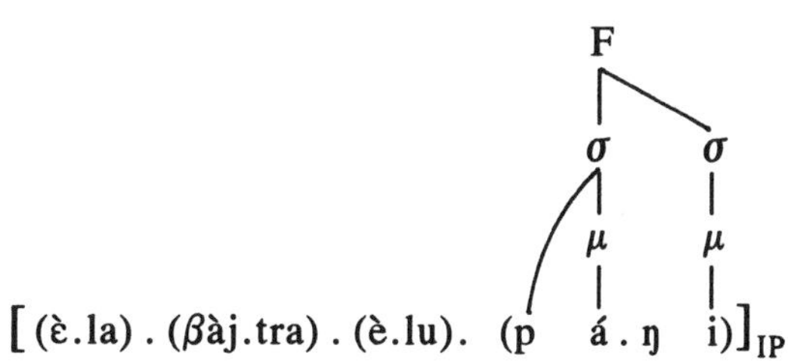

The relevant portion of the initial representation in (26a) reflects the output of the lexical component: a bimoraic foot built on a single heavy syllable. The first iteration of the disyllabic template required by (24a) cannot simply begin by counting the first two syllables from right to left, thereby embracing *pan* and the preceding syllable *lo* into a trochaic foot, because such move would entail an undesirable stress shift onto the latter, producing the incorrect *(*ló.pan*). If, on the other hand, we were to enforce preservation of lexical prominence in *pan*, and still count from right to left, as dictated by (24a), the wrong output would again be obtained, since the resulting foot would be iambic: (*lo.pán*), not trochaic, in violation of (24a). The obvious way to ensure the construction of a syllabic trochee is to map the appropriate left-headed disyllabic template (15a) rightwards, as in (26b), taking monosyllabic *pan* as its head, and an additional syllable (a catalectic syllable) initially unlinked to any segmental material as its weak node to the right. The representation in (50b) also reflects the application of phrasal stress (24b) in the usual manner, yielding the expected prominence on the first syllable of the last foot. Finally, the empty syllable node in (26b) has been filled through optional epenthesis, which simply inserts the features of the default vowel, as in (26c) (where the operation of mid-vowel raising has been factored in), with concomitant resyllabification of the final consonant as the onset of the phonetically-realized catalectic syllable.

To summarize the essence of my analysis so far, I have proposed that there is a requirement in Galician that the metrical head of the intonational phrase be a binary foot, as dictated by (24a). In words with either penultimate or antepenultimate stress (cf. types (22b-d) above), the bimoraic trochee constructed at the lexical level is also bisyllabic and thus will be readily promoted to the head of the intonational phrase by (24b). In oxytonic consonant-final words (type (22a)), however, the foot bearing lexical stress is monosyllabic. The only viable alternative compatible with foot construction (24a) is to build the metrical head of the corresponding intonational phrase on a degenerate foot. Under these circumstances, a catalectic syllable is called upon to repair a potential violation of foot binarity, and thus such violation is avoided at the relevant (abstract) level of representation. The empirical interest of the Galician data is that satisfaction of foot binarity is also required, albeit optionally, in the more concrete level of phonetic representations.

It should be clearly understood that foot binarity is not an absolute requirement. Degenerate feet will be constructed in nonhead positions within the intonational phrase whenever a conflict arises between the preservation of lexically-assigned stress and the left-to-right iteration of foot construction (24a). This is shown for the sentence *quero que lle dés pan* (phonetically, with optional epenthesis: [kɛ́.ru. ki. ǰi. dés. pá.ŋi]) 'I want you to give him/her (some) bread' in (27), where the monosyllabic word *dés* 'you give-SUBJ' forms a foot by itself. Crucially, such form is not the head of the intonational phrase in (27) and thus binarity need not be enforced:

(27)

```
                                  x
  (x   .)   (x  .)   (x)    (x   .)
   σ   σ     σ  σ     σ      σ   σ
[ kɛ̀ . ru .  kì . ǰi .  dès .  pá . ŋi ] IP
```

The fact that optional epenthesis may be realized only on the head of the intonational phrase, and nowhere else, need not be stipulated; it follows from a universal principle, commonly known in the literature on extrametricality as the *peripherality condition* (cf. Hayes 1980, 1995, Harris 1983, 1992, Halle and Vergnaud 1987, Roca 1992). Extrametrical segments (i.e., those that are systematically ignored by stress rules) are licensed only in the periphery (right or left edge) of some prosodic domain. Recall that in the analysis of Galician word stress illustrated in (22) extrametricality is afforded exceptional status, in that it comes into existence only when triggered by a special diacritic excluding the last mora from the domain of stress. In much recent work on Spanish stress in which an appeal to extrametricality has been made, the practical role of this notion has been to mark lexical exceptionality on stress placement (see Harris 1992 for further discussion). In other languages, such as Latin, extrametricality of the final syllable is totally predictable, and thus naturally assigned by rule. Since, as already mentioned, catalexis can be readily considered the formal counterpart of extrametricality, I find *a priori* no compelling argument against the notion that catalectic elements be also subject to this condition. Given this characterization, any non-final element in the intonational phrase (e.g., *dés* in (27)) will be ineligible for catalexis.

The reader may have noticed by now that the analysis of foot structure based on syllabic trochees at the phrasal level (24a) is at odds with what may be considered the standard analysis of (postlexical) secondary stress in Spanish, first advocated in Roca (1986), and adhered to by Halle and Vergnaud (1987), which instead posits the construction of syllabic iambs, also in a left-to-right iteration. Since the patterns of secondary stress and rhythm in Galician are in all relevant respects identical to those of Spanish, which of the two alternatives turns out to be the correct one is open to empirical verification. However, given the availability of the garden-variety of repair mechanisms in a standard metrical analysis, such as stress clash resolution (foot reversals, prominence deletion, etc.), and constraints ensuring the preservation of previously constructed metrical structure (see Halle 1990, Halle and Kenstowicz 1991, Harris 1991a), the two foot construction alternatives are probably equally well-equipped to adequately account for the organization of phrasal prominence in Galician.

We can easily establish, however, that (24) has an immediate edge over its competitor. For if foot construction at the phrase level is assumed to be iambic, then the basic insight we have gained so far would inevitably be lost: that optional epenthesis is the phonetic exponent of foot binarity —the universal unmarked option— at a more abstract level of representation. In particular, under an account positing syllabic iambs, the last word of the intonational phrase *pán* in (26) above, would form a perfect iamb with the preceding syllable, as shown in (28); foot binarity is thus satisfied within the relevant prosodic domain, and therefore the motivation for inserting an epenthetic vowel is no longer obvious.

(28)

```
                                  x
(x)  (.   x)   (.   x)  (.   x)
 σ    σ    σ    σ    σ    σ    σ
[ɛ̀ . la . βàj . tra . ɛ̀ . lu . páŋ ] IP
```

The above analysis not only provides a principled explanation to the instances in which optional epenthesis applies (i.e., in consonant-final oxytones); it also predicts without any stipulation those instances in which epenthesis does *not* occur. Hence, in all words exhibiting surface penultimate or antepenultimate lexical stress (cf. (22b-d) above), the bimoraic foot constructed lexically is also bisyllabic, and thus foot binarity will be optimally satisfied at the postlexical level in the relevant instances. This result follows directly from our formal characterization of catalexis as implementing syllabic binarity on the foot heading the intonational phrase at an abstract level of representation. In essence,

I am claiming that by virtue of instilling phonetic substance into the catalectic syllable, postlexical epenthesis can be conceived of as the optional manifestation of an abstract linguistic property —binarity of foot structure— in surface represention s.

An additional piece of evidence can be given in support of an analysis of optional epenthesis as the phonetic manifestation of a catalectic syllable. As in Spanish, vowel sequences in Galician are subject to a sandhi rule whereby an unstressed high vowel is desyllabified and adjoined to the syllable headed by an immediately adjacent nonhigh vowel. Following Roca's (1991) analysis of Spanish, I refer to this process as *syllable merger*. As illustrated in (29), where some illustrative alternations between high vowels and glides are given, syllable merger applies both within and across words.[18]

(29)	a.	*sa.*[í]*r*	'to leave'	vs.	*sa*[j]*.ré.mos*	'we will leave'
		ba.[ú]*l*	*'trunk'*	*vs.*	*ba*[w]*l.cí.ño*	'little trunk'
	b.	*dous* [i]*n.vér.nos* 'two winters'		vs.	*no* [j]*n.vér.no* 'in the winter'	
		dez [u]*.ni.fór.mes* 'ten uniforms'		vs.	*lé.va* [w]*.ni.fór.me* '(s)he is wearing a uniform'	

In colloquial Moañés speech, syllable merger applies regularly to postvocalic unstressed tense mid vowels whenever the conditions for syllable merger are met, as shown in (30). This seems to suggest that at the relevant point in the derivation in which merger applies, the mid vowel in question has already undergone raising.

(30)	*e.l*[a. é]*n.tra*	'she is entering'	vs.	*e.l*[a j]*n.tróu*	'she entered'
	e.l[a. ó]*.lla*	'she is looking'	vs.	*e.l*[a w]*.llóu*	'she looked'

The formal statement of the desyllabification process involved in syllable merger appears to require a rule such as (31). Independent principles will ensure that the high vowel linked to the second mora, being the least sonorous within the resulting complex nucleus, will be realized as a glide (see Zec 1988, Dunlap 1991, ch. 4, Rosenthall 1994: 133-ff.):

(31) *Syllable merger*

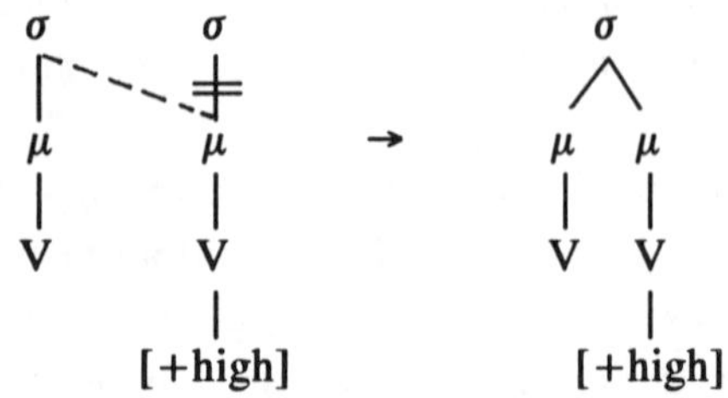

(mirror image)

Remarkably, the vowel inserted word-finally by optional epenthesis always preserves its syllabicity, as shown in (32). This generalization has no exceptions: it holds independently of style or speech tempo.[19]

(32) *bó* ~ *bó.*[i] (cf. **bó*[j]) 'good-MASC'
cú ~ *cú.*[i] (cf. **cú*[j]) 'buttocks'
ca.fé ~ *ca.fé.*[i] (cf. **ca.fé*[j]) 'coffee'
d.omi.nó ~ *do.mi.nó.*[i] (cf. **do.mi.nó*[j]) 'dominoes'

The inalterability of the optional vowel in relation to syllable merger can be accounted for in a number of ways. In a strictly derivational approach, for example, the epenthetic vowel can easily be prevented from undergoing desyllabification by means of extrinsic ordering. Namely, syllable merger would fail to apply to the optional final vowel if it counterfeeds vowel epenthesis. As indicated earlier, vowel raising always applies to the output of epenthesis, turning it into [i]. Given these assumptions, we obtain derivations such as those in (33) for the two representative examples from (32) *bo* 'good-MASC' and *café* 'coffee', where only the relevant steps in the derivation are shown.

(33)

	UR's:	/bo/	/kafe/
1)	*Syllabification*:	bó	ka.fe
2)	*Stress*:	bó	ka.fé
3)	*Syllable merger*:	—	—
4)	*Optional epenthesis*:	bó.e	ka.fé.e
5)	*Mid-vowel raising*:	bó.i	ka.fé.i

Unfortunately, however, such an analysis relies on brute force. It provides no valuable insight for the fact the epenthetic vowel remains unaffected by syllable merger. Of course, the reason for such inalterability effect is evident: by merging with the preceding syllable, the very purpose of catalexis —that of enforcing foot binarity— would be defeated. It appears that these facts are more amenable to an alternative couched in the optimality framework, whereby a foot binarity constraint imposed on the head of the intonational phrase simply dominates whatever other constraints are responsible for syllable merger. An optimality account of optional epenthesis is beyond the scope of this paper (see Colina, this volume, section 4.3, for such an analysis).

A final clarification should be made regarding optional epenthesis. Just as in Spanish (Harris 1980, 1985b, 1991b, 1991c), there is a morphological well-formedness constraint on the shape of Galician words requiring that a {VC} word-marker template be located to the right of the stem, on the outermost layer of morphological structure, as shown in (34). The V position will be filled by the gender morpheme, an operation carried out by a morphological spell-out rule (*gender marker realization*) that specifies this vowel as [o] for the masculine and [a] for the feminine. The C position, on the other hand, will be realized in plural forms, where the plural morpheme will in the default case be spelled out as /s/. In taking this approach, I follow closely the proposals made by Harris (1980, 1985b, 1991b) for Spanish. This issue will be discussed in more detail in section 3 in our analysis of lexical (obligatory) epenthesis.

(34) $[[\ \ldots\ ]_{\text{Stem}}\ \text{V C}]_{\alpha}$ (where α = Noun or Adjective)

In particular, I follow Harris (1991b), who proposes that Spanish consonant-final words, such *pan* 'bread', *papel* 'paper', and so on, are lexically marked as exceptions to the rule of gender marker realization. In addition, words that end in *-e* in surface forms, such as *parte* 'part', *lume* 'fire', etc, are also exceptions to the marker realization rule. In the latter forms, the final vowel is absent in underlying structure: whenever a stem-final consonant cannot be parsed by core syllabification rules, lexical epenthesis is called in to fill the V position in the word-marker template (34) with the default vowel features. This means that in addition to the syllable structure considerations, lexical epenthesis effectively contributes eliminating lexical exceptionality in the word-marker template. By contrast, when the stem in such forms ends in a syllabifiable consonant (e.g., *pan* 'bread') the V position in the word-marker template remains unassociated to any segmental material at the lexical level. These are precisely the cases in which optional epenthesis may apply in Galician (provided, of course, that the stress pattern of the word is oxytonic). By appearing sequentially after the stem, the optional final vowel will in effect overlap with the word-marker position in surface forms. However, the particular position of the epenthetic vowel with regard to morphological structure is formally quite distinct in both cases, as clearly brought out in the representation of *parte* 'part' ([pár.ti]) and *pan* 'bread' (phonetically [pa.ŋi] with optional final [i]), as illustrated in (35) (*St* = Stem; ω_m = morphological word; ω_{pr} = prosodic word):

(35) a. $\Big[\Big[[\text{párt}]_{St}\ \text{i}\ \Big]_{\omega_m} \Big]_{\omega_{pr}}$

b. $\Big[\Big[[\text{páŋ}]_{St} \Big]_{\omega_m}\ \text{i}\ \Big]_{\omega_{pr}}$

In *parte* (35a) (underlyingly /part/), the final [i], inserted by lexical epenthesis, is anchored in the word-marker position, just between the stem boundary and the morphological word boundary. In *pan* (35b), on the other hand, the final [i] inserted by optional epenthesis, is located outside the morphological structure of the word, appended to its right edge as some sort of phonological clitic within the corresponding prosodic word.

The evidence for the structural distinction suggested in (35) is compelling. We saw in section 1 that optional epenthesis can apply to plural forms (cf. (14) above). As expected, the insertion of the optional epenthetic vowel here is conditioned by the familiar metrical constraint that also operates in singular forms; the final product must be a paroxytonic stress pattern. Recall that lexical epenthesis may apply in the plural forms of all stress-final words ending in the consonants /s, l, r/, effectively rendering them paroxytonic, and hence ruling out the possibility of optional epenthesis, as seen in (36):

(36)	a.	singular	plural	
		már	*má.res* ~ **má.re.s*[i]	'sea'
		més	*mé.ses* ~ **mé.se.s*[i]	'month'
		pa.pél	*pa.pé.les* ~ **pa.pé.le.s*[i]	'paper'

On the other hand, words ending in a stressed vowel (including a falling diphthong) or /n/[20] generally select the allomorph {s} in the plural, as in (37). Lexical epenthesis does not occur in such cases. By contrast, optional epenthesis *may* apply to these forms: plural formation does not alter their syllable count, and so they remain oxytonic in the plural.

		singular	plural	
(37)	a.	*bó*	*bós* ~ *bó.s*[i]	'good-MASC'
		réi	*réis* ~ *réi.s*[i]	'king'
		ca.fé	*ca.fés* ~ *ca.fé.s*[i]	'faith'
		bo.cói	*bo.cóis* ~ *bo.cói.s*[i]	'big barrel'
		do.mi.nó	*do.mi.nós* ~ *do.mi.nó.s*[i]	'dominoes'
	b.	*pán*	*páns* ~ *pán.s*[i]	'bread'
		ir.mán	*ir.máns* ~ *ir.mán.s*[i]	'brother/sister'
		le.gón	*le.gón* ~ *le.gón.s*[i]	'hoe'
		al.ma.cén	*al.ma.céns* ~ *al.ma.cén.s*[i]	'warehouse

Since, as already noted in section 1, the plural morpheme invariably occupies the most peripheral position on the right edge of morphological structure, it follows that the vowel inserted postlexically in the plural forms in (37) cannot occupy the word-marker position, and thus it necessarily lies outside the right boundary of the morphological word.

3 Word-final epenthesis in Galician as rule inversion

In this section I consider the evidence for epenthesis in Galician within a historical dimension, and turn to characterize it as a type of sound change commonly known as *rule inversion* (Vennemann 1972). It is argued that the grammar of Modern Galician contains a rule of lexical epenthesis, which obligatorily inserts a vowel word-finally whenever a lexical stem ends in an unsyllabifiable consonant or consonant sequence. This is a first stage in the process of rule inversion. Given the well-known fact that Galician did undergo a rule of word-final apocope, I will attempt to show that the medieval apocope rule has been reinterpreted as one of epenthesis in the synchronic grammar of Modern Galician. Furthermore, by supplying —albeit optionally— the vowel that historically had been lost by apocope, optional epenthesis is viewed as a second historical step in rule inversion, one which entails almost a complete reversal of the medieval situation. If this analysis can be upheld, then additional evidence is provided in favor of the view that the optional word-final vowel is the result of optional insertion.

Rule inversion can be characterized as a special case of lexical restructuring (Vennemann 1972: 210). The simplest and most common type of restructuring occurs when a set of surface forms derived by the operation of a phonological rule at a certain historical stage are reanalyzed as the underlying ones in a subsequent stage. In the process, the rule in question is dropped from the grammar, resulting in grammar simplification. Lexical restructuring appears to be almost inevitable in sound changes involving absolute neutralization (i.e., when a rule obliterates an underlying opposition in all contexts; cf. Kiparsky 1982). Since absolute neutralization does not result in phonological alternations, there is no direct evidence in the language for postulating surface forms that differ from underlying ones. A typical example is the sound change that turned the voiceless labiovelar fricative /ʍ/ into the back round glide /w/ in certain English dialects (see King 1969). As a result, words like *where*, *whale*, etc. became homophonous with *wear*, *wail*. Children acquiring these dialects would never hear the sound [ʍ], and therefore they would have no reason to suppose that surface [w] is derived from any source other than underlying structure.

Consider two alternating forms A and B, and a phonological rule R_i that carries out the structural change $A \rightarrow B$ in context C_i in the synchronic grammar at some historical point. Rule inversion occurs when the surface form B, derived by R_i in that grammar, is reanalyzed as the underlying representation by the next generation of speakers, such that now the same output forms are obtained by a different rule R_j, whose structural change can be characterized as the inverse of R_i (hence the term *rule inversion*) in C_i's complementary set of environments. Inversion resembles lexical restructuring in that: a) a set of phonetic representations are reanalyzed as the basic ones; and b) such a reanalysis is justified by general considerations on formal simplicity. Unlike lexical restructuring, however, rule inversion does not reduce the number of rules in the phonological component; instead, it is induced by some simplification in the internal structure of the grammar; for example, one that leads to the elimination of opacity in surface representation.

Among the various types of rule inversion discussed by Vennemann, those determined by purely phonological factors typically involve the reanalysis of a rule of deletion by one of epenthesis.[21] Two examples from British English discussed in Vennemann (1972) will serve as a brief illustration of consonant deletion being inverted to consonant insertion. The first one concerns a rule in Middle English whereby the final /n/ of the indefinite article *an* was deleted when the following word began in a consonant, thus resulting in alternations such as Modern English *an old man* vs. *a kind man*. The second example consists in a rule that deleted /r/ both word-finally and before a consonant in certain dialects, producing [r]~∅ alternations such as *The wate*[r] *is cold* vs. *He drunk the water* [wɔtə]). Vennemann produces evidence indicating that inversion has occurred in both cases. He shows that the same phonetic outputs can be generated in a simpler manner by replacing a rule of deletion by one of epenthesis, thereby providing evidence for rule inversion.

Let us turn now to the historical evidence in favor of rule inversion in Galician. It should be mentioned at this point that the general facts about apocope in Old Galician[22] are very similar, though not identical, to those of Old Spanish. Since Spanish apocope has been studied much more extensively and in greater depth of detail, it will be useful to compare the historical developments in both languages.[23]

In order to frame the discussion about apocope in Old Galician, it would be useful to mention a historical development that affected the consonantal system of the language around the 11th century, before the beginning of the literary period.[24] As other Hispano-Romance varieties, the consonant inventory of Old Galician contained the dental affricates /tˢ, dᶻ/ (deriving mainly from Latin /k, t/ followed by a front vocoid) in phonemic contrast with their fricative apico-alveolar counterparts /s, z/. The former pair deaffricated, turning into the corresponding dental fricatives /ş, ẓ/ at some point before the emergence of the first Old Galician documents (Azevedo Maia 1986: 438-440). In the ancestor of Moañés, as in other dialects of Western Galician, earlier distinctions in point of articulation and voicing were subsequently neutralized. As a result, /s/ is at present the single reflex of all four former sibilant phonemes.[25]

Most varieties of Hispano-Romance underwent a rule of apocope during the preliterary period, which involved the loss of word-final /-e/ after a certain class of consonants. Initially, apocope was an optional rule, and it apparently remained that way until at least the 13th century. Documents dating back to the middle of this century still exhibit some variation in the presence of final /-e/ in the relevant cases.

Two additional facts should be noted about medieval apocope. First, the deleted /-e/ in nouns and adjectives derives, quite generally, from the Latin third declension marker *-e-*. This vowel became word-final upon the loss of the accusative desinence *-m* (*-em* > *-e*). And second, deaffrication of /t^s, d^z/ into /s, z/ in Old Galician must have preceded the emergence of apocope, since final /-e/ is still optional in the earliest texts; the spelling conventions used in these documents clearly indicate that deaffrication had already been accomplished when apocope was still an optional rule (cf. Azevedo Maia 1986: 438-ff.).

Optional deletion of final /-e/ in Galician must have started around the middle of the 11th century. In its original form the process took place when word-final /-e/ was preceded by a single consonant belonging to the class of anterior coronals (see García de Diego 1909: 23-25, Azevedo Maia 1986: 435, 524), arguably the least marked type of consonants in syllable-final position (cf. Clements 1990). Excluded from this set, however, were the oral stops /t, d/, after which apocope did not occur, at least initially, as well as the trill /r̄/. Such failure is hardly surprising: the historical evidence from Galician strongly indicates that at no synchronic stage in its historical development from Latin were either oral stops or trills allowed in syllable-final position in native words.

The underlying consonantal inventory of Old Galician at the point in which the optional apocope rule first emerged is shown in (38). Apocope applied at this stage only when final /-e/ was preceded by one of the underlying consonants contained inside the box.

(38)

obstruents	p	t	č	k
	b	d	ǰ	g
	f	[s, ş]	š	
	v	[z, z̧]	ž	
sonorants	m	[n]	ñ	
		[l]	λ	
		[r]		
		r̄		

(Boxed segments shown in brackets.)

As stated earlier, the phonological conditions favoring the /-e/ deletion in the history of both Galician and Spanish were very similar. There is, however, at least one interesting difference between the two. The correspondences in (39) illustrate the constraints imposed on apocope in both languages.

(39)		Latin	Spanish	Galician	
	a.	*MESE*	*mes*	*mes*[26]	'month'
		AD TRANSVERSE	*a través*	*a través*	'through'
		RADICE	*raíz*	*raiz*	'root'
		FEROCE	*feroz*	*feroz*	'ferocious'
	b.	*PANE*	*pan*	*pan*	'bread'
		RATIONE	*razón*	*razón*	'reason'
		MELE	*miel*	*mel*	'honey'
		SALE	*sal*	*sal*	'salt'
		AMORE	*amor*	*amor*	'love'
		DOLORE	*dolor*	*dor*	'pain'
	c.	*VITE*	*vid*	*vide*	'grapevine'
		SITE	*sed*	*sede*	'thirst'
		SALUTE	*salud*	*saúde*	'health'
		CIVITATE	*ciudad*	*cidade*	'town'
		MERCEDE	*merced*	*mercede*	'mercy'
	d.	*FALCE*	*hoz*	*fouce*	'sickle'
		CALCE	*coz*	*couce*	'kick'
		CALICE	*caliz*	*couce*	'chalice'
		FASCE	*haz*	*feixe*	'bundle'
		PISCE	*pez*	*peixe*	'fish'
	e.	*NEVE*	*nieve*	*neve*	'snow'
		PRINCIPE	*príncipe*	*príncipe*	'prince'
		TIMET	*teme*	*teme*	'(s)he fears'
		**BUFE*	*bofe*	*bofe*	'lung'
		**COMBATTE*[27]	*combate*	*combate*	'combat'
		TURRE	*torre*	*torre*	'tower'
		FOLLE	*fuelle*	*fol*	'bellows'
		NOCTE	*noche*	*noite*	'night'
		FUGIT	*huye*	*fuxe*	'(s)he flees'
		AXE	*eje*	*eixe*	'axle'

f.	*SERPE*	*sierpe*	*serpe*	'snake'
	FORTE	*fuerte*	*forte*	'strong'
	SORTE	*suerte*	*sorte*	'luck, fate'
	ISTE	*este*	*iste*	'this one-MASC'
	PESTE	*peste*	*peste*	'plague'
	COMITE	*conde*	*conde*	'count'
	PONTE	*puente*	*ponte*	'bridge'
g.	*UB(E)RE*	*ubre*	*ubre*	'udder'
	DUPLU	*doble*	*doble*	'double'
	LEP(O)RE	*liebre*	*lebre*	'hare'
	SEMPER	*siempre*	*sempre*	'always'
	UT(E)RE	*odre*	*odre*	'wineskin'
	PATRE	*padre*	*pai*	'father'
	ALACRE	*alegre*	*alegre*	'happy

As shown in (39), in both Galician and Spanish apocope took place after a single anterior coronal, whether a fricative obstruent (39a), or a sonorant (39b). The three general contexts in which final /e/ was preserved in both Galician and Spanish are illustrated in (39e-f): (i) after labials, the voiceless dental /t/, the trill /r̄/, and nonanterior coronals (i.e., palatals), as shown in (39e);[28] (ii) after biconsonantal clusters of falling sonority (39f); and (iii) after consonantal sequences of rising sonority, whether primary or derived historically by syncope of a posttonic nonlow vowel (39g). Unlike Spanish, however, Galician did not undergo apocope after /d/ (derived in most cases by voicing of intervocalic /t/), as seen in (39c). Nor was /-e/ lost after a coronal obstruent preceded by a glide (derived by a variety of historical processes), as illustrated in (39d). The preservation of final -e in the latter context can be explained in a straightforward manner, since otherwise apocope would have left a glide-consonant sequence in word-final position, a combination disallowed by general syllable structure conditions on possible codas in Old Galician. In Spanish, on the other hand, the particular historical evolution of the Latin consonant clusters in (39d) yielded conditions perfectly compatible with apocope, and therefore these items regularly underwent the rule (cf. note 28).

Around the 12th century, and due to a variety of sociolinguistic factors (see Lapesa 1951, 1975), the prevailing constraints on apocope in Hispano Romance were relaxed. In Old Spanish, the rule's scope was optionally extended to include certain environments, such as those in (39e) and (39f), which earlier had been exempted from apocope, as illustrated by the Old Spanish forms in (40).[29] In short, apocope now applied after any single consonant, irrespective of point of articulation (40a), and also after consonant clusters of decreasing sonority (40b). This expansion of the apocope rule to a larger set of environments is traditionally known as *extreme apocope*.

(40)

a.	*quiçab* ~ *quiçabe*	'may be'	*call* ~ *calle*	'street'
	princep ~ *princepe*	'prince'	*vall* ~ *valle*	'valley'
	nief ~ *nieve*	'snow'	*noch* ~ *noche*	'night'
	nuef ~ *nueve*	'nine'	*lech* ~ *leche*	'milk'
	deleyt ~ *deleyte*	'pleasure'	*dix* ~ *dixe*	'I said'
	siet ~ *siete*	'seven'	*adux* ~ *aduxe*	'I added'
	torr ~ *torre*	'tower'	*linax* ~ *linaxe*	'lineage'
	lueñ ~ *lueñe*	'afar'	*duc* ~ *duque*	'duke'
b.	*allend* ~ *allende*	'beyond'	*verd* ~ *verde*	'green'
	cond ~ *conde*	'count'	*cort* ~ *corte*	'court'
	infant ~ *infante*	'child'	*muert* ~ *muerte*	'death'
	gent ~ *gente*	'people'	*trist* ~ *triste*	'sad'
	valient ~ *valiente*	'brave'	*huest* ~ *hueste*	'soldier'
	romanz ~ *romanze*	'ballad'	*humilt* ~ *humilde*	'humble'

At this historical point, the apocope process was probably determined in part by phonetic environment: there seems to have been a statistical preference for the rule to apply more often before a vowel-initial word (as in the phrase *delant o detrás* 'in front or behind'), where the final *-t* of *delant* was readily resyllabified as an onset to the following syllable: *de.lan.t o. de.trás* (Harris-Northall 1991: 34).

Some scholars regard extreme apocope as an essentially foreign trait that became a prestigious norm in the speech of the educated elites during the 12 and

13th centuries, adopted either from the contact with the many Gallo-Romance and Catalan settlers who moved to central and western Spain during the 12th and 13th centuries, or from literary works from Gallo-Romance authors who at the time were widely admired and imitated in these areas of Spain. Whether it was also present in the speech of the lower social classes, and, if it did, just how widespread it was in popular speech, still remains a matter of dispute.

Among the extralinguistic factors that played a role in the spread of extreme apocope, geographical location was an important one. The process had become firmly established both in Catalan (Badía Margarit 1951: 169-71), spoken in the easternmost areas of the Iberian Peninsula, and in Gallo-Romance. In both regions, word-final /-e/ and /-o/ were regularly lost. The operation of apocope in Catalan and Gallo-Romance was subject to the familiar universal sonority constraint, requiring that the resulting syllable final cluster be of falling sonority. Naturally, apocope was blocked in these two languages whenever, as a result, a sequence with a rising sonority profile would have been created in word-final position.

In Old Spanish, extreme apocope never reached the status of an obligatory rule. Furthermore, the deletion of final /-e/ was by far more frequent than that of final /-o/; /-a/ was rarely (if ever) apocopated. The spread of extreme apocope gradually diminished from east to west within the Iberian Peninsula (Catalán 1971). Towards the end of the 13th century, extreme apocope becomes rarer in Castilian documents, perhaps with the sole exception of those written in the easternmost regions, presumably because of their close contact with Aragonese and Catalan. Interestingly, the demise of extreme apocope in Castile during the 13th century coincided with the decline of French and Catalan cultural influence (Lapesa 1951). From this point onwards, the occurrence of word-final /-e/ in Old Spanish basically reverted to the stage depicted in (39), namely, it surfaced after consonant clusters, and after single consonants other than /d, s, n, l, r/. Such distribution has largely prevailed until modern times.

In its spread from east to west, extreme apocope must have reached Old Galician towards the end of the 12th century, but it was governed by constraints of a more restrictive type than those prevailing in Old Spanish. To be sure, it targeted almost exclusively word-final /-e/ —rarely /-o/— when preceded by either a single dental stop (quite generally /d/), as in (41a),[30] or by a biconsonantal group of falling sonority, the second member of which was also a dental stop, as in (41b) (García de Diego 1909: 24, 44, Azevedo Maia 1986: 524). Unlike Old Spanish, deletion of final /-e/ in Old Galician did not occur after noncoronals. This suggests that coda position did not license point of articulation features in Old Galician (cf. Goldsmith 1989, 1990).

(41)	OGal.	MGal.	
a.	*sed, set ~ sede*	*sede*	'thirst'
	verdat ~ verdade	*verdade*	'truth'
	abbat ~ abbade	*abade*	'abbot'
	her(e)dat ~ her(e)dade	*herdade*	'inheritance'
	auctoridat ~ auctoridade	*autoridade*	'authority'
b.	*gent ~ gente*	*gente*	'people'
	font ~ fonte	*fonte*	'fountain'
	ferament ~ feramente	*feramente*	'fiercely'
	grand ~ grande	*grande*	'big'
	mort ~ morte	*morte*	'death'
	sort ~ sorte	*sorte*	'luck, fate'

As in Old Spanish, extreme apocope in Old Galician was an optional rule; it is not uncommon to find both the apocopated and unapocopated variants of a given form in the same document (Azevedo Maia 1986: 524).[31] Around the 14th century, the optional deletion illustrated in (41) became rare in Old Galician, coinciding with the decline of Gallo-Romance cultural influence, eventually reaching a point in which the distribution of word-final [-e] in the synchronic grammar essentially reverted to the situation originally found in the 12th century, before the emergence of extreme apocope. Such is roughly the distribution we also find in modern Galician shown in (42); namely, [-e] is generally absent in words ending in a consonant that belongs to the set /s, n, l, r/ (42a), and present in the complementary set of environments: after dentals and /r̄/ (42b), after palatals (42c), after noncoronals (42d), and after biconsonantal (or larger) clusters, whose sonority profile is either falling (42e) or rising (42f) (the relevant grapheme-to-sound correspondences in Galician are as follows: *qu* = [k], *gu* = [g], *x* = [š], *ll* = [ǰ], *ch* = [č], and *z* = [s] or [θ], depending on the dialect):

(42)

a.	*lápis*	*'pencil'*	*b.*	*metade*	'half'
	rapaz	'child'		*vontade*	'will'
	xoven	'young'		*leite*	'milk'
	mel	'honey'		*noite*	'night'
	fol	'belows'		*torre*	'tower'
	fogar	'hearth'		*borre*	'ash'
c.	*feixe*	'bundle'	d.	*ceibe*	'free'
	ferruxe	'rust'		*rape*	'monk fish'
	talle	'bodice'		*lume*	'fire'
	detalle	'detail'		*fame*	'hunger'
	foche(s)	'you were'		*xefe*	'chief'
	escabiche	'marinade'		*desaugue*	'gutter'
	peche	'closing'		*zoque*	'clog'
e.	*(aqu)este*	'this one'	f.	*cadavre*	'corpse'
	(d)onde	'where'		*febre*	'fever'
	fonte	'fountain'		*arbre*	'tree'
	lonxe	'far'		*sempre*	'always'
	sorte	'luck, fate'		*xofre*	'sulfur'
	dengue	'pelerine'		*alpendre*	'stable'
	palanque	'fence'		*milagre*	'miracle'

Having exposed some of the relevant historical details about apocope, I would like to argue that an adequate analysis of the facts in (42) requires a lexical rule of epenthesis, and not one of apocope. I conclude from this that at some historical point in the development of Galician, this language must have undergone a process of rule inversion, whereby the medieval rule of /-e/ deletion was replaced by one of *e*-insertion. In this analysis, then, the underlying shape of a form such as *metade* 'half' in (42b) would be /metad/ and a lexical rule would insert the surface [-e] ([-i] in Moañés).

It should be clear at this point that there are *two* types of final epenthesis in Galician. One is the optional rule of epenthesis discussed in section 1. Words ending in /s, n, l, r/, such as those in (42a), undergo optional epenthesis. On the other hand, if an account of word-final *-e* in (42b-f) in terms of rule inversion is correct, then the final vowel in these forms is to be accounted for by insertion of a second type: obligatory epenthesis.

In addition to the optional vs. obligatory status of these two epenthesis types, they are crucially different in three other respects. First, optional epenthesis must be postlexical, since it is partially conditioned by syntactic factors, as will be shown in the next section. Obligatory epenthesis, on the other hand, is a typical word-level rule. Second, optional epenthesis is constrained by metrical factors, in that it does not apply whenever a marked stress pattern would result, as we have already observed. Although it ultimately eliminates word-final close syllables, the motivation for optional epenthesis is not critically determined by syllable structure. Understandably so; it applies after the set of only consonants that may occupy the coda position in Galician. Stress facts, on the other hand, do not play a role in lexical epenthesis, but syllable well-formedness constraints certainly do. Lexical epenthesis conspires to make sure that all underlying word-final consonants and consonant clusters that are otherwise disallowed in coda position word-finally (namely, those other than the set /s, n, l, r/) are incorporated into syllable structure, as the onset of the new syllable created by the inserted vowel.

In summary, *e*-epenthesis in (42a) is optional, it belongs to the postlexical level, it is metrically conditioned, and it applies in a syntactically-determined prosodic domain: the intonational phrase. Lexical epenthesis is obligatory, it has the morphological word as its domain, and it is invoked in order to enforce syllable structure constraints required in the lexical domain.

It will be useful at this point to review the underlying consonant inventory of modern Galician in note 5, repeated here as (43); where the consonants that are not commonly followed by [-e] are shown inside the box:

(43)

obstruents	p	t	č	k
	b	d	ǰ	g
	f	(θ) s	š	(x)
sonorants	m	n	ñ	
		l		
		r		
		r̄		

Consider now an analysis of the facts in (42) based on the assumption that apocope has remained a synchronic rule in the grammar of Galician since medieval times. According to this hypothesis, all the items in (42) are represented with an underlying word-final /-e/, and then it is apocopated in (42a) by rule (44). Such rule states that [e] is deleted after a coronal anterior consonant which is either a voiceless fricative or a nontense sonorant ([−tense] excludes /r̄/, which can be distinguished from its corresponding flap by virtue of being specified with the feature [+tense]; see Cressey 1978 for Spanish).

(44)

$$e \rightarrow \emptyset \;/\; V \left[\begin{matrix} +\text{cor} \\ +\text{ant} \\ \left\{ \begin{matrix} \begin{bmatrix} -\text{son} \\ +\text{cont} \end{bmatrix} \\ \begin{bmatrix} +\text{son} \\ -\text{tns} \end{bmatrix} \end{matrix} \right\} \end{matrix}\right]_1^1 \;\_\_\_\; \#\#$$

The view that the synchronic grammar of Spanish contains an apocope rule similar (though not identical) to (44) was firmly held among generative Spanish phonologists, especially during the 1960's and 1970's (see Foley 1965, Harris 1969, 1970, Cressey 1978, 1980),[32] although some early dissenting voices suggested that an alternative based on epenthesis provided a more adequate account of the facts in question (Saltarelli 1970, Contreras 1977). Three basic arguments were forwarded by the supporters of an apocope rule in Modern Spanish. The first is that by positing an underlying final /-e/ in items such as those in (42a) greater formal simplicity would be achieved in the statement of the plural allomorphy. Much as in Galician, the most common plural allomorphs in Modern Spanish are {-s} (45a), {-es} (45b-c), and {∅} (zero) (45d). The overwhelming majority of Spanish words belong to the paradigms in (45a-b).

(45)	a.	sing.	plur.	
		casa	*casas*	'house'
		gata	*gatas*	'cat-FEM'
		libro	*libros*	'book'
		gato	*gatos*	'cat-MASC'

b.	sing.	plur.	
	pan	*panes*	'bread'
	mar	*mares*	'sea'
	mes	*meses*	'month'
	papel	*papeles*	'paper'
	nariz	*narices*	'nose'
	ciudad	*ciudades*	'city'
c.	*parte*	*partes*	'part'
	bote	*botes*	'boat/bounce'
	grande	*papeles*	'big'
	sobre	*sobres*	'envelope'
d.	*lunes*	*lunes*	'Monday'
	tesis	*tesis*	'thesis'
	análisis	*análisis*	'analysis'
	parálisis	*parálisis*	'paralysis'

Assuming that words in (45b-c) end in /-e/ in underlying forms, then we would have the derivations in (46), representative of the plural surface forms of the items in (45) (the relevant morpheme boundaries in (46) are indicated by a hyphen; both the singular and plural forms of a consonant-final word, such as *pan*, are given for expository purposes; the degemination of two identical consonants in the derivation of *lunes* can be easily motivated by independent principles in Spanish):

(46)

	UR's:	/kasa-s/	/pane/	/pane-s/	/parte-s/	/lunes-s/
1)	*Stress*:	kása-s	páne	páne-s	párte-s	lúnes-s
2)	*Apocope*:	—	pán	—	—	
3)	*Degemination*:	—	—	—	—	lúnes
	Output:	kásas	pán	pánes	pártes	lunes

An extrinsic ordering of the stress rule before the apocope rule, as done in (46), is critical for the second argument adduced in favor of the apocope análisis; namely, that the postulation of an underlying final /-e/ simplifies the statement of stress assignment. In Spanish, unmarked stress falls on the penult in vowel-ending words, and on the final syllable in consonant-final words. Both antepenultimate stress in vowel-final words (*cálido* 'warm', *teléfono* 'telephone', etc.), and penultimate stress in consonant-final words (*útil* 'useful', *azúcar* 'sugar', etc.) are exceptional. If stress assignment precedes apocope in the derivation, as in (46), then surface consonant-final words such as *papel* would actually be vowel-final (/papele/) at the point in which stress is assigned, thus matching the paroxytonic pattern of vowel-final words (cf. (45a)). Likewise, consonant-final forms marked with penultimate stress such as *útil*, would actually be proparoxytones for stress purposes, since when stress applies the final vowel is still present (/utile/), making them formally identical to vowel-final words with antepenultimate stress, such as *cálido*. In short, by positing an underlying final /-e/ in consonant-final forms, the argument goes, the vast majority of Spanish words fall into two general stress patterns: penultimate stress, the unmarked type, and antepenultimate stress, the marked one.

The problem with such approach is that there is no reason to suppose that stress formally interacts with apocope in any obvious way. Yet the analysis in (46) requires that stress be crucially ordered before apocope, otherwise no simplification would be gained in the formulation of stress assignment. In short, the apocope hypothesis claims trochaic stress for consonant-final words, even though such pattern never appears in surface forms. A further —and seemingly undesirable— consequence of an apocope analysis would be the implicit claim that Spanish is not sensitive to syllable weight, since evidence for weight sensitivity derives almost exclusively from consonant final oxytones, and all such items would contain a trochaic foot at the relevant point in the derivation in which stress is assigned.

A third argument invoked in favor of apocope in Spanish involves the rule of *velar softening*, which turns stem-final underlying /k/ into [θ] ([s] in American Spanish) and /g/ into [x] (through an intermediate stage [š]) when followed by a front vowel /i, e/ in the following suffix, as illustrated in (47).

(47)	a.	*ápi*[θ]*-e*	'tip, apex'	*api*[k]*-al*	'apical'
		de[θ]*-ena*	'group of ten'	*dé*[k]*-ada*	'decade'
		sedu[θ]*-ir*	'to sedduce'	*sedu*[k]*-ción*	'seduction'
		medi[θ]*-ina*	'medicine'	*médi*[k]*-o*	'doctor'

b.	*cónyu*[x]-*e*	'spouse'	*conyu*[γ]-al	'conjugal'
	Bel[x]-*ica*	'Belgium'	*bel*[γ]-*a*	'belgian'
	prote[x]-*er*	'to protect'	*prote*[k]-*tor*	'protector'
	diri[x]-*ir*	'to direct'	*dire*[k]-*tor*	'director'

There are a number of lexical items, however, which appear to undergo some sort of velar softening in spite of the fact that the stem is not followed by a front vowel in surface forms, as shown in (48).

(48)	a.	*vo*[θ]	'voice'	*vo*[k]-*al*	'vocal'
		cervi[θ]	'cervix'	*cervi*[k]-*al*	'cervical'
	b.	*perdi*[θ]	'partridge'	*perdi*[γ]-*ón*	'pellet'
		nari[θ]	'nose'	*nari*[γ]-*udo*	'large-nosed'

According to the apocope account, the presence of velar softening in words in the first column in (48) is straightforward given the assumption that the base morpheme is followed by /-e/ in underlying forms. Clearly, then, the postulation of the underlying final /-e/, coupled with extrinsic ordering, will ensure that velar softening takes a *free ride* on items such as those in (48). The derivations of the items *apice* 'apex (/apik-e/), tip' and *voz* 'voice' (/bok-e/), shown in (49), would be almost identical, except that *apice* would have to be lexically marked as an exception to apocope:

(49)	*UR's*:	/apik-e/	/bok-e/
1)	*Stress*:	ápik-e	bók-e
2)	*Velar softening*:	ápiθe	bóθe
3)	*Apocope*:	—	bóθ
	Output:	ápiθe	bóθ

There are several problems with the velar softening argument. First, for many speakers the semantic relatedness of some of the pairs such as those in (47)-(48) is anything but obvious, and thus such alternations appear to be better handled by means of allomorphy rules or via rules (see Hooper 1976). Second, if the change of a velar stop /k/ into an interdental [θ] can (metaphorically) be described as *softening*, the alternation between a voiced velar stop /g/ (realized as the spirant [γ]) and the voiceless velar counterpart [x] in (47b) can hardly be characterized in the same way. Indeed, there is some serious questions as to whether they constitute manifestations of the same phonological process. Related to this issue is a third objection. Notice that unlike (47), in (48) both [k] and [γ] alternate with [θ]. If the relevant items in (48b) have in fact undergone the same formal process as those in (47b), it is not immediately clear why the result of applying such process to /g/ should result in [θ] in the former, but [x] in the latter. Finally, the existence of pairs such as those in (50) pose a serious challenge to the analysis embodied in (49). The final *e's* in these items do not trigger velar softening; yet there is simply no reason —whether morphological, phonological, or otherwise— to suspect that they are any different from those in (47), which do trigger such rule.

(50)	a.	*enfo*[[k]-*e*	'focus'	*fo*[k]-*al*	'focal'
		to[k]-e	'touch'	*to*[k]-*ar*	'to touch'
		true[k]-e	'exchange'	*tro*[k]-*ar*	'to exchange'
		estan[k]-*e*	'pool, pond'	*estan*[k]-*ado*	'stagnant'
	b.	*plie*[γ]-*e*	'fold'	*ple*[γ]-*ar*	'to fold'
		despe[γ]-*e*	'take off'	*despe*[γ]-*ar*	'to take off'
		li[γ]-*e*	'date'[33]	*li*[γ]-*ón*	'womanizer'
		meren[g]-*e*	'meringe'	*meren*[γ]-*ado*	'whipped (milk)'

Evidently, then, data such as (50) would have to be viewed as lexical exceptions to velar softening. In sum, the apocope hypothesis is manifestly at odds with the empirical fact that the velars preceding word-final /-e/ in (50) do not undergo softening.

Next, let us consider briefly the essence of the first two arguments for positing underlying /-e/ on the claim that an apocope account results in simplification of plural allomorphy and stress assignment.

From the perspective of recent metrical theories, an apocope analysis clearly does not provide a formally simpler account of stress in consonant-final words.[34] For example, given the assumption that primary stress in Spanish is built on a moraic trochee laid on the right edge of a word (Dunlap 1991), as suggested earlier for Galician, it would be completely indifferent whether an item such as *papel* 'paper' contains an underlying final vowel (/papele/), as claimed by the apocope hypothesis, or whether such vowel is absent from underlying forms (/papel/), as in an non-apocope account: the algorithm (21) will invariably assign lexical stress to the appropriate vowel in such items, as shown in (51) (where, as earlier, step (i) reflects morification, and step (ii) foot construction; of course, the output of foot construction in (51a) would subsequently be subject to apocope, yielding [papél], as desired):

(51) a.

```
                                         F
                                         |\
                  μ  μ μ            μ   μ μ
         (i)      |  | |    (ii)    |   | |
/papele/  →     p a p e l e   →    p a p é l e
```

b.

```
                                         F
                                         |\
                  μ  μ μ            μ   μ μ
         (i)      |  | |    (ii)    |   | |
/papel/   →     p a p e  l    →    p a p é  l
```

As for the claim that apocope simplifies the statement of plural allomorphy, it can be shown that an alternative in terms of epenthesis provides an equally simple formal characterization of plural formation in Spanish, and so the point about simplicity clearly becomes a moot one. To illustrate this, consider the account of Spanish noun and adjective plurals proposed in Harris (1980, 1985b, 1991b), which I have briefly introduced earlier. Following Harris, I assume that Spanish plural formation is constrained by three basic principles, which I state in a slightly modified form in (52) (the reader will recall that clause (52a) has already been introduced earlier in (34)).

(52) a. $[[\ \ldots\ ]_{\text{Stem}}\ \text{V C}]_{\alpha}$ (where α = Noun or Adjective)

b. [+plural] → [s]

c. In noun and adjective plurals, associate the segment [s] with the rightmost C position in the prosodic template.

In general, the template's V-slot in (52a) correlates with grammatical gender. When the prosodic units of the VC template are realized in surface forms, they are variably known as *word-markers* (Harris 1985b, 1991b), *terminal elements* (Harris 1983, Crowhurst 1992a), or simply *desinences* (Roca 1989). Word marker realization, a lexical redundancy rule already discussed, provides phonetic substance to the gender morpheme: [a] for the feminine, and [o] for the masculine (see Harris 1991b: 44-45). Rule (52a) states that the canonical (unmarked) morphological shape of Spanish words must satisfy a prosodic well-formedeness constraint, requiring that a VC template —which we may call the *word-marker template*— be placed on the right of the stem, in the outermost layer of morphological structure, as shown in (52a).[35] In singular forms, the C-slot of the word-marker template remains unassociated to any segmental material; therefore, it will be stray-erased, and thus will not be realized in surface structure. However, it does acquire phonetic content in the plural. First, the redundancy rule (52b) spells out the morphological feature [+plural] as [s]. And second, the plural word marker [s] inserted by (52b) associates to the available C slot in the lexical template by (52c). The principles in (52) can be better illustrated with some representative examples (most of them from (45) above, repeated here under (53)). Each item in (53) is shown with its relevant morphological structure, including its corresponding word-marker(s) (note that in underived words, such as those in (53), the stem coincides with the actual root).

(53)		singular		plural		
	a.	*libro*	[[libr]o]	*libros*	[[libr]os]	'book'
	b.	*cruce*	[[cruc]e]	*cruces*	[[cruc]es]	'crossing'
	c.	*pan*	[[pan]∅]	*panes*	[[pan]∅ s]	'bread'
	d.	*parte*	[[part]∅]	*partes*	[[part]∅ s]	'part'
	e.	*lunes*	[[lun]es]	*lunes*	[[lun]es]	'monday'

The form in (53a) represents the default morphological word shape. The remaining words in (53) exhibit some sort of idiosyncratic behavior with respect to the canonical shape. In (53b), the word-final *-e* is contained in the underlying form, and thus it will associate to the V-slot provided by the word-marker template; unlike *libro*, however, gender realization will fail to apply to *cruce* since the final vowel is already specified in the lexical entry, and lexical redundancy rules such as marker realization, cannot act in a feature-changing manner. Forms in (53c-d), on the other hand, bear a diacritic that marks them as exceptions to the word-marker realization rules; whenever present, the surface word-marker [-e] in these items is always the result of lexical (obligatory) epenthesis. Finally, (53e) comprises a small number of lexical items in which both word-marker positions in the template have already been occupied in underlying representations. These considerations are summarized in the following typical derivations of the items in (53):

(54)

```
a.  C V C C V      (i)   C V C C V   C     (ii)   C V C C V  C
    | | | | |       →    | | | | |   |      →     | | | | |  |
   [[l i b r] o]        [[l i b r] o + s]        [[l i b r] o + s]

b.  C C V C V      (i)   C C V C V   C     (ii)   C V C C V  C
    | | | | |       →    | | | | |   |      →     | | | | |  |
   [[c r u c] e ]       [[c r u c] e + s]        [[c r u c] e + s]

c.  C V C          (i)   C V C V C         (ii)   C V C V C
    | | |           →    | | |   |          →     | | | | |
   [[p a n]   ]         [[p a n]  + s]           [[p a n] e + s]

d.  C V C C        (i)   C V C C V C       (ii)   C V C C V  C
    | | | |         →    | | | |   |        →     | | | | |  |
   [[p a r t]   ]       [[p a r t]  + s]         [[p a r t] e + s]

e.  C V C V C      (i)   C V C V C         (ii)   C V C  V C
    | | | | |       →    | | | | |\         →     | | |  | |
   [[l u n] e  s]       [[l u n] e  s + s ]      [[l u n] e  s]
```

Step (i) in all the examples in (54) subsumes the satisfaction of the principles stated in (52), including plural formation and gender marker realization (whenever applicable). Step (ii) reflects the operation of epenthesis where relevant (i.e., cases (54 c-d)). The linking by (54b) of the last [s] (the segmental exponent of the plural) to the C-slot position of the word-marker template in (54e) yields two identical segmental matrices associated with one C-slot, a configuration which is formally nondistinct to one segmental matrix liked to one C-slot, and so the former representation is converted to the latter by universal convention (see Harris 1980: 19).

The upshot of the analysis in (52)-(54) is that there is no need for variable plural exponence in an epenthesis type of account, since the plural morpheme is consistently /-s/. Since the facts about plural formation and stress in Galician are, in all the relevant details, identical to those found in Spanish, such considerations can be extended to the former in arguing against apocope.

To recapitulate, I have pointed out several objections that can be raised against apocope, and suggested that its epenthesis counterpart enjoys equal advantages in terms of formal simplicity. But so far, little evidence has been provided for a rule of word-final epenthesis. Indeed, it can be argued that the latter alternative is not only formally simpler than its competitor; in addition it can be solidly motivated on independent grounds in both Spanish and Galician.

Consider the range of cases that have been linked to lexical epenthesis in Spanish (cf. Harris 1980, 1985a, 1987), summarized in (55). Here, epenthesis ensures compliance with two quite distinct, but equally basic, constraints in Spanish. We have already discussed the first one: the epenthetic vowel provides the default segmental content to the vocalic position in the canonical word-marker template (52a). The second is of a purely prosodic nature: in all four different types of epenthesis illustrated in (55), the function of the inserted [e] (shown in bold, for clarity) is to provide a syllabic support to otherwise unsyllabifiable consonants, thus ensuring that they will survive in phonetic representations.[36]

(55)

	Latin	Spanish		English	Spanish
a.	*SPONGIA*	***e**sponja*	'sponge'	*spray*	***e**sprey*
	STELLA	***e**strella*	'star'	*standard*	***e**stándar*
	SPHERA	***e**sfera*	'sphere	*stress*	***e**strés*
	SCHOLA	***e**scuela*	'school'	*ski*	***e**squí*

b.	*in+spirar*	'to breathe in'	vs.	*espirar*	'to breath out'
	in+scribir	'to enroll'	vs.	*escribir*	'to write'
	hemi+sferio	'hemisphere'	vs.	*esfera*	'sphere'
	yugo+slavo	'Yugoslav'	vs.	*eslavo*	'Slav(ic)'
	de+slabonar	'to unlink'	vs.	*eslabón*	'link'
	con+streñir	'to oppress'	vs.	*estreñir*	'to constipate'
	pre+scindir	'to do without'	vs.	*escindir*	'to split, divide'

c.	*fratr+icida*	'fratricide'	vs.	*frater+nal*	'fraternal'
	piedr+a	'stone'	vs.	*peder+nal*	'flint'
	abr+ir	'to open'	vs.	*aber+tura*	'opening'
	cubr+ir	'to cover'	vs.	*cober+tura*	'cover'
	libr+e	'free'	vs.	*liber+tad*	'freedom'
	sacr+o	'holy'	vs.	*sacer+dote*	'priest'

d.	sing.	plur.			sing.	plur.	
	mar	*mares*	*'sea'*	*vs.*	*mora*	*moras*	'mulberry'
	sol	*soles*	*'honey'*	*vs.*	*sola*	*solas*	'alone-FEM'
	pan	*panes*	*'bread'*	*vs.*	*pana*	*panas*	'corduroy'
	mes	*meses*	*'month'*	*vs.*	*mesa*	*mesas*	'table'
	red	*redes*	*'net'*	*vs.*	*rueda*	*ruedas*	'wheel'

In the transition from Latin to Spanish, and quite generally to all other Western Romance languages, the vowel [e-] was epenthesized initially in words beginning with /s/ plus consonant, as shown by the correspondences in (55a). The adaptation of lexical items recently borrowed from English, with an analogous word-initial /#sC-/ sequence, indicates that the rule has remained productive. In (55b) word-initial [e] alternates with [∅] when a prefix is added to the right of the stem. In (55c) the same alternation obtains when a root-final /r/ is preceded and followed by a consonant. Finally, the left columns in (55d) illustrate the [∅] ~ [e] alternation found in singular/plural forms discussed earlier. A proponent of epenthesis would argue that the rule is needed independently in order to account for the alternating forms in (55).

I will not address here the issue of whether the most adequate mechanism to represent vowel epenthesis consists of syllable-building rules (as in Harris 1983, 1989a, 1989b, Hualde 1991a) or a template-matching procedure coupled with directionality (Itô 1989, Crowhurst 1992). Clearly, there must be some principle in Spanish ensuring that [e] is inserted to rescue phonological segments that otherwise cannot be incorporated into syllable structure. It is only with the assumption of such principle that an uniform account of the [∅] ~ [e] alternations in (55) can be provided. In an apocope analysis, on the other hand, the systematic relationship between the word-final [-e] in (45c) and the epenthesis processes illustrated in (55) no longer exists, and a linguistically significant generalization would inevitably be missed.

Let us suppose at this point for expository convenience that the formal principles assumed to be at work in lexical epenthesis are syllable-building rules of the type proposed in Harris (1983, 1989a, 1989b) and Hualde (1991a). I further assume with Harris (1985a, 1987) that insertion of [-e] at the lexical level involves the two operations in (56). The first step consists in the insertion word-finally of a vocalic mora, represented by an X-slot associated to the feature [–consonantal, as in (56a). In a subsequent step, this mora is assigned the features of [e] by a default rule of Spanish (56b) (the circled X-slot represents a prosodic position unaffiliated to syllable structure):

(56) a.

$$\begin{array}{ccccccc} \emptyset & \rightarrow & X & / & \textcircled{X} & \underline{\quad\quad} &]_{\omega} \\ & & | & & | & & \\ & & [-\text{cons}] & & [+\text{cons}] & & \end{array}$$

b.

$$\begin{array}{ccc} X & \rightarrow & X \\ | & & | \\ [-\text{cons}] & & [\text{e}] \end{array}$$

The syllabification rules of Spanish are given in (57):

(57) a. *Nucleus assignment and syllable projection*:
Assign a nucleus (N) node to segments specified as [–cons]. Project N′ (rhyme) and N″ (syllable).

b. *Onset formation*:
Attach a prenuclear [+consonantal] segment to the N″ node. A second consonant may be incorporated under certain conditions.

c. *Coda adjunction*:
Adjoin a postnuclear consonant to the N′ node. /s/ may be adjoined as a second member word-internally.

An illustration of the rules in (57) applying to an item subject to lexical epenthesis is given in (58) for the Spanish word *parte* 'part':

(58) a. *Underlying representation*: /part/

b. *Syllabification rules* (57a-c):

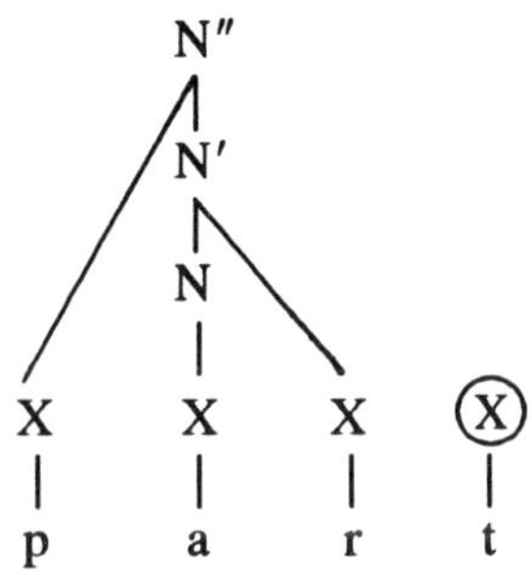

c. *Insertion of a syllabic mora* (56a):

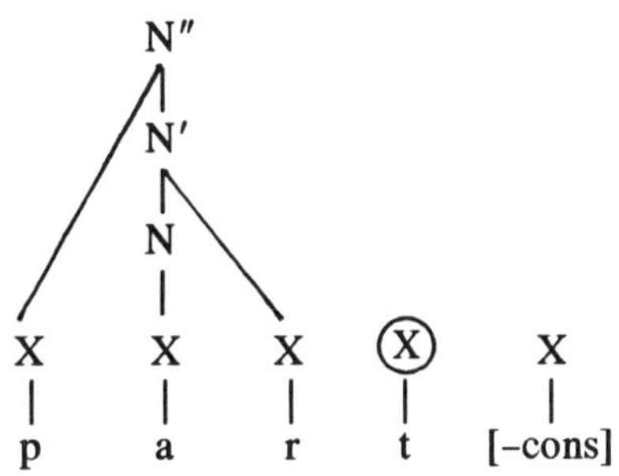

d. *Assignment of default vowel features* (56b):

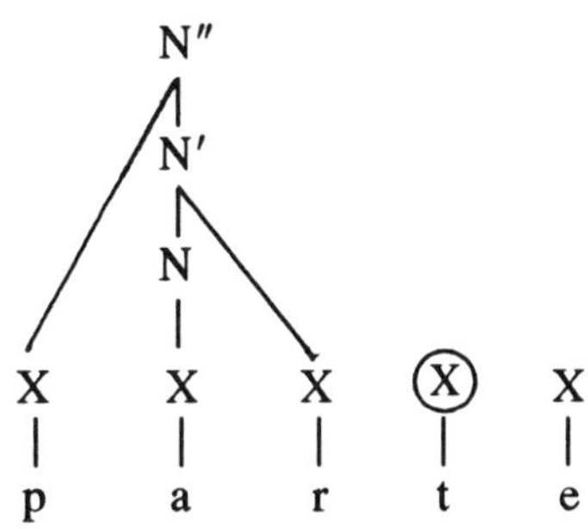

e. *Reapplication of syllabification rules* (57a-b):

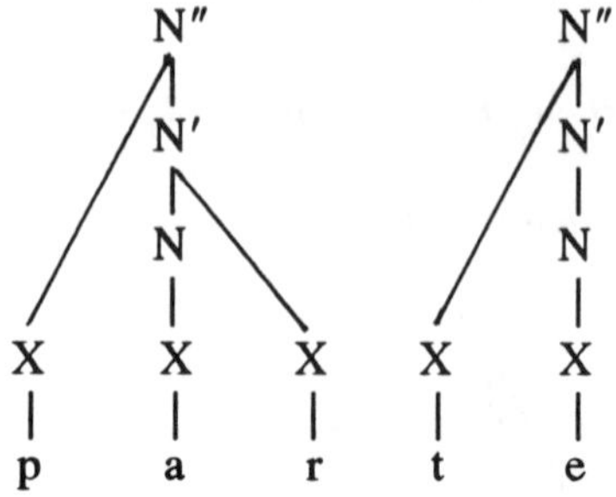

I would like to show now that an analysis in terms of epenthesis is formally simpler than an apocope alternative on another front. I turn to Galician in order to illustrate this point. As usual, very similar considerations would apply to Spanish. A serious problem for an apocope account in Galician is posed by the existence of a sizable number of words, such as those shown in (59), in which the structural description of the apocope rule (44) is met, and yet the final vowel is obligatorily retained in surface forms.

(59)	a. *bule*	'(s)he hastens'	*prefere*	'(s)he prefers'
	repele	'(s)he repels'	*fire*	'(s)he wounds'
	cose	'(s)he sows'	*coce*	'(s)he cooks'
	tose	'(s)he coughs'	*produce*	'(s)he produces'
	b. *fale*	'I speak-SUBJ'	*chore*	'I cry-SUBJ'
	esfole	'I skin-SUBJ'	*more*	'I live-SUBJ'
	pase	'I pass-SUBJ'	*sone*	'I wipe my nose-SUBJ'
	case	'I marry-SUBJ'	*trone*	'it thunders-SUBJ'
	c. *cine*	'cinema'	*crise*	'crisis'
	pene	'penis'	*dose*	'dosis'
	perene	'perennial'	*análise*	'analysis'
	prole	'descendants'	*parálise*	'paralysis'
	mole	'large mass'	*cruce*	'crossing'
	curare	'curare'	*doce*	'twelve'
	folclore	'floklore'	*trece*	'thirteen'
	envase	'container'	*enlace*	'link'
	base	'basis'	*apéndice*	'appendix'

The two classes in (59a-b) are essentially open-ended. They comprise the vast majority of verb forms whose root ends in /s, n, l, r/. The [-e] is retained in both the third person singular of the present indicative (59a) and the first and third person singular of the present subjunctive (59b). Indeed, final [-e] is preserved in most such verb forms, irrespective of the nature and number of the preceding consonant(s).[37] As a consequence, an apocope analysis would require the additional complexity that the rule be made sensitive to nonphonological information, so that it applies only to nonverb forms. But this move still does not render apocope regular, since nonverb forms such as those in (59c) would have to bear an arbitrary diacritic that marks them as exceptions to apocope. In short, apocope would have to be substantially lexicalized. An epenthesis account has the advantage that none of these difficulties arise, and thus no exceptionality needs to be recorded: all the items in (56) are of the (53b) type, and thus contain a word-final vowel in underlying structure, in contrast with those in (53c-d), which do not.

Selective lexical exceptionality to a given rule creates phonological opacity, in the sense that there are lexical items which do not undergo the rule even though they meet the rule's conditions. It is widely accepted by now that the presence of opaque forms may be a factor in sound change; *ceteris paribus*, language learners will tend to eliminate opacity from surface structure, often by means of a restructuring of underlying forms (Kiparsky 1982). If apocope was in fact a productive rule in Galician, then we would expect that children would make overapplication mistakes, producing apocopated forms such as [fál] instead of *fale* 'I speak-SUBJ' in (59b), *bul* for *bule* '(s)he hastens' (59a), and so on. As far as I have been able to determine, these mistakes are never made by children learning Galician as a first language.

Two additional facts need to be considered in support of lexical epenthesis. One of them is historical. At some point around the end of the 14th century, those speakers of Galician whose grammar contained (albeit optionally) an extreme apocope process had to switch to one in which word-final [-e] appeared obligatorily after a consonant other than /s, n, l, r/. For the next generation of speakers, the empirical justification for postulating an epenthesis rule based on syllable structure at this point is transparent: final [-e] appears whenever a word-final consonant (or consonant cluster) is not licensed by general syllable wellformedness conditions.

The second argument is synchronic. In modern standard Galician, [e] is inserted in foreign loans that end in an unacceptable consonant or consonant group. The examples in (60), most of which have been borrowed from English, are cited in Costa Casas et al. (1988: 42):[38]

(60)	a.	*clube*	'club'	*quiosque*	'kiosk'
		filme	'film'	*cheque*	'check'
		iogurte	'yogurt'	*fraque*	'tuxedo'
		iate	'yacht'	*coque*	'coke (coal)'
		Franforte	'Frankfurt'	*Nova Iorque*	'New York'
		sanduíche	'sandwich'	*Iraque*	'Iraq'

In view of the preceding considerations, it seems unlikely that the synchronic grammar of modern Galician contains a rule of lexical apocope. The facts rather support lexical epenthesis.

To summarize, in this section I have argued that Galician has a lexical rule of final [-e] epenthesis. It has been determined that this rule is obligatory, and that its phonological operation is determined exclusively by phonotactic constraints. In this respect, it differs from the process of optional epenthesis discussed in section 1, in which no syllable structure constraints appear to be at work. Given the fact that Galician had a rule of apocope during the Middle Ages, I conclude that the language has undergone a process of rule inversion, and thus the principles of the synchronic grammar that account for the distribution of word-final [-e] in Galician, (whether obligatory or optional), clearly do not represent a direct continuation of the state of affairs found in early medieval Ibero-Romance. In section 2, a number of arguments have been given in support of the epenthetic nature of this vowel in the synchronic grammar.

The historical sequence of events that leads from Old Galician to the present minimally consists of five basic stages. A brief synopsis of the five historically ordered synchronic grammars is depicted in (61) for the modern Galician words *sol* 'sun' and *fonte* 'fountain' (the effects of mid-vowel raising in Moañés has been factored in for Grammar 5):

(61)	*Underlying forms*:	*Phonetic forms*:
Grammar 1:	/sole/	[sóle]
	/fonte/	[fónte]
Grammar 2:	/sole/	[sóle] and [sól] (by apocope)
	/fonte/	[fónte]
Grammar 3:	/sole/	[sóle] and [sól] (by apocope)
	/fonte/	[fónte] and [fónt] (by (extreme) apocope)
Grammar 4:	/sol/	[sól]
	/font/	[fónte] (by lexical epenthesis)
Grammar 5:	/sol/	[sól] and [sóli] (by optional epenthesis)
	/font/	[fónti] (by lexical epenthesis)

Consider in more detail the scenario suggested in (61). As discussed earlier, towards the end of the 12th century Galician acquired an optional rule deleting final /e/ after the set /s, n, l, r/. We may refer to the grammar of the language before the apocope rule was added as Grammar 1. In a subsequent stage, Grammar 2 contained an optional rule of apocope, would have produced two distinct outputs for the same underlying form, depending on the optional application of such rule. At a subsequent point (Grammar 3), apocope was extended to words in which final [-e] was preceded either by a dental or a cluster of two coronals the second member of which was a dental. Crucially, there was a later stage at which surface forms without the final vowel were interpreted as more basic, the other one being derived by a rule of epenthesis (Grammar 4). Finally, Grammar 5 reflects the situation in modern Galician, where optional [-e] may occur word-finally even after the consonants regularly licensed to occupy the coda position, as indicated in section 1.

Grammars 4 and 5 differ from Grammars 2 and 3 in that they contain a rule of epenthesis instead of a rule of apocope and its lexicon contains consonant-final words such as /sol/. For speakers with Grammars 4 and 5, underlying forms contain a final consonant. This implies that any rules affecting these consonants could affect the derived vowel-final forms as well. When the language acquired the rules of nasal velarization and /s/-apicalization, these rules spread to the alternants with an epenthetic final vowel from the more basic consonant-final forms. Thus, the difference between Grammars 2 and 3 on the one hand, and Grammars 4 and 5, on the other, becomes apparent. The epenthetic vowel could also be generalized to contexts where it did not belong historically, including the position after the plural morpheme, as witnessed by forms such as *irmans-e*, occurring in present-day Galician (Grammar 5). We may ask what could have caused the reanalysis from Grammar 3 to Grammar 4. A sensible answer could be that for those items presenting an alternation, consonant-final variants had become more frequent than those with final-vowel. One way this could have happened is by a progressive restriction on forms with final /e/ to the phrase-final environment, as we find nowadays.

If the account in (61) is correct, then one may readily conclude that Galician epenthesis represents a case of rule inversion, one which has not received much previous attention, but which in view of the empirical evidence appears particularly compelling.

4 Conclusion

This paper has studied in detail the facts about Galician word-final epenthesis. I have determined, first, that the optional final vowel is not present in underlying forms, but is rather inserted by a rule of epenthesis. As empirical support for this hypothesis, a number of facts were examined related to the interaction of optional epenthesis and two other processes Galician: nasal velarization and /s/-apicalization. Second, it has been suggested that the optional epenthetic vowel can be better viewed as the phonetic manifestation of a catalectic syllable, introduced to satisfy foot binarity at the (postlexical) level of the intonational phrase. And third, I have argued that historically word-final epenthesis, both the lexical and the optional types, constitutes a case of rule inversion, since in an older stage of the language (the Middle Ages) the grammar of Galician contained a rule of final apocope. Rule inversion initially came about through a process of reanalysis involving that postulation of (obligatory) lexical epenthesis in words whose stem ended in a consonant (or sequence of consonants) other than /s, n, l, r/, many of which had originally undergone extreme apocope in the medieval period. As for optional epenthesis we know next to nothing about the precise historical point it emerged in Galician dialects. Nevertheless, by insertion of a final vowel in precisely those words that had initially undergone the non-extreme type of apocope (i.e., those ending in /s, n, l, r/), optional epenthesis can be viewed as generalizing the scope of rule inversion to the vast majority of the Galician lexicon.

Notes

* A preliminary version of this paper was presented, in collaboration with José Ignacio Hualde, at the *Annual Meeting of the American Association of Teachers of Spanish and Portuguese*, held in Cancún, Mexico, in August of 1992, although the present paper bears little resemblance to that initial version. José Ignacio has been instrumental in providing me with valuable insights on several issues discussed in this paper, and I would like to gratefully acknowledge his contribution. I also thank Sonia Colina, Carlos Eduardo Piñeros, and Dale Hartkemeyer for their comments. The responsibility for any errors or misconceptions is exclusively my own. This work was partially funded by a Tinker Foundation Foreign Field Research Travel Grant, awarded by the Latin American Studies Program at the Ohio State University. I dedicate this paper to the memory of my father.

1 For arguments in favor of an epenthesis-based analysis of word-final [-e] in Spanish, see Harris (1985, 1987, 1989a).

2 Moaña's population is about 20.000, and it is located in the Morrazo Peninsula, in the southwest corner of the Galician region, about 30 kilometers north of the Portuguese border. The town stretches for over ten kilometers along the north shores of the Vigo Bay (*Ría de Vigo*), about three nautical miles away from this city by ferry crossing.

3 Optional final epenthesis, traditionally known as *paragoge*, is not exclusive to Galician; it also occurs in certain dialects of European Portuguese (see, for example, Williams 1938: 112, Sá Nogueira 1958: 174-176, Nunes 1969: 73). Sá Nogueira, for example, mentions that in the Algarve region an epenthetic vowel may also be

introduced optional in vowel-final words: *pe* 'foot' may become *pei* (1958: 176). It is my own observation that optional epenthesis also occurs in several areas of the northwestern region of Portugal, roughly from the city of Oporto to the Galician border.

4 Mid vowel raising accounts for alternations such as *v*[é]*nto* 'wind' vs. *v*[i]*ntoada* 'strong wind', *b*[ó]*tas* 'you throw' vs. *b*[u]*tar* 'to throw'.

5 Words are given in standard Galician orthography followed by their corresponding phonetic transcription. For expository convenience, syllable boundaries are indicated with a period for all items. The symbol [ɟ̶] stands for a voiced dorso-palatal fricative obstruent, the spirant allophone of the underlying palatal affricate obstruent /ǰ/; [ʂ] represents the apico-alveolar allophone of /s/ in syllable final position. For completeness, the underlying vowel and consonant inventories of standard Galician are as follows:

(i) *Vowels:*

i			u
e			o
	ɛ	ɔ	
	a		

(ii) *Consonants*:

p	t	č	k
b	d	ǰ	g
f	θ, s	š	
m	n	ñ	
	l		
	r, r̄		

A feature of Moañés shared by other Western Galician varieties is the lack of /θ/; all instances of this phoneme in standard Galician have corresponding /s/ in Moañés. In addition, in this dialect [g] is in complementary distribution with the voiceless velar fricative [x]: in native words, [g] occurs only after nasals; in all other contexts it has been replaced by [x], a sound change that probably took place in some areas of Galicia around the 18th century (see Pensado and Pensado Ruíz 1983).

6 Other Galician varieties appear to present epenthesis also in the case of nonoxytonic consonant-final words (García de Diego 1909: 72, and Carballo Calero 1979: 119. It is not clear to what extent optional epenthesis is allowed in non-oxytones, since both authors give only one (and the same) example: *fácil(e)* 'easy'. Such an insertion of an epenthetic vowel in proparoxytones is disallowed in Moañés Galician.

7 "It is not easy to know whether one is dealing with the conservation of the etymological vowel or with a later paragogic development" [My translation, FMG].

8 The data in (2) reflect a moderately slow speech style. In faster registers, the nasal is actually coarticulated; it bears simultaneously a velar point of articulation and one it assimilates from a following consonant (see Martínez-Gil 1991, 1993).

9 Cf. Trigo Ferre (1988) for languages unrelated to Galician in which velar is also the default point of articulation.

10 Cf. Harris (1989a, 1989b), Hualde (1991a) for more detailed discussion on the application of this theory to syllabification in Spanish.

11 There is but one single exception to this statement, the indeterminate feminine article *unha* 'a, one-FEM' (as well as its derivatives *algunha* 'any-FEM', *nigunha* 'not any-FEM', etc.), which invariably surfaces as [ú.ŋa] (see Martínez-Gil 1991, 1993 for further details).

12 As noted earlier (cf. note 5), some Galician dialects, including the recognized standard, have a distinction between /s/ and /θ/, as in northern Iberian Spanish. In a large area of Galicia, however, there is only one phoneme /s/ corresponding to these two. Moañés belongs to this last group. We have observed already that this dialect presents both [s] and [ʂ], but they occur as simple allophones of a single phoneme /s/.

13 Evidently, the default status of the velar nasal [ŋ] and the apical sibilant [ʂ] in Moañés is at variance with the Trubetzkoy's observation (1969) that the unmarked value emerges whenever some phonological processes results in the neutralization of some underlying contrast.

14 As expected, the final /s/ in the plural forms *meses*, *xueces* in (10b) is apical, since it occurs in syllable-final position.

15 For an analysis of lexical stress in Spanish that appeals to catalexis, see Nouveau (1994).

16 In phonetic forms, this constraint is violated in Spanish in a handful of proparoxytonic (generally, Latin or Greek) loans with a heavy final syllable: *régimen* 'regime', *análisis* 'analysis', *parálisis* 'paralysis', etc. It is interesting to note that in Galician the final consonant in these loans has been deleted, as can be seen in the corresponding items *réxime*, *análise*, *parálise*.

17 Words with oxytonic stress (arguably the most marked type of stress in Galician), such as *mamá* 'mummy', *café 'coffee'*, *dominó 'dominoes'*, etc., could easily be analyzed as being lexically preassociated to a mora. Applied to such forms, morification would result in a vowel sharing two moras (i.e. a long vowel), which would be immediately simplified into a single one by general principle in the language.

18 For clarity, in (29) and in subsequent examples in this section, primary stress is indicated for all the relevant data, whether or not it is registered in conventional spelling.

19 The observation about the failure of the optional epenthetic vowel to undergo desyllabification is made in some standard descriptive studies of Galician (e.g., Carballo Calero 1979: 123).

20 It should be recalled that in most Galician dialects, the sequence /ns/ is allowed as the word-final coda, provided that the /s/ is the plural morpheme.

21 There appears to be an intriguing asymmetry in the directionality of rule inversion which still awaits explanation. The relevant examples examined by Vennemann involve rules of deletion being reanalyzed as insertion. Vennemann himself (1972: 218) admits that he cannot find any examples reflecting the opposite direction, namely, a rule of epenthesis which has been reanalyzed as one of deletion, although it is not immediately obvious why this logical possibility should be ruled out.

22 Most historians have considered Galician and Portuguese as varieties of the same language until around the 14th century. For this reason, they are traditionally referred to as *Galician-Portuguese*. Towards the beginning of the 15th century, Galician and Portuguese already show some noticeable phonological differences (see Carballo Calero 1979, Azevedo Maia 1986, chapters 1 and 3). I use the term *(Old) Galician* to refer to the variety spoken to the north of the Miño river, the modern political boundary between Galicia and Portugal.

23 See Lapesa (1951, 1975), Catalán (1971), Montgomery (1975), Allen (1976), Harris-Northall (1991).

24 The earliest documents available from Old Portuguese were written towards the end of the 12th century. According to Williams (1938: 13) they "mark the historical beginning of Old Portuguese." Among the texts from Galicia and northern Portugal collected by Azevedo Maia (1986), the earliest dates back to half a century later, about the middle of the 13th century.

25 According to Harris-Northall (1992), in Old Spanish the dental affricates /t^s, d^z/ also underwent neutralization in both manner of articulation and voicing when located in coda position, thus becoming the dental fricative [ş], but the distinction was kept in onset position until at least the 15th century.

26 The unapocopated form *messe* is found in Galician medieval poetry (García de Diego 1909: 44).

27 From Latin COMBATTUERE.

28 Due to a variety of historical reasons, certain consonants or consonant clusters in Galician did not develop into palatals, as they did in Spanish (cf. Spanish *fuelle, noche* vs. Galician *fol, noite* in (39e). Conversely, other consonant clusters became palatals in Galician (cf. *peixe, feixe* in (39c)), but not in Spanish.

29 In (40), both the apocopated and unapocopated Old Spanish forms are given. In (40a), *ch* = [č], *x* = [š], and *ll* = [λ].

30 Notice the medieval devoicing of /d/ word-finally was recorded in the spelling of the apocopated forms shown in (41a).

31 Apocope in plural forms whose stem ends in a nasal, such as *pans* (< *panes*) illustrated in (14b) above, occurred around the 15th century (Azevedo Maia 1986: 661). This development bears no relationship to medieval extreme apocope.

32 Harris (1995) has reinstated the idea of an underlying final vowel, but this time, it is specified only as a vowel slot in the prosodic skeleton: the underlying form of *papel*, for example, would be /papel-V/. Clearly, such view would imply the return to some sort of apocope rule.

33 The sense of 'date' for the word *ligue* is, in the popular speech of teenagers in Peninsular Spanish, that of 'a date with a girl'. On the other hand, *ligón* can probably be better glossed as 'a boy that successfully dates a lot of girls'.

34 Within the linear generative framework, Contreras (1977) forcefully argues against the idea that apocope simplifies the analysis of stress assignment in Spanish.

35 The view that nominals must satisfy the prosodic constraint of ending in a VC template is articulated in more detail in Harris (1985b, 1991b). Notice, furthermore, that in stems that end in a consonant (or consonant cluster) which cannot be incorporated to the preceding coda because it would violate syllable structure conditions in Spanish, the V slot in the template effectively acts ensure an optimal syllabification of the segmental content of the stem (see the discussion related to (53) and (54) below).

36 Notice, however, in contrast with (55c), that if the second of two stem-final consonants is an obstruent, when it becomes trapped between two consonants, as the consequence of adding a consonant-initial suffix, it is stray-erased, as shown by the forms in the right column of (i):

(i)	*escul*[p]+*ir*	'to sculpt'	vs.	*escul+tura*	'sculpture'
	absor[β]+*er*	'to absorb'	vs.	*absor+ción*	'absorption'
	mo[β]+*er*	'to move'	vs.	*mo+ción*	'motion'
	un[x]+*ir*	'to anoint'	vs.	*un+ción*	'anointment'
	distin[g]+*ir*	'to distinguish'	vs.	*distin+to*	'distinct'

37 There are three common exceptions to the use of final [-e] as marker of third person singular in verb forms of the present indicative: *pon* '(s)he puts', *ten* '(s)he has', and *ven* '(s)he comes'.

38 By contrast, the Moañés dialect opts for deletion of the final consonant in some of these items: *clu* 'club', *iogúr* 'yogurt', *fra* 'tuxedo', *Franfor* 'Frankfurt', *Nova Ior* 'New York', and so on.

References

Alcina Franch, Juan, and José Manuel Blecua. *Gramática española*. Barcelona: Ariel.

Allen, J. H. D. Jr. 1976. Apocope in Old Spanish. In *Estudios ofrecidos a Emilio Alarcos Llorach*, 1.15-30. Oviedo: Universidad de Oviedo.

Alonso, Dámaso. 1962. *La fragmentación fonética peninsular*. Madrid: Consejo Superior de Investigaciones Científicas.

Alvarez, Rosario, Xosé L. Regueira, and Henrique Monteagudo. 1989. *Gramática galega*, 2nd ed. Vigo, Spain: Galaxia.

Archangeli, Diana. 1984. *Underspecification in Yawelmani Phonology and Morphology*. Doctoral dissertation, MIT.

Archangeli, Diana. 1988. Aspects of underspecification theory. *Phonology* 5.183–207.

Archangeli, Diana, and Douglas Pulleyblank. 1986. *The Content and Structure of Phonological Representations*. Ms., University of Arizona and University of Southern California.

Archangeli, Diana, and Douglas Pulleyblank. 1989. Yoruba vowel harmony. *Linguistic Inquiry* 20.173-217.

Azevedo Maia, Clarinda de. 1986. *História do Galego-Português: Estado linguístico da Galiza e do Noroeste de Portugal desde o século XIII ao século XVI*. Coimbra: Instituto Nacional de Investigação Científica.

Baehr, Rudolf. 1970. *Manual de versificación española*. Madrid: Gredos.

Badía Margarit, Manuel. 1951. *Gramática histórica catalana*. Barcelona: Noguer.

Broselow, Ellen. 1982. On predicting the interaction of stress and epenthesis. *Glossa* 16, 115-132.

Burzio, Luigi. 1994. *Principles of English Stress*. New York: Cambridge University Press.

Carballo Calero, Ricardo. 1979. *Gramática elemental del gallego común*, 7th ed. Vigo, Spain: Galaxia.

Catalán, Diego. 1971. En torno a la estructura silábica del español de ayer y del español de mañana. *Sprache und Gesichte. Festschrift für H. Meier*. München: Fink. (Reprinted in Catalán 1989, 77-104).

Catalán, Diego. 1989. *El español: orígenes de su diversidad*. Madrid: Paraninfo.

Clements, George N. 1990. The role of sonority in core syllabification. In *Papers in Laboratory Phonology I*, ed. John Kingston and Mary Beckman, 283–333. New York: Cambridge University Press.

Contreras, Heles. 1977. Epenthesis and stress assignment in Spanish. *University of Washington Working Papers in Linguistics* 3.9-33.

Costa Casas, Xoán Xosé, María dos Anxos González Refoxo, César Carlos Morán Fraga, and Xoán Carlos Rábade Castiñeira. 1988. *Nova Gramática para a aprendizaxe da língua*. La Coruña, Spain: Vía Láctea.

Cressey, William. W. 1978. *Spanish Phonology and Morphology: A Generative View*. Washington D. C.: Georgetown University Press.

Cressey, William W. 1980. Sobre la abstracción en fonología y ciertos fenómenos del castellano. In *La estructura fónica de la lengua castellana: fonología, morfología, dialectología* ed. Jorge Guitart and Joaquín Roy, 113-137. Barcelona: Anagrama.

Crowhurst, Megan. 1991. *Minimality and Foot structure in Metrical Phonology and Prosodic Morphology*. Doctoral dissertation, University of Arizona (Distributed by Indiana University Linguistics Club, 1992).

Crowhurst, Megan. 1992a. Diminutives and augmentatives in Mexican Spanish: a prosodic analysis. *Phonology* 9.221-253.

Crowhurst, Megan. 1992b. The minimal foot and epenthesis in Sierra Miwok. Ms., University of Texas, Austin.

Dalbor, John. 1980. *Spanish Pronunciation: Theory and Practice* (2nd. ed.). New York: Holt, Rinehart and Winston.

Dunlap, Elaine. 1991. *Issues in the Moraic Structure of Spanish*. Doctoral dissertation, University of Massachusetts at Amherst.

Fernández Rei, Francisco. 1990. *Dialectoloxía da lingua galega*. Vigo, Spain: Edicións Xeráis de Galicia.

Foley, James. 1965. *Spanish Morphology*. Doctoral dissertation, MIT.

García de Diego, Vicente. 1909. *Elementos de gramática histórica gallega*. Burgos: Hijos de Santiago Rodriguez (Reprinted in 1984, as Supplement 23 of *Verba*, Santiago de Compostela: Universidade de Santiago de Compostela.).

Giegerich, Heinz J. 1985. *Metrical Phonology and Phonological Structure: German and English*. New York: Cambridge University Press.

Goldsmith, John. 1989. Autosegmental licensing, inalterability, and harmonic application. In *Papers from CLS 23: Parasession on Autosegmental and Metrical Phonology*, ed. C. Wiltshire, R. Graczyk, and B. Music, 116-133. Chicago: Chicago Linguistic Society.

Goldsmith, John. 1990. *Autosegmental and Metrical Phonology*. Cambridge, Mass.: Blackwell.

Halle, Morris. 1990. Respecting metrical structure. *Natural* Language and Linguistic Theory 8.149-176.

Halle, Morris, and Jean-Roger Vergnaud. 1987. *An Essay on Stress*. Cambridge, Mass.: MIT Press.

Halle, Morris, and Michael Kenstowicz. 1991. The *Free Element Condition* and cyclic versus noncyclic stress. *Linguistic Inquiry* 22.457-501.

Harris, James W. 1980. Non-concatenative morphology and Spanish plurals. *Journal of Linguistic Research* 1.15-31.

Harris, James W. 1983. *Syllable Structure and Stress in Spanish: A Nonlinear Approach*. Cambridge, Massachusetts: MIT Press.

Harris James W. 1984a. Autosegmental phonology, lexical phonology, and Spanish Nasals. In *Language Sound Structure*, ed. Mark Aronoff and Richard T. Oehrle, 67-82. Cambridge, Mass.: MIT Press

Harris, James W. 1984b. Theories of phonological representation and nasal consonants in Spanish. In *Papers from the XIIth Linguistic Symposium on Romance Languages*, ed. Philip Baldi, 153-168. Philadelphia: John Benjamins.

Harris, James W. 1984c. La espirantización en castellano y la representación fonológica autosegmental. *Working Papers in Linguistics* 1.149-167, Universitat Autónoma de Barcelona.

Harris, James W. 1985a. Spanish diphthongization and stress: a paradox resolved. *Phonology Yearbook* 2.31-46.

Harris, James W. 1985b. Spanish word markers. In *Current Issues in Spanish Phonology and Morphology*, ed. Frank H. Nuessel Jr. Bloomington, Indiana: Indiana University Linguistics Club.

Harris, James W. 1987. Epenthesis Processes in Spanish. In *Studies in Romance Languages*, ed. Carol Neidle and Rafael Núñez-Cedeño, 107-122. Dordrecht: Foris.

Harris, James W. 1989a. Sonority and syllabification in Spanish. In *Studies in Romance Linguistics*, ed. Carl Kirschner and Janet DeCesaris, 139–153. Philadelphia: John Benjamins.

Harris, James W. 1989b. Our present understanding of syllable structure in Spanish. In *American Spanish Pronunciation*, ed. Peter C. Bjarkman and Robert M. Hammond, 151–169. Washington D.C.: Georgetown University Press.

Harris, James. 1991a. With respect to metrical constituents in Spanish. *Current studies in Spanish linguistics*, ed. Héctor Campos and Fernando Martínez-Gil, 447-473. Washington D.C.: Georgetown University Press.

Harris, James W. 1991b. The exponence of gender in Spanish. *Linguistic Inquiry* 22.27-62.

Harris, James W. 1991c. The form classes of Spanish substantives. *Yearbook of Morphology*, ed. G. Booij and J. van Marle, 65-88. Boston: Kluwer.

Harris, James. 1992. Spanish stress: the extrametricality issue. Bloomington: Indiana University Linguistics Club.

Harris, James W. 1993. Integrity of prosodic constituents and the domain of syllabification in Spanish and Catalan. In *The View from Building 20*, ed. Kenneth Hale and Samuel J. Keyser, 177–193. Cambridge, Mass.: MIT Press.

Harris, James. 1995. Projection and edge marking in the computation of stress in Spanish. *The Handbook of phonological theory*, ed. John Goldsmith, 867-887. Cambridge, Mass.: Blackwell.

Harris-Northall, Ray. 1991. Apocope in Alfonsine texts: a case study. In *Linguistic Studies in Medieval Spanish*, ed. Thomas Cravens and Ray Harris-Northall, 29-38. Madison, Wisconsin: The Hispanic Seminary of Medieval Studies.

Harris-Northall, Ray. 1992. Devoicing, deaffrication, and word-final *-z* in Medieval Spanish. *Hispanic Linguistics* 4:245-274.

Hayes, Bruce. 1980. *A Metrical Theory of Stress Rules*. Doctoral dissertation, MIT. (Revised version published in 1981 by the Indiana University Linguistics Club).

Hayes, Bruce. 1985. Iambic and trochaic rhythm in stress rules. In *Proceedings of the Berkeley Linguistics Society 11: Parasession on Poetics, Metrics, and Prosody*, ed. M. Niepokuj, M. VanClay, V. Nikiforidou, and D. Jeder, 429-446. Berkeley: Berkeley Linguistics Society.

Hayes, Bruce. 1987. A revised parametric metrical theory. In *Proceedings of NELS 17*, ed. J. McDonough, and B. Plunkett, 274-289. Amherst, Mass.: Graduate Linguistic Student Association.

Hayes, Bruce. 1989. Compensatory lengthening in moraic phonology. *Linguistic Inquiry* 20.253-306.

Hayes, Bruce. 1995. *Metrical Stress Theory: Principles and Case Studies*. Chicago: University of Chicago Press.

Hooper, Joan B. 1976. *An Introduction to Natural Generative Phonology*. New York: Academic Press.

Hualde, José Ignacio. 1991a. On Spanish syllabification. In *Current Studies in Spanish Linguistics*, ed. Héctor Campos and Fernando Martínez-Gil, 475-493. Washington D. C.: Georgetown University Press.

Hualde, José Ignacio. 1991b. Unspecified and unmarked vowels. *Linguistic Inquiry* 22.205-209.

Inkelas, Sharon, and Draga Zec. 1990. *The Phonology-Syntax Connection*. Chicago: The University of Chicago Press.

Inkelas, Sharon, and Draga Zec. 1995. Syntax-phonology interface. In *The Handbook of Phonological Theory*, ed. John Goldsmith, 535-549. Cambridge, Mass.: Blackwell.

Itô, Junko. 1989. A prosodic theory of epenthesis. *Natural Language and Linguistic Theory* 7.217-59.

Kenstowicz, Michael. 1986. Notes on syllable structure in three Arabic dialects. *Revue Québécoise de Linguistique* 16.101-128.

King, Robert. *Historical Linguistics and Generative Grammar*. Englewood Cliffs, New Jersey: Prentice-Hall.

Kiparsky, Paul. 1982. *Explanation in Phonology*. Dordrecht: Foris/

Kiparsky, Paul. 1991. Catalexis. Ms., Stanford University.

Kiparsky, Paul. 1985. Some consequences of lexical lexical phonology. *Phonology Yearbook* 2.85-138.

Ladd, D. Robert. 1986. Intonational phrasing: the case for recursive prosodic structure. *Phonology Yearbook* 3.311-340.

Lapesa, Rafael. 1951. La apócope de la vocal en castellano antiguo: Intento de explicación histórica. *Estudios dedicados a Menéndez Pidal*, II, 185-226. Madrid: Centro Superior de Investigaciones Científicas. (Reprinted in Lapesa 1985, 167-197).

Lapesa, Rafael.1975. De nuevo sobre la apócope vocálica en castellano medieval. *Nueva Revista de Filología Hispánica* 24.13-23. (Reprinted in Lapesa 1985, 198-208).

Lapesa, Rafael. 1985. *Estudios de historia lingüística española*. Madrid: Paraninfo.

Levin, Juliette. 1985. *A Metrical Theory of Syllabicity. Doctoral dissertation, MIT.*

Lipski, John. This volume. Spanish word stress: the interaction of moras and minimality.

Maia, Clarinda de Azevedo. 1986. História do Galego-Português. Coimbra: Instituto Nacional de Investigação Científica.

Martínez-Gil, Fernando. 1991. The insert/delete parameter, redundancy rules, and neutralization processes in Spanish. In *Current Studies in Spanish Linguistics*, ed. Héctor Campos and Fernando Martínez-Gil, 495-571. Washington D. C.: Georgetown University Press.

Martínez-Gil, Fernando. 1993. Galician nasal velarization as a case against structure preservation. In *Proceedings of Berkeley Linguistics Society 19*, ed. Josua S. Guenter, Barbara A. Kaiser, and Cheryl C. Zoll, 254-267. Berkeley: Berkeley Linguistics Society.

McCarthy, John, and Alan Prince. 1986. *Prosodic Morphology*. Ms., University of Massachusetts and Brandeis University.

McCarthy, John, and Alan S. Prince. 1993. *Prosodic Phonology 1: Constraint Interaction and Satisfaction*. Ms., University of Massachusetts at Amherst, and Rutgers University.

McCarthy, John, and Alan S. Prince. 1995. Faithfulness and reduplicative identity. In *Papers in Optimality Theory* (University of Massachusetts Occasional Papers 18), ed. Jill Beckman, Laura Walsh Dickey, and Suzanne Urbanczyk, 225-384. Amherst, Mass.: University of Massachusetts Graduate Linguistic Student Association.

Menéndez Pidal, Ramón. 1962. *El dialecto leonés*. Oviedo: Diputación de Oviedo.

Michelson, Karin. 1981. Stress, epenthesis, and syllable Structure in Mohawk. In *Harvard Studies in Phonology*, 2.311-353, ed. G. N. Clements. Bloomington, Indiana: Indiana University Linguistics Club.

Michelson, Karin. 1988. *A Comparative Study of Lake-Iroquoian Accent*. Boston: Kluwer.

Montgomery, Thomas. 1975. La apócope en español antiguo y la 'ī' final latina. *Studia Hispanica in Honorem R. Lapesa* 3.351-362. Madrid: Gredos.

Navarro Tomás, Tomás. 1948. *Manual de entonación española*. New York: Hispanic Institute.

Navarro Tomás, Tomás. 1956. *Métrica español*. Syracuse, N. Y.: Syracuse University Press.

Navarro Tomás, Tomás. 1966. *Estudios de fonología española*. New York: Las Américas Printing Company.

Navarro Tomás. Tomás. 1977. *Manual de pronunciación española*, 19th ed.. Madrid: Consejo Superior de Investigaciones Científicas.

Nespor, Marina, and Irene Vogel. 1986. *Prosodic Phonology*. Dordrecht: Foris.

Nouveau, Dominique. 1994. Catalexis in word stress: evidence from Spanish and Dutch. In *Proceedings of the Thwelfth est Coast Conference on Formal Linguistics*, ed. Erin Duncan, Donca Farkas, and Philip Spaelti, 51-66. Stanford, California: Center for the Study of Language and Information.

Nunes, José Joaquim. *Compêndio de gramática histórica portuguesa*, 7th. ed. Lisboa: Livraria Clásica Editora.

Paradis, Carole. 1988a. On constraints and repair strategies. *The Linguistic Review* 6.71-97.

Paradis, Carole. 1988b. Towards a theory of constraint violations. *McGill Working Papers in Linguistics* 5.1-44.

Paradis, Carole. 1993. Ill-formedness in the dictionary: a source of constraint violation. *Canadian Journal of Linguistcs/Revue Canadienne de Linguistique* 38.215-234.

Paradis, Carole, and Darlene LaCharité. 1993. *Constraint-based Theories in Multilinear Phonology*. Special issue, *Canadian Journal of Linguistcs/Revue Canadienne de Linguistique* 39.

Pensado, José L. and Carmen Pensado Ruíz. 1983. *'Gueada' y 'geada' gallegas*. Supplement 21 of *Verba*. Santiago de Compostela: Universidade de Santiago de Compostela.

Pitau, Massimo. 1972. *Gramatica del sardo-nuorese*. Bologna: Pàtron.

Prince, Alan, and Paul Smolensky. 1993. *Optimality Theory: Constraint Interaction in Generative Grammar*. Ms., Rutgers University, New Brunswick, and University of Colorado, Boulder.

Quilis, Antonio. 1973. *Métrica española*. Madrid: Alcalá.

Rice, Keren. 1987. On Defining the intonational phrase: evidence from Slave. *Phonology Yearbook* 4.37-59.

Real Academia Española. 1982. *Esbozo de una nueva gramtica de la lengua espaola*. Madrid: Espasa Calpe

Roca, Iggy. 1986. Secondary stress and metrical rhythm. *Phonology Yearbook* 3.341-370.

Roca, Iggy. 1989. The organization of grammatical gender. *Transactions of the Philological Society* 87.1-32.

Roca, Iggy. 1991. Stress and syllables in Spanish. *Current studies in Spanish linguistics*, ed. Héctor Campos and Fernando Martínez-Gil, 599-635. Washington: Georgetown University Press.

Roca, Iggy. 1992. Constraining extrametricality. *Phonologica 1988*, ed. Wolfgang U. Dressler, H. C. Luschutzky, O. E. Pfeiffer, and J. R. Rennison, 239-248. New York: Cambridge University Press.

Roca, Iggy. This volume. On the role of accent in stress systems: Spanish evidence.

Rodríguez Castellano, Lorenzo. 1954. *Aspectos del bable occidental*. Oviedo: Instituto de Estudios Asturianos.

Rosenthall, Sam. 1994. *Vowel/Glide Alternation in a Theory of Constraint Interaction.* Doctoral dissertation, University of Massachusetts at Amherst.

Sá Nogueira, Rodrigo de. 1958. *Tentativa de explicação dos fenómenos fonéticos em português*, 2nd. ed. Lisboa: Livraria Clásica Editora.

Saltarelli, Mario. 1970. Spanish plural formation: apocope or epentehsis? *Language* 48.89-96.

Saltarelli, Mario. This volume. Stress in Spanish and Latin: where phonology meets prosody.

Selkirk, Elisabeth O. 1984. *Phonology and Syntax: The Relation Between Sound and Structure*. Cambridge, Mass.: MIT Press.

Selkirk, Elisabeth O. 1995. Sentence prosody: intonation, stress, and phrasing. In *The Handbook of Phonological Theory*, ed. John Goldsmith, 550-569. Cambridge, Mass.: Blackwell.

Steriade, Donca. 1995. Underspecification and markedness. In *The Handbook of Phonological Theory*, ed. John Goldsmith, 114-174. Cambridge, Mass.: Blackwell.

Trigo Ferre, Rosario L. 1988. *On the Phonological Derivation and Behavior of Nasal Glides*. Doctoral dissertation, MIT.

Trubetzkoy, N. S. 1969. *Principles of Phonology* Berkeley: University of California Press.

Vennemann, Theo. 1972. Rule inversion. *Lingua* 29.209-242.

Veiga Arias, Amable. 1976. *Fonología gallega.* Valencia: Editorial Bello.

Williams, Edwin. 1938. *From Latin to Portuguese*. Philadelphia: University of Pennsylvania Press.

Zec, Draga. 1988. *Sonority Constraints on Prosodic Structure*. Doctoral dissertation, Stanford University. (Published by Garland, New York, 1994).

IV Portuguese

10

Some remarks about stress in Portuguese

ERNESTO D'ANDRADE

1. Introduction

During the past forty years, many important aspects of Portuguese phonology have been investigated from the perspective of different theoretical frameworks. Research on vowels includes studies on neutralization, epenthesis, harmony in the nominal and verbal systems, sandhi phenomena, diphthongization, reduction, deletion, and nasalization. Work on glides has been done regarding nasalization, glide/vowel and glide/obstruent alternations. In the area of consonants, there has been investigation into liquid velarization and vocalization, nasal assimilation and deletion, velar softening, dental stop assibilation, spirantization of voiced obstruents, aspiration of /s/ (in Brazil), and distribution and realization of /r/ (mainly in Brazil). The following represent other areas of research: word stress (primary, secondary, and echo stresses), syllable types and structure, phrasal stress (and destressing), cliticization, word compounding phenomena, and morphophonology of evaluative (diminutive and augmentative) suffixes.[1]

Word stress, the focus of this paper, is probably the only topic that has been systematically studied from all perspectives by grammarians, philologists, and linguists, since the 16th century.

The present paper will first present stress in general and its status in linguistic theory. Then the history of studies on stress will be reviewed. Taking the 1970s as a point of departure, a summary of stress studies in Brazil and Portugal will be presented. Finally, Brazilian and European Portuguese will be contrasted.

2. Stress in phonological theory

The analysis of stress in the SPE framework became widely accepted, among other reasons, because in most cases the distribution of stressed and unstressed syllables could be described by a small set of rather simple rules. Nevertheless, to consider stress, [± stress], identical to other distinctive features was to take it as a property of all segments (including stops and fricatives, for example). However, stress has properties that distinguish it from other features. It has no invariant phonetic indices. Sometimes, increased duration of the stressed syllable or vowel enhances the perception of stress; other times, it is reflected by the reduction of a vowel. In other instances native speakers' judgments and perceptions are essential. In addition to the lack of precise and uniform phonetic correlates, stress also differs from other features: (i) by the fact that, in many languages, it requires discriminations beyond the binary level, while phonological rules only allow for two values [+] and [-]; (ii) by its distance effects, since in many languages (e.g. Portuguese) a given syllable is stressed due to its position in the word or in the phrase, and not because of its internal constituency. In many languages stress involves the repetition of a base model, sequences of a stressed syllable and an unstressed syllable (or vice-versa), resulting in syllable stress due to position, not because of an inherent property. However, there are also cases in which a syllable has inherent stress, either because of its weight or some arbitrary property of the lexical unit. Should a language accept multiple stress per word, one is always perceived as more prominent than the others. Finally, the main stress in a phrase will always be the main stress of one of its constituents, never a secondary stress.

Stress is not a distinctive feature like [± ant] or [± nasal] but rather an abstract relation of prominence. Therefore in order to analyze the stress system of a given language, we must consider stress not to be an inherent property of syllables. In other words, stress corresponds to an autonomous level of representation relative to the segmental chain.

The Autosegmental Theory gave rise to new perspectives on stress. The first autosegmental attempt to describe stress was an analysis in terms of foot trees and binary metrical constituents. Besides explaining main stress, this analysis tried to take into account different degrees of stress among different syllables of the word. For example, Andrade (1983, 1988) found such an analysis insufficient. Because of the difficulties caused by trees, a metrical grid on which the feet heads of the trees were projected had to be associated. Passing to an analysis in terms of trees and grids soon made trees superfluous.

The metrical grid introduced by Liberman (1975) became an integral part of any analysis of stress systems. For every language, the base parameters for building a grid are directionality (Left - Right, or Right - Left) and prominence of the first element (prominent or not). However, two perspectives have emerged among phonologists. Some phonologists believe that the first element corresponds to a trough (a weak beat) or to a peak (a strong beat), without it being necessary to recognize the existence of metrical constituents. Stress is then basically a rhythmic phenomenon. Other phonologists assume that the sequence of stressed and unstressed syllables is due to the existence of binary metrical constituents (feet) that are left or right headed. In this case, stress reflects the grouping of positions in the grid into constituents with a commanding element, or head. Another difference between these two perspectives resides in the treatment of stress clash. In the 'grid only' theory, stress clash is produced by additional rules while in the 'grid and constituents' model, stress clash is directly generated when syllables are assigned to metrical constituents (feet). The most dominant pattern consists of avoiding stress clash though, exactly what the 'grid only' theory does by default.

A further development of the 'grid and constituents' theory is what is called 'parentheses correspondence and edge parameters.' Halle (1990) considers that the grid may be marked before constituent construction by two types of mechanisms: either a given syllable may have a pre-assigned asterisk in line 1 or a metrical parenthesis may be inserted. Parentheses correspondence marks the opposite edge of the constituent which is marked with the parenthesis, and the edge marking parameter shows the place and order for the other parentheses.

Idsardi (1992) abandons parentheses correspondence because he considers it to be redundant. Halle and Vergnaud (1987) consider parentheses the result of grouping metrical positions into headed constituents. For Idsardi, parentheses play an even more important role; constituent building is processed in several stages and is the product of rules and conventions that act at different points in the derivation.[2]

3. Stress in Portuguese

3.1 Historical background: before the 20th century

Fernão de Oliveira is the obligatory point of departure. In his preface to the third edition of Fernão de Oliveira's grammar, Sá Nogueira (1936) writes: "A gramática de Fernão de Oliveira's Grammar (1536) foi a primeira que se publicou em português; foi a primeira que se publicou do português e em português; foi a primeira que se publicou do português e de um português; e foi a primeira que se publicou do português e em Portugal" ('Fernão de Oliveira's Grammar (1536) was the first published in Portuguese, by a Portuguese, in Portuguese and in Portugal').

In chapter xxix, Oliveira indicates the conditions, derived from spelling, under which words are stressed on the last, the penultimate, or the antepenultimate syllable, recognizing that "nesta pequena obra não ha lugar para falar mais particularidades e não somẽnte nos verbos / mas tambẽ nos nomes e em outras partes ha hi eiçeições (p. 62)" ('in this small work there is no place to speak about peculiarities, not only in verbs but also in the other grammatical categories where there are exceptions'). From chapter xxviii (*On Stress*) we must note his statement that "os lugares deste açento de que falamos são entre nos a vltima syllaba ou penultima: ou antepenultima: daqui para tras o nosso esprito nem orelhas não consintem auer açento e a nação ou gente que outra cousa pode sentir e cõsentir não se cõforma com nosco nẽ a musica do nosso ouuido e do seu e hũa e conforme (p. 58)" ('stress falls on the last, the penultimate or the antepenultimate syllable. From there backwards, neither our spirit nor our ear allows for stress, and the nation or people who can accept it are not like us; the music of our and their ears is not alike')

João de Barros (1540:63-4) simply tells us that "toda sílaba tem três açidentes: número de lêteras; espáço de tempo; açento álto ou baixo" ('every syllable has three properties: number of letters, space of time, and high or low stress'). He could have analyzed the rules of syllable stress and quantity in Portuguese by giving versified examples, but he did not because "isso ę degradádo destes nossos reynos: ficará esta matęria para quando o uso ô requerer" ('that is degrading in our kingdom. This matter will be treated when usage requires it').

For Contador de Argote (1725:287), "Enclitica he aquella particula, ou palavra, que perde o seu tom, e o poem na ultima syllaba da palavra antecedente, se he capaz delle" ('enclitic is that particle or word that loses its tone, which goes on to the last syllable of the preceding word if it can bear it'), and tone "He um certo geyto, ou diversidade de som, com que pronunciamos a mesma palavra, ou particula" ('is a certain way or sound diversity with which we pronounce the same word or particle'). "The particles *Me*, *Te*, *etc.* lose their own tone and become enclitics because they are right after the verb." (1725:289)

Madureira Feijó (1824:17-20) says that "Accento he aquelle tom, que na pronunciaçaõ das palavras faz cada huma das vogaes junta com outras letras, a que chamamos Syllaba. Porque em humas se levanta a voz, ferindo com mais força o ar; em outras se deprime, ou abate; e em outras nem se deprime, nem se levanta totalmente, mas fica em meio tom" ('stress is that tone which in the pronunciation of words makes each vowel, together with other letters, into what we call a syllable. Sometimes the voice raises, hitting the air more strongly, and other times it gets depressed, or knocks down, and still other times it does not get totally depressed or raised but remains in a half tone'). All other references to stress are related to graphic diacritics. Note, though, the acute accent, called "agudo, porque assim como toda a cousa aguda he a que sobe para cima, tambem este tom he o que mais sobe na pronunciação" ('acute, because as everything that raises is acute, so this tone is the most raising in pronunciation').

Francisco Brou (1875:150) only speaks about stress when defining verse as "a forma de elocução sujeita a determinado numero de syllabas e a certa disposição de accentos predominantes donde resulta uma cadencia aprazivel" ('the form of elocution subject to a given number of syllables and the right disposition of prominent stresses from which a pleasant cadence results').

Epifânio da Silva Dias (1870:159) claims that in prosody "Ha ainda um certo numero de regras geraes, sobretudo relativas ao logar do accento; mas, na maior parte, ou só se podem dar olhando á sua origem, e por isso não teem logar n'um livro da indole do nosso, ou são demasiado conhecidas para que seja necessario, para nacionaes, gastar tempo em apontá-las" ('there is a certain number of general rules, mainly related to stress placement, but in their majority they cannot be given without reference to history—for this reason they have no place in a book like ours—or they are too well known by native speakers, which makes it unnecessary to spend time in stating them').

António da Costa Duarte (1877:21) defines stress as "o tom da voz mais ou menos elevado e forte na pronunciação das syllabas" ('the more or less raised and strong tone of voice in syllable pronunciation'), and he states that "todos os vocabulos tem uma syllaba de som forte e predominante" ('every word has a syllable with a strong and prominent sound'). He distinguishes brief syllables from long syllables and says, "mas como uma syllaba pode ser *longa*, por gastar o tempo de duas breves, e com tudo não ser aguda; segue-se que ha muita differença entre a Quantidade e o accento das syllabas" ('but, as a syllable may be *long*, because it takes the time of two brief ones without being acute, it follows that there is a great difference between quantity and syllable stress').

According to Adolfo Coelho (1896:25-6), stress "póde ser *principal* (*tonico*) ou *secundario*. Uma palavra tem sempre, com excepção das chamadas *enclíticas*, accento tonico e póde ter um ou mais accentos secundarios. Em *musical* o accento principal está em *cal* e ha um accento secundario em *mu*... Na historia das linguas o accento é de grande importancia, porque quando elle consiste em augmento d'intensidade contribue notavelmente para a conservação das syllabas que comprehende; quando consiste em augmento de elevação dá á linguagem chatacter rhytmico e parece condicionar diversas alterações de vogaes e ainda de consoantes" ('may be main (tonic) or *secondary*. A word, except for the so called enclitics, always has main stress and it may have one or more secondary stresses. In *musical* 'musical' main stress is in *cal* and there is a secondary stress in *mu* ... In the history of languages stress is a very important factor because when it consists of an increase of intensity, it contributes remarkably to the preservation of the syllables involved, and when it consists of an increase of raising it gives the language a rhythmic character as well as the conditioning of several vowel and consonant alterations').

The most interesting author is undoubtedly Gonçalves Viana by whom we may cite three works showing that his position on the subject did not remain the same. Viana (1883:60-67) posits a few rules for word stress placement, but his position about secondary stress (and echo stress) is not very clear. On one hand, he says that "les syllabes qui précedènt la tonique sont toujours atones, à moins que le mot ne soit d'une longueur extrême. Le mot portugais *contribuição* n'a qu'un accent, sur la syllable *-ção* qui le termine" ('syllables preceding the main stressed one are always unstressed, unless the word is very long. The Portuguese word *contribuição*, 'contribution', has only one stress, on the final syllable *-ção*') On the other hand, in a footnote, he states that "lorsque, par la longueur du mot ou la difficulté de prononcer plusieurs voyeles atones de suite, on place l'accent secondaire sur quelque syllabe prétonique, le plus souvent sa place est différente de l'anglais ex. Portugais *constìtuiçáo*, anglais *cònstitútion* (p. 62)." ('when due to the length of the word or the difficulty in pronouncing a sequence of several unstressed vowels, we place the secondary stress on a pretonic one. Most often, its place is different from English, ex. Portuguese *constìtuiçáo*, English *cònstitútion*') Notice that *constituição* and *contribuição* have the same number of syllables.

Viana (1892:84-87) indicates a series of rules about the main stressed syllable, but he tells us nothing about secondary stress, except that "chama-se também *predominante* o acento mais forte, e dominantes os outros, com relação ás syllabas átonas que acompanham as dêste modo accentuadas" (p. 15) ('the strongest stress is also known as *predominant*; other instances of stress are called *dominant* in relation to the unstressed syllables that accompany them').

In Viana (1903:28-9) the most explicit references to stress are found. After giving some rules for the location of word stress, he recognizes that "Dans les mots polysyllabiques, outre l'accent principal, il y a toujours des accents secondaires frappant les syllabes antétoniques.... On peut donner comme règle générale que, devant la syllabe prédominante il ne peut y avoir plus de deux syllabes complètement atones" ('for each polysyllable, besides the main stress, there are instances of secondary stress on pretonic syllables ... We may say as a general rule that before the predominant vowel, there can be no more than two completely unstressed syllables'). Besides this kind of secondary stress, that is "subjectifs et peuvent affecter des voyelles pleines ou des voyelles réduites..., parce qu'ils sont dus à la structure des mots, à leur longueur, ..., il y a aussi des accents secondaires, dépendant de la signification, plutôt objectifs" ('subjective and may affect plain vowels as well as reduced vowels..., because they are due to word structure, word length etc., there are also rather objective instances of secondary stress that are dependent on meaning'). The distinction first noted by Viana between subjective and objective secondary stresses corresponds to the distinction that will be made here between echo stress, dependent on main stress, and secondary stress, independent of main stress.

3.2 Twentieth century

3.2.1 Before the seventies

Leite de Vasconcelos (1901:76) only informs us that "Portuguese words may be monosyllabic or polysyllabic. Monosyllabic words are naturally oxytons when they are isolated. Polysyllabic words may be oxytons, paroxytons and proparoxytons."

For J. J. Nunes (1969:30-1) "Among the syllables that compose words there is one of higher intensity—it is the so called *tonic*—in relation to which the others are unstressed," and every "word has a tonic stress, even if there are some that may lose it when they are pronounced together with the one that follows or precedes them. The same happens with *proclitics* and *enclitics*, as we see in *já lhe dei*, 'I already gave him/her', and *dei-lhe*, 'I gave him/her', where *lhe* is proclitic in the first case and enclitic in the second case. Besides the stressed syllable, there are polysyllables in which another syllable is raised by voice, often with an intensity not inferior to that one—that stress is called *secondary*. We observe it, among others, in these words: *váidade* 'vanity', *sólteiro* 'bachelor', *cègáda* 'masquerade', *pátetice* 'silliness', *pègada* 'footprint', *pàzada* 'stroke of shovel', etc." It seems there is a confusion here between secondary stress, non-neutralized unstressed vowels, and vowel position in the word. Regarding secondary stress in Latin, he confirms that "according to what we have already noticed, Portuguese also manifests the existence of this stress in words with more than two syllables."

Morais Barbosa (1965:218) provides a good example of a structuralist view on stress, stating "concerning the place of stress in a word, nothing except tradition determines it in today's synchrony."

In Brazil, Said Ali (1966) considers the existence of degrees of atonicity, but it is Mattoso Câmara (1970) who tries to describe and predict the environments in which the different degrees of atonicity may occur. According to Nascentes (1942:24), "words with more than three syllables present one or more secondary stresses besides main stress" and, above all, "secondary stress falls, generally, every two syllables."

3.2.2 After the seventies

3.2.2.1 Brazil

Yvonne Leite (1974), presents a treatment of stress in Brazilian Portuguese in a critically descriptive and historical perspective. Most importantly, the author discards the possibility that syllable weight plays a role in stress assignment. Norma Fernandes (1976) provides a description of the acoustic correlates of stress in the Brazilian Portuguese of São Paulo. Iara Costa's (1978) dissertation analyzes certain stress shifts in Portuguese within the model of generative phonology. Major (1985) provides an acoustic analysis of Brazilian Portuguese without a clear phonological theory. Moraes (1986, 1987) gives an acoustic-perceptive study and description of the acoustic correlates of word stress, respectively.

Helênio de Oliveira (1989), contrary to the other works cited, concentrates on word destressing in Portuguese. In his chapter on 'gradation of atonicity', he proposes that a 'rhythmic rule' is responsible for the prominence of certain syllables that do not bear main stress.

Massini (1991) analyzes stress in Portuguese in an essentially phonetic manner. Some aspects of the analysis are provided in the 'Massini-Abaurre framework,' similar to that of Selkirk (1980) .

Bisol (1994) sets out to describe the stress system of Brazilian Portuguese in metrical terms, though she considers Portuguese a quantity-sensitive language. For example, heavy, or closed, syllables are obligatorily stressed. This is why *café*[3] 'coffee,' is stressed on the last syllable; a closed syllable ending in a consonant which is not phonetically present but found in derived words, such as *cafezeiro* 'coffee plant'. The problem is that if we have *cafezeiro* we also have *cafeeiro* 'coffee plant', with no consonant and *cafeteira* 'coffee-pot', with a different consonant. We also have *chá* 'tea', *chaleira* 'tea-pot', *chazeiro* 'tea lover', with /l/ and /z/ and not /t/ and /z/ as in the first case. Positing that loan words such as *chalé* 'chalet' and *robô* 'robot' have a final /t/ can only be motivated because, in the first case there is a *-t* in French orthography, but not pronunciation, and in the second case, there is a *-t* in Czech orthography and pronunciation. But what consonant can we assume for *avô* 'grandfather', or *chaminé* 'chimney'? Since stress falls on the last syllable of the stem in over seventy-five percent of the words, independently of both the number of syllables and whether the last syllable is open or closed, it is hard to accept quantity as a conditioning factor for stress.

The fact that stress never falls further leftward than the penultimate syllable of the stem is an argument in favor of analyzing stress in demarcative terms.

3.2.2.2 Portugal

Mateus (1977) presents an analysis of stressed and unstressed vowels within an SPE framework which is more detailed than Andrade (1977) and recognizes, as does Mattoso Câmara (1970), four degrees of stress for vowels not bearing main stress.

(1) *General rule for Verbs:*

$$V \rightarrow [+\text{ stress}] \;/\; \_\_((CoV)CoV)Co\#]V$$

(2) *General rule for Noun and Adjectives:*

$$V \rightarrow [+\text{ stress}] \;/\; \_\_C_0VC_0\#]_{N,\,A}$$

Two additional rules must apply to forms marked in the lexicon as exceptions: one for words stressed on the last syllable and one for words stressed on the antepenultimate syllable.

Mateus (1983), adopts a non-SPE framework to refer to different types of boundaries between word formatives when describing word stress in Portuguese. Andrade (1983, 1988) analyzes stress in Portuguese within the constituents-only, or trees-only, theory.

Delgado-Martins (1986), though not limited to phonological matters, is an interesting work concerned with different degrees of stress in Portuguese from a perceptive phonetic point of view.

Andrade and Viana (1988, 1989) explain the right-left rhythmic wave of Portuguese in terms of a 'grid and constituents' analysis and show the existence of main stress echoes in every even syllable to the left of the main stress syllable. Echo stresses present themselves as a rhythmic curve, a rhythmic principle of alternation between strong and weak beats. In the vast majority of cases, echoes are phonetically marked by the relative duration of the syllables that occupy each of the positions. Besides echo stress there may also be a non-rhythmic secondary stress in initial position.

Pereira (1990) provides an analysis of the Portuguese nominal system within Metrical Phonology, following Selkirk's (1980) proposal. The importance of this work is limited because it is only a partial study with questionable validity, considering that Selkirk (1984) abandons her earlier proposals. Pereira (1993) studies stress in Portuguese using what may be called 'Parentheses Correspondence.'

Andrade and Laks (1992a, 1992b, 1993) present the Portuguese stress system in 'grid only' terms and propose that the word stress pattern in Portuguese be described by means of lexical marking and a stress principle. In this way, final, penultimate and antepenultimate stress in Portuguese is adequately described by the application of two parameters: rhythmic wave and anchoring. It is nevertheless necessary to assume that, on the one hand, defective class markers are associated with a rhythmic position and, on the other hand, certain morphemes may be associated with a lexical trough.

The morphological composition of words is as follows:

(3) *Nouns:*

$$[\text{Root}]_1, ([\text{Class}]_2, [\text{Number}]_3)_{N\ A}$$

(4) *Verbs:*

$$(\text{CL})_0, [\text{Root}]_1, (\text{Class})_2, ([\text{TM}]_3, (\text{PN})_4), (\text{CL})_5)_V$$

Except in the case of a lexical trough, the absence of a class marker in nouns and adjectives implies that stress falls on the final syllable. In other words, stress will be final only if nouns or adjectives do not show a class marker. In this way, we can say that the alternation between final and penultimate stress in nouns and adjectives is morphologically conditioned by the absence or presence of a class marker. Such is not the case for verbs. The absence of a tense marker has no effect on stress position. In order to verify what has just been said, compare the following pairs of words:

(5) a. pap<u>á</u> /p<u>a</u>pa b. at<u>a</u>ca / atac<u>a</u>va
'dad/Pope, porridge' '(it, (s)he) attacks' / '(it, (s)he) attacked'

In the first pair, the absence of a class marker in the first word induces final instead of penultimate stress. In the second pair, both verb forms exhibit stress on the penultimate syllable, even though the first form has no tense marker.

The principles and parameters underlying word stress in Portuguese are these given in (6) - (8):

(6) *The Portuguese Rhythmic Principle:*

Rhythmic wave, trough - edge, right anchoring, first edge strong

(7) *Parametrization:*

In L_0, P(erfect) G(rid), right - left, trough, first edge strong.

(8) *The Anchoring Principle:*

The wave anchors to the first position corresponding to its initial beat; in the absence of such a position, it anchors to the right limit of the word.

In this way, when a word has no lexical trough the rhythmic wave anchors to the right limit of the word. However, when a word has lexical troughs the rhythmic wave anchors to the first trough it finds, which corresponds to its initial beat.

One of the effects of the Anchoring Principle is that when the word has a lexical trough, the positions to its right are not affected by the rhythmic wave. This is due to the fact that the wave anchors to the trough and spreads from right to left. By default, the positions to the right are troughs. On the other side, note that if a word has more than one lexical trough, the rhythmic wave may stress one of them if it is in an odd position in relation to the wave anchoring point. For example, in *atómico* there are two lexical troughs; the wave anchors to the first one (/i/); the second trough (/o/), is turned into an edge by the wave. The final /o/ is a trough by default.

4. Brazilian Portuguese

It would be strange if word stress placement were different in Portugal and Brazil. The term 'placement' is used because the phonetic cues associated with stress may not be the same in both varieties. Although two varieties of a language may show differences in stress placement for some words (for example, *púdico* / *pudico* 'chaste', *leucemia* / *leucémia* 'leukemia' in Portuguese, and similar contrasts between British English and American English), a language in which two dialects present different stress systems does not seem possible. Such a criterion would lead us to wonder how many languages there are in Cape Verde since two different stress systems, one for the Sotavento Islands, and another for the Barlavento Islands, apparently are in use.

A notorious difference between European and Brazilian Portuguese is that in spite of sharing the same stress system, the position of stress varies dialectically in some words. In Portugal, words like *rapto* 'kidnapping' / 'I kidnap', *ritmo* 'rhythm' / 'I give the rhythm', *indigno* 'unworthy' / 'I become indignant', for example, may be noun or verb forms without being distinguished by stress placement, as in *cômputo* / *computo* 'count'/ 'I count', *divórcio* / *divorcio* 'divorce' / 'I get divorced', *júbilo* / *jubilo* 'exultation' / 'I exult', *último* / *ultimo* 'ultimate' / 'I terminate.' In Brazil, on the other hand, nouns and verbs are always distinguished, as in *rápito* / *rapito* 'kidnapping' / 'I kidnap' *rí[t]/[č]imo* / *ri[t]/[č]ímo* 'rhythm' / 'I give the rhythm' and *indí[g]ino* / *indi[g]íno* 'unworthy' / 'I become indignant', with noun forms stressed on the antepenultimate syllable and verb forms stressed on the penultimate syllable.

If epenthetic vowels are lexical troughs, then why is stress not on the same place in both forms? If, on the other hand, epenthetic vowels are not lexical troughs, why is stress not on the same place in both forms?

Consider the representations of *rapto*$_N$ and *rapto*$_V$, in Portugal.

(8)

```
*  .          *  .
*  *          *  *
rapto N       rapto V
```

Since there is no lexical trough, stress is obligatorily on the same syllable in both forms. If the representations were:

(9)

```
 . * .        . * .
 * * *        * * *
rapito N     rapito V
```

then the result for Brazilian Portuguese should be *rapíto* in both cases, with the noun form incorrectly stressed. In the framework adopted here, the solution for these cases is very simple. Epenthetic vowels are lexical troughs and as such the representation of *rapto* $_N$ is:

(10)

```
 * * *
rapito N
```

which, once the grid is built, will give the result:

(11)

```
 * . .
 * * *
rapito N
```

Since there are no lexical troughs in the verb forms, the only result the grid can produce is:

(12)

```
                          . * .
 * * *                    * * *
rapito V       ⇒         rapito V
```

The second case in which there is stress variation between Portugal and Brazil concerns a small group of words in which a phonetic segment is phonologically interpreted in different ways. So, in Portugal *desag[ú]a*, 'it flows into', and *enxag[ú]a*, '(s)he rinses', with [u] stressed, but *desag[wá]r*, 'to flow into' and *enxag[wá]r*, 'to rinse' are realized with a [w]. It is assumed here that these words contain a /u/ that may be stressed or semivocalized. In contrast, in

Brazil, both *deság[w]a* and *enxág[w]a,* as well as *desag[w]ar* and *enxag[w]ar* are realized with a [w]. There are two possible reasons for this: the speaker may simply suppose that the word contains /w/, a glide that can not be stressed; or s/he may interpret [w] as part of the preceding labialized consonant.

In conclusion, the stress system of all Portuguese dialects obeys one set of principles and parameters, independently of the phonetic cues that each variety of the language may manifest.

Notes

1 Many of the aspects cited here are also pointed out for Spanish in Harris (1995:867).

2 This paper will not discuss stress assignment from the perspective of Optimality Theory or Harmonic Phonology.

3 In order to facilitate reading, the stressed vowels of the examples in Portuguese are underlined.

References

Ali, Said. 1966. *Gramática Secundária da Língua Portuguesa.* São Paulo: Ed. Melhoramentos.

Andrade, Ernesto d.' 1977. *Aspects de la Phonologie (Générative) du Portugais.* Lisbon: Instituto Nacional de Investigaçõ Cientifica.

Andrade, Ernesto d.' 1983. L'Accent de Mot en Portugais. University of Lisbon, ms.

Andrade, Ernesto d.' 1988. O Acento de Palavra em Português. *Colloquium on Spanish, Portuguese and Catalan Linguistics,* ed. J. Staczek. Washington DC: Georgetown University Press.

Andrade, Ernesto d.' and Bernard Laks. 1992a. Na Crista da Onda. *Actas do VII Encontro da Associação Portuguesa de Linguística.* Lisbon: APL.

Andrade, Ernesto d', and Bernard Laks. 1992b. Word Stress in Portuguese. *Colloquium on Portuguese Linguistics.* GLOW. Lisbon.

Andrade, Ernesto d', and Bernard Laks. 1993. Surfing the Wave: Word Stress in Portuguese. University of Lisbon and University of Paris VIII, ms.

Andrade, Ernesto d', and M. Céu Viana. 1988. O Ritmo e o Acento em Português. *Actas do II Encontro Regional da Associação Portuguesa de Linguística em Homenagem ao Professor L. F. Lindley Cintra.* Lisbon: APL.

Andrade, Ernesto d', and M. Céu Viana. 1989. Ainda sobre o Acento e o Ritmo em Português. *Actas do IV Encontro da Associação Portuguesa de Linguística,* 3-16. Lisbon: APL.

Barbosa, Jorge Morais. 1965. *Études de Phonologie Portugaise*. Lisbon: Junta Nacional de Investigações do Ultramar.

Barros, João de. 1540. *Gramática da Língua Portuguesa*. (ed. Maria Leonor. C. Buescu, 1971). Lisbon: Publicações da Facultad de Letras da Universidade de Lisboa.

Bisol, Leda. 1994. The Stress in Portuguese. *Actas do Workshop sobre Fonologia*, 19-32. Lisbon.: Associação Portuguesa de Linguística.

Brou, Francisco P. 1875. *Grammatica Particular ou Estudos sobre as Principaes Difficuldades da Lingua Portuguesa*. Lisbon: Typographia Progressista.

Câmara, Joaquim Mattoso. 1970. *Estrutura da Língua Portuguesa*. Petrópolis: Vozes.

Coelho, F. Adolfo. 1896. *A Lingua Portuguesa*. Oporto: Magalhães e Moniz.

Contador de Argote. 1725. *Regras da Lingua Portuguesa*. Lisbon: Officina de Musica.

Costa, Iara B. 1978. *O Acento em Português; Estudo de Algumas Mudanças no Modelo da Fonologia Gerativa*. Master Dissertation, Campinas.

Delgado-Martins, M. Raquel. 1986. *Sept Etudes sur la Perception*. Lisbon: INIC

Dias, Epiphânio da Silva. 1870. *Grammatica Practica da Lingua Portuguesa*. Oporto: Tip. do Jornal do Porto.

Duarte, A. da Costa. 1877. *Grammatica Philosophica da Lingua Portuguesa*. Maranhão: Antonio P. Ramos d'Almeida.

Fernandes, Norma H. 1976. *Contribuição para uma Análise Instrumental da Acentuação e Intonação em Português*. Master Dissertation, São Paulo.

Halle, Morris. 1990. Respecting Metrical Grid. *NLLT* 8.

Halle, Morris, and Jean-Roger Vergnaud. 1987. An Essay on Stress. Cambridge, Mass.: MIT Press.

Harris, James. 1995. Projection and Edge Marking in the Computation of Stress in Spanish. *A Handbook of Phonological Theory*, ed. by J. Goldsmith, 856·-887. Blackwell, Oxford.

Hayes, Bruce. 1981. *A Metrical Theory of Stress Rules*. Bloomington. Indiana: IULC.

Idsardi, William. 1992. *The Computation of Prosody*. Doctoral dissertation, MIT.

Laks, Bernard. 1993. La Constituance Revisitée. *De Natura Sonorum*, ed. B. Laks e M. Plénat. Paris: Publications de l'univ. de Vincennes (Paris VIII).

Leite, Yonne. 1974. *Portuguese Stress and Related Rules*. Doctoral dissertation, University of Texas, Austin.

Leite de Vasconcelos, J. 1901. *Esquisse d'une Dialectologia Portugaise*. (2nd ed. 1970). Lisbon: Centro de Estudos Filológicos.

Libermann, Mark. 1975. *The Intonational System of English*. Bloomington, Indiana: IULC.

Madureira Feijó. 1824. *Orthographia ou Arte de Escrever e Pronunciar com Acerto a Lingua Portugueza*. Lisbon: Martin Irmãos.

Major, Roy. 1985. Stress and Rhythm in Brazilian Portuguese. *Language* 61.259-82.

Massini, Gladys. 1991. *A Duração no Estudo do Acento e do Ritmo em Português*. Master dissertation, Campinas.

Mateus, M. Helena. 1977, (2nd edn. 1982). *Aspectos da Fonologia Portuguesa*. Lisbon: Centro de Linguística da Universidade de Lisboa.

Mateus, M. Helena. 1983. O Açento de Palavra em Português: uma Nova Proposta. *Boletim de Filologia* 28.211-229.

Moraes, João. A. de. 1986. Acentuação Lexical e Acentuação Frasal em Português: um Estudo Acústico-perceptivo. *2° Encontro Nacional de Fonética e Fonologia*. Brasília.

Moraes, João. A. de. 1987. Correlats Acoustiques de l'Accent de Mot en Portugais brésilien. Proceedings of the 11th Int. Cong. of Phonetic Sciences. Vol. 3:313-316. Talin: Academy of Sciences of the Estonian SSR, USSR.

Nascentes, Antenor. 1942. Prosódia. *O Idioma Nacional*. São Paulo: Comp. Editora Nacional.

Nunes, José J. 1969. *Compêndio de Gramática Histórica Portuguesa*. Lisbon: Livraria Clássica Editora.

Oliveira, Fernão de. 1536. *Grammatica da Lingoagem Portuguesa*. R. de Sá Nogueira, (ed.), (1933). Lisbon: José Fernandes Júnior.

Oliveira, Helênio de. 1989. *Atonização de Vocábulos em Português e Regras Afins*. Doctoral Dissertation, Univ. Federal do Rio de Janeiro.

Pereira, M. Isabel. 1990. *Da Prosódia: Análise da Evolução do Conceito de Prosódia e das Diferentes Abordagens Linguísticas das Questões Prosódicas*. Master dissertation, Lisbon.

Pereira, M. Isabel. 1993. Questões de Acento. *Actas do VIII Encontro da Associação Portuguesa de Linguística*. 418-430. Lisbon: APL.

Prince, Alan. 1983. Relating to the Grid. *Linguistic Inquiry* 14.19-100.

Prince, Alan. 1990. Quantitative Consequences of Rhythmic Organization. *Papers from the 26th Regional Meeting*, vol. 2. Chicago: Chicago Linguistic Society.

Selkirk, Elisabeth. 1980. On the Role of Prosodic Categories in English Word Stress. *Linguistic Inquiry* 11.563-605.

Selkirk, Elisabeth. 1984. *Phonology and Syntax*. Cambridge. Mass.: MIT Press.

Viana, A. R. Gonçalves. 1903. *Portugais: Phonétique et Phonologie. Morphologie. Textes*. Leipzig: Teubner.

Viana, A. R. Gonçalves. 1973. *Estudos de Fonética Portuguesa*. Lisbon: Imprensa Nacional-Casa da Moeda.

11

On the prosody and intonation of Focus in European Portuguese*

Sónia Frota

0 Introduction

The relation between Focus and prosodic phenomena has a long tradition in generative literature. In earlier works, stress and intonation are taken to be the defining features of Focus, and are conceived as properties of surface structure which determine interpretation. Chomsky (1971) and Jackendoff (1972) represent this view: the former defines Focus as "the intonation center of surface structure" (Chomsky 1971: 201), and the latter states that stress is the criterion for Focus assignment and the Focus marker "contains a feature marking the pitch contour" to be "syntactically" associated with the focused constituent (Jackendoff 1972: 234, 262). Such a theory of Focus assignment would become inconsistent with later developments in generative grammar: on the one hand it plays with phonological features as if they were *in* syntax; and on the other, it conceives semantic interpretation as being directly triggered by stress and intonation. Yet, it undoubtedly captures the basic intuition that, at least in English-type languages, phonological phenomena are the key to Focus.

From the 1980s onward, work on the phonological component of grammar has accounted for that basic intuition in two major ways: (i) the intonational phonology account, and (ii) the prosodic phonology account. The touchstone of (i) has been nucleus placement or, more generally, pitch accent distribution (cf. work by Ladd 1980, Gussenhoven 1984, Beckman and Pierrehumbert 1986, Grice 1995, Féry 1993, among others). As for (ii), the main issue has been how Focus determines phonological phrasing (Cho 1990, Kanerva 1990, Selkirk and Chen 1990, Vogel and Kenesei 1990, Zec and Inkelas 1990). Languages like English, German, Dutch, or Italian are well-documented in the body of work related to (i), whereas languages like Hungarian, Hausa, Chinese, or Korean are mainly discussed in the research on (ii). This does not mean, of course, that both accounts are unrelated (or unrelatable), nor that the authors assume some kind of principled distinction between them, as clearly shown by Hayes and Lahiri's (1991) account of Bengali, which explicitly unifies the prosodic and intonational phonology frameworks.

This paper attempts to provide an account of the phonology of Focus in European Portuguese (hereafter EP). My aim is to describe in formal terms how Focus is expressed by phonological means. To accomplish this aim I will use both the theory of the Prosodic Hierarchy developed by Selkirk, Nespor and Vogel, Ladd, and others, and the theory of Intonation developed by Pierrehumbert, Ladd, Gussenhoven, Grice, and other authors in this research tradition. The analysis proposed addresses the following areas: evidence for phonological constituent structure in EP, prominence assignment at phrasal level, and the phonology of declarative intonation. Consequences for a cross-linguistic understanding of the phonology of Focus will be tentatively explored.

The analysis presented here is based on data taken from the speech of three EP native speakers of the Lisbon area (the author is one of them), checked against the speech of three other speakers of the same variety. To my knowledge, this is the first attempt at a formal characterization of the prosody and intonation of Focus in EP.

1 Prosodic structure

A cross-linguistic survey of evidence for phonological domains shows that segmental rules are among the strongest arguments for the Prosodic Hierarchy theory, while suprasegmental properties have generally been dealt with to a lesser extent (cf. Nespor and Vogel 1986, Hayes 1990, Nespor 1993, among others). However, prosodic structure can be taken not only to define the domains of phonological rules, but also the points of association of the tunes of a melody and the input to a representation of rhythm (as in Nespor and Vogel 1989, or Nespor 1990 for rhythmic evidence, and Hayes and Lahiri 1991, or Ladd 1992b for intonational evidence).

In the search for evidence for prosodic phrases in EP, the various types of properties —both segmental and suprasegmental— were taken into account (cf.

Frota 1995a, 1996). Since I am interested in the prosodic structure above the word level, particularly in the Phonological Phrase (ϕ) and the Intonational Phrase (I) domains, which have been shown to be at stake when Focus and phrasing are the issue (see section 1.2), I will limit the following discussion to these two phrasal domains. In the analysis of the data, I am assuming the basic cross-linguistic algorithms for ϕ- and I-formation, and the possibilities for ϕ- and I-restructuring presented in Nespor and Vogel (1986) and in much subsequent work.

1.1 The Phonological Phrase and the Intonational Phrase in EP

Our results show that prosodic phrasing in EP has two main characteristics, both with interesting consequences to prosodic hierarchy theory: (i) the absence of positive evidence for ϕ; (ii) the presence of evidence for some recursivity in prosodic structure.

The analysis of a large group of sandhi phenomena known to apply across words shows that they are sensitive to phonological phrasing; namely, that they form a cluster of domain juncture or domain span rules bounded by the I domain.[1] These rules do not refer to ϕ in any way; neither does ϕ define the domain of application or the domain-internal juncture relevant to the phenomena in question. Let us take Fricative Voicing as a first illustration of these results.

In EP the word-final fricative /s/ becomes voiced when it is followed by a word-initial vowel. As can be seen from the sentences in (1), Fricative Voicing applies across any two words when its segmental context is present, except across an I-boundary.[2]

(1)

a. [[a*s* aluna*s* africana*s*]$_{\phi}$ [ofereceram caneta*s*]$_{\phi}$ [ao*s* amigos]$_{\phi}$]$_{I}$
   the students African gave pens to-the friends
   'The African students gave pens to their friends'

b. [a*s* alunaS]$_{I}$ [até onde sabemoS]$_{I}$ [[obtiveram]$_{\phi}$ [boa*s* avaliações]$_{\phi}$]$_{I}$
   the students as far as (we) know got good marks
   'The students, as far as we know, got good marks'

This can be expressed by means of the rule in (2) (for the purposes of this paper, the difference between an I^{max} domain and an I domain will not be discussed, since the crucial point is the presence of an I and not a ϕ-type boundary).[3]

(2) $$\begin{bmatrix} +\text{cont} \\ +\text{ant} \\ +\text{cor} \end{bmatrix} \rightarrow [+\text{voice}] \ / \ [\ldots [\ldots \_\_]_w \, [V \ldots]_w \ldots]_{I\,max}$$

The processes of Vowel Deletion and Consonant Degemination involved in Syllable Degemination exhibit an analogous behavior. This phenomenon is described in the literature as follows: when the final syllable of w_1 is equal or very similar to the initial syllable of w_2, the final vowel of the former is deleted, the two consonants become a geminate, and they may finally reduce to one consonant.[4] As the examples in (3) show, complete Syllable Degemination applies across words that belong to the same I. The ϕ-boundary is, again, not relevant.

(3) a. [[o meu pai]$_\phi$ [herdou]$_\phi$ [um cam*po* poluído]$_\phi$]$_I$
the my father inherited a field polluted
'My father inherited a polluted field'
(cam**po** poluído → cam**p** poluído → campoluído)

b. [[o cam*po*]$_\phi$ [podia estender-se]$_\phi$ [até ao ribeiro]$_\phi$]$_I$
the field could go-itself up to-the river
'The field could go up to the river'
(cam**po** podia → cam**p** podia → compodia)

c. [o camPO]$_I$ [poluído mas recuperável]$_I$ [foi uma boa aquisição]$_I$
the field polluted but recoverable was a good buy
'The field, polluted but recoverable, was a good buy'
(cam**po** poluído ↛ *campoluído)

These facts can be captured by the rules in (4).

(4) a. $\begin{matrix} V \\ [\alpha \text{high}] \end{matrix} \rightarrow \emptyset \; / \; [\ldots[\ldots C_a \_\_]_w \; [C_a \begin{matrix} V \\ [\alpha \text{high}] \end{matrix} \ldots]_w \ldots]_{I\,max}$

b. $C_a \rightarrow \emptyset \; / \; [\ldots[\ldots \_\_]_w \; [C_a \ldots]_w \; \ldots]_I$

Three additional (and clearly distinct) processes of vowel adjacency resolution, namely, Vowel Merger, Vowel Deletion, and Semivocalization, tell the same story: they are all bounded by the I-domain.[5]

Vowel Merger applies in a sequence of two words within the same I: if w_1 has a word-final vowel *a* ([ɐ]) and w_2 has an identical word-initial vowel, the two vowels are changed into the low vowel [a]. The sentences in (5) illustrate the application of this rule.

(5) a. $[[$*a* alun*a*$]_\phi$ $[$*a*ceitou$]_\phi$ $[$o emprego$]_\phi$ $[$no restaurante$]_\phi$ $]_I$
the student-FEM accepted the job at-the restaurant
'The student accepted the job at the restaurant'

b. $[$*a* *a*lunA$]_I$ $[$após o exame$]_I$ $[$foi para a discoteca$]_I$
the student-FEM after the exam went to the disco
'The student, after the exam, went to the disco'

Vowel Deletion eliminates a sequence of two different adjacent vowels—one word-final; the other word-initial—within the same I. Finally, Semivocalization converts the high vowels /i/ and /u/ into glides when followed by another vowel within the same I.[6] That these rules exhibit a pattern analogous to Vowel Merger can be seen in the examples in (6).

(6) a. $[[$o músic*o* africano$]_\phi$ $[$cantou$]_\phi$ $[$várias canções$]_\phi$ $]_I$
the musician African sang several songs
'The African musician sang several songs'

b. $[[$o músic*o*$]_\phi$ $[$aceitou$]_\phi$ $[$o emprego$]_\phi$ $[$no restaurante$]_\phi$ $]_I$
the musician accepted the job at-the restaurant
'The musician accepted the job at the restaurant'

c. $[$o músicO$]_I$ $[$após a audição$]_I$ $[$saltou para a plateia$]_I$
the musician after the audition jumped to the audience
'The musician, after the audition, joined the audience'

In these examples, the segmental context and the domain of application of the corresponding rules are both present; therefore, either of the rules applies, as in (6a-b). If, however, the domain of application of the rules is not met, their application is blocked, as in (6c).

The three rules of vowel adjacency resolution are formulated in (7).

(7) a. *Vowel Merger*:

$$\begin{matrix} V_a\ V_a \\ [-\text{high}] \end{matrix} \rightarrow \begin{matrix} V \\ [+\text{low}] \end{matrix} \ / \ [\ldots[\ldots\_\_]_w\ [\_\_\ldots]_w \ldots]_{I\,\max}$$

b. *Vowel Deletion*:

$$V_a \rightarrow \emptyset \ / \ [\ldots[\ldots\_\_]_w\ [V_b\ldots]_w \ldots]_{I\,\max}$$

c. *Semivocalization*:

$$\begin{bmatrix} +\text{high} \\ \alpha\,\text{back} \\ \alpha\,\text{round} \end{bmatrix} \rightarrow [-\text{syll}] \ / \ [\ldots\_\_\ V \ldots]_{I\,\max}$$

To sum up so far, the sandhi phenomena observed provide strong evidence for the Intonational Phrase domain in EP. By contrast, they provide no segmental evidence for the Phonological Phrase domain. This property of phrasing in EP is independently confirmed by other types of evidence.

The application of rules (7b-c) seems to be constrained by rhythmic restrictions. Namely, the rules do not apply when an ill-formed rhythmic configuration would result, and a potential readjustment is not available.[7] However, rhythmic restrictions in EP pattern in an unexpected way, as the examples in (8) illustrate (where syllables bearing lexical stress in the relevant items are shown in capitals).

(8) a. [[o vesTId*o* ÂMbar]$_\phi$ [foi vendido]$_\phi$]$_I$
the dress amber was sold
'The amber dress was sold'
(vestid[w]âmbar; cf. *vestidâmbar)

b. [[o dançaRInO]$_\phi$ [Ama]$_\phi$ [a bailarina russa]$_\phi$]$_I$
the dancer-MASC loves the ballerina Russian
'The dancer loves the Russian ballerina'
(*dançarin[w]ama, *dançarinama)

Assuming that in EP (and arguably in any language), clashes tend to be avoided, the creation of ϕ-level clashes seems to be more constrained than the creation of lower level clashes. The reason for this unusual pattern is the impossibility of readjusting a ϕ-level clash, as suggested in Frota (1996): EP does not exhibit a clear strategy of clash resolution, unlike English or Italian, which are more resourceful languages at the ϕ-level (cf. Nespor and Vogel 1986, Nespor 1987). The results of a specific study on clash resolution in EP confirm this idea, as there is a clear difference between the situation that holds within ϕ and across ϕ: in the former case there is systematic lengthening of the first stressed vowel involved in the clash, whereas in the latter case there is no such effect (nor any other effect; cf. Frota 1995c). Therefore, EP seems to have a way of introducing enough distance (lengthening being its physical correlate) between clashing stresses within ϕ, but not across ϕ.

Another piece of evidence for this analysis comes from the results of a study on pre-boundary lengthening in EP, which reveal the absence of contrastive final lengthening at ϕ-boundaries, as shown by the fact that there is no difference between the lengthening found at ϕ-boundaries and that found at word boundaries. By contrast, pre-boundary lengthening is a feature of I-boundaries (cf. Frota 1995b).

Additional evidence for the *invisibility* of the ϕ-domain in EP comes from intonation: in this language the ϕ-domain, in neutral utterances, is also tonally *invisible*; i.e., such domain is not marked either by pitch accents or by a boundary tone. The opposite situation characterizes the I domain, which is always tonally marked at least by a pitch accent and a boundary tone (see section 2.1). These intonational properties of I are a strong argument for I-recursivity in EP: only by postulating a recursive prosodic structure of the kind proposed in Ladd (1992b) can both the intonational and the segmental facts of EP be accounted for. The Intonational Phrase is always the domain of an intonation contour, but both the internal and the external I-boundaries of a recursive Intonational Phrase (I^{max}) may define the domain of phonological rules in EP. The processes involved in Syllable Degemination described above are a case in point: Vowel Deletion is bounded by an I^{max}-boundary, while Consonant Deletion is bounded by any I-boundary (see the rules in (4) above).[8] I will not discuss this property of phrasing in EP any further here, since it does not bear crucially on the relation between phrasing and Focus. (For a detailed discussion of the case for prosodic recursivity in EP, the interested reader is referred to Frota 1996).

To summarize, ϕ invisibility in EP is matched by compelling evidence for the Intonational Phrase domain. The existence of such an asymmetry does not mean that evidence for ϕ is absent in EP. In fact, the clash situation results reported above can be interpreted as some kind of (negative) evidence for ϕ, suggesting that this level is distinct from the word level. However, the invisibility of ϕ has to be considered a property of EP prosody, as opposed to languages like Bengali, Greek, French, Italian, or English, and probably closer to languages like Dutch or German.[9]

1.2 Focus and phonological phrasing

That Focus can have an effect on phonological phrasing is well documented in the literature on prosodic phonology. Although various proposals have been made to account for such an effect in the literature, some of them poorly motivated, it seems evident that in the large majority of cases Focus affects phrasing at either the I-level or at the ϕ-level. Hungarian is a language in which Focus affects phrasing at I-level (cf. Vogel and Kenesei 1990). In Hausa, on the other hand, the Focus' effect on phrasing takes place at the ϕ-level (cf. Zec and Inkelas 1990). In EP, as I presently show, Focus does not obligatorily change phonological phrasing.

Due to the clear properties of the I domain in EP, the assessment of a Focus effect at this level poses no difficulties. I will use the segmental evidence for I discussed in section 1.1 above, and illustrate the facts with the process of Fricative Voicing (see section 1.1 above; the other sandhi rules discussed show the same behavior). As can be seen from the examples in (9), in which focused constituents are capitalized, Focus does not block the application of the rule; indeed, Focus does not lead to the placement of an I-boundary either at the right edge (9b and c), or at the left edge of the focused constituent (9d).[10]

(9) a. [[a*s* aluna*s*]$_{\phi}$ [ofereceram]$_{\phi}$ [a*s* rosa*s*]$_{\phi}$ [ao monitor]$_{\phi}$]$_{I}$
b. [[A*S* ALUNA*S*]$_{\phi}$ [ofereceram]$_{\phi}$ [a*s* rosa*s*]$_{\phi}$ [ao monitor]$_{\phi}$]$_{I}$
c. [[a*s* aluna*s*]$_{\phi}$ [ofereceram]$_{\phi}$ [A*S* ROSA*S*]$_{\phi}$ [ao monitor]$_{\phi}$]$_{I}$
d. [[a*s* aluna*s*]$_{\phi}$ [ofereceram]$_{\phi}$ [a*s* rosa*s*]$_{\phi}$ [AO MONITOR]$_{\phi}$]$_{I}$
the students-FEM gave the roses to-the teacher
'The students gave the roses to the teacher'

The assessment of a Focus effect on phrasing at ϕ-level is much less straightforward. Since the only cue to the ϕ category I have been able to find is the contrast between within-ϕ and across-ϕ in clash situations (see 1.1 above), I will use it as a diagnostic for Focus-changing phrasing. Some representative examples are given in (10) (syllables bearing lexical stresses are shown in italics and focused constituents are capitalized).

(10) a. O poeta cantou [uma ma*nhã* *âm*bar]$_\phi$
the poet sang a morning amber
'The poet sang an amber morning'

b. [O ga*lã*]$_\phi$ *an*da de porsche
the romantic lead goes by Porsche
'The romantic lead drives a Porsche'

c. O poeta cantou [uma MA*NHÃ* *âm*bar]$_\phi$

d. O poeta cantou [uma MA*NHÃ* angeli*cal*]$_\phi$
the poet sang a morning angelical
'The poet sang a beautiful morning'

A clash situation such as that in (10a) is dealt with by introducing enough distance between the two clashing stresses, an operation effected by lengthening the first stressed vowel. By contrast, the clash type illustrated in (10b) seems to remain unresolved (see section 1.1 above). If Focus indeed led to the introduction of a ϕ-boundary, we would expect (10c) to group with (10b) —with a ϕ-boundary between the clashing nuclei— and not with (10a). However, this is clearly not the case, since in (10c) there is lengthening of the first stressed vowel. It could be argued that in this case lengthening is due simply to Focus, and not to a strategy for resolving the clash. There is a difference, however, between (10c) and (10d) which indicates that this argument in fact does not hold: in (10d) there is Focus, but no clash, and the lengthening on the first stressed vowel is noticeably shorter than in (10c). These facts suggest that Focus does not affect phonological phrasing at the ϕ-level.

To conclude this section, three properties have been shown to characterize the relation between Focus and phrasing in EP: (i) Focus does not affect the building up of Intonational Phrases; i.e. there is no need for a specific clause in the I-formation algorithm to account for Focus (unlike in Hungarian); (ii) Focus does not affect the construction of Phonological Phrases, i.e. there is no need for a specific clause in the ϕ-formation algorithm to account for Focus (unlike in Hausa); (iii) there is no evidence whatsoever for a *Focus level* or a *Focal Phrase* as a new prosodic category intermediate between ϕ and I (unlike in Chichewa, according to Kanerva 1990). In other words, EP is a language in which Focus has neither a direct nor an obligatory effect on prosodic structure.

1.3 Focus and relative prominence

Although the phonetic nature of stress phenomena has long been a matter of some discussion, experimental work on EP has shown that duration and energy are reliable correlates of word stress: the vowel bearing lexical stress is phonetically realized with longer duration and higher energy (cf. Delgado Martins 1977, Andrade and Viana 1988). My own instrumental research has shown that focused constituents present the same kind of correlates: a consistent durational and energy effect on the stressed vowel of the focused element (cf. Frota 1991, 1993, and 1995c). Focus thus seems to be a kind of stress-related phenomenon at the phrasal level. If we assume that stress is a feature of the phonological organization of utterances —as is generally assumed in the prosodic/intonational phonology framework— an account of the abstract prominence patterns of utterances has to include and account for the relation between Focus and prominence. Some basic guidelines for such an account will be discussed below.

In EP phrasal stress is characterized by final prominence. Thus, the default prominence pattern in the language is *weak-strong*. At the Phonological Phrase level, the rightmost non-clitic word is assigned the value *strong* (*s*) and all its sister nodes are assigned the value *weak* (*w*), a trait of all right-recursive languages (cf. Nespor and Vogel 1986:168).[11] At the Intonational Phrase level, the label *s* is assigned to the rightmost ϕ within I, as in Italian, or Bengali (to cite two of the many final prominence languages discussed in the literature).[12] In EP, argument structure does not seem to play a role in the assignment of phrasal stress, (unlike Dutch, German, or English --cf. Gussenhoven 1984, 1992).

The examples in (11) illustrate how prominence is assigned in EP.

(11) a.
w w w s
w s s w s w s
[[As americanas]$_\phi$ [ofereceram]$_\phi$ [a enciclopédia]$_\phi$ [ao jornalista]$_\phi$]$_I$
the Americans-FEM gave the encyclopedia to-the journalist
'The Americans gave the encyclopedia to the journalist'

b.
w w s
w s s w w s
[[As americanas]$_\phi$ [ofereceram-na]$_\phi$ [ao jornalista]$_\phi$]$_I$
the Americans-FEM gave-it-FEM to-the journalist
'The Americans gave it to the journalist'

c.
w s
w w s s
[[A minha carteira]$_\phi$ [desapareceu]$_\phi$]$_I$
the my wallet disappeared
'My wallet is missing'

d.
w s
w s s w
[[O presidente]$_\phi$ [demitiu-se]$_\phi$]$_I$
the chairman resigned-himself
'The chairman has resigned'

Examples (11b) and (11d) show how the clitics *na* and *se* fail to be assigned ϕ prominence even in the rightmost position of ϕ.[13] In (11c) and (11d) we have equivalent examples to the ones discussed by Féry (1993) for German and Gussenhoven (1984) for Dutch. However, unlike in German or Dutch, I-prominence in EP is assigned to the predicate (the rightmost ϕ) and not to the argument (in these cases, the subject).

One could object that since in EP ϕ is an invisible category in prosodic structure, the assignment of ϕ relative prominence is simply a theoretical stand. While this objection could be justified for neutral utterances, it certainly does not hold for marked ones. On the one hand, in emphatic speech, where stresses are intensified and thus become clearly audible, such peaks of prominence occur precisely in the places predicted by phrasal prominence assignment. On the other hand, in utterances in which a focused constituent is in non-final phrasal position, there is a prominence-changing effect that can only be understood if contrasted with the default prominence pattern.

Following many other authors (such as Féry 1993, Hayes and Lahiri 1991, Ladd 1980, forthcoming), I am assuming that languages have neutral, default prominence patterns. These patterns occur when no particular constituent is focused in the utterance, namely, in *news sentences* or *citation forms*. When a particular constituent is focused, neutral prominence gives way to marked prominence.

The following examples illustrate marked prominence assignment in EP.

(12) a.
```
        w              w          S              w
    w     s            s        w   s         w      s
```
[[As alunas]$_\phi$ [ofereceram]$_\phi$ [as rosas]$_\phi$ [ao monitor]$_\phi$]$_I$

'The students gave THE ROSES to the teacher'

b.
```
    w                               w                 s
    S    w   w                 w      s          w       s
```
[[Todas as alunas]$_\phi$ [ofereceram flores]$_\phi$ [ao monitor]$_\phi$]$_I$

'ALL the students gave flowers to the teacher'

c.
```
        w             S       w              w
    w     s           S       w           w    s
```
[[As alunas]$_\phi$ [ofereceram flores]$_\phi$ [ao monitor]$_\phi$]$_I$

'The students GAVE flowers to the teacher'

In (12a) the constituent [as rosas] is focused and therefore I-prominence is assigned to this phrase, not to the rightmost phrase within I. (12b) also shows early prominence assignment, but at the ϕ-level: the quantifier [todas] attracts Focus and is therefore the stressed element in its phrase. In (12c) the verb is focused, exemplifying a case of early prominence at both ϕ and I-level.[14]

So far, marked prominence looks like early assignment of prominence: in a final-prominence language, a *s-w* pattern conveys Focus. The question arises as to what the *w-s* pattern actually conveys. In quite a number of languages this pattern seems to be ambiguous: it can either reflect neutral stress or marked stress (i.e., Focus).[15] This ambiguity has to do with the fact that a *w-s* pattern conveying default prominence and a *w-s* pattern conveying Focus are realized in the same manner. In accordance with the general principles of prosodic organization, a pitch accent is associated with the prominent element; thus prominence is realized by a certain pitch contour. In any event, in this type of language, such pitch accent is the same in either case. German, Dutch, and English are examples of ambiguous languages as far as the *w-s* prominence pattern is concerned (cf. Féry 1993, Ladd 1980).[16] EP, by contrast, seems to lack such ambiguity.

The sentences in (13) illustrate a case in which neutral prominence and Focus prominence appear to be expressed by the same prominence pattern: the label *s* is assigned to the rightmost constituent.

(13) a. w w w s
w s s w s w s
[[As americanas]$_{\phi}$ [ofereceram]$_{\phi}$ [a enciclopédia]$_{\phi}$ [ao jornalista]$_{\phi}$]$_{I}$
'The Americans gave the encyclopedia to the journalist'

b. w w w S
w s s w s w s
[[As americanas]$_{\phi}$ [ofereceram]$_{\phi}$ [a enciclopédia]$_{\phi}$ [ao jornalista]$_{\phi}$]$_{I}$
'The Americans gave the encyclopedia TO THE JOURNALIST'

However, (13a) and (13b) are clearly distinct, both perceptually and acoustically. Moreover, they are necessarily different, as (13b) means that *the American females gave the encyclopedia to the journalist, and not to someone else*, whereas (13a) means that *it so happened that the American females gave the encyclopedia to the journalist*, and neither can convey the meaning of the other. That the two sentences are realized differently can thus be interpreted as the result of some difference in their phonological organization. I will put forward the hypothesis that this difference resides in the prominence pattern. Neutral prominence (the *w-s* pattern) and Focus prominence (whether *S-w* or *w-S*) are *always* two distinct categories. Thus the similarity between the two *w-s* patterns is only apparent. As stress is the basic organizing principle for tune-text association (cf. Beckman and Pierrehumbert 1986, Pierrehumbert and Beckman 1988, Hayes and Lahiri 1991, Ladd 1992a, among many others), both patterns trigger pitch accent association. However, as neutral prominence (*w-s*) is categorically distinct from Focus prominence (*w-S*), the two patterns are expected to be differently realized, e.g. picking up distinct (unambiguous) tonal realizations. A similar lack of ambiguity has been found in other languages, Bengali being a well-known example (cf. Hayes and Lahiri 1991:63-64).[17]

To sum up, the relation between Focus and prominence in EP seems to be best accounted for by setting up a distinction between neutral prominence and Focus prominence. In this view, Focus is phonologized as a stress feature of the phonological organization of utterances. The presence of this feature, as predicted by general principles of tune-text association, has consequences on the intonational patterns of EP.

2 Intonation

Work on intonation in the last fifteen years has been characterized by the appearance of studies on different languages which are comparable because they share a number of basic assumptions. These assumptions form the core of a theory of intonation that has been able to deal with a wide range of facts in an increasing number of languages. I will not attempt to outline here the basic assumptions of intonational phonology theory, nor discuss the cross-linguistic advantages of such a theory (cf. Ladd 1992a, forthcoming). I take the view that intonation is a sequence of categorically distinct units which are associated with prominent elements in the segmental string or with edges in the prosodic phrase. These units are the phonologically relevant local events in the pitch contour. The contour located between them is phonologically unspecified. For purposes of illustration, the notation I will use for tonal events is that developed by Hayes and Lahiri (1991). This notation distinguishes between starred tones (T*) and unstarred tones (T), and also between ϕ-level boundary tones (Tp) and I-level boundary tones (Ti).

2.1 Standard declarative intonation in EP

Instrumental work on EP declarative intonation consistently describes a contour made up of an initial rise and a final fall. Between these initial and final events, pitch draws a more or less straight line in which nothing seems to happen (Delgado Martins and Lacerda 1977, Martins 1986, Viana 1987, Frota 1991). An illustration of the standard declarative contour is given in Fig. 1:

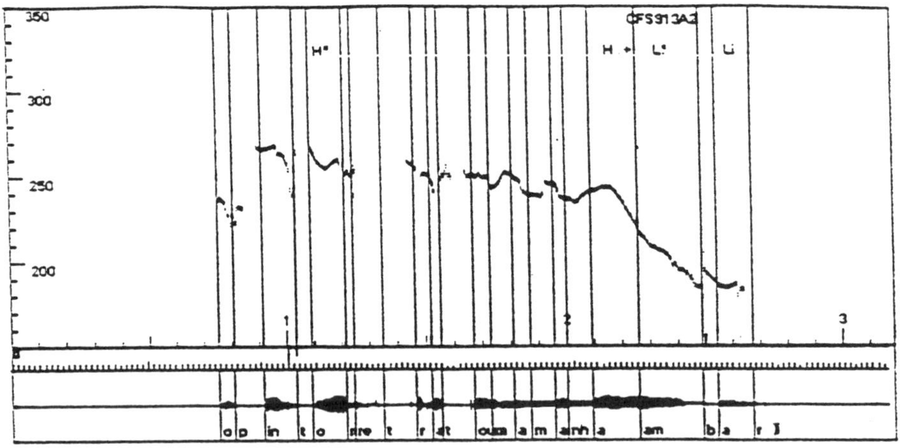

Fig. 1. Pitch contour and speech wave for the utterance *O pintor retratou uma manhã âmbar* 'The artist painted an amber morning.'

Viana (1987) is the first account of EP intonation in which some of the assumptions of the intonational phonology framework are used. Building on the work by Viana, Frota (1993) proposes to account for the declarative contour by the tune H* H+L* L_i. (Such proposal, however, diverges from Viana 1987 in some crucial aspects, such as the organized articulation between tonal events, prominence patterns and prosodic structure, the notion and the role played by association and alignment, and the introduction of underspecification). Thus the contour of the sentence presented in Fig. 1 has the tonal representation in (14).

(14)

```
              w           w                 s
         w    s           s     w        w  s
        [[O pintor]φ [retratou]φ [uma manhã  âmbar]φ ]I
              |                              |      |
              H*                            H+L*    Li
```

The neutral declarative tune can be analyzed into nuclear and prenuclear parts.[18] The nuclear pitch accent H+L* and the boundary tone L_i are the tonal events which define the declarative tune. In an utterance with at least two stressed syllables, a prenuclear accent is also expected to occur: the unmarked declarative prenuclear accent is H*, associated (but not always aligned) with the first stressed syllable of an Intonational Phrase.[19] As Phonological Phrases in EP do not have tonal properties in the unmarked cases, there is only one prenuclear accent per I in neutral declarative intonation (versus what happens in English, or in a more extreme case, in Bengali). Therefore, in addition to (14), both (15a) and (15b) have the neutral declarative tune.

(15) a.
s
[[Casaram]$_\phi$]$_I$
H+L* L_i
(they) married
'They got married'

b.
w w s
w s w s
[[As alunas]$_\phi$ [comeram caramelos]$_\phi$]$_I$
H* H+L* L_i
the students-FEM ate candies
'The students ate candies'

Since in EP not all phrasal prominence or phrasal boundaries in prosodic structure have to be signalled intonationally, but only I-level prominence and I-level boundaries, / T* Ti / is the minimum allowed phonological specification for a tune in this language. There is, however, the option of introducing additional pitch accents in the declarative contour, as (16) illustrates.[20]

(16) [[As alunas]$_\phi$ [emprestaram livros]$_\phi$ [às amigas]$_\phi$]$_I$

	L*+H		L*+H	H+L*
	the students-FEM	lent	books	to-the friends-FEM

'The students lent (the) books to their friends'

When introduced, these pitch accents are associated to the ϕ-level prominent elements, as predicted by the general principles of tune-text association, and make *visible*, perceptually as well as acoustically, the prosodic phrase that they intonationally signal; however, no clear change of meaning is apparently introduced.

2.2 The intonation of Focus

If a Focus is present in the utterance, the declarative contour shows local (and sometimes also global) differences from the neutral H* H+L* L_i tune. Two situations are possible, according to the nature of the Focus information present in the utterance: (i) there are lexical or syntactic elements associated with Focus; (ii) Focus relies solely on prosodic means (i.e. *free Focus*).

Utterances with quantifiers (like *all*), focusing adverbs (like *only*), or contrastive dislocation exemplify the first situation. These utterances are characterized by the presence of a higher number of pitch accents. The sentences in (17) and their respective pitch contours (see Fig. 2 below) illustrate this fact.[21]

(17) a.

w	w	S	w	w	s
		w			s

[[As alunas todas]$_\phi$ [ofereceram-lhe orquídeas]$_\phi$]$_I$
the students-FEM all gave-him orchids
'ALL the students gave him orchids'

b.

w	w	S	w	w	s
		w			s

[[As alunas todas]$_\phi$ [ofereceram-lhe rosas]$_\phi$]$_I$
the students-FEM all gave-him roses
'ALL the students gave him roses'

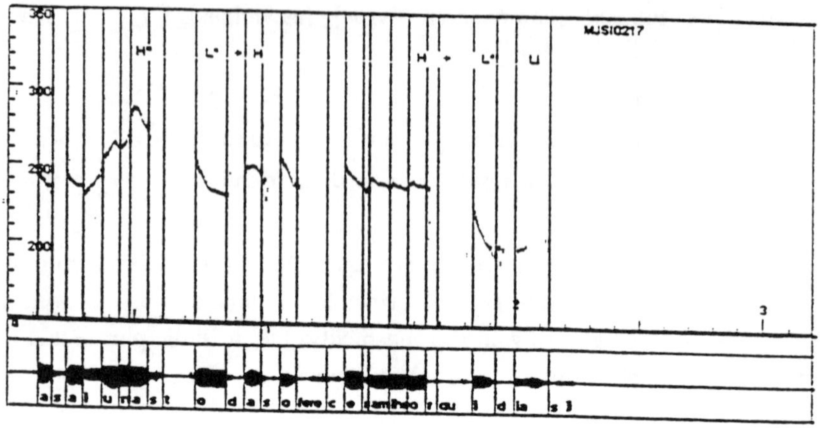

Fig. 2a

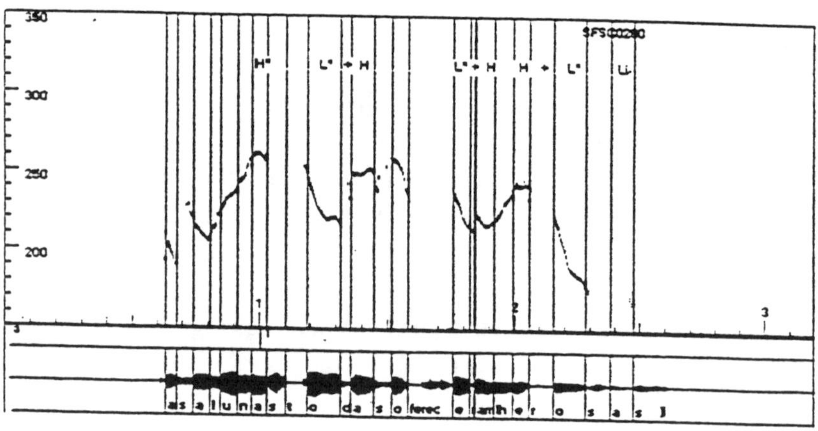

Fig. 2b

Fig. 2. F_0 contours and speech waves for the utterances: (a) *As alunas todas ofereceram-lhe orquídeas*; and (b) *As alunas todas ofereceram-lhe rosas*.

The relevant descriptive generalization seems to be the following. A constituent which bears lexical/syntactic related Focus information obligatorily gets a T*. This tone assignment accounts for the higher number of tonal events in the utterances with these constituents. However, we have seen that in neutral declaratives it is also possible to introduce additional pitch accents (see section 2.1). What, then, is the difference between neutral declaratives with additional pitch accents and the kind of utterances under discussion? Whereas in neutral declaratives additional tonal events are merely *optional* and occur where predicted by neutral prominence assignment, in utterances with lexical/syntactic related Focus information a pitch accent is *obligatorily* associated with the constituent that conveys such information, and it occurs where predicted by Focus prominence assignment.

The second type of situation related to the presence of Focus in the utterance is one in which Focus is signalled solely by prosodic means. In this case, although the tonal features are the same as in the neutral declarative —an initial high and a high immediately followed by a low— there is a systematic difference in the timing of the H+L, correlating with a difference of meaning: an L aligned with the stressed vowel of the prominent constituent expresses a neutral declarative; an H so aligned expresses Focus. Fig. 3 shows an example of this contrast. The pitch contour of the utterance in (15a) above is presented in (a), which could be a *natural* answer to *E o Roberto e a Maria?* 'What about Rob and Mary'?, whereas (b) reflects the Focus contour, unacceptable as an answer to the same question, but an adequate answer to a question such as *Eles separaram-se?* 'Did they split up?.'

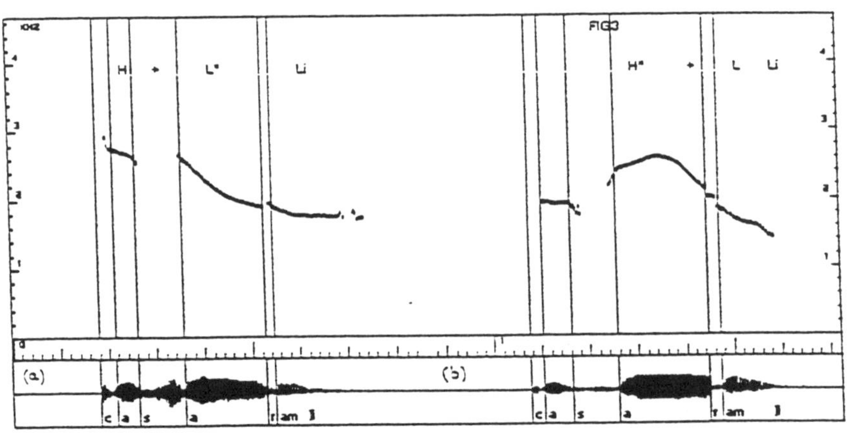

Fig. 3. F_0 contour and speech wave for the utterance *Casaram*: (a) neutral contour; and (b) Focus contour.

Further illustration of this systematic difference in the alignment of the H+L sequence is provided by the sentences in (18) and their respective pitch contours (see Fig. 4 below). These sentences should be contrasted with their neutral declarative version presented in (14) and Fig. 1 above.

(18) a.
w w S
w s s w w S
[[O pintor]$_\phi$ [retratou]$_\phi$ [uma manhã âmbar]$_\phi$]$_I$
| |
H*+L L_i

b.
w w S
w s s w S w
[[O pintor]$_\phi$ [retratou]$_\phi$ [uma manhã âmbar]$_\phi$]$_I$
| |
H*+L L_i

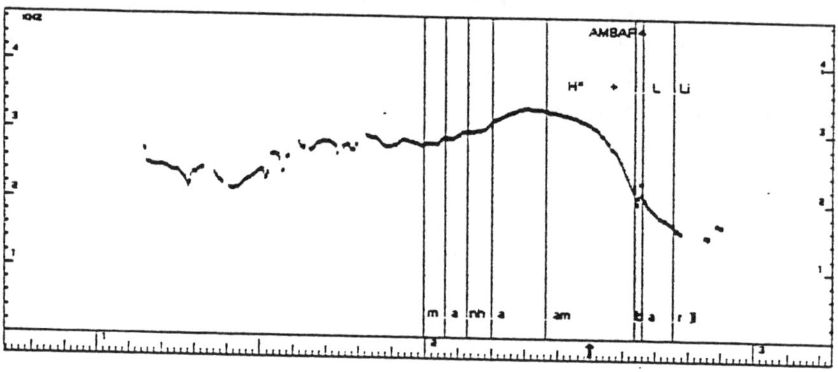

Fig. 4a

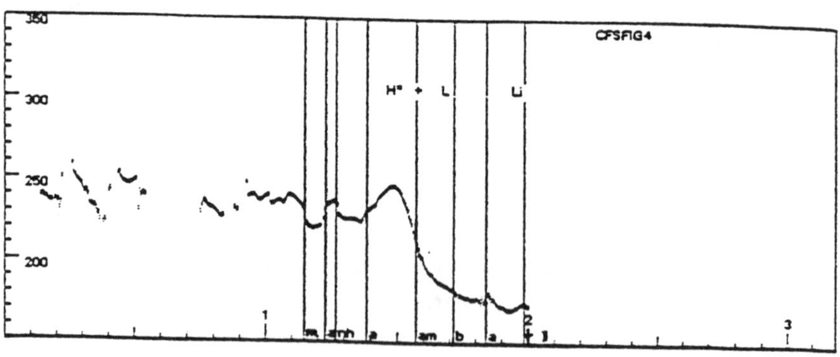

Fig. 4b

Fig. 4. F_0 contour for the utterance *O pintor retratou uma manhã âmbar*: (a) *âmbar* is focused; (b) *manhã* is focused.

Since in (14) and (18) nuclear stress falls on a syllable adjacent to another stressed syllable (*maNHÃ ÂMbar*), these are interesting cases for looking at the H+L alignment. In the neutral contour, nuclear stress falls on *ÂMbar* (see (14)) and therefore the L of the H+L nuclear pitch accent is aligned with the stressed syllable (see Fig. 1). In (18a) *ÂMbar* is focused and thus nuclear stress also falls on this element, but the H of the nuclear H+L is now aligned with the stressed syllable (see Fig. 4 (a)). Finally, if the focused element is *maNHÃ* as in (18b), nuclear stress falls on this element, and the H is thus aligned with its stressed syllable, while the L is reaching its target on the next syllable (see Fig. 4 (b)), just as in (14). However, both the prominence patterns and the tonal sequences in (14) and (18b) are crucially different.

It seems clear that the difference in alignment reflects an underlying difference in association: H+L* is the neutral declarative nucleus, while H*+L is the Focus nucleus. The following examples demonstrate that the distribution of Focus pitch accent is not restricted to late nuclei. As shown by the examples in (19) and their corresponding patterns in Figure 5, nuclear stress is realized by the tonal sequence H*+L, irrespective of the particular locus of Focus prominence.

(19)

a. w w S w

w s s w s w s

[[As alunas]$_\phi$ [ofereceram]$_\phi$ [as rosas]$_\phi$ [ao monitor]$_\phi$]$_I$

'The students gave THE ROSES to the teacher'

b. S w w w

w s s w s w s

[[As americanas]$_\phi$ [ofereceram]$_\phi$ [a enciclopédia]$_\phi$ [ao jornalista]$_\phi$]$_I$

the Americans-FEM gave the encyclopedia to-the journalist

'THE AMERICANS gave the encyclopedia to the journalist'

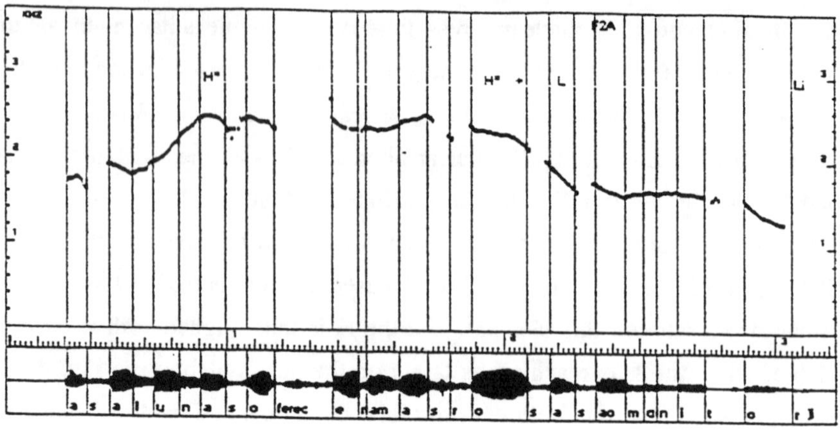

Fig. 5a

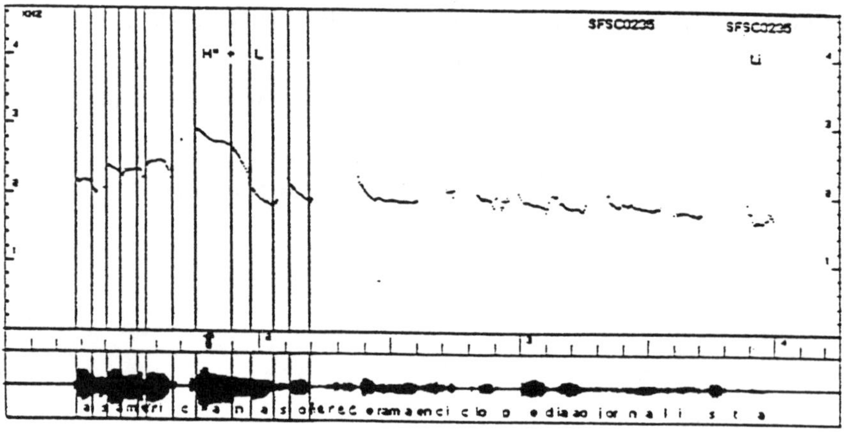

Fig. 5b

Fig. 5. F_0 contours and speech waves for the utterances: (a) *As alunas ofereceram* AS ROSAS *ao monitor*; and (b) AS AMERICANAS *ofereceram a enciclopédia ao jornalista*.

Before concluding the intonational description and analysis of utterances in which Focus relies solely on prosodic means, one question has yet to be addressed; namely, isn't the raising of the H tone a relevant tonal effect associated with Focus in EP?[22]

The raising of the H is a well-documented fact in the literature on a number of languages (cf., for example, Pierrehumbert and Beckman 1988: 7), and is what Viana (1987: 74, 144-146) takes to be the main tonal feature of Focus in EP.[23] Although I agree that the raising of the H may exist in the Focus nucleus, my data show that this raising is subject to variation from speaker to speaker, and within various renditions of the same sentence by the same speaker. Furthermore, the raising is clearly optional, as some of the examples given above illustrate (cf. Fig. 3). These facts suggest that the raising of the H tone (and consequently, its larger fall) is an optional and gradient feature which the Focus nucleus may show, probably linked to a gradience of emphasis. What is not a matter of *plus/minus* but rather of *yes/no* are the timing differences in alignment, which I claim are the basis of a categorical distinction between two pitch accents: H+L* and H*+L.

In conclusion, the intonation of Focus in EP is adequately captured by the following generalization: a T* is associated obligatorily to the focused constituent labelled *S* in prosodic structure, either at the ϕ-level or at the I-level. In the latter case, this T* is the nuclear accent of the utterance. If this is an utterance in which there is nothing else to focus but the phonological means of conveying it, this T* is the Focus nucleus H*+L. Unlike English, Dutch, or German, and like Bengali or Standard Italian, in European Portuguese there is no ambiguity between neutral accent (i.e. *broad Focus*) and Focus accent (i.e. *narrow Focus*).

3 The phonology of Focus

It has been shown in this paper that a framework in which utterances have a phonological organization provides an adequate account of the phonology of Focus phenomena in EP. As stated, information related to such organization includes: (i) a phonological constituent structure (the prosodic phrases characterized by various segmental and suprasegmental properties); (ii) phrase-level abstract prominence patterns; and (iii) categorically distinct intonational features. Prosodic structure plays a central role in this approach as both relative prominence and intonational features are related to prosodic constituents in permissible ways according to the phonological constituent structure. The existence of a set of principled relations — for example, if *w-s* is the prominence pattern of a given prosodic phrase *X*, pitch accent association within the phrasal domain of *X* picks up first the strongest stress (i.e., the *s* of that domain) — does not entail that the various dimensions are strictly dependent. To the contrary, *phrasing*, *stress*, and *accent* can be seen as different independent dimensions, although related in structured and meaningful ways.

Both the theory of the prosodic hierarchy and the theory of intonation (in Pierrehumbert's research tradition) face the challenge of providing a universal descriptive framework. In the final section of this paper, Focus, phrasing, stress, and accent in a number of languages will be considered, and some suggestions for a cross-linguistic approach to the phonology of Focus will be tentatively put forward.

3.1 A cross-linguistic view: where does EP stand?

In the previous discussion we have seen that Focus in EP does not change prosodic phrasing. The literature on prosodic structure provides us with reports on Focus effects on phrasing which can be said to follow two main directions: (i) Focus determines phrasing at its basic level; i.e., Focus phenomena have to be taken into account in the building up of phonological constituents (cf. Vogel and Kenesei 1990, or Zec and Inkelas 1990); (ii) a Focus effect on phrasing (if and when it arises) is a *restructuring* effect, i.e. a derived phenomenon (cf. Beckman and Pierrehumbert 1986, for English). EP is another member of the second group.

Hungarian or Hausa can be cited as examples of languages which show a basic —and therefore strictly obligatory— Focus effect on phrasing. In these languages, Focus is part of the information to be processed by the phrasing algorithms. The Phonological Phrase algorithm proposed for Hausa in Zec and Inkelas (1990: 370), reproduced in (20), is an illustration of this effect.

(20) *Phonological Phrase Algorithm*

a. Prominent elements are mapped into their own ϕ.

b. From the bottom up, branching nodes are mapped into ϕ's.

c. No two phonological words on opposite sides of an XP boundary may be phrased together to the exclusion of any material in either XP.

Each clause of the algorithm operates only on unphrased material; Focus, together with branchingness and maximal projections, is taken into account.

In languages like English, Italian, or Bengali, Focus is absent from the type of information accessed by the basic phrasing algorithms. These languages take into account only notions such as *lexical head*, *maximal projection*, *direction of recursivity*, or *c-command*, as illustrated by the Phonological Phrase algorithm proposed in Nespor and Vogel (1986:168), repeated here in (21).

(21) *Phonological Phrase algorithm* (ϕ domain)

> The domain of ϕ consists of a C which contains a lexical head (X) and all C's on its nonrecursive side up to the C that contains another head outside the maximal projection of X.

In these languages, the kind of effect Focus has on phrasing is best expressed by restructuring phenomena which affect, and therefore presuppose, default phrasing (Focus restructuring in English, as proposed in Kenesei and Vogel 1993 and reported in Kleinhenz 1994, is such an example).

I believe that the difference just described is not a trivial one. The way in which the phonology of Focus has been accounted for in the literature is revealing in this respect. As already noted (see the introduction to this paper), languages like Hausa and Hungarian put emphasis on phrasing, and segmental/lexical phenomena play a major role among the arguments that support phrasing dependency on Focus. By contrast, in languages like English or Italian the emphasis is put on prominence and intonation, and stress and accent phenomena are the kind of evidence that is taken to support a presumed effect of Focus on phrasing. In the latter group of languages, the metrical and intonational means of conveying Focus are given a crucial role.

The fact that in the second group of languages a presumed effect of Focus on phrasing may be stronger or weaker would seem to suggest that languages differ in a continuum, instead of a two-way fashion, as I am proposing. For example, according to Kenesei and Vogel's 1993 *Focus restructuring*, English would show a stronger Focus effect than EP, which seems to show no effect at all. However, if accenting/deaccenting are not taken as almost synonyms with (and the sole evidence for) phrasing/dephrasing and —perhaps more importantly— if other (non-phonological) properties of the languages are taken into account, the case for the classification suggested here may be further strengthened.

3.2 The syntax-phonology interface: evidence for two major types of languages

There is an interesting correlation between the kind of Focus/phrasing relation found in a language and its morpho-syntactic properties concerning Focus. Focus affects the building up of phonological phrasing in languages in which stress and intonation alone do not suffice to mark a constituent as focused. This situation arises because the language has some Focus morphology (i.e. Focus has to be conveyed by a morpheme or particle whose placement identifies the focused element) and/or syntax (i.e. Focus is conveyed through a particular structural relation, as the focused element has to occupy a particular structural position). Hausa and Hungarian, together with Aghem, Basque, or Korean, are examples of languages in which Focus is *morpho-syntactic* (cf. Horvath 1986: 123-124, Hyman 1979, Zec and Inkelas 1990, Vogel and Kenesei 1990, Cho 1990). Focus does not affect the building up of phrasing in languages in which there is no clear and visible evidence for any Focus morphology or syntax. In these languages, stress and intonation alone suffice to mark a constituent as focused. Languages in which Focus is *phonological* include English, German, Dutch, Italian, and EP (cf. Nespor and Vogel 1986, Horvath 1986: 93-94, Féry 1993, Gussenhoven 1984, Zwart 1993, Grice 1995, Frota 1993, 1994).[24]

Generally, Focus discourse-configurational languages (in the sense of Kiss 1995: 6) can be expected to show similar phonological consequences associated with Focus. As Focus is formally marked either by special morphology, by a structural Focus position, or by both, the fact that it has to be taken into account in the phrasing algorithms seems a natural consequence in a theory which presupposes some morpho-syntactic input to phonological phrasing. Moreover, it is not surprising, under our assumptions that the phonology of Focus shows different properties in non-discourse-configurational languages (i.e., not *phrasing* effects, but rather *stress* and *accent* effects).[25]

I hope to have been able to show that in the observed correlation between morpho-syntactic properties and the properties of the phonology of Focus lies an interesting and fruitful course of research. In the realm of the Iberian languages, Basque and Catalan, considered to be discourse-configurational languages (cf. Horvath 1986: 123-124 and Kiss 1995: 6, 20-23), would be a test for the proposals put forward in this paper. As for broader cross-linguistic testing, an enormous empirical challenge stands ahead of us. In some cases, the relevant morphological and syntactic observations are not available; in other instances, a more systematic investigation of the phonology of Focus seems to be called for in future research.

Notes

* I would like to thank Bob Ladd and Marina Nespor for helpful comments on this paper. Carlos Gussenhoven has also commented on a first outline of the paper. My audiences at the University of Nijmegen and at the University of Amsterdam (February, 1995), to whom prior versions of this work were presented, have contributed with useful suggestions. Bob Ladd has given me the kind permission to cite his forthcoming book on intonational phonology, and Marina Vigário has allowed me to use some of the materials of her research on the prosody of focusing adverbs. A different version of this paper was presented at the *International Conference on Interfaces in Linguistics* held in Oporto, November, 1995).

1 In Sá Nogueira (1938), Andrade (1977), Cunha and Cintra (1984), and Andrade and Viana (1993) the phenomena here considered are described as operative across words. Only in the first of these works there are a few examples of cases in which some of the phenomena are favored against cases in which they are not favored, but no account of such differences is suggested.

2 In these and all the remaining examples, the application of a given rule is indicated by italics; small caps indicate that the rule in question does not apply. Although the absence of segmental evidence for ϕ makes it difficult to know if ϕ restructuring is a possibility in EP, the prosodic structure presented in the examples assumes that the type of restructuring found in Italian and English is also an available option in EP. Nothing in this assumption undermines the basic distinction between what happens within and across an I-boundary.

3 (2) is a reformulation of the rule (8b) in Frota (1993), which in turn was based on Andrade (1977: 212, rule (53)).

4 A detailed description of the phenomenon is found in Sá Nogueira (1938).

5 The vowel adjacency resolution phenomena have had a long history of short descriptive references in the literature, starting with Oliveira (1536). Sá Nogueira (1938) is aware of the complexity of these phenomena. It is this apparently unruled complexity that emerges from Andrade and Viana's (1993) description of external sandhi phenomena involving adjacent vowels. In my knowledge, the fact that the different processes of vowel adjacency resolution are sensitive to the structural configuration of the words involved, was first explicitly stated in the literature on EP in Frota (1995a). However, a detailed phonetic analysis of the vowel adjacency resolution processes remains yet to be done, and it may bring new insights into the findings reported and discussed in Frota (1995a, 1996).

6 Semivocalization is a domain span rule, but here only its external sandhi application is of relevance.

7 Note that as vowel adjacency resolution rules affect syllabic nuclei, restrictions related to stress and rhythm are to be expected (cf. Nespor 1987). In the case of Vowel Merger (which affects two nuclei), word stress on either of the vowels blocks the rule, while in the case of both Vowel Deletion and Semivocalization only word stress on the first vowel has a blocking effect.

8 I take the I^{max}-domain as the Intonational Phrase domain dominated by the prosodic category of the immediately higher level.

9 For the first group of languages the existence of ϕ-level rules and other ϕ-level phenomena (e.g. final lengthening, tonal marking) is well established (cf. Nespor and Vogel 1979, 1982, 1983, 1986, Condoravdi 1990, Hayes and Lahiri 1991, Arvaniti 1994, Grice 1995). The same does not seem to be true for Dutch and German, according to van Donzel (1994, and p.c.) and Kleinhenz (1994, 1995).

10 (9a) is a neutral sentence; i.e. none of the constituents is particularly highlighted (the terms *unmarked accent*, *unmarked stress pattern*, *normal stress*, *neutral accent*, or *broad Focus* are used by various authors to refer to sentences like (9a)). (9b-d), on the contrary, are marked sentences. For example, (9d) is a natural response (in the sense of Chomsky 1971 and Jackendoff 1972) to a question like *Have they given the roses to the doctor?*, while (9a) is not.

11 According to Nespor (1994), this straight connection between direction of recursivity and the prominence pattern supports the hypothesis that "the two syntactic parameters of head directionality and direction of recursivity are set on the basis of phonological characteristics of language".

12 I-final prominence seems to be the overwhelming pattern in the languages studied. In fact, I do not know of any language with I-initial prominence.

13 In this respect EP is like Standard Italian, and unlike French and certain Italian dialects in which clitics do get stressed in this position (cf. Nespor and Vogel 1986: 155-157).

14 The examples in (12) are taken to mean the following: (a) it was the roses (and not the books or any other gifts) that the (female) students have given the teacher; (b) all the students (and not just a few, or any specific group of them such as *five*, *American*, or *literature* students) have given flowers to the teacher; (c) the students have given (and not sold) flowers to the teacher.

15 As was already referred in footnote 10, the terminology on stress patterns and Focus is varied and sometimes confusing. For example, *neutral stress* and *broad Focus* on the one hand, and *marked stress* and *narrow Focus* on the other, are generally equivalent. Some authors even use the term *neutral Focus* to refer to *broad Focus* (cf. Hayes and Lahiri 1991). For the sake of clarity, I will keep the term Focus only for marked stress and use neutral or default stress for the unmarked pattern.

16 It is not clear to me if in these languages other intonational features (e.g. downstep, pitch range) are not possible cues to prominence patterns in such a way as to disambiguate between *w-s* as neutral stress and *w-s* as Focus. If this is indeed a possibility, maybe the account of prominence assignment here suggested for EP could be extended to these languages.

17 In Vigário (1995) ϕ-level neutral and marked prominence assignment is looked at in detail. I believe that Vigário's results are essentially compatible with the approach developed here (and first hinted in Frota 1993).

18 Although Pierrehumbert's original framework of intonation analysis does not include tune internal structure, several authors in Pierrehumbert's research tradition make either crucial use of the nucleus/head distinction (e.g. Ladd 1992b and forthcoming, Féry 1993, among others), or consider it useful from a descriptive point of view (e.g. Hayes and Lahiri 1991). Ladd (forthcoming) proposes to replace the term *head* by *prenuclear contour*, or *prenuclear accent(s)*.

19 Late alignment characterizes the prenuclear H* in a way similar to the prenuclear high accent in English (cf. Silverman and Pierrehumbert 1990). The factors conditioning the gradient differences in the alignment of the H* in EP remain, however, unstudied.

20 The example is taken from Vigário (1995: appendix II, file mjmi0038). According to this author, two different pitch accents may be optionally introduced in the prenuclear stretch of declarative tunes: L*+H and H+L*.

21 For exemplification and discussion of other types of lexical/syntactic related Focus information, the reader is referred to Frota (1993) (for contrastive dislocation), and to Vigário (1995) (for a detailed analysis of the intonation of focusing adverbs and negation).

22 In fact, another question remains to be addressed. Does the Focus nucleus display the property of deaccenting the material to the right, as apparently suggested by figure 5? The available data provides no straightforward answer to this question; although deaccenting is a possible strategy in EP, it is also true that in the same instances of early nucleus a post-focal secondary accent may be present (see Vigário 1995 for a similar observation). This issue certainly deserves further investigation.

23 It is important to note that Viana does not consider at all the issues of alignment and association in her analysis.

24 Japanese and Bengali were pointed out to me as potential counterexamples to the two major types of languages view by C. Gussenhoven (p.c.). In these languages Focus is taken to have strong effects on phrasing (cf. Pierrehumbert and Beckman 1988, Hayes and Lahiri 1991), and apparently there is no Focus morphology or syntax. However, a closer look seems to indicate that neither of them is a true counterexample. On the one hand, Japanese has Focus particles syntactically linked with the focused element (cf. König 1991), which may indicate the presence of some Focus morphology. On the other hand, according to Beckman and Pierrehumbert (1986: 268), the phonetic effects after a focused word in Japanese may be interpreted either as a consequence of dephrasing or as a consequence of accent subordination to the focused word. As for Bengali, the absence of morphological or syntactic Focus marking seems to be a fact, but the way in which Focus affects phrasing does not make Bengali a *morpho-syntactic* language: according to Hayes and Lahiri (1991:92), Focus does not directly affect default phonological phrasing; instead, it acts as a restriction on restructuring of phonological phrasing.

25 If I am on the right track, phonological evidence for including a language in the phonological type can be taken as evidence against an analysis which instantiates Focus as a functional syntactic projection in that language. EP seems to be clearly a phonological language in this regard. Therefore, although Old Romance showed properties of morphological and structural Focus marking (cf. Uriagereka 1992), an analysis such as Martins (1992a, 1992b, 1994a, 1994b), who proposes a kind of structural Focus position in EP, is challenged by phonological counter-evidence.

References

Andrade, Ernesto. 1977. *Aspects de la phonologie (generative) du portugais.* Lisboa: Publicações do Centro de Linguística da Universidade de Lisboa, Instituto Nacional de Investigação Científica.

Andrade, Ernesto, and M. C. Viana. 1988. Ainda sobre o acento e o ritmo em português. *Actas do IV Encontro da Associação Portuguesa de Linguística*, 3-15. Lisboa: Faculdade de Letras da Universidade de Lisboa.

Andrade, Ernesto, and M. C. Viana. 1993. Que horas são às (1)3 e 15?. *Actas do VIII Encontro da Associação Portuguesa de Linguística*, 59-66. Lisboa: Faculdade de Letras da Universidade de Lisboa.

Arvaniti, Amalia. 1994. Acoustic features of Greek rhythmic structure. *Journal of Phonetics* 22.239-268.

Beckman, Mary, and Janet Pierrehumbert. 1986. Intonational structure in Japanese and English. *Phonology Yearbook* 3.255-310.

Cho, Young-mee Y. 1990. Syntax and phrasing in Korean. *The Phonology-Syntax Connection*, ed. Sharon Inkelas and Draga Zec, 47-62. Chicago: University of Chicago Press.

Chomsky, Noam. 1971. Deep structure, surface structure,and semantic interpretation. *Semantics: An Interdisciplinary Reader in Philosophy, Linguistics and Psychology*, ed. D. Steinberd and L. Jakobovits, 183-216. New York: Cambridge University Press.

Condoravdi, Cleo. 1990. Sandhi rules of Greek and prosodic theory. *The Phonology-Syntax Connection*, ed. Sharon Inkelas and Draga Zec, 63-84. Chicago: University of Chicago Press.

Cunha, Celso, and Luis L. Cintra. 1984. *Nova gramática do português contemporâneo.* Lisboa: Edições Sá da Costa.

Delgado Martins, Maria R. 1977. *Aspects de l'accent en portugais. Voyelles toniques et atones.* Doctoral dissertation of 3rd cyclem, University of Strasbourg.

Delgado Martins, Maria R., and Francisco Lacerda. 1977. Para uma gramática da entoação. Paper given at the *Congresso de Filologia e Linguística*, Rio de Janeiro.

Donzel, Monique van. 1994. Stress shift in the Nederlands. Master's thesis, ATW/Fonetiek, Leiden University.

Féry, Caroline. 1993. *German Intonational Patterns.* Tübingen: Niemeyer.

Frota, Sónia. 1991. *Para a prosódia da frase: quantificador, advérbio e marcação prosódica (somente alguns tópicos em foco).* Master's thesis, University of Lisbon.

Frota, Sónia. 1993. On the prosody of Focus in European Portuguese. *Proceedings of the Workshop on Phonology*, 45-66. Lisboa: APL.

Frota, Sónia. 1994. Is Focus a phonological category in Portuguese? *Proceedings of Console I*, ed. P. Ackema and M. Schoorlemmer, 69-86. The Hague: Holland Academic Graphics.

Frota, Sónia. 1995a. Os domínios prosódicos e o português europeu: fenómenos de sandhi. *Actas do X Encontro da Associação Portuguesa de Linguística*, 221-237. Lisboa: Colibri.

Frota. Sónia. 1995b. Acoustic features of prosodic phrases in European Portuguese. Ms., University of Lisbon.

Frota, Sónia. 1995c. Clashes and prosodic domains in European Portuguese. *Proceedings* 19.93-107, Institute of Phonetic Sciences, University of Amsterdam.

Frota, Sónia. 1996. Prosodic phrases and European Portuguese: in search of evidence. *Proceedings of Console III*, 47-69. Leiden: Sole.

Grice, Martine L. 1995. *The Intonation of Interrogation in Palermo Italian: Implications for Intonation Theory*. Tübingen: Niemeyer.

Gussenhoven, Carlos. 1984. *On the Grammar and Semantics of Sentence Accents*. Dordrecht: Foris.

Gussenhoven, Carlos. 1992. Sentence accents and argument structure. *Thematic Structure: Its Role in Grammar*, ed. I. M. Roca, 79-106. Berlin, Dordrecht: Foris Publications.

Hayes, Bruce. 1990. Precompiled Phrasal Phonology. *The Phonology-Syntax Connection*, ed. Sharon Inkelas and Draga Zec, 85-108. Chicago: University of Chicago Press.

Hayes, Bruce, and Aditi Lahiri. 1991. Bengali intonational phonology. *Natural Language and Linguistic Theory* 9.47-96.

Horvath, Julia. 1986. *Focus in the theory of grammar and the syntax of Hungarian*. Dordrecht: Foris Publications.

Hyman, Larry (ed.) 1979. *Aghem Grammatical Structure (with Special Reference to Noun Classes, Tense-Aspect and Focus Marking)*. Los Angeles, California: Dept. of Linguistics, University of Southern California.

Jackendoff, Ray. 1972. *Semantic Interpretation in Generative Grammar*. Cambridge, Mass.: MIT Press.

Kanerva, Jonni M. 1990. Focusing on phonological phrases in Chichêwa. *The Phonology-Syntax Connection*, ed. Sharon Inkelas and Draga Zec, 145-161. Chicago: University of Chicago Press.

Kenesei, István, and Irene Vogel. 1993. Focus and phonological structure. Ms., University of Delaware.

Kleinhenz, Ursula. 1994. *Focus and Phrasing in German*. Arbeitspapiere des Sonderforschungsbereichs 340. Stuttgart/Tübingen.

Kleinhenz, Ursula. 1995. Domain typology and the phonology/syntax interface. Paper given at the *International Conference on Interfaces in Linguistics*, University of Oporto.

Kiss, Katalin (ed.) 1995. *Discourse Configurational Languages*. New York: Oxford University Press.
König, Ekkehard. 1991. *The Meaning of Focus Particles: A Comparative Perspective*. London, New York: Routledge.
Ladd, D. Robert. 1980. *The Structure of Intonational Meaning: Evidence from English*. Bloomington, Indiana: Indiana University Press.
Ladd, D. Robert. 1992a. An introduction to intonational phonology. *Papers in Laboratory Phonology II - Gesture, Segment, Prosody*, ed. G. J. Docherty and D. R. Ladd, 321-334. Cambridge: Cambridge University Press.
Ladd, D. Robert. 1992b. Compound prosodic domains, ms. University of Edinburgh.
Ladd, D. Robert. forthcoming. *Intonational Phonology*. New York: Cambridge University Press.
Pierrehumbert, Janet, and Mary Beckman. 1988. *Japanese Tone Structure*. Cambridge, Mass.: MIT Press.
Martins, Ana M. 1992a. Clitic placement from Old to Modern European Portuguese. Unpubl. ms., University of Lisbon.
Martins, Ana M. 1992b. Focus and clitics in European Portuguese. Paper given at the *Graduate Students Conference*, University of Maryland.
Martins, Ana M. 1994a. A colocação dos clíticos e a relevância da categoria Sigma. Paper given at the *International Meeting on Portuguese*, University of Lisbon.
Martins, Ana M. 1994b. *Clíticos na história do Português*. Vol. 1. Doctoral dissertation, University of Lisbon.
Martins, Fernando. 1986. *Entoação e Organização do Enunciado*. Master's thesis, University of Lisbon.
Nespor, Marina. 1987. Vowel degemination and fast speech rules. *Phonology Yearbook* 4.61-85.
Nespor, Marina. 1990. On the separation of prosodic and rhythmic phonology. *The Phonology-Syntax Connection*, ed. Sharon Inkelas and Draga Zec, 243-258. Chicago: University of Chicago Press.
Nespor, Marina. 1993. Phonology between words and phrases. Paper given at the *Workshop on Phonology*, University of Coimbra.
Nespor, Marina. 1994. Setting syntactic parameters at a prelexical stage. *Proceedings of ABRALIN XXV*.
Nespor, Marina, and Irene Vogel. 1979. Clash avoidance in Italian. *Linguistic Inquiry* 10.467-482.
Nespor, Marina, and Irene Vogel. 1982. Prosodic domains of external sandhi rules. *The Structure of Phonological Representations*, Part I, ed. Harry van der Hulst and Norval Smith, 225-255. Dordrecht: Foris.
Nespor, Marina, and Irene Vogel. 1983. Prosodic structure above the word. *Prosody: Models and Measurements*, ed. Anne Cutler and D. Robert Ladd, 123-140. Berlin: Springer.
Nespor, Marina, and Irene Vogel. 1986. *Prosodic Phonology*. Dordrecht: Foris.

Nespor, Marina, and Irene Vogel. 1989. On clashes and lapses. *Phonology* 6.69-116.

Oliveira, Fernão. 1536/1975. *A gramática da linguagem portuguesa*, 4th ed. Lisboa: Imprensa Nacional, Casa da Moeda.

Sá Nogueira, Rodrigo. 1938. *Elementos para um tratado de fonética*. Lisboa: Imprensa Nacional.

Selkirk, Elisabeth, and Tong Shen. 1990. Prosodic domains in Shanghai Chinese. *The Phonology-Syntax Connection*, ed. Sharon Inkelas and Draga Zec, 313-337. Chicago: University of Chicago Press.

Silverman, Kim, and Janet Pierrehumbert. 1990. The timing of prenuclear high accents in English. *Papers in Laboratory Phonology I: Between the Grammar and Physics of Speech*, ed. John Kingston and Mary E. Beckman, 72-106. New York: Cambridge University Press.

Uriagereka, Juan. 1992. A focus position in Western Romance. Paper given at the *15th GLOW Conference*, Lisbon.

Viana, M. C. 1987. *Para a síntese da entoação do português*. Dissertação para acesso à categoria de Investigador Auxiliar, Centro de Linguística da Universidade de Lisboa, INIC.

Vigário, Marina C. 1995. *Aspectos da prosódia do Português Europeu: estruturas com advérbios de exclusão e negação frásica*. Master's thesis, University of Lisbon.

Vogel, Irene, and István Kenesei. 1990. Syntax and semantics in phonology. *The Phonology-Syntax Connection*, ed. Sharon Inkelas and Draga Zec, 339-363. Chicago: University of Chicago Press.

Zec, Draga and Sharon Inkelas. 1990. Prosodically constrained syntax. *The Phonology-Syntax Connection*, ed. Sharon Inkelas and Draga Zec, 365-378. Chicago: University of Chicago Press.

Zwart, Cornelius J. W. 1993. *Dutch Syntax: A Minimalistic Approach*. Doctoral dissertation, University of Groningen.

12

On the interplay of morphology, prosody and faithfulness in Portuguese pluralization

ALFONSO MORALES-FRONT AND D. ERIC HOLT

1 Introduction

In this paper we demonstrate that, in spite of its surface array of manifestations, Portuguese pluralization is systematic and unitary at its root. That is, we shall show that the plural of *papel* 'paper', for example, is *papeis* because there is a change of underlying /l/ to surface [j] and because the plural morpheme is concatenated to the stem. However, this work does not aim to provide yet another analysis in which a base form is mapped to a surface form through a set of unrelated rules. Instead, we adopt the constraint-based Optimality Theory (Prince and Smolensky 1993), and focus on explaining the surface phonological alternations related to pluralization as the logical result of keeping morphology and prosody as simple as possible.

Our central assertion is that the morphology involved in pluralization is as simple as it can be: the plural morpheme must be realized segmentally as /s/ and must occur at the right edge of the word. Most of the alternations arise when these demands of morphology must be upheld while meeting other prosodic restrictions. Morphology requires the presence of the plural morpheme /s/, and prosody requires the well-formedness of syllabic and metrical constituents. In this paper we show how this specific case of conflict between morphology and prosody is resolved at the expense of segmental faithfulness to the input form.

There are a number of interesting aspects of Portuguese plural formation that have launched a considerable amount of investigation from different theoretical approaches (see section 3 for a review). The first area of debate is the determination of the underlying forms. Are *-s* and *-es* allomorphs? If this is not a case of lexicalized alternation, then the alternation between *-e* and *-es* must be either a case of synchronic epenthesis or lenition. In Portuguese, plural formation intersects with consonant gliding and nasalization—with concomitant deletion of the nasal (e.g. /papel+s/[1] → [papejš] and /irman+o+s/ → [irmãw̃]). Moreover, in different previous analyses, many processes have been considered in relation to pluralization. These are, among others, denasalization, tensing, centralization, deletion, epenthesis, softening, analogy, and diphthongization. Our view is that this proliferation of processes is the result of approaching the problem from within a procedural framework. When considered from a constraint-based perspective, the relationship between the different surface realizations emerges, and a greater level of explanation is attained. The processes intersecting with pluralization do not stem from independent or unrelated rules, as previously proposed, but are the result of striving to accommodate, at the expense of faithfulness, morphological and prosodic constraints.

2 Data

We begin this section with a presentation of the basic data under consideration. First are words that end in a vowel or (nonnasal) glide, which present the simplest case of pluralization:

(1) Words with a final vowel- and nonnasal glide:

casa	*casa+s*	'house(s)'
coisa	*coisa+s*	'thing(s)'
pau	*pau+s*	'stick(s)'
rei	*rei+s*	'king(s)'

Here we see that the plural marker /-s/ is concatenated to the singular form, with no further changes taking place that concern us here.

Next are words that end in a consonant:

(2) Words ending in /s/ with penultimate stress:

simples	*simples*	'simple'
ourives	*ourives*	'goldsmith(s)'
lápis	*lápis*	'pencil(s)'
pires	*pires*	'saucer(s)'

íris	*íris*	'iris(es)'
gratis	*gratis*	'free'
caos	*caos*	'chaos(es)'
oásis	*oásis*	'oasis/oases'
ônibus	*ônibus*	'bus(es)'

This is a near exhaustive list of words of this type, which have identical surface forms for both the singular and plural.

In (3) are words ending in /s/ that are stressed on the ultimate syllable. Here we see that the plural forms surface with [eš], not simple [š]:

(3) Words ending in /s/ with final stress:

português	*português+es*	'Portuguese'
mês	*mês+es*	'month(s)'
gas	*gas+es*	'gas(es)'

Words ending in /-r/ behave like the forms in (3), showing final [eš]:

(4) Words ending in /-r/:

mar	*mar+es*	'sea(s)'
bar	*bar+es*	'bar(s)'
favor	*favor+es*	'favor(s)'
cor	*cor+es*	'color(s)'
flor	*flor+es*	'flower(s)'
lar	*lar+es*	'home(s), hearth(s)'
luar	*luar+es*	'moonlight(s)'

Words ending in /l/ constitute another class. The /l/ is velarized to [ɫ] in Continental Portuguese in syllable-final position, as in the singular forms, but is vocalized to [j] word-finally before the plural morpheme /-s/. Additionally, we observe three types of alternations in the plural:

For words ending in stressed *-al*, *-el*, *-ol*, *-ul*, /l/ becomes a glide. The plural form ends in [jš]:

(5) Words ending in stressed *-al*, *-el*, *-ol*, *-ul* ([ɫ ~ j]):

hospital	/ospital/	[os.pi.táɫ]	'hospital'
hospitais	/ospital+s/	[os.pi.tájš]	'hospitals'
hotel	/otel/	[o.téɫ]	'hotel'
hoteis	/otel+s/	[o.téjš]	'hotels'
farol	/farol/	[fa.róɫ]	'headlight'
farois	/farol+s/	[fa.rójš]	'headlights'
paul	/paul/	[pa.úɫ]	'swamp'
pauis	/paul+s/	[pa.újš]	'swamps'

If the final vowel is /i/, however, there are two possible further alternations. In (6) we see that there is lowering of unstressed /i/ to [e], and that a falling diphthong surfaces (only a representative example is shown in full phonetic form):

(6) Unstressed /-il/ is realized in the plural as [ejš] ([iɫ ~ ejš]):

fácil	/fásil/	[fá.siɫ]	'easy'
fáceis	/fásil+s/	[fá.sejš]	'easy pl.'
lábil	*lábeis*		'labile'
fóssil	*fósseis*		'fossil(s)'
frágil	*frágeis*		'fragile'
dócil	*dóceis*		'docile'
ágil	*ágeis*		'agile'

Note, however, that when the final /i/ is stressed this change is not possible:

(7) Stressed /-il/ realized in the plural as [íš] ([íɫ ~ íš]):

subtil	/subtil/	[subtíɫ]	'subtle'
subtís	/subtil+s/	[subtíš]	'subtle pl.'
fuzil	*fuzís*		'rifle(s)'
funil	*funís*		'funnel(s)'
canil	*canís*		'kennel(s)'
imbecil	*imbecís*		'imbecile(s)'

The last major class of data is those words that end in the nasal diphthong [ãw̃] in the singular. The principal difficulty in analyzing these cases is that in the plural they show one of three forms, which depend both historically and synchronically on the Latin etymological root. The need to posit input forms that are identical or similar to the Latin etyma has been established by Saciuk (1970), Brasington (1971), St. Clair (1971), Mira Mateus (1975) and Brakel (1979), and is due to the numerous alternations that require the original morphological form be present. Below are the relevant data:

(8) Morphological alternations requiring positing of underlying nasal consonant (representative samples):

a. [ãw̃] ~ [ãw̃š] (<Lt. -anu(s))

irmão *irmãos* 'brother(s)' (cf. *irmanar* 'link')
cristão *cristãos* 'Christian(s)'

b. [ã] ~ [ãš] (< Lt. -ana(s))

irmã *irmãs* 'sister(s)'
alemã *alemãs* 'German(s), fem.'
cristã *cristãs* 'Christian(s), fem.'

c. [ãw̃] ~ [õj̃š] (< Lt. -one(s))

patrão *patrões* 'patron(s)' (cf. *patronato* 'patronage')
limão *limões* 'lemon(s)'
leão *leões* 'lion(s)'

d. [oa] ~ [oas] (< Lt. -one(s))

leoa *leoas* 'lioness(es)' (cf. [bõ] ~ [boa], [leãw̃] ~ [leoa])

e. [ãw̃] ~ [ãj̃š] (< Lt. -ane(s))

pão *pães* 'bread(s)' (cf. *panificar* 'make bread')
cão *cães* 'dog(s)'
capitão *capitães* 'captain(s)'

3 Previous analyses

3.1 Unmarked pluralization

The data in (1) are unproblematic since we see the simple concatenation of the plural marker /-s/. All previous accounts agree on this much, and so this will not be addressed further.

3.2 Identical forms

Beginning with the data in (2), those words with identical forms in both the singular and plural like *simples*, there is disagreement in analysis among previous authors. For instance, Williams (1962:126) cites historical evidence that these are cases of haplology, while the earliest synchronic analyses of these forms is given by the structuralist Mattoso Câmara (1970, 1972). He proposed that there is a zero plural allomorph that is added to words that end in an atonic syllable already ending in /s/. This quite unexplanatory account is bettered by Andrade (1977). Andrade argues that the plural marker /-s/ is uniformly added to all base forms, with a concomitant degemination rule for the forms in (2). This is shown below:

(9) simples + /s/ → simpless → simples

For analogous data in Spanish, Harris (1980) proposes a similar approach. Adapting work done in templatic morphology, Harris posits the following general template for the plural forms of nouns and adjectives:

(10) $[[\ldots]_{Root}\ V\ C\ ]_{Word}$

Thus, a noun or adjective of the type Sp. *dosis* 'dose' has the identical plural form because of its morphological structure [[dos] i s] (cf. *dosificar* [[[dos] ifik]ar]), and the V C portion of the template in (10) is satisfied by the exceptional Terminal Element /is/. As in Andrade's analysis, the plural morpheme is concatenated to the base form, but is then merged under identity with the stem-final /s/.

An analysis using the template in (10) does not seem able to account for all of the Portuguese data above in (2). *Simples*, *caos* and *gratis* do arguably have morphological structure that would satisfy the template in (10) (cf. *simpleza* [[[simpl]ez]a], *caótico* [[[kao]tik]o], *gratuito* [[[grat]uit]o]), but for the majority of the above forms we cannot reasonably posit such morphological structure. Finally, Lipski (1973) notes that these words are quite exceptional, and assumes that native speakers would have difficulty in pronouncing *[V́...Vsis], since the final syllable of Portuguese paroxytones is very weakly articulated and is often dropped. Furthermore, he assumes that these forms already sound like plurals, so no plural ending is added.

3.3 Apocope versus epenthesis

Next, for the class of words exemplified in (3) and (4), those that show [eš] in the plural, many previous accounts have assumed that these base forms underlyingly possess the /e/ seen in the plural form (cf. for example, Hensey 1968, Mattoso Câmara 1970, Saciuk 1970, St. Clair 1971, Brasington 1971, Andrade 1977). Then, /e/ is either apocopated in the singular forms, or surfaces when the plural marker *-s* is added. These authors assume the Latin Stress Rule, so this /e/ also serves to regularize the stress of consonant-final words as underlyingly penultimate. Lipski (1973:76) argues against the apocope hypothesis, reasoning that such an analysis is undesirably abstract. Instead, he assumes that there is epenthesis of /e/ in the plural forms, because the simple addition of *-s* would yield the impermissible sequences **-ls* **-rs* **-zs* **-ss*. He states (p. 77) that this epenthesis is merely part of a general tendency toward making Portuguese a CV language (Brazilian Portuguese is the case Lipski addresses, but this is also true of Continental Portuguese). As for stress assignment, he assumes that the generalization native speakers make is that words ending in a consonant take final stress.

3.4 /l/-final words

For words ending in /l/, those in (5)-(7), early accounts (Mattoso Câmara 1970, St. Clair 1971:94, Andrade 1977) assumed that these forms underlyingly end in /e/, which is either apocopated in the singular forms as in (3) and (4) or provides the structural environment for a rule of intervocalic loss of /l/. Such accounts assume that it is the underlying /e/ that undergoes glide formation once the /l/ is lost and is in contact with another vowel. This crucially requires the extrinsic ordering of the apocope rule after the intervocalic /l/-deletion rule, and such ordering should be eliminated if possible, given the lack of independent evidence for it. Likewise, an analysis that does not posit an underlying /e/ that never surfaces in the singular is preferable to an analysis that does. Furthermore, for the singular/plural pairs under discussion, the /e/ would *always* surface in the plural as the palatal glide [j], so there is really *no* evidence that supports an analysis requiring /e/ in the base forms.

Lipski (p. 78) notes that aside from playing a crucial role in the analysis these authors give of pluralization, this supposedly general rule of 'lateral loss' does not occur in Portuguese. In fact, there are thousands of words with intervocalic /l/, and even the type of words under discussion here contain /l/ intervocalically in forms other than the plural, such as *canal* ~ *canículo* '(little) canal', *papel* ~ *papelão* 'paper ~ cardboard', etc. Both Lipski (1973) and Agard (1984) assume that /l/ directly becomes [j] in the plural, and not that there is intervocalic loss of /l/ with concomitant glide formation of /e/.

The gliding of /l/ to [j] in Continental Portuguese is usually not related in the literature to the processes of vocalization and velarization of /l/ in syllable-final position. We note in passing that Lipski (p. 76) cites *[-ls] as an impermissible sequence, a restriction he uses to motivate epenthesis, as in *males* and *cônsules*, the only two exceptions to the loss of /-l-/, but not as motivation for gliding. On his account then, we would expect forms like **papeles* instead of *papeis*.

One author who does propose an explicit analysis of the vocalization of /l/ in the plural in Brazilian Portuguese (BP) (not Continental Portuguese, CP) to both [w] and [j] is Girelli (1988). Although his proposal employs an elaborate and quite unorthodox X'-theory of syllable structure, many of his ideas are fairly readily translated into the constraint-based approach adopted here. His principal claim relevant to the current discussion of /l/ is that in BP, syllable-final /l/ is realized within the nucleus, and so surfaces either as [w], before a pause or some consonant other than [š], or as [j], when the liquid is a sister to [š] within the nucleus (p. 147). He also assumes that those features whose values vary depending on the realization of /l/ as [w] or [j] are unspecified, and only filled in by other marking conventions. Though not identical, this general approach is consistent with the proposal of Inkelas (1995) with regard to underspecification and lexicon optimization in Optimality Theory.

Other facts that must be accounted for are the other alternations seen in (6) and (7). For (6), e.g. *fácil* ~ *fáceis*, both Mattoso Câmara and Andrade assume that from the base form /fasile/ there is loss of /l/, raising of /e/, dissimilation of /i/ to [e], and then glide formation of [i] to [j]. For (7), e.g. *subtil* ~ *subtís*, Mattoso Câmara assumes that from /subtile/ the /l/ is suppressed in the plural (/subtil/:

*subti(l)s = [subtíš]), while Andrade argues that there is elision of /l/, raising of /e/ to [i], and subsequent merger. The interaction of these rules is complex, and their relative ordering is simply stipulated. Since the rules and rule interaction posited above for (6) are so problematic, Lipski (p. 78) claims that these forms are "completely irregular...for obvious reasons, no attempt has ever been made to derive them in a principled way." In spite of the limited number of examples and Lipski's warning, we will later present our analysis, which will account for the regularity of the /-il/ ~ [ej] alternation, even if the number of words is reduced.

3.5 The nasals

There has been a long debate, at least since the early 1940s, regarding the phonological status of nasal vowels in Portuguese. The discussion centers around whether these vowels are underlyingly /Ṽ/ or /VN/ sequences. Proponents of the phonemic status of nasal vowels[2] prefer this non abstract analysis of the phonology of these vowels. On the other hand, advocates of the /VN/ analyses[3] prefer this proposal on morphological grounds. That is, a common underlying form containing /VN/ is attributed to the root in related forms such as *som* [sõ] 'sound', *sonoro* [sunoru] 'sonorous', *origem* [oriʒẽj̃] 'origen', *originar* [oriʒinar] 'originate' (Mira Mateus 1975:46, cited in Parkinson 1983).

Other evidence also supports the VN analysis.[4] First, with respect to the distribution of the allophones of /r/, the same variant that occurs after a heterosyllabic consonant also occurs after a nasal vowel: Is[X]ael 'Israel', pal[X]ar 'to chat', gen[X]o 'son-in-law' (Mattoso Câmara 1953:93, 1977:70). Second, prefinal heavy syllables are never skipped by the stress rule, and nasalized vowels in penultimate position followed by a consonant pattern the same way; that is, *rápido* 'rapid' is perfectly normal, but nonce **rápindo* is impossible (Reighard and Almeida 1983). This suggests that the rhyme in question is heavy. Third, nasal vowels do not occur in syllables closed by an oral consonant (Cintra 1962:26-31), which can be explained by assuming that only one rhyme consonant is allowed in Portuguese (Wetzels 1991:82, Mattoso Câmara 1953, 1972, Mascherpe 1970:68-9, López 1979:111, Azevedo 1981:38, 90; see also the appendix). Fourth, word-final nasal vowels are resistant to deletion or contraction (Mattoso Câmara 1953), which follows from their underlying VN, not Ṽ, status, since only after further rules changed VN to VṼ would the nasal vowel meet the description for sandhi phenomena to take place (Wetzels 1991:81; this argument is challenged by Parkinson 1983:168-71). Fifth, the diphthongization of final /-ẽ/ to [ẽj̃], as in *bem* [bẽj̃] 'well', is more straightforwardly explained as a process that alters the final segment of a two-segment sequence (Parkinson 1983:161). Sixth, the variable realization of nasality, e.g. *finca* 'farm' [fĩĩka ~ fĩñka ~ fĩŋka] (Cagliari 1981:85, cited in Wetzels p. 81) is easily explained by the VN analysis as either the loss of the consonantality of the nasal or as its assimilation to a neighboring segment. Lastly, phonetic studies indicate that the nasal vowels of Portuguese are different from those found in French, for instance. That is, there is nasalization mainly on the second half of the vowel, which according to the VN analysis, corresponds to the slot occupied by the underlying nasal (Trigo 1993:388-89 cites Lacerda and Strevens 1956, Lacerda and Head 1952, Morais Barbosa 1965, Mira Mateus 1975:94 and Stevens, Andrade and Viana 1988; Morais Barbosa 1965 cites Louro 1954-55:242).

Given the various phonetic realizations of the underlying sequence, the issue arises as to the exact nature of this nasal segment. Early accounts assumed it was the neutralized nasal archiphoneme /-N/ (e.g. Mattoso Câmara 1970); others assumed that it is some sort of transitional element (Lacerda and Hammarström 1962:123, Louro 1954-55:242, both cited in Morais Barbosa 1983:84-85) or a 'relaxed *n*...like a glide, a transition sound from the vowel to the following occlusive' (translated from Morais Barbosa 1983:87). In generative accounts, this segment has received many names: it is the *mora-nasal* with no place of articulation of McCawley (1968:84), the *anusvara* of Trigo (1988:123), and is an 'incomplete segment' lacking a Place of Articulation (PA) according to Wetzels (1991:77); Girelli (1988:133) assumes that this segment is unspecified for the feature [consonantal]. The ultimate phonetic realization of the nasal consonant depends on what processes affect this segment (loss, assimilation, etc.). When the preceding vowel in nasalized, it is often assumed that the nasal element has undergone nucleation, forming a complex nucleus analogous to the structure of a diphthong (Parkinson 1983:158). Similar structure is proposed by Girelli (p. 133). Wetzels (p. 88) comments that it should not be surprising to see nasal consonants in the nucleus given the relative ease with which they become syllable peaks (though they do not in Portuguese). Trigo (1988:123), though discussing Gbe, in the spirit of de Chene and Anderson (1979) also assumes that the change from V+N to Ṽ results from the shifting of the nasal glide from coda to nuclear position (this then triggers monophthongization in Gbe from ṼṼ to Ṽ).

Evidence supporting the nucleation of /n/ comes from the data concerning the breaking of hiatus (Parkinson 1983:163): e.g., *sim, é*, 'yes, it is', is pronounced [sĩ^{ɨ} ε], analogous to *é, é* [ε ^{j}ε] 'it is, it is'. Thus, there is no evidence to show that the nasal is in coda position, since if it were, we would expect *sim, é* to be realized as *[si.nε], contrary to fact. The resyllabification data is thus consistent with the proposal that the nasal comes to be part of the syllable nucleus, having moved from the coda position that other consonants occupy.

Lastly, there is additional data cited from Brandão de Carvalho (1988) that is consistent with nucleation: compare the pairs *pesco* 'I fish' [pɛ̆š k^{o}] / *pescar* 'to fish' [pəš 'kar] and *meto* 'I put into' ['me t^{o}] / *meter* 'to put into' [mə 'ter] with the pairs *deito* 'I lay, spread' [dɐy t^{o}] / *deitar* 'to lay, spread' [dɐy 'tar] and *sento* 'I sit' [sẽn t^{o}] / *sentar* 'to sit' [sẽn 'tar]. Here we see that both atonic open syllables and atonic syllables closed by /-s/ undergo reduction, while in those syllables closed by a glide or nasal there is no such reduction. This may be attributed to their both having a complex nucleus. See further discussion in section 3.4, and fn. 12.

4 A constraint-based analysis

In this section we elucidate the analysis we propose, showing that the various surface realizations are the result of the interaction of a set of morphological, prosodic and faithfulness constraints.

4.1 Theoretical preliminaries

Optimality Theory ('OT', Prince and Smolensky 1993) posits that a grammar is a set of ranked 'soft' or violable constraints. A component called the Generator (GEN) produces a set of candidate output forms whose satisfaction of the constraints is determined in parallel by the Evaluator (EVAL). The optimal output form *minimally violates* the set of constraints that define the grammar under study; that is, a surface form may not satisfy all the constraints of a language, yet still be optimal or preferable to others that violate higher-ranked constraints.

Sample tableaux are given in (11) and (12) that visually illustrate how an OT grammar functions. The assumed underlying form is given in the upper left cell of the tableau and potential output forms are listed as candidates in the first column. Across the top of the tableau are the universal constraints whose relative importance in a given language is indicated by the ranking they are given; the more dominant a constraint the further left it appears in the tableau. An asterisk indicates a violation of a constraint, and an exclamation point indicates that a violation is 'fatal', that is, that this particular violation is the reason the candidate output is eliminated from consideration when compared to the optimal output. ☛ indicates the optimal candidate, i.e., the actual output for the language.

(11)

/input/	Constraint 1	Constraint 2
Candidate output 1	*!	
☛ Candidate output 2		**

(12)

/input/	Constraint 1	Constraint 2
Candidate output 1	*	**!
☛ Candidate output 2	*	*

In (11) Candidate output 1 violates Constraint 1, and because Candidate output 2 does not violate Constraint 1, Candidate 1 is eliminated from consideration. For (11) then, Candidate output 2 is optimal, as indicated by ☛, even though it incurs two violations of lower-ranked Constraint 2. In (12) both Candidates violate Constraint 1, and the determination of optimality is effected by the satisfaction of Constraint 2. Here, Candidate 1 twice violates Constraint 2, while Candidate 2 only violates it once. Hence, the fatality of the second violation of Constraint 2 is indicated with '!'. Optimal Candidate 2 is likewise indicated by ☛.

An important group of constraints that comprise the grammar of a language is the faithfulness family of constraints, which regulates the relation of features and structures between underlying representations and their surface manifestations.

Here we will assume a Correspondence interpretation of the faithfulness constraints. In a Correspondence-based approach to faithfulness the familiar PARSE constraint may be redefined as follows:

(13) MAX-IO (INPUT-OUTPUT):

Every element of the input has a correspondent in the output.

(McCarthy and Prince 1995:264)

This constraint is satisfied when all the elements in the input correspond to elements in the output. In derivational terms this would amount to the requirement that no information from the input be lost, deleted, unparsed, transformed or destroyed.

Similarly, a Correspondence-based version of FILL is that in (14):

(14) DEP(ENDENCY)-IO:
Every element of the output has a correspondent in input.
(McCarthy and Prince 1995:264)

As with FILL, this constraint is violated when there are elements in the output that are not part of the input. In derivational terms this would mean no epenthesis or insertion of elements.

Finally, the IDENTITY family of constraints enforces identity between the feature values in the two corresponding strings:

(15) IDENT(ITY)-IO [F]
Output correspondents of an input [γF] are also [γF].
(McCarthy and Prince 1995:264)

Apart from these constraints demanding faithfulness between input and output, we wish to introduce morphological constraints that directly affect the realization of the plural morpheme. We will employ the cover term MORPHOLOGY for these constraints, but will not enter into precise formalization here.[5] One of these constraints controls the phonological form of the plural morpheme and establishes a correspondence relation between the morpheme and the segment /s/; another determines the location of this morpheme as the right edge of the Prosodic Word.

(16) MORPH(OLOGY) (informal definition):
The plural morpheme is /s/ and is realized at the end of the word.

4.2 The unmarked case of pluralization

As mentioned in sections 2 and 3.1, all previous studies assume that for words ending in a vowel or nonnasal glide, /-s/ is simply concatenated to the singular form to form the plural. In OT, this concatenation is not the result of a rule, but is instead one of the possible outputs of GEN. Then, EVAL must select the candidate with an /-s/ concatenated at the right edge of the word as the optimal candidate for a plural form. For our analysis, it is the effect of MORPH that selects the correct candidate in cases of unmarked pluralization. With the constraints presented we can account for the first set of data in (1):

(17) Vowel- and nonnasal glide-final words:

casa casa+s 'house(s)'

/casa + s/	MORPH	MAX	DEP
☞ casas			
casaes			*!
casa	*!	*	
casap	*!		
cassa	*!		

For the unmarked examples all relevant prosodic constraints are satisfied in the optimal candidate, so no further complication needs to be noted in this regard. It is worth indicating that regardless of the ranking of these three constraints the optimal candidate is always *casas*. This set of data was unproblematic for all previous accounts and it is still unproblematic on our account.

4.3 Identical singular/plural pairs

Why is the plural of *simples* 'simple' *simples*, rather than *simpless*? Obviously, what is "wrong" with this expected "regular" output is the sequence of two identical segments. The Obligatory Contour Principle (OCP) (see, among others, Goldsmith 1976) disallows such a sequence.

(18) OCP

Identical adjacent elements are disallowed at the melodic level.

Still we might expect that the result of concatenating *-s* to a word-final /s/ would be the long segment ([š:]). In this case, there would be no OCP violation since all the melodic nodes are shared and only the two mora units remain in the output.

(19) simples + s → simple s

... | | Λ

μ μ   μ μ

This kind of candidate would violate *LONG (see Rosenthall 1994, and others, for the more specific *LONG-V).

(20) *LONG
Long segments are not allowed.

Since the output is neither long nor a sequence of identical segments we can assume that *LONG and OCP are dominant constraints.

The simplification of *s*+*s* → [š] could also be a case of tier merger up to the level of the mora; alternatively, it could be argued that since inflectional morphemes are ignored by the stress system, they do not carry a mora. In any of these cases, the output would neither be long nor would violate the OCP. In this case, the constraint affected is *MULTIPLE CORRESPONDENCE:

(21) *MULTIPLE CORRESPONDENCE (*MC)
Elements of the input and output must stand in a one-to-one correspondence relationship with each other.
(Lamontagne and Rice 1995:218)

The kind of structure that this constraint targets is exemplified in (22):

```
(22)        simples + s     INPUT
                   \ /
             simples        OUTPUT
```

Finally, there are two further possibilities that need to be considered: (i) the plural morpheme is not parsed; (ii) the final /s/ of the stem is not parsed.

Graphically, these last two options can be depicted as in (23):

```
(23) Option (i)          Option (ii)
       simples + s         simples + s
        ...    |   |         ...    |   |
        simples  ø          simpleø   s
```

On our analysis, the first option is a violation of MAX and MORPH because the plural morpheme does not have a correspondent in the output string. The second option violates MAX but satisfies MORPH.

Because all plurals end in /s/ in Portuguese, we will assume that MORPH is undominated. Next, the ranking posited between Max and DEP follows from the observation that in general the language favors epenthesis over deletion to avoid problems of syllabification (e.g., /piknik/ → [pi.kə̱.nikə̱]). Vowel length, which had been contrastive in Latin, was lost in Late Latin due to a constraint reranking by which *LONG became stronger than MAX. Finally, the ranking of DEP with respect to *MC seems problematic, however, because in order to account for identical singular and plural pairs we would need to posit that DEP dominates *MC.

(24)

/simples + s/	OCP	MORPH	*LONG	MAX	DEP	*MC
simpleses					*	
☞ simples s s						*
simplesø		*!		*		
simpleøs				*!		
simples:			*!			
simpless	*!					
simplest		*!				
simplesi		*!				

However, it is obvious that the same set of constraints with the same ranking could not derive the data in (3), where we have cases of words ending in /-s/ with final stress. *Português* has the plural form *portuguêses* not **português*. In order to get plural *portuguêses*, we would need a ranking reversal of DEP and *MC. This possibility is to be rejected for two reasons: (i) allowing constraint reversals considerably weakens the OT machinery, since it forces us to give up assumptions central to the theory (see Inkelas, Orgun and Zoll 1995); and, (ii) treating this problem as a reversal for exceptional cases would miss the generalization that all of these exceptions, apart from ending in /s/, also have final stress.[6]

The key difference between the examples in (2) and those in (3) is the location of stress. We have then, a peculiar situation were the plural form is predictable from stress. However, since stress is not underlyingly specified, there must be some difference in the lexical entry able to predict both the difference in stress pattern and the concomitant difference in pluralization. As mentioned above, an analysis based on morphological structure (along the lines of what Harris 1980 proposes for Spanish) is not viable in Portuguese. Our position here is that coda consonants in Portuguese are moraic, meaning that they are included in the computation of stress assignment. This accounts for the fact that in consonant-final words the unmarked pattern is ultimate stress, as Lipski says (see the end of section 3.3). In this setting, a word such as *simples* has a marked stress pattern. Our contention is that this markedness has to do with the fact that the final /s/ fails to project a mora. Then, the situation we want to explain is that the merging of the final /s/ with the plural *-s* is preferred only when the final /s/ is not associated to a mora in the singular. The plural morpheme is arguably never associated to a mora, since it never alters the location of stress of the singular form. This fact can be interpreted as the result of a constraint specifically banning the association of the plural morpheme to a mora. We will refer to this constraint as *MORA-PL. This allows us to solve the problem of the ranking between DEP and *MC. In agreement with general tendencies of the language, we postulate that merger of compatible segments is the preferred option. However, when the result of merger is not well-formed, epenthesis (or some featural change) has the opportunity to apply. This is reflected in the ranking *MORA-PL » DEP » *MC.

(25)[7]

/portuges +s/	MORPH, OCP	*MORA-PL	*LONG	MAX	DEP	*MC
☞ portug[é]ses					*	
portug[é]s ∧ s s		*!				*
portug[é]øs				*!		
portug[é]sø	*!			*		
portug[éš:]			*!			
portug[é]ss	*!					
portug[é]set	*!				*	
portug[é]si	*!					

In the case of *simples*, *MORA-PL does not have a bearing on any of the candidates, and the effect of the normal setting of the language that favors fusion emerges.

(26)

/simples + s/	MORPH, OCP	*MORA -PL	*LONG	MAX	DEP	*MC
s[í]mpleses					*!	
☞ s[í]mples s s						*
s[í]mpleøs				*!		
s[í]mplesø	*!			*		
s[í]mple[s:]			*!			
s[í]mpless	*!					
s[í]mplesi	*!					*
s[í]mplest	*!					

The data in (4) (words ending in /r/ taking the plural [eš], e.g., *favor* ~ *favores*) are identical to the data in (3), and so nothing needs to be added to the order of the constraints. The final consonant is moraic and distinct from the morpheme /s/ that is added, and consequently merger is not possibile. Nonetheless, in the following tableau we add a new constraint. A suboptimal candidate such as *favors* shows that there are syllabic constraints dominating DEP and MAX. This is confirmed by the general tendency of Portuguese to solve syllabification problems by epenthesis (e.g., *club* borrowed in CP as [klúbə], *picnic* as [pikəníkə] etc.; BP shows epenthetic [i]). It is clear that we are dealing here with limitations on what segments Portuguese allows in coda position.[8] Nevertheless, the correct implementation of coda limitations is again tangential to our concern here. We will refer to these limitations with the general label SYLL. Candidates that receive a mark for SYLL contain ill-formed syllables.

(27)

/favor + s/	MORPH	SYLL, *MORA -PL	*LONG	MAX	DEP	*MC
☞ favores					*	
favors		*!				
favort	*!	*				
favori	*!					
favorø	*!			*		
favoøs				*!		

So far, the stated constraints and the proposed ranking account for the data in (1)-(4). To simplify the exposition of the illustrations, we omit MORPH from further discussion and tableaux, given that we do not have evidence that it is ever dominated in Portuguese (i.e., plurals end without exception in [š]). Accordingly, we will no longer take into account candidates that violate MORPH since they cannot be optimal. We will further tend to omit from discussion constraints not playing a direct role in the computation of the optimal candidate.

4.4 Vocalization and velarization of /l/

The set of data in (5)-(6) contains examples of plurals of words that end in /l/. We repeat here one example of each group for ease of reference.

(28)	*hotel*	/otel/	[o.téɫ]	'hotel'
	hoteis	/otel+s/	[o.téjš]	'hotels'

Notice the alternations between /l/ and [ɫ] word-finally, and more importantly, between /l/ and [j] in the plural. We need to explain what eliminates candidates such as [o.télš] or [o.téɫš] from contention. As we shall see, this follows from syllable structure constraints.

(29) Words ending with unstressed /il/ realized in the plural as [ejš]:

fácil	/fasil/	[fá.siɫ]	'easy'
fáceis	/fasil+s/	[fá.sejš]	'easy pl.'

Here the question is why [ijš] should be suboptimal. Clearly, the answer has to make reference to the OCP.

(30) Words ending with stressed /il/ realized in the plural as [íš] (not [éjš]):

fuzil	/fusil/	[fu.zíɫ]	'rifle'
fuzis	/fusil+s/	[fu.zíš]	'rifles'

Here again we have an OCP-related problem. However, in this case, the optimal candidate merges the sequence [íj] to [í] instead of lowering the first element ([éjš]). Why in this case is merging better than lowering?

For each of these questions our analysis will provide an explanation. First, though, we need to discuss what the observed alternations have in common.

4.4.1 Velarization and gliding as nucleation

The possibilities of alternation of final /l/ may seem unrelated if we see them as transformations (/l/ → [j] and /l/ → [ɫ]). However, these two processes begin to converge when we realize that behind the names *velarization* and *gliding* what we have is two different manifestations of nucleation (Colman 1983, Parkinson 1983, Girelli 1988). For the present analysis we want to show that a tendency toward nucleation results in [j] or [ɫ] depending on the phonological context.

Let us start by stating that the vocalization of /l/ is not an uncommon process. Within the family of Romance languages, examples are abundant. Walsh (1995) gives Balearic Catalan as an example, and cites the alternation between Standard Catalan *alba* 'sunrise' with Balear Catalan *aube* (from Alcover and Moll 1968). Von Essen (1964) cites the change from Late Latin /l/ to [u] in Provençal when final; Portuguese syllable-final /l/ acquires a strong velar component and approaches [u] in CP, and actually is [w] in BP; the same change occurs in French, e.g. Lat. *caballo* 'horse' > Fr. *cheval, chevaux*; *ascultat* 'listen' > *écoute*; *alba* > *aube*, etc.[9] Syllable-initially, /l/ may also become [j], as in the change in Italian of Latin *Cl* sequences: *plenu* 'full' > *pieno*, *clave* 'key' > *chiave*, *glande* 'acorn' > *ghiande*, *flamma* 'flame' > *fiamma*, etc. Expanding our view beyond Romance, we see the change from /l/ > /i/ in syllable-final position as well, as in the Bavarian dialect of German: *Holz* 'wood' is [hoits], and in the Munich dialect /l/ has been completely changed to [i], e.g. *foisch* 'false' and *hoib* 'half' (Sütterlin 1916:121, cited in von Essen 1964). This occurs synchronically in Cibaeño Spanish as well (see Guitart 1989), where *él* 'he', e.g., is pronounced [ey] in all contexts. In West Polish [w] is traced to [ɫ], as in [ɫan] > [wan] 'field', and a similar phenomenon occurs in the Low German dialect of Vierlanded, where, for instance, *hell* 'clear, light' was pronounced [hew], *School* 'school' is [šewʊ], *kalf* 'calf' is [kawf] (von Essen 1964). Finally, Walsh (1995) gives further examples from Polish, where /l/ > /w/ in all positions (Walsh cites Carlton 1991), and Trigo (1988:69) cites /kšaɫt/ → [kštawt] 'shape', and other examples. This same alternation occurs in Mehri (southern Arabian Semitic) in coda position: [ɬo:leθ] 'third (masc.)' vs. [ɬewθe:t] 'third (fem.)' (Johnston 1975, cited by Walsh). The Portuguese data, then, represent neither a surprising nor isolated case.

We follow Lipski (1973) in assuming that the loss of /l/ in the Portuguese cases is not 'intervocalic', and so we reject the claim that the input contains a final /e/, which would then be either apocopated (in the singular) or glided (in the plural).

To account for this vocalization we adopt here an assumption tacitly made by Girelli (1988), and explicitly made by Colman (1983:32-33). That is, 'vocalization' is to be understood as the loss of consonantal properties, a consonantal sound thus becoming a (more) vocalic one. Colman assumes that vocalization is really 'nucleation', whereby a (possibly lenited) consonantal (now approximant) allophone moves into the nucleus. The restructuring created by the nucleation brings about vocalization. Colman further assumes (p. 34) that if the nuclear pattern that results does not match an existing template, and the vocalized element cannot remain in the coda, it may be lost. Evidently, this is only sometimes the case in Portuguese since the segment is either velarized, vocalized or lost.

We assume that /l/ is forced into the nucleus when it is followed by a tautosyllabic consonant (the [l] and the following consonant in *maldad* 'evil', *palrar* 'to chat', etc. are heterosyllabic) because in this situation it cannot occupy coda position.[10] For BP, it appears that the limitations on the coda may be formulated quite generally, simply disallowing any consonant in the coda, as Girelli explicitly assumes, since in syllable-final position /l/ is always vocalized to [w] or [j]. This stronger limitation on the possibilities of the coda also explains why nearly all consonant clusters in BP are eliminated by epenthesis, as in *obter* 'to obtain' [ob i téX], *enigma* 'enigma' [enig i ma], *admirar* 'to admire' [ad i miráX], etc. For CP, /l/ is merely strongly velarized to [ɫ] in syllable-final position, but is vocalized to [j] when it occurs next to the plural /-s/ (showing that the CP coda is just slightly more permissive). Velarization of /l/ may be viewed as an intermediate realization between [l] and [w]. As Sproat and Fujimura's (1993) experimental phonetic data show, all [l]s contain both coronal and dorsal articulations. The difference between the so-called 'light' and 'dark' [l]s is the position each occurs in syllable structure, with the vocalic dorsal component having an affinity with the syllable nucleus.[11] This velarization is particularly strong in CP because the secondary dorsal PA is actually incorporated into the nucleus. This is the preliminary stage Colman discusses before complete nucleation occurs. This next step is the realization of /-l/ in BP as [w], since fewer coda consonants are permitted, and so the primary CPlace coronal node is eliminated. In both BP and CP, however, the coronal Place of Articulation of plural /-s/ must be maintained (as a result of MORPH). Our position is, then, that [ɫ] is a case of partial nucleation that follows from coda avoidance. While in CP this partial nucleation seems to be enough when [ɫ] is the only segment in the coda, it is clearly not sufficient in BP, or in CP when the /s/ from the plural can only dock to the same coda position. In that sense we can say that the presence of the plural morpheme pushes the /l/ into the nucleus.[12]

4.4.2 Analysis of lateral nucleation

In order to keep our representations simple, we will subsume the previous discussion of syllable structure constraints under the label SYLL. Again, examples that would violate constraints that govern syllable well-formedness (specifically coda constraints) are assigned a mark under this constraint. Likewise, the following examples include the constraints IDENT introduced above in (15). Below we show how the data in (5) (words ending in stressed *-al, -el, -ol, ul*) is accounted for with the same constraint ranking, provided that IDENT is ranked below DEP:

(31)

/otel + s/	SYLL	MAX	DEP	IDENT
(h)otelš	*!			
(h)oteɫš	*!			*
☞ (h)otejš				*
(h)oteøš		*!		
(h)oteleš			*!	

Thus, we now can explain why *hot*[elš] and *hot*[eɫš] are not optimal: these candidates violate Portuguese coda well-formedness constraints. Other candidates still competing for optimality are eliminated by the faithfulness constraints, ranked in Portuguese as MAX » DEP » IDENT. In this situation, the change of value for the feature [lateral] turns out to be the least marked option. Without the feature [+lateral] the segment is able to be realized as a glide in the nucleus.[13]

Next, for the set of data in (6), where we see that unstressed *-il* is realized as [ejš] in the plural, it is obvious that candidate [facijš] is discarded by the OCP.

(32)

facil + s	OCP	SYLL	*LONG	MAX	DEP	*MC	IDENT
facilš		*!					
faciłš		*!					*
☞ facejš							**
faci:š			*!				*
facijš	*!						*
faciøš				*!			
facileš					*!		
faciš (i l)						*!	*

As with the words in (5), here the morphological requirements (MORPH) can only be upheld when /l/ is realized in the nucleus as a glide. The special situation here is that this glide clashes with the high vowel that has nowhere else to dock but to the same nucleus. In this example, IDENT must be crucially ranked below *MC, implying that changing feature values of the underlying form is a preferred strategy to fusion even when the outcome of the fusion would be well formed.

Finally, the special case of words ending in stressed *-il* (the data in (7)) must be taken into account. As it stands, the proposed set of constraints fails to select the correct plural form [fuziš] (from /fuzil+s/) over the competing candidate [fuzeiš]. Again, the key difference between [fá.sił] ~ [fá.sejš] and [fu.zíł] ~ [fu.zíš] is stress location. It has been repeatedly observed in the phonological literature that stressed vowels are more resistant to any kind of alternation than their non-stressed counterparts. Evidence for this observation can be found within the language in the pattern of reduced and full vowels that correspond to stressed and unstressed vowels. One way to interpret vowel reduction is to assume that, in general, vowels have a tendency to be reduced (to be mid and central). However, this process of reduction is blocked when the vowel carries main stress. The blocking of this tendency to reduce vowels, and the blocking of the /i/ ~ [e] alternation at hand, can be seen as the result of a constraint of the HEAD-CORRESPONDENCE family, (for related discussion of the tendency for the head to resist change, see Alderete 1995, Kenstowicz 1995, Itô, Kitagawa and Mester 1995, McCarthy 1995; for vowel reduction, see Alderete 1995):

(33) HEAD(PRWD)-IDENT[F]

Correspondent segments in the head[14] of the PrWd agree in value for the feature (α). (Adapted from Alderete 1995:14)

This is an identity type of faithfulness constraint that requires that the features in the input agree with the features in the output. However by ranking HEAD-IDENT constraints above all other IDENT constraints we can account for the fact that the head features are more resistant to alteration. Again, since we do not have evidence in our data showing that the features of the head are altered we will represent HEAD(PRWD)-IDENT(α) as undominated. Now we can demonstrate that [fuzíš] is better than [fuzeiš]. Furthermore, since fusion is preferred to epenthesis, [fuzíš] is better than [fuzileš]:

(34)

fuzil + s	H-IDENT, OCP	*LONG, SYLL	MAX	DEP	*MC	IDENT
fuzílš		*(S)!				
fuzíɫš		*(S)!				*
fuzéjš	*(H)!					*
fuzí:š		*(L)!				*
fuzíjš	*(OCP)!					*
fuzíøš			*!			
☞ fuzíš ∧ i l					*	*
fuzíleš				*!		

4.5 Nasals

Vowel nasalization is quite systematic when a stressed vowel is followed by a nasal.[15] We assume that nasalization is a process of assimilation of the vowel to a following nasal. This assimilation is limited to stress vowels because nasal vowels are not allowed in unstressed position. In many cases, nasalization of the vowel is complemented by apparent deletion or gliding of the nasal. As discussed in section 3.5, we argue that nasal loss and gliding should be interpreted as nucleation. This puts /n/ gliding or loss and /l/ gliding or velarization at the same level. This is a desired result because now the relation between these processes and pluralization emerges quite naturally, and is entirely consistent with the data from Brandão de Carvalho discussed in section 3.5 and fn. 12. It simply makes sense that if the grammar reacts to the concatenation of /s/ to a word ending in /l/ by pushing the lateral into the nucleus, the tendency should be the same when /s/

is concatenated to any other word-final consonant. Nasal loss, nasal gliding, lateral gliding and lateral velarization are examples of the grammar resorting to nucleation. However, as we saw above, when /-s/ is concatenated to /r/ (or some instances of /s/) at the end of a word, the optimal result shows epenthesis instead of nucleation (*mar* ~ *mares*). This can be explained in OT if the nucleation of /r/ and /s/ (and any other consonant other than /n/ and /l/ as well) entails stronger violations than epenthesis, while at the same time epenthesis is worse than the adjustments required for the nucleation of /n/ and /l/.

As we saw in the previous section when discussing lateral gliding, nucleation can be readily related to a lateral not being able to be parsed into a well-formed coda. Similarly, nasals not allowed in a coda are better realized as glides in the nucleus (e.g., /pans/ → [pãj̃s]). However, the role of coda conditions is not evident in examples such as /irman+o/ → [irmãw̃] or /irman+o+s/ → [irmãw̃s]. Here syllabification should be able to assign the nasal to an onset that would form a syllable with the following vowel. Nonetheless, we interpret this alternation as the result of nucleation, instead of as deletion as in traditional accounts.[16]

4.5.1 Nucleation of onset nasals

To explain /irman+o/ → [irmãw̃] we need to posit a constraint, other than coda limitations, that can push the coronal nasal towards the preceding syllable. Our contention is that *STRUCTURE (see Prince and Smolensky 1993:25, fn. 13) is the constraint behind this kind of nucleation.

(35) *STRUCTURE (*STRUC)
Structure should be constructed minimally.
(Prince and Smolensky 1993:25, fn. 13)

Up to this point, nucleation has surfaced as gliding or velarization (for laterals). However, it is not clear that the glide in [irmãw̃] is the surface manifestation of the nasal. Instead, we posit that the nasal is totally merged with the vowel, allowing for the gliding of the final /o/. The following figure illustrates the correspondence relationship between input and output elements in a similar fashion to the representations we are using in the tableaux.

(36)
```
i r m ã w
      /\ |
     a n o
```

Since Portuguese has nasal vowels, the merging of the nasal with the previous vowel is a possibility that avoids unnecessarily adding an extra syllable. Thus, as long as *STRUC is ranked above *MC we obtain the kind of merging in (36).

However, with just *STRUC we would not be able to explain why merging does not take place if the preceding vowel is unstressed (cf. *irmanar*). Furthermore, there are a number of other peculiarities about the merging of nasals that deserve some consideration. For instance, merging does not happen if the nasal is not coronal (cf. /cam+a/ → [kãma], *[kãa], *[kã] 'bed'; /puɲ+o/ → [pũɲo], *[pũo] 'fist'). This limitation to coronal nasals is expected if only coronals are unspecified for PA. It is true that there are a handful of exceptions to the generalization that coronal nasals are always totally merged into the nucleus (e.g. *cana* [cãna], *[cãa] 'sugar cane'). However, most of these exceptions derive from Latin geminate /nn/, and may be handled in a manner similar to that discussed in fn. 8. Moreover, nucleation may be blocked if the coronal nasal is followed by a consonant (cf. /kaNp+o/ → [kãmpo] ~ [kãpo] 'field'). Here, the variability indicates resistance to nucleation effected by interference of nasal assimilation. Assimilation and nucleation may enter in conflict, canceling out each other and giving rise to free variation. The interplay of nucleation and assimilation is made evident by the specific array of possibilities of variation for *finca* 'farm' [fĩĩka ~ fĩñka ~ fĩŋka] (Cagliari 1981:85, cited in Wetzels p. 81).

A peculiarity of nasals that is not easy to explain is that in their tendency to group with the preceding vowel they may be totally merged or surface as a glide. If nucleation can trigger either gliding or total merging we must be able to predict under what circumstances one or the other is optimal. In the following figure we illustrate the context of gliding and merging:

(37)	*Gliding*		
a.	/pan/	[pãw̃]	'bread'
	/pan+s/	[pãj̃s]	'breads'
	Total Merging		
b.	/irman+o/	[irmãw̃]	'brother'
	/irman+o+s/	[irmãw̃s]	'brothers'

The generalization is that gliding takes place only at the end of the word and before the plural morpheme.

Our claim here is that what controls whether gliding or total merging is optimal is the constraint WEIGHT-TO-STRESS.

(38) WEIGHT-TO-STRESS (Σ=$\mu\mu$)
The head of the PrWd must be bimoraic.

Several authors (Repetti 1989, Morales-Front 1994, Holt (in preparation), among others) have noticed that there is a tendency in Romance languages for a tonic nucleus to be bimoraic. In some Italian dialects this tendency may give rise to long vowels, and in Spanish it may be responsible for diphthongization. This kind of correlation between stress and complex nuclei is also at the base of nasal nucleation in Portuguese when a tonic nucleus attracts a following nasal.

As noted in fn. 14, we assume that the head of the PrWd is the vocalic nucleus. Consequently, a moraic coda would not satisfy WEIGHT-TO-STRESS; only a long vowel or a diphthong in the nucleus does. As formulated, Σ=$\mu\mu$ explains why the attraction of the nasal to the previous nucleus happens only when that nucleus carries the main stress. This constraint must be ranked below *LONG since we do not want all tonic vowels to be long. Similarly, it must rank below DEP to avoid generalized diphthongization. As shown in the following tableau, the glide surfaces when merging would not satisfy WEIGHT-TO-STRESS.

(39)

/pan/	SYLL	*LONG	MAX	Σ=$\mu\mu$	IDENT
pan				*!	
pã Λ an				*!	
pãã		*!			
☞ pãw̃					*

WEIGHT-TO-STRESS favors the nasal surfacing as a glide because in that realization it contributes to the weight of the nucleus. However, this gliding is not always possible. With an input such as /irman+o/, if the nasal were realized as a glide and parsed with the nucleus of the preceding syllable ill-formed syllable structure would ensue (*[ir.mãw.o]). Parsing the glide into the onset would not help because it would still clash with Portuguese syllable structure (or sonority) restrictions that disallow a glide as the only member of an onset. Likewise, in words such as /kamp+o/, gliding would conflict with assimilation (*[kãw̃.po]).[17] Since an assimilated nasal and not a glide is what surfaces we have to conclude that assimilation is more important. Finally, a word such as /kam+a/ does not have the kind of nasal (unmarked PA) that can be realized as a glide. Gliding can take place at the end of a word because in this position there is no lexical nasal assimilation and therefore no conflict. It can also arise before the palatal segment of the plural since in this case there is no conflict between assimilation and gliding. That is, both constraints can be satisfied simultaneously, as in, e.g., [pãj̃š].

4.5.2 Nucleation of onset nasal: the analysis

Having argued that WEIGHT-TO-STRESS and *STRUC are the constraints behind what we have termed "onset nucleation", we provide here an explanation of the data that falls under this label. For masculine plurals the following set of alternations has to be accounted for: (repeated from (8))

(40)	[ãw̃] ~	[ãw̃š]:	(< Lt. -anu(s))	
(=(8a))	*irmão*	/irman+o/	[irmãw̃]	'brother'
	irmãos	/irman+o+s/	[irmãw̃š]	'brothers'
(41)	[ãw̃] ~	[õj̃š]	(< Lt. -one(s))	
(=(8c))	*patrão*	/patron/	[patrãw̃]	'patron'
	patrões	/patron+s/	[patrõj̃š]	'patrons'
(42)	[ãw̃] ~	[ãj̃š]	(< Lt. -ane(s))	
(=(8e))	*pão*	/pan/	[pãw̃]	'bread'
	pães	/pan+s/	[pãj̃š]	'breads'

Synchronically, each group has a different plural form but an unexpected uniform ending [ãw̃] for the masculine singular. As indicated, each of the groups can be traced to different Latin endings: *-anu, -one, -ane*. In Late Latin those endings were arguably *-ano, -on* and *-an,* which are the underlying forms posited for our analysis.

From these underlying forms the correspondences between base and surface form are as represented in (43):

(43) /an+o/ /on/ /an/ → [ãw̃]

/an+o+s/ → [ãw̃š] /on+s/ → [õj̃š] /an+s/ → [ãj̃š]

We first illustrate how Σ=μμ triggers nucleation in examples such as /irrman+o/ → [irmãw̃].

(44)

/irman+o/	SYLL, *LONG	MAX	DEP	Σ=μμ	*MC	IDENT
ir.mã.n o | | | a n o				*!		
ir.mã. o Λ | an o	*!			*	*	
☞ ir.mãw̃ Λ | an o					*	*
ir.mãã.n o \\| | | a n o			*!		*	
ir.mã. ø Λ | an o		*!		*	*	

The most faithful candidate to the input (*irmano*) fails because the stressed nucleus is not heavy. Additionally, this tableau shows that Σ=μμ must crucially outrank *MC. Among the candidates that do not violate Σ=μμ, the one with total merging of the nasal into the previous vowel and gliding of the final /o/ results optimal. We follow here Girelli's assumption with regard to the underspecification of nasals that they are unspecified for the feature [consonantal] because of the morphological alternations given in (8). As previously mentioned, this is consistent with Inkelas' (1995) arguments that only features that alternate are underspecified.

The alternation of the corresponding feminine form can be accounted for in similar terms. The difference here is that the final vowel cannot form a glide. Instead, since it is identical to the vowel preceding the nasal it can be merged. As argued above, *STRUC is ranked above *MC.

(45)

/irman+a/	SYLL, *LONG	MAX	DEP	Σ=μμ	*STRUC	*MC	IDENT
ir.mã.n a | | | a n a				*	*!		
ir.mã.w̃a | | | a n a	*!			*	*		*
ir.mã n ø | | | a n a		*!		*			
ir.mãã.n a \\| | | a n a	*!		*		*		
☞ ir.mã /|\\ ana				*		*	

Both [irmãna] and [irmã] violate Σ=μμ; consequently, what determines the outcome is that the former has an extra syllable (*STRUC), while for the latter the next violation is the more lowly-ranked *MC.

For the plural, the addition of /s/ to the coda does not affect the number of marks incurred by each candidate.

(46) /irman+o+s/ [irmãw̃s̃] 'brothers'

/irman+o+s/	SYLL, *LONG	MAX	DEP	Σ=μμ	*STRUC	*MC	IDENT
ir.mã.n o s | | | | a n o s				*!	*		
ir.mã. o s /\\ | | an o s	*!			*	*	*	
☞ ir.mã w̃s /\\ | | an o s						*	*
ir.mãã.n o s \\| | | | a n o s	*!		*		*		
ir.mã ø s /\\ | | an o s		*!		*		*	

(47)

/irman+a+s/	SYLL, *LONG, OCP	MAX	DEP	Σ=μμ	*STRUC	*MC	IDENT
ir.mã.n a s | | | | a n a s				*	*!		
irmã.w̃a s | | | | a n a s	*!			*	*		*
irmã.n ø s | | | | a n a s		*!					
irmãã.n a s \\| | | | a n a s	*		*!		*	*	
ir.m ã a s |\\ | | ana s	*!		*			*	
☞ ir.mã s /|\\ | ana s				*		*	*

4.5.3 Nucleation of coda nasals

One detail that must be discussed before moving on to additional tableaux illustrations is the realization of the nasal as a back or front glide. This alternation can be observed in (37) where we have the same underlying nasal realized as [w̃] in the singular and [j] in the plural. Consider also the following set of examples from Trigo (1993:380):

(48)	*fin	>	f[ĩ]	'end'
	*atún	>	at[ũ]	'one'
	*pan	>	p[ɐ̃w̃]	'bread'
	*ándan	>	ánd[ɐ̃w̃]	'they go'
	*montón	>	mont[ɐ̃w̃]	'heap'
	*también	>	tamb[ɐ̃ỹ]	'also'
	*vírgen	>	vírg[ɐ̃ỹ]	'virgin'
	*ánden	>	ánd[ɐ̃ỹ]	'they go (subjunctive)'

If [ĩ] and [ũ] are contractions from [iỹ] and [uw̃], then, we can make the generalization that when there is no assimilation to a following consonant, a nasal not specified for PA assimilates to the preceding vowel. That is, it is realized as a front glide when preceded by a front vowel, and as a back glide when preceded by a back vowel.[18] We do not want to have this assimilation apply to any preceding vowel because nasals in an onset do not become dorsal following dorsal vowels (i.e. *fo[ŋ]ema). The domain where assimilation to the vowel occurs is the nucleus.

(49) VOWEL-AGREEMENT (V-AGR):
Members of a complex nucleus share Place of Articulation features.

However, this alternation between front and back realizations is not maintained when the nasal is followed by the consonant of the plural morpheme [š]. In this context, the nasal systematically surfaces with a palatal place of articulation that agrees with the consonant:

(50) a. /patron+s/ [patrõȷ̃š] 'patrons'
b. /pan+s/ [pãȷ̃š] 'breads'

We mentioned above that (50) is the only context where nasal assimilation and gliding are compatible. The fact that a front glide emerges even if preceded by a back vowel (50b) is an indication that assimilation to the consonant has a higher ranking than V-AGR. Assimilation to the following consonant can be formalized as follows:

(51) CONSONANT-AGREEMENT (C-AGR):
Two adjacent consonants must share Place of Articulation features.

We know that V-AGR cannot dominate IDENT (cf. /pan+s/ → p[ãȷ̃š], *p[ẽȷ̃š]); we also know that C-AGR dominates V-AGR (cf. /pan+s/ → p[ãȷ̃š], *p[ãw̃š]) and that C-AGR dominates Σ=μμ (cf. [kãmpo] *[kãwpo]).

(52) /pan+s/ [pãȷ̃š] 'breads' (= data in (8e))

/pan+s/	SYLL	C-AGR	Σ=μμ	IDENT	V-AGR
p[ãnš]	*!		*		
p[ãš]			*!		
☞ p[ãȷ̃š]				*	*
p[ãw̃š]		*!		*	
p[ẽȷ̃š]				**!	

The singular form has the crucial difference that since there is no consonant following the nasal, C-AGR is not relevant.

(53) /pan/ [pãw̃] 'breads'

/pan/	SYLL	C-AGR	Σ=μμ	IDENT	V-AGR
p[ãn]			*!		
p[ã]			*!		
p[ãj̃]				*	*!
☞ p[ãw̃]				*	
p[ẽj̃]				**!	

The proposed ranking can also account for /patron+s/ → [patrõj̃s̃]:

(54)

/patron+s/	SYLL	C-AGR	Σ=μμ	IDENT	V-AGR
patr[õnš]	*!		*!		
patr[õš]			*!		
☞ patr[õj̃š]				*	*
patr[õw̃š]		*!		*	
patr[ẽj̃š]				**!	

For the masculine singular we must recall that the first vowel of a nasal diphthong is pronounced as a central low vowel ([patrɐ̃w̃] instead of [patrõw̃]). This is an unexpected result because our constraints would predict [patrõw̃] as the optimal output:

(55)

/patron/	SYLL	C-AGR	Σ=μμ	IDENT	V-AGR
patr[õn]			*!		
patr[õ]			*!		
patr[õj̃]				*	*!
☞ patr[õw̃]	*!			*	
patr[ãw̃]				**!	
patr[ẽj̃]				**!	

Of the candidates given above [patrõw̃] is optimal. However, as mentioned in the discussion of the data in (48), the final phonetic output is a diphthong with a centralized version of the back vowel, [ɐ̃w̃]. An additional option given by many previous accounts is that the alternations /on/ → [ɐ̃w̃] and /an/ → [ɐ̃w̃] are a result of analogical influence from the most frequent alternation /ano/→ [ɐ̃w̃]. In either case, the analysis proposed above may be maintained. This completes the discussion of this complex data[19]

5 Conclusion

We hope to have fulfilled the initial goal of reaching a deeper understanding of how the realizations of the plural result from contrasting demands within the grammar. We have shown that there is no need to complicate the lexicon with allomorphs. We have also seen that the morphological process of pluralization is a simple and transparent process of concatenation: without exception /-s/ is concatenated to the end of a singular word to create the plural. Nor does the heavy load of our analysis fall on the grammar, as was the case for previous analyses where there was a proliferation of rules; if all the constraints employed in our analysis are universal, then there is no added complexity. Finally, we have been able to accommodate all of the intersecting processes without having to appeal to any kind of amendment of the basic assumptions of Optimality Theory. It is only the interaction of contrasting demands from morphology, prosody and faithfulness that account for the surface alternations that take place in Portuguese when the plural marker /-s/ is concatenated to the end of a word.

Appendix

Portuguese syllable structure. In this section we outline the structure of the syllable in Portuguese, or more specifically the rhyme constituent, since the onset is not pertinent to the pluralization alternations analyzed here.

While in Latin any consonant (stop, fricative, nasal or liquid) could appear post-vocalically, and /s/ could follow this consonant, Portuguese (and other Romance languages) had a tendency to reduce and/or eliminate closed syllables through a variety of historical processes such as palatalization, affrication, simplification of geminates and consonant groups, vocalization, monophthongization, etc. (Mattoso Câmara 1972:46, Porzio Gernia 1976, Lloyd 1994, etc.). The result is that in Modern Portuguese consonant clusters do not occur syllable- or word-finally (Mascherpe 1970:68-9, cited in Girelli 1988:93; Azevedo 1981:90). Any CC group will necessarily be heterosyllabic, with the C closing the syllable limited to *r, n, l, s* (López 1979:114, Mattoso Câmara 1972:49, Azevedo 1981:38, etc.), or making a generalization, only by sonorants and *s* (Wetzels 1991:82).[20] This has led to the following syllable template, which maximally allows one coda position, which must be filled by either a sonorant or a sibilant (Wetzels, p. 82; López, p. 111):

```
a)         R            *C            R
          / \           / \          / \
          N C                        N   C
         / \ |                       |   |
     (m) a j š                   (r) e   š (to)
   (fás) e j š                   (c) u   r (so)
                                 (c) a   ɫ (do)
                                 (r) e   n (da)
```

This template also provides an explanation for why nasal vowels in Portuguese do not occur in syllables closed by an oral consonant, of the type *[kõp.tar], since there are not sufficient structural positions for the /VN/ necessary to yield [Ṽ].[21] In a word like /transporte/, we would have both /n/ and /s/ in the coda, which is impermissible according the template in (a), and so the [nasal] specification is parsed in the nucleus. In the case of /kampo/, assimilation yields variable results. Likewise, /-l/ is either velarized to [ɫ] as a result of partial incorporation into the nucleus (as in CP), or is completely absorbed into the nucleus, i.e. is vocalized, yielding [w] (as in BP). These cases, then, are better described as complex nuclei.[22]

With regard to the vowels and glides that may occupy the nucleus, we note that the vastly predominant type of diphthong is of falling sonority, VG, whose first member may be of any quality:[23]

(b) diphthongs		example		gloss	
iw	-	*riu*	-	'laughed/3p sg'	-
ew	ej	*deu*	*dei*	'gave/3p sg'	'I gave'
ɛw	ɛj	*céu*	*anéis*	'sky'	'rings'
aw	aj	*mau*	*pai*	'bad'	'father'
-	ɔj	-	dói	-	'hurt/3p sg'
ow	oj	*sou*	*boi*	'be/1p sg'	'steer'
-	uj	-	*fui*	-	'we went'

(from Mattoso Câmara 1972:53)

Rising, GV, diphthongs are unstable in Portuguese, and may always be pronounced in hiatus (Azevedo, p. 68); that is, for such sequences there is free variation between [V.V] and [GV] (Mattoso Câmara 1972:55).

Finally, nasal diphthongs are one of three types, always VG (listed in decreasing order of frequency):

(c)	*ão* [ãw̃]	*pão*	'bread'
	ãe [ãj̃]	*mãe*	'mother'
	õe [õj̃]	*põe, limões*	'put/3p sg', 'lemons'

Notes

1 At the end of a word /s/ is pronounced [š] in Portuguese. Since this palatalization affects all words ending in /s/, and not only the plural morpheme, we posit /s/ as the underlying form.

2 Hall 1943a,b; Sten 1944, Rogers 1954, Hammarström 1954, 1962a,b; Head 1965, Pontes 1965, Back and Mattos 1971-72, Back 1973, Tláskal 1980.

3 Trager 1943a,b; Reed and Leite 1947, Mattoso Câmara 1953, 1970, 1972; Morais Barbosa 1962, 1965, 1983; Malmberg 1971, and from within generative accounts, Saciuk 1970, Brasington 1971, St. Clair 1971, Mira Mateus 1975, Brakel 1979, Parkinson 1983, Girelli 1988, Brandão de Carvalho 1988, Wetzels 1991, Trigo 1993. Parkinson 1983 actually maintains a hybrid position that nasal vowels are underlyingly of the form /VN/, which is subsequently transformed to a diphthong on the surface. Given his acceptance of the underlying /VN/ status of nasal vowels, for our present purposes we can classify his approach with the second groups of authors. Girelli 1988 takes a similar approach, which will be discussed further below. For more detailed discussion of the issues involved, the reader is referred to Vandresen 1975, Parkinson 1983 and Wetzels 1991.

4 Much of the following discussion is based on Wetzels 1991:81-82, with additional arguments from Parkinson 1983:171-72, Brandão de Carvalho 1988:245-46, and the authors they cite.

5 For the time being, until an elaborate version of how to treat allomorphy and morpheme concatenation in OT is available, we will appeal to (16). One likely formalization would be to state the phonological form of a morpheme as a correspondence constraint and its position as an alignment constraint; this would be in agreement with the general functioning of OT and has the potential advantage of predicting some cases of phonologically controlled allomorphy just when these constraints are dominated. In any case, nothing in the present analysis crucially relies on the correct formalization of (16). All we need for the present analysis to hold is any constraint, set of constraints, rule or

stipulation with the same results as (16). For treatments of allomorphy in OT, see Mester 1994, Tranel 1996, Russell 1995 and Yip 1995.

6 The option of considering these examples with identical singular and plural forms as completely irregular has been adopted in previous analyses. As mentioned, Lipski 1973:79 has the following to say about these cases: "words ending in *-s* with unstressed final syllable, are quite exceptional, constituting at most half a dozen examples. Historically, these words once had a regular ending in *-es*, losing the ending through a process of haplology to yield the present forms (cf. Williams, 1962:126). Synchronically, there has been no attempt at restoring a regular plural form, for the final syllable of a Portuguese proparoxytone is very weakly articulated, often dropped; thus, an ending such as * *V́...Vsis* would ordinarily reduce to *V́...Vs*."

7 We omit from discussion candidates such as [simpléses], with penultimate stress, given that such plural forms alter the stress pattern of the singular form. This is something that never happens and may be due to prespecification. If prespecification is involved, then a high ranking of Max(Σ) would disqualify candidates that do not show the stress in the same syllable where it is prespecified.

8 See the appendix for a discussion of Portuguese syllable structure.

9 Sletsjöe 1971 dates this change in French to the 8th and 9th centuries.

10 *Solsticio*, *perspectiva*, and a handful of other words are apparent exceptions to this statement. However, as Mattoso Câmara 1972:49 notes, these are cases of morpheme concatenation to a bound stem with initial 'impure' /sC/: [sol + stisio], [per + spektiva].

11 For a more thorough discussion of all factors that influence the realization of /l/, the reader is referred to Sproat and Fujimura 1993.

12 There is additional evidence that lends support to the claim that /l/ (at least the vocalic dorsal element) occupies the nucleus, not the coda. (Interestingly, the same evidence extends to /N/, as well.) The data come from Brandão de Carvalho 1988:244-245, and lend credence to the vocalization-as-nucleation hypothesis ([°] represents a reduced high back vowel):

(a)	meto = ['me t°]	/	meter = [mə 'ter]	'I put (into) / to put (into)'
	levo = ['lɛ v°]	/	levar = [lə 'var]	'I raise / to raise'
	cozo = ['ko z°]	/	cozer = [k° 'zer]	'I cook / to cook'
	voto = ['vɔ t°]	/	votar = [v° 'tar]	'I vote / to vote'
(b)	desço = ['deš s°]	/	descer = [dəš 'ser]	'I descend / to descend'
	pesco = ['pɛš k°]	/	pescar = [pəš 'kar]	'I fish / to fish'
	gosto = ['goš t°]	/	gostar = [g°š 'tar]	'I like / to like'
	gosto = ['gɔš t°]	/	gostar = [g°š 'tar]	'like (noun) / to like'

(c)	verto = ['ver t^o]	/	verter = [vər 'ter]	'I pour / to pour'
	perco = ['pɛr k^o]	/	perder = [pər 'der]	'I lose / to lose'
	mordo = ['mor d^o]	/	morder = [m^{o}r 'der]	'I bite / to bite'
	corto = ['kɔr t^o]	/	cortar = [k^{o}r 'tar]	'I cut / to cut'
(d)	deito = ['dɐy t^o]	/	dietar = [dɐy 'tar]	'I lay, spread / to lay, spread'
	coimo = ['koy m^o]	/	coimar = [koy 'mar]	? / ?
(e)	relva = ['Rɛɫ vɐ]	/	relvar = [Rɛɫ 'var]	grass, lawn / ?
	volto = ['vɔɫ t^o]	/	voltar = [vɔɫ 'tar]	'I return / to return'
(f)	sento = ['sẽn t^o]	/	sentar = [sẽn 'tar]	'I sit / to sit'
	conto = ['kõn t^o]	/	contar = [kõn 'tar]	'I count / to count'

If we compare (a-c) with (d-f), we observe that the mid vowels in a syllable closed by /-s/, /-r/ are reduced in atonic position, as are simple vowels in open syllables ((a) above), while the mid vowels closed by glides, /-l/ and /-n/ are maintained. Brandão de Carvalho attributes the like behavior of syllables ending in /-l/, /-n/ and diphthongs as evidence suggesting that in (e,f), just as in (d), there is a complex nucleus. Parkinson 1983:159 reaches the same conclusion (with the exception of /-l/, which he does not address): oral diphthongs, nasal monophthongs and nasal diphthongs all have the structure of a diphthong or complex syllable nucleus.

13 We are aware of the discussion concerning the possibly privative status of the feature [lateral] (Steriade 1995), and of Walsh's 1995 assertion that there exists no such feature. (Walsh argues instead for the feature [liquid].) The resolution of this discussion is not strictly relevant to our analysis here.

14 Here we will make the noncrucial assumption that the stressed vowel is the head of the PrWd.

15 It has been noticed that nasalization correlates strongly with stress. Consider, as an example, the alternation in verbal forms adduced by Vandresen (1975:87):

	['ɐ̃]mo	'I love'
	['ɐ̃]mas	'you love'
but	[a'mɐ̃]mos	'we love'

We are aware that many other factors (which will not be discussed here) may affect nasalization. There are examples where nasalization correlates with stress but only if both phenomena are cyclic. Perini (1971) (cited by Leite 1974:73) notes the contrast between c[a]*mính+a* 'he walks' and c[ɐ̃]*m+ính+a* 'small bed'. Nonetheless, Leite also notes that many dialects do not have this kind of contrast. The correlation between stress and nasalization also fails in cases were we find nasal vowels in atonic position (e.g. [bẽ 'nẽnẽ]). Finally, a difference should be made between optional and non-optional nasalization or even between different degrees of nasalization (see Ladefoged 1967).

16 The traditional interpretation is that the nasal deletes in intervocalic position when the first vowel carries the primary stress of the word; then the final /o/ becomes a glide. Obviously, this kind of analysis would clash with monotonicity and parallelism, two basic assumptions of OT.

17 One might wonder why *[kãw̃po] does not satisfy assimilation. If one assumes the articulator group hypothesis in which [continuant] is located under PA (Padgett 1992, 1994, and others), then the assimilated nasal will be [-cont], but the two segments of [w̃p] disagree for this feature. Another reason could be that [labial] is a vocalic PA for [w] while assimilation is computed with respect to the consonantal PA.

18 This generalization is blurred by a phonetic neutralization that renders the initial vowel of a nasal diphthong as the centralized low vowel [ɐ̃]. For this restriction in diachronic development, see Mattos e Silva 1991:76.

19 We still have not treated the data in (8d), *leoa* ~ *leoas*. This feminine singular/plural pair is interesting only in that it shows loss of nasalization (from /leon + a/). Since there are no [õã] sequences or dipthongs in the language (see the appendix), the nasal is completely effaced.

20 Azevedo (p. 89) cites words with obstruent-final syllables, even [-continuant] ones, but these are always broken up by epenthesis in Brazilian Portuguese (BP), and are frequently elided in Continental Portuguese (Mâttoso Câmara 1953:79, 1972:48-9). In the case of epenthesis in BP, an otherwise unattested stress pattern obtains, with the ante-antepenultimate syllable receiving stress in some cases: /ritmiko/ [rí ti mi ku]. The epenthetic vowel apparently is transparent here; we leave this for further research. See Alderete 1995 for a typology of 'degree of participation' that epenthetic segments may show in other prosodic patterns.

21 The case of Lt. COMPUTARE > *comptar* > Sp., Port. *contar*, suggests that this situation is resolved by eliminating the obstruent, thus maintaining the nasal consonant, which is more closely related to the nuclear vowel. Compare Spanish and Portuguese, however, in their treatment of /-ns/. /transportar/ is often [tras.por.tar] in Spanish, but is [trã(n)s.por.tar] in Portuguese, since the nasal may incorporate into the nucleus in Portuguese, but not Spanish; that is, there can be (phonetically audible) nasal vowels in the one language, but not the other.

22 Girelli (p. 64). He extends this to the case of /r, s/ in BP using an X'-notation of syllable structure.

23 Except */ɔw/, which is unexplained.

References

Agard, Frederick B. 1984. *A Course in Romance Linguistics, Volume 1: A Synchronic View*. Washington, D.C.: Georgetown University Press.

Alcover, Antoni and Fransesc Moll. 1968. *Diccionari Català-Valencià-Balear* 1. Spain: Palma de Mallorca.

Alderete, John. 1995. Faithfulness to prosodic heads. Paper presented at The Derivational Residue in Phonology. Tilburg University. October 5-7, 1995. Rutgers Optimality Archive.

Andrade Pardal, Ernesto d'. 1977. *Aspects de la Phonologie (générative) du Portugais*. Lisboa: O Centro de Linguistica da Universidade de Lisboa.

Azevedo, Milton M. 1981. *A Contrastive Phonology of Portuguese and English*. Washington, D.C.: Georgetown University Press.

Back, Eurico and G. Mattos. 1971-1972. *Gramática Construtural de Língua Portuguesa*. Two vols. São Paolo: FTD.

Back, Eurico. 1973. São fonemas as vogais nasais do português? *Construtura* 4.297-317.

Barbosa, Osmar. 1967. *Dicionário de Flexão das Palavras*. Rio de Janeiro: Biblioteca Línguas Vivas.

Brakel, C. A. 1979. A gramática gerativa e a pluralização em português. *Boletim de Filologia* 25.55-96.

Brandão de Carvalho, Joaquim. 1988. Nasalité et structure syllabique en portugais et en galicien: approche non linéare et panchronique d'un problème phonologique. *Verba* 15.237-263.

Brasington, R. W. P. 1971. Noun pluralization in Brazilian Portuguese. *Journal of Linguistics* 7.151-177.

Cagliari, Luiz Carlos. 1981. *Elementos de fonética do português brasileiro*. MA thesis, Universidade Estadual de Campinas.

Carlton, Terence R. 1991. *Introduction to the Phonological History of the Slavic Languages*. Columbus, Ohio: Slavica Publishers.

Cintra, Geraldo. 1962. Ensaios sôbre a estrutura do português de Brasil. *Estudos* 1.17-31.

Colman, Fran. 1983. 'Vocalisation' as nucleation. *Studia Linguistica* 37.30-48.

de Chene, Brent E. and Stephen R. Anderson. 1979. Compensatory lengthening. *Language* 55.505-535.

Girelli, Carl Anthony. 1988. *Brazilian Portuguese Syllable Structure*. Doctoral Dissertation, University of Connecticut.

Goldsmith, John. 1976. *Autosegmental Phonology*. Doctoral Dissertation, Massachusetts Institute of Technology. (Distributed by the Indiana University Linguistics Club: Bloomington).

Guitart, Jorge M. 1989. Concatenation-stratum phonology (nee lexical phonology) and a Dominican dialect of Spanish. *American Spanish Pronunciation: Theoretical and Applied Perspectives,* ed. Peter C. Bjarkman and Robert M. Hammond, 187-195. Washington, D.C.: Georgetown University Press.

Hall, Robert A. 1943a. The unit phonemes of Brazilian Portuguese. *Studies in Linguistics* 1.1-6.

Hall, Robert A. 1943b. Occurrence and orthographic representation of phonemes in Brazilian Portuguese. *Studies in Linguistics* 2.6-13.

Hammarström, Göran. 1954. Review of Holger Sten 1944. Les particularités de la langue portugaise. *Revista do Laboratório de Fonética Experimenta* 2.158-162. Coimbra: Universidade de Coimbra.

Hammarström, Göran. 1962a. Review of José Gonçalo Herculano de Carvalho 1958. *Fonologia mirandesa. Romance Philology* 15.350-356.

Hammarström, Göran. 1962b. Discussion of Morais Barbosa 1962. *Proceedings of the Fourth International Congress of Phonetic Sciences*. Helsinki, 1961. 709. The Hague: Mouton.

Harris, James W. 1980. Noncatenative morphology and Spanish plurals. *Journal of Linguistic Research* 1.15-33.

Head, Brian F. 1965. *A Comparison of the Segmental Phonology of Lisbon and Rio de Janeiro*. Doctoral Dissertation, University of Texas, Austin.

Hensey, Fritz. 1968. Questões de fonologia gerativa: as regras de pluralização. *Estudos Linguísticos* 3.1-10.

Holt, D. Eric. In preparation. Constraint Interaction in the Development of Syllable Structure from Latin to Spanish and Portuguese. Doctoral Dissertation, Georgetown University.

Inkelas, Sharon. 1995. The consequences of Optimization for underspecification. *Proceedings of the 24th North East Linguistics Society*. Amherst, Massachussetts: Graduate Linguistics Student Association.

Inkelas, Sharon, Cemil Orhan Orgun and Cheryl Zoll. 1996. Exceptions and static phonological patterns: cophonologies versus presepecification. Rutgers Optimality Archive, ms.

Itô, Junko, Yoshihisa Kitagawa and Armin Mester. 1995. Prosodic faithfulness and Correspondence: Evidence from a Japanese argot. To appear in *Journal of East Asian Linguistics*.

Johnstone, T. M. 1975. The Modern Southern Arabian Languages. *Afroasiatic Linguistics* 1.93-121.

Kenstowicz, Michael. 1995. Base-identity and uniform exponence: Alternatives to cyclicity. Massachusetts Institute of Technology, ms. Rutgers Optimality Archive.

Lacerda, Armando de and Brian F. Head. 1962. Análise de sons nasais e sons nasalizados do Português. *Revista do Laboratório de Fonética Experimental*, 6.5-70. Coimbra: Universidade de Coimbra.

Lacerda, Armando de and Göran Hammarström. 1952. Transcrição fonética de português normal. *Revista do Laboratório de Fonética Experimental* 1.119-135. Coimbra: Universidade de Coimbra.

Lacerda, Armando de and P. Strevens. 1956. Some phonetic observations using a speech-strecher. *Revista do Laboratório de Fonética Experimental* 3.5-16. Coimbra: Universidade de Coimbra.

Ladefoged, Peter. 1967. Linguistic Phonetics. *UCLA Working Papers*.

Lamontagne, Greg and Keren Rice. 1995. A Correspondence account of coalescence. *Papers in Optimality Theory*, ed. Jill N. Beckman, Laura Walsh Dickey and Suzanne Urbanczyk, 211-223. University of Massachusetts Occasional Papers in Linguistics 18. Amherst, Massachussetts: Graduate Linguistics Student Association.

Leite, Yvonne de Freitas. 1974. *Portuguese Stress and Related Rules*. Doctoral Dissertation, University of Texas, Austin.

Lipski, John M. 1973. The surface structure of Portuguese: plurals and other things. *Linguistics: An International Review* 111.67-82.

Lloyd, Paul M. 1994. Contribution to the study of the syllable structure of Old Spanish. Paper presented at the Modern Language Association meeting. San Diego, California. December 28, 1994.

López, Barbara Stradt. 1979. *The Sound Pattern of Brazilian Portuguese (Carioca Dialect)*. Doctoral Dissertation, University of California, Los Angeles..

Louro, José Inês. 1954-55. Estudo e clasificação das vogais. *Boletim de Filologia* 15.215-248.

Malmberg, Bertil. 1971. La structure phonétique de quelques langues romanes. *Phonétique générale et romane*. 301-342. The Hague & Paris: Mouton.

Mascherpe, Mario. 1970. *Análise comparativa dos sistemas fonológicos do inglês e do português*. São Paolo: Cadeira de Linguia e Literatura Inglesa. Faculdade de Filosofia, Ciencias e Letras de Assis. Distribuidores: Livraria Francesa.

Mattos e Silva, Rosa Virgínia. 1991. *O purtuguês arcáico: fonologia*. São Paolo: Contexto.

Mattoso Câmara, Joaquim. 1953. *Para o estudo da fonêmica portugesa*. Rio de Janeiro: Simões.

Mattoso Câmara, Joaquim. 1970. *Estrutura da língua portuguesa*. Petrópolis, RJ: Voces.

Mattoso Câmara, Joaquim. 1972. *The Portuguese Language*. Trans. by Anthony J. Naro. Chicago: University of Chicago Press.

McCarthy, John J. 1995. Extensions of faithfulness: Rotuman revisited. University of Massachussetts, Amherst, ms. Rutgers Optimality Archive.

McCarthy, John J. and Alan Prince. 1995. Faithfulness and reduplicative identity. *Papers in Optimality Theory*, ed. Jill N. Beckman, Laura Walsh Dickey and Suzanne Urbanczyk, 249-384. University of Massachusetts Occasional Papers in Linguistics 18. Amherst, Massachussetts: Graduate Linguistics Student Association.

McCawley, James D. 1968. *The Phonological Component of a Grammar of Japanese*. The Hague: Mouton.

Mester, R. Armin. 1994. The quantitative trochee in Latin. *Natural Language and Linguistic Theory* 12.1-61.

Mira Mateus, Maria Helena. 1975. *Aspectos da Fonologia Portuguesa*. Lisboa: O Centro de Estudos Filológicos.

Morais Barbosa, Jorge. 1962. Les voyelles nasales portugaises: interprétation phonologique. *Proceedings of the Fourth International Congress of Phonetic Sciences*. Helsinki, 1961. 691-708. The Hague: Mouton.

Morais Barbosa, Jorge. 1965. *Etudes de phonologie portugaise*. Lisboa: Junta de Invetigações do Ultramar.

Morais Barbosa, Jorge. 1983. *Etudes de phonologie portugaise*. 2nd ed. Evora: Universidade de Evora, Divisão de Línguas e Literatura.

Morales-Front, Alfonso. 1994. *A Constraint-based Approach to Spanish Phonology*. Doctoral Dissertation, University of Illinois, Urbana-Champaign.

Padgett, Jaye. 1992. Stricture and Nasal Place Assimilation. Linguistic Research Center report LRC-92-08. University of California, Santa Cruz. In revised form in *NLLT* (1994).

Parkinson, Stephen. 1983. Portuguese nasal vowels as phonological diphthongs. *Lingua* 61.157-177.

Perini, M. 1971. The process of nasalization: Evidence from Portuguese. University of Texas, Austin, ms.

Pontes, Eunice. 1965. *Estrutura de Verbo no Português Coloquial*. Petrópolis: Vozes.

Porzio Gernia, María Luisa. 1976. Tendenze strutturali della sillaba latina in età arcaica e classica. *Scritti in onore de G. Bonfante*, 757-779. Brescia: Paideira Editrice.

Prince, Alan and Paul Smolensky. 1993. Optimality Theory: Contraint Interaction in Generative Grammar. Rutgers University and University of Colorado, Boulder, ms.

Reed, David W. and Yolanda Leite. 1947. The segmental phonemes of Brazilian Portuguese. *Phonemics: A Technique for Reducing Languages to Writing*, ed. Kenneth L. Pike, 194-202. Ann Arbor: University of Michigan Publications.

Reighard, J. and A. de Almeida. 1983. /R/ en début et en fin syllabiques dans les dialects portugaises. *Revue de l'Association Québécoise de Linguistique* 3.177-186.

Repetti, Lori. 1989. The Bimoraic Norm of Tonic Syllables in Italo-Romance. Doctoral Dissertation, University of California, Los Angeles.

Rogers, Francis M. 1954. Review of Mattoso Câmara 1953. *Language* 30.503-509.

Rosenthall, Sam. 1994. Vowel/Glide Alteration in a Theory of Constraint Interaction. Doctoral Dissertation, University of Massachusetts, Amherst.

Russell, Kevin. 1995. Morphemes and candidates in Optimality Theory. University of Manitoba, ms. Rutgers Optimality Archive.

Saciuk, Bohdan. 1970. Some basic rules of Portuguese phonology.. *Studies Presented to Robert B. Lees by his Students*, ed. Jerrold M. Sadock and Anthony Vadek, 197-222. Papers in Linguistics Monograph Series 1. Edmonton and Champaign: Linguistic Research, Inc.

Sletsjöe, Leif. 1971. La vocalisation du *l* et les formes *as* et *des* en ancien français. *Sprache und Geschichte: Festschrift für Harri Meier zum 65 Geburtstag*, ed. Eugenio Coseriu and Wolf-Dieter Stempel, 449-458. Munich: Fink.

Sproat, Richard and Osamu Fujimura. 1993. Allophonic variation in English /l/ and its implications for phonetic implementation. *Journal of Phonetics* 21.291-311.

St. Clair, Robert N. 1971. The Portuguese plural formation. *Linguistics: An International Review* 68. 90-102.

Sten, Holger. 1944. Les particularités de la langue portugaise. *Travaux du Cercle de Linguistique de Copenhague 2*. Copenhagen: Munskgaard.

Steriade, Donca. 1995. Underspecification and markedness. *The Handbook of Phonological Theory*, ed. John Goldsmith. 114-174. Oxford: Basil Blackwell.

Stevens, K.N., Andrade, A. and M.C. Viana. 1988. Perception of vowel nasalization in VC contexts: A cross-language study. Paper presented at the Annual Meeting of the Acoutical Society of America.

Sütterlin, Ludwig. 1916. Lautbildung.

Tláskal, Jaromir. 1980. Remarques sur les voyelles nasales en portugais. Zeitschrift für Phonetik, *Sprachwissenschaft und Kommunikationsforsching* 33.562-570.

Trager, George L. 1943a. Note on Hall 1943a. *Studies in Linguistics* 1.6.

Trager, George L. 1943b. Note on Hall 1943b. *Studies in Linguistics* 2.12-13.

Tranel, Bernard. 1996. French liaison and elision revisited: a unified account within Optimality Theory. *Aspects of Romance linguistics: Selected Papers From the Linguistic Symposium on Romance Languages XXIV*, ed. Claudia Parodi, Carlos Quicoli, Mario Saltarelli and María Luísa Zubizarreta. Washington, D.C.: Georgetown University Press.

Trigo, R. Lorenza. 1988. On the Phonological Derivation and Behavior of Nasal Glides. Doctoral Dissertation, Massachusetts Institute of Technology.

Trigo, R. Lorenza. 1993. The inherent structure of nasal segments. *Phonetics and Phonology 5: Nasals, Nasalization and the Velum,* ed. Marie K. Huffman and Rena A. Krakow, 369-400. New York: Academic Press.

Vandresen, Paolino. 1975. O vocalismo português: implicações teóricas. *Revista Brasileira de Linguística* 2.80-103.

von Essen, Otto. 1964. An acoustic explanation of the sound shift [ɫ] > [u] and [l] > [i]. *In Honour of Daniel Jones: Papers Contributed on the Occasion of His Eightieth Birthday 12 September 1961*, ed. David Abercrombie, et al, 53-58. London: Longmans.

Walsh Dickey, Laura. 1995. The Phonology of Liquids. Doctoral Dissertation, University of Massachusetts, Amherst. Defense Draft, November 8, 1995.

Wetzels, W. Leo. 1991. Contrastive and allophonic properties of Brazilian Portuguese vowels. *New Analyses in Romance Linguistics (LSRL 18, 1988)*, ed. Dieter Wanner and Douglas Kibbee, 77-99. Philadelphia: Benjamins.

Williams, Edwin B. 1962. *From Latin to Portuguese: Historical Phonology and Morphology of the Portuguese Language*. Philadelphia: University of Pennsylvania Press. First edition 1938.

Yip, Moira. 1995. Identity avoidance in phonology and morphology. University of California, Irvine, ms. Rutgers Optimality Archive.

13

Apocope and Lenition in Portuguese

WAYNE J. REDENBARGER

0. Introduction

Continuing progress in process-oriented approaches to Morphological Theory has created an opportunity for a salutary integration of the principles of generative morphological theory with those of Lexical Phonology (LexP). The present study examines the relation between the putative shape of certain underlying verb and noun stems in Portuguese and the set of Word Formation Rules (WFRs) and Phonological Rules (P-rules) which operates upon their output. This rule interaction sheds light on the structure of these components and provides new insights into certain morphological and phonological problems, calling into question our previous understanding of these phenomena in Portuguese.

The form of this paper will be first to provide an overview of the structure of the integrated morphological and phonological model used herein, followed by a statement of the conventional wisdom regarding Portuguese *-e* apocope and *-l-* lenition. Our integrated WFR cum LexP model will then be used to examine three competing analyses of the phenomena in question, distinguished by differing assumptions regarding the underlying stems. The paper will end with a summary and discussion of conclusions.

1. Overview of the structure of the integrated model

The present study employs a process morphology model derived from the one exemplified in Stephen Anderson's 1992 book *A-Morphous Morphology* (hereafter A-MM). Anderson's major new work broadens and refines his 'Extended Word and Paradigm' model (see Spencer 1991 § 6.5.2). We agree with Anderson that it is an improvement on the line of inquiry begun by Aronoff (1976) not to accept the primacy of words in morphological theory. We concur that 'it is not words but stems that function as the base of Word Formation Rules' (A-MM.71). This present study employs three improvements on Anderson's model.

The first of our proposed modifications derives from the observation in Halle and Marantz (1993) that Anderson was not required to postulate morpheme features; rather he could have merely redefined the morpheme (p. 112). We shall do precisely that and refer to abstract concepts such as PL (plural) and PAST as 'morphemes', designating them with capital letters.[1] This does not damage our ability to retain the process morphology concept of WFRs which realize such morphemes as phonological strings, e.g. PAST → [z]. The left side of the WFR in this case is a morpheme; the right side is a phonological segment on a branch, as indicated by the double brackets.

The second major point where we shall diverge from A-MM is in the ability to refer to boundary elements or 'edges' designated by double brackets. This work accepts the arguments and adopts the usage developed in Halle and Mohanan (1985) and Mohanan's (1986) *The Theory of Lexical Phonology* (hereafter TLP). The reader is referred to these works (especially TLP.129). The retention in our model of traditional edge information is in direct opposition to Anderson's new proposal to 'replace explicit reference to boundary elements in the interior of a domain' by replacing them with metaconditions on rules (TLP.248).

Note that we are using unlabelled branches, i.e., the only morphological information available to the P-rules is edge information. In this way, we obviate the ability to 'look back' to the previous derivational history of the form beyond its branching within that stratum.

We also consider the kind of modular organization reflected in A-MM (p. 254) to be wholly compatible with the kinds of strata suggested in TLP. We shall therefore make use of modular layers of rules and employ the standard Bracket Erasure Convention at the end of each stratum. This ensures that the internal morphological information created by the action of the WFRs at each level are available only to the P-rules of that stratum.

Finally, we diverge from A-MM and retain the position of TLP that a lexical stratum may or may not be cyclic (cf. TLP.47 vs. A-MM.248). Despite cyclicity having been a primary motivation for the original arguments regarding rule organization (Kiparsky 1982), there is clear evidence that the lexical strata of certain heavily morphologized languages like Latin are non-cyclic (see Redenbarger forthcoming). Therefore, we follow Halle and Mohanan and do not assume cyclicity in any stratum.

The goal of these modifications to A-MM is to better integrate the generalizations of LexP with those of process morphology.

2. Specifics of the model

In the Halle-Mohanan LexP model, phonological rules are partitioned into strata. Some operate within the lexicon and others afterwards or 'postlexically', continuing the practice begun with the first work on Lexical Phonology (Kiparsky 1982). An important difference with the TLP model, however, is that the strata are not obligatorily undetermined regarding cyclicity; rather they are presumed to be non-cyclic until proven otherwise (Mohanan 1986:47).

The several boundary symbols of SPE (=, +, #, ##, etc.) are replaced by one single type of branching structure. That branching information is only available to the P-rules within the stratum in which they were generated by a WRF, since the branches are aggregated at the end of each stratum by the (internal or ⟧⟦) Bracket Erasure Convention (BEC, cf. TLP.23). Thus, distinctions in representation which would have been denoted by different boundary symbols in SPE are indicated in exactly the same manner in the TLP model (cf. 1a and 1b).

(1a)	kæt+z	ri=du	hat#ʃat
(1b)	⟦kæt⟧⟦z⟧	⟦ri⟧⟦du⟧	⟦hat⟧⟦ʃat⟧

The double brackets are notational devices equivalent to a branching structure of the following shape:

(2)

kætz
/\\
kæt z (TLP.128)

It is the action of WFRs that creates the branching structures of each stratum. The branching structures are thus available only within their stratum of operation, being erased at the end of the stratum by the BEC.

As indicated above, we concur with the arguments presented in Anderson (1992 §3.5) and therefore consider the first stratum's input to be stems plus morphological information. Both in A-MM and in the modified WFR cum P-rules model used in this paper, only the stem will arrive from the lexicon in the form of a phonological representation, sometimes labeled a 'lexeme' (Halle and Marantz 1993:129).

In contrast, the associated morphological information is abstract. Since this information (e.g. PL, PAST, etc.) constitutes our redefined morpheme, all rules that manipulate it (e.g. agreement in gender or number, etc.) will have taken place before the input string is sent to the morphological cum phonological strata. Underlying morphological abstractness is a feature common to our model and A-MM. The important distinction is that in our model the word 'morpheme' refers to an abstract meaning entity. These morphemes are realized or converted to phonological representations via the action of WFRs.

In the A-MM model, this morphological information takes the form of 'features' which remain behind even after the WFRs have operated. In our model the capitalized morphological information is rewritten in the Chomsky (1957) 're-write rule' sense: the abstract entity is replaced by phonological information. When a WFR operates, an additional branch in the Halle-Mohanan LexP framework is created. Thus, in the plural of the example above, the WFR cum P-rules will operate as:

(3) Input String — [kæt] PL
Affixation stratum
WFR: PL → [z] — [kæt] [z]
(no P-rules apply)
] Erasure — [kætz]
Post Lexical stratum
P-rule: Ob → [-voi] / [-voi] __] — [kæts]

The environment for the PLex P-rule of voicing assimilation makes crucial use of the environment / __] (word-final position). Had the rule been applicable in the previous affixation stratum, it would have ambiguously meant 'internal branch final' as well as 'word-final'. Only after all internal] boundaries have been erased, in the postlexical stratum, can notions such as 'word-initial' or 'word-final' be invoked.[2]

The WFRs and P-rules would then apply in the following type of arrangement:

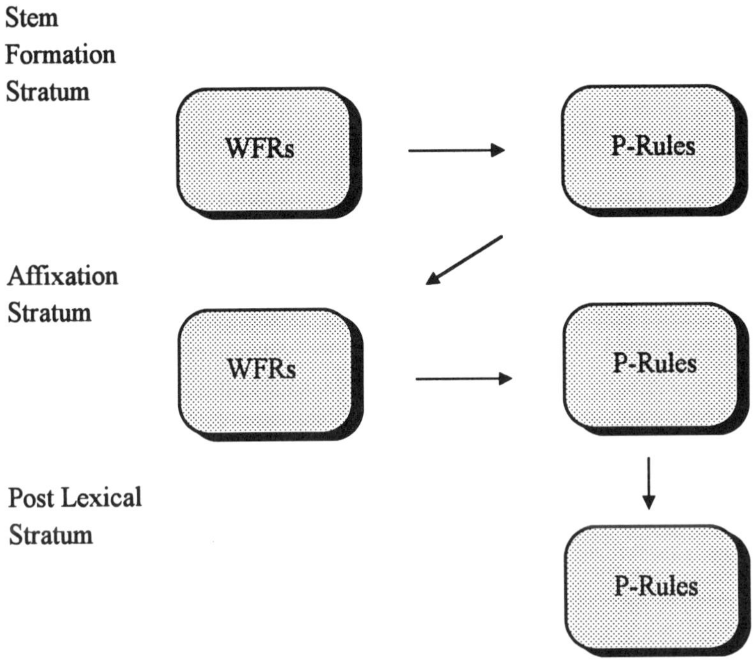

In this non-cyclic model, one-way arrows indicate that all of the WFRs of a module apply before passing their results on to the associated phonological rules for the given stratum. The job of the P-rules in each stratum is to resolve the incompatibilities created by the WFRs of that stratum. When they function postlexically they are phrasal sandhi rules, but the rules of earlier strata perform internal sandhi.

Thus, our primary modifications to the A-MM model are:

1) use abstract morphemes rather than morphological features;
2) retain all branching or 'edge' information until the end of each stratum;
3) make no a priori presumptions regarding the cyclic nature of any stratum.

There is one more important point regarding ordering. The view adopted here is that there exist ordered lists of rules inside of ordered modules or strata. It is true that there are a number of binary WFR rule pairs where a restricted environment applies first and the second subrule rewrites the given morpheme as 'elsewhere' if that first environment is not met. However, with the use of abstract morphemes and actually re-writing them, the elsewhere concept falls out automatically and no meta-principle on rule applications to block reapplication is required. 'Elsewhere' cases cannot reapply when the special case has earlier applied because the morpheme has been rewritten and is no longer part of the input string.

Interestingly, there seem to be few, if any, such instances in the P-rules. We therefore suggest that to whatever extent the Panninian 'Elsewhere Principle' (Kiparsky 1973) comes into play, it operates as a metatheoretical principle which may predict why pairwise WFRs have the extrinsic order they do. Except for that case, the rules are extrinsically ordered, as are all P-rules where the principle does not appear to apply. The ordering of the strata automatically imposes extrinsic order on the overall rule system. We shall assume that the notion is general and therefore posit that within the WFRs and P-rules there is extrinsic order as well.

The combination of extrinsic order and the formulation of WFRs as non-word-driven re-write rules handles both the problem of morpheme order in what are sometimes called paradigmatic slots as well as the double application problem discussed in Halle and Marantz (1993 §3). To use a computational metaphor, the set of abstract morphemes attached to a lexeme can be considered one unordered property list, that being the label which LISP programmers use to refer to that type of data structure. If the rule set is extrinsically ordered and the WFR rule which realizes SUBJ → **[a]** precedes the rule which specifies that 2ND → **[s]**, the following results are obtained automatically:

1) The paradigmatic statement that the subjunctive marker precedes the person marker is captured;

2) The absence of a subjunctive marker in the indicative is not a 'zero-morph'; the form simply did not have SUBJ in its input string. Therefore, it is merely a case of a re-write rule which did not apply since there was no SUBJ morpheme in the input string. In short, 'indicative' is but a piece of English prose used to refer to a form which has no SUBJ morpheme in the input string. The word 'indicative' itself has no theoretical status. The same would hold for 'present', 'active' and others;

3) As noted above, the double application problem of A-MM requires a special metatheoretical principle to block double application of less marked rules after the more complex case has already applied (A-MM §5.3.2). This is due to Anderson's retention of input morphological features, even after the application of

WFRs (see the criticism in Halle and Marantz 1993:130 of the A-MM position in this regard);

4) The use of a binary feature to distinguish three categories is automatically forbidden (i.e. plus, minus, and neither) (see Halle and Marantz 1992, example 6). Our model is binary; a given input string will either contain a particular morpheme such as SUBJ or it will not. This problem will be seen as parallel to the intentional use of phonological features in the same way by underspecification phonologists; in our model the structure of morphological marking precludes ternary marking. In the integrated model used here, for purposes of exposition, the abstract capitalized morphemes are concatenated in the order in which the rules are going to realize them to facilitate comprehension of the rule application order.

Note that in this model there is a process which inserts the general theme vowel marker (TV) in all forms marked for person (all finite verb forms). This rule is followed by lexical table rules such as:

(4) TV → V1 / [fal] __

Rule 4, which operates during the stem formation stratum, means 'the general theme vowel marker is rewritten as the first conjugation marker after the stem [fal]'. This situation dictates that categorical statements about rules which apply to the entire class of verb forms can only be made in the stem formation stratum, since TV will be rewritten before the end of the stratum, and thus the derivational history cannot later be retrieved. To put it another way, use of the notion of TV to condition a rule or rules must be done in the WFRs of the same stratum.

This case arises in Portuguese when verb stems are laxed but there is no laxing in e.g. feminine nouns which may ultimately have the same morphological and phonological shape as first conjugation verbs (see Redenbarger 1982 for an SPE formulation and below for a reformulation). The conditioning environment in our model is simply /__TV. This approach obviates the need for labeled brackets (cf. TLP §5.2.1). It also explains the point of having a TV marker, thereby answering the questions posed in A-MM §5.2.1. Recall that TVs are stem level affixes and are not part of the original stem. Consider the Latin form [lawd] 'praise'. This root gets a TV (later realized as V1, ultimately [ā]) when it has verb markers following, as in [lawdās] 'praises', but receives a declension class marker (DM) instead (later realized as N3, ultimately [ø]) on its way to becoming the Gen sg. noun [lawdis] 'of praise'.

In an integrated model such as ours, when the TV marker is rewritten in phonological form the morpheme itself is rewritten, thus it does not remain in feature form thereby allowing 'looking back'. This formalism captures the correct generalization. That is, in voicing assimilation involving a word-final *-z*], the P-rule has only phonological and edge information to work with. For instance, whether that segment came from an original verb, possessive, or noun plural marker (distinct morphemes all realized as [s] in English) the phonological rule treats them alike once the WFRs have operated.

Under this account, Halle and Marantz's position that 'morphology must include a theory of features that determines when they must cluster in morphemes and when they may surface in separate terminal elements ... [e.g.] the feature "CONJ1" in ... Latin' (1993:133) is not required. The approach taken here to determine in which stratum a WFR rule belongs is to examine:

1) the ordering needed to realize the phonological material in the proper linear order to build from the inside out, i.e., TVs before SUBJ, and

2) the phonological rules appropriate to each stratum.

In summary, the surest way to determine in which stratum a given morpheme is realized is to see which set of P-rules it feeds. In a WFR cum LexP model, there is no need for an additional principle to predict such cases because system coherence, including the simple order of the phonological realizations, will handle such matters. We now turn to such an example in Portuguese.

3. Portuguese apocope and lenition: The conventional wisdom

Diachronic facts: In the process of language change, new phonological rules tend to be added at the end of the rule system (King 1969:42). This is because socio-rules are ordered after binary phonological rules, and it is these variable rules which ultimately undergo binary phonologization, thus constituting the source of new phonological rules, i.e., the generative formulation of the 'transfer problem' (Labov 1972, 1994 § 'D'). This process often obscures the work of the rules of previous strata by overwriting their collective output. Additionally, it causes rules which were once late at a particular synchronic stage of the language to be gradually forced down earlier into the system. The ultimate case of this process is when once surface-true postlexical phonological rules are pushed down and ultimately morphologized (see Anderson 1992 §13.2 and references therein).

It is an important fact of Latin that in its entire rule system there is no WFR or P-rule dependent on the knowledge of either syllabification or word stress (see

Redenbarger forthcoming). Even Latin clitics, such as *-que* and the Latin prefixes which are found in a stratum following the word level postlexical rules precede syllabification and stress assignment. In short, these two rules can be ordered directly before the phrasal sandhi stratum. For this reason, Latin stress and syllabification are wholly surface true with no later rules to overwrite their output.

However, this is not the case in the Romance group, including the Hispano-Romance (H-R) daughters. Several new rules arise in the H-R daughters which are dependent on knowledge of prior stress placement. One obvious case is Castilian diphthongization which makes crucial use of stress placement: diphthongization must be ordered after stress.

Another H-R innovation, also crucially ordered after stress, leads to the crux of the contemporary Portuguese problems to be dealt with in this paper: word-final *-e* apocope which is defined in rule system terms as the addition of a postlexical rule deleting e̲]. As the examples in (5) demonstrate, in both Old Castilian and Old Portuguese, word-final *-e* apocope operated regularly after [r] and [l].

	Latin	*Castilian*	*Portuguese*	
(5a)	a.mā́.ɾe	a.máɾ	a.máɾ	'love' INF
(5b)	(h)os.pi.tā́.le	(h)os.pi.tál	(h)os.pi.tál	'hospital'(sg.)

Through the action of a productive penultimate stress rule plus this subsequent *-e* apocope rule, a set of forms arose whose singulars show stress on the final syllable even though the penultimate vowel received the stress at the point in the derivation when the regular stress rule applied.

In the plurals, where a final plural marker [s] kept the /e/ from being postlexically word-final, e] did not suffer apocope since the segment did not meet the rule's structural description requiring the segment to be word-final. Hence, many pairs of the following type developed:

(6) *underlying*	*Old Castilian*	*Old Portuguese*	
[pɾofesore]	pro.fe.sóɾ	pro.fe.sóɾ	'teacher' (sg.)
[pɾofesore][s]	pro.fe.só. ɾes	pro.fe.só.ɾes	'teacher' (pl.)

It is the interaction of this apocope process with two other classic innovations in diachronic Portuguese phonology that causes even further divergence of the Old Portuguese and Old Castilian paradigms.

Specifically, there is another diachronic Portuguese innovation to the effect that intervocalic /l/ is deleted. When this new rule interacts with the above *-e* apocope rule, the following results are obtained:

(7) *underlying*	*Old Castilian*	*Old Portuguese*	
[sol■o]	sólo	soo > só [sɔ́]	'alone'
[vɔl■o]	vʷɛ́lo	voo > vó	'flight'
[ospitale]	os.pi.tál	os.pi.tál	'hospital' (sg.)
[ospitale■s]	os.pi.tá.les	os.pi.tắʲs	'hospital' (pl.)

The final Portuguese plural form in (7) shows the additional effect of the glide formation process operating on an intermediate (postlexical) representation of : [ospitaes] → [ospitắʲs] (see Morales-Front and Holt this volume).

In short, the plural forms undergo intervocalic /l/ deletion but the singulars do not, due to *-e* apocope which leaves /l/ in absolute word-final position.

Note that another Old Portuguese voiced coronal, /n/, is also deleted intervocalically at about the same time that the *-l-* lenition rule is added to the end of the rule system. This may have occurred possibly as late as the tenth century (Boyd-Bowman 1980:90). It sometimes, but not always, leaves behind nasalization on the preceding vowel.

(8) *underlying*	*Old Castilian*	*Old Portuguese*	
[tene■re]	tenér	teer > tér	'have' INF
[sona■re]	sonár	soár	'sound' INF
[lan■a]	lána	lã́	'wool'

The interesting aspect is the interaction of these rules at the time the rule was being phonologized diachronically. For example, in the third person singular of [tene], it is crucial to know whether to drop the final *-e* while there is still a preceding underlying /n/ required to correctly condition the *-e* apocope rule. Doing so destroys the environment required for the /n/ to delete intervocalically. Conversely, we must know whether to delete the intervocalic /n/ first. This precludes the final /e/ from deleting by removing the conditioning preceding /n/. Apocope and lenition are in the classic mutually bleeding order. Like the *-l-* lenition case above, the correct answer is that *-e* apocope operates first allowing [tɛne] → [tɛn] which in turn undergoes syllable-final nasal deletion with concomitant nasalization of the preceding vowel postlexically.

(9) *underlying*	*Old Castilian*	*Old Portuguese*	
[tɛne]	tʲɛne	tẽ	'has'
[tɛne][mos]	tenemos	temos	'we have'

Old Portuguese additionally innovates with a rule of final stressed [aN] diphthongization to the effect of:

(10) á N] → ɐ̃́ w]

Rule (10) further obscures the underlying form in such a way that the underlying oral /a/ surfaces in neither the singular nor the plural of this form:

(11) *underlying*	*Old Castilian*	*Old Portuguese*	
[alemane]	a.le.mán	a.le.mɐ̃́w	'German' (sg.)
[alemane][s]	a.le.ma′nes	a.le.mɐ̃́ʲs	'German' (pl.)

The set of additional Portuguese innovations converts an original situation of transparency much like the one which still exists in modern Spanish, into one in which the underlying form is quite obscured. The key insight is that the rules apply (and presumably entered the phonology) in that particular order.

It must also be noted that Spanish, while it did not add the kinds of additional phonological rules which Portuguese did, instead sporadically applied the *-e* apocope rule to a broader range of environments, for example, after 'ungrouped' /d/:

	(12) *Latin*	*Old Castilian*	*Old Portuguese*	
	[veritate]	verdad	verdade	'truth'
but	[parte]	parte	parte	'part'

This phenomenon leads us to the last part of our discussion: the current day synchronic system, which has to deal with the consequences of all this history.

4. The contemporary system

While it is true that the morphological and phonological patterns which each generation of children must master exist as the result of the history of the language, it does not follow that contemporary language learners will necessarily posit rules which recapitulate the history of the language. In this case, it is the standard analysis of Spanish to ascribe the /e/ which appears in plurals, such as the *profesor* - *profesores* examples above, to the WFR realizing the plural marker, rather than to the noun stem itself. This analysis solves some problems, but it creates others. It is 'less abstract' in that some linguists presuppose that having underlying representations be as close to the surface forms is a desideratum, even if it means substantial complications of the rule system in exchange.

4.1 Spanish

If for Spanish one puts /e/ into the plural marker, allowing the underlying stem to look like the singular, then in exchange one must have two WFRs in exchange to realize the different plural markers: one for the cases where the *-e* has formerly been deleted, and *-s* for the others. Putting the /e/ into the special case of the plural marker WFR means that there is no underlying final vowel in forms such as *profesor*, thus the standard penultimate stress rule pervasive in Spanish phonology will be unable to correctly assign stress in all such cases. Therefore, the stress rule must be complicated and a sub-case created to assign final syllable stress only in cases where the /e/ was diachronically deleted

While the loss of clean rule generalizations is painful, the consideration which seems to force this unfortunate solution is the lack of any compelling synchronically productive rule which might motivate the abstract underlying *-e* stem representation. In cases when an underlying *-e* stem is posited in forms other than nouns, there are no alternations. For example, the verb stems show a perfectly stable *-e*:

(13) [p^{w}ɛde] 'he can' [v^{w}ɛle] 'he flies'

Barring any alternation, attempts to posit an underlying *-e* in noun stems would require a synchronic *-e* deletion rule, but doing so to productively generate the noun system would generate erroneous forms in the verb system.

4.2 Portuguese

The following types of synchronic nouns in Portuguese are consistent with productive apocope:

(14)	hospital	hospitais	'hospital(s)'
	rapaz	rapazes	'boy(s)'
	professor	professores	'teacher(s)'

Notice that the problematic Spanish *-d(e)* examples noted above pose no problem for an abstract analysis of the same phenomena in Portuguese. Portuguese has 3sg. [pɔde] 'he can' just as Spanish has [p^{w}ɛde] but this poses no problem. Portuguese did not expand the scope of the historical *-e* apocope rule to include the environment 'after ungrouped /d/' in nouns, unlike Spanish (recall contemporary Port. *verdade*, vs. Span. *verdad*, etc.). Therefore, we exclude stops from our set of conditioning segments and retain only the voiced coronal continuants.

Similarly, the problematic Spanish [v^{w}ɛle] example has no diachronically surviving intervocalic /l/ in Portuguese: the underlying stem is [voa] and is regular. Invervocalic /l/ deletion took place centuries ago and the evidence suggests a simple '*l*-less' reanalysis of the present underlying forms, thus the retention of final /e/ after a vowel is equally unremarkable.

The most convincing argument of all is that in Portuguese it is clear that there is a productive phonological process which would provide the kind of synchronic motivation which was wholly lacking for a productive rule of Spanish apocope. Specifically, during the medieval period of Portuguese phonology there were no devoicing rules of the type which decimated the Castilian obstruent series (see Boyd-Bowman 1980:10-11); thus the voiced coronal continuant /z/, which did not survive in Spanish, survived in Portuguese, thereby creating a set of Portuguese verbs stems whose verb stems end in *-ze*. These verbs show synchronic *-e* apocope just as the *hospital* and *professor* forms do. The theme vowel itself apocopates after /z/ in 3sg. present indicative verb forms of the second conjugation.

(15)	faz$\underline{\underline{e}}$r	faz$\underline{\underline{e}}$mos	faz$_{=}$	'does'
	traz$\underline{\underline{e}}$r	traz$\underline{\underline{e}}$mos	traz$_{=}$	'brings'
	diz$\underline{\underline{e}}$r	diz$\underline{\underline{e}}$mos	diz$_{=}$	'says' etc.

(cf. Spanish *hace*, etc. These cases cannot be solved by an alternative choice of underlying form since we are dealing with a clearly productive theme vowel here.)

Not only is this apparently strong evidence for Portuguese synchronic *-e* apocope after /z/, but in Portuguese, unlike Spanish, the process is productive after /r/ as well:

(16)	querer	queremos	quer_	'wants'
cf.		professores	professor_	'teacher(s)'

This is a wholly productive process in Modern Portuguese. It is not just that there are no nouns which end in /re/ or /ze/, but there are no second conjugation verbs whose root final consonant is /r/ or /z/ in which the theme vowel *-e*] does not undergo apocope.

Portuguese would appear to have synchronically productive *-e* apocope alternations which can be formalized using only phonological and edge information. It has also eliminated a major group of counterexamples to *-l-* lenition such as *vo(l)ar*. Under this approach modern Portuguese stress still appears to be late and transparent, like Latin, and the WFRs for pluralization avoid the necessity of an /es/ subcase, like Spanish, for those cases where the original final *-e* has been lost. Unfortunately, the situation is not that simple, as we shall see in the detailed discussion of the following three sections.

4.2.1 Analysis 1: SPE-type

There are many surface counterexamples to intervocalic *-l-* lenition in Portuguese if the modern synchronic rule posited merely recapitulated the diachronic facts, for example:

(17) alegre 'happy' eleger 'elect' etc.

Thus, from the time of the earliest generative analyses (Mateus 1975), the contemporary rule was restricted so that lenition operated only across morpheme boundaries. This avoids generating erroneous outputs in examples such as those cited immediately above, i.e., *eleger* would be *eleg + e + r* , and the intervocalic /l/ would fail to suffer lenition. The SPE view then was that forms like *hospitais* would lose the /l/ in their underlying stem only when intervocalic and across a morpheme boundary.

While the diachronic restructuring of the Latin [vɔla] forms as Portuguese [voa] forms mentioned above saves us from a problematic set of counterexamples to the *-l-* lenition rule, other intractable examples do exist. It has been observed (Redenbarger 1978) that a class of non-deleting -V/V- examples exists constituting counterexamples to any simple synchronic *-l-* lenition formulation, even one specifying '+ boundaries'. These examples arise as a result of changes in the system which have taken place since the medieval rule's productive stages.

Specifically, some of the most common verbs in the language such as *falar* 'to speak', *calar* 'to hush', etc. quite obviously have a surface intervocalic /l/ in all of their regular forms.

(18)	falar	falamos	fala	etc.
	'to speak'	'we speak'	'speaks'	
	calar	calamos	cala	etc.
	'to hush'	'we hush'	'hushes'	

Every one of these counterexamples to the SPE-type *-l-* lenition rule cited above has an /l/ both intervocalically and across a morpheme boundary, e.g.:

(19) /fal + a + mos/ 'we speak' etc.

These verbs did not suffer the results of the diachronic innovation of lenition because they did not contain intervocalic *-l-* at the time the rule operated, for example:

(20) fab(u)lare > fablar(e) > falar
callar(e) > calar

Since children have no inherent knowledge of the history of the language, modern day Portuguese learners evidently simply posit an *-l-*, and do not delete it. These counterexamples have been known for years, yet no SPE analysis could handle them.

In short, the productivity of modern day *-l-* deletion seems questionable, at least within the capabilities of the SPE framework to express it, yet the plurals of the *hospital* type examples presuppose it.

4.2.2 Analysis 2: WFR cum P-Rules: The Abstract Solution

Consider the following putative derivations for the *hospital* - *hospitais* examples cited above.[3] Note that within each stratum WFRs precede P-rules as shown in the flow chart on p. 447:

(21)

Input String	[ospital]	[ospital] PL
Stem Formation		
WFR: ø → NCM /]__ Gender	[ospital] NCM	[ospital] NCM PL
WFR: NCM → N3 / [ospital]__	[ospital] N3	[ospital] N3 PL
WFR: Lex Table: NCM → [e]	[ospital] [e]	[ospital] [e] PL
P-r: (none apply)		
] Bracket Erasure	[ospitale]	[ospitale] PL
Affixation		
WFR: PL → [s]		[ospitale] [s]
P-r: Intervocalic *-l-* Lenition		[ospita e] [s]
] Bracket Erasure		[ospitaes]
PostLexical Stratum		
P-r: Syllabification	[os.pi.ta.le]	[os.pi.ta.es]
P-r: Penultimate Stress	[os.pi.tá.le]	[os.pi.tá.es]
P-r: e → ø / [C+voi+cont+cor] __	[os.pi.tál]	
P-r: Glide Formation		[os.pi.tá^{j}s]
P-r: Syl Fin l → w	[os.pi.tá^{w}]	
P-r: Syl Fin Palatalization	[oʃ.pi.tá^{w}]	[oʃ.pi.tá^{j}ʃ]

Under this analysis, noun stems like *hospital* belong to Noun Class 3 (N3). This marker is realized as [e], just as N1 is realized as [a], and N2 as [o]. We refer to the input form [ospital] as a noun 'root' and to the output of the stem formation stratum [ospitale] where the 'root' has been aggregated with the noun class marker vowel as a noun 'stem'. There is a unified penultimate stress rule, ordered before apocope of the underlying word-final /e/. When the stem final /e/ is not realized in word-final position (due to the realization of the [s] plural marker), *-e* does not apocopate, feeding *-l-* lenition. Note that word final /l/ changes to [w] in contemporary Brazilian Portuguese and to velar [ɫ] in modern Continental Portuguese. This is what we call the abstract analysis.

There are some insuperable problems with this analysis as well, despite its reformulation in terms of contemporary process morphology and level-ordered phonology. Specifically, the *-l-* lenition rule cannot be properly formulated (note that it was only stated in prose in the derivation above). The reason is that the only time the lenition rule knows that the [e] realization of N3 is on a separate branch (i.e., 'across a + boundary') is in the stem formation stratum. At the end of that stratum, the][is lost due to Bracket Erasure and the united stem is passed on to the affixation stratum.

However, if the lenition rule (/l/ → ø / V__][V) is put in the affixation stratum, it will no longer be applicable because the stem formation '][' will no longer be there. Unfortunately, the option to merely delete /l/ intervocalically is not viable because there are many root internal VlV sequences (noted above) which preclude that solution.

Nor can the problem be solved by moving lenition to the stem formation rules where the][is available because deletion of root final /l/ would result in all the forms of the noun. The contextual information which conditions the deletion according to the following segment has not yet been realized and will not be realized until the operation of the rules of the following stratum at which time the][will be gone.

In short, the abstract formulation has structural counterexamples, and the process morphology cum phonology solution constrains the rules so that the *-l-* lenition rule cannot be formulated.

4.2.3 Analysis 3: WFR cum P-rules: The concrete solution

The same morphology cum phonology model used for the previous solution will be employed here, but now without the assumption that the underlying noun stem is *-e*] final. That is, let us now assume that the synchronic situation is quite different from the diachronic facts in this regard as well. We can retain the formulation of the lenition rule: /l/ → ø / V__][V , provided we also posit the N3 class as having a 'zero' marker instead of the [e] posited earlier.[4] Consider the following derivations under this new set of assumptions:

(22)

Input String	[ospital]	[ospital] PL
Stem Formation		
WFR: ø → NCM /]__ Gender	[ospital] NCM	[ospital] NCM PL
WFR: NCM → N3 / [ospital]__	[ospital] N3	[ospital] N3 PL
WFR: Lex Table: NCM → [ ]	[ospital] [ ]	[ospital] [ ] PL
P-r: (none apply)		
][Bracket Erasure	[ospital]	[ospital] PL
Affixation		
WFR: PL → [es] / C __		[ospital] [es]
P-r: l → ø / V__][V		[ospita] [es]
][Bracket Erasure		[ospitaes]
PostLexical Stratum		
P-r: Syllabification	[os.pi.tal]	[os.pi.ta.es]
P-r: Stress / C __]	[os.pi.tal]	
P-r: Penultimate Stress		[os.pi.ta.es]
P-r: e → ø / [C+voi+cont+cor] __	. . . .	
P-r: Glide Formation		[os.pi.ta^{j}s]
P-r: Syl Fin l → w	[os.pi.ta^{w}]	
P-r: Syl Fin Palatalization	[oʃ.pi.ta^{w}]	[oʃ.pi.ta^{j}ʃ]

Note the interesting result that the post-lexical apocope rule no longer plays a role in the derivation of these forms. If no [e] is ever added to form an *-e* final noun stem then there is no *-e* to apocopate . Similarly, with the WFR for N3 now realized as zero, the same noun stem situation without *-e* arises in the *rapaz - rapazes*, and *professor - professores* forms as well.

Note also the necessary bifurcation of the PL WFRs into a special case after consonants and another simple [s] case elsewhere. While this complication of the WFRs is certainly not preferable, note that this concrete solution solves the above discussed *fala-* counterexamples with no further modification required.

(23)	
Input string	[fal] 1ST PL
Stem Formation	
WFR: ø → TV /]__PERSON	[fal] TV 1ST PL
WFR: TV → V1/ fal]__	[fal] V1 1ST PL
WFR: V1 → [a]	[fal] [a] 1ST PL
P-Rules: (none apply)	
] Erasure	[fala] 1ST PL
Affixation	
WFR: 1ST PL → [mos]	[fala] [mos]
P-r: l → ø / V__] V	. . . .
] Erasure	[falamos]
PostLexical	
P-r: Pre Nas Tensing	[falɐmos]
P-r: Syllabification	[fa.lɐ.mos]
P-r: Stress	[fa.lɐ́.mos]
P-r: Fin Syl Unstr Raisg	[fa.lɐ́.mus]
P-r: Syl Fin Palatalization	[fa.lɐ́.muʃ]

The earliest generative formulations used SPE '+ boundary' formalism. The generalization that the only time lenition operated was across a morpheme boundary was captured, however, the counterexamples cited above were equally across a morpheme boundary (eg., / fal + a + mos / 'we speak').

Notice that by modern process morphology and phonology standards, the representation with plusses was inappropriately merging structures now considered to be in different strata. The $+ a$ structure is a theme vowel and is part of the process of forming the verb stem which is realized in the stem formation stratum. In contrast, the $+ mos$ structure is a person-number marker not affixed until the following stratum. In a process WFR cum P-rule model there is no point in the derivation when both pieces of branching/boundary information are present in the derivation at the same time. This is an inherent problem of the early SPE framework viz., the lack of stratum or module differentiation inherent in the use of the '+' boundary within that model (see TLP.129-130).

Here, the final formulation of the *-l-* lenition rule is posited:

(24) l → ø / V __] V

The rule must be a P-rule of the affixation stratum where it will be fed by a two part pluralization WFR, one of which generates [es]. It is a consequence of the stratal modularization of the rule set that the sequence -Vl▮a-, in the derivation of all *falar* forms will not provide the context for the application of lenition because in those forms the Vl▮V sequence will occur only in the stem formation stratum. By the time that string is handed on to the affixation stratum, the internal bracket will have been erased and the sequence will be -Vla]-. This long-standing problematic counterexample to *-l-* lenition is finally explained by a contemporary model of WFRs and P-rules, which partitions the rule sets into strata, combined with a concrete analysis of the noun stems.

There is an additional set of counterexamples to the abstract solution which come from well-known verbs but which to my knowledge have not been previously adduced with regard to this problem. I refer to the forms of *valer*, including the third singular present indicative form *vale*.

These forms have the verb stem [val▮e] during the stem formation stratum aggregating to [vale] by the end of the stem formation module, just as we saw with the *fala*-type forms. In short, they have the same final phonological shape as the putative underlying representation we had originally considered for *hospital*(e), and would have that shape from the affixation stratum onwards. This is an additional demonstration that the sequence *-ale*] cannot be posited for the N3 stems since these verb forms clearly demonstrate that this sequence does not undergo *-e* apocope. In this model, P-rules cannot see the morphological source of the phonological segments on which they operate, so they cannot distinguish a verb form from a noun form.

There are additional examples where *-e* apocope must not apply when *-e* is preceded by an /l/. However, we still have a productive deletion rule which deletes *-e* when the segment preceding it is an /r/ or a /z/, i.e., the *quer-* forms where [kɛɾe] becomes [kɛɾ] ([kɛh]) word finally, and the *faz* forms where [faze] becomes [faz] ([faʲʒ]), as discussed above.

In short, what had earlier appeared to be a viable argument based on the existence of an apparently synchronically productive *-e* apocope rule is now seen to be untenable for additional reasons. The *-e* apocope rule works only after /r/ and /z/, not after /l/. The reason nouns have no final /e/ after /l/ is the distribution created by the history of the language. The result at some time in the past was an analysis of at least the *-le* nouns of the N3 class as underlyingly final '*-e*-less' rather than their being synchronically *-e* final and undergoing productive deletion. When one considers all the data cited above, it is clear that whatever process is deleting /e/ in *quer-* and *faz-* could not be extended to delete word-final /e/ in *-le*] sequences, thus broadly motivating the abstract noun system analysis. It would appear that Portuguese acts in the same concrete way as Spanish.

The other item requiring attention in the underlying 'athematic' solution for nouns like *hospital - hospitais* is that there is an affixation stratum rule deleting the first vowel in V▮V sequences. This rule accounts for the loss of the theme vowel in both the first person singular of the present indicative and in all of the forms of the present subjunctive. Thus:

(25)

Input	[fal] SUBJ 1ST PL	[val] 1ST PL
Stem Formation Stratum		
WFR:	[fal] TV SUBJ 1ST PL	[val] TV 1ST PL
WFR:	[fal] V1 SUBJ 1ST PL	[val] V2 1ST PL
WFR:	[fal] [a] SUBJ 1ST PL	[val] [e] 1ST PL
P-Rules: none apply		
▮Bracket Erasure	[fala] SUBJ 1ST PL	[vale] 1ST PL
Affixation Rules		
WFR: SUBJ → [e] /a]__	[fala] [e] 1ST PL	
WFR: 1ST PL → [mos]	[fala] [e] [mos]	[vale] [mos]
P-rule: l → ø / V__▮V		
P-rule: V → ø / __▮V	[fal] [e] [mos]	
▮Bracket Erasure	[falemos]	[valemos]
Post Lexical Rules		
4 rules	[fa.lémuʃ]	[va.lémuʃ]

While the *fala-* forms do not have the same phonological shape as the *vale-* forms underlyingly, the *falemos* present subjunctives become identical to the *valemos* indicatives after the application of the above V▮V deletion rule in the affixation stratum. More importantly, the *falemos* form could well undergo (inappropriately) the Vl▮V deletion rule needed in the plural forms of *hospitais* since the ▮ boundary will be in place in their forms once the SUBJ marker is realized during the affixation stratum.

The crucial difference between the *falemos* and *valemos* forms is that the latter form has no ▮ boundary in an *-l* ▮ V- sequence at any time in the affixation stratum as the *-l-* lenition rule requires. This difference, however, is not the case with the *fale* Present Subjunctive forms of *fala-*. Note that the WFR which realizes SUBJ as [e] is an affixation stratum rule. Thus, the affixation stratum *-l-* lenition rule can operate on its output.

The solution is to ensure the order of application of rules is V_l_] V, lenition operating before the V]V deletion rule, as indicated in the parallel derivations above. The vowel which had been attached by WFR originally in the stem formation stratum will be correctly deleted in the case of a following [V sequence, i.e., first person singulars and all present subjunctives, but there will be no stripping of *-l*] to provide additional and incorrect applications to the forms of *fala*, etc.

There is one final problem with the *-e* apocope rule. It cannot simply be postlexical, requiring no] information. There are many subjunctives from the [a] theme conjugation which constitute surface counterexamples. For example, the subjunctive of *mora-* has the phonological form [more] postlexically, but it does not apocopate final *-e*.

On the other hand, when we consider this rule as a member of the P-rules of the affixation stratum, remember that our brackets are not 'labeled'. A ']' is a ']' and the environment /__] can equally signal branch-final as well as word-final. If the rule merely specifies /__], then it will inappropriately delete all of the theme vowels in all forms of *querer*, *fazer*, etc. since the representation *-ze*] or *-re*] will frequently appear (though only branch-finally within that stratum). Consider these examples:

(26) [kɛɾe]mos] → *[kɛr]mos]
[faze]mos] → *[faz]mos], etc.

It turns out that Jakobsen's "Signe Zéro" (1939) is the conditioning environment. There are two WFRs which realize morphemes as zero: 1) the 3sg. morpheme, and 2) the 1sg. morpheme in special cases. That latter pair of rules is:

(27) 1ST → [ ] /] X V] __
1ST → [o]

Recall that the WFRs do two things: (1) produce phonological segments where there were only abstract morphemes before, and (2) create branching structures on which these phonological segments are placed. The question of when to prune empty branches has been studied since Ross' (1967) dissertation. In this case, the branch, though phonologically empty, is clearly required. The rule is:

(28)

$$\begin{bmatrix} C \\ +\text{cont} \\ +\text{voi} \\ -\text{lat} \\ -\text{cor} \end{bmatrix} \quad \begin{matrix} e \\ \downarrow \\ \emptyset \end{matrix} \quad]\,[\,]$$

Results of the application of this rule are:

(29)

Input	[keɾ]	3RD	[val]	3RD
Stem Formation				
WFR: TV insertion	[keɾ] TV	3RD	[val] TV	3RD
WFR: Vb Stem Laxing	[kɛɾ] TV	3RD		
WFR: Lex Table	[kɛɾ] V2	3RD	[val] V2	3RD
WFR: V2 → [e]	[kɛɾ] [e]	3RD	[val] [e]	3RD
no P-rules apply				
] Erasure	[kɛɾe]	3RD	[vale]	3RD
Affixation Stratum				
WFR: 3RD → [ ]	[kɛɾe]	[ ]	[vale]	[ ]
P: e apocope	[kɛɾ]	[ ]		
] Erasure	[kɛɾ]		[vale]	
Post Lexical				
4 rules	[kɛ́x]		[vá.li]	

The specific exclusion of laterals with the [-lat] provision in the *-e* apocope rule (see above) keeps *vale* from incorrectly becoming **val.*

5. Summary

The necessity to exclude *-l(e)* noun stem cases to avoid erroneous derivations with the *vale-* verb forms forces us to reassess the original apparent generality of the apocope rule. Recall that the diachronic facts are such that the apparent loss of word-final /e/ after all voiced coronal continuants was so widespread that the distribution of data motivated positing a productive synchronic rule. Thus, in conjunction with the equally evident productivity of the *-l-* lenition rule and the support provided by that process for an underlying *-e]* final noun solution, we considered a contemporary synchronic solution reflecting the diachronic generality.

However, we now see that, just as we earlier had to give up the abstract underlyingly *-e*] final noun stem solution due to contemporary counterexamples to the *-l-* lenition process, the *-e* apocope process turns out to be synchronically unlike the diachronic facts as well. While the contemporary *quer* and *faz* 3sg. forms look like the historical facts, the *vale* forms are counterexamples. The apocope rule, therefore, must be restricted not to delete the word-final /e/ after /l/ in verbs. However, without that possibility in our synchronic system, the entire *hospital - hospitais* noun stem alternation which we originally used as a primary motivation for our synchronic analysis does not work because we cannot delete the word-final *-e*] after an /l/.

In summary, the orthography of modern Portuguese attempts to represent the history of the language; however, this is not consonant with the current linguistic system. It is easily explained to a student by saying:

All of the words which now end in a voiced coronal continuant used to have an underlying final *-e* in their stem. If you count that final *-e* vowel when you count vowels for stress, then stress is transparently penultimate. If that principle fails to make the correct prediction, stress is then considered exceptional. Then and only then must you use an explicit written stress mark in the official orthography, e.g.:

(30)	fala [fá.la],	falamos [fa.lɐ́.muʃ]	hospital [os.pi.tá^{w}]
vs.	avó [a.vɔ́]	câmara [k ɐ́.ma.ɾa]	fácil [fá.si^{w}]
	'talks'	'we talk'	'hospital'
	'grandfather'	'camera'	'easy'

(Forms like *hospital* demonstrate the assumed *-e* apocope rule, whereas forms such as *fácil* are considered exceptional and require a written stress mark even though surface penultimate). In the plurals, the underlying *-e* can be seen, e.g.:

(31)	professor ~ professores	rapaz ~ rapazes, etc.
	'teacher' 'teachers'	'boy' 'boys'

Even when the rule which deletes *-l-* between vowels causes the *-l-* to go away when it is intervocalic in the plural, you will still see the underlying *-e* where it is respelled as '*i*', given that diphthongs like [Vj] are spelled '*Vi*' in Portuguese by spelling convention:

(32) hospital ~ hospitais papel ~ papeis lençol ~ lençois
'hospital' 'hospitals' 'paper' 'papers' 'sheet' 'sheets'

In short, all one needs to know to determine when to use a written stress mark is that words ending in /l/, /r/, or /z/ had a final *-e*, and that you must count that final vowel before you zap it.

That's all there is to it, at least for the Portuguese 101 students. However, that piece of orthographic practice representing common wisdom regarding Portuguese simply cannot be maintained synchronically for modern Portuguese. We have seen in the sections above that the phonological environment required to write the *-l-* lenition rule proves that the *hospital* type nouns do not have an underlying stem in *-e*], and that thus the WFR for PL realization is actually two subrules: (1) a special case and, (2) a general elsewhere case, like Spanish. We have also seen that *-l-* lenition is not even surface true due to forms such as *fala* and many others. Instead, the lenition rule has been pushed down into the system and now requires branching information and careful rule ordering for it to operate correctly. It has greatly evolved from a formerly surface true fact.

In addition, we now see that the *-e* apocope rule required to delete the *-e*] in singular forms cannot be generally formulated once there is an awareness of counterexamples such as *vale*. There is system internal evidence that the *hospital* type nouns do not have a stem-final /e/, but even if there were not, a rule could not delete it given the conditioning branching requirements of synchronic *-e* apocope.

In the end, we have two cases of stress and we have *-e*-less nouns, both of which look much like the standard Spanish solution. The promise of an abstract modern Portuguese solution as good as the orthographic stress system appears simply intractable, and the possibility of one unified rule each for stress and pluralization is equally unworkable.

In the early days of generative phonology, it was suggested that synchronic generative solutions were simply recapitulations of a language's history. The modern Portuguese case clearly demonstrates that while rules may come and go, at a later stage, a language's rule system can come to bear rather little resemblance to the diachronic happenings by which it acquired its present morphological and phonological patterns.

Notes

1 See Anderson (1992 §3.4) for a full discussion of binary morphemes versus morpheme features.

2 See Mohanan (1986:128) for detailed discussion of this fundamental notion of Lexical Phonology.

3 Note that in our WFR cum LexP system the abstract morpheme PL is attached to the plural form. The singular differs in that it has the same stem but with no plural morpheme. This is to capture the fact that plurals are not formed from singulars but both are formed from stems plus (or perhaps absent any) associated morphemes.

4 Recall that we still need NCM markers since the N1 markers in [a] and the N2 markers in [o] are not affected by this change in our hypothesis regarding the realization of the N3 marker.

References

Anderson, Stephen R. 1992. *A-Morphous Morphology*. Cambridge Studies in Linguistics 62. Cambridge: Cambridge University Press.

Aronoff, Mark. 1976. *Word Formation in Generative Grammar*. Cambridge, Mass.: MIT Press.

Boyd-Bowman, Peter. 1980. *From Latin to Romance in Sound Charts*. Washington, DC: Georgetown University Press.

Chomsky, Noam. 1957. *Syntactic Structures*. Le Havre: Mouton.

Halle, Morris and Alec Marantz. 1993. Distributed morphology and the pieces of inflection. *The View from Building 20*, ed. Kenneth Hale, and Samuel Jay Keyser. Cambridge, Mass.: MIT Press.

Halle, Morris and Karuvannur P. Mohanan. 1985. Segmental phonology of Modern English. *Linguistic Inquiry* 16.57-113.

Jakobson, Roman. 1939. Signe Zéro. *Selected Writings* 2.211-19. The Hague: Mouton.

King, Robert D. 1969. *Historical Linguistics and Generative Grammar*. Englewood Cliffs, NJ: Prentice-Hall.

Kiparsky, Paul. 1973. 'Elsewhere' in phonology. *A Festschrift for Morris Halle*, ed. Stephen R. Anderson and Paul Kiparsky, 93-106. New York: Holt, Rinehart, and Winston.

Kiparsky, Paul. 1982. Lexical morphology and phonology. *Linguistics in the Morning Calm*, ed. I.S. Yang, 3-91. Seoul: Hanshin.

Labov, William. 1972. The internal evolution of linguistic rules. *Linguistic Change and Generative Theory*, ed. Robert P. Stockwell and Ronald K.S. Macaulay. Bloomington: Indiana University Press.

Labov, William. 1994. *Principles of Linguistic Change*. Oxford: Blackwell.

Mateus, Maria Helena Mira. 1975. *Aspectos da Fonologia Portuguesa*. Lisbon: Centro de Estudos Filológicos.

Mohanan, Karuvannur P. 1986. *The Theory of Lexical Phonology*. Dordrecht: D. Reidel.

Redenbarger, Wayne J. 1978. Review of *Aspectos da fonologia portuguesa*, by Maria Helena Mira Mateus. *Language* 54.949-952.

Redenbarger, Wayne J. 1982. *Articulator Features and Portuguese Vowel Height*. Cambridge, Mass.: Harvard University.

Redenbarger, Wayne J. In preparation. *The Synchronic Morphology and Phonology of Latin*.

Ross, John R. 1967. *Constraints and Variables in Syntax*. Doctoral dissertation. MIT.

Spencer, Andrew. 1991. *Morphological theory: Word structure in generative grammar*. Oxford: Blackwell.

V Spanish

14

The interface between inherent and structural prominence in Spanish*

Paloma García-Bellido

1 Introduction and theoretical background

An important insight in the understanding of the relationship between tone and segment in natural languages is that they enter in two types of relations (Goldsmith 1976). A segment may have a lexical tone (inherent relation) or acquire one, given by some higher organizational structure (structural relation).

(1) a. Inherent relation b. Structural relation

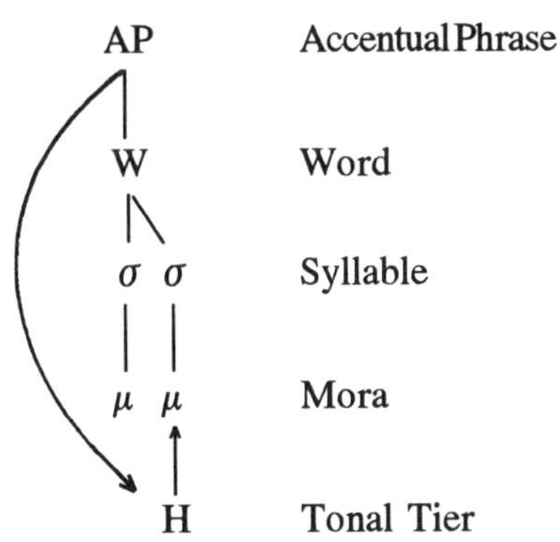

The inherent structure in (1a) is generally understood to be an 'accent' and used systematically by tone languages. 'Accent' is a bottom-up formal property (prominence) with which some mora may participate in higher organizational structures. In (1a), μ can be interpreted as having an inherent accent by virtue of imposing a fixed autosegmental tonal shape (Pulleyblank 1986, Hyman and Katamba 1993). If the inherent specific tone is replaced by an asterisk $\mu*$ (Goldsmith 1982a) or by a left- or right-bracket projection on the edge of its rhyme (Halle and Idsardi 1995), this configuration may also be interpreted as an accented mora. The structural relation in (1b) is usually understood as being prominently used by stress languages. The top–down relation is a formal property (prominence) which some moras acquire from higher organizational structures (Beckman 1986, Pierrehumbert and Beckman 1988). In (1b) the relation between the tone–bearing element μ and a H tone is a structural relation since the tone that the μ acquires is provided by a prosodic category AP and therefore is predicted from the hierarchical configuration in which μ occurs (*labelled metrical trees* in Liberman and Prince 1977, *prosodic categories* in Selkirk 1980, *grids* in Prince 1983, and *bracketed grids* in Hammond 1986, Halle and Vergnaud 1987, Hayes 1995, and Halle and Idsardi 1995).

Some linguists have tried to give a genesis of *accent* and *lexical stress* based in the interaction of these two types of relations. For the former, Clements and Goldsmith (1984) suggest that inherent tone sequences such as LH or HL have been reanalyzed in some Bantu languages as being binary domains where at most one tone is made structurally prominent (T*), creating a culminative domain: L* H, or H* L, or L H*, or H L*. The value of this T* tone links with the new inherently accented mora $\mu*$ (Goldsmith 1982a). In the so-called *pitch–accent languages*, like Swedish, there are two types of *dynamic stress* or *bitonal pitch–accents*: H*L and HL* (Pierrehumbert and Beckman 1988, §8.4). The genesis of word accent or *lexical stress* in the so-called *delimitative stress languages*, that is, languages which have main stress on the edges of a domain, is taken up by Hyman (1977) suggesting that a neutral declarative intonation structure may be reanalyzed as an accentual structure on the edge. Thus, the intonation pattern for medial phrase boundaries in French consists of a H boundary tone on the right edge accompanied by a final lengthening. A word in isolation in an utterance will then acquire the same tonal–durational structure.

In other words, the position of stress in a French word is explained by the existence in the same language of the same pitch contour at a higher organizational intonation level.

A challenge in current phonological theory is to find general principles which explain how these two types of prominence interact in languages.[1] Recent work by Pierrehumbert and Beckman (1988) has brought to the phonologist's attention striking tonal organizational similarities between languages considered to be pitch-accent languages, such as Japanese, or tonal languages like Hausa, and languages classified as stressed languages, such as English. Tonal phenomena involving inherent and structural relations seem, for these authors, to have a subset of identical properties. These findings reveal that previous language classifications in terms of the triad tonal/pitch-accent/stress are probably misleading since all of them have in more or less degree the two types of relations described in (1). It seems that both tonal relations given in (1) and their interaction play a pivotal role in the understanding of prosodic phenomena of natural languages.

Perhaps the most enlightening approach to the interaction of these two types of prominence is found in recent work on the organization of tone in tonal structures. Experimental work on intonation has isolated three basic alignment types of tones: a pitch accent tone, T*, a phrase accent tone, T–, and a boundary tone, T% (Beckman and Pierrehumbert 1986, Pierrehumbert 1980, Pierrehumbert and Beckman 1988). Each type of tone has a different relation to the text and a specific function. For instance, in (2) T* is a nuclear element and has a culminative function (Trubetzkoy 1969). T* aligns with a lexical accent in the text (Goldsmith 1981). The tones introduced by T– and T% do not need to be phonologically associated to segmental material but to intonational nodes; they have a delimitative function. The Intermediate Phrase in English contributes a postnuclear delimitative tone T–. The Intonation Phrase (Major Phrase) contributes a postnuclear Boundary tone T%. In (2) the tonal melody corresponds to a neutral declarative answer to a question such as 'What is this?':

(2)

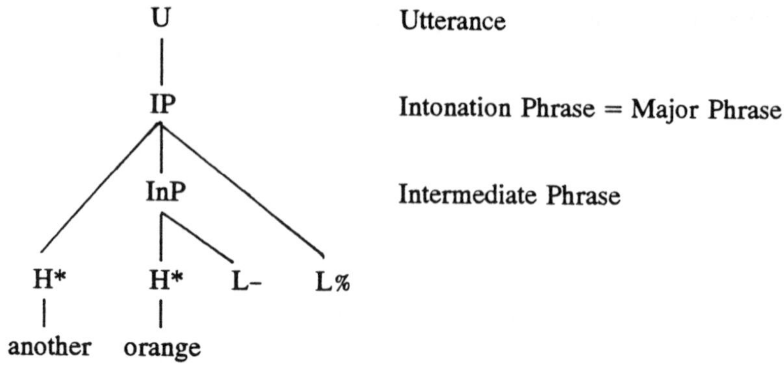

In Figure 1, the alignment of the melody with the text is shown using a fundamental frequency line (from Pierrehumbert 1980: 148).

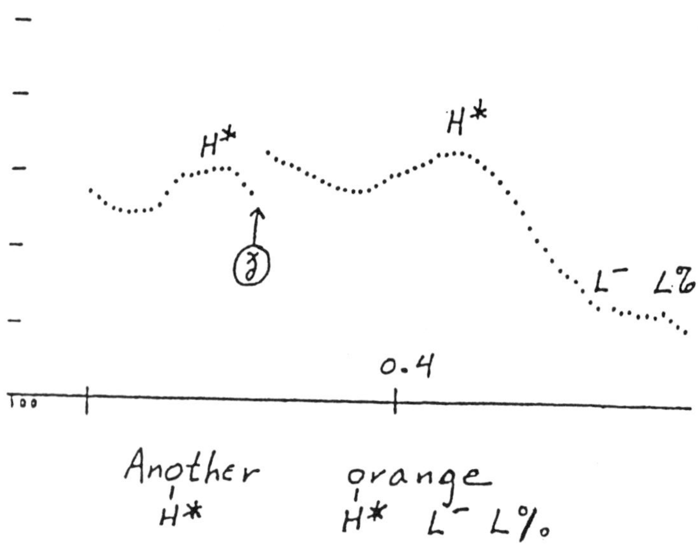

Fig. 1. The alignment of the melody with the text is shown using a fundamental frequency dotted line. H* is a tonal peak representing a pitch accent; L is a low value in the fundamental frequency line. L- represents a phrase accent tone, and L% a boundary tone. (From Pierrehumbert 1980: 148, 1.2.A)

Structures such as (2) are hierarchical U > IP > InP. However, there is no agreement on how many levels of prosodic constituency are allowed crosslinguistically (see Selkirk 1984, Selkirk 1995, Ladd 1986, Pierrehumbert 1980, Nespor and Vogel 1986).

1.1 The case of Spanish

1.1.1 Inherent accent and the morphological structure of the word

In Spanish, morphemes can contain inherently accented elements (μ*) or be inherently unaccented (for verb morphemes, see Roca 1992; for nominal morphemes, see García-Bellido 1994). The last μ* of the last accented morpheme is tonally prominent iff it occurs within the last three syllables of the word, as illustrated in ((3i)b), ((3ii)b), and ((3iii)b) below. I will first discuss which morphemes have an inherent prominence (*) in the Spanish word.

The morphological word is inflected. The morphological structure of the Inflected Word ($\{...\}_{IfW}$) includes an Inflectional Stem ($\{ | ... |_{IfS} \}_{IfW}$) followed on the right by inflectional morphemes ($\{ | ... |_{IfS} ... \}_{IfW}$). The inflectional stem contains derivational morphemes ($\{ | [...]_D |_{IfS} ... \}_{IfW}$).

Two accentual properties make verbal words (verbs) different from nominal words (nouns, adjectives, adverbs). Firstly, while nominal inflectional morphemes are unaccented: *$\{ | [\text{termin}]_D |_{IfS}$ ó* + $\text{s}\}_{IfW}$ 'end + Nominal Class + PL'; verbal inflectional morphemes can either be accented or unaccented: Verbal $\{ | [\text{termin}]_D |_{IfS}$ ó* $\}_{IfW}$ 'end + PRET IND 3SG', $\{ | [\text{termin}]_D |_{IfS}$ á*+r$\}_{IfW}$ 'end + Thematic Vowel + INF', $\{ | [\text{termin}]_D |_{IfS}$ á* + ba+ mos$\}_{IfW}$ 'end + Thematic Vowel + IMP IND + 1PL', Nominal: $\{ | [\text{términ}]_D |_{IfS}$ o + s$\}_{IfW}$ 'end + Nominal Class + PL'.[2]

Secondly, when the inflectional section of the word contains only unaccented inflectional morphemes, nominal and verbal words have different accentual properties. In the verbal word, prominence can be lexically predicted since it always falls on the last syllable of the inflectional stem but never before that syllable: {| [termí*n]$_D$ |$_{IfS}$ o}$_{IfW}$ 'end + PRES IND + 1SG', {| [termí*n]$_D$ |$_{IfS}$ e + mos}$_{IfW}$ 'end + PRES SUBJ + 1PL' (Andalusian dialects; see Mondéjar 1970). In the nominal word, inherent accent is not restricted to occurring only on the last syllable of the inflectional stem. Inherent accent in nominal words can occur on the penultimate syllable of the inflectional stem: {| [azú*car]$_D$ |$_{IfS}$ e s}$_{IfW}$ 'sugar + PL' or on the last syllable of the inflectional stem: {| [autocá*r]$_D$ |$_{IfS}$ e s}$_{IfW}$ 'coach + PL'. In the set of inherently accented nominal morphemes with accent on the last syllabic vowel of the inflectional stem, there is a subset which can be lexically predicted. When the IfS ends in a nonsyllabic palatal segment (quite generally, the glide [j] or the voiced obstruent [ǰ]), inherent accent is restricted to fall only on the last syllabic vowel of the inflectional stem: {| [carí*cj]$_D$ |$_{IfS}$ a + s}$_{IfW}$ 'caress + Nominal Class + PL', {| [[democrá*]$_D$ cj]$_D$ |$_{IfS}$ a + s}$_{IfW}$ 'democracy + Nominal Class + PL', {| [amarí*ǰ]$_D$ |$_{IfS}$ o + s}$_{IfW}$ 'yellow + Nominal Class: MASC+ PL'.

A complementary set of cases, for which no linguistic evidence of inherent accent is found when they occur in isolation in an utterance, are assumed here to receive no inherent accent, but only structural prominence provided by the intonational domain (3).

Each T of the AP is aligned with the last three moras (Tone-Bearing Units, henceforth *TBU*) which must be heads in their weight structure on the right edge of a IfW (McCarthy and Prince 1994). The tone value of T* links its structural value to the tone value of the rightmost accented mora in the alignment domain.[3] If there is no accented mora, the value of T* links to the tone value of the leftmost mora in the alignment domain (Pierrehumbert 1993). I follow Yip (1989) in representing the association of the TBU with its pitch feature via an intermediate node called the Tonal Root Node. Since in Spanish the tone value of the segment is either * or empty, the mora will always bear the tone value provided by the structural domain. A tonic word in isolation in a neutral declarative utterance will always show a peak on the fundamental frequency line. This can be represented by giving a structural H to the value of the T*, through a ternary Accentual Phrase (AP).

(3) *The Interface between inherent and structural prominence.*

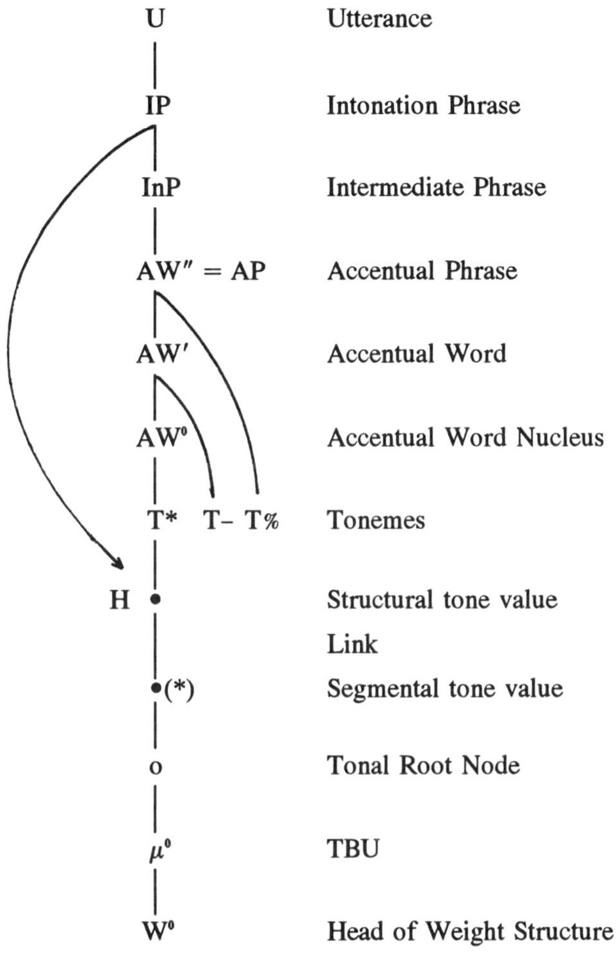

(i)	μ^0	a. $\{\acute{\mu}^0\}_{\text{IfW}}$	b. $\{\ldots\acute{\mu}^{0}*\}_{\text{IfW}}$
(ii)	μ^0	a. $\{\acute{\mu}^0\,\mu^0\}_{\text{IfW}}$	b. $\{\ldots\acute{\mu}^{0}*\,\mu^0\}_{\text{IfW}}$
(iii)	μ^0	a. $\{\ldots\acute{\mu}^0\,\mu^0\,\mu^0\}_{\text{IfW}}$	b. $\{\ldots\acute{\mu}^{0}*\,\mu^0\mu^0\}_{\text{IfW}}$
		Structural	Inherent + Structural

All monosyllabic and bisyllabic nominals are in principle unaccented unless there is linguistic evidence to the contrary. For instance, {útil} 'useful' and its plural {útiles}, may both be unaccented. Since the derived word {inútil} 'useless' does not have antepenultimate stress, then we conclude that {ú*til} is accented on the *u* just as its plural counterpart. Polysyllabic nominal words such as {régimen} 'regime', {regímenes} 'regime+PL,' {déficit}'deficit', {metrópoli} 'metropoli', {democrático} 'democratic', {demócrata} 'democrat' are structurally prominent. Under our analysis, if the inflected word {democrá*tico} were inherently accented, then we would expect the word {democra*ta} to bear structural prominence on the accented mora: {democrá*ta}. Since {demócrata} has prominence only in the antepenultimate, we must conclude that none of these words is inherently accented. If the IfS of both |[[demo]crat]| and |[[demo]crat]ic]| are unaccented, then we predict that they will have only structural prominence and therefore will have tonal prominence on the antepenultimate in a neutral declarative utterance.

Structural prominence is accommodating English borrowings: {guásinton} 'Washington', {mánchester} 'Manchester', {jáguar} 'Jaguar', and even preferring antepenultimate prominence to penultimate {macnámara} 'MacNamara'. All cases in (3a) are cases of structural prominence. All cases in (3b) are of structural and inherent prominence. Here the AP aligns with an inherently accented word.

I will show in this paper that in Spanish at least three different types of relations between T* and the text can be found at the intonational level (4a, b, c). A first type of relation (4a) aligns the tone values of an Accentual Phrase AP with the tone values of the last three tone bearing-units of an Inflected Word in the utterance. T* is linked to the rightmost inherently accented mora of the Inflected Word as in (4a). (4a) represents a linking relationship between the value of an inherent accented mora μ* and the tone value received from the toneme T* in the intonational structure. The phonetic tone value assigned to the T* in the utterance, here represented as a node •, will contain the tone value that the mora will receive.

(4) a.

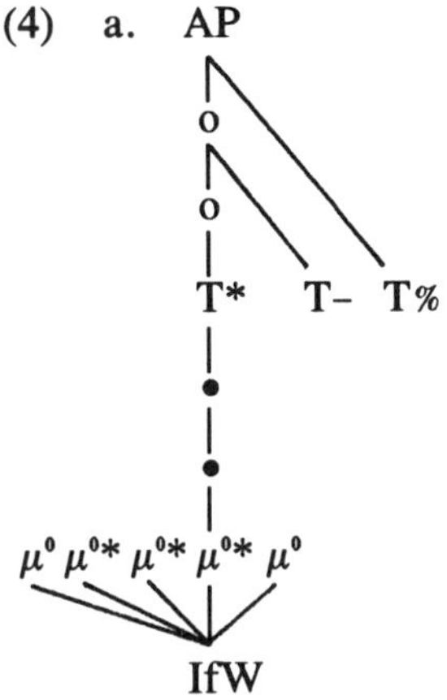

co lo ca ré mos
(we) place-FUT-1PL
'we will place'

b.

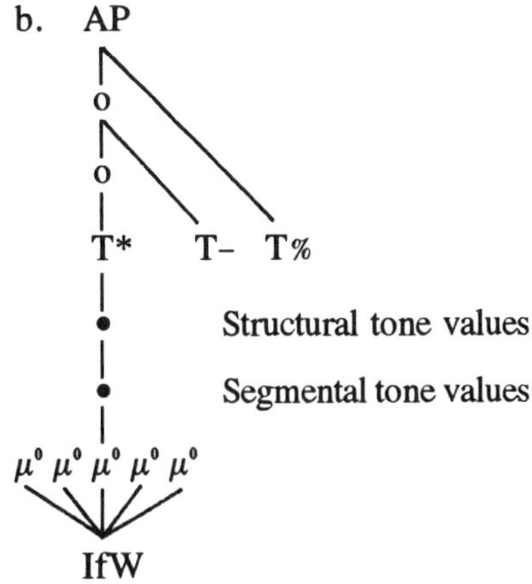

te le fó ni co
'telephonic'

c.

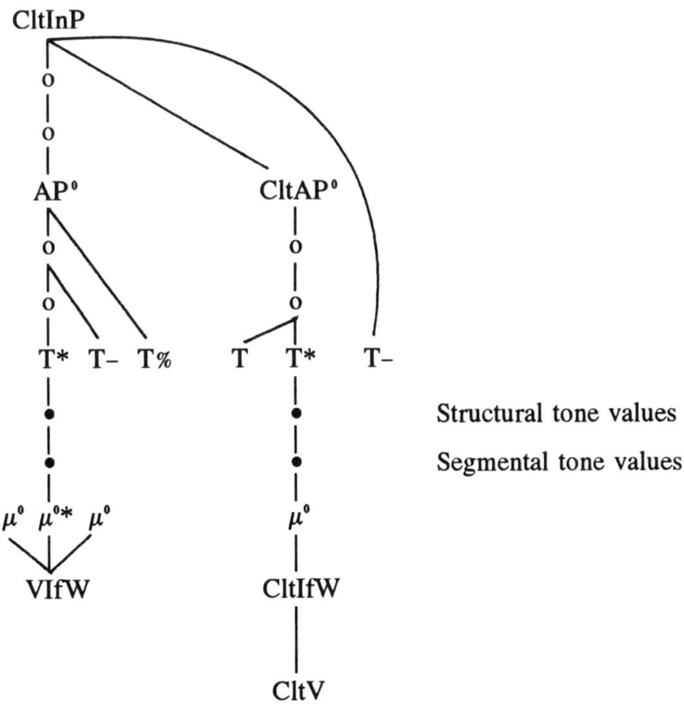

co ló que lò...
'(you formal) place it...!

The second type of relation (4b) aligns an AP with the last three moras of the Inflected Word and links T* to the letmost unaccented mora in the ternary domain. Finally, the third type, (4c), links an unaccented word, such as a clitic, to an edge pitch accent T* provided by the Clitic Intermediate Phrase (CltInP). The bitonal edge CltAP^{o} (T T*) aligns its T's with the last two moras of the Clitic Verb Phrase which contains clitic material in enclitic position. This alignment cannot be successful if any one of its moras is already linked. The right edge T* of the CltInp links with the edge mora of the Clitic Verb (CltV). Cases (4b) and (4c) show that prominence in Spanish may only be structural. When structural prominence can link to an inherent prominence, it produces a prominence match as in (4a) (Goldsmith 1982a). If the structural prominence T T* cannot find two non-linked moras to align with, by default T* will not link to any mora and the tonal structure will be cancelled. In this respect, the edge AP introduced at the end of an enclitic operation in the syntax functions as a delimitative AP, marking the end of a syntactic constituent. In Spanish, proclitic syntactic adjunction does not have an intonational delimitative effect.

The last two cases are particularly relevant to a hierarchical intonational theory, since they show that at an intonational level the location of prominence can only be structural, given the fact that it cannot be predicted from the presence of an inherent accent. In (4c), clitics which do not have inherent accent become prominent by virtue of being adjoined to the right edge of an AP associated to a VIfW in the syntax. Similar edge effects have been found in English. Selkirk (1995) analyzes the prominence on *bàm*, which is on the first syllable of the second constituent in ((*grêen*) (*bàmboo tábles*)), to a Phrase Edge Prominence. Crucially if *bamboo* is not on the left edge of a constituent, as in ((*grêen bambòo*) (*tábles*)), then Edge Prominence cannot apply, even though there is rhythmic clash. In the same way, in Spanish a clitic which does not have inherent prominence will be assigned structural prominence if it lands on the right edge of the verb, but not if it occurs on the left edge of the verb: ¡*que lo colóque*! 'have him place it!' (cf. *¡*que ló colóque*!).

Following the lexicalization theory of Hyman (1977), it is assumed here that a ternary intonational structure, such as the AP in (3), is the hierarchical lexicalization of a structure such as (2). In (2), there is a delimitative tone, such as a phrase accent tone T−, provided at the InP level, and a boundary tone T%, added at the Intonational Phrase level. The delimitative Ts provided by the IP and the InP are not represented in (3).

The remainder of the paper is divided into three sections. In section 2, I will sketch the basic structure of the utterance in Castilian Spanish following recent work on the hierarchical intonational framework outlined above. The phrase accent tone T- and the boundary tone T% will be discussed in that context. The crucial role of the culminative function of the Spanish AP will be argued to be responsible for the single prominence in (4a) and other compound phenomena. In section 3, the evidence for a clitic edge prominence and its effects will be discussed. In section 4, I will argue against any configurational properties for inherent prominence, and propose instead edge-oriented accent generalizations (the descriptions D1 and D2 in section 4 below) which are controlled by either particular morphemes or by morphological categories in a specific morphological domain (cf. (25c) below). Here, inherent prominence is morphological, and inherited historically, while structural prominence is intonational. Therefore, in this analysis prominence is not assumed to result from a 'stress' algorithm (see Harris 1995 for a different view). It will be concluded that whether a morpheme is accented or not and where it(s) accent(s) is/are placed is a historical legacy which has to be memorized. The location of structural prominence in the inflected word is totally predictable when it occurs in isolation in an utterance and therefore does not need to be memorized.

It will be briefly discussed that the simplicity displayed by a direct linking between inherent and intonational prominence should be preferred, on language-particular and on theoretical grounds, to two other approaches where the T* of an InP links to the head of a right-headed conflated metrical structure where several rules have been applied in succession.

2 The structure of the Spanish utterance

Traditional phonetic accounts of the Castilian Spanish utterance point out that an Utterance (U) can contain many Intonation Phrases (*grupos fónicos*; Navarro Tomás 1968, Quilis 1975, Martínez Celdrán 1984).[4] The minimal utterance U must contain one nuclear Intonation Phrase IP*. The IP* in a neutral declarative utterance starts with a rising pitch (L% H*) which culminates on the first pitch accent. In a neutral declarative utterance, there is a falling pitch (H*L- L%) from the last accented syllable, up to the end of the utterance.[5]

(5)

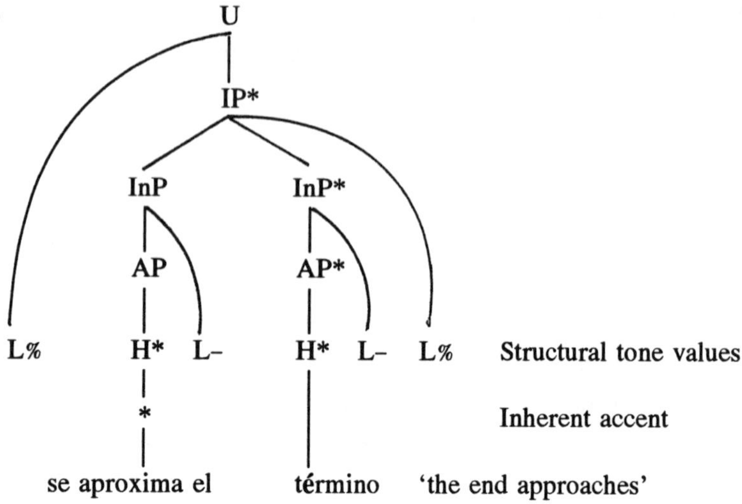

Navarro Tomás (1968) observes that there may be a fall of pitch between accented syllables. This effect is captured in this framework by the presence of the phrase accent T–, introduced by the InP. The pitch of the T* in a structure like (5) varies in some predictable way in a neutral declarative utterance: the second H* subordinates. This type of subordination has been found in Japanese, Hausa, and English (Beckman and Pierrehumbert 1986 and Pierrehumbert and Beckman 1988), and also in Basque (Elordieta, this volume). According to these authors a sequence HLH can trigger phonetic subordination or *catathesis*. Each language parametrizes at the point in time in which catathesis starts in the sequence. I will assume here, until more research is done on this topic, that the subordination phenomena found in Spanish in contexts like (5) are triggered by catathesis applying at the IP level.

All Spanish phoneticians agree that an IP* can have different melodies expressing different meanings (Navarro Tomás 1968, Quilis 1975, Martínez Celdrán 1983). The most classical example is yes/no questions. It is reported that when an IP is made into a question, it is clearly different from a neutral declarative IP, since it has a falling pitch followed by a rising pitch at the end. A typical melody in a yes/no question contains an initial rise until reaching the first pitch accent, followed by a falling tone from the initial pitch accent up to the last pitch accent, where it rises. A hierarchical representation is given in (6).

(6)

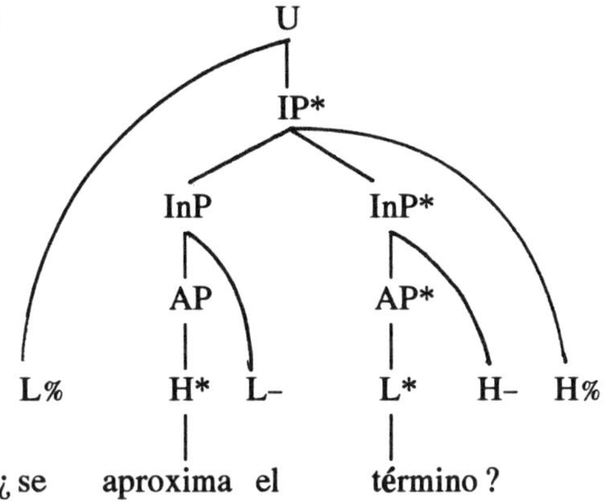

The last pitch accent is the locus where the L* links. When two IPs are gathered in an utterance, the prefinal IP usually displays a High boundary tone H%, which marks the utterance as incomplete.

(7) (T% (T* T- T* T- H%)$_{IP}$ (T* T- T* T- L%)$_{IP*}$)

((si se aproxima el tren)$_{IP}$ (yo me escondo)$_{IP*}$)$_{U}$

((yo me escondo)$_{IP}$ (si se aproxima el tren)$_{IP*}$)$_{U}$

'if the train approaches, I hide'

'I hide, if the train approaches'

I will show now that several constraints (semantic-syntactic, morphological, prosodic-phonetic) restrict the class of words that can land in an AP* domain.

The following data shows that a semantic-syntactic constraint selects which words can occur in AP*.

(8) a. – ¿Quién ha chillado? 'Who has screamed?'
– él 'He'

b. – ¿A quién le has chillado? 'To whom have (you) screamed?'
– *le 'Him'

In (8) both answers have a monosyllabic utterance; yet only the pronoun *él*, but not a clitic, is licensed in the AP*. In general an utterance must have as a member of its AP* a subset of all possible words (Navarro Tomás 1968,

§167–171, Quilis 1981). This subset comprises only the class of lexical projections with a descriptive content. Functional projections such as clitics, determiners, conjunctions, and some prepositions, function prosodically at the intonational level as do suffixes in the morphology. They need the presence of a lexical projection with descriptive content.

Observe now the following dialogue where the same semantic–syntactic constraint applies.

(9) a. – Juan había ido a casa. 'Juan had gone home'.

b. – *Sí, había / Sí, lo hizo. 'Yes, (he) had / Yes, (he) did it'

In (9b) the auxiliary verb is accented inherently; yet it cannot be licensed in the AP*, since it is a functional projection which does not have a descriptive meaning. Therefore, the property of being inherently accented is not sufficient to be licensed in an AP*.

A morphological constraint restricts the class of possible expressions which can be licensed in an AP*. An AP* has to include both the inflectional stem (IfS) (represented below with |...|) and its inflectional material, constituting then a well-formed Inflected Word (IfW) (represented below with {...}). This morphological constraint on the set of words licensed in AP* accounts for the ungrammaticality of (10b).

(10) a. – ¿Cómo está la pizza? 'How is the pizza?'
– { | Buen | $_{\text{IfSt}}$ a}$_{\text{IfW}}$ 'Good + Nominal Class: FEM'

b. –* | Buen | $_{\text{IfS}}$ 'Good'

In (10b) the answer contains a lexical projection with an intensional meaning (Chierchia and McConnell 1990), an adjective without its Nominal Class; hence its failure to appear in an AP*.

From the data analyzed in the above examples, one may conclude that if a word can be licensed in an AP*, then it must be the case that it can be licensed in any AP. On the other hand, the auxiliary, which is not licensed in a nuclear AP* position such as in (9b), may occur in any nonnuclear AP position by virtue of being accented inherently. In consequence, the auxiliary is licensed in a nonnuclear position such as in (9a).

A prosodic–phonetic constraint is responsible for the grammaticality of {él} in (8a). In order for an utterance to be able to be expressed phonetically in an utterance there must be in Spanish at least one tone-bearing unit linked to its AP*, namely, the head of a weight structure. This is a necessary and sufficient condition at the prosodic–phonetic level, as (8a) shows. This prosodic–phonetic constraint follows from the seemingly universal fact that in order for an utterance to be audible, some tone-bearing unit needs to be present so that the phonetic tone value of T* can be expressed. Other languages such as Arabic set the minimum to two heads (Hayes 1995). The T* of the AP* aligns with the only available tone-bearing unit, and links to it to produce a monosyllabic well-formed utterance, as in (11) below.

If the interpretation of intonational prominence in Spanish is obtained by virtue of linking the value of T* in an AP* < InP* <IP* < U with at least one nuclear mora of an inflected content word, then the prominence of such inflected monosyllabic words is predictable by a universal phonetic principle. In other words, the prominence of a monosyllabic word in an intonational construction does not need to be inherent in the inflected word, since it can be structurally given by the intonational phonetic structure.

This explains why in an utterance in Spanish, a word in isolation always has at least one prominent syllable. The specific tone that the syllable bears depends on the assignments given at higher levels. As a consequence, in a yes/no question the prominent mora linked to the nucleus of the AP* will be L*, but in a neutral declarative utterance it will be H*.

(11)

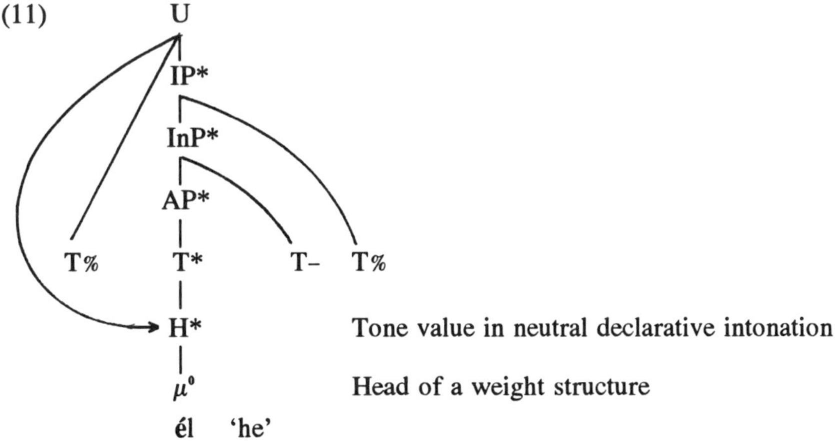

Structural prominence assignment is found in languages like Japanese, where accentual phrases may contain no accented words (Pierrehumbert and Beckman 1988). The Accentual Phrase in that language assigns a fixed H tone to the leftmost unaccented word in the AP, and this tone links to the second mora (1b). In Spanish the U assigns a H tone to an unaccented content word in a neutral declarative utterance by virtue of having a Nuclear T* linked to a mora. How this assignment is obtained in polysyllabic unaccented words is a matter that will be discussed in section 4.

I will now suggest that the fact that not all inherent prominences surface at the intonational level follows from the assumption that the AP in Spanish has a culminative property: at most one tone value in at most one pitch accent T* can occur in any given AP^0 < AP′ < AP″, and the linking of its T* value can only occur with at most one mora, as illustrated in (12a-b). Since the alignment and linking of an AP^0 described above for (3) operates with respect to the right edge of an IfW, nothing except culminativity prevents the value of the T* from spreading leftward to each accented mora in the AP″ domain. Languages that lack a culminativity constraint in a given prosodic intonational domain can in principle have the value of the structural H in T* spread to all inherently accented moras in the domain. In Nguni languages there is no culminativity in the AP″, and therefore the H of its T* must also link to the inherent tone at the begining of the AP″. In this language, spreading of the structural H value affects the intervening moras up to the inherent one: /úku-namathelisa/ → ${}_{AP''}$(úkúnámá(thélisa)$_{AP^0}$). In Zulu, whose AP″ is constrained by culminativity, only the structural H is phonetically present: /úku-namathelisa/ → ${}_{AP''}$(ú-ku-nama(thélisa)$_{AP^0}$) (see Odden 1995: 471). This explains why in Spanish T* links only to one mora in an AP″.

(12)	a.	* * * {|[coloc]|a+rí a+mos} 'place+ThV+COND+1PL' ('we would place')	* * {|[[algodon] cít]|o} 'cotton+DIM+Nominal class'
	b.	* * {|[coloc]|á+r} 'place+ThV+INF' ('to place')	* {|[algodón]|} 'cotton'

The culminative property of the AP″ explains the following data taken from Navarro Tomás (1968, §167) where the first word does not have a tonal prominence. The boundary tones of the AP⁰ are not represented in (13)

(13) a. i. Señor Martínez (* on Señor, * on Martínez) 'Mr Martínez'

ii. Maria José (* on Maria, * on José) 'María José'

iii. patas arríba (* on arríba) 'legs up'

iv. casa de mi pádre 'my father's house'

b. i. buen hómbre 'good man'

ii. gran pícaro 'big rascal'

c.

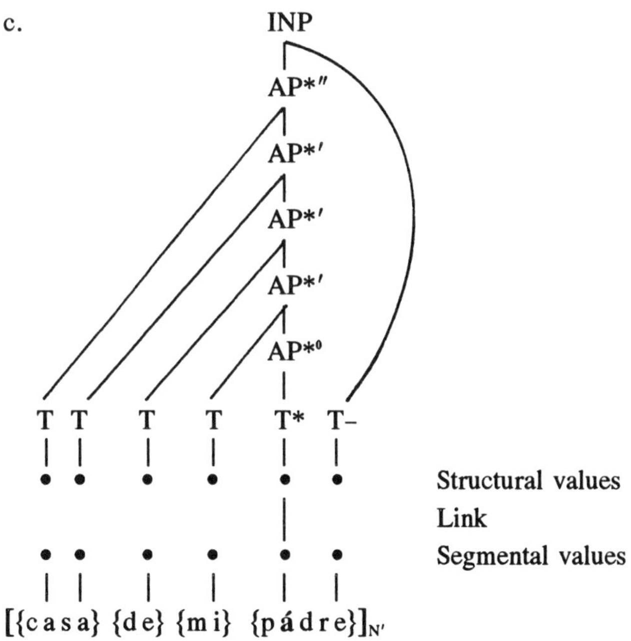

The first words in (13a) (*Señór*, *María*, *pátas*, *cása*) can all be licensed in AP* positions, while the first words in (13b) (*gran*, *buen*) cannot. Culminativity only guarantees that as a result of the alignment of the AP″ with the right edge of the rightmost IfW, as described for (3) above, only one mora will carry the value of the T*. According to this alignment, *casa de mi padre*$\}_{IfW}$ could have structural prominence on the antepenultimate: *casademípadre*}. Since this is not the case, in order to explain examples like (13aiv, 13bi), the linking of the T* in the AP″ needs to be constrained so that it is circumscribed to link inside the rightmost IfW. It follows, then, that all monosyllabic, disyllabic, and trisyllabic words are not accented unless there is evidence to the contrary. Any material proclitic to T* in the AP⁰ in (13) is recursively adjoined to the left of the AP⁰, as illustrated in (13c). None of the accents in (13ai-ii), which will be adjoined in the AP″ intonational domain, except the last one, will reflect any tonal peaks, regardless of their inherent prominence, behaving therefore in the same way as the inherently accented morphemes in (12).

I have argued that the set of possible phonetic expressions licensed in an AP″ in Spanish is restricted by several constraints. Each constraint (syntactic-semantic, morphological, prosodic and phonetic) contributes to the licensing of linguistic expressions in an AP* < InP* < IP* < U. The nonaudible property of inherent accent is explained by a culminativity property that AP″ has in Spanish.

3 Clitic prominence

It has been observed that when clitics are suffixed to the verb the rightmost clitic of the clitic sequence may acquire secondary prominence (Navarro Tomás 1917: 381-382, 385).[6]

(14)	búscalò	'look for it!'
	búscamelò	'look for it on my behalf!'
	búscasemelò	'look for it for him on my behalf!'

More precisely, Navarro Tomás (1917, 1968) points out that if there is a nuclear antepenultimate prominence in isolation in the utterance, then the last syllable is always longer than the nuclear one. This observation for Spanish data supports similar observed facts in other languages where the boundary tone T% lengthens the last syllable (Beckman and Pierrehumbert, 1986). In (15), two similar words are given.

(15) a. búscalò 'look for it!'

b. níscalo 'type of edible mushroom'

The *o* in (15a) and the *o* (15b) are longer than the most prominent vowel in the word (Navarro Tomás 1916, 1917, 1968 §178). However, in the *o* of (15b) there is no perceived prominence. This shows that duration cannot be the sole parameter for the recognition of prominence in Spanish. If it were, we would expect the last syllable in (15b) to have nuclear prominence. Further evidence that there is prominence only on the antepenultimate syllable in (15b), and that there is prominence on the last syllable of (15a), is provided by questions. When these two words are questioned, the L* links with the *o* in (15a) and the *i* in (15b), but not with the final syllable in (15b). This can be explained if L* links with the last perceived pitch accent of the IP.

It has also been observed that the clitic does not receive prominence if it lands next to a nuclear prominence (Roca 1986).

(16) a. buscádlo 'look for it (you-PL informal)'

b. *buscádlò

For this author, secondary stress applies from right to left constructing right-headed feet. Exhaustiveness requires a degenerate right-headed foot to be created on the clitic in (16b). By assuming that a Clash Deletion Rule deletes a secondary stress after the primary stress, the secondary stress on the last syllable in (16b) is deleted yielding (16a).

In the present framework, since a clitic is not licensed in isolation in an utterance, it is not licensed either in the nuclear position of the AP″ (17b). The structure in (17a) is impossible since the AP⁰ must contain only one T* which aligns with the rightmost word, and links inside it. (17a) is illformed since it contains two T*.

(17)

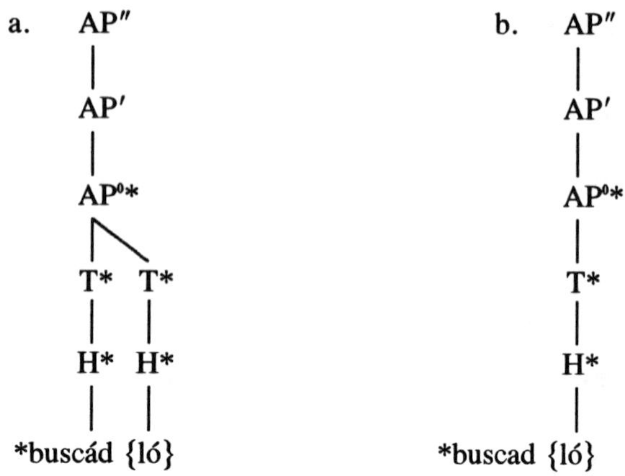

Since clitics have a perceived pitch accent when enclitic in the same VP, I will assume that the most likely representation can be the one given in (18), where the CltInp is not subject to culminativity but each of its AP″ members is.

(18)

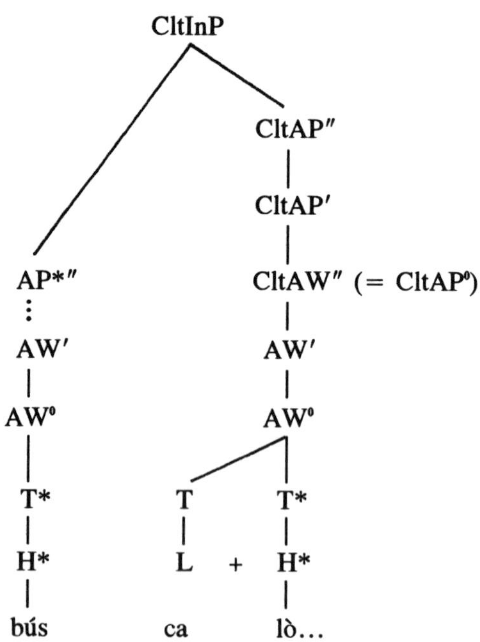

The configuration of the CltAP⁰ in (18) exhibits a binary alignment with the last two moras. Note that although *-ca* has been aligned with the T% of AP⁰*, it is realigned with the T of CltAP⁰. In this respect, this framework allows for a syllabic mora to be realigned. In other words structural overlapping is possible. The general principles of alignment only ban crossing alignments and prohibit the alignment with a linked syllabic mora. For evidence in other languages, see Garcia-Bellido (1994). The proper alignment explains that when a clitic is adjoined to a verb with penultimate prominence, as in (15a), a pitch T* can be linked. Notice that in this configuration an unstressed syllable is flanked by two prominences: HLH. The pitch contour then can be interpreted as containing a nuclear pitch H* followed by a bitonal pitch-accent L+H* (Beckman and Pierrehumbert 1986). The insertion of the bitonal pitch accent triggers catathesis, subordinating the pitch of the clitic. It is then the presence of an alignment site for the T of the bitonal pitch accent which licenses the insertion of the Right Edge Prominence Pitch. The pitch accent has, then, a delimitative function, rather than a culminative function like in (16a). From the stipulation in (13c), it follows that any sequence of clitics before the last clitic will be recursively adjoined to CltAP′, and thus will not receive any pitch accent.

Evidence for the presence of the structural prominence of the clitic in (18) is provided by comparing two minimal pairs. In (19) there are three prominences. Primary tonal prominence is indicated as (´), and a secondary as (`) in these examples.

(19) a. $((\text{Sí})_{AP})_{InP}\ ((\text{salè})_{AP}\ (\text{a Ìdo})_{AP})_{InP}$
'yes, (I) put salt over Ido'

b. $((\text{Sísa}\ )_{AP}(\text{lè})_{AP})_{InP}\ ((\text{a Ìdo})_{AP}\ )_{InP})$
'you (informal) steal something from Ido!'

In Figures 2a and 2b there are three peaks aligned, respectively, with the *i* of *si*, the *e* of *sale*, and the *i* of *Ido*. The last two peaks show a falling prominence triggered by the presence of a LH* after the first H*. In Figure 2b the valley between the clitic and the *i* of *Ido* corresponds to the Phrase accent L- of the first InP which spreads over the preposition. In Figure 2a the prominence of the verb in the past is maintained on to the preposition. There is a L- tone after the peak of the -éá which can be interpreted as a Phrase accent L- marking the limit between the CltInP *salè* 'put+PAST (salt)' and the verb complement InP *a Ìdo* 'over Ido'. The falling tone on the last syllable corresponds to the phrase accent of the last InP* and the Boundary tone of the IP*.

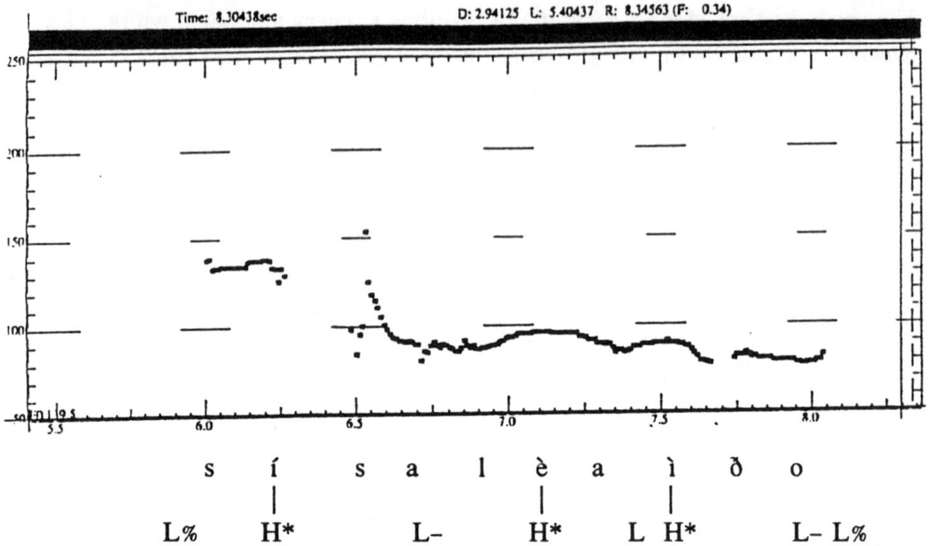

Fig. 2a. Fundamental frequency line aligned with the Spanish sentence in (19a) *Sí, salè a Ìdo* 'yes, (I) put salt over Ido'.

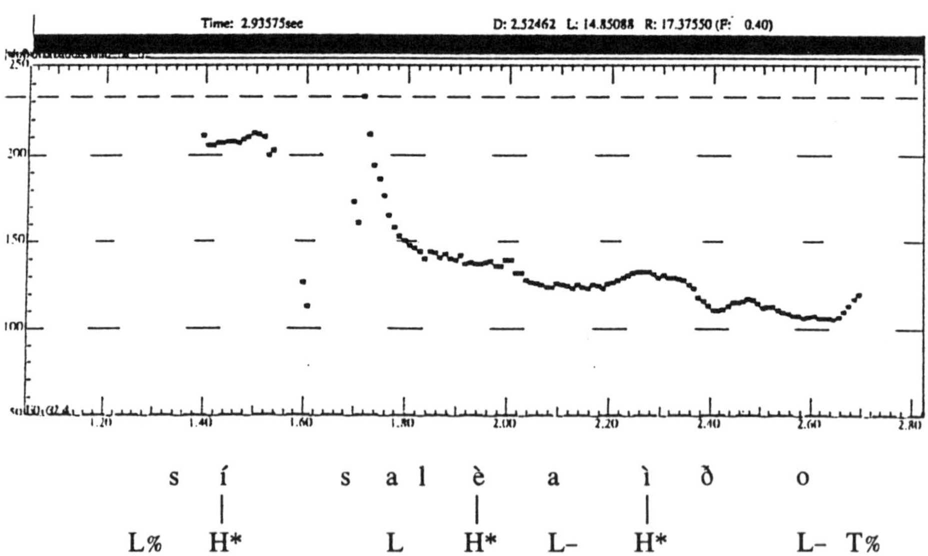

Fig. 2b. Fundamental frequency line aligned with the Spanish sentence in (19b) *Sísalè a Ìdo* 'you (informal) steal something from Ido!'

A hierarchical structure for Figure 2a is given in (20a), and one of Fig. 2b is represented in (20b):

(20) a. b.

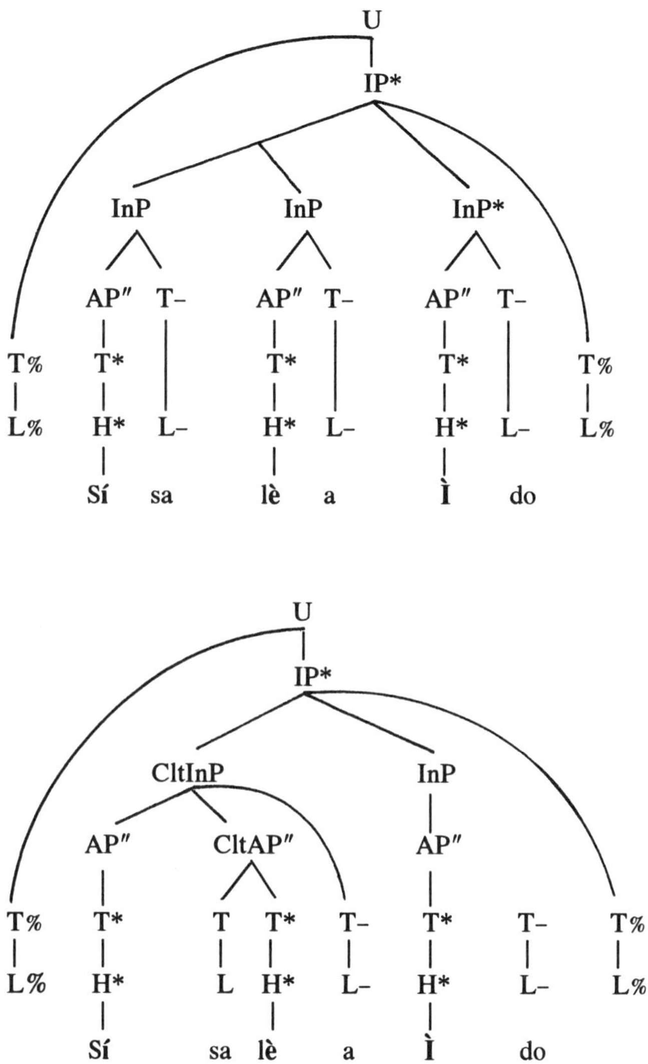

If the clitic had not been accented in (20b), then we would have had an F_0 drop over *le*, just as that shown over *se* in Figure 3. This utterance: '*Sisa se ha ido*' 'Sisa herself has gone' has a clitic *se* in proclitic position adjoined to a verb.

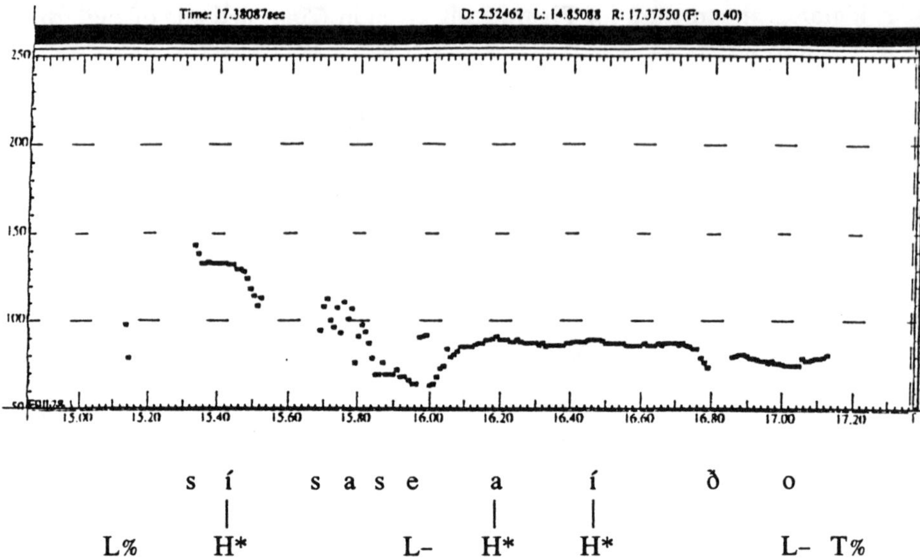

Fig. 3. F_0 line aligned with the Spanish sentence *Sísa se ha ído*.

In Figure 3 there are only two peaks. The first peak H* aligns with *Si* of *Sisa*, and the second peak H* aligns with the fused accents of the two verbs. The phrase accent T- of the first InP has a L- tone which aligns with the clitic. The second peak after the clitic creates the catathesis configuration H* L-H*. In (21) there is a hierarchical representation of Figure 3.

(21)

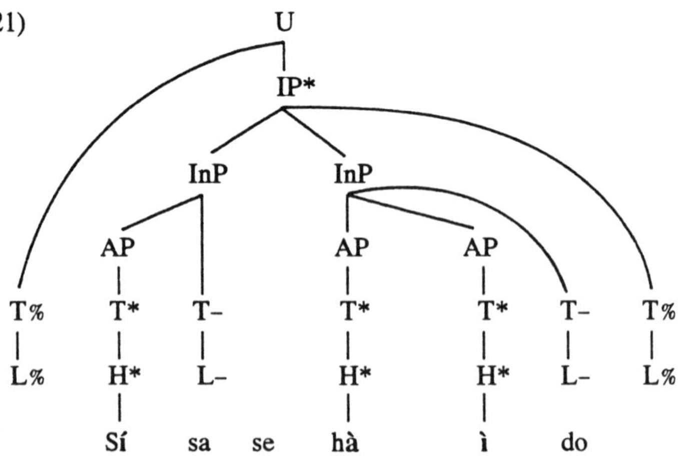

Further evidence for the presence of the pitch accent in the clitic comes from the blocking of Glide Formation in the examples of (20). In (21) the quality of the vowel of the clitic *se* is clearly a glide [j]. No similar interpretation can be given to the accented clitic *le* or the accented past morpheme *-e-* in (20).

The crucial fact is that if a clitic is preposed to its verb it remains unaccented and like any unaccented element it can acquire the phrase accent of the previous InP. In this case no peak should be expected. When the clitic is postponed, a bitonal delimitative pitch accent is structurally given to mark the end of a V domain with encliticized clitics. This structural bitonal pitch accent aligns with the rightmost clitic word in the InP iff some unaccented mora can align between both accents in the CltInP domain.

These findings support recent studies on the perception of Spanish word stress (Solé Sabater 1984). This author shows that pitch, duration and loudness may all contribute to the perception of word stress. However, pitch is the most important in isolation and in combination with the others. This result agrees with earlier studies on the nature of Spanish stress (Quilis 1981, §12.11). The *Gramática de la Real Academia Española* (1973: 64, fn. 1) attributes to tone the major function in stress recognition. Navarro Tomás (1968, §183) points out that tone and amplitude generally coincide but the main tone of the word is higher than the tone of the rest of the syllables in the word.[7] Bolinger and Hodapp (1961: 47) state that tone is the most important element while duration and loudness are secondary factors. They suggest that stress is perceived as falling or rising pitch contours in the intonation phrase. In the opinion of Spanish phoneticians such as Quilis (1981: 328) in the question *¿ya ha venido*? 'has (he) arrived yet?', stress is perceived in the syllable *ni* because it has a falling pitch followed by the rising pitch of the unstressed *do*. Contreras (1963) and Quilis (1971) further support the tonal nature of stress in Spanish.

4 Segmental prominence assignment

In the preceding section, I have shown that InP contributes a T- and IP a T%. This T% lengthens the final vowel. In this section I assume, given the evidence of both T- and T% in the IP of the intonational structure in Spanish, that the structure of the AP⁰ is the intonational lexicalized version of the structure of culminative and delimitative tones in the Spanish IP. I will argue here that the structural prominence assigned by this structure must be distinguished from the segmental prominence assigned at the morphological level. I will contend that there is only one type of nondelimitative intonational AP⁰, which I will call the *Intonational Foot* (22b). I will show that if segmental prominence (μ*) is obtained via an alignment between a prosodic Foot (F) and a Weight Foot (WF), then Spanish needs seven different dubious types of prosodic feet and five equally dubious types of WF (see (23b) below). One of these feet F is theoretically unconstrained, since it must be formed by using improperly syllabified prosodic material (F5). Adscribing to the simplicity criterium, I will conclude that segmental prominence in Spanish is not theoretically predictable using a set of well-defined universal Foot structures, and therefore is probably memorized for each morpheme. Within the set of morphemes which have segmental prominence, there are only two possible locations for an accent (*): either the rightmost or the penultimate syllabic mora. This is probably the historical result of maintaining the location of the Latin prominence using instead a morphological accentual system. However, at the Inflectional Stem level, two generalizations can be found in the lexicon. First, if the Inflectional Stem is verbal, then the rightmost syllabic mora must be segmentally prominent. Secondly, if the Inflectional Stem is nominal, and ends in a nonsyllabic palatal segment, then the rightmost syllabic mora is segmentally prominent. These two generalizations do not follow from any synchronic linguistic principle that I am aware of, and therefore they could be simply the result of historical generalizations whose precise formulation I leave open for future discussion (cf. García-Bellido 1994). The interface between intonational and lexical prominence can be summarized as in (22) for a nondelimitative AP⁰, i.e. one which is not CltAP⁰ (see (18) above):

(22) a. Align an AP^0 with the right edge of the IfW domain (}). From right to left, align the value of each T with the value of each μ. The value of T* links with at most one value of at most one μ^0 (Culminativity) in the IfW domain ({}): either the rightmost aligned $\mu^{0}*$, or else the leftmost aligned μ^0.

b. Example:

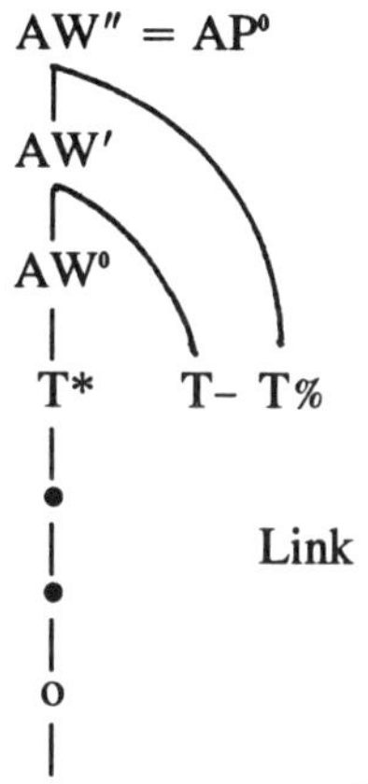

	Link	Structural	Inherent + Structural
(i)	$\mu^0(*)$ }	$\{\acute{\mu}^0\}$	$\{\ldots\acute{\mu}^{0}*\}$
(ii)	$\mu^0(*)$ μ^0 }	$\{\acute{\mu}^0\ \mu^0\}$	$\{\ldots\acute{\mu}^{0}*\ \mu^0\}$
(iii)	$\mu^0(*)$ μ^0 μ^0 }	$\{\ldots\acute{\mu}^0\ \mu^0\ \mu^0\}$	$\{\ldots\acute{\mu}^{0}*\ \mu^0\ \mu^0\}$

In (22b) W″ does not project moras from the Onset, but it does in Pirahã (Everett 1988). I will use curly brackets {...} for the inflected word domain, while square brackets [...] will be used to indicate any other morphological domain. The alignment of the AP^0 with an unaccented word is given in (23a). Represented in (23b) are seven different types of alignments of a Prosodic Foot (F), broken into syllables (Hualde 1991), with Weight Feet broken into moras. In (23c), two lexical generalizations are given for Spanish: (i) only some members of any given morphological class in the lexicon are subject to F//WF alignment; (ii) the segmental assignment of prominence (*) to a mora picks the leftmost μ^0 in the alignment. If Weight Feet are understood to be Metrical Feet (MF) once one mora is designated to be the prominent one in the structure, then every WF becomes a MF. Metrical feet have been categorized into types: moraic trochee (MF1, 2, 4), moraic iamb (MF3), syllabic trochee (MF6), and orphan moraic/syllabic iamb/trochee (MF7) (Hayes 1995). It becomes apparent that the alignment of canonical WF with prosodic material of F is not easy to define for Spanish due to two theoretical problems.

The first problem is the alignment of WF5. The alignment of a nonsyllabic mora in WF4 or WF1 follows from universally accepted principles of mora projection (Hayes 1995). This alignment is theoretically compatible with the presence of a C associated to a Rhyme (N′) in F4 and F1 (García Bellido 1989). However, the projection of a mora for a nonsyllabic palatal glide in WF5 is clearly problematic for the understanding of well-formed metrical feet. If a palatal glide projects a mora, even though there is no head of the structure, its syllabic trochaic foot is not a well-formed structure, since the W^0 of its right branch does not have a nuclear root to associate with. In other words, since glides are not licensed as heads of prosodic or metrical structures, F5 and WF5 are formed on ill-formed structures. Secondly, it also becomes apparent that the postulation of feet like WF7 to predict segmental prominence in Spanish is not without problems. If the concept of heaviness is responsible in the literature for the moraic segmental assignments of morphemes associated to WF1, WF2, WF3, WF4, and the notion of binary foot is the basis for the syllabic trochee associated to WF6, then it becomes theoretically problematic to allow for WF7. Degenerate feet on a right edge are always found as a result of a leftover in a rightward scanning (Hayes 1995). It is clear that this is not the case in Spanish. A newly created morpheme with a sequence like VCVCV] entering the lexicon has probably the same chances in Spanish of being accented in the penultimate, the final syllabic vowel, or remaining unaccented in the morphological domain. If this is proven to be correct, then the problematic alignment of F7//WF7 is equivalent theoretically to the memorization of the position of the $\mu^{0}*$ with respect to the right morphological edge. This can be done with a description D1 where] represents any non IfW domain:

> D1: The rightmost μ^0 in a morphological domain [...] is prominent for some morphemes.

Since the description D1 does the same job as WF1, WF2, WF3, WF4, and WF5, then only WF6 is a possible legitimate metrical candidate for metrical foot alignment. However, there is evidence in Spanish that even the postulation of

WF6 for metrical alignment is empirically problematic. The word [cara*cte*r] 'character' has two accents. If the segmental prominence were achieved through foot alignment, then either WF7 or WF6 would align, but not both. Therefore foot alignment cannot predict the Spanish empirical facts. A description such as D2, where] represents any non IfW domain:

> D2: The second rightmost μ^0 in a morphological constituent [...] is prominent for some morphemes

can account for F6 cases and the doubly accented ones. D1 and D2 should be preferred since they predict data that alignment cannot.

The theoretical problems raised by the alignment of prosodic configurations in the Spanish lexicon leads us to conclude that segmental prominence is memorized via location descriptions such as D1: μ^0*] for some morphemes and D2: μ^0*μ^0(*)] for other morphemes. The conjunction of D1 and D2 correctly predicts that both descriptions can be true for a given morpheme. This result is in line with research done in Pierrehumbert (1993), who shows that heads may function as locations, not as prosodic categories.

(23) a. *Alignment and link of an intonational structure with an unaccented IfW*:

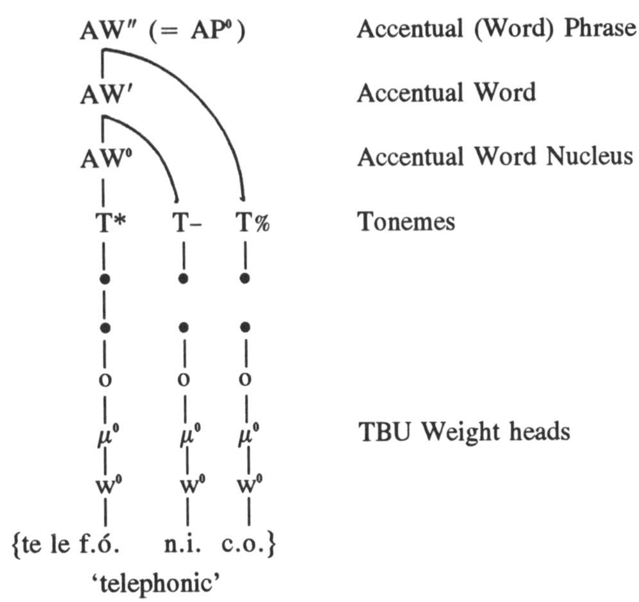

b. *Alignment of weight structure with prosodic syllabic feet in the morphological domain*:

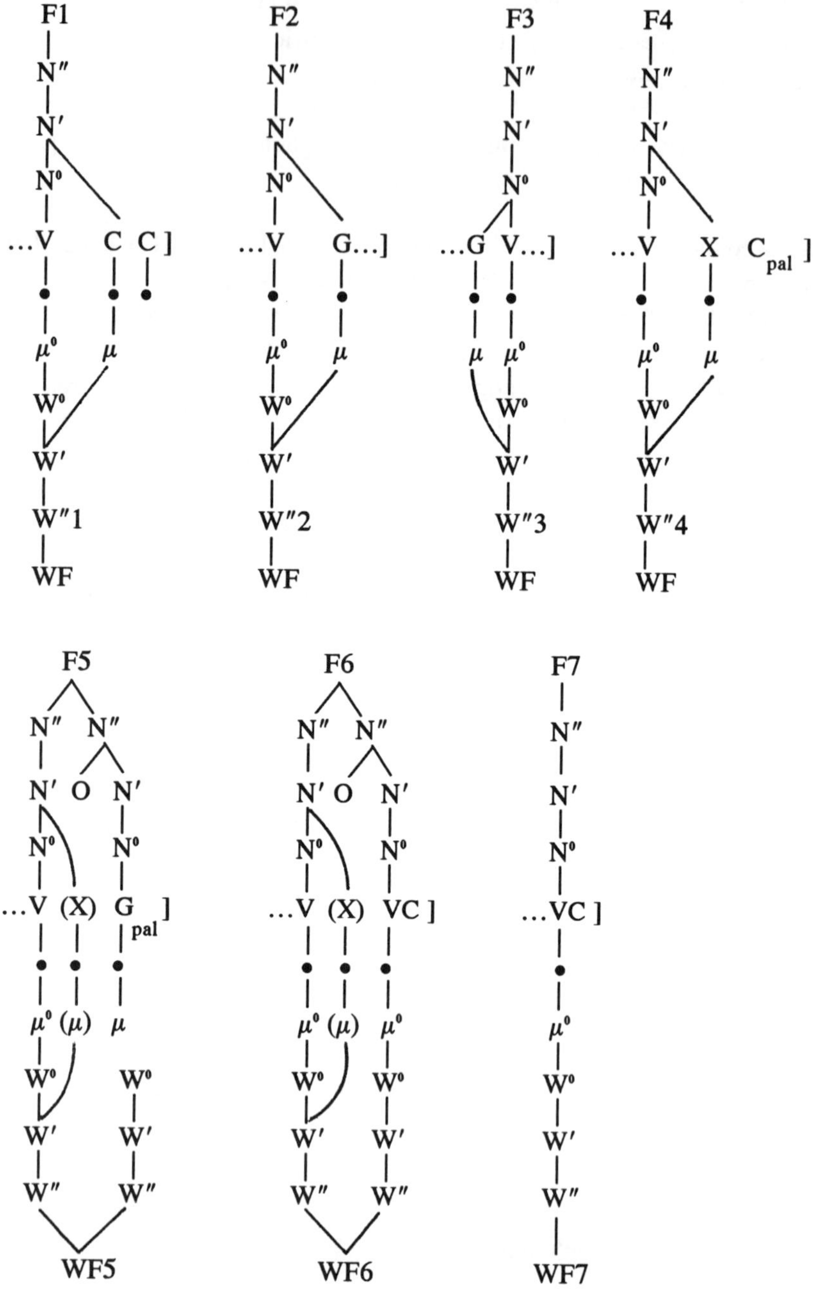

c. *Assignment of segmental prominence*:

(i) Not every member of a morphological class has alignment F//WF.

(ii) The leftmost μ^0 in WF is assigned accent $\overset{*}{\underset{\mu^0}{|}}$, and WF → MF.

d. *Examples*:

F1:	[garg–.**án**.–t]a	'throat'
F2:	[ac–.**éj**.–t]e	'oil'
F3:	[id–.j**ó**.–t]a	'idiot'
F4:	[cab–.**á**.**ǰ**–]o	'horse'
F5:	[car–.**í**.cj–]a	'caress', [camp.**én**.d.**j**–]o 'compendium'
F6:	[az–.**ú**.c.a.–r]	'sugar', [car–.**ác**.t.e.–r] 'character'
F7:	[algod–.**ó**.–n]	'cotton'

The simplicity of the alignment displayed between an intonational foot and a sequence of μ^0's idiosynchratically accented, is argued here, provides further support against a configurational approach to morpheme prominence as sketched, for the sake of the argument, in (23b, c). The different properties of (23a-b) are summarized in (24) and discussed subsequently.

(24)	*Intonation foot: properties*	*Prosodic foot: properties*
(i)	Domain of alignment: IfW	roots, derivational and inflectional morphemes, inflectional stems
(ii)	Maximal alignment: three TBU	ternary
(iii)	Type: nondegenerate	± degenerate
(iv)	Terminal nodes: T* / T– / T%	V/G/C
(v)	Prominence: left	left/right
(vi)	Alignment with: μ^0	μ^0 / μ
(vii)	Type of inclusion: total	partial

All μ^{0} in (23b) are obtained from alignment with the prosodic foot and can be achieved by universal sonority principles (Kiparsky 1979).

While in the intonation level it can be predicted that the head is always on the left of the alignment, in the prosodic foot, there is no such prediction since in F3 the head is right (24iv, vi).

In (23) both AP° and the prosodic foot have at least one μ^{0}. However, while the terminals in the AP° can align only with μ^{0}, the terminals in the prosodic feet can also align with nonhead moras (24vi). In that respect the former structure is a homogeneous alignment while the latter is a heterogeneous one.

In (23b) all feet are degenerate feet at the F level, except F5 and F6, and subsequently acquire accent by (23ii). Antepenultimate prominence in (25a) would have to be obtained with some additional ternary syllabic alignment. In the intonational foot there is only one unique ternary type (24iii). If the AP° could be degenerate, then it would predict that the last unaccented inflection had to be prominent, yielding **coloc+a+mós* 'place+ThV+ PRES+1SG', **chocolat+it+ó+s* 'chocolat+DIM+INFL+INFL'.

In (23b) not every member of a morphological class can align with a WF (partial inclusion, and therefore acquire accent by (33c). Antepenultimate assignment could be done by any ternay structural algorithm. For instance, not every Tense-Mood-Aspect morpheme has segmental prominence (25b) (cf. [ba] 'Past-Ind-Impf' vs. [í.a] 'Past-Cond-Impf').

While in (23b) the alignment of the feet is partial, in (23a) it is total. Every member of a given IfW class, such as N, V, Adj, and Adv, can align with a nondelimitative AP°. In that respect (23a) is of total inclusion while (23b) is of partial inclusion (24vii).

Finally, while the AP° has as its domain of alignment the Inflected Word, morphological feet have as their domain of alignment either the root or the derivational morpheme or the inflectional stem (24i). Some illustrative examples are shown in (25).

(25) a. *Roots and derivational morphemes represented between* [...]:

		accented +foot alignment	unaccented -foot alignment
D1	F1:	[garg-.**á**n.-t]a 'throat'	{[fr**ó**m.is.t]a} 'Fromista'
D1	F3:	[id-.j**ó**.t]a 'idiot'	{[al**í**k.wo.t]a} 'proportional'
D2	F6:	[az-.**ú**.c.a.-r] 'sugar'	{[d**é**f.i.c.i.t]} 'deficit'
D1	F7:	[carb-.**ó**.-n] 'coal'	{[**á**rb.o.l]} 'tree'
		[alel-.**í**.-] 'gilliflower'	
		[carbon-.**í**.-k]o 'coal+DIM'	{[carb**ó**n.i.k]o} 'carbonic'
		[in-.**ó**.k.w-]o 'harmless'	{[ven.tr**í**l.o.k.w]o} 'ventriloquist'

b. *Inflectional morphemes*:

		accented +foot alignment	unaccented -foot alignment
D2	F6:	colocar[-.**í**.a.-] 'place+COND'	coloc**á**[b.a.] 'place+IMPERF'
D1	F7:	coloqu[-.**é**.-] 'place+PRET 1SG	s**ú**p[.e.] 'know+PRET 1SG'
		coloqu[-.**é**.-]mos 'place+PRES SUBJ+1PL' (Castilian)	col**ó**.qu[.e.]mos 'place+PRES SUBJ+1PL' (Andalusian)[8]

c. *Inflectional stems represented between |...|*

(i) All verbal Inflectional stems have, without exception, prominence on the rightmost μ^0 at the IfS level:

D1: |colóc|o 'place PRES 1SG'

(ii) All nonverbal inflectional stems have, without exception, prominence on the rightmost μ^0 if it is followed by a palatal (glide or consonant) in the same domain:

D1: |acéjt|e 'oil'

D1: |cabáǰ|o 'horse'

D1: |compéndj|o 'compendium'

D1: |democrácj|a 'democracy'

The inflectional stem is the last domain before the inflectional morphemes are added to form an inflectional word IfW. The morpheme $[\text{fabric}]_N$ 'factory' and its verbal counterpart $[\text{fabric}]_V$ 'to manufacture' are unaccented. When the verb enters the IfS level (25ci) its last head-mora becomes prominent.

The generalization in (25ci) accounts for the exceptionless observation in all dialects of Spanish by which prominence in an inflected verb never occurs on the penultimate syllable of the inflectional stem. Each morphological constituent brings its accentual property, either in its final syllable, via D1, or in the penultimate syllable, via D2. At the IfS level, the unaccented |[[democrac] j]| is accented following (25cii). The generalization in (25cii) is a constraint applying at the IfS level. Supposing there are counterexamples to (25cii), such as |[gwal.dís.nej]| 'Walt Disney', |[u.rú.gwáj]| 'Uruguay', then a morpheme (in brackets) such as [a.céj.t]e (23d) will belong to D1, and the morpheme [j] in [de.mo.crá.c]j]a] will also belong to D1. However, [gwal.dís.nej] and [u.rú.gwaj] will belong to D2. No constraint (25cii) would be needed any longer.

There remains a final important issue in Spanish morphological prominence. Observe the following data. In (26) there are two types of paradigmatic prominence. On the right-hand side all prominences are columnar, since they fall on the same syllable of the same morpheme while on the left-hand side, the prominence is not columnar since it does not fall on the same locus of the same morpheme.

(26)	*Noncolumnar*	*Columnar*
a.	+Verbal IfW	
	Castilian	*Argentinean*
	* * {|colóc| [a] s} 'place PRES IND 2SG'	* * {|coloc| [á] s} 'place PRES IND 2SG'
	* * {|coloc| [á] mos} 'place PRES IND 1PL'	* * {|coloc| [á] mos} 'place PRES IND 1PL'
b.	–Verbal IfW	
	* * {|carácter|} 'character'	* {|cadáver|} 'cadaver'
	* * {|caractér| es} 'character+PL'	* {|cadáver| es} 'cadaver+PL'
	* {|ómicron| } 'omicron'	* {|carbón|} 'coal'
	* {|omicrón|es} 'omicron+PL'	* {|carbón| es} 'coal+PL'

In noncolumnar paradigms, the T* of the AP^0 fails to link with the rightmost inherent prominence of the Inflected Word if this accent is on the rightmost syllable of IfW. This is clearly an idiosyncratic situation in the Spanish lexicon which is governed by individual morphemes. It is again a historical legacy of Latin. In Latin, the accent on the edge of the word could not be expressed if there was another syllabic mora in the word preceding the accent to which T* could link. As in Latin, in all the cases where the accented mora has failed to link with T* in Spanish, this accented mora is the last syllable of the IfW. It can be said that these morphemes prohibit their accents from surfacing in their alignment with an AP* through a well-formedness condition.[9]

(27) *Well-formedness Condition for some morphemes*:

The rightmost accent is absorbed iff it occurs on the right edge of the IfW.

The well-formedness condition (27) imposed by some lexical items accounts for the fact that the mora, once its accent has been absorbed, will be treated as a nonaccented mora and therefore will align with T%. T* then has to link to the rightmost accented mora μ^{0}* (this time ex-second accent), as usual. If no accent is present to link with, the third unaccented mora will receive intonational prominence (*ómicron*). This approach predicts that words which are always antepenultimate: ***régimen*** 'regime' ***regímenes*** 'regime+PL' are lexically unaccented, and therefore will display a noncolumnar prominence in their paradigms. As expected, they will receive prominence by linking the third unaccented mora to the T* in the AP^{0}.

I have shown that in Spanish morphological inherent prominence is different from intonational structural prominence. Spanish has unaccented morphemes (no inherent prominence) and accented morphemes (inherent prominence) via D1 and D2. When accented words align with the AP^{0}* their rightmost accent will receive intonational prominence if this accent is within the last three syllable positions in an IfW. If no accent is in that ternary domain, the intonational prominence will be given maximally to the third unaccented syllable. Some morphemes absorb their accent just in case they occur on the right edge of the word. I have suggested that the ternary intonational structure is a lexicalization of the structure of the IP* in the same language which requires, after the culminative accent T*, a Phrase accent T–, and a boundary tone T%. The effects of these two Ts in IP* have been discussed in previous sections.

The simplicity of this approach to explain the interface between lexical and intonational prominence has to be evaluated with other alternatives. I assume some familiarity with the rules, principles, and parameters of metrical theory. In Halle and Idsardi (1995) it is suggested that languages which have lexical accent or are sensitive to quantity have a parenthesis projected on line 0.[10] I will use asterisks for both cases and place them under the text.

(28)

```
Line 0   Project: L    x  x   x          x  x   x  x    x(x# avoided
                       re gi men         re gi me nes
                              *                     *   heavy
                       ------------------------------
         Edge: RLR     x  x)  x          x  x   x) x
                       re gi men         re gi me nes
                       ------------------------------
         ICC: L        (x  x)  x         x (x   x) x
                       re gi men         re gi me nes
                       ------------------------------
         Head: L        x                  x
                       (x  x)   x        x (x   x) x
                       re gi  men        re gi me nes
                       ------------------------------
Line 1   Edge: RRR      x)                 x)
                       (x  x)  x         x (x   x) x
                       re gi men         re gi me nes
                       ------------------------------
         Head: R        x                  x
                        x)                 x)
                       (x  x)  x         x (x   x) x
                       ré gi men         re gí me nes
```

After Conflation, the secondary stresses disappear, leaving only primary stress. Now consider the following derivation when a nominal lexical item brings an inherent prominence on its last syllable.

(29)

Line 0	Project: L	x x x al go don *	x x (x x al go do nes * *	x(x# avoided heavy
	Edge: RLR	x x) x al go don	x x (x) x al go do nes	
	ICC: L	(x x) x al go don	(x x (x) x al go do nes	
	Head: L	x (x x) x al go don	x x (x x (x) x al go do nes	
Line 1	Edge: RRR	x) (x x) x al go don	x x) (x x (x) x al go do nes	
	Head: R	x x) (x x) x *ál go don	x x x) (x x (x) x al go dó nes	

In this framework, all accented morphemes which have an accent on the last syllable of the inflectional stem and do not have phonetic inflection in the singular will have to be exceptions to the general x(x#, since their accented syllable attracts stress on the edge of the IfW: {|algodón|} 'cotton'; {|convóy|} 'convoy'; {|marroquí|} 'Moroccan'. This exemption can apply only in the singular but has to be prevented from applying in the plural otherwise *{algodonés} would be wrongly stressed. Moreover, not all morphemes accented on the last syllable can be exceptions, since that would wrongly predict that words such as *{caractér}, or *{omicrón} have prominence on the last syllable (see (27b) above). Notice that Avoid x(x# is independently required not only in cases like (28) but also for stressing monosyllables.[11]

A more formal problem is that in this approach some stipulations have to be implemented in the general theory in order to avoid bad bracketings such as that illustrated in (30):

(30) Line 0 Project: L x x (x exempt from Avoid x(x#
al go don
*
Edge: RLR x x()x

In (30), a right bracket has been inserted to the left of the rightmost x. Some stipulation has to be provided to avoid misplacing brackets.

In Halle and Vergnaud (1987) and Roca (1992) lexical accent is encoded as a special mark (#) on line 1, and is subject to the Faithfulness Condition by which lexical accents have to be heads of a foot. This approach also needs additional theoretical stipulations (García-Bellido 1994). Since feet are built from bottom to top when the lexical accent is called on line 1, it can land on three different positions: over the recessive position of the foot (31i), on the head of the foot (31ii), or over an extrametrical position (31iii).

(31) (i) x #
(x x) (ii) x#
(x x) (iii) x #
(x x)<x>

Iff the lexical accent is on line 1 before the foot is built, some additional theoretical stipulations should be added to block binary foot formation, and to ensure degenerate foot formation instead. In all cases the accent would need to form a foot on its own, so that it can bear main stress or be extrametrical, or be secondary stress, and therefore be able to be conflated.

None of these problems is encountered in the approach proposed here. The linking of an inherent accent with T* and the assignment of phonetic prominence given by the intonational structure is, on theoretical and language-particular grounds, simpler than the other two alternatives. In these approaches metrical structures are used to create a primary stress which will later be linked to the Intermediate Phrase. Under the proposal suggested here, no metrical structure needs to intervene between the linking of the inherent prominence with the T* It is expected that more research on these lines would shed some light on the interface between inherent and intonational prominence in natural languages.[12]

Notes

* I would like to thank Jennifer Cole, John Coleman, John Goldsmith, and Janet Pierrehumbert for their comments and encouragement through the initial stages of this paper. Special thanks to Andrew Slater for making the recordings and printings. I am indebted to Fernando Martínez-Gil and two other contributors to this volume for their comments. All mistakes, as usual, are mine.

1 See for example work by Goldsmith in Bantu and Northern Iroquoian languages (Goldsmith 1982b, Goldsmith and Sabimana 1989). Goldsmith suggests that H tone in these languages links with the head of a binary organizational structure.

2 In these and subsequent examples, vowels that bear a perceived primary or secondary tonal prominence in an utterance are represented in boldface. I utilize phonetic symbols to indicate the high glides [j] and [w], as well as the voiced obstruent [ĵ], rather than using the conventional spelling, whenever any of them is the final segment in a derivational stem. In order to avoid orthographic confusions, the palatals are indicated in boldface. To simplify matters, the various manifestations of the voiced palatal obstruent are indicated here with one single symbol [ĵ]. For Spanish syllabification, see Hualde (1991).

3 It is conceivable that both T* and μ* have an autosegmental node where the phonetic values, structural and inherent respectively, are expressed, as in (i) below:

(i)

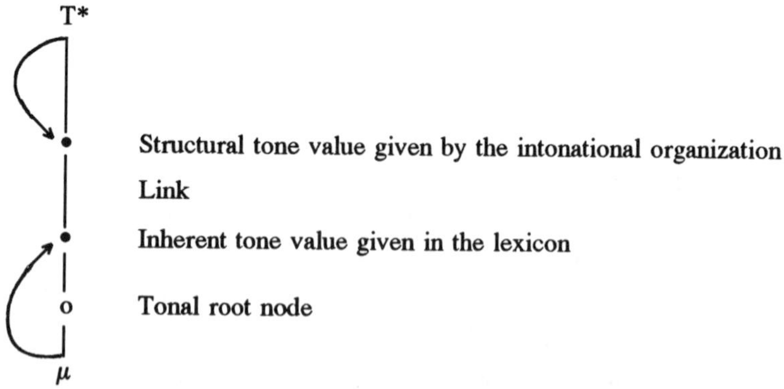

Since only one value out of two is phonetically expressed, it might be interesting to see which are the principles that languages use to allow one, but not the other, to surface (Goldsmith 1984). So, for instance, tonal languages might always impose the inherent value while nontonal languages might always impose their structural value (see Frota 1994 for European Portuguese; see also Nespor and Vogel 1986 for Italian and Greek, which have inherent and structural prominence; see Nespor and Vogel 1996 for French, Italian dialects of Viozene and Southern Calabria, which also exhibit structural prominence). In our approach for Spanish, the mora has no particular inherent tonal value, unlike in tonal languages or in Japanese, where the lexically accented mora is always HL. In Spanish if μ is made prominent in the lexicon, it is inherently accented. The lexically accented mora assigns as lexical tone value the accent *, as Goldsmith (1982a) suggests. In order to simplify representations, I will not represent the segmental tonal value node and the Tonal Root node throughout the paper except when required.

4 The IP is the domain for some important phonological rules such as Continuant Spreading (Mascaró 1984), Nasal Assimilation (Harris 1984) and Resyllabification (Harris 1983). For intonational studies of a Venezuelan dialect in a Pierrehumbert framework see Sosa (1991).

5 It has been reported in work done in the last twenty years or so that languages such as French, English, Dutch, Finnish, Japanese, and a large number of African languages, have a fundamental frequency declination effect in an intonation group manifested as a downdrift in pitch (Pierrehumbert 1973). There is no published study on pitch declination in Spanish, but work in progress by Prieto (1995) el al. point to an accent-by-accent decay or *downstep* in Mexican Spanish, together with a *final lowering,* and even a *final fall*, the latter consisting in a drastic pitch lowering in utterance-final position. The lowering domain in Mexican Spanish is the final pitch accent. The psychological reality of the last pitch has been confirmed in Pierrehumbert (1980), where she reports that when two stressed syllables are physically different in pitch, the second being lower than the first, speakers normalize for declination, judging the second stressed syllable higher than it actually is. This lack of correspondence between mental representations and F_0 values may be responsible for the same effect in clitics at the end of an utterance in Spanish. Informal experiments that I have myself carried out show that utterance-final clitics do not trigger a substantial rise in pitch; yet native speakers *hear* a prominence in the last clitic. Furthermore, in questions containing a clitic at the end of an utterance, this clitic marks the location where the rising pitch starts, thus showing the behavior of a proper pitch accent.

6 Although a clitic at the end of the utterance is perceived with prominence, it does not show a significant rise in the fundamental frequency line (see note 5). However, the rise is present in non utterance-final position, as will be shown in this paper.

7 "En la pronunciación de las palabras aisladamente consideradas coinciden en líneas generales el tono y el acento de intensidad, recayendo de ordinario el tono normal sobre la misma sílaba que lleva el acento y pronunciándose por debajo de este tono, con inflexión ascendente o descendente, según los casos, las demás sílabas de la palabra." (Navarro Tomás 1968: 214–215).

8 See Mondéjar (1970).

9 Following on the lines of the representation given in note 3, absorption can be represented as (i). The accent is moved away from the inherent value node; therefore the T* cannot see it since T* does not have access to the Tonal Root node.

(i)

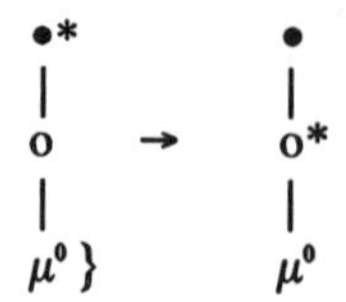

The term absorption is borrowed from Case theory in current Government and Binding theory.

10 For a recent alternative to Spanish stress in Halle and Idsardi's framework see Harris (1995), where examples such as (29) are not discussed.

11 See the discussion that Halle and Idsardi (1995) have on monosyllabic words in Latin where x(x# is preferred to (x# to force monosyllabic words, such as *qua*: 'which', to project their lexical accent.

12 Languages with antepenultimate prominence could be reflecting a case of ternary lexicalized intonational structure. The discussion in Everett (1988) for Pirahã, where extrametricality has to be revoked before main stress is applied, may follow the same lines of T* linking outlined for Spanish. In Pirahã, T* links to the heaviest syllable of the final three syllables, otherwise to the rightmost in a intonational structure such as T% T–T*. Apparently, Pirahã has rising intonation (Everett, personal communication).

References

Beckman, Mary E. 1986. *Stress and Non–Stress Accent*. Dordrecht: Foris.

Beckman, Mary E., and Janet B. Pierrehumbert. 1986. Intonation structure in Japanese and English. *Phonology Yearbook* 3.255–309.

Bolinger, Dwight L., and M. Hodapp. 1961. Acento melódico. Acento de intensidad. *Boletín de Filología* 13.33–48. Universidad de Santiago de Chile.

Chierchia, G. and G. McConnell. 1990. *Meaning and Grammar*. Cambridge, Mass.: MIT Press.

Clements, George N., and John Goldsmith. 1984. Introduction. *Autosegmental Studies in Bantu Tone*, ed. G. N. Clements and J. Goldsmith, 1–17. Dordrecht: Foris.

Contreras, Heles. 1963. Sobre el acento en español. *Boletín de Filología* 15.223–237. Universidad de Santiago de Chile.

Frota, Sonia. 1994. Is Focus a phonological category in Portuguese? *Proceedings of Console I*, ed. P. Ackema and M Schoorlemmer, 69-86. The Hague: Holand Academic Graphics.

Everett, Daniel L. 1988. On metrical constituent structure in Pirahã. *Natural Language and Linguistic Theory* 6.207–246.

García-Bellido, Paloma. 1989. Aspectos recientes de la fonología autosegmental. Las palatales en español. *Lenguajes Formales y Lenguajes Naturales* 4.1.309-328.

García-Bellido, Paloma. 1994. Parasitic heads in metrical theory. Ms., University of Oxford.

Goldsmith, John. 1976. *Autosegmental Phonology*. Doctoral dissertation, MIT. (Published in 1979 by Garland Press, New York).

Goldsmith, John. 1981. English as a tone language. *Phonology in the 1980s*, ed. D. Goyvaerts. Ghent: Story-Scientia.

Goldsmith, John. 1982a. Accent system. *The Structure of Phonological Representations* (vol. I), ed. Harry van der Hulst and Norval Smith, 47–63. Dordrecht: Foris.

Goldsmith, John. 1982b. The rise of rhythmic structure in Bantu. *Phonologica 1984*, ed. W. Dressler et al., 65–78. New York: Cambridge University Press.

Goldsmith, John, and Firmard Sabimana. 1989. The Kurundi verb. *Modèles en tonologie*, ed. Francis Jouanettt, 19–62. Edition du CNRS 1989.

Halle, Morris, and Jean-Roger Vergnaud. 1987. *An Essay on Stress*. Cambridge, Mass.: MIT Press.

Halle, Morris, and William Idsardi. 1995. General properties of stress and metrical structure. *The Handbook of Phonological Theory*, ed. John Goldsmith, 403–443. Cambridge, Mass.: Basil Blackwell.

Hammond, Michael T. 1986. The obligatory-branching parameter in metrical theory. *Natural Language and Linguistic Theory* 4.185–228.

Harris, James W. 1983. *Syllable Structure and Stress in Spanish. A Nonlinear Analysis*. Cambridge: MIT Press.

Harris, James W. 1984. Autosegmental phonology, lexical phonology and Spanish nasals. *Language Sound Structure*, ed. Mark Aronoff and Richard T. Oehrle, 67-82. Cambridge, Mass.: MIT Press.

Harris, James W. 1995. Projection and edge marking in the computation of stress in Spanish. *The Handbook of Phonological Theory*, ed. J. Goldsmith, 867-887. Cambridge, Mass.: Blackwell.

Hayes, Bruce. 1995. *Metrical Stress Theory. Principles and Case Studies*. Chicago: The University of Chicago Press.

Hyman, Larry (ed.). 1977. On the nature of linguistic stress. *Studies in Stress and Accent. Southern California Occasional Papers in Linguistics* 4.37–82.

Hyman, Larry, and Francis Katamba. 1993. A new approach to tone in Luganda *Language* 69.34–67.

Hualde, José I. 1991. On Spanish syllabification. *Current studies in Spanish Linguistics*, ed. Héctor Campos and Fernando Martínez-Gil, 475-493. Washington D. C.: Georgetown University Press.

Kiparsky, Paul 1979. Metrical structure is cyclic. *Linguistic Inquiry* 10.421–441.

Ladd, D. Robert. 1986. Intonational phrasing: the case for recursive prosodic structure. *Phonology* 3.311–340.

Liberman, Mark and Alan Prince. 1977. On stress and linguistic rhythm. *Linguistic Inquiry* 8.249–336.

Martínez Celdrán, Eugenio. 1984. *Fonética*. Barcelona: Teide.

Mascaró, Joan. 1984. Continuant spreading in Basque, Catalan and Spanish. In *Language sound structure*, ed. Mark Aronoff and Richard T. Oehrle, 287-298. Cambridge, Mass.: MIT Press.

McCarthy, J. and A. Prince. 1994. Generalized alignment. *Yearbook of Morphology*, 79-153.

Mondéjar, José. 1970. *El verbo andaluz. Formas y estructuras*. Madrid: Consejo Superior de Investigaciones Científicas.

Navarro Tomás, Tomás. 1916. Cantidad de las vocales acentuadas. *Revista de Filología Española* 3.387–408.

Navarro Tomás, Tomás. 1917. Cantidad de las vocales inacentuadas. *Revista de Filología Española* 4. 371–388.

Navarro Tomás, Tomás, 1968. *Manual de pronunciación española*. Madrid: Consejo Superior de Investigaciones Científicas.

Nespor, Marina, and Irene Vogel. 1986. *Prosodic Phonology*. Dordrecht: Foris.

Odden, D. 1995. Tone: African Languages. *Handbook of Phonological Theory*, ed. J. Goldsmith, 444-475. Cambridge, Mass.: Basil Blackwell.

Pierrehumbert, Janet B. 1973. The perception of fundamental frequency declination. *Journal of the Acoustic Society of America* 66.2.363-369.

Pierrehumbert, Janet B. 1980. *The Phonology and Phonetics of English Intonation*. Doctoral dissertation, MIT. (Distributed by Indiana University Linguistics Club, Bloomington, Indiana, 1987.)

Pierrehumbert, Janet B. 1993. Alignment and prosodic heads. *Proceedings of the Eastern States Conference on Linguistics*. Ithaca, N.Y.: DMLL Publications, Cornell University, 367-381.

Pierrehumbert, Janet B., and Mary E. Beckman. 1988. *Japanese Tone Structure*. Cambridge, Mass.: MIT Press.

Prieto, Pilar. 1995. Pitch downstep in Spanish. Ms., AT&T Bell Laboratories.

Prince, Alan. 1983. Relating to the grid. *Linguistic Inquiry* 14.19–100.

Pulleyblank, Douglas. 1986. *Tone in Lexical Phonology*. Dordrecht: Reidel.

Quilis, Antonio 1971. Caracterización fonética del acento en español. *Travaux de Linguistique et de Littérature* 9.53–72.

Quilis Antonio 1975. Las unidades de entonación. *Revista Española de Lingüística* 5.261–279.

Quilis, Antonio. 1981. *Fonética acústica de la lengua española*. Madrid: Gredos.

Real Academia Española 1973. *Esbozo de una nueva gramática de la lengua española*. Madrid: Espasa Calpe.

Roca, Iggy. 1986. Secondary stress and metrical rhythm. *Phonology* 3.341–370.

Roca, Iggy. 1992. On the sources of word prosody. *Phonology* 9.267–287.

Selkirk, Elisabeth. 1980. The role of prosodic categories in English word stress. *Linguistic Inquiry* 11.563–605.

Selkirk, Elisabeth. 1984. *Phonology and Syntax: the Relation Between Sound and Structure*. Cambridge, Mass.: MIT Press.

Selkirk, Elisabeth, 1995. Sentence prosody. *The Handbook of Phonological Theory*, ed. John Goldsmith, 550–569. Cambridge, Mass.: Basil Blackwell.

Solé Sabater, M–J. 1984. Experimentos sobre la percepción de acento. *Estudios de Fonética Experimental* 1.131–242.

Sosa, Juan manuel. 1991. *Fonetica y fonologia de la entonacion del español hispanoamericano*. Doctoral dissertation. University of Massachusetts, Amherst.

Trubetzkoy, N. S. 1969. *Principles of Phonology*. (Translated by Christiane A. M. Baltaxe.) Berkeley: University of California Press.

Yip, Moira. 1989. Contour tones. *Phonology* 6.149-174.

15

Variability, multilectalism, and the organization of phonology in Caribbean Spanish dialects

JORGE M. GUITART

1. Introduction

Variability in phonology refers to the fact that a word may be pronounced differently on different occasions, even though the segments of the word are always in exactly the same phonetic environment. One example would be a word that ends in a consonant which is sometimes pronounced, sometimes not, despite the fact that the surrounding sounds are the same in every case.

Like other natural languages, Caribbean Spanish dialects show variability, especially in the pronunciation of consonants in coda position, the part of the syllable following the vowel or syllabic nucleus. It is precisely the pronunciation of coda consonants that is characteristic of Caribbean Spanish and certain other dialects that are not in this geographic region, but are related historically to Caribbean dialects (e.g., those of Panama and the Atlantic coast of Colombia). Not only are the phenomena affecting coda consonants in Caribbean Spanish of considerable interest in themselves, but also of great interest is the fact that the phenomena are variable. Linguists who have studied variability in Caribbean Spanish have assumed that it is due to the alternation of procedures belonging to the same phonological system, with this alternation being largely determined by factors outside the grammar. The view that I would like to advance here is that variability is an effect of the alternation of procedures belonging to different phonological systems, and this alternation is an effect of the uneven control that speakers have over those systems.

I will attempt to show that the phonetic behavior of Caribbean speakers with regard to coda consonants supports the following assumptions:

a) Any Caribbean Spanish speaker who shows variability in the pronunciation of coda consonants has acquired more than one phonological system;

b) Caribbean Spanish speakers do not normally display equal control over the different phonological systems that underlie their pronunciation;

c) Uneven control is the cause of the variability observed and is manifested in the imperfect match between allophones and styles, a situation similar to that observed among second language learners and second language users who have fossilized;

d) Uneven control leads the average Caribbean speaker to switch from one phonological system to another in the course of speech, even midword, accounting for the variability observed for a given segment.

The specific organization of the phonology of Caribbean Spanish dialects is not at issue here. At present there are challenges to the long-held view that a generative phonology must contain phonological rules of a transformational nature. The challengers' view is that phonology is constraint-based rather than rule-based. But whether phonology is a set of rules applying in a derivational fashion or a set of constraints applying at once, a theory of phonological competence must contend in a principled way with the fact of variability. We will see shortly that variability poses a problem for any phonological model that assumes that speakers have only one phonological system for every language they speak.

2. Dropping, Neutralization, and Simplification of Coda Consonants in Caribbean Spanish

Caribbean Spanish is characterized by frequent manifestations of certain phonetic phenomena affecting consonants in coda position. In some instances a coda consonant is not pronounced at all. This phenomenon has been called *deletion* in rule-based phonology. I will refer to it here as *dropping*. Dropping of /s/ and /d/ in word final position is quite common, e.g., [kompá] for *compás*, 'beat', [mitá] for *mitad*, 'half'. Other coda consonants are dropped, but less frequently. Nasals may sometimes be represented by a nasalization without any oral gestures taking place, e.g., [bẽ] for *ven*, 'come'. The tap /r/ may be dropped when it is the infinitival morpheme, e.g., [komé] for *comer*, 'to eat'. Dropping is less common word-internally. One example would be [dotór] for *doctor*, 'doctor'.

I am assuming here that any phonological system that is part of the grammar of a natural language includes two levels of representations: a phonetic level and an underlying level, and any theoretical model of such a system must be formulated in terms of these two levels. Now, Caribbean Spanish has coda consonants in underlying representation, since morpheme-ending consonants that have been dropped in coda position appear when the same morpheme is not at the right edge of a word, e.g., [kompáse] for *compases*, 'beats', [mitáde] for *mitades* 'halves', [benían] for *venían*, 'they were coming', [koméremo] for *comeremos*, 'we will eat'. Another indication that coda consonants are present at the underlying level comes from the facts of variability: the same speaker may pronounce two different tokens of the same consonant-ending word and drop the consonant in only one instance, even within the same utterance, e.g., [dó, dós mése] for *dos, dos meses*, 'two, two months.'

The other phonetic phenomena affecting coda consonants in Caribbean Spanish can be subsumed under the label *phonetic neutralization*. Two phonologically distinct segments belonging to the same natural class are phonetically neutralized when both have exactly the same phonetic representation. In coda position in Caribbean Spanish this representation can be either a) a sound that is identical in its distinctive features to an onset allophone of one of the segments, e.g., both /l/ and /r/ may be pronounced [l], or b) a sound that in its distinctive features is unlike any of the onset allophones of the segments in question, e.g., both /s/ and /f/ may be pronounced [h].

Perhaps the most conspicuous instances of phonetic neutralization in coda position in Caribbean Spanish are the following:

a) both voiceless fricatives /s/ and /f/ may be realized as the glottal fricative [h], a phenomenon referred to as *aspiration*; e.g., [áhta] for both *asta*, 'flagpole' and *afta*, 'canker sore';

b) both liquids /l/ and /r/ may have the same manifestation, either by being realized as the palatal glide, [y], a phenomenon referred to as *liquid gliding* or *vocalization*, as happens in the Cibaeño dialect of Dominican; e.g., [séyda] for both *celda*, 'cell' and *cerda*, 'bristle', or by lateralizing /r/, a phenomenon known as *lateralization*, as happens in different dialects throughout the Caribbean; e.g., [álma] for both *alma*, 'soul' and *arma*, 'weapon', or by assimilating both /l/ and /r/ to the following onset, as happens in some Cuban dialects, e.g.; [púgga] for both *pulga*, 'flea' and *purga*, 'purge';

c) nonvelar stops and nasals may be realized as velar, a phenomenon referred to as *velarization*, observed for example among Cubans and Venezuelans; e.g., [péksi] for *Pepsi(Cola)*, [égniko] for *étnico*, 'ethnic', [iŋno] for *himno*, 'anthem', [alemáŋ] for *alemán*, 'German (masculine)'.

The fact that coda consonants in Caribbean Spanish are phonetically neutralized only in a variable way (e.g., sometimes *arma* and *himno* are pronounced [arma] and [ímno] by the same speakers who may pronounce them as [álma] and [iŋno]) indicates that consonants still contrast in coda position at the underlying level.

Because both dropping and phonetic neutralization reflect apparent trends, however unfulfilled, towards a simpler phonological system, I will use the term *simplification* in the remainder of the paper to refer globally to both dropping and all phenomena subsumed under phonetic neutralization.

3. The Mixing of Radical and Conservative Realizations in Caribbean Spanish

Given that coda consonant simplification is highly frequent in Caribbean Spanish, an interesting question is whether Caribbean Spanish is evolving toward a phonological system that has no coda consonants. The phenomena subsumed under phonetic neutralization perhaps reflects a trend toward some sort of compromise between retention and elimination in which there would still be coda consonants, but only one per class (as Chela Flores (1986) has hypothesized), i.e., one stop, which would be velar; one nasal, which would also be velar; one fricative, which would be laryngeal; and one liquid, which perhaps would be lateral. Or maybe there would be no liquids in coda position (cf. liquid gliding).

There is evidence that simplification was already occurring in Caribbean Spanish more than four centuries ago (see Boyd-Bowman 1975) and a good question is why no Caribbean Spanish dialect presents a simpler system after all this time. What has prevented Caribbean speakers from reducing the inventory of coda consonants or from getting rid of coda consonants altogether?

One factor inhibiting the formation of a simpler consonant system for Caribbean Spanish may be the influence of orthography on pronunciation. The Spanish orthographic system reflects the phonological system of Castilian, a dialect where dropping and neutralization are not nearly as extensive as in Caribbean Spanish. For example, there is no dropping of word-final /s/ in Castilian, no neutralization involving /s/ and /f/, and no liquid neutralization of the kind that occurs in Caribbean Spanish.

If we refer to phonetic realizations showing simplification as *radical* and to realizations that do not show simplification as *conservative*, we can say that Caribbean Spanish is considerably more radical than Castilian. At the same time, since, as we have seen, the phonological contrast between segments affected by dropping and neutralization still exists at the phonological level, the underlying representation of lexical items in Caribbean Spanish apparently does not differ greatly from that of Castilian. Presumably, awareness of the orthographic code (whether conscious or unconscious) leads literate speakers to both preserve distinctness in coda consonant representations at the phonological level and realize these consonants as their nonsimplified versions, at least part of the time. Precisely one interesting aspect of Caribbean Spanish pronunciation is that speakers 'mix' radical and conservative realizations of the same underlying coda consonants, with the radical realizations being more frequent overall. However, in certain contexts, for example, in formal speech, the opposite may occur and conservative realizations may be more frequent than radical ones.

4. The Phonological Characterization of Coda Consonant Simplification in Caribbean Spanish

Assume for the moment that to each particular dialect there is only one grammar, containing one and only one phonological system. I believe that all generative phonologists who think that phonology is rule-based and at least some phonologists who reject rules entirely in favor of constraints—including the proponents of Optimality Theory (henceforth OT), to mention what appears to be the most widely accepted constraint-based approach—would share two assumptions regarding the form of the phonological system. The first assumption is that the phonological system includes elements, and principles and procedures, with the principles and procedures determining the shape of elements in actual pronunciation. The second assumption is that the elements affected by some of those procedures are underlying lexical items containing phonological information which remains invariable in synchronic use. That is to say, at least until a language changes with respect to the phonological content of a given lexical item, the underlying representation of a morpheme remains the same, even if the morpheme is pronounced in different ways when it combines with other morphemes in words or phrases.

How would the facts of coda consonant simplification in Caribbean Spanish be characterized in a model based on those two assumptions? For the sake of simplicity, let me refer only to the characterization of word-final consonant dropping. In what follows I would like to show how word-final dropping has been characterized in rule-based phonology and how it must be characterized in OT. For each model I will show how its characterization of consonant dropping fails to account for the facts of Caribbean Spanish if it is maintained that each particular dialect contains one and only one phonological system.

5. Coda Consonant Dropping in Rule-based Phonology

The characterization of word-final dropping in rule-based phonology is done by positing a rule of deletion, a phonological transformation operating upon an underlying form that contains the consonant. The rule specifies that an underlying consonant in coda position will not have any phonetic representation. Every word-final consonant in Caribbean Spanish meets the structural description of such a rule. (For rule-based descriptions of Caribbean Spanish phonological phenomena see for example Guitart 1976, Núñez Cedeño 1980, and Zamora and Guitart 1988.)

The problem is that in actual pronunciation Caribbean Spanish speakers do not drop word-final consonants automatically. Data from numerous variability studies on Caribbean Spanish show that for any group of speakers, dropping never occurs one hundred percent of the time, even in spontaneous, unguarded speech. This is true, for instance, of word-final /s/ (See Cedergren 1973, Terrell 1979, and Alba 1982b for data from three different Caribbean Spanish dialects). In a certain number of instances the rule of deletion fails to apply to segments that meet its structural description. There is no explanation, internal to the grammar, for why the rule does not apply.

Since, in a rule-based phonology, the form of phonetic representations is determined primarily by rules, when deletion does not apply to a word-final consonant, other rules have applied instead. Consider the case of word-final /s/. It may be deleted, but it may also be aspirated, i.e., pronounced as [h], or it may be pronounced as [s]. When /s/ is aspirated instead of deleted, a rule of aspiration has applied. The rule of deletion and the rule of aspiration refer to the same type of segment in the same phonetic environment. There is no grammar-internal explanation for why sometimes one rule applies instead of the other. There also is no grammar-internal explanation for why sometimes neither rule applies and /s/ is realized as [s]. In the latter case, there must be a rule specifying that the segment is pronounced as a voiceless alveolar fricative in coda position. Therefore, there are at least three rules that inexplicably alternate in their application to the same segment in the same context. None of these three rules is descriptively adequate when all the possibilities for /s/ are taken into account.

Suppose we constrain the application of each one of these rules to a different 'style' of pronunciation defined in terms of speed and relative self-monitoring, and say that deletion occurs only in very fast unguarded speech, aspiration in moderately fast speech that is also unguarded, and retention in slow, careful speech. The problem with this solution is that Caribbean Spanish speakers sometimes delete or aspirate /s/ in slow speech in formal situations (e.g., when reading words aloud from a list) and retain /s/ in unguarded speech (see Ma and Herasimchuk 1971). The construct of style is unable to correct the deficiency of the rules in question.

6. Coda Consonant Dropping in OT

Like other constraint-based models, OT does not contain phonological transformations, i.e., rules that may insert or delete segments or change feature values. Rather, there is a set of phonological constraints common to all natural languages, and these constraints act as filters in the relationship between underlying representations and surface forms. Constraints in OT may be positive or negative. A positive constraint is, for example, 'syllables must have onsets', expressed as Onset. A negative one is 'syllables must not have codas', expressed as *Coda. In OT, the phonological portion of a grammar consists primarily of two components, a generator, GEN, and an evaluator, EVAL. Constraints belong in the latter. Given an underlying form (consisting of one or more morphemes containing phonological information), GEN simultaneously generates an unordered set of *candidates* for surface form and these candidates are the input to EVAL. EVAL, which includes the set of constraints, evaluates the different candidates, but the constraints do not apply serially, as rules would in a rule-based approach. Rather they apply simultaneously, in parallel fashion. On the other hand, constraints are always ranked in a hierarchy. A higher constraint exerts a greater influence than a lower constraint in the evaluation process. For any particular language, ranking is fixed and invariable, but ranking varies from language to language. This implies that ranking is parametrized. Suppose A, B, and C are constraints. One language may show the ranking A > B > C (A is ranked over B which is ranked over C.) In another language the ranking may be B > C > A; in a third language the ranking may be C > A > B, etc. It may be the case that some constraints are highly ranked in every language. For instance, it is possible that Onset and *Coda rank highly in all languages, since all languages have CV syllables.

Of all the candidates generated by GEN and evaluated by EVAL, only one is identical to the surface form. This is the *optimal candidate*. The other candidates will be eliminated because they violate some significant constraint. However, the optimal candidate may violate constraints. For instance, there are surface forms that contain syllables of the V or VC types. Both types of syllable violate Onset and VC violates *Coda. The crucial difference between the optimal candidate and the candidates that did not `make it' to the phonetic surface is that the unsuccessful candidates violated more highly ranked constraints than those violated by the optimal candidate. To illustrate, suppose that in a language, Onset is ranked higher than *Coda, and suppose that the underlying morpheme is /popol/. GEN generates, among others, the candidates pop.ol and po.pol for this morpheme. Now pop.ol violates Onset because the second syllable does not have an onset, and it also violates *Coda because the second syllable has a coda. But po.pol does not violate Onset, though it does violate *Coda. The optimal candidate is po.pol because it did not violate the higher constraint Onset. Now, Onset constitutes for unsuccessful pop.ol the *fatal constraint*, meaning the constraint whose violation rules out a candidate as the optimal candidate.

Sometimes, all candidates violate the same constraints and the same low optimality is decided on the basis that one candidate shows fewer violations. Consider the following example, which incidentally illustrates how consonant dropping can be handled in OT. Suppose that a Caribbean Spanish speaker pronounces the word *inglés*, 'English'—the masculine adjective—as [in.glé]. This is a single-morpheme word. However, its underlying representation must be /ingles/, since the same speaker says [in.gle.sa] for *inglesa*, the feminine adjective. GEN generates several candidates for the surface form of *inglés*, among them [in.glé] and [in.glés]. There are other candidates, e.g., [ing.lé], [i.nglé], [i.ng.l.é.s], [ing.lé.s], [ing.lés], etc., all of which will meet some fatal constraint, but I will skip the details for the sake of simplicity. Now, [in.glés] and [in.glé] both violate Onset and *Coda, but the form without final /s/ shows only one violation of *Coda whereas the form ending in /s/ shows two violations. And that is why the form without /s/ is the optimal candidate and is the one that is realized in the phonetic surface (for OT in general see Prince and Smolensky 1993, and for an OT treatment of Spanish phenomena see Morales-Front 1994.)

In general, if a language does not have coda consonants (for example, as in the case of Hawaiian), it means that *Coda is ranked higher in that language than constraints that would not disallow coda consonants. In such a language, if any two forms, X and Y, generated by GEN for a given underlying form, Z, are identical, except that Y has an additional final consonant (e.g., X is *papa* and Y is *papak*) then X will be the optimal candidate—it will be the surface representation of Z—and Y will be fatally constrained by *Coda.

The OT model would account nicely for coda consonant dropping in Caribbean Spanish, were it not for the variable nature of dropping. An invariable ranking showing *Coda higher adequately describes every instance of word-final consonant dropping but is descriptively inadequate for the cases in which the same word is pronounced with a consonant at the end.

7. A Thought Experiment about Bilinguals and Bilectals

Suppose now that a native speaker of a language that has no coda consonants, let me call it L-a, acquires successfully another language, L-b, after having acquired L-a. That is to say, L-b is the second language (henceforth L2) of this speaker. Now, L-b has coda consonants in word-internal position but not in word-final position. Suppose that in L-b the word *mu* means 'house', *ka* means 'ware' and the plural morpheme is *i*. Suppose further that 'houses' is pronounced *mumi* and 'houseware', which is a single word, as in English, is pronounced *mumka* . Given these facts, both rule-based phonologists and OT phonologists would agree that in L-b the underlying form of the morpheme for *house* is /mum/. A rule based-phonologist would say that Language B has a word-final consonant deletion rule, whereas an OT phonologist would say that constraints are ranked in L-b in a way that allows codas word-internally but not word-finally. In spite of these differences, rule-based phonologists and OT phonologists would agree that an L-a/L-b bilingual possesses two different grammars and therefore two different phonological systems. When the successful L2 learner speaks L-b, s/he does not use the grammar of L-a, but rather the grammar of L-b, which is why she never mispronounces, *mumka* as *[muka].

Suppose now that another native speaker of L-a acquires L-b as an L2, but not as well as the first one, because s/he can communicate adequately in L-b, s/he has a foreign accent when s/he speaks it. For instance, s/he tends to pronounce 'houseware' as *[muka] instead of [mumka]. However, s/he does not do this all the time and sometimes pronounces the same word correctly. Suppose we assume that whenever s/he speaks Language B s/he uses a single grammar. Within a rule-based framework we would have to say that when s/he says *[muka] for *mumka*, a rule of deletion has applied, and so the singular phonology of her/his nonnative-like version of L-b includes this rule, which actually does not belong in the native inventory of L-b. But we would have no system-internal explanation for the cases in which s/he pronounces the word correctly. Within the OT framework, we would have to say that in the incorrect pronunciation, *[muka] for *mumka*, constraints are ranked so as to disallow codas. Suppose an OT phonologist, who assumes that the underlying representation of the word in question is /mumka/, knows only of cases in which the speaker says *[muka]. The OT phonologist will have to say that the speaker has acquired a ranking that disallows codas. However, since for any single phonological system ranking is fixed and invariable, the same OT phonologist would have no explanation for the cases where the same speaker says, correctly, [mumka].

Now suppose that this not-so-successful L2 learner has internalized two distinct phonological systems for L-b. This means that s/he has two different grammars of L-b. These two grammars may or may not share the same lexicon, morphology, or syntax. One of these grammars shows no phonological influence from L-a but the other one does. The speaker has imported from L-a principles and procedures that disallow coda consonants. This speaker in a sense speaks two varieties of Language B, one allowing word-internal coda consonants and one not. I will refer to these varieties as *lects* rather than dialects, because their relative use is not necessarily associated with living in a given geographical location or belonging to a certain social class. Lect 1 is the one that is closer to Language A. Lect 1, like L-a, does not have coda consonants. Lect B does have coda consonants, but only word internally. Our L2 learner with a variable accent is *bilectal*, in addition to being bilingual.

Now, if you prefer a rule-based framework, you can say that Lect 1 contains a coda deletion rule that applies to codas regardless of their position within a word, and Lect 2 contains a different deletion rule whose structural description specifies word-final position as the environment of application. In other words, the rule inventories of Lect 1 and Lect 2 are different. If you prefer the OT framework, you can say that in Lect 1 constraints are ranked so as to disallow coda consonants in any position, but in Lect 2 they are ranked so as to disallow them only at the right edge of a word. That is to say, in L1 and L2 constraint ranking has been parametrized differently.

Now suppose that L-b encodes the phrase 'ceramic houseware' in a single word, *akmumka*, where the morpheme for 'ceramic' is *ak*. Native speakers of L-b pronounce the word invariably as [ak.mum.ka]. However, our imperfect L2 learner shows at least three pronunciations for *akmumka*. In a very few instances s/he pronounces the word correctly, other times says [a.mu.ka], dropping both codas, and sometimes says [ak.mu.ka], dropping only the second coda. Sometimes s/he "hypercorrects" and says [ak.mum.kam]. But let me focus on the pronunciation [ak.mu.ka]. The speaker applies the procedures of Lect 2 (the farther from her/his native L-a) to the first syllable, but applies the procedures of Lect 1 (the closer to her/his native L-a) to the second syllable. That is to say, the speaker switches between lects in the middle of a word. This is akin to bilinguals switching between languages within an utterance and even within a sentence—the phenomenon known as *code-switching* (see Poplack 1980). The switching between lects in midword is an instance of *phonological code-switching.*

Consider now that bilinguals who code-switch regularly at the syntactic level are normally not what some linguists have called *balanced bilinguals.* Rather they are what I will call *imperfect bilinguals.* Imperfect bilinguals have a dominant language, which is usually their native language, called the first language, or L1, which they speak with native-like ability. In their other language, their L2, which is their nondominant language, they show some degree of phonological deviation (they have a 'foreign accent') as well as some degree of deviation regarding other parts of the grammar (sentences that are incorrect by native standards).

There are some significant facts to be noted about the linguistic behavior of the average code-switcher. Some of these facts pertain to syntax and some to phonology. First, consider that code-switchers are able to keep the two languages syntactically distinct even in conversation, since whenever switching is not intrasentential, at least simple sentences are entirely either in L1 or L2. Furthermore, switchers use in their L2 syntactic structures that do not exist in their L1. These structures are either unlike, identical, or similar in some degree to those of L2 as spoken natively. Consider also that code-switchers show sounds in their L2 that do not exist in their L1. These sounds are either unlike, identical, or similar in some degree to those of L2 as spoken natively. Furthermore, switchers may show phonological procedures in their L2 that do not exist in their L1. For instance, native speakers of Spanish flap the coronal stops *t* and *d* when speaking American English as an L2.

The facts just cited strongly suggest that imperfect bilinguals who code-switch have acquired at least two different grammars and at least two different phonological systems. There are no grounds to suppose that code-switchers have a single grammar and therefore a single phonology. There are also no grounds to suppose that they have a single phonology shared by two different grammars.

It would be possible to calculate the relative frequency with which a code-switcher uses each language in relation to a number of extragrammatical factors, such as the situation that the speaker is in, the topic being discussed, and the sex, social class, and educational level of the speaker. The results of these calculations would tell us a great deal about the use of language in society, but they would tell us nothing about the system or systems that underlie the switcher's knowledge. However, if the focus is on the relationship between the observable facts of language use and the equally observable facts of topic, situation, social class, etc., it is irrelevant to ask how many grammars the speaker has internalized or whether the speaker switches between grammars or simply between procedures within a single grammar.

Regarding phonological alternations within a single language, the assumption of those primarily interested in the relationship between language use and extragrammatical factors is that monolingual speakers who know only one dialect of a given language know only one grammar. This is precisely the position of quantitative sociolinguists, or linguists operating under the framework developed by William Labov and his followers (see Labov 1972, Silva Corvalán 1989), whom I will refer to as *Labovians* here. To my knowledge, Labovians who have analyzed the pronunciation of Caribbean Spanish have assumed that any person who speaks a single dialect of Caribbean Spanish (whether described geographically or socially) is not, in my terms, bilectal, but is instead *monolectal*, possessing only one grammar.

Labovians do not recognize the possibility that a Caribbean Spanish speaker who speaks only one dialect may be switching between two different phonological systems when s/he says, for example, [as.beh.to] for *asbesto*, 'asbestos', where the first coda is not simplified but the second coda is (cf. our imaginary example [ak.mu.ka]).

8. Variability and Procedural Failure

Labovians have characterized variability in terms of *variable rules*. These are not rules, but statistical statements about the probability of each allophone occurring in relation to a number of linguistic and extralinguistic factors. Consider the simplification of /s/ in Caribbean Spanish. Labovians say that there is a variable S with three manifestations, [s], [h] and [Ø], the latter, the 'zero' allophone, signifies the absence of the segment (in my terms, the case in which /s/ is dropped). However, some Labovians have referred to two rules that serve to characterize the two manifestations of /s/ simplification. These rules are called Aspiration and Deletion. Cedergren (1983) proposes that the two rules are as shown in (1) rather than as shown in (2):

(1)	a.	s → h
	b.	s → ø
(2)	a.	s → h
	b.	h → ø

The analysis in (1) is preferred by Labovians because it is less abstract and it is based entirely on the facts. The analysis in (2) involves an intermediate abstract step, an [h] that is never manifested on the phonetic surface but it is posited to be the input to Deletion. Labovians speak of deletion and aspiration as processes. Therefore the rules in (1) are regarded as dynamic mechanisms, not simply as expressions of static relations between an underlying form and its different phonetic manifestations. On the other hand, there is no attempt within the Labovian framework to find explanations for why the processes of deletion or aspiration alternately fail. However, Labovians do not think of variability in terms of procedural successes or failures. Rather, they regard the alternation between conservative and radical realizations as a manifestation of the inherently variable character of human language. On the other hand they also regard such an alternation as a symptom of competing diachronic trends. One trend is towards changing the present pronunciation system and another towards leaving it unchanged. If a given alternation disappears historically, it is because an entire speech community has adopted a new system.

But the status of coda consonants in Caribbean Spanish is peculiar because variability shows stability rather than change, as Labov himself points out is the case of /s/ (See Labov 1994:595). This stability is in need of an explanation, but to my knowledge, Labovians studying Caribbean Spanish have not furnished one.

Within the Labovian framework it would be possible to say that there are at least three competing diachronic trends in Caribbean Spanish manifested in variability. There is a trend toward the elimination of coda consonants, and there is an opposite trend toward retention without phonetic neutralization. The third trend is to retain codas but to apply processes such as aspiration, lateralization, etc., leading to phonetic neutralization. However, for Labovians these trends do not manifest the existence of competing systems within one speaker but only the existence of competing processes within a single system. The lack of recognition of the possibility of competing systems within the same speaker on the part of Labovians may be related to their lack of interest in grammar as a model of competence and their interest in relating linguistic performance (in our case, actual pronunciation) to extralinguistic facts of a social and historical nature through the cataloging and quantification of surface phenomena.

9. The Variable Nature of Variability Factors

In considering the possibility that Caribbean Spanish speakers may be in possession of more than one phonological system, it is important to look at certain data provided by the Labovian analysis of Caribbean Spanish variability. Labovians have determined the probability of occurrence of both conservative and radical manifestations of the same segment in relation to a number of factors. Some of these factors are extralinguistic (including those of a social nature) and some are purely linguistic. Among extralinguistic factors are those that pertain to qualities of the speakers themselves and to their social circumstances, e.g., their sex and educational level. One purely linguistic factor considered by Labovians is the phonetic environment in which a given sound occurs in terms of characteristics of neighboring sounds.

For Labovians, one very important extralinguistic factor in variability is *formality*. This refers both to the situation that a speaker is in and the topic that s/he or she is talking about. In some Labovian studies, degree of formality has been related to certain tasks speakers are asked to perform. Formal situations have included reading words from a list, reading a text, and discussing a formal topic. Informal situations have included discussing an informal topic and engaging in spontaneous conversation. The frequency rate of phenomena such as /s/ aspiration and /r/ lateralization in Caribbean Spanish dialects have been found to be relatively lower in situations that Labovians classify as formal and relatively higher in situations they classify as informal. (See, e.g. Ma and Herasimchuk 1971, Lafford 1986.)

Among other factors affecting the probability that a given allophone may occur are speakers' social class and level of education. It is important here to refer to the phenomenon of stigmatized pronunciation. When a certain phonetic process makes words depart from standard pronunciation (which normally is that of the more educated and affluent people in the society), such a process becomes socially stigmatized; it is 'bad' to pronounce words that way. Labovian studies have repeatedly found that the probability of occurrences of stigmatized sounds is lowest among upper class speakers and increases to the point that it is highest among lower class speakers. As would be expected, there is also a negative correlation between the occurrence of stigmatized processes and the level of education. In Caribbean Spanish, simplification phenomena have been shown to be more frequent among the lesser educated and the lower classes. (See, e.g., Alba 1990.)

Another factor considered by Labovians has been gender. Studies on different language groups have shown that men and women who speak the same language natively pronounce it differently. In some cases women have shown to be more innovative than men (See, Fontanella de Weinberg's 1979 study of a non-Caribbean Spanish dialect). In other cases they have shown to be more conservative. For instance, Rojas (1982) found that Cibaeño Dominican women engaged in liquid gliding less than men.

Moving on to purely linguistic constraints, it has been found that word-final dropping of /s/ in Caribbean Spanish is less frequent when the vowel beginning the next word is stressed than when it is unstressed (see, e.g., Alba 1982b) and it has also been found that word-final /s/ dropping is less frequent when the word is toward the beginning of a sentence than when it is toward the end (see Poplack 1979.)

Consider now that the effect of any given factor on variability is itself variable. To illustrate, Caribbean Spanish studies show that speakers do not refrain from simplification in formal contexts. For example, Ma and Herasimchuk's (1971) Puerto Rican subjects lateralized /r/ and aspirated /s/ even when reading from a list of words. Take now the factor of sex. Cibaeño Dominican males glide liquids more than women, but women also glide them (See Rojas 1982). And if we attend to the criteria of education and social class, we see that educated, upper-class speakers do not refrain from aspirating or dropping /s/ (see Lafford 1982). Moving on to linguistic factors, Caribbean speakers tend to aspirate and drop word-final /s/ less when the word that follows begins with a stressed vowel than when the initial vowel is weakly stressed, but simplification occurs before weakly stressed vowels as well (see Alba 1982b). And word-final /s/ dropping occurs more when the word is not at the beginning of a sentence, but it also may occur at the beginning of a sentence (see Poplack 1979). In short, no factor invoked by Labovians as influencing pronunciation stops simplification one hundred percent of the time.

We can think of formality, upper class status, and strong stress as factors that are only partially successful in *inhibiting* simplification. Conversely, we can think of informality, lower class status, and weak stress as factors that are only partially successful in *facilitating* simplification, given that coda consonants are not simplified one hundred percent of the time in informal situations, by lower class speakers, or before weakly stressed vowels.

10. Variability and Control Among Caribbean Spanish Speakers

Suppose now that a native speaker of Caribbean Spanish who lives in a Spanish-speaking community refrains from simplifying any coda consonants while reading a list of words aloud. This is not an imaginary possibility. It would be the expected behavior of radio and TV announcers in Caribbean Spanish countries and Caribbean Spanish communities in the United States, e.g., in Cuban Miami (I would like to add that Caribbean Spanish announcers, anchor persons and reporters who do not engage at all in coda consonant simplification can be seen and heard daily on Univisión, a TV network in the United States broadcasting exclusively in Spanish).

Recall that reading aloud constitutes a formal situation in the Labovian framework. The behavior of media speakers is atypical of the *average* Caribbean speaker as reflected in Labovian data, since the incidence of nonsimplified allophones in formal situations never reaches one hundred percent for any group (see Ma and Herasimchuk 1971, and Lafford 1982). Why are announcers able to inhibit simplification one hundred percent of the time? One possible answer is that they have achieved this through training. They exhibit total *control* over the conservative mode of pronunciation of coda consonants.

Consider now the relationship between control and the notion of *style*, as normally used in sociolinguistic parlance. Styles in sociolinguistics are modes of speaking according to the relative formality of social contexts. A formal situation calls for a formal style, and an informal situation for an informal style. In formal styles speakers are more linguistically conservative than in informal styles. Native speakers of a language are said to be in control over the stylistic range of their native language, i.e., knowing when to be conservative and when not, according to situation. In contrast, nonnative speakers do not have such a control.

11. Similarities between Caribbean Spanish Speakers and L2 Learners

Linguists who have applied the Labovian model to the study of nonnative pronunciation (e.g., Tarone 1988) have noticed that the pronunciation of nonnative speakers shows variability, with one important aspect of it being that nonnatives may be phonologically conservative in informal situations but nonconservative in formal situations, contrary to what is expected of natives. Within the sociolinguistic model of second language acquisition, successful acquisition occurs when the learner gains control over the stylistic range.

Caribbean Spanish announcers who are capable of refraining totally from simplification in a formal situation resemble successful L2 learners who have attained mastery over the stylistic range. In contrast, the average Caribbean Spanish speaker, who shows nonconservative forms in formal situations and conservative forms in informal situations, resembles a second language learner who has not yet achieved mastery over style.

There is another significant way in which Caribbean Spanish speakers resemble second language learners with respect to the conservative mode: the control over the conservative mode of pronunciation increases with schooling. The frequency of conservative realizations is positively correlated with the number of years that an individual spends in school (see Alba 1990). However, education does not grant automatic control over the conservative mode of pronunciation, as seen in the fact that simplification is never reduced to zero at the highest level of schooling. The average educated speaker still shows no absolute control over the conservative mode. It is safe to assert that the average Caribbean speaker, even if highly educated, is unable to speak conservatively at will.

I would like to provide anecdotal support for this assertion from the experiences of several educated Caribbean Spanish-speaking individuals known to me who have been instructors of Spanish as an L2 in the United States. It is generally assumed in the pedagogy of L2 Spanish in the U.S. that students should be taught a conservative pronunciation without simplification. In addition, among educated speakers in the Spanish-speaking world, simplification carries low prestige and Caribbean Spanish-speaking instructors report being ridiculed by colleagues from conservative-speaking countries for engaging in simplification. This situation and the demands of pedagogy lead to attempts on the part of Caribbean Spanish-speaking instructors to modify their pronunciation in the classroom as well as around their colleagues. However, these instructors report that it is impossible for them to pronounce conservatively at all times, either before their students or their colleagues.

12. Control and Fossilization in L2

Recall the imaginary L2 learner of a language that allows codas in word internal position but disallows them word-finally. Recall also that the native language of the same learner does not allow codas at all, which is why the learner does not pronounce word-internal codas when s/he should, though sometimes s/he does pronounce them, i.e., her/his pronunciation of word-internal codas is variable. Recall how I presumed this learner to be bilectal and bound to switch grammars in midword, i.e., engage in phonological code-switching. Suppose now that this learner mispronounces coda consonants variably for the rest of her/his life. In my terms s/he continues to be bilectal in L2 and continues to switch between Lect 1 and Lect 2 in speech. In Labovian terms s/he presents a stable case of variability.

Consider now that the case of my imaginary L2 speaker is very much like that of the average L2 speaker in real life. Most L2 learners never gain absolute mastery over the phonology of their L2, retaining a foreign accent all their lives. The average L2 learner "fossilizes" with respect to phonology at some stage in his/her interlanguage development (see Selinker 1972). That is to say, in Labovian terms, L2 phonological variability becomes stable past a certain point in the development of the learner's interlanguage. What also becomes stable is the lack of control over style, which is perpetuated for as long as the learner speaks L2. Variability is then an effect of the lack of control on the part of L2 speakers. But what is it exactly that the average L2 speaker has no control over? The answer is that such a speaker has no control over the use or non-use of the different lects of L2 that s/he or she has internalized.

13. A Hypothesis on the Acquisition of Caribbean Spanish as a First Language

The parallelism between L2 learners and Caribbean Spanish speakers with respect to variability and control would seem to be limited by the fact that in the case of a monolingual Caribbean Spanish speaker the language is acquired natively. Think of a child acquiring a Caribbean Spanish dialect. S/he has no phonological system to start with, so we cannot talk about two lects, one being more like a native lect than the other. But suppose the same child acquires first the simplest, least marked system that is consistent with the data. Since consonant dropping is so common, the child constructs a phonology that has principles and procedures assuring that no coda consonants appear on the phonetic surface. The child's *first lect* allows no coda consonants. But just like a child growing up in a multilingual environment is capable of becoming multilingual, the Caribbean Spanish-speaking child is capable of becoming multilectal and indeed will become so. There are data to which the child is exposed that contradict the no-coda hypothesis, but rather than modifying the phonology of the first lect, the child constructs a second phonology that allows coda consonants. However, the principles and procedures of such a phonology require the types of simplification that I have subsumed under phonetic neutralization. Later, on the basis of the relatively infrequent incidence of conservative pronunciation, i.e., nonsimplification, the child constructs a third phonology that is the most marked with respect to coda consonants. It is over this grammar that the average Caribbean Spanish speaker has least control.

In other words, the average Caribbean Spanish speaker is at least trilectal, with respect to phonology, and has at least three autonomous phonological modules. The possibility is open that the three (or more) phonological modules are part of a grammar that has only one lexicon and single modules for morphology, syntax, and semantics.

If we look at Caribbean Spanish multilectalism within the framework of a rule-based phonology, we can say that lects differ in their rule inventories. For instance, the phonology of the most conservative lect contains neither Aspiration or Deletion, the phonology of the most radical lect contains Deletion but not Aspiration, and the phonology of the lect allowing simplified codas contains Aspiration but not Deletion. No lect contains both rules since they are incompatible. On the other hand if we look at multilectalism within the OT framework we can say that lects differ in the way that the same universal constraints are ranked. In the phonology of the most radical lect *Coda is ranked higher than other constraints that would allow coda consonants, while in the phonology of the most conservative lect *Coda is ranked lower than those other constraints. And in the phonology of the lect that shows simplified codas, constraints are ranked so as to allow for instance liquid lateralization and nasal velarization, which are disallowed by the ranking of constraints in the other lects.

14. Differential Ability among Multilectals

As happens among bilinguals who have acquired their two languages sequentially rather than simultaneously, there exists among multilectals different degrees of mastery over the system that was not acquired first. As is well known, a few bilinguals are balanced, showing 'native-like' control over L2. On the opposite side of the spectrum there are individuals who have only a rudimentary knowledge of their L2. In the middle of the spectrum is the average bilingual, who certainly does not show 'native-like' control over L2. Similarly, among multilectals, relatively few individuals show control over their most conservative lect. Among these would be the Caribbean Spanish radio and TV announcers who do not simplify coda consonants at all, at least not when they are before a microphone. It is a good question whether these individuals are so phonetically conservative when they are not at their jobs. In my experience, there are media announcers from Caribbean Spanish countries who also speak conservatively away from their jobs. Apparently, as can happen to bilinguals, there are multilectals who, either consciously or unconsciously, acquire greater control over the conservative lect at the expense of the more radical lects. Such individuals sound conservative at all times, regardless of situation. At the opposite end of the spectrum there must be individuals practically incapable of using the most conservative lect. In the middle are perhaps the most numerous group of multilectals. These are the ones who normally engage in phonological code-switching, regardless of situation, though they will use the conservative lect more in formal situations and the radical lects more in informal situations.

Phonological code-switching adequately describes all cases in which Caribbean Spanish speakers alternate between simplification and nonsimplification within the same utterance and even within the same word, as in, for example, [as.béh.to] for *asbesto*, 'asbestos'. Phonological code-switching is the normal mode of pronunciation for the average Caribbean Spanish speaker, and it is perhaps the basis for the internalization of competing grammars on the part of children.

15. Summary and Conclusions

I have proposed here that variability in Caribbean Spanish coda consonants is an effect of the uneven control that speakers have over at least three different phonological systems they have acquired. The most radical of these does not allow coda consonants, the most conservative does, and does not allow codas to be simplified. A third lect allows simplified coda consonants. The lack of control over the most conservative lect resembles that shown by bilinguals over their weaker language. During acquisition the Caribbean Spanish child is presented with conflicting information about codas, and first internalizes a system that is least marked with respect to codas (no codas) and lastly internalizes the most marked system (one with codas that cannot be simplified). Some speakers are able to gain control over the most conservative lect but most speakers never attain such control, engaging frequently in phonological code-switching and giving variability a 'stable' appearance.

References

Alba, Orlando (ed). 1982a. *El Español del Caribe: Ponencias del VI Simposio de Dialectología.* Santiago de los Caballeros: Departamento de Publicaciones de la Universidad Católica Madre y Maestra.

Alba, Orlando. 1982b. Función del acento en el proceso de elisión de la /s/ en la República Dominicana. In Alba 1982a, 15-26.

Alba, Orlando. 1990. *Variación Fonética y Diversidad Social en el Español Dominicano de Santiago.* Santiago de los Caballeros: Pontificia Universidad Católica Madre y Maestra.

Boyd-Bowman, Peter. 1975. A sample of Sixteenth Century 'Caribbean' Spanish Phonology. *Colloquium on Spanish and Portuguese Linguistics*, ed. William Milán, John J. Staczek, and Juan C. Zamora, 1-11. Washington, D.C: Georgetown University Press.

Cedergren, Henrietta J. 1973. *The interplay of Social and Linguistic Factors in Panama.* Doctoral dissertation, Cornell University.

Cedergren, Henrietta J. 1983. Sociolingüística. *Introducción a la Lingüística Actual*, ed. Humberto López Morales, 147-65. Madrid: Editorial Playor.

Chela Flores, Godsuno. 1986. Las teorías fonológicas y los dialectos del Caribe Hispánico. In Núñez Cedeño, Páez Urdaneta and Guitart, 21-30.

Fontanella de Weinberg, Beatriz. 1979. *Dinámica Social de un Cambio Lingüístico.* Ciudad de México: Universidad Nacional Autónoma de México.

Guitart, Jorge M. 1976. *Markedness and a Cuban Dialect of Spanish.* Washington, D.C.: Georgetown University Press.

Lafford, Barbara A. 1986. Valor diagnóstico social del uso de ciertas variantes de /s/ en el español de Cartagena, Colombia. In Núñez Cedeño, Páez Urdaneta, and Guitart, 53-74.

Labov, William. 1972. *Sociolinguistic Patterns.* Philadelphia: University of Pennsylvania Press.

Labov, William. 1994. *Principles of Linguistic Change: Volume I: Internal Factors.* Cambridge, MA: Blackwell Publishers.

Ma, Roxana, and Eleanor Herasimchuk. 1971. The linguistic dimensions of a bilingual neighborhood. *Bilingualism in the Barrio*, ed. Joshua Fishman, Robert L. Cooper and Roxana Ma, 347-464. Bloomington: Indiana University Press.

Morales-Front, Alfonso. 1994. *A Constraint-based Approach to Spanish Phonology.* Doctoral dissertation, University of Illinois, Urbana-Champaign.

Núñez Cedeño, Rafael. 1980. *La Fonología Moderna y el Español de Santo Domingo*. Santo Domingo: Editorial Taller.

Núñez Cedeño, Rafael, Iraset Páez Urdaneta and Jorge M. Guitart (eds.) 1986. *Estudios sobre la Fonología del Español del Caribe*. Caracas: Ediciones La Casa de Bello.

Poplack, Shana. 1979. *Function and Process in a Variable Phonology*. University of Pennsylvania dissertation.

Poplack, Shana. 1980. Sometimes I'll start a sentence in Spanish y termino en español: Toward a typology of code-switching. *Spanish in the United States: Sociolinguistic Aspects*, ed. Jon Amastae and Lucía Elías-Olivares, 230-63. Cambridge: Cambridge University Press.

Prince, Alan, and Paul Smolensky. 1993. *Optimality Theory: Constraint Interaction in Generative Grammar*. Rutgers University, New Brunswick and University of Colorado, Boulder, ms..

Rojas, Nelson. 1982. Sobre la semivocalización de las líquidas en el español cibaeño. In Alba 1982a, 273-87.

Selinker, Larry. 1972. Interlanguage. *International Review of Applied Linguistics* 10.209-31.

Silva Corvalán, Carmen. 1989. *Sociolingüística: Teoría y Análisis*. Madrid: Editorial Alhambra.

Zamora, Juan C., and Jorge M. Guitart. 1988. *Dialectología Hispanoamericana: Teoría, Descripción, Historia.* Salamanca: Publicaciones del Colegio de España, 2nd. edition.

16

There is no imperative paradigm in Spanish*

JAMES HARRIS

1 The basics

What is an imperative? Presumably, any physically possible human vocalization, or even a silent gesture, could serve pragmatically to command or request. However, grammarians and —more importantly— native speakers of Spanish single out a special set of verb forms as "imperatives", all of which permit or require second person reference. For example, all of the following expressions can have imperative illocutionary force, but only in (1c) is the verb a member of the special grammatical set of imperatives:[1]

(1) a. *¡sin mentir!*
without to-lie
'no lying!'

b. *quiero que digas la verdad*
I-want that you-say the truth
'I want you to tell the truth'

c. *di la verdad*
'tell the truth'

Each stem in the special imperative set manifests several different inflectional forms, yet —remarkably— there are no imperative paradigms in Spanish in the usual sense. That is, there is no set of inflectional affixes and/or internal modifications that characterize all and only the imperative forms of a given stem. Rather, the imperative forms of regular verbs in Spanish show a strange pattern of homophony with independently occurring indicative and subjunctive forms.

I show in (2) the imperative forms of the completely regular verb *pas-* 'pass' and in (3) those of the highly irregular verb *v-/vay-/fu-/Ø-* 'go':[2]

(2) a. affirmative; b. negative

	sing	plu	sing	plu
1pers	*	*pasemos*	*	*pasemos*
2pers	*pasa*	*(pasad)*	*pases*	*(paséis)*
3pers	*pase*	*pasen*	*pase*	*pasen*

(3) a. affirmative; b. negative

	sing	plu	sing	plu
1pers	*	*vamos*	*	*vayamos*
2pers	*ve*	*(id)*	*vayas*	*(vayáis)*
3pers	*vaya*	*vayan*	*vaya*	*vayan*

The first surprise in (2-3) is that there are different sets of forms for affirmative and negative imperatives, a characteristic of no other set of verb forms in Spanish. Further, hardly any "imperative" form is exclusively that; the pattern of homophonies with forms in nonimperative paradigms is shown in (4):

(4) a. affirmative; b. negative

	sing	plu	sing	plu
1pers	*	subjn/indic	*	subjn
2pers	indic/imper	(imper)	subjn	(subjn)
3pers	subjn	subjn	subjn	subjn

As shown, third person singular and plural affirmative and all negative imperative forms are identical to the corresponding (same person and number) present subjunctive forms. First person plural affirmative imperatives are also identical to the corresponding subjunctives, with the exception of *vamos*, which is identical to the corresponding present indicative form. For all imperatives with regular stems, the second person singular affirmative is identical to the third (not second!) person singular present indicative; in a handful of verbs (see below) these imperatives are special (distinct from 3pers sing pres indic). Finally, Iberian dialects have one exclusively imperative form in both regular and irregular verbs, namely, second person plural.

The upshot is that Latin American dialects appear to have no regular imperative form that is not borrowed from some other paradigm, and Iberian dialects have only one (2pers plu).[3]

All forms used as imperatives in Spanish have one thing in common, namely, second person semantic content.[4] This falls out as follows. For first person, singular imperatives do not exist, as indicated in (2-4); first person plural imperatives have only an "inclusive" interpretation, that is, as 'speaker(s) and addressee(s)'. The case of morphological second person was described just above. Semantically third person imperatives do not exist; forms occupying third person singular and plural slots are those used with nonintimate 'you', *usted* and *ustedes*, which are formally third person despite their second person reference.[5]

This study investigates what we can learn from this odd situation about the organization of grammar. I claim —following current purely syntactic studies— that certain main verbs in semantically imperative sentences are syntactically imperative while others are syntactically subjunctive; and furthermore —departing from all the current literature— that among the main verbs that are syntactically imperative, some are morphologically imperative while others are morphologically subjunctive. If these claims are correct, they provide empirical support for the theory of Distributed Morphology,[6] which provides the appropriate formal grammatical interface principles that allow a given verb form to be semantically and syntactically imperative but morphologically subjunctive, among other possibilities.

We turn now to the phenomenon of clitic placement, a particularly instructive aspect of the syntactic behavior of imperatives. Clitic behavior in fact constitutes the centerpiece of arguments concerning mood in the syntactic studies referred to below:[7]

		verb-clitic affirm imperative	clitic-verb other
(5)	a.	*Pasa-me-lo* Pass it to me	*Me-lo-pasa* (indic) He is/you are passing it to me
			No me-lo-pases (neg imper) Don't pass it to me
	b.	*Pasemos-lo* Let's pass it	*Quizá lo-pasemos* (subjunct) Maybe we'll pass it
			No lo-pasemos (neg imper) Let's not pass it
	c.	*Pase(n)-lo* Pass it	*Quizá lo-pase(n)* (subjunct) Maybe you'll (pl) pass it
			No lo-pase(n) (neg imper) Don't pass it

As shown, clitics are obligatorily postverbal in affirmative imperatives but obligatorily preverbal with all other person-marked hosts. The same is true in cases of clitic "climbing", as is illustrated in (6), where *lo* has climbed from its position as complement of *haciendo* 'doing' to be hosted by a higher verb:

	affirm imper	indic/subjunct/neg imper
(6)	*Sigue-lo haciendo (tú)* Keep on doing it	*Lo-sigue haciendo* He/you keep(s) on doing it
	Siga(n)-lo haciendo (usted/ustedes) Keep on doing it	*Quizá lo-siga(s/n) haciendo* Maybe he/you/they'll keep on doing it
		No lo-siga(s/n) haciendo Don't keep on doing it

The fact that the affirmative imperative verb forms in (5) and (6) are overtly identical to the horizontally paired indicatives, subjunctives, and negative imperatives shows that the surface position of clitics is not determined by the verb form itself but rather by whether the clause is semantically imperative or not and syntactically negative or not. There are two syntactic points to be retained from (5) and (6): (a) negative imperatives have the syntax of nonimperatives though the former are semantically no less imperative than affirmative imperatives; and (b) all affirmative imperatives have the same syntax, though some have imperative morphology and others have subjunctive morphology.[8]

I can now outline the main points of my proposals, which I articulate more fully in the following section.

(a) The fact that imperatives, regardless of their overt form, are syntactically distinct from other forms is attributed to a syntactic property that I notate as the abstract operator IMP. This syntactic property is present in all and only the sentences whose verbs exhibit the syntactic behavior of imperatives.

(b) Since negation is syntactic/semantic in nature, and since negative (semantic) imperatives have the syntax of nonimperatives as illustrated in (5-6), IMP occurs syntactically only in affirmative clauses. Semantic imperatives are syntactic subjunctives elsewhere.

(c) The verbs of most sentences with the operator IMP are systematically homophonous with subjunctives. This morphological generalization is stated as a readjustment rule in the Morphological Structure Component of the grammar that interprets the operator IMP as the morphological feature [imp] in second person syntactic imperatives and as [subj] in all other syntactic imperatives.

These points are summarized in (7) for quick reference:

(7)

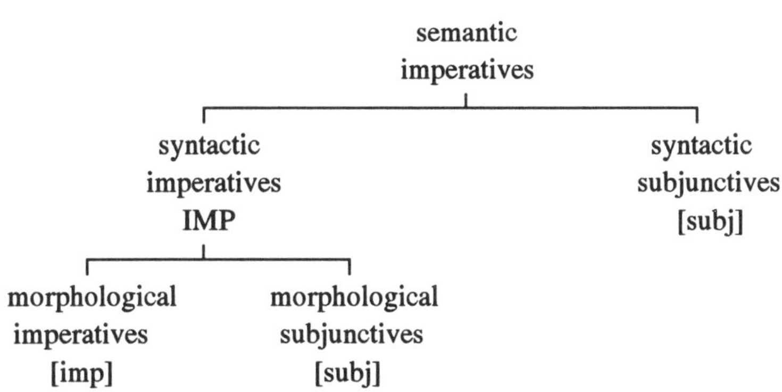

Again, all and only morphologically second person forms in syntactically/semantically affirmative clauses are morphological imperatives.[9] There are two sources of subjunctive morphology in the semantic class of imperatives: (a) the syntactic requirement that semantic imperatives be syntactic subjunctives in negative clauses; (b) the morphological requirement that syntactic imperatives (in affirmative clauses) be morphological subjunctives unless they are second person.

A further point: regular second person singular affirmative forms aren't literally "borrowed" from indicative paradigms; rather, these imperatives are homophonous with third person singular indicatives because these two sets of forms share two morphological properties: (a) they both employ the maximally unmarked or "default" verb stem and (b) neither manifests any overt phonological realization of person and number.

I will now make these proposals more precise.

2 Analysis

I adopt as theoretical framework a version of Distributed Morphology, which postulates an autonomous Morphological Structure Component (MS).[10] In familiar terms, MS is an input-output (interpretive) device that takes the output of the Syntactic Component as input and produces from it an output that is fed to the Phonological Component. In terms of Chomsky (1993, 1994), the MS component comes into operation on the Phonological Form (PF) branch of the computational system at the "spell-out" point. MS contains two ordered subcomponents: a set of rules and the Vocabulary. The rules subcomponent consists of operations that modify minimally the structure and content of syntactic output representations (which are simultaneously transmitted unaltered to Logical Form for semantic interpretation). The Vocabulary is a list of lexical entries from which phonological matrices and other information are copied onto morphological terminal nodes. Vocabulary insertion is strictly "feature filling"; that is, phonological and morphological information is added to the terminal nodes supplied by the MS rules but the features already present in them cannot be altered.

The terminal elements of syntax are specified for all and only the properties that play a role in syntax (e.g. syntactic category, case, tense, mood, aspect, number, etc., in Spanish, but not conjugation/declension class). The terminal elements of MS, on the other hand, are specified for the features essential to the phonological instantiation of morphemes (e.g. conjugation or declension class, case, tense, etc.). MS rules thus convert syntactic properties into morphologically relevant features where necessary, or remove them.

Returning to Spanish, Laka (1990) provides an explicit general theory of the syntax of negation, with copious data from Spanish, among other well-studied languages. Key proposals that have a bearing on syntactic properties of Spanish affirmative and negative sentences that are understood as imperatives are illustrated in (8):[11]

(8)

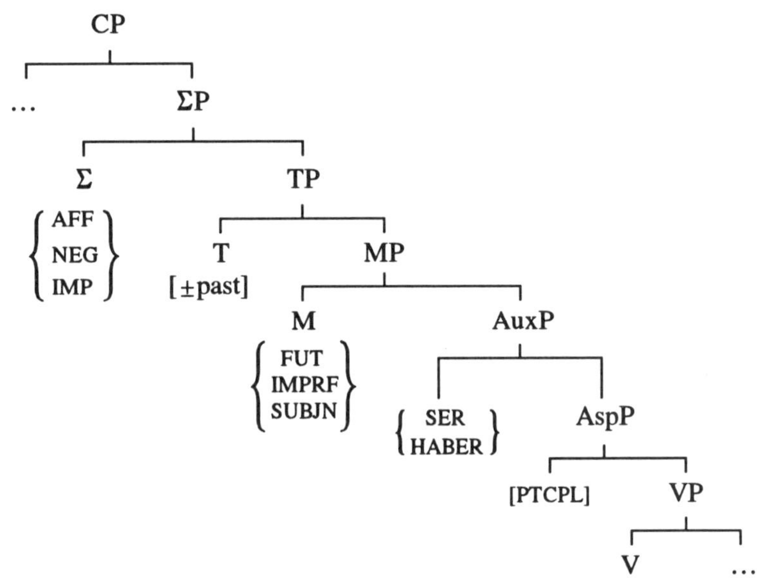

The functional category ΣP (Σ reminds us of "speech act") may be projected between CP and TP.[12] The possible heads of ΣP include the sentential operators AFF(irmation, *sí*), NEG(ation, *no*), and IMP(erative) in Spanish. The T(ense) feature [±past] is generated under the head of TP; and SUBJN=subjunctive is one of the possible heads of MP (M for Modal, or more traditionally, "mood"). Thus Laka's explanation for the syntactic incompatibility of IMP and negation —that is, the systematic exclusion of imperative verb forms in negative sentences understood as imperatives— is that IMP and NEG are mutually exclusive dependents of Σ. On the other hand, there is no incompatibility between NEG and SUBJN, which can be freely generated under Σ and M, respectively. Hence Spanish is free to employ the (present) subjunctive as the "irrealis" mode compatible with the semantics of negative imperative sentences.[13]

Other syntacticians, notably Rivero (1994a, 1994b, 1994c), dispute certain details of Laka's analysis but solidly agree on the basic premise that NEG and IMP are syntactically incompatible while NEG and SUBJN are not.[14]

Laka's and Rivero's analyses are instructive for what they omit as well as for what they include. In neither work do we find an explanation for the fact that only morphologically second person verb forms used in affirmative imperative sentences are morphologically imperative.[15] Laka does not mention this fact. Rivero calls imperatives other than second person "true imperatives in syntax" but "surrogate in morphology", and she leaves their explanation to "future research" (Rivero 1994c, sec. 2.5). These omissions are neither surprising nor fortuitous in purely syntactic investigation. To see why, take *ven* vs. *venga* as concrete examples. Both words mean 'come', and both are used in affirmative imperative speech acts directed to a singular 'you'; *ven* is the "intimate" form of address (subject *tú*) and *venga* is the "nonintimate/distant" form (subject *usted*). Morphologically, *ven* is imperative but *venga* is subjunctive. It is hardly clear why motivation for this choice of morphology should be sought in syntax. Nor can syntax be expected to explain why the corresponding "intimate" plurals have imperative morphology (*venid*) in Spain but subjunctive morphology (*vengan*) in Latin America. These are wrinkles in the morphology of the various dialects of Spanish, not in their syntax. I will now show how the relevant generalizations can be located naturally and straightforwardly in the MS component of their grammars.

For background I illustrate in (9) the operations of MS in the derivation of Spanish verb forms that are marked for person and number.[16] The example is first person plural *ra*-past subjunctive. In this form, derivational and inflectional constituents are phonologically instantiated with maximal transparency, that is, unobscured by morphological and/or phonological processes that make the constituency of certain other forms less obvious.

(9)

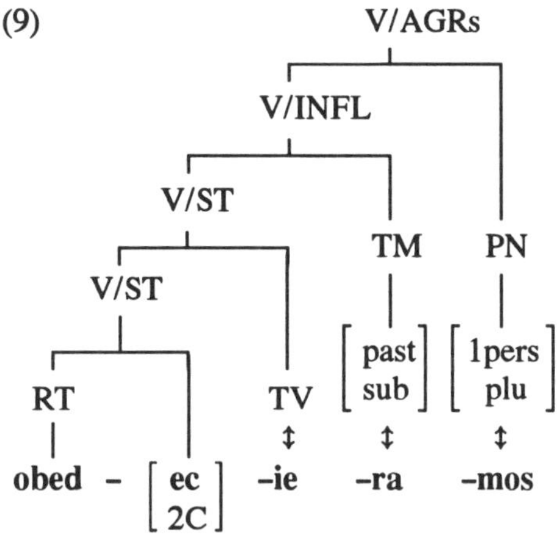

AGRs = subject agreement

INFL = inflection for tense, etc.

ST = stem

TM = tense/mood, PN = Φ-features

RT = root, TV = theme vowel

↕ = Vocabulary insertion

2C = second conjugation

Starting at the bottom left, the RT=root is a bound form with no determinable category (cf. *obed+iente* 'obedient'), from which the suffix *-ec* forms a verb stem that belongs to the so-called "second conjugation". Conjugation class is a lexical property of stems/suffixes that form verbs; together with other purely morphological information (e.g. finiteness, tense, mood in verbs; derivational suffixes in deverbal forms), conjugation class determines the TV=theme vowel (which may in fact be a diphthong, as shown, or zero in some cases) and certain other morphological properties. Conjugation class has no syntactic relevance: there is no syntactic behavior peculiar to one particular class. Thus the TV constituent in (9) is not present in syntactic representations; rather, it is generated in MS as a result of purely morphological wellformedness conditions.[17]

The inflectional morphemes in (9) are tense/mood and person/number.[18] Though Laka's proposed distribution of T(ense) and M(odal) or mood elements in (8) has been questioned,[19] let us suppose for the sake of argument that it is correct in relevant respects. It does not follow that there must be corresponding separate T and M constituents in morphological structure. One of the most securely established types of operations in the rules subcomponent of MS is "morphological fusion", whereby independent structurally adjacent syntactic terminals are combined into a single morphological terminal (the traditional "portmanteau" morpheme). This formal operation is illustrated schematically in (10):

(10) $$[T]\quad[M]\quad\Rightarrow\quad\begin{bmatrix}T\\M\end{bmatrix}$$

Rule (10) forms a single tense-mood terminal in MS out of two separate T and M morphemes inherited from syntax. Thus the morphological structure illustrated in (9), which is well motivated on purely morphological grounds, is in no way compromised by the fact that tense and mood clearly enjoy a degree of syntactic autonomy and are presumably separate functional projections in syntactic structure. The same is true, *mutatis mutandis*, of the ΣP projection and of person and number.

I now address the central fact that remains unaccounted for on Laka's and Rivero's accounts, namely, that even affirmative semantic/syntactic imperatives contain morphologically subjunctive verb forms in certain cases. Rule (11) is the key:

(11)
$$\text{IMP} \rightarrow \left\{ \begin{array}{ll} \text{[imp]} & /\_\_\ \text{[2pers]} \\ \text{[subj]} & \text{(default)} \end{array} \right\}$$

This MS readjustment rule interprets the abstract syntactic operator IMP of (8) —or its equivalent in any alternative syntactic story— as the morphological feature [imp] in second person forms and as morphological subjunctive elsewhere. After the application of (11) and Vocabulary insertion in MS, semantic/syntactic affirmative imperative forms like those shown in (2) fill out the hierarchical structure of (9) with the content illustrated in (12):

(12) a. Second person singular b. Second person plural

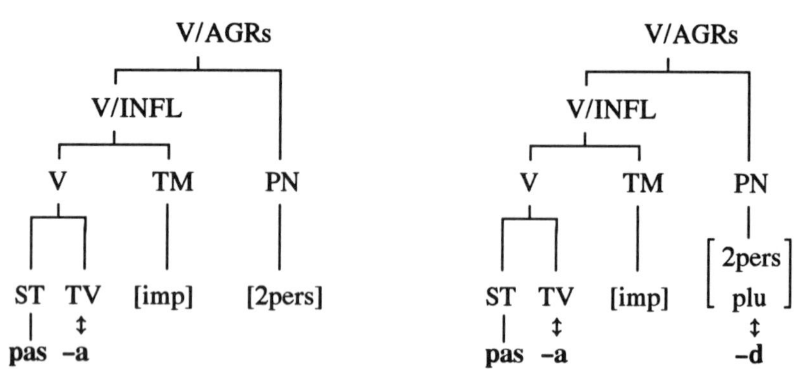

(12) (cont.)

c. Third person (plural)

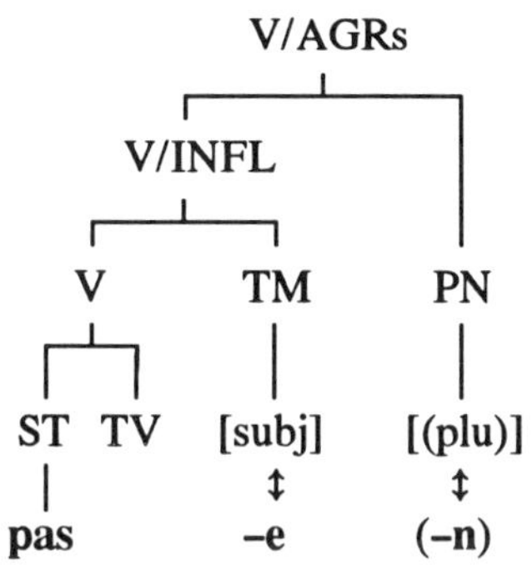

The stem *pas-* belongs to the unmarked ("first") conjugation, whose TV constituent is /a/ when realized overtly. Rule (11) introduces [imp] in (12a,b) and [subj] in (12c). Vocabulary insertion (see immediately below) provides a phonological realization for the TM terminal in (9) and (12c) but not in (12a,b).[20] Similarly, the Vocabulary inserts phonological material in the PN terminal in (9) and (12b) but not in (12a), and in (12c) iff the feature [plu] is present.

I give in (13) a suggestive fragment of the Vocabulary list in the MS of Spanish that contains entries relevant to (9) and (12). A few other entries are included to facilitate illustration of the principles that govern insertion.[21]

(13) Morphological Structure Component: Vocabulary

a. TV ↔ ie / [mC]__X (X = certain deriv. and infl. suffixes)[22]

$$\text{i} \;/\; \left\{ \begin{array}{l} \text{[mC]\_\_Y} \\ \text{[3C]\_\_} \end{array} \right\} \quad \text{(Y = other deriv. and infl. suffixes)}$$

e / [2C]__

a

(13) (cont.)

b. TM ↔ ra / [___, pst, subj]

{ a / [mC] [___, pst, imperf]
  ba [___, pst, imperf] }

{ a / [mC] [___, subj]
  e [___, subj] }

c. PN ↔ mos / [___, 1pers, plu]

{ d / [imp] [___, 2pers, plu]
  is [___, 2pers, plu] }

{ Ø / [imp] [___, 2pers]
  s [___, 2pers] }

n / [___, plu]

Vocabulary insertion obeys the condition that the indexical/contextual features of vocabulary items must be a subset of the features in terminal nodes. Vocabulary items are in fact characteristically underspecified with respect to terminal nodes, and their indexical/contextual features impose a partial ordering within sublists in accordance with the familiar universal Paninian principle of "more complex takes precedence".[23] For example, the second PN item *-d* of (13c) can be inserted into the PN terminal of (12b), where the contextual requirement of *-d* is met, but not into the PN node of (12a) because the indexical features {2pers, plu} of *-d* are not a subset of {2pers} in (12a). Moreover, although {2pers} is compatible with (technically, *not distinct from*) {2pers, plu}, the PN of (12b) cannot be phonological zero (the entry two lines below *-d*) since *-d* takes priority by Paninian disjunctivity, leaving zero for (12a). By the same token, the next-to-last PN entry *-s*, the realization of second person singular in the unmarked case, cannot be inserted in (12a), since the Paninian principle gives priority to the PN entry Ø, whose more complex contextual/indexical features are found in (12a).

Let us turn to the topic of irregular imperatives. The special cases in which the second person singular affirmative imperative does not coincide phonologically with the third person singular present indicative are shown in (14):

(14)	imper ≠	indic	(infinitive)	
	di	*dice*	*(decir)*	'say, tell'
	haz	*hace*	*(hacer)*	'do, make'
	pon	*pone*	*(poner)*	'put, place'
	sal	*sale*	*(salir)*	'leave, go out'
	sé	*es*	*(ser)*	'be'
	ten	*tiene*	*(tener)*	'have'
	val	*vale*	*(valer)*	'be valid/worth'
	ve	*va*	*(ir)*	'go'
	ven	*viene*	*(venir)*	'come'

These imperatives are special in two ways: (i) they all lack the TV of regular imperatives (among other forms), and (ii) many have other stem peculiarities, namely, *di* lacks the final consonant of the default stem *dic-*; *ten* and *ven* lack the diphthong that is expected when these stems are stressed (cf. indicative *tiéne* and *viéne*); in the case of *sé* 'be' and *ve* 'go',[24] these verbs exhibit such extensive stem suppletion that it is not obvious what imperative to expect.[25]

Neither type of anomaly is unique to irregular imperatives. Athematicity is seen in other regular and irregular verb forms, for example, participles such as *escri-to* 'written', *muer-to* 'died', *ro-to* 'broken', and so on. And there are athematic deverbal derived words, for example *describ-/descrip-ción* 'describe/description'.[26] In principle, athematicity can be formalized as adding cases like those shown in (15) to Vocabulary sublist (13a):

(15)	TV ↔ Ø /	X ___ [imp] [-plur]	(X=list of stems in (14))
		Y ___ [ptcpl]	(Y=list of stems)
		Z ___ W	(other cases)

Alternative formalizations of athematicity are possible, but I will not discuss them since nothing crucial to imperatives hangs on the choice.

The second anomaly in (14) is similarly only one instance of a widespread phenomenon. The deviant imperative stems *di*, *ve*, *sé*, *ten*, and *ven* are those of verbs that have other phonologically unpredictable, morphologically selected stem shapes in other contexts. Furthermore, many verbs with regular imperatives have similarly deviant stem shapes in other forms. For example, I list in (16a) all of the morphologically selected allomorphs of the stem of *decir*, and in (16b) all those of the stem of *saber* 'to know', which does not figure in (14):

(16)

a.

/di/ :	{ [imp] [-plu] / future, conditional }
/dig/ :	1pers sing pres indic, pres subjunct
/dix/ :	preterit, *ra* and *se* past subjunct
/dič/ :	participle
/dik/ :	certain derived forms
/dis/[27]	(default)

b.

/se/ :	1pers sing pres indic
/sep/ :	pres subjunct
/sup/ :	preterit, *ra* and *se* past subjunct
/sap/ :	certain derived forms
/sab/	(default)

The imperatives in (14) lead to no unique insight into the general phenomenon of stem allomorphy, which can be studied profitably only in a broader context. Having illustrated the phenomenon, I move on.

The negative counterparts of the forms in (14) are identical to the second person singular present subjunctive in each case (irregular, as it happens), as expected.

The plural counterparts are more instructive. Consider Iberian dialects first, where the parenthesized forms with the PN suffix *-d* illustrated in (2a) and (3a) are used as second person plural affirmative imperatives. The *-d* plural imperative of every verb in (14) is regular; indeed, no Spanish verb at all has an irregular *-d* plural imperative, whatever irregularity might be displayed elsewhere. For these forms, the default stem is always used, as in infinitives.[28] One technical consequence of this seemingly banal generalization deserves mention: the feature [-plural] (or some other formal rendition of "singular") must be used in (15) to block its application (in whatever formal interpretation) to plural imperatives. The point is interesting in that there are few if any other generalizations in Spanish in which singularity must be explicitly specified; that is, in which plurals rather than singulars systematically embody the unmarked/default case. Thus only weak motivation can be found in Spanish for abandoning the restrictive and hence *a priori* attractive claim that singularity is registered formally as absence of the privative feature [plural].[29]

In Latin American dialects, to whose morphology the feature cluster [2pers, pl] is totally alien,[30] *-d* plural imperative forms do not occur; the only plural imperatives are first and third person, which must be morphologically subjunctive. There is obviously no general prohibition against the combination of [2pers] and plurality in overt morphology —witness Iberian Spanish and many other languages. The complete absence of this combination in Latin American Spanish morphology is due to the MS "impoverishment" rule (17):[31]

(17) [2pers, pl]
↓
Ø

This rule deletes [2pers] in any morphological terminal that also contains the feature [pl], leaving no person feature at all. This is the formal counterpart of "third person", the default person in Spanish (and presumably universally). The fact that rule (17) operates in MS in Latin American —but not Iberian— Spanish is of paramount importance: rule (11), which governs the distribution of imperative and subjunctive morphology, refers to the feature [2pers]. The effect of rule (11) is modulated by the prior operation of rule (17): since (17) removes [2pers] in plurals, (11) automatically assigns imperative morphology to singular semantic/syntactic imperatives but subjunctive morphology to plurals. Consequently, in Latin American dialects, semantic/syntactic second person plural imperatives are not only morphologically third person but morphologically subjunctive as well. These results escape the range of purely syntactic analysis like Laka's and Rivero's, but they follow directly from a grammar in which (17) feeds (11).

3 Conclusion

The meticulous survey of traditionalist, structuralist, and generativist literature on the inflection of Spanish verb forms presented in Ambadiang (1993) should convince anyone that the problem with this complex set of data —like any other— is that it can be described in a vast number of ways that cannot be immediately rejected on *a priori* grounds. Discussion becomes interesting only when and to the extent that a restrictive theory, supported empirically by (perhaps few but compelling) crucial cases, radically reduces the available descriptive options. The present study focusses on the inflection of verb forms used in sentences understood by native speakers as imperatives, which is examined from the theoretical perspective of Distributed Morphology.[32]

The main challenge to a principled account of this material lies in the seemingly arbitrary pairing of imperative and subjunctive in syntax and morphology. For example, *sepa* 'know' and *vaya* 'go' (and their plurals *sepan* and *vayan*) are unmistakably subjunctive in their morphology; but these forms have a syntactic property unique to imperatives among person-marked forms, namely, they take enclitic pronouns in affirmative sentences understood as imperatives. This challenge is not seriously addressed in the syntactic literature with which I am familiar;[33] it is the central issue in the present study. Accordingly, rule (11), which determines the distribution of overt imperative and subjunctive morphology in imperative sentences, is the central formal mechanism. The total descriptive apparatus employed is minimal: only rule (11) and one or two Vocabulary items, depending on dialect, are required only for imperatives; all other devices are obviously needed in one guise or another for other aspects of Spanish derivational and inflectional morphology.

As we saw above, purely syntactic accounts of Spanish imperatives abruptly fall silent just when discussion of overt morphology would be appropriate. This is no accident; it is just at that point that well motivated syntactic proposals are no longer possible. In Distributed Morphology, on the other hand, as we also saw, it is possible to carry the story forward, essentially by calling a morphological spade a spade.

The inflectional characteristics of Spanish imperatives also present a challenge to affix-based lexicalist theories of Morphology,[34] in which word formation applies pre-syntactically and all information relevant to a word's syntax must appear in the root node of that word's constituent structure tree ("complex symbol") via "percolation" or else be provided by redundancy rules that supply unmarked feature values. It remains to be demonstrated by proponents of affix-based theories that these two devices are able to furnish the syntactically required features of Spanish verb forms in imperative sentences on the basis of their overt affixes, which, as described in detail above, are essentially either those of subjunctive forms or zero.

Notes

* With the conventional caveat, I gratefully acknowledge help of one kind or another from Morris Halle, Itziar Laka, Alec Marantz, Rolf Noyer, María-Luisa Rivero, and Esther Torrego.

1 I use standard orthography, which will not seriously mislead any reader, in all examples.

2 Second person plural forms are parenthesized in (2-3) and subsequently to indicate that they occur only in Iberian dialects. In Latin American dialects, there is no second person plural morphology at all —in verbs or any other forms. In these dialects, all syntactic/semantic second person plural items are realized morphologically as the corresponding third person (default) plural form. For example, *vieron su casa* (literally 'saw-plural unmarked-possessor house') is ambiguously 'they saw their house', 'they saw your (pl) house', 'you (pl) saw their house', or 'you saw your (pl) house' (and other, irrelevant readings). A formal account of this property of Latin American dialects is given in Harris (1994a).

3 See previous note.

4 Is this a semantic universal? Does an imperative illocutionary act entail addressing a second person at least implicitly?

5 See note 2 regarding second person plural. Singular *usted* has the same status in both Iberian and Latin American dialects: it means 'you (distant)' —as opposed to *tú* 'you (intimate)'— but is morphologically third person in every way.

6 See Noyer (1992) for background and Halle and Marantz (1993, 1994) for a detailed exposition of the theory of Distributed Morphology. Harris (1993, 1994a, 1994b, 1996) contain arguments from Catalan and Spanish in support of the theory.

7 For the reader's convenience I set off clitics with dashes not used in standard orthography (and I suppress written accent marks thereby rendered superfluous).

8 Further discussion here of the position of clitic pronouns in semantic/illocutionary imperatives in Spanish (the same in Iberian and Latin American dialects) would not be productive since there is no strong consensus in the recent literature regarding the syntax of Romance clitics in general (cf. Kayne 1991, Rivero 1994c, and references therein).

9 Reminder: these forms are second person singular (subject *tú*) and plural (subject *vosotros*, Spain only), and no others.

10 Cf. references in note 6.

11 One-bar level category symbols are omitted to save space.

12 T(ense)P(hrase) can be taken as equivalent to the IP of Pollock (1989) and much related work.

13 Past tense is excluded on semantic grounds in both affirmative and negative imperative sentences.

14 I take no stand on the relative merits of Laka's and Rivero's analyses where they diverge. The points on which they agree are important to the present discussion; their disagreements are not. I have chosen to illustrate Laka's claims in (8) because these particular details are useful below. Bosque (1994) and Zanuttini (1991) are useful works on negation in Romance languages.

15 Reminder: overt first and third person forms must be morphologically subjunctive, as shown in (2-7).

16 I intend to give a more detailed treatment of Spanish verb inflection in Harris (in preparation); for the moment I merely make certain general observations regarding the division of labor between syntax and morphology.

17 Harris (1996, section 3 and Appendix). Stems carry class information lexically as an abstract diacritic mark, not as phonological features of the TV (Harris 1973, 1975, 1980, 1987). For example, consider first conjugation *edi*[t]-/*edi*[t]*or* 'edit/editor' vs. third conjugation *emi*[t]-/*emi*[s]*or* 'emit/emitter'. The *t-s* alternation is associated with third, but not first, conjugation stems precisely in forms where there is no overt TV. These facts, like many others, make it clear that "conjugation class" does not coincide with or reduce to the phonological properties of some vowel, at any level of representation. I emphasize this point because it has not always been appreciated in the literature (cf. Ambadiang 1993, chapter 5).

18 Infinitives, participles, and gerunds lack these morphemes but have their own respective suffixes. This issue is discussed at length in Harris (1996).

19 Rivero (1994b, 1994c).

20 Alternatively, the formative *-e* in (12c) might be viewed as the realization of the first conjugation TV in the morphological environment /___[subj]. The issue is not crucial to present concerns; cf. Harris (in preparation).

21 *Caveat lector:* (13) is oversimplified for the sake of brevity. Harris (in preparation) gives more detail.

22 [mC] = "marked conjugation class", that is, second and third.

23 No ordering is imposed on entries that do not stand in a subset relation. For example, in (13b) neither of the first two TM entries *ra* and *a* is a proper subset of the other; thus they are not ordered, and need not be since they never compete for insertion into the same morphological terminal node. The same is true of the first two PN entries in (13c), etc.

24 The latter is accidentally homophonous with the expected imperative *ve* 'see'.

25 Phonetic zero for the stem of the imperative of 'go' (as in its infinitive *ir*) would entail that no audible form could be uttered!

26 Compare thematic *exhib-*/*exhib-i̱-ción* 'exhibit/exhibition'.

27 /diθ/ in many dialects in Spain. In all dialects, the stem vowel is /e/ when the immediately following syllable has [í].

28 Elementary textbooks use the infallible mnemonic "replace the *-r* of the infinitive with *-d*"; thus *decir*/*decid*, *hacer*/*haced*, *ir*/*id*, and so on.

29 Reformulations of the first case of (15) are of course logically possible —for example, requiring that [imp] not be followed by any phonological material in the word— but such alternatives lack independent motivation, apparently; that is, their only function would be to deny that [plural] can be a binary feature.

30 See note 2.

31 See the references in note 10 for discussion of morphological impoverishment in general and of the role of rule (17) in Spanish.

32 Distributed Morphology is restrictive in the first instance because it must meet clear boundary conditions set independently by syntax on the one hand and by phonology on the other, and in the second instance because it countenances the minimal range of formal mechanisms compatible with empirical necessity.

33 Rivero and Terzi (to appear), which reached me when the present study was already in press, is also silent on this matter.

34 DiSciullo and Williams (1987), Lieber (1980, 1991), Selkirk (1982), and Williams (1981).

References

Ambadiang, Théophile. 1993. *La morfología flexiva*. Madrid: Taurus Ediciones, Santillana, S.A.

Bosque, Ignacio. (to appear). La negación y el principio de las categorías vacías. *Nueva Revista de Filología Hispánica* 41.

Chomsky, Noam. 1993. A minimalist program for linguistic theory. *The View from Building 20*, ed. Kenneth Hale and S. Jay Keyser, 1-52. Cambridge, Mass.: MIT Press.

Chomsky, Noam. 1994. Bare phrase structure. *MIT Working Papers in Linguistics, Occasional Papers* 5. Cambridge, Mass.: MIT Department of Linguistics.

DiSciullo, Anna, and Edwin Williams. 1987. *On the Definition of Word*. Cambridge, Mass.: MIT Press.

Halle, Morris and Alec Marantz. 1993. Distributed morphology and the pieces of inflection. *The View from Building 20*, ed. Kenneth Hale and S. Jay Keyser, 111-76. Cambridge, Mass.: MIT Press.

Halle, Morris and Alec Marantz. 1994. Some key features of distributed morphology. *MIT Working Papers in Linguistics*, Vol. 21, ed. Andrew Carnie and Heidi Harley, 275-88. Cambridge, Mass.: MIT Department of Linguistics and Philosophy.

Harris, James. 1973. Las formas verbales de segunda persona plural y otras cuestiones de fonología y morfología. *Revista de Lingüística Teórica y Aplicada* 11.31-60.

Harris, James. 1975. Aspects of Spanish verb morphology. *Studies in Romance Linguistics*, ed. M. P. Hagiwara, 44-60. Ann Arbor: University of Michigan.

Harris, James. 1980. Lo morfológico en una gramática generativa; alternancias vocálicas en las formas verbales del español. *La estructura fónica de la lengua castellana*, ed. Jorge M. Guitart and Joaquín Roy, 141-99. Barcelona: Anagrama.

Harris, James. 1987. The accentual patterns of verb paradigms in Spanish. *Natural Language and Linguistic Theory* 5.61-90.

Harris, James. 1993. The morphology of Spanish clitics. *Evolution and Revolution in Linguistic Theory: Essays in Honor of Carlos Otero*, ed. Héctor Campos and Paula Kempchinsky, 168-197. Washington, DC: Georgetown University Press.

Harris, James. 1994a. The syntax-phonology mapping in Catalan and Spanish clitics. *MIT Working Papers in Linguistics*, Vol. 21, ed. Andrew Carnie and Heidi Harley, 321-53. Cambridge, Mass.: MIT Department of Linguistics and Philosophy.

Harris, James. 1994b. El traslado de pluralidad en los pronombres clíticos del español. Paper presented at *III Encuentro de Lingüística del Noroeste*, Universidad de Sonora, Hermosillo, México, 16-18 November, 1994.

Harris, James. 1996. The syntax and morphology of class marker suppression in Spanish. *Grammatical Theory and Romance Languages*, ed. Karen Zagona, 99-122. Amsterdam: Joh Benjamins.

Kayne, Richard. 1991. Romance clitics, verb movement and PRO. *Linguistic Inquiry* 22.647-86.

Laka, Itziar. 1990. *Negation in Syntax: on the Nature of Functional Categories and Projections*. Doctoral dissertation, MIT.

Lieber, Rochelle. 1980. *The Organization of the Lexicon*. Doctoral dissertation, MIT.

Lieber, Rochelle. 1991. On percolation. *Yearbook of Morphology* 2.95-138.

Noyer, Rolf. 1992. *Features, Positions, and Affixes in Autonomous Morphological Structure*. Doctoral dissertation, MIT.

Pollock, Jean-Yves. 1989. Verb movement, Universal Grammar, and the structure of IP. *Linguistic Inquiry 20*.365-424.

Rivero, María-Luisa. 1994a. Clause structure and V-movement in the languages of the Balkans. *Natural Language and Linguistic Theory* 12.63-120.

Rivero, María-Luisa. 1994b. On indirect questions, commands, and Spanish quotative **que**. *Linguistic Inquiry* 25.547-54.

Rivero, María-Luisa. 1994c. Negation, imperatives, and Wackernagel effects. *Rivista di Linguistica* 6.91-118.

Rivero, María-Luisa and Arhonto Terzi. (to appear). Imperatives, V-movement, and logical mood. *Journal of Linguistics* 31.

Selkirk, Elisabeth. 1982. *The Syntax of Words*. Cambridge, Mass.: MIT Press.

Zanuttini, Raffaella. 1991. *Syntactic Properties of Sentential Negation: a Comparative Study of Romance languages*. Doctoral dissertation, University of Pennsylvania.

17

Spanish word stress: the interaction of moras and minimality

JOHN M. LIPSKI

1 Introduction

1.1 Stress assignment has benefitted from the largest single share of the research paradigm on Spanish (phonology (cf. Halle and Vergnaud 1987; Harris 1983, 1991, 1992, forthcoming; Roca 1988, 1991; Den Os and Kager 1986 for representative analyses). Leaving aside technical details, the principal bones of contention are (i) the nature and extent of extrametricality (e.g. of consonants, vowels, entire syllables); (ii) the domain of stress assignment (word, derivational stem, etc.); (iii) quantity sensitivity or the lack thereof. Less frequently mentioned in the context of Spanish stress assignment, but crucial in order to situate Spanish phonology in a universal perspective, is (iv) the extent to which Spanish metrical structures can be accommodated in proposed universal typologies of foot-types and relative markedness of specific configurations.

1.2 The present remarks are offered as a contribution to the first, third, and fourth points. It will be claimed below that extrametricality in Spanish stress assignment plays a far lesser role than in most contemporary proposals, being limited in effect to final consonants in those consonant-final words in which stress does not fall on the final syllable. Under the assumption that extrametricality, like any other formal expression of exceptionality, should be eschewed whenever possible, this severe reduction of extrametricality is highly desirable. Quantity sensitivity also plays a more diminished role than suggested by recent studies. Spanish did not inherit the Latin Stress Rule directly, and syllable weight is relevant only in the last two syllables of a word. The interaction between metrical parameters and Spanish stress has changed significantly during the evolution from Classical Latin to modern Spanish. With very few exceptions, Spanish stress is based on (a slightly modified version of) the moraic trochee (Hayes 1985, Harris 1992, Dunlap 1991).

2 General principles of Spanish stress assignment

2.1 By nearly all modern accounts of Spanish stress assignment (cf. Harris 1983, 1991, 1992; Roca 1988, 1991), Spanish metrical feet are left-headed (trochaic), and iteratively formed from right (end of the word) to left, thus accounting for the predominant penultimate stress. In a recent modification, Harris (1992) postulates that word-final vowels are regularly extrametrical. Spanish vowel-final words with penultimate stress in effect end in a monosyllabic foot, for purposes of initial metrical assignment, while words with antepenultimate stress end in a bisyllabic (trochaic) foot. Within this framework, penultimate stress in vowel-final words follows from a stress-assigning algorithm which assigns main stress at the right edge of the metrical domain. Left-headed binary constituents (trochaic feet) are then formed from right to left, on the remaining material. Word-final inflectional consonants are extrametrical, accounting for regular penultimate stress in plurals such as *libros* 'books,' as well as in verb forms such as *hablas* 'speak (2s.),' *hablan* 'speak (3pl.),' etc. Other final consonants are not extrametrical, so that the basic rule assigning stress at the right edge of the metrical domain correctly assigns final stress. Consonant-final words with penultimate stress, as well as (vowel-final) words with antepenultimate stress are handled by an identical mechanism; such words are lexically-marked exceptions to the rule assigning stress to the right edge of the relevant domain. The only remaining part of the stress-assigning algorithm is the (iterative) formation of left-headed feet; hence a trochee will be formed at the right edge of the metrical domain. For a word ending in a metrical consonant, this results in penultimate stress, while in vowel-final words, antepenultimate stress results.

2.2 This use of extrametricality is significantly different from the proposals in Harris (1983), the seminal application of metrical theory to Spanish stress assignment. In the latter, antepenultimate stress was effected by making the **penultimate** syllable extrametrical. Since extrametricality is only possible at the periphery of the relevant domain, this requires the decomposition of the corresponding words into 'stem' and 'word-marker,' with extrametricality applying at the periphery of the former domain. Non-final stress in consonant-final words follows from the extrametricality of the final consonants involved. The 'dual' use of extrametricality has been challenged by several investigators, and was replaced in Harris (1992) by a single use of extrametricality (word-final vowels), which is peripheral by any definition.[1]

2.3 Harris (1992) avoids most of the needless complexities and exceptions of earlier theories. The model makes predictions of relative markedness of stress configurations which accord with both statistical distributions and native speakers' intuitions regarding 'typical' Spanish words. However, once quantity sensitivity is added to the model, some internal inconsistencies emerge, which motivate the search for additional refinements, and a more detailed study of quantity sensitivity in modern Spanish.

3 Quantity sensitivity in the models of Harris (1983, 1992)

3.1 Quantity sensitivity has been built into most generative models of Spanish stress assignment. Harris (1983) noted that words with antepenultimate stress could not have a branching rhyme in the penult: **teléfosno*, **átasca*, **retrópiolo*, etc. Most native speakers find such nonce forms to be ill-formed. Similarly, words ending in a falling diphthong must have final stress: *carey* 'tortoise' and *mamey* 'type of fruit' are allowed, but **cárey*, **mámey* are not. These observations were generalized to the notion that 'weak nodes cannot branch.' In a counterproposal, Roca (1988) cites the Spanish place name *Frómista*, and assimilated Anglicisms such as *Wáshington* and *Mánchester* in defense of the claim that quantity sensitivity no longer exists in Spanish, if it ever did (i.e. past the Late Latin stage). Harris (1992) is justifiably skeptical about the relevance of foreign borrowings in determining the phonological structure of Spanish, especially in view of the widespread rejection by native speakers of nonce-forms like **teléfosno*, **dinósauro*, etc. Moreover, the overwhelming statistical preference for antepenultimate stress with light penults, with at most 1-2 exceptions in any single dialect of Spanish, is powerful evidence in favor of quantity sensitivity; similar quantitative trends have been accepted as evidence of Obligatory Contour Principle constraints against co-occurrence in such languages as Arabic (e.g. McCarthy 1986) and Javanese (Mester (1986).

3.2 Harris (1992) brings the issue of Spanish quantity sensitivity within the framework of moraic phonology: stress is assigned to the penultimate (metrical) mora, if it is a syllable head. This revised claim brings both dividends and difficulties. Among the advantages is an instant account of the impossibility of proparoxytones with branching (bimoraic) penults: the first of the two morae of the penultimate syllable must receive stress, thus precluding stress assignment any further to the left. This also accounts for the impossibility of words like **cáricia*, with a rising diphthong in the final syllable. Words ending in a falling diphthong such as *carey* must receive final stress, since the final semivowel cannot be extrametrical. This explains the impossibility of penultimate (or antepenultimate) stress in words ending in a falling diphthong. The requirement that the stressable mora be a syllable head permits forms like *farmacéutico* 'pharmacist,' *vástago* 'scion,' and *náufrago* 'shipwrecked person.' Although Harris does not explicitly discuss this extension of bimoraicity (except to illustrate why the above words are allowed), this model allows both monomoraic and bimoraic syllables to serve as the head of a bisyllabic foot.

3.3 Consonant-final words with penultimate stress, such as *túnel* 'tunnel,' *cóndor* 'condor,' etc. are handled by a subtle interpretation of the Spanish multi-stage syllabification algorithm (cf. Harris 1989a). It is claimed, in effect, that these final consonants are not syllabified at the time the initial stress-assigning algorithm is applied. However, if all final consonants are unsyllabified at the time the original stress-assigning algorithm applies (and Harris 1992: 37 is explicit in this regard: 'word-final consonants cannot make branching rhymes for (lexical) stress rules'), then there is no ready accounting for final stress, e.g. in *papel* 'paper,' *disfraz* 'disguise,' *cortés* 'courteous,' etc. For these words, Harris (1992: 36) only makes oblique reference to the original proposal, that of assigning stress to the right edge of the metrical domain. Similarly, if the stressing of the penultimate metrical mora is a rule rather than a tendency (or a permitted combination), then there is no accounting for penultimate stress in vowel-final words (which, in this model, end in an extrametrical vowel, hence mora) that contain a light penult. Such stress, rather than being maximally unmarked (as in the original proposal), is somehow exceptional, in need of additional justification. In Harris (1992)'s account of quantity sensitivity, the left-headed bimoraic requirement represents a window or filter, rather than a template which must be exactly filled. At the same time, while correctly accounting for certain excluded combinations, the introduction of quantity sensitivity complicates the theory, in previously straightforward cases of penultimate stress in vowel-final words and final stress in consonant-final words.

4 Trochaic feet within a moraic framework

4.1 At the outset of research into the metrical structures involved in stress assignment, it was assumed that complete symmetry obtained between right-headed (iambic) and left-headed (trochaic) feet, in both quantity-sensitive and quantity-insensitive systems. Hayes (1985) demonstrated that iambic systems are more frequently quantity-sensitive, often exhibiting vowel lengthening under stress, while trochaic systems are more frequently quantity-insensitive, with intensity rather than length being the primary concomitant of stress. From this standpoint, Spanish might be predicted to be quantity-insensitive, both because of its clearly trochaic rhythm and since noticeable lengthening of stressed vowels does not normally occur. Among quantity-sensitive feet, the combination [L, H] or [μ [$\mu\mu$]] is preferred for iambic feet, while the combination [L L] or [μ μ] is the preferred trochaic type. Hayes (1985), Prince (1992), and others have proposed the '(bi)moraic trochee' for quantity-sensitive systems. This template can be satisfied either by a bisyllabic foot [[μ] μ], or by a single heavy syllable $[\mu\mu]_\sigma$. The strongest versions (e.g. McCarthy and Prince 1986), categorically disallow a trochaic foot of the form [[$\mu\mu$] μ], i.e. a heavy syllable followed by a light syllable. Other versions (e.g. Prince 1992) propose that [H, L] trochees, while not categorically excluded, are highly marked and disfavored.

4.2 Spanish stress assignment is consistent with the moraic trochee, as already adumbrated by Harris (1992) and Dunlap (1991). However, the bimoraic trochee is not compatible with extrametricality of final vowels and the unsyllabified status of final consonants: the existence of words like *casa* 'house,' *mañana* 'morning,' etc. (presumably with a single metrical mora) together with words like *casta* 'caste,' *carta* 'letter,' etc. would imply that monomoraic feet are not only tolerated in Spanish, but are even preferred. This goes against the comparative evidence analyzed by Prince (1992), who ranks monomoraic [L] feet at the very bottom of the scale of acceptability. If final vowels are extrametrical, then Spanish would allow monomoraic feet without restrictions, and a statistical sweep of the Spanish lexicon would probably reveal that [μ] or [L] feet are at least as frequent as [[$\mu\mu$]] or [H] feet.

5 Secondary accents and quantity sensitivity in Spanish

5.1 The issue of quantity sensitivity in Spanish is also tied to the assignment of secondary stresses. Harris (1983) offered a model in which primary and secondary stresses are assigned via a single algorithm, essentially creating trochaic feet from right to left (but with the apparently unconstrained option of having 'ternary' or dactylic feet word-internally, possibly through stress retraction). Many immediate responses to Harris (1983) made similar claims. Roca (1986) offered evidence that secondary stress in Spanish is assigned after primary stress, in a separate process. In turn, Harris (1992), modifying the model of Halle and Vergnaud (1987), allows for erasure of the secondary stresses originally created as part of the alternating trochaic grid structure; the secondary stresses which emerge on the surface presumably are derived as per Roca (1986).

5.2 Harris (1992) establishes quantity sensitivity as a criterion for the assignment of primary stress, but the remainder of his stress-assigning algorithm only refers to the creation of binary trochaic feet from right to left. Implicitly, quantity sensitivity is shown to be crucial only in the rightmost foot. Although Spanish does exhibit various patterns of secondary stress, these are of an alternating sort (with a possible alternative of simply giving a secondary stress to the word-initial syllable in polysyllabic words). Nothing in the observed patterns of Spanish secondary stress suggests a correlation with syllabic quantity. At the same time, the alternating non-final trochees formed in the models of e.g. Harris (1983, 1992), Halle and Vergnaud (1987), etc. are subsequently erased or conflated, thus making the entire question of quantity sensitivity of non-final feet for stress assignment a moot point.

5.3 Irrespective of whether or not secondary stresses in Spanish are formed as part of the initial iterative foot formation process, a look at the Spanish lexicon reveals that reducing the issue of quantity sensitivity to a statement such as 'weak nodes cannot branch' (e.g. Harris 1983) only accounts for penultimate and final syllables. The well-formedness of hundreds of words with branching rhymes in pretonic syllables makes it clear that more is at stake than a simple yes-no answer to the question of quantity sensitivity. Assuming right-to-left iterative formation of trochaic feet, branching rhymes in non-final feet would be found both as the head of non-terminal feet (e.g. *astronómico* 'astronomical,' *artificio* 'artifice'), and as non-heads (e.g. *Anastasio*, *envoltura* 'wrapping'). Harris (1983: 122) offers the initial suggestion that quantity sensitivity only affects strong feet (i.e. dominated by the strong node of the word tree), and cites Hayes (1980) as a theoretical antecedent. However, nothing in Hayes' work directly corresponds to the notion that quantity sensitivity is something which is turned 'on' and 'off' within the expanse of a single word.[2]

5.4 In addition to the existence of branching rhymes in what would be the weak branch of non-final trochaic feet, several Spanish dialects exhibit compensatory lengthening phenomena which suggest that iterative foot formation is not part of the basic stress-assigning algorithm. One case involves compensatory vowel lengthening in Cuban Spanish, following loss of word-internal preconsonantal /s/ (Hammond 1986; Núñez Cedeño 1987, 1988a, 1989). Assuming that final vowels are not extrametrical, if the foot $[[\mu\mu]\ \mu]$ or [H L] were less 'harmonic' than the bimoraic trochee [L L], vocalic CL should be highly disfavored in words like *bosque* [bo:ke] 'forest,' since complete elision of the /s/ should increase the harmonicity of the foot. Contrary to these expectations, vocalic CL regularly occurs in such words.[3] Moreover, if foot formation were iterative, words such as *talismán* and *protestante* would contain a recessive bisyllabic trochee, with a heavy second syllable: $[\mu,\ \mu\mu]$. This is highly disfavored as a trochee; indeed, Prince 1992 and others strictly exclude trochees of the form [L, H]. Even if it were accepted, for purposes of argument, that Spanish allows such 'backwards' trochees, since such combinations are highly disharmonic, vocalic CL should seldom or never occur following loss of /s/ in such words. Quite to the contrary, loss of the coda consonant and concomitant loss of the associated mora would have a harmonic effect, and should be favored. However, this prediction is not borne out, and CL freely occurs in these words.[4]

5.5 A closely related phenomenon is hypercorrect /s/-insertion in vernacular Dominican Spanish (cf. Núñez Cedeño 1986, 1988b). Essentially, epenthetic /s/ is inserted as a coda consonant in open syllables, the same environment in which syllable-final /s/ is routinely lost in Dominican Spanish. The hypercorrect /s/ can appear in any coda position, except in the penultimate syllable of proparoxytones: **párpasdo*, **teléfosno*, etc. It also is barred from syllables which are already bimoraic: **harsto*, **cansto*, except word-finally, where, e.g. *flors* < *flor* 'flower' can occur.[5] The epenthetic /s/ is frequent in the stressed syllable of paroxytones, which, if Spanish metrical structures were quantity-sensitive, would represent the disharmonic shift [L L] > [H L]: *isno* < *ino* < *himno* 'hymn,' *dipusta* < *diputa* < *disputa* 'dispute,' *yusca* < *yuca* 'yucca,' etc.[6] Moreover, if Spanish words contained iterative trochaic feet, epenthetic /s/ in the second syllable of words like *invistado* < *invitado* 'guest,' *afestado* < *afetado* < *afectado* 'affected,' would strongly contravene the Weak Branching Constraint by turning a $[[\mu]\ \mu]$ trochee into $[[\mu]\ \mu\mu]$. Like Cuban vocalic CL, Dominican /s/-epenthesis suggests that iterative foot formation does not occur in Spanish.

5.6 Non-iterativity of foot formation is compatible with parameterized models of stress assignment (e.g. Hayes 1985, 1987; Hammond MS; Crowhurst 1992). Other Spanish dialects exhibit harmony processes conditioned by the existence of a single foot. Certain Montañés/Bable dialects studied by Hualde (1989b) exhibit harmony processes which extend from the final vowel up to and including the stressed vowel. In other dialects, harmony only obtains between a final vowel and the stressed vowel; this process targets the head of the metrical foot. In this dialect cluster, harmony to the left of the stressed vowel is sporadic or nonexistent, regardless of the pattern of secondary accents. This suggests that only a single metrical foot is created, which in turn channels the effects of [-ATR] and height harmony.

Eastern Andalusian dialects exhibit vowel harmony (cf. Lieber 1987, Zubizarreta 1979), in which [-ATR] spreads leftwards from a final vowel, originally following the loss of a final consonant (typically /s/). In the great majority of instances, spreading of [-ATR] does not spread to the left of the tonic vowel, once more indicating that only a single metrical foot is in place, through which the harmonic process operates.

6 Reassessing Spanish quantity-sensitivity: minimality parameters

6.1 Hayes (1985, 1992), McCarthy and Prince (1986), Prince (1992), etc. claim that the only type of trochaic foot possible in quantity-sensitive systems is the bimoraic trochee $[\mu\ \mu]$. This template can be satisfied either by a bisyllabic foot $[[\mu]\ \mu]$, or by a single heavy syllable $[\mu\mu]_\sigma$. These same theories disallow $[[\mu\mu]\ \mu]$ trochees. Spanish, however, provides large numbers of paroxytones with heavy penults, filling a trimoraic [[$\mu\mu$] μ] template; dialectal data which manipulate the moraic structure show no signs of eliminating this configuration in favor of a more 'harmonic' bimoraic trochee. Moreover, Spanish proparoxytones with heavy stressed syllables (e.g. *álgebra*) arguably include as many as four morae in a single foot. The discrepancies between the Spanish data (and Spanish has never been regarded as an 'exotic' language) and well-reasoned foot typologies require additional inquiry. The details of Spanish foot formation are best handled by parameterizing the requirement that head and foot templates be completely filled.

6.2 Crowhurst (1992) establishes a repertoire of universally available foot templates, in which headedness is not yet assigned. One of the universal templates is [$\mu\mu$ μ], which generates all Spanish (primary stress) feet. In quantity-sensitive systems, the $Head_{min}$ parameter can be set either to **Off** (requiring a bimoraic head) or **On** (allowing a monomoraic head). Similarly, the $Foot_{min}$ parameter can be set to **Off** (requiring a minimally bimoraic foot) or **On** (allowing a monomoraic foot).

In Spanish, $Head_{min}$ is normally set to **On**, allowing monomoraic heads such as *cama* 'bed,' *casa* 'house.' However, $Foot_{min}$ is set to **Off**, requiring a minimally bimoraic foot, which can be satisfied either by a single heavy syllable [$\mu\mu$] (e.g. *papel*, *carey*), or via penultimate stress, if the final syllable is light (*casa*, *carta* 'letter'). The full range of Spanish feet is: [$\mu\mu$], [[μ] μ] and [[$\mu\mu$] μ]. The parametric settings are:

(1)

Template:	[$\mu\mu$ μ]
Directionality:	right to left
Headedness:	left
Iterativity:	non-iterative
Minimal structure:	
$Foot_{min}$:	off
$Head_{min}$:	on

We also assume that foot construction is **maximally binary**.[7]

6.3 The proposed model generates all and only the set of Spanish stress patterns. Words ending in a final heavy syllable (e.g., falling diphthong, or non-inflectional consonant) fully fill the bimoraic foot template. The first step is association of the template to the right edge of the metrical domain:

(2) ***Associate template***:

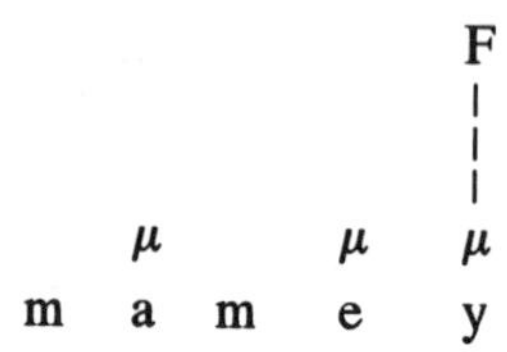

The next step is maximization of the foot. Since in Spanish the $Foot_{min}$ parameter is set to **Off**, a minimal foot must contain at least two morae (in words ending in a semivowel or consonant, the preceding mora must be incorporated in any case, in order to ensure the presence of a syllable head):

(3) ***Maximize foot***:

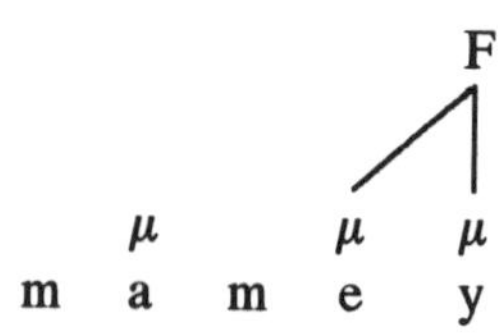

The final step is projection of the head. Since Spanish sets the $Head_{min}$ parameter to **On**, a head can consist of a single mora. However, in words ending in a heavy syllable, with the syllable head coming first, both morae are incorporated into the head:

(4) ***Project head***:

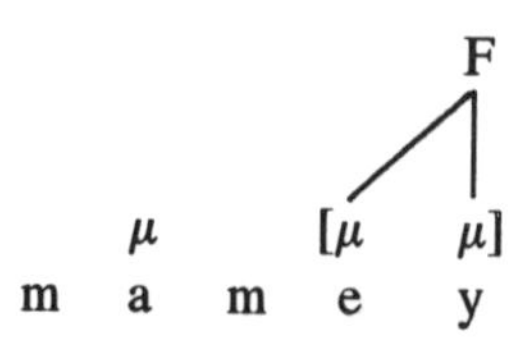

Penultimate stress is impossible in such words, since the foot template is fully satisfied by taking only the final two morae into account. Penultimate stress would result in a branching recessive node, which is universally prohibited. Words like *túnel*, *cóndor*, etc. contain an extrametrical final consonant. The impossibility of **cárey*, **mámey*, etc. is presumably due to the fact that the final segment is **semivocalic** rather than consonantal. This is an idiosyncrasy of Spanish grammar, and does not follow directly from universal phonological principles.

6.4 The derivation of penultimate stress in words ending in a vowel or extrametrical consonant is straightforward. Taking as an example *bola* 'ball,' the first step is association of the template to the right edge of the word:

(5) ***Associate template***:

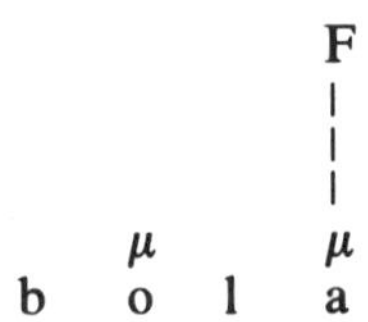

Since this single mora does not satisfy the minimally bimoraic requirement of $Foot_{min}$ = **Off**, foot maximization will incorporate the preceding mora:

(6) ***Maximize foot***:

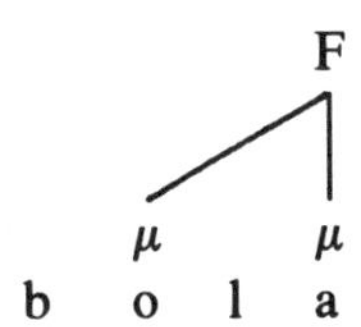

Finally, since $Head_{min}$ = **On** allows for a monomoraic head, projection of the head will target the penultimate syllable:

(7) ***Project head***:

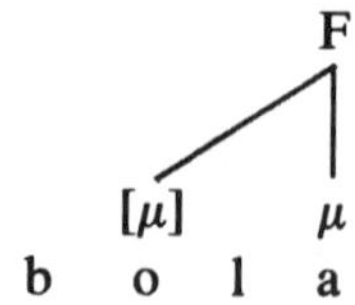

If the penultimate syllable is bimoraic (heavy), as in *basta* 'suffice (3s.),' the derivation proceeds in the same fashion. Association of the template will target the final mora; foot maximization will incorporate not only the preceding mora (associated to an element in the coda), but also the accompanying syllable head; head projection will embrace both morae of the penultimate syllable:

(8)

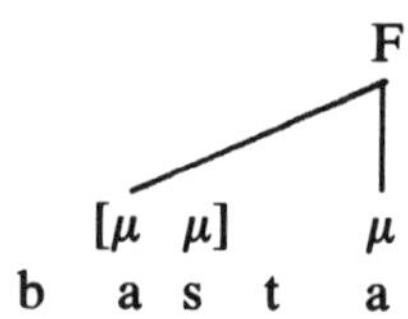

6.5 Assuming the minimality parameter settings given above, antepenultimate stress cannot be generated at all. The bimoraicity required by the Spanish foot template will be exhaustively satisfied by the final syllable of words ending in a heavy syllable, and by the penultimate syllable of vowel-final words. Harris (1983, 1992) and others have generated Spanish antepenultimate stress through liberal use of extrametricality. However, within the parameterized minimality framework, antepenultimate stress, which by any account must carry some sort of lexical mark, involves the parameter setting $Head_{min}$ = **Off**. This requires a bimoraic head. It is thus not coincidental that antepenultimate stress is incompatible with heavy penultimate or final syllables (modulo the occasional extrametricality of final consonants, as in *régimen*). Antepenultimate stress can be generated only in words of three or more syllables which (i) bear the lexically altered parameter setting $Head_{min}$ = **Off**, and (ii) have light syllables in both the penult and final positions. Consider a typical derivation (*teléfono* 'telephone'):

(9) ***Associate template*:**

***Maximize foot*:**

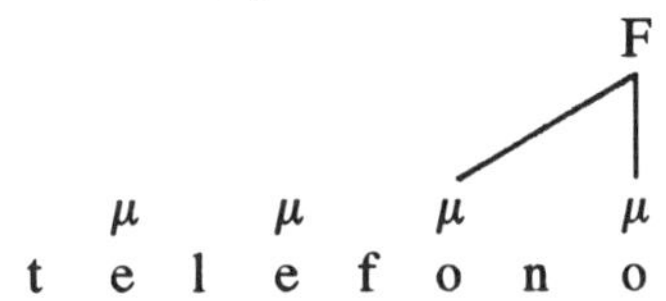

***Project head*:**

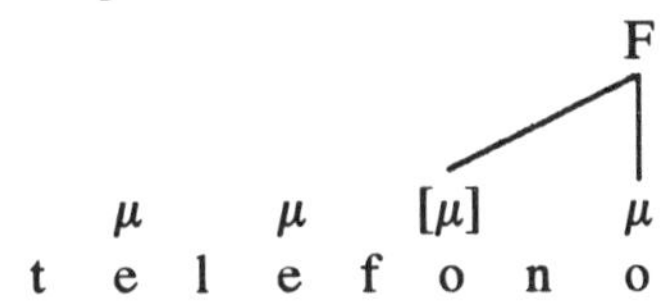

***Satisfy head*:**

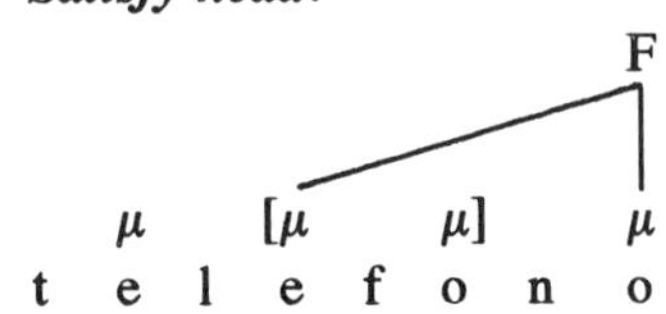

Finally, proparoxytones with heavy antepenults (e.g. *vástago*, *álgebra*, etc.) receive a similar derivation. The template is originally associated to the final mora; projection of the head incorporates the penultimate vowel, but satisfaction of the bimoraicity requirement for the head requires incorporation of an additional mora. However, the immediately preceding mora is a coda consonant, so the syllable head must also be incorporated, giving a foot with four morae:

(10)

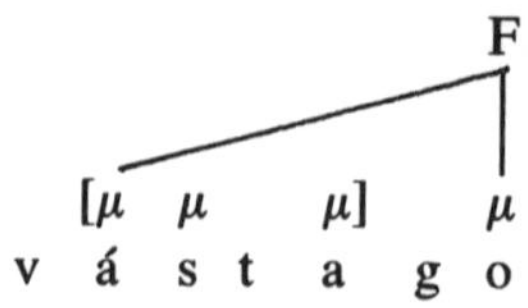

This is not an indictment of the trimoraic [$\mu\mu$ μ] template, since the incorporation of the coda consonant and its accompanying mora is required by the principles of prosodic licensing (e.g. Itô 1986). The mora associated with the coda consonant cannot be licensed except by a syllable node, which in turn requires the presence of a syllable head, thereby necessitating the presence of the immediately preceding vowel. Halle, O'Neil and Vergnaud (1993: 530) observe that 'Stressable elements are the head vowels of syllables *and the immediately following rhyme segment*, if any' [emphasis in original]. Dunlap (1991: 19) calls this condition the Head Prominence Relation: 'If stress is assigned anywhere in a syllable, it will be realized on the syllable head.' In the general case, this exoneration holds of all mora-counting templates, as part of the condition of 'prosodic integrity' (cf. Crowhurst 1992: 26 and the references therein), a prohibition against splitting a syllable between two different feet.

6.6 The most marked set of Spanish words susceptible to a stress-assigning algorithm are non-verbal forms ending in a stressed vowel: *rubí* 'ruby,' *café* 'coffee,' *maní* 'peanut,' *dominó* 'domino(es),' etc. All such words are of extra-Romance origin, and exhibit considerable variability in plural formation. Grammatical treatises usually decree that the plural is formed by adding *-es*, except for *mamá*, *papá*, *sofá* and words ending in stressed *-é*. In practice, variant forms are more frequently heard, especially in vernacular speech; typical alternatives include zero plurals, plurals in *-s*, and plurals in *-ses* (e.g. *cafeses* '[cups of] coffee,' *manises* 'peanuts'). In the present model, such words are lexically marked for $Foot_{min}$ = **On**, allowing a monomoraic foot, which together with the usual Spanish setting of $Head_{min}$ = **On** ensures that stress falls on the final vowel. Plurals in *-es* and *-ses* have the effect of creating a bimoraic foot. In Harris (1992: 44), the exceptionality of these forms is handled by lexically marking them so that the final vowel is not extrametrical. Harris (1983) had noted that the stems of such words end in a vowel, and contain no class marker; it may be, as suggested by Harris (1992) and others, that exceptional stress is at least partially predictable based on this morphological peculiarity.

7 Historical excursus: stress and quantity sensitivity in Classical Latin

7.1 Modern Spanish stress is often described as a direct heir of the (Classical) Latin Stress Rule. However, the differences between Spanish and Latin stress assignment are as significant as the similarities; modern Spanish stress assignment cannot be an unbroken continuation of Latin patterns. Quantity sensitivity disappeared in late Latin, and played no role in Old Spanish stress assignment. At some point during the medieval period, quantity sensitivity again came to characterize Spanish stress assignment, as a result of several independent sound shifts in the language. Quantity sensitivity in modern Spanish is considerably less evident than it was in Latin, and a combination of foreign borrowings and ongoing sound changes may once more return Spanish to the ranks of languages in which stress assignment is quantity-insensitive. It is therefore instructive to trace the rise and fall of quantity sensitivity in the transition from Latin to modern Spanish, as this enterprise promises to shed some light on the interaction between parametric settings and learnability.

7.2 Hayes (1987: 277) cites Latin stress as a typical example of a non-iterative moraic trochee, although Hayes (1985) had come close to suggesting that all trochaic stress systems are quantity-insensitive. Prince (1992), while showing little affinity for [H L] ($[[\mu\mu]\ \mu]$) trochees, acknowledges the widespread existence of such feet in Latin proparoxytones (assuming extrametricality of final syllables in Latin). Prince accounts for the Latin Stress Rule (which produces, e.g. *ín.te.<ger>* vs. *per.fec.<to>*) as exhibiting the harmonic preference of [H L] feet over [L]. If stress were to fall on the penultimate syllable of *integer*, a monomoraic foot would result. Presumably, *spá.tu.<la>*, with its [L L] foot structure, would be harmonically preferable to proparoxytones with closed stressed syllables; however, Prince cites no evidence of phonological processes in Latin which might facilitate the change from [H L] to [L L].

7.3 In the parametric minimality framework, Latin stress assignment shared with modern Spanish the use of a $[\mu\mu\ \mu]$ template, as well as the parametric settings $Foot_{min}$ = **Off**, $Head_{min}$ = **On**. These settings require a minimally bimoraic foot, while allowing a monomoraic head. Since final syllables were extrametrical, template satisfaction began with the penultimate syllable. If this syllable was heavy (bimoraic), both the head and the foot requirements were satisfied, and a monosyllabic bimoraic trochee was formed. Modulo extrametricality, this is the same process as in modern Spanish words ending in a heavy syllable (e.g. *mamey*, *papel*). Latin words with a light penult required incorporation of the preceding syllable head to satisfy the bimoraic foot condition. This is the same configuration that occurs in modern Spanish vowel-final words. In Latin, since the final syllable was extrametrical, this automatically resulted in antepenultimate stress. If the antepenult was also light, a bimoraic $[[\mu]\ \mu]$ foot resulted.[8] If the antepenult was heavy, the same requirement of prosodic integrity required incorporation of the syllable head (in the case of a syllable with a coda consonant), or the entire prosodic structure of the syllable head (in the case of a long vowel). In these cases, a $[[\mu\mu]\ \mu]$ foot resulted.[9] Consider the derivation of a word like *spatula*:

(11) ***Associate template***:

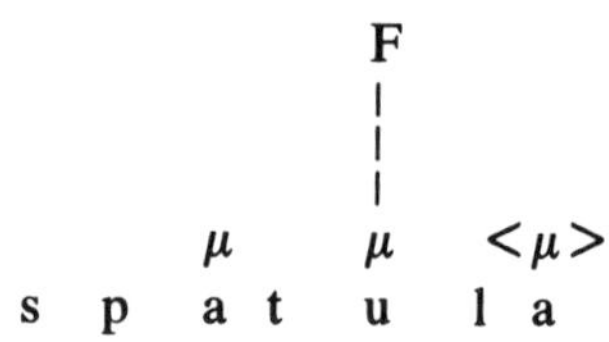

Maximize foot:

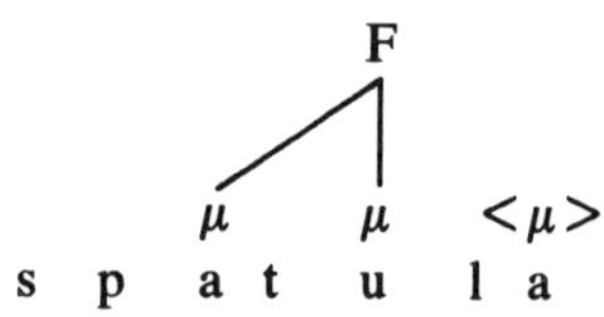

Project head:

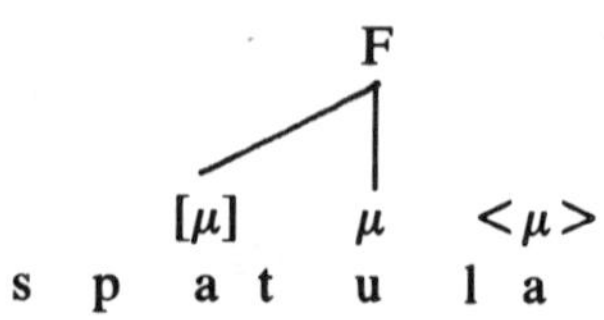

In words with a light penult and heavy antepenult (*integer*), a similar derivation ensues:

(12) ***Associate template***:

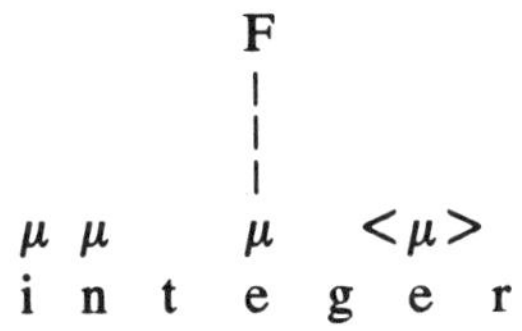

Maximize foot:

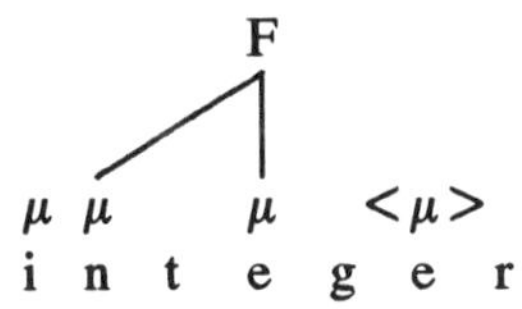

Project head:

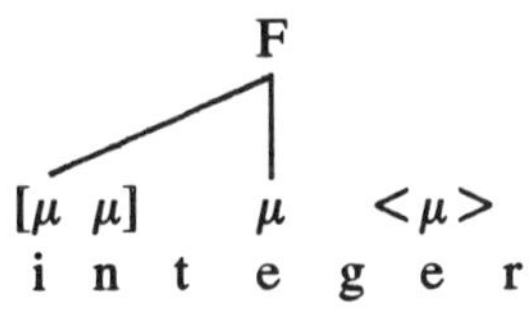

7.4 The critical difference between Spanish and Latin foot formation lies in the fact of final syllable extrametricality in Latin, and the metrical relevance of (most) final syllables/morae in modern Spanish proparoxytones are also characterized by the lexical diacritic $Head_{min}$ = **Off**, an option that did not exist in Latin, but which indirectly reflects Latin antepenultimate stress. Finally, Latin contained no proparoxytones with heavy penults, which would be the equivalent of Spanish consonant-final paroxytones (e.g. *túnel*, *árbol*). In other respects, the processes were identical. Both Spanish and Latin use the [μμ μ] foot template, both require a minimally bimoraic trochee, and both allow for a monomoraic head. It would seem, from looking only at the two diachronic endpoints, that at some intermediate stage, final syllables lost their extrametricality and entered into the moraic count for foot formation. Obviously, the process was not as simple as merely 'turning off' extrametricality. What really happened was a complete loss of quantity sensitivity before Spanish emerged as a separate language, followed by later events which targetted Old Spanish final syllables, and which created a new system of quantity sensitivity in which final syllables play a central role.

7.5 Earlier treatments of Latin stress assignment have usually made direct or indirect reference to moraic structure, without focusing on the interplay of minimal structure parameters and foot formation. Implicit in many descriptions was the idea that the Latin Stress Rule made penultimate stress the default: stress the penult unless it was a light syllable, in which case stress the antepenult. The inference is that heavy syllables themselves attract stress, and it is therefore unclear why antepenultimate stress should be preferred in Latin words whose antepenult was also light. It also does not explain why a heavy syllable in the pre-antepenult cannot attract stress (cf. Basbøll 1989). Beginning at least as far back as Jakobson (1936), a moraic-based stress assignment rule was proposed: disregarding the final syllable, stress the (syllable head of the) penultimate mora of the word. Allen (1973: 177-8) comes closer to the contemporary notion of minimal structure by proposing an 'accentual matrix,' a span of one heavy or two light syllables, in which the accent will fall. For Allen, 'the accent occupies the last matrix in the word, exclusive of the final syllable ...' (cf. also Vincent 1988). However, this proposal does not directly account for antepenultimate stress in words with a heavy antepenult, such as *ínteger*. Jakobson's proposal, to stress the syllable head of the penultimate mora, is descriptively adequate, but needs to be fitted against contemporary typologies of universal foot templates.

8 Quantity sensitivity in old and modern Spanish

8.1 Spanish differs prosodically from its Latin antecedents in two fundamental ways. First, distinctive vowel and consonant length has disappeared.[10] There is no longer a direct encoding between the mora count and the precise temporal duration of the segmental string. Spanish 'heavy' syllables are exclusively those closed by a consonant or containing a semivowel; the physical duration is often less than that of a long vowel. Most of the (relatively rare) quantity-sensitive trochaic stress systems studied by Hayes (1985, 1987), Prince (1992), etc. contain distinctively long vowels. In fact, quantity-sensitive trochaic systems with distinctive vowel length are relatively rare, and those based on a $[\mu\mu\ \mu]$ template are even fewer.[11] This leads to phenomena such as trochaic shortening, described by Prince (1992) for English. This contrasts with quantity-sensitive iambic systems, in which gemination of a consonant is a frequent means of achieving a maximal head (cf. Crowhurst 1992: chap. 2). The fact that bimoraic vowels (and consonants) are not present in Spanish inherently weakens the system of quantity sensitivity, in comparison with other languages in which phonological weight is openly manifested in both vowel and consonantal length distinctions.

8.2 Spanish stress assignment shows none of the instability or variation which might be expected of a highly marked configuration. Nothing suggests that children acquiring Spanish pass through less 'marked' configurations en route to acquiring the correct patterns –e.g., there is no tendency to assign antepenultimate stress to polysyllabic words with light penults (see Hochberg 1987, 1988).[12] Modern Spanish stress assignment is a hybrid system, combining both quantity-sensitive and quantity-insensitive components. All Spanish morphological phenomena use prosodic templates in which only syllables, not morae, are the key elements (cf. Crowhurst 1992, Lipski forthcoming). Only in cases where a heavy syllable could conceivably appear in the weak node of a trochaic foot does quantity sensitivity enter into the picture, in a negative fashion. Even here, the extent to which quantity sensitivity actively overrides the syllabic template is open to discussion. Spanish tolerates loanwords in which antepenultimate stress is combined with heavy penults; while loanwords do not constitute a basis for rejecting quantity sensitivity, they do suggest the transitional status of the last redoubt of Spanish quantity-sensitivity: the prohibition against antepenultimate stress with branching penults (and of penultimate stress in words ending in a falling diphthong). Spanish consonant-final paroxytones (e.g. *árbol*) end in a stressed syllable followed by an unstressed heavy syllable, which regardless of proposed extrametricality, provides a ready model for a [H H] or [L H] trochee.

8.3 In the transition from Latin to Spanish, the disappearance of distinctive vowel length concurrently made the old Latin Stress Rule opaque. The fact that certain words with open penultimate syllables had antepenultimate stress while others had penultimate stress became a purely arbitrary lexical marking, which ultimately led to orthographic conventions indicating unexpected stress patterns. In Latin, word-final syllables were always extrametrical for purposes of stress computation, but the initial stages of Old Spanish exhibited neither quantity sensitivity nor extrametricality. Spanish had inherited the Latin stress patterns, but quantity sensitivity had disappeared, as witnessed by the lack of a bilateral correlation between antepenultimate stress and a light penult. Old Spanish contained vast numbers of words with penultimate stress and light (vowel-final) syllables, and this configuration became the default. Antepenultimate stress was no longer predictable, but was rather a lexical exception. It was observationally true that Old Spanish contained no proparoxytones with branching penults, but this type of negative evidence would be difficult if not impossible to be naturally learned as part of the language acquisition process. At the same time, nearly all non-inflectional final consonants had disappeared. These events motivated a gradual shift toward penultimate stress as the unmarked –indeed highly preferred– Spanish pattern.

8.4 At this stage in the development of Spanish, there were only two stress patterns: penultimate stress (in words which ended in a vowel or an inflectional consonant), and antepenultimate stress (also in vowel-final words), inherited directly from Latin. Some of the latter words eventually gravitated toward penultimate stress, while the opposite shift occurred less frequently. There was no direct test of residual quantity sensitivity in the form of potential proparoxytones with heavy penults. There was no source of words which might trigger a prohibition against antepenultimate stress with a branching penult. Nothing suggests that native speakers of Old Spanish were aware of the purely statistical fact that no proparoxytone had a penultimate syllable with a branching rhyme. Awareness of the impossibility of such proparoxytones would constitute 'negative evidence' of the most questionable sort, and there was no positive evidence which pointed to quantity sensitivity. Thus there was no sense in which a heavy syllable 'attracted' stress. Many words with antepenultimate stress gravitated toward penultimate stress, a process which had begun in late Latin and perhaps even earlier. At the same time, widespread syncopation of posttonic vowels in proparoxytones created an ever-larger stock of paroxytones, furthering the momentum in favor of penultimate stress as the unmarked option. In this system, the foot template was bisyllabic [σ σ], but the minimality parameters remained the same as in Latin: $Foot_{min}$ = **Off** (requiring a bisyllabic trochaic foot), and $Head_{min}$ = **On**, allowing monomoraic heads (e.g. in words like *mañana*). As in modern Spanish, words with antepenultimate stress were lexically marked for $Head_{min}$ = **Off**, requiring bimoraic or heavy syllables as heads, in this case, spread over two syllables. The only difference between old and modern Spanish is that Old Spanish used a quantity-insensitive syllable-based template, which could therefore only be satisfied by counting syllables, and not morae. In late Latin and Old Spanish, final stress in words ending in heavy syllables was not regularly available; only bisyllabic feet were acceptable, and therefore the quantity of the individual syllables was irrelevant.

8.5 Word-final stress in Spanish did not become an option until widespread apocope of final vowels (beginning around the 11th-12th centuries) in originally paroxytonic words created a new stress category for Sp: consonant-final oxytones: *amore* > *amor* 'love,' *razone* > *razón* 'reason,' etc. Final apocope in words with antepenultimate stress created another new category: paroxytones ending in non-inflectional consonants (e.g. *árbole* > *árbol*). At this juncture, Spanish had expanded the possibilities of (non-verb) word stress to encompass the 'three-syllable window' which characterizes the modern language. There were no legitimately Spanish words ending in a stressed vowel (except for verb forms, which require a morphologically-informed stress analysis —but cf. Harris 1987, 1989b), so that in a very real sense Spanish had developed a stress system in which the first heavy syllable, counting leftward from the end of the word, 'attracted' stress. However, unlike Arabic (which contains a similar conditioning environment), or Latin (modulo final syllable extrametricality), in Spanish the checking normally stopped at the penultimate syllable, resulting in default paroxytonic accent. In this scenario, extrametricality of certain final consonants became a necessary concomitant, to account for penultimate stress in words like *árbol* and *régimen*. However, unlike Latin, no vowels/syllables were extrametrical.

8.6 The (re-) introduction of quantity sensitivity into Spanish meant that the foot template shifted from the bisyllabic [σ σ] back to the moraic template [$\mu\mu$ μ] which had existed in Latin. The parameter settings characterizing Latin and Old Spanish remained unchanged: $Foot_{min}$ = **Off** (requiring at least a bimoraic syllable), and $Head_{min}$ = **On**, allowing a monomoraic head. The only readjustment occasioned by the creation of new stress configurations was the substitution of a moraic foot template for a syllabic template. This is a minimal shift, consistent with the subtle change in accentual patterns occasioned by the development of consonant-final oxytones. These words define the major point of difference between the syllable-based and mora-based templates. Oxytones were simply not possible under the Old Spanish bisyllabic template, while in the later, quantity-sensitive stage, all (excluding extrametricality in a handful of words such as *árbol*, *túnel*, etc.) and only bimoraic final syllables attracted stress. At the same time, if the final syllable was light, all (but not only) heavy penults attracted stress. These data constitute sufficient positive evidence to deduce quantity-sensitivity, with stress assigned to the first of the final two syllables (counting right to left) which was heavy, or to the penult by default. Words with antepenultimate stress were, then as now, exceptional, in requiring 'more' metrical structure. In such words, bimoraicity is not sufficient; three morae (or four, in the case of words like *álgebra*) are needed to make an acceptable foot. A parameter setting of $Head_{min}$ = **Off** is easily learnable from such words.

Proparoxytones such as *vástago*, *álgebra*, etc. actually group four morae into the metrical foot, in apparent violation of even the [$\mu\mu$ μ] template. However, this violation is more apparent than real, since the third mora from the end is a coda consonant, incapable of being a syllable head and therefore receiving stress. In such circumstances, the syllable head must be incorporated into the foot, regardless of the total number of morae. The same phenomenon occurred in Latin, which freely admitted proparoxytones with heavy antepenults. Thus, the possibility of a foot with four morae is a normal consequence of stress assignment, and does not violate the fundamental trimoraic template. In the realm of template satisfaction, consonantal morae are treated with more flexibility than vocalic morae, since in Spanish, no consonant can form a syllable head. The absolute number of morae present in a prosodic template must be tempered by the overriding need to couple the template with well-formed and fully licensed syllables, which in turn necessitate the first available vowel, counting from right to left. A word like *carey* fully satisfies the trochaic template, thus making penultimate stress impossible. On the other hand (assuming that prevocalic glides are in the rhyme/nucleus, just as postvocalic glides), penultimate stress is possible in words ending with a rising diphthong: *tapia*. Although the two morae of the final syllable satisfy the minimally bimoraic requirement for a well-formed Spanish foot (word), the leftmost mora cannot be a syllable head, thus requiring that the next available syllable head (the preceding vowel) become the head of the trochaic foot.

9 Is modern Spanish losing its quantity sensitivity?

9.1 The preceding remarks have postulated that Old Spanish inherited the late Latin quantity-insensitive trochaic stress system, in which such facts as the impossibility of antepenultimate stress with a branching penult were largely irrelevant and not learnable through positive evidence. An independent prosodic innovation, large-scale final vowel apocope, not only created numerous consonant-final words with final stress, but in the process created a new quantity-sensitive stress system, in many ways significantly different from its Latin predecessor, and not logically descending from the latter. In the transition from Latin to modern Sp, quantity sensitivity has disappeared and then reappeared again, suggesting that the phonological equilibrium responsible for the bases of the stress system is relatively fragile, and is susceptible to alteration by independent phonological changes. It is therefore of interest to consider developments which could return Spanish to a quantity-insensitive stress system. This question is particularly relevant since in contemporary Spanish, the only exceptionless evidence of quantity-sensitivity, and negative evidence at best, is the impossibility of non-final stress in words ending in falling diphthongs, and of antepenultimate stress in words with a heavy penult. In other respects, the general rule that the first heavy syllable counting from the right edge receives stress has enough exceptions as to possibly open the door to a weakening or removal of the requirement of quantity-sensitivity.13

9.2 Spanish contains many consonant-final words with penultimate and occasionally even antepenultimate stress (e.g. *árbol*, *túnel*, *régimen*). Many of these words have very high frequencies of occurrence, form part of the core vocabulary, and in no way strike native speakers of Spanish as strange or exceptional (except for the presence of an orthographic accent). Spanish has also absorbed many words ending in a stressed vowel, largely geographical names of non-Hispanic origin but also a residue of elements introduced into Peninsular Spanish centuries ago (e.g. *Bogotá*, *Panamá*, *caló*, *capó*, *baladí*, *sefardí*, etc.). It is increasingly difficult to dismiss oxytonic stress in vowel-final words as a marginal idiosyncrasy to be swept away by the liberal assignment of 'extrametricality.' Spanish routinely accommodates proparoxytones with heavy penults, including place and personal names such as *Wáshington*, *Mánchester*, *Wínchester*, etc., apparently without significant difficulties of pronunciation (as opposed, e.g. to the nearly total inability to cope with borrowed words beginning with /s/ + CONSONANT). Such words are still regarded as foreign, and since Spanish has never exhibited a tendency to convert penultimate stress into antepenultimate stress, it is impossible to observe the spontaneous creation of new proparoxytones within Spanish[14]

9.3 Modern Spanish has no words ending in a falling diphthong with penultimate stress, and many Spanish speakers reject forms like **mámey*, **cáray*, etc. However, there does not appear to be a systematic reason why Spanish should not have such words, as witnessed by the occasional pronunciation *cónvoy*, instead of the more usual *convoy*. In Peninsular Spanish dialects retaining second person plural verb forms, unstressed final *-ais* and *-eis* routinely occur (e.g. *hablastais* 'you {pl.} spoke' *comisteis* 'you {pl.} ate'), and in those Peninsular dialects which combine use of these forms with loss of final /s/ (e.g. much of eastern Andalusia, Alicante, Murcia, Extremadura, etc.), unstressed final falling diphthongs do occur. In Latin America, popular Chilean Spanish combines *voseo* forms retaining the etymological diphthong with loss of final /s/, thus giving rise to combinations such as *séai(s)*. Similar combinations are found in Maracaibo, Venezuela, and residually in the rural Spanish of western Panama. Vocalization or 'liquid gliding' of syllable-final /l/ and /r/ in the Dominican Cibao region often elides final /l/ and /r/ after an unstressed vowel (e.g. *revólver* > *revóive* 'pistol'), but occasionally produces final unstressed falling diphthongs. Finally, Spanish does not demonstrate a major aversion to borrowed names ending in unstressed falling diphthongs, such as *Bólchoi*, *Dísney*, etc.

9.4 Contemporary Spanish is becoming ever more cosmopolitan, absorbing words from a variety of languages as well as regional dialects of Sp; the language may be poised on the verge of a return to quantity-insensitivity. In such a new system, trochaic stress would be the default in vowel-final words, and final stress would be the default in consonantal-final words; any deviations from this pattern would be lexically-marked exceptions. Some idiolects may have achieved this state of affairs already, particularly in areas characterized by bilingualism with languages exhibiting greater prosodic flexibility. For example, many bilingual Sp-English speakers in the United States do not share the strong aversion to quantity-sensitive violations, such as proparoxytones with heavy penults. The combination of circumstances reviewed above may actually create dialect differences, between quantity-sensitive (e.g. more conservative, isolated) dialects, and quantity-insensitive (more cosmopolitan, and/or in a bilingual environment) dialects. This is a promising area for future research.[15]

10 Summary and conclusions

The preceding remarks yield the conclusion that contemporary models of Spanish main stress are substantially correct, but require some additional refinements in order to avoid both under- and overgeneration, and to fit Spanish into universal typologies of metrical structures.[16] The principal conclusions can be summarized as follows:

(1) Spanish main stress assignment is non-iterative.

(2) The only extrametrical elements in Spanish are word-final consonants in consonant-final words with non-final stress.

(3) Spanish stress assignment is quantity-sensitive, but this is computed only in the final two syllables.

(4) Spanish quantity sensitivity is not a direct continuation of the Latin Stress Rule, but is rather an independent development, coming after a quantity-insensitive stage represented by late Latin and Old Spanish.

(5) Spanish requires that all feet be minimally bimoraic, and a single moraic trochee is formed at the right edge of a word.

(6) Antepenultimate stress is effected by a lexically-specific requirement that the head of the metrical foot be bimoraic, thereby requiring incorporation of the antepenultimate syllable. Vowel-final oxytones are lexically marked to allow a monomoraic foot.

(7) Coda consonants are automatically incorporated into the feet whenever it is necessary to target the nuclear vowel of the syllables to which they belong.

Notes

1 A slightly different approach was developed independently by Inkelas (1990: 180f.):

a. Terminal elements are invisible

b. Final Stress Rule (FSR): stress final syllable in domain

The terminal elements are essentially the final vowels which follow the derivational stem; thus *mesa* is [[mes]a], *aspirante* is [[aspirant]e], *animal* is [animal], etc. Inkelas' proposal automatically accounts for final stress in words like *papá*, *Perú*, *caló*, etc., which do not contain a terminal element, and which are therefore affected by the FSR. This is an advantage over Harris's model, in which stressed final vowels are handled stipulatively. Inkelas handles antepenultimate stress via the lexical prespecification of a foot, together with stray syllable adjunction: 'adjoin an unstressed syllable to a preceding nonbranching foot' (p. 182). This lexical diacritic gives no account for the paroxytonic restrictions noted by Harris (1983).

2 Hayes (1980) hints that Spanish is not quantity-sensitive, and Hayes (1985: 440) makes this claim explicitly for Spanish secondary stress. However, this does not exclude the possibility that Spanish primary stress is assigned via a quantity-sensitive metrical structure, as claimed by Harris (1983). Hayes (1992: 93) says of Spanish that 'the stress pattern is basically the Latin type, but with degenerate words allowed,' but Hayes (1992: 94) states categorically that 'Main stress in Spanish is phonemic, though it can be predicted to a fair extent by complex lexical rules, whose character continues to be debated ...' In any event, the schema proposed for Spanish by Hayes (1992: 93) would seem to require antepenultimate stress in words of 3 or more syllables, with a light penult. This is because Hayes assumes final syllable extrametricality in Spanish, as in Latin, while disallowing degenerate feet (and also disallowing trimoraic trochees of the form $[[\mu\mu]\ \mu]$. Thus:

$$\ldots - \smile <\sigma> \# \quad \rightarrow \quad \ldots \overset{(x)}{-} \smile <\sigma> \#$$

where (x) represents a bimoraic monosyllabic trochee. However, Spanish does not require antepenultimate stress in words like *bosquejo*, *cartero*, *tembleque*, *astilla*, etc.

3 If it were assumed, once again for purposes of argument, that word-final vowels were extrametrical, then a word like *bosque* would end in a monosyllabic, bimoraic trochee $[\mu\mu]$. Assuming the scale of harmonicity of Prince (1992), vocalic CL could be seen as preserving the preferred [H], instead of the highly disharmonic [L] or monomoraic foot. In this case, however, the vast number of Spanish vowel-final words with a light penult, e.g. *cama*, *casa*, etc., would be without explanation.

4 Another common occurrence in several Caribbean dialects (including much of the Caribbean coast of Colombia, central Cuba, and occasionally the Dominican Republic) is loss of syllable-final liquids /l/ and /r/ combined with gemination of a following consonant: *porque* > *pocque* 'because,' *salga* > *sagga* 'leave (imp.),' *curba* > *cubba* 'curve,' etc. Word-internally, since gemination represents the same sort of mora-conserving CL as vocalic CL occasioned by loss of /s/, similar contradictory predictions obtain if iterative trochaic foot formation and the disharmonicity of a [H L] foot are presumed. For example, gemination is quite frequent at the end of the first syllable of bisyllabic paroxytones (this being statistically one of the most frequent instances of the environment in question): *algo* > *aggo* 'something,' *porque* > *pocque*, *tarde* > *tadde* 'late,' *puerta* > *puetta* 'door,' etc. Gemination in words like *desammado* < *desalmado* 'without a soul,' *musummán* < *musulmán* 'Moslem,' *anaqquista* < *anarquista* 'anarchist,' etc. is also incompatible with iterative foot formation, since a a strongly disfavored [μ, $\mu\mu$] trochee would be preserved by liquid gemination.

5 In New Mexico Spanish, another /s/-weakening dialect (although not as extreme as Caribbean Sp), the present writer has observed hypercorrect epenthetic /s/ in *burla* > *bursla*.

6 In the case of stressed word-final vowels, the addition of an epenthetic /s/ creates a more desirable bimoraic foot [$\mu\mu$]. Thus while loss of a syllable-final consonant creates a possibly more unmarked open syllable, epenthetic /s/-addition in the syllabic coda increases the mora count in favor of a harmonically more preferred foot-type. This development is consistent with the incorporation of Spanish stressed syllables into a prosodic foot.

7 A somewhat different approach to quantity-sensitive stress assignment in Spanish comes from Dunlap (1989). She accepts Hayes' (1987) moraic trochee, together with the extrametricality of most word-final vowels, and inflectional consonants. However, she computes moraicity with respect to the *derivational stem*, essentially the word minus the final vowel. Thus in a word like *calabaza* 'pumpkin,' the morphological analysis is [[kalabas]a]. In Dunlap's interpretation, the final syllable of the derivational stem is /bas/, which is bimoraic. The moraic trochee is satisfied by this syllable, and penultimate stress results. Words with antepenultimate stress (e.g. *sábana* 'sheet') also mark the final mora (of the derivational stem) as extrametrical. Thus *sábana* is morphologically and metrically [[saba(n)]a]; the last metrizable syllable is the monomoraic /ba/, so the requirement of the moraic trochee requires incorporation of the preceding syllable into the foot. This proposal is problematic for several reasons. First, it presupposes a resyllabification following stress assignment which fundamentally alters the syllabic constituency, hence the moraicity, of certain consonants. This is inconsistent with contemporary notions of prosodic invariability

during a derivation. Moreover, by positing that a consonant which ultimately emerges in the onset of the final syllable is coda-final at some earlier stage, a word like *caspa* 'dandruff' must be analyzed as [[kasp]a], with a completely impossible coda cluster. Any analysis which posits structurally disallowed combinations at the underlying level is highly suspect. Presumably, a word like *alegre* 'happy' has the structure [[alegr]e], in which case two consonants would change their constituency, going from an impossible coda cluster to a normal onset cluster. In any event, a word like *caspa* or *alegre* would contain a trimoraic syllable at the point of stress assignment, so something 'more' than a moraic trochee would be required. As an additional complication, the two words would be underlyingly indistinguishable in terms of moraic structure, despite the fact that superficially one contains a heavy syllable (presumably 'attracting' or at least constraining stress), while the other contains a light syllable. If antepenultimate stress results from the extrametricality of the final mora of the derivational stem, then a word like *abismo* 'abyss' could not have antepenultimate stress, since the two remaining morae of the virtual syllable /bism/ form the moraic trochee. However, this same line of reasoning should exclude antepenultimate stress in a word like *álgebra*, whose final virtual syllable would be /gebr/, which even after extrametricality would contain two morae: /geb/. In proparoxytones such as *vástago* and paroxytones such as *carta*, a trimoraic syllable should result, which cannot be easily reconciled with the requirement of a moraic trochee. For the reasons just elaborated, the constituency-shifting model of Dunlap (1989) still falls short of accounting for Spanish stress assignment, although providing an early insight into the moraic sensitivity of Spanish foot formation. Dunlap (1991) provides a more consistent mora-based model, which avoids many of the morphological infelicities of the earlier study.

8 Hayes (1987), in proposing the moraic trochee, allows for a slight relaxation of the claim that quantity-sensitive stress assignment cannot be iterative. This comes from Hayes (1987: 279) algorithm for moraic trochee formation:

Form $(\underset{m\ m}{x\ \ .})$ if possible, where $(\underset{m\ m}{x\ \ .})$ is either $(\underset{\smile\ \smile}{x\ \ .})$ or $(\underset{-}{x})$; otherwise form $(\underset{\smile}{.})$

The monomoraic foot (.) is by definition stressless, whereas a stressed moraic trochee can be either monosyllabic (x) (a single heavy syllable) or bisyllabic (x .) (two light syllables). In applying this notion to Latin stress assignment, Hayes (1987: 282) defines the algorithm as 'from right to left, construct moraic trochees non-iteratively (i.e. until a stress is assigned).' Thus for Hayes iterativity entails assignment of more than one stressable (i.e. headed) foot. Given that Latin final syllables are extrametrical, a word with a heavy penult will satisfy the (x) template, giving penultimate stress. A word with light penult and light antepenult will satisfy the (x .) template, giving antepenultimate stress. A word with a light penult and heavy antepenult requires the (non-iterative) formation of two feet; the rightmost is a stressless (.) foot, and to the left comes a monosyllabic moraic trochee:

```
(x  .) (.)
 μ  μ   μ
 i  n t e g <e r>
```

This model clearly cannot account for the full range of contemporary Spanish stress patterns. Paroxytones with light penults (e.g. *casa*, *todo*, etc.) could only be analyzed as bimoraic if the final vowel is regarded as metrical. A word like *caspa* would then be analyzed as (x) (.). However, if final vowels are metrical, then antepenultimate stress can never be generated, since a moraic trochee requires at most two syllables. If the final vowel is regarded as extrametrical, then words like *casa* could only be handled by an ad hoc mechanism, for example default assignment of stress to a monomoraic foot in the absence of additional moraic material. Similarly, the impossibility of antepenultimate stress with a heavy penult is handled as in Latin: the penultimate syllable forms a bimoraic trochee. However, just as in Latin, antepenultimate stress is predicted for all words of three or more syllables in which the penult is light; this sharply contradicts observed Spanish patterns, in which paroxytonic stress is strongly preferred. Within Hayes' theory, the recourse to the stressless monomoraic foot (.) until a moraic trochee can be parsed provides an overly powerful generative device. It is impossible **not** to find a moraic trochee (providing of course that at least two morae are available), as long as otherwise unparsable monomoraic syllables can be set aside as belonging to stressless feet (cf. also Prince 1992: 390, fn. 13; Kager 1989: 5-6). Hayes (1992: chap. 6) relaxes the prohibition against iterative assignment of moraic trochees, allowing for such formation in certain languages.

9 Prince (1992: 363) offers the model of Harmonic Parsing: 'In the directional sweep (RL, LR) of foot-parsing, build the *best* foot, the one with the maximum *R*[hythmic] *H*[armony] –from the materials available at the moment of parsing.' Prince's ranking of harmony (for trochaic systems) is [L L], [H] > [H L] > [L]. When applied to Latin, Prince's harmonic parsing provides the same results as Hayes's moraic trochee, but without the requirement of an additional stressless foot. Assuming final syllable extrametricality, harmonic parsing will form a [H] foot on a penultimate heavy syllable, thus assuring penultimate stress. A word (of more than two syllables) with a light penult (e.g. *spátula*) will be parsed into a more harmonic [L L] foot, rather than the least harmonic [L]. Finally a word like *íntegre* will be parsed into a [H L] trochee, harmonically less desirable than [L L] but still possible. Like the moraic trochee, harmonic parsing should generate antepenultimate stress in all polysyllabic Spanish words with a light penult, which does not happen.

10 Although old or modern Spanish contains a handful of words in which identical adjacent vowels appear (e.g. *leer*, *loor*, and proper names like *Saavedra*, *Caamaño*,

etc.), these typically do not receive a lengthened pronunciation except in artificial diction (when an actual bisyllabic pronunciation may be attempted).

11 Crowhurst (1992) lists only Old English, Chugash and Cayuvava, all of which are subject to alternative analyses.

12 Both diachronically and in popular speech at the synchronic level, there is a well-documented tendency toward conversion of antepenultimate stress to penultimate stress (e.g. *océano* > *oceano*, etc.). Otero (1986), however, makes precisely the opposite claim, namely that shifts from penultimate to antepenultimate stress are more characteristic of the evolution of Spanish (Roca 1990 disputes some of the Otero's data). For Otero, antepenultimate stress is unmarked, providing that the penultimate syllable is not heavy. Otero believes that Spanish basically continues the Latin Stress rule, except that in Latin all final rhymes are extrametrical, while in Spanish only the final consonants of derivational stems are regularly extrametrical. This is not the appropriate place to discuss Otero's counterproposals, but if his observations on stress retraction are indeed characteristic of contemporary Spanish, then the 'new' (i.e. post-medieval) Spanish quantitative stress system may be gravitating toward a general setting of $Head_{min}$ = **Off**, requiring all metrical heads to be bimoraic.

13 Cf. Roca (1990) for some illuminating proposals on the historical development of Spanish stress, from Latin antecedents. Roca (1990) continues to affirm that modern Spanish is quantity insensitive, citing the large number of exceptions to any approximation of the Latin Stress Rule (e.g., consonant-final paroxytones, vowel-final oxytones), the lack of distinctive vowel length, and the ease with which foreign proparoxytones like *Mánchester* are accepted into Spanish. However, he concedes (p. 160) that 'some evidence that the constraint has had and probably still has some synchronic force in Spanish does however exist.' Roca's alternative solution (p. 161) is: '... interpreting the diachronic residue of Latin quantity sensitivity in the synchronic Spanish system as a redundancy.' This procedure is instantiated by a redundancy rule that blocks an otherwise general stress retraction rule just in case the penultimate rhyme is branching (or contains a palatal consonant). This is merely begging the question, however; postulating a quantity-sensitive constraint to a general rule is just a restatement of quantity sensitivity. In other respects, Roca's theory fares well in accounting for a wide range of regular and seemingly irregular Spanish data, and is deserving of more detailed consideration than can be afforded here.

14 Núñez Cedeño (1986) observes that hypercorrect /s/-insertion in vernacular Dominican Spanish never occurs in the penultimate syllable of proparoxytones: **sábasdo*, **órgasno*, etc. For what it is worth, the present writer has observed occasional hypercorrect /s/ in this context, in Caribbean Spanish dialects and in New Mexico Spanish. These occurrences are sporadic and very rare, but when combined with the growing store of borrowed proparoxytones with heavy penults, as well as

vowel-final oxytones, this may signal the first glimpses of an eventual return to a quantity-insensitive stress system, in which the bisyllabic template [σ σ] is primordial, but in which extrametricality and other forms of exceptionality play a greater role. This state of affairs should not be surprising, given that the absorption of borrowed words from a variety of sources has been instrumental in determining the intricacy and complexity of stress assignment in languages such as English and Dutch (cf. Kager 1989).

15 The present study is compatible with the quantity-sensitive trimoraic trochee (the Germanic Foot) postulated by Dresher and Lahiri (1991) to account for Old English data: 'From left to right, build binary, quantity-sensitive left-headed trees whose left branch contains at least two moras.' The combination of binarity and a bimoraic head means that each foot will have at least two syllables; it will have three if the first syllable is light, since the following syllable will have to be incorporated as part of the (branching) head. Given the left-to-right parsing, Germanic feet can actually contain four morae: [[L H] L] (e.g. *cyninga*), etc. Although sharing with the moraic trochee of Hayes (1987) the requirement of a bimoraic head, the Germanic foot differs from the bimoraic trochee in its required binarity. A syllabic sequence H L would be parsed (left-to-right) as [H] [L] (where the second foot is degenerate) under a moraic trochee analysis; the same sequence would be parsed into a single Germanic foot: [[H] L]. Historically, the Germanic foot eventually became opaque, but the requirement of binarity became transferred from the foot to the stressed syllable, requiring that the latter be bimoraic. The present analysis has proposed that Spanish shares with Old Germanic the binarity requirement (except in the case of word-final heavy syllables). However, heads are not required to be bimoraic in Spanish, except in the case of words with antepenultimate stress. Since Spanish foot construction takes place from right to left, in the normal case no Spanish foot will have more than three morae. A final sequence ...H will be parsed ...[H]; a combination ...L L will be footed as ...[[L] L], a sequence ...H L will be footed as [[H] L], etc. However, since Spanish has $Foot_{min}$ = **Off**, if the final syllable is light, the penultimate syllable must necessarily become the head, thus making for a trimoraic foot. Only in words for which $Head_{min}$ = **Off**, requiring a bimoraic head, does a configuration isomorphic to the Germanic foot appear: ...L L L is parsed [[L L] L], and ...H L L is parsed [[H L] L], with four morae in the latter foot.

16 The trimoraic [H L] template proposed by Dresher and Lahiri (1991) for Old English, as well as the examples examined by Crowhurst (1992) all involve cases where trimoraicity was maintained even when the requirement that each branch of a foot dominate a syllable head need not be invoked. In other words, bimoraicity of the head was frequently satisfied by a long vowel, with some vowels even lengthening under stress (much as occurs in modern Italian). Spanish, on the other hand, is based on the bimoraic trochee, and incorporates a third mora into the foot only when this

represents a non-syllabic element, semivocalic nuclear segment or coda consonant. In words with penultimate stress, there is no overwhelming tendency towards a $[[\mu\mu]\ \mu]$ foot (although at the same time there are no general processes which actively change a [H L] foot to [L L]). The extra mora in trimoraic feet is in a sense accidental, required only in order to ensure that each syllable will have a head consisting of a vocalic nucleus. This is different from the situation in Old Germanic, in which trimoraic trochees were actively selected for. Despite the existence of trimoraic feet, Spanish is still characterized by the bimoraic trochee template. The bimoraic template could be easily maintained if coda consonants received their accompanying mora via the Weight by Position (WP) rule, applying after the initial foot formation. Processes such as vocalic CL are low-level phonetic processes, and conserve moraic structure precisely because they operate after WP has assigned morae to coda consonants. This would be ideal from the point of view of universal typologies, but runs into trouble on two fronts. First, it would not account for default final stress in consonant-final words; the mora associated with the final consonant must be in place prior to foot formation. At the same time, there would be no excluding antepenultimate stress in words with coda consonants in the penultimate syllable. Thus, even if Spanish does have a WP rule, all morae associated with coda consonants must be in place before footing occurs. This does not eliminate the need to postulate a $[\mu\mu\ \mu]$ template, but the fact that low-level processes such as CL preserve a trimoraic structure does not constitute evidence that trimoraic feet are preferred in Spanish.

References

Allen, W. S. 1973. *Accent and Rhythm.* New York: Cambridge University Press.

Basbøll, Hans. 1989. Phonological weight and Italian raddoppiamento fonosintattico. *Rivista di Linguistica* 1.5-31.

Crowhurst, Megan. 1992. *Minimality and Foot Structure in Metrical Phonology and Prosodic Morphology*. Ph. D. dissertation, University of Arizona. Distributed by Indiana University Linguistics Club.

Den Os, Els and René Kager. 1986. Extrametricality and stress in Spanish and Italian. *Lingua* 69.23-48.

Dresher, B. Elan and Aditi Lahiri. 1991. The Germanic foot: metrical coherence in Old English. *Linguistic Inquiry* 22.251-286.

Dunlap, Elaine. 1989. The role of sonority in Spanish stress assignment. *WECOL* 89, volume 2.94-102.

Dunlap, Elaine. 1991. *Issues in the Moraic Structure of Spanish*. Ph. D. dissertation, University of Massachusetts.

Espinosa, Aurelio. 1925. Syllabic consonants in New Mexican Spanish. *Language* 1.109-118.

Halle, Morris, Wayne O'Neil, and Jean-Roger Vergnaud. 1993. Metrical coherence in Old English without the Germanic foot. *Linguistic Inquiry* 24.529-539.

Halle, Morris and Jean-Roger Vergnaud. 1987. *An Essay on Stress*. Cambridge: MIT Press.

Hammond, Michael. 1984. *Constraining Metrical Theory: a Modular Theory of Rhythm and Destressing*. Ph. D. dissertation, distributed by Indiana University Linguistics Club.

Hammond, Michael. 199X. Metrical theory and learnability. Unpublished manuscript, University of Arizona.

Hammond, Robert. 1986. En torno a una regla global en la fonología del español de Cuba. *Estudios sobre la fonología del español del Caribe*, ed. Rafael Núñez Cedeño, Iraset Páez Urdaneta, Jorge Guitart, 31-39. Caracas: La Casa de Bello.

Harris, James. 1983. *Syllabic Structure and Stress in Spanish*. Cambridge: MIT Press.

Harris, James. 1987. The accentual patterns of verb paradigms in Spanish. *Natural Language and Linguistic Theory* 5.61-90.

Harris, James. 1989a. Sonority and syllabification in Spanish. *Studies in Romance Linguistics*, ed. Carl Kirschner and Janet Decesaris, 139-153. Amsterdam: John Benjamins.

Harris, James. 1989b. How different is verb stress in Spanish? *Probus* 1.241-258.

Harris, James. 1991. With respect to metrical constituents in Spanish. *Current Studies in Spanish Linguistics*, ed. Héctor Campos and Fernando Martínez-Gil, 447-473. Washington: Georgetown University Press.

Harris, James. 1992. Spanish stress: the extrametricality issue. Bloomington: Indiana University Linguistics Club.

Harris, James. 1995. Projection and edge marking in the computation of stress in Spanish. *A handbook of Phonological Theory*, ed. John Goldsmith, 867-887. Cambridge, Mass.: Blackwell.

Hayes, Bruce. 1980. *A Metrical Theory of Stress Rules*. Ph. D. dissertation, MIT. Revised version published in 1981 by the Indiana University Linguistics Club.

Hayes, Bruce. 1985. Iambic and trochaic rhythm in stress rules. *BLS* 11.429-446.

Hayes, Bruce. 1987. A revised parametric metrical theory. *NELS* 17.274-289.

Hayes, Bruce. 1989. Compensatory lengthening in moraic phonology. *Linguistic Inquiry* 20.253-306.

Hayes, Bruce. 1989. 1992. *Metrical Stress Theory: Principles and Case Studies*. Unpublished MS, University of California, Los Angeles.

Hochberg, Judith. 1987. Acquisition data and phonological theory: the case of Spanish stress. *BLS* 13.

Hochberg, Judith. 1988. First steps in the acquisition of Spanish stress. *Journal of Child Language* 15.273-292.

Hualde, José I. 1989a. Delinking processes in Romance. *Studies in Romance Linguistics*, ed. Carl Kirschner and Janet DeCesaris, 177-193. Amsterdam: John Benjamins.

Hualde, José I. 1989b. Autosegmental and metrical spreading in the vowel-harmony systems of northwestern Spanish. *Linguistics* 27.773-805.

Idsardi, William. 1992. *The Computation of Prosody*. Ph. D. dissertation, MIT.

Inkelas, Sharon. 1990. *Prosodic Constituency in the Lexicon*. New York: Garland. Revised version of Ph. D. dissertation, Stanford University, 1989.

Jakobson, Roman. 1936. Ueber die Beschaffenheit der prosodischen Gegensätze. *Selected Writings*, vol 1, 254-261. The Hague: Mouton.

Kager, René. 1989. A metrical theory of stress and destressing in English and Dutch. Dordrecht: Foris.

Lieber, Rochelle. 1987. *An Integrated Theory of Autosegmental Processes*. Albany: State University of New York Press.

McCarthy, John. 1986. OCP effects: gemination and antigemination. *Linguistic Inquiry* 17.207-63.

McCarthy, John and Alan Prince. 1986. *Prosodic Morphology*. MS, University of Massachusetts and Brandeis University. To be published by MIT Press.

McCarthy, John and Alan Prince. 1990. Foot and word in prosodic morphology: the Arabic broken plural. *Natural Language and Linguistic Theory* 8.209-283.

Mester, Armin. 1986. *Explorations in Tier Structure*. Ph. D. dissertation, University of Massachusetts.

Núñez Cedeño, Rafael. 1986. La /s/ ultracorrectiva en dominicano y la estructura silábica. *Actas del II Congreso Internacional sobre el Español de América*, ed. José Moreno de Alba, 337-347. Mexico: Universidad Nacional Autónoma de México.

Núñez Cedeño, Rafael. 1987. Alargamiento vocálico en cubano: re-análisis autosegmental. *Actas del VII Congreso de ALFAL (Asociación de Lingüística y Filología de América Latina)*, t. I, 623-630. Santo Domingo: ALFAL.

Núñez Cedeño, Rafael. 1988a. Alargamiento vocálico compensatorio en el español cubano: un análisis autosegmental. *Studies in Caribbean Spanish Dialectology*, ed. Robert Hammond, Melvyn Resnick, 97-102. Washington: Georgetown University Press.

Núñez Cedeño, Rafael. 1988b. Structure-preserving properties of an epenthetic rule in Spanish. *Advances in Romance Linguistics*, ed. David Birdsong, Jean-Pierre Montreuil, 319-335. Dordrecht: Foris.

Núñez Cedeño, Rafael. 1989. CV phonology and its impact on describing American Spanish pronunciation. *American Spanish Pronunciation, Theoretical and Applied Perspectives*, ed. Peter Bjarkman, Robert Hammond, 170-186. Washington: Georgetown University Press.

Otero, Carlos P. 1986. A unified metrical account of Spanish stress. *A Festschrift for Sol Saporta*, ed. Michael Brame, Heles Contreras, Frederick Newmeyer, 299-332. Seattle: Noit Amrofer,

Prieto, Pilar. 1992a. Morphophonology of the Spanish diminutive formation: a case for prosodic sensitivity. *Hispanic Linguistics* 5(1-2).169-205.

Prieto, Pilar. 1992b. Truncation processes in Spanish. *Studies in the Linguistic Sciences* 22(1).143-158.

Prince, Alan. 1992. Quantitative consequences of rhythmic organization. *CLS* 26(2).355-398.

Repetti, Lori. 1989. *The bimoraic Norm of Tonic Syllables in Italo-Romance*. Ph. D. dissertation, University of California, Los Angeles.

Repetti, Lori. 1991. A moraic analysis of *raddoppiamento fonosintattico*. *Rivista di Linguistica* 3.307-330.

Roca, Iggy. 1986. Secondary stress and metrical rhythm. *Phonology Yearbook* 3.341-370.

Roca, Iggy. 1988. Theoretical implications of Spanish word stress. *Linguistic Inquiry* 19.321-350.

Roca, Iggy. 1990. Diachrony and synchrony in word stress. *Journal of Linguistics* 26.133-164.

Roca, Iggy. 1991. Stress and syllables in Spanish. *Current Studies in Spanish Linguistics*, ed. Héctor Campos and Fernando Martínez-Gil, 599-635. Washington: Georgetown University Press.

Vincent, Nigel. 1988. Non-linear phonology in diachronic perspective: stress and word structure in Latin and Italian. *Certamen Phonologicum*, ed. Pier Marco Berinetto and Michele Loporcaro, 421-432. Torino: Rosenberg & Sellier.

Zubizarreta, María Luisa. 1979. Vowel harmony in Andalusian Spanish. *MIT Working Papers in Linguistics* 1.1-11.

18

On the Spanish depalatalization of /ɲ/ and /ʎ/ in rhymes.

CARMEN PENSADO*

> Vos defendéis el desdén,
> todos vencerle queremos;
> vos decís que esto es razón:
> permitíos el festejo.
>
> Agustín Moreto, *El desdén con el desdén*

Both synchronic experimental evidence and the diachronic behavior of the alternants /ɲ/—/n/ and /ʎ/—/l/ suggest that coda depalatalization was never a productive rule. Synchronic variants are linked by their shared semantic content and show only analogical semiproductivity. Furthermore, morphophonologically opaque relationships in the lexicon tend to be substituted by transparent ones. All this suggests that, contrary to what is generally assumed, phonological similarity may play a major role in the organization of the mental lexicon.

1. It is a well known fact of Spanish phonology that words cannot end in palatal consonants.[1] Therefore, [ɲ] and [ʎ] in word-final position are hard to pronounce for native speakers. Foreign words containing them are adapted by various means. Final [ɲ], spelled <ñ>, may be depalatalized to [n]. Catalan loanwords —which are the main source for final [ɲ]— may also be adapted through a spelling pronunciation of Catalan <ny> as [ni]: *Company, Alemany, Fortuny*. Final *-ll* is usually depalatalized: *Maravall, Coll, Urgell*. Given these facts it is hardly surprising to find alternants like those in (1):

(1) *Depalatalization in word-final position*
a. Word internal [ʎ] vs. word-final [l]

ella, ello	él
aquella, aquello	aquel
doncella	doncel
clavellina	clavel
utillaje	útil

b. Word internal [ɲ] vs. word-final [n]

doña	don
desdeñar	desdén

Palatals are also forbidden in syllable-final position, where we find matching alternants (most of them opaque to some degree):

(2) Depalatalization in coda

a. [ʎ] in the syllable-onset vs. [l] in coda:

bello	beldad
caballo	cabalgar
calle	Caldefranco, Caldevilla
castillo	Castilblanco, Castildevides
valle	Valdejimena, Valcuevo

b. [ɲ] in the syllable-onset vs. [n] in coda:

ceñir	cinta
plañer, plañir	planto
teñir	tinte
uñir (dial.)	yunta
empeñar	prenda
reñir	rencilla
tañer	tangible

In order to account for these forms, Harris (1983: 51, 53) posited two sister rules depalatalizing consonants in a rhyme:

(3) Depalatalization rules

$$\begin{array}{c} N \rightarrow n \\ | \\ R \end{array} \qquad\qquad \begin{array}{c} L \rightarrow l \\ | \\ R \end{array}$$

As Harris shows, an interesting property of these rules is that there are cases where depalatalization applies in syllable-initial position. The plural of *doncel* is *donceles*, not **doncelles*. Harris uses this phenomenon to argue for the need of the cycle. The morphological structure of this pair of words would be the following:

(4) Analysis of *doncel, -es, doncella, -as* in Harris (1983)

	Singular	*Plural*
Masculine	$[\text{doncel}]_N$	$[[\text{doncel}]_N\ \text{es}]_N$
Feminine	$[\text{doncell} + \text{a}]_N$	$[\text{doncell} + \text{a}]_N\ \text{s}]_N$

Syllabification would apply twice: in the inner cycle it would assign coda status to *doncel*. In the next cycle, after bracket erasure, *donceles* would be resyllabified as an onset.[2]

For the sister rule of *ñ*-depalatalization there is an absolute minimal pair: *desdén* has the plural *desdenes*, but *desdeñes* also exists as the second person singular present subjunctive of *desdeñar*. Plural *desdenes* would be explained the same way as *donceles*. For *desdeñes,* Harris proposes the following structure: $[[\text{desdeñ} + \text{a}]_V\ \text{es}]_V$ where *a* is the theme vowel of *desdeñar* which is deleted in the derivation. Palatal *ñ* is syllable-initial throughout and cannot depalatalize.

This neat analysis has met with great success. It has been repeatedly used by Kiparsky (1982: 145, 1985: 91) and is given as an example in Carstairs-McCarthy (1992: 66). Even though I am aware that James Harris himself would no longer subscribe to it (personal communication), it has become a sort of classic, so it may be worthwhile to verify whether speakers do analyze these words as they are supposed to.

2. There is another way to look at the problem. The distribution we encounter in the examples studied by Harris is the most frequent one in morphophonological alternants. There is no allomorphy in inflection (either verbal, *desdeñes*, or nominal, *donceles*), we find allomorphy in derivation (*desdén—desdeñar*). Why should we expect pl. **doncelles*, or subj. **desdenes* at all? Actually, the cycle was applied to segmental morphology in order to justify this kind of distribution. But we can take this reasoning further: what is the need of the cycle when inflection seems perfectly faithful to surface forms? Do speakers actually set up abstract bases such as *desdeñ-* in order to account for derivational regularities *(desdén / desdeñar)* at the cost of complicating inflection *(desdenes)*? Are non-alternating forms systematically processed?

2.1. Several tests were designed in order to find out whether an abstract analysis is psychologically real for Spanish speakers (see Appendix). The subjects were 53 young adult native speakers of Spanish (mostly Castilian), undergraduate students of Spanish Philology. Even though these data are too sketchy to be conclusive, they were clear enough to indicate the major trends in speakers' behavior. A surprising result is that some of the answers are completely unexpected: they are incompatible with generalizations inferred from the existent lexicon. We will be focusing on these highly suggestive "impossible" answers.

The first test was designed in order to see whether speakers, when confronted with the evidence of alternating nonce words, would use the alternants productively and whether they would do so according to the above-mentioned rules. Subjects were shown six (6) sets of two drawings showing an animal-like creature, and a machine to make it. They were told that the drawings represented the future mascot for some company and the machine that manufactured it. Each of the creatures was given a name: a noun of CVCVCVC structure and final stress. The manufacturing process was named by a related verb in *-ar* (the productive inflectional class in Spanish). Except for the first case, each noun-verb couple showed a morphophonological alternation actually attested in the Spanish lexicon (/ʎ/— /l/, /r/—/s/, /r/—/l/, /ɲ/—/n/, /au/—/o/). After studying the first set of drawings, subjects were shown three additional sets of drawings: the first one with two mascots, the second with several mascots, and the third with many mascots. Each of the drawings had a descriptive phrase, with a gap in the relevant places for the subjects to fill in the noun or the verb root. Suffixes were already given. The subjects were split in two groups. Half of them where shown first the verb and then the noun and, for the questions, first the plural of the noun, then an adjective in *-oso* and, lastly, an *-ado* participle. The other half were shown the noun first and then the verb. As for the questions, they were asked first to give the plural, then the -ado participle and last the -oso adjective. Considering the alternants at issue, /ʎ/— /l/ and /ɲ/—/n/, we could expect to find depalatalization in plurals and palatals in -ado participles. Real evidence should come from -oso derivatives, which could be linked either to the noun or to the verb. The suffix *-oso*, which is very frequent (ca. 500 entries) and productive, is overwhelmingly noun-based. Nevertheless, there are some *-oso* adjectives built on verbal roots.

We would expect a pattern *desdén* — *desdeñoso*, with a nominal base and showing allomorphy. If speakers actually used the postulated analysis, they should make the relevant connection and use it consistently. Conversely, the order of the stimuli should be of little consequence.

In a second test, speakers were given a list of fifty-seven (57) Spanish words. They were told that all were derived from other Spanish words, and were asked to provide them. The list was dictated (to minimize reading errors) and subjects were given approximately ten (10) seconds to answer. Except for three control items, all words could be potentially connected to bases showing different alternants. Nine items had an -oso suffix, which, as we said, is predominantly noun-based, and 8 items an -al suffix. Both are very productive and show several morphophologogical alternants. If speakers were using the postulated rules, we would expect to find a consistently nominal base for *-oso* and for *-al*, not a verbal one. Obviously, this test presupposes that Aronoff's (1976) *Unitary Base Hypothesis* does not work (cf. Rainer 1992: 110-111). Notice that, no matter whether we presuppose that the lexicon consists of lists of words or of lists of morphemes, no theory of morphology and the lexicon would want to miss the systematicity of the relationship between *desdén* and its palatal cognates. A word-based model such as the one in Aronoff (1976), for instance, would postulate *desdén* as a base-form, plus rules relating final *-n* to intervocalic *ñ*. A morpheme-based one, such as Lieber's (1981), would postulate an abstract root *desdeñ-* and a rule depalatalizing it in word-final position.

In a third test, speakers were given derived words and were asked to define them, if possible, with a related word. Otherwise, with any other kind of explanation. This test ought to show whether the relevant base items were actually known to the subjects and if they were seen as derivationally or just semantically related. If the standard analysis were true, we would expect speakers to capture the relevant derivational relationships. Answers should be almost identical to the ones shown in Test 2.

In a fourth test, speakers were asked to coin new derivatives for *don* and for *él,* in order to see whether intervocalic /ɲ/ and /ʎ/, which appear in inflection, would show up in derivation also, as the standard analysis would predict.

To summarize, if the abstract analysis were true we would expect that:

- Speakers would be aware of the alternants and connect them derivationally.
- Alternants would be rule-governed; base forms and rules would be consistently hypothesized; the base form would be one and the same for the entire

word family; rules would be productive and suffix behavior would be systematic; and nonce forms would behave just like existing words.

3. The results obtained from the responses to the tests were strikingly different from what the standard analysis would lead us to think:

As shown by the results of Test 1 (see (5)), speakers showed a tendency to disregard allomorphy, in spite of the fact that they were given evidence for it.[3]

(5) Presence/absence of allomorphism in nonce words for Test 1

	enapil	enapillar	tipacol	tipacorar	siparén	sipareñar	tomirel	taumirelar
n.a.	1	1			3	4		
yes	12	6	19	9	19	11	24	7
no	14	18	5	14	5	10	1	15

As shown by the results in the second row, there was a strong tendency to disregard allomorphy. However, what is really striking is the fact that the presence or absence of allomorphy is conditioned by the order of the stimuli. In the order *enapil, enapillar, -es, -ado, -oso* (abbreviated as "enapil"), responses showing allomorphy are in the majority. Conversely, in the order *enapillar, enapil, -es, -oso, -ado* (presented as "enapillar"), elimination of allomorphy was the rule. In order to understand the reason for this behavior it is necessary to further analyze the responses to Test 1.

In most cases, plurals, following the nominal root, showed no palatals (43 *enapiles*, 46 *siparenes*). However, there were also several cases of plurals with palatals (*enapilles, sipareñes*). It is interesting to note that speakers who formed plurals with palatals also used palatals in participles and *-oso* derivatives. This means that these subjects did not realize that there was any alternation at all and simply forgot that the nouns were *siparén,* and *enapil*, without palatals. That is to say, plural formation showed no allomorphy (as in *desdén—desdenes* or *doncel—donceles,* and unlike *él—ellos*).

As for verbal inflection, only two (2) subjects built the participles on the nominal root and then recalled the verbal root for *-oso* derivatives. All others either forgot the verbal root completely (8 for *enapil*, 19 for *enapillar*, 4 for *siparén*, 9 for *sipareñar*) or they built participles on verbal roots either with or without allomorphy in the other categories: 14 for *enapil*, 6 for *enapillar*, 14 for *siparén*, 10 for *sipareñar*. That makes an overwhelming majority of results showing no allomorphy in verbal inflection.

The behaviour of *-oso* derivatives was striking (see (6) below). In nonce words, we would expect that speakers would apply their internalized rule... provided that they realized that there were alternants. Nevertheless, *-oso* was simply formed on the nearest stimulus. Next to *-ado,* it was built on the verbal form. Oddities such as *-adoso, -aoso* prove it even more clearly.

(6) Derivatives in *-oso* for the *ll / l* and the *ñ/n* alternants.

(a) In the order *enapil, enapillar, -es, -ado, -oso,* (b) in the order *enapillar, enapil, -es, -oso, -ado.*

(a)		(b)	
enapilloso	14	enapiloso	17
enapiladoso	1	enapilloso	6
enapilaoso	1	enapiloroso	1
enapiloso	8	invalid	1
enapiloso/enapilloso	1		
enapilleoso	1		
invalid	1		

(c) In the order *siparén, sipareñar, -es, -ado, -oso,* (d) in the order *sipareñar, siparén, -es, -oso, -ado*

(c)		(d)	
sipareñoso	12	siparenoso	9
sipareñadoso	1	sipareñoso	7
siparadoso	1	sipare-oso	1
sirapiñoso	1	sipariñoso	1
sipareneoso	1	sirapeñoso	1
siparenoso	7	sirapiñoso	1
sirapenoso	1	sirapenoso	1
siparoso	1	siraperoso	1
invalid	1	siparoso	1
		siparosa	1
		invalid	2

When it is next to plural *-es*, the *-oso* derivative is built on the nominal root, and this leads to across the board elimination of allomorphy (see (7)). This is the cause for the reversed patterns of allomorphy shown above in (5).

(7) Bases for *-oso* and presence/absence of allomorphism. Results based on the nearest stimulus are shown in **boldface**.

<table>
<tr><th colspan="3">no allomorphism</th><th colspan="3">allomorphism</th></tr>
<tr><td></td><td>inf.base</td><td>nom. base</td><td>inf. base</td><td>part. base</td><td>nom. base</td></tr>
<tr><td>enapil</td><td>5</td><td>8</td><td>1</td><td>9</td><td>2</td></tr>
<tr><td>enapillar</td><td></td><td>19</td><td colspan="2">6</td><td></td></tr>
<tr><td>siparén</td><td>1</td><td>4</td><td>1</td><td>13</td><td>2</td></tr>
<tr><td>sipareñar</td><td>1</td><td>9</td><td colspan="2">9</td><td></td></tr>
<tr><td>tipacol</td><td>1</td><td>4</td><td>1</td><td>13</td><td>5</td></tr>
<tr><td>tipacorar</td><td></td><td>14</td><td colspan="2">9</td><td></td></tr>
<tr><td>tomirel</td><td></td><td>1</td><td>2</td><td>16</td><td>6</td></tr>
<tr><td>taumirelar</td><td>1</td><td>14</td><td colspan="2">5</td><td>2</td></tr>
</table>

Inconsistency in postulating either a verbal base or a nominal base is also true in the behavior of each individual speaker. Only 10 out of 23 subjects (in the order verb—noun) and 11 out of 25 (in the order noun—verb) gave consistent responses (either a verbal or a nominal base for *-oso* in all five items). Furthermore, consistent responses in the order *-ado* — *-oso* were mostly verb-based. Conversely, in the order *-es* — *-oso* they were noun-based. This implies that consistency does not seem to be a property of each subject's grammar, but an accident brought about by this particular task.

Summing up, the alternants showed no productivity. Base-forms were not consistently postulated and suffix behavior was not systematic. Instead of rules, what we find is analogy based on the nearest stimulus. The results of the other tests confirm these conclusions.

When asked to provide derivatives for *don* and for *él* (where allomorphy includes inflectional categories), speakers showed a marked tendency towards derivation based in /l/, /n/, as shown by the results of Test 4 in (8).

(8) Results of Test 4: (a) 'tratar de don', (b) 'la cualidad de ser él'

donear	25	elidad	18
doñear	12	eleidad	17
donear/doñear	1	eleidad/elidad	2
dondear	8	eldad	3
doñeo	1	eleidad/eldad	1
donedear	1	eloidad	2
dononear	1	ellidad	2
dontear	1	eledad	1
		elleidad	1
		ilidad	1
		leidad	1

Here analogical coining was expected, but nevertheless it is striking to find analogical "monsters" such as *dondear* (based on *uste+dear*), *donedear* (on *ust+edear*) or *dontear* (on *tu+tear*) or *eloidad* (on *y+oidad*). This implies that speakers showed little care in splitting up words. Instead of using semantic criteria or even mere economy of analysis, they just tried to make derivatives that copied the largest conceivable amount of phonological material in the base (what Bybee and Moder (1983) called *product-oriented schemas*).

In Tests 2 and 3, where the task was to point out bases for derivation, speakers were split between *desdén* and *desdeñar* as possible bases for *desdeñoso*. When they were asked to provide a definition for *desdeñoso,* speakers showed a higher percentage of responses involving *desdén* than *desdeñar* (see (9)).

(9) Results of Test 3. Definitions for *desdeñoso*

desdén	29
desdeñar,que desdeña, etc.	20

When asked to provide a base for *desdeñoso*, there was a higher percentage of *desdeñar,* (see (10)).

(10) Results of Test 2. Base for *desdeñoso*

desdeñar	23
desdén	21
desdeño	3
desdeñ	1
desde	1

These results confirm the plausibility of a verbal base for *desdeñoso* as Rainer (1993: 112, 648) already suggested with syntactic arguments. The rate of responses involving *desdeñar* is highly significant given the fact that, as mentioned, *-oso* is overwhelmingly noun-based. In the two relevant cases in Test 2 where *-oso* derivatives could be related either to a verbal or a nominal root, *desdeñoso* and *temeroso,* speakers showed a tendency for verbal bases which, in these particular cases, happen to be more transparent (see (11)).

(11) Results of Test 2. Base for *temeroso*

temor	29
miedo	1
temeridad	1
temer	19

Notice that if this phonological interpretation is correct, *temeroso* is analyzed as *temer+oso*, an odd derivation based on the whole infinitive, not on the verbal root.[4] These results are confirmed by similar tendencies involving the suffix *-al.* In spite of the fact that *-al* builds adjectives exclusively on nouns and adjectives, seven (7) subjects mentioned *perjudicar* as the base for *perjudicial*, an "impossible" answer. The phonological motivation for this result is confirmed by two (2) erroneous base-forms of *perjudicio*. Analogously, as a base for *judicial*, the more transparent *juicio* (22 responses) was preferred to both to *juez* (20) and *justicia* (3), the bases suggested by Rainer (1993: 400).

Regarding words in Test 3 where the /ʎ/—/l/ and the /ɲ/—/n/ alternants are in word-internal position but the semantic relatedness persists, subjects did not show any significantly different behavior (*pace* Mascaró 1990: 479). Most of them knew the words and related them derivationally. Notice that, once more, transparent bases are preferred whenever possible (as for *tinte*, see (12)).

(12) Results of Test 3 for words with alternants in syllable-final position: (a) definitions for *beldad,* (b) definitions for *tinte*

(a)		(b)	
bello, -a, belleza (base)	29	tinta, tintar, tintorería	23
belleza (semantic correlate)	7	teñir, tiñe	15
various	6	various	5
n.a	8	n.a.	2

4. How can we interpret these results? First, speakers seem to be aware of the alternants in their lexicon when they are sufficiently transparent (as shown in the results of Tests 2 and 3). However, this does not predetermine them to capture easily the alternants in nonce words (Test 1). Similar results regarding diphthongization in Spanish verbal paradigms were obtained by Bybee and Pardo (1981).

Semantic relatedness is not enough for derivational relatedness, as shown by the slight difference between responses to Test 3, where speakers were asked to define words, and Test 2, where they were asked to find bases for derivatives. Speakers show a tendency to relate semantically similar words that also show a certain degree of phonological similarity. However, in order to consider them as true bases for derivation, the degree of phonological opacity must be smaller.

Bases chosen for derivation are not the ones that could be chosen on grammatical criteria (e.g., the semantically most simple, the one statistically normal for a given suffix, etc.). In Test 1, when speakers were asked to inflect or derive new forms on given bases, they did so on the basis of the nearest stimulus. This meant inconsistent behaviour of derivational categories (i.e. no meaning-based regularities) contrary to Bybee and Pardo's (1981) results for inflection.

This tendency is not as prominent in the real lexicon as in nonce words. There is a way to explain this divergence if we follow the connectionist models in conceiving morphophonological regularities as lexicon-based, and not as rule-based (cf. Rumelhart and McClelland 1986, Bybee 1988; see MacWhinney 1994, for a recent survey of these approaches). In the lexicon, the regularities are based on connections between existing words. Speakers cannot regroup them as they wish. However, in nonce words speakers are not hampered by the weight of the existing connections and they can react exclusively on phonological stimulus.

To answer our first set of questions, we have gathered evidence showing that speakers do not process non-alternating forms, even if they are linked in a word-family which shows allomorphy and the relationship is perceived. Morphophonology seems to be structured in such a way that processing is minimized: alternants are not sorted out unless it is inevitable. In the cases shown, all inflection is processed through simple suffix addition. Derivation tends to avoid allomorphy whenever it is possible: in coining new words and in choosing among possible derivational relationships.

In other words, in spite of the fact that depalatalization is surface true, in the isolated word, it does not behave as a morphophonological rule in Spanish. But this is not a new fact about contemporary Spanish morphophonology. Probably depalatalization was never a true rule.

5. Other evidence for the irregular characteristics of depalatalization comes from its historical behavior. As we shall see, depalatalization was never a regular phonological change in Spanish. Furthermore, most of the existing alternants were not created by depalatalization, but by an unrelated process, non-palatalization, or by simple borrowing. Depalatalization was never productive.

Obviously, the input of depalatalization are word and syllable-final /ɲ/ and /ʎ/ but regularly these consonants failed to appear in such positions. In word-final position they could have arisen through the loss of final vowels, especially of final *-e*; however in Old Spanish —in contradistinction to Catalan or French— apocope took place only under very strict conditions: after single alveolar consonants. Apparently, in all other contexts final *-e* was not lost. Most potential instances of word-final palatal consonants show final vowels instead: *cerralle* arch. 'cerco, lo que ciñe o rodea', *fuelle*, *muelle*, *armuelle* 'planta quenopodiácea' (< HOLU MOLLE). This is the historical reason for the palatal in *desdeñe* (3rd sg. subj.).

Only for a short period in Medieval Spanish final *-e* could be optionally dropped after any single consonants (and some clusters) potentially leading to word-final palatals. This happened even with *-o,* and *-a* in connected contexts, (see (13)).

(13) Loss of final *-a, -o* (data from Menéndez Pidal 1944: §49. 3., Lapesa 1951: 174)

First member of a compound: *cabelprieto* 'cabello+prieto' (*JRuiz* 1485d)
Titles: *donn Endrina* 'doña+Endrina' (*JRuiz* 669a) *don Elvira* 'doña+Elvira' *(Cid)*
First names before patronimics: *Nun* 'Nuño', *Fortún* 'Fortuño', *Ordón* 'Ordoño', *Tel* 'Tello'

These apocope processes are the only internal source leading to the alternants shown above in (1). However, apocope in these forms always remained optional. For instance, in Schede's (1987) rich corpus of verbal forms, apocope does not show up at all in the relevant subjunctives of the 1st conjugation (e.g., *apelle, asañe, calle, dañe*). The only instances of apocope are *sal/sale* / *salle* (pres.) and *sal* / *sale* / *salle* (imperative) of archaic *sallir;*[5] and *tuelte* 'tuelle+te', with a clitic pronoun, correlating nicely with other instances of apocope in closely connected sequences.

Another related problem is that we cannot ascertain whether word or syllable-final clusters were already single palatal consonants by the time of syncope and apocope. Word-final /ɲ/ could arise from the Vulgar Latin clusters NJ, NG, as in *lueñe*. But the main source for word-final /ʎ/, /ɲ/ are geminate -LL-, -NN-. As for word internal position, syllable final /l/, /n/ could originate from late syncope between -LL-, -NN-, and a following consonant. However, evidence from other clusters demonstrates that, in those positions, palatalization simply failed to take place. Take, for instance, the results of Latin -ULT- in word or syllable-final position where, instead of the regular outcome /tʃ/, we find the intermediate stage /j(t)/: MULT(U) > *muy* (proclitic, before a consonant), VULTURE > *buitre* / MULTU > *mucho, much* (late apocope before a vowel) (see Harris-Northall (1990: 64-65)).[6]

As for the sources of /ɲ/ and /ʎ/, there is no evidence for palatalization of geminate -NN- and -LL- in word-internal position (Pensado 1984: 309, 314): *PULLETRU > *potro*, COLLOCARE > *colgar*, FOLLICARE > *holgar*, POLLICARE > *pulgar*, GEMELLICARE > *remelgar*, CABALLICARE > *cabalgar*, *HINNICLARE > *relinchar*, GALLICU > *galgo*. Arguably, they simplified before palatalizing. In word-final position, our data are not very clear. Word-final *-l* and *-n* could just as well be interpreted as the result of degemination. The above mentioned tendency to avoid apocope could be explained alternatively as due to the effect of a preceding geminate (this effect can be detected even for -SS- which seems to have simplified much earlier: O.Sp. *messe,* Mod. Sp. *mies* < MESSE). It seems that palatalization of LL, NN was still a productive process in the Golden Age. This is the simplest way to account for variable palatalization of *ll* < *r+l* in sandhi in rhymes such as *cabello/cogello* (see Pensado 1993 for further arguments). Therefore, it would be just as reasonable to assume that orthographic <-ll>, attested in the definite article (masc. *ell olio, ell estudio, ell otro,* and "feminine" *ell alma*) was simply a geminate (see Pensado, forthcoming). According to the standard interpretation, ILLU(D), ILLA(M) (Mod.Sp. *lo, la)* simplified to **elo*, **ela*, **elos*, **elas,* but ILL(E) gave both *el* and palatal *ell.* Oddly enough, this implies that palatalization in the paradigm of the article would have taken place only in final position, where palatals were disfavored. Assuming that orthographic <ell> is just a phonetic archaism with preservation of the Latin geminate is phonetically more plausible. Notice that there seem to be no attested instances of pronominal <ell>, which would have made sense in a paradigm showing palatalization *(ella, ellos, ellas)*.

To complicate the matter further, in Old Spanish and, much more frequently, nowadays, there are also alternants showing both /ɲ/, /ʎ/ and /n/, /l/ (and even /ʎ/—/l/—/li/) in intervocalic position vs. /n/, /l/ in word-final position, see (14). These alternants originate from Latin LJ, NJ and had a different distribution: palatal allomorphs occurred only in some derivatives of a certain base form. There was no allomorphy in inflection.

(14) Derivational alternants with intervocalic /ɲ/, /ʎ/ — /l/, /n/— (/li/) vs. final /l/, /n/

/ɲ/, /ʎ/	/l/, /n/	/li/	/-n/
gallego	Galicia		
Gran Bretaña	británico		
Alemaña	alemánico		alemán
Bretaña			bretón
Cataluña			catalán, catalanidad, catalanismo, catalanista
ordeñar	ordenar		orden
millón, millar	milenio, milésima	miliarea	mil

In summary, most cases of "final depalatalization" were actually instances of non-palatalization. All the remaining cases are loanwords. This is the case of *desdén* and *doncel* (borrowed from the Provençal of courtly literature). Other cases of Provençal or Catalan loanwords are *refrán* (Prov. *refranh*), *sostén* (Prov. *sostenh*), and Medieval forms such as *domén* (found in *Fuero de Avilés*, < Prov. *domenh*), and *entall* (< Prov. *entalh*). There is no evidence that these borrowings ever had any palatal allomorphs.

There are also some dialectal borrowings. Latin -AGINE gave Castilian *-én* (through a sequence of changes *-ain* > *-ein* > *-én*, where final *-n* did not palatalize). Western dialects (Leonese and Galician) hypercharacterized the (feminine) suffix for gender and the resulting form -AGINA gave regularly *-aña* (Cast. *sartén* / Gal. *sartaña*, Cast. *provena* 'mugrón de la vid' / Leon. (Zamora) *probaña*). Even though these variants do not coexist in any dialect, the standard may accept them, showing alternants such as *herrén* 'forraje de avena, cebada, trigo, centeno y otras plantas que se da al ganado' / *herreñal, herrenal* 'terreno en que se siembra el herrén'.

All this means that synchronic alternants arose in two different forms (see (15)).

(15) Historical sources for final "depalatalization"

word-internal	word-final non-palatalization	word-final depalatalization
pie/ ʎ/es	pie/l/	
lue/ ɲ/e		lue/n/

Since final depalatalization was never a full-fledged rule of Spanish phonology, it never followed the standard historical development of phonological rules (which commonly start as postlexical to become lexical at a later stage).

Nevertheless, its two diachronic origins could have been synchronically reinterpreted as a single (lexical) depalatalization rule. In both cases there were alternant forms either through different context-dependent diachronic evolution, or —in isolated instances such as *desdén / desdeñar, herrén / herreñal* — through contrast between inherited forms and borrowings. In contrast to Modern Spanish, Medieval Spanish allowed allomorphy in plurals (see, e.g. *pie / piedes*, in *Siesta de Abril*). However, as in Modern Spanish, speakers seem to have missed the relevant generalization. Instead, they treated the alternants as lexical idiosyncracies. This is shown by a conspiracy of different changes eliminating allomorphy.

5.1. Most Medieval forms showing apocope restored their final vowels and consonants became palatal again. Restoration was systematic when the lost vowel was *-a, -o,* and also, not surprisingly, in verb-forms: Class. Sp. *lueñe*, Mod. *cabello, doña, ermitaño* (vs. Med. *ermitán*), *atañe, bulle*. The only remaining word, *piel*, acquired a new plural, *pieles*, thereby eliminating allomorphy. Only the personal pronoun, demonstratives, *don / doña,* and *doncel / doncella,* retained their alternants. These alternants may have been treated as suppletive, as they are today (cf. the results of Test 4). The result of these phenomena is a drastic reduction of allomorphy.

Depalatalization also decayed in loanword adaptation, where adding a support vowel, *-e,* to preserve palatals became the usual strategy: *dalle* (Prov., Cat. *dall)* 'guadaña', *detalle* (Fr. *dètail), gobernalle, gobernallo* (Cat. *governall*), *talle* (Fr. *taille*), *ventalle* 'abanico' (Cat. *ventall*), *zolle, azolle* 'pocilga' (Arag., Nav., Cat. *(la) soll*). This trend even lead to anti-etymological palatals: *retuelle* Sant. 'especie de red para pescar', *retel* 'arte de pesca para cangrejos consistente en un aro con una red en forma de bolsa' (maybe from Mozarabic *retewél*, Leyden Glossary). Today, depalatalization is common once again: *champán* (Fr. *champagne*).

5.2. Another possibility was to coin alternative derivatives showing no allomorphy in order to eliminate the troublesome loanword. This is what happened when foreign *desdén* entered the native family of *desdeñar*. Various native alternative forms were coined (*desdeñanza, desdeño*), none of which succeeded in catching on.

5.3. We do not find evidence of any productivity of the alternants. Many of those forms which alternate synchronically were never created from variants showing allomorphism. For instance, dialectal *herreñal* comes from *herreña*, not from *herrén*, and *desdeñoso* comes from archaic *desdeño*. As indicated above, depalatalized loanwords (*refrán, sostén*) never show any palatal variants either in inflection or in derivation (*refranes, refranero, sostenes, sostener*). Obviously, loanwords which preserve their palatals do not show any derivatives with allomorphy either: *detalle, detalles, detallar)*.

Allomorphy only occurs when either inherited words and borrowings or multiple borrowings from different languages converge. Once more, this process did not lead to productivity. One can find allomorphism only by grouping together different (though etymologically related) word-families. It is highly doubtful that these families are derivationally related through a common form, since their semantic relationship is always opaque.

(16) Synchronic distribution of allomorphic variants /n/,/l/ vs. /ɲ/, /ʎ/ in derivation

non-palatal	palatal
don Covadonga, Busdongo (place-names) doncel duende	dueña: dueñesco, doñear, doñeador dueño: doñeguil 'señoril' doñaguil Sal. 'clase de aceituna' doñegal, doñigal 'clase de higo'
novel novela: novelón, novelar, novelizar, novelable, novelador, novelero, novelería, novelista, novelística, novelesco	novillo: novillejo, novillada, novillero

cascabel: cascabelear, cascabeleo, cascabelada, cascabelero cascabelillo 'variedad de ciruela'	cascabillo 'cascabel de sonar', 'cascarilla que contiene el grano de trigo o cebada', cúpula de la bellota' cascabullo Sal. 'cúpula de la bellota'
mantel: mantelado, mantelería, manteleta, mantelete mantelo	mantilla: mantellina, mantilleja mantillo: mantillón
herpil 'saco de red de tomiza, con mallas anchas, destinado a portear paja, melones, etc.'	arpillera 'tejido por lo común de estopa muy basta, con que se cubren cosas para defenderlas del polvo y del agua.', arpillar Méj. 'cubrir con arpillera', arpillador, arpilladura
orden: ordenación, ordenadamente, ordenado, ordenador, ordenamiento, ordenante ordenando ordenada ordenanza: ordenancista	ordeñar: ordeñadora
mil: milhombres, milhojas, milgran, milenrama, milamores, milmillonésimo, milpiés, milrayas milésima, milésimo milenio, milenarista, milenarismo, milenario miliárea, miligramo, mililitro, milímetro	milla millar: millarada millón: millonada, millonario, millonésimo.
pastel: pastelear, pasteleo, pastelería, pastelero, pastelillo, pastelista, pastelón, empastelar, empastelamiento	pastilla: pastillero

We find allomorphy only in *miliar, miliario* 'dícese de la columna, piedra, etc., que antiguamente indicaba la distancia de mil pasos' (related to *milla* in its second meaning 'medida para las vías romanas, de ocho estadios o mil pasos de cinco pies romanos, equivalente a cerca de un cuarto de legua').

Unsurprisingly, the only word-family where allomorphy is significant is that of *piel*. Even in this case, there is a tendency for derivatives to eliminate alternants which are semantically unjustified. Instead of *pelleja* 'ramera', depalatalized *peleja* is found in Medieval Spanish (*Alex* O). Today, *pelejo* 'pellejo' is vulgar in Almería. Conversely, a back-formation *pello,* 'especie de zamarra fina' (instead of *piel*) was extracted from *pellón* 'vestido talar antiguo que se hacía regularmente de pieles'. A derivative, *pielero,* 'el que compra pieles crudas o comercia con ellas', was coined directly from *piel.* All compounds show *-l-*: *peliagudo, peliblando, pelicorto, peliduro, pelilargo, pelirrojo, pelirrubio.* The evolution of the verb *pelar* is also relevant. Its first definition according to the *Real Academia Española* (1992) is still 'cortar, arrancar, quitar o raer el pelo', which was the original Latin meaning of PILARE, from PILUM (Sp. *pelo*). Its third definition, 'despellejar, quitar la piel a un animal' comes from a Vulgar Latin extension of the original meaning also found in other Romance languages. In recent times, it has actually entered the family of *piel,* in spite of the fact that it does not show the expected diphthong in inflection (it is nevertheless inflected *yo pelo* < PILO, not ****yo pielo*). This was shown by the answers to Test 3. Out of 49 answers, 25 defined *pelar* as 'quitar la piel' or a similar phrase, classifying this as a definition with a word of the same family. Only 8 subjects defined *pelar* as 'quitar el pelo'.[7]

Allomorphy is also minimized by the tendency of derivatives to build their own families, independent from *piel* (17).

(17) Lack of allomorphic variants in the sub-families of *piel*

pellejo, pelleja 'piel quitada del cuerpo del animal': pellejuelo, pellejazo, pellejudo
pellón: pellote, pello
peletero 'persona que tiene por oficio trabajar pieles finas o venderlas' (Fr. pelletier): peletería
pelleta 'pelleja': pelletería, pelletero, Pellitero (family-name)
pelleja 'ramera'
pellejo 'cuero cosido para contener líquidos': pellejería, pellejina, pellejuela
pellejero 'persona que tiene por oficio adobar o vender pieles', pellijero,
pelliza 'prenda de abrigo hecha o forrada de pieles finas': sobrepelliz
pellica 'cobertor de cama hecho de pellejos finos, pellico hecho de pieles finas y adobadas, piel pequeña adobada', pellico 'zamarra de pastor', pelliquero
apellar 'untar y adobar la piel sobándola, para que reciba bien los ingredientes del color que se le quiere dar'.
traspillarse 'desfallecer, extenuarse'.

6. From the evidence gathered, we must conclude that there is no rule of depalatalization, and that there never was any. Of course, one can always reply that historical evidence is not relevant for synchronic analysis and that the behavior of speakers can be attributed to performance. All this may be true, but then we need an explanation for the fact that all past and present speakers are such incompetent performers.

Otherwise, we are forced to admit that a regular variation in surface lexical forms does not imply an underlying connection. The lexicon is organized in small sections, linked by both semantic and formal surface analogy. Semantically related words which are phonologically different tend to be stored separately. These results are at odds with what is universally assumed for the organization of derivation, which is supposed to be semantically based. As Marchand (1963: 220) states: "Content must be the final criterion of derivational relationship for any pair of words."

Actually, if the standard conception were true, one would expect morphophonological rules either to generalize or fade away homogeneously across the lexicon, according to morphological categories. In the long run, there would be a progressive regularization of morphophonology in the lexicon. Obviously this is not true. Morphophonological rules in the lexicon tend to split up following formal, not semantic, regularities. This happens in spite of the fact that morphophonological regularities are quite unmotivated from a morphological point of view, given their phonological origin. The diachronic result is that opacity in form leads to opacity in meaning.

According to Dressler (1985: §10.8.3.i and following), inflected forms tend towards biuniqueness between form and meaning (diagrammaticality): the same form tends to signal the same meaning. Inflection shows a tendency to link transparency of morphosemantic relationships to transparency of morphotactic relationships. Rules would tend to be diagrammatic and antidiagrammatic ones would tend to inversion or lexical fading or, at least, morphophonological rules would tend to appear in marked categories. This leads to systematically preferred base—derived relationships built on semantic principles of markedness and cognitive priority (see Bybee and Brewer (1980) for an interpretation of historical changes in Spanish morphophonemics following these principles). On the other hand, also following Dressler (1985), words tend to become lexicalized in derivation (i.e. stored as wholes), so that full semantic or morphotactic transparency are much less important. The more lexicalized words are, the more reference to lexical factors rules must have (i.e., exceptions).

However, Dressler does not explain how all this scenario comes about. In his model synchronic derivation may play two roles: one "generative" in inflection, another "interpretive" in derivation. Even in this interpretive function, Dressler assumes for rules a base-derived relationship which is unidirectional, semantically based, and unique (Dressler 1985: §10.8.3.5.1.). Links between words would be substantially identical in inflection and in derivation. If derivation in the lexicon is based on the same principles as in inflection, the tendency toward irregularity and the degrading of rules into analogy patterns (suppletion) are hard to explain.

On the contrary, if the unanalyzed word tends to take priority over single morphemes, this implies that processing within the lexicon is radically different: derivation has surface phonological analogy as its main ingredient, it tolerates a certain degree of semantic complexity, and it is non-unique.[8]

APPENDIX

Test 1.

a. Describir las siguientes situaciones:

1.Esto es un babacor   Esta es una máquina de babacorar
1b. Esto son dos _________s   Esto está bastante _______ado
Esto es muy _________oso

Same with: enapil—enapillar, minacús—minacurar, tipacol—tipacorar, siparén—sipareñar, tomirel—taumirelar.

b. Describir las siguientes situaciones:

1.Esta es una máquina de babacorar   Esto es un babacor
1b. Esto son dos _________s   Esto está bastante _______oso
Esto está muy _________ado

Same with: enapillar—enapil, minacurar—minacús, tipacorar—tipacol, sipareñar—siparén, taumirelar—tomirel.

Test 2.

Las palabras siguientes se derivan de una base (como *panadería* de *pan*). Escribir la base correspondiente en el espacio en blanco que hay a su derecha.
acción, acrobático, afeminar, aguzar, albuminal, analizar, apologético, apuesta,

ascenso, calamitoso, campista, celestial, científico, compromiso, conyugal, correcto, cosmopolizante, cúprico, desdeñoso, despierto, dificultar, digestión, eclipsar, electricista, entenebrecer, escultórico, fundamental, helvético, herboso, hospedar, imperial, infinidad, judicial, láctico, mágico, naufragar, paralizar, parentesco, paternal, pedagógico, pedregoso, pellejo, perjudicial, pescozón, piadoso, pleonástico, portugués, princesa, prodigioso, resplandor, sarcástico, serpentino, sinóptico, temeroso, universitario, vergonzoso, vertiginoso

Test 3.

Algunas palabras se pueden definir con una perífrasis basada en una palabra de la misma familia.

Por ejemplo: **panadería**: sitio donde se vende **pan**
calamitoso: que causa **calamidades**

Imaginar —si parece posible— una definición de este tipo (columna 1) para las palabras siguientes. Si no fuera posible, proponer otro tipo de definición (p.ej. **panadería**: tahona, **calamitoso**: catastrófico, que causa desgracias) en la columna 2.

Cuando no se conozca el significado de alguna palabra, se debe proponer una "definición" imaginaria marcándola siempre con una interrogación (?)

Words: doncellez, desdeñoso, tinte, abatismo, beldad, milla, clavellina, catalán, doñear, inquilino, pelar.

Test 4.

Se trata de **crear** palabras:

a. Si *tutear* es 'tratar de tú' y *ustedear* 'tratar de usted', ¿cómo se dirá 'tratar de don'?

Escribir la contestación en el espacio en blanco:

b. Si *yoidad* es un tecnicismo del lenguaje filosófico que quiere decir 'la cualidad de ser yo' ¿cómo se dirá 'la cualidad de ser él'?

Escribir la contestación en el espacio en blanco:

Notes

* This research was partly funded through *Acción Integrada Hispano Austriaca* 1994, 18B. My students of *Introducción a la Filología Románica* (2nd semester, 1994/1995) willingly answered the tests for this study and discussed the results. My son Víctor and Fernando Sánchez Miret volunteered for the pilot version of the tests. They all proved to be excelent specimens of that precious creature: the native speaker. The conclusions reached are mine, as are all errors and inaccuracies, but they are the source of the data. This paper could never have been written without their cooperation. Additional thanks go to W.U. Dressler for his bibliographical advice and to Julián Méndez Dosuna, who corrected an earlier version of this paper and made many interesting suggestions.

1 Unless otherwise stated, words are taken from the Real Academia Española (1992) dictionary and from Corominas and Pascual (1980/91), either directly of with the help of Bosque and Pérez Fernández (1987). The definitions are those of Real Academia Española (1992), and the abbreviations for the names of Old Spanish texts those of Corominas and Pascual (1980/91).

2 Postlexically, word final -l and -n palatalize before word initial palatals. We will not be further concerned with this context-dependent palatalization. I am grateful to Maria Rosa Lloret for drawing my attention to this phenomenon.

3 Results in the tables may not add up to 54 (the total number of subjects) due to a varying number of blank responses.

4 Diachronically, *temeroso* comes from Lat. TIMOROSUM with dissimilation in the sequence o—o.

5 *Salir* is the etymological form, *sallir* is an analogical generalization of the palatalized forms *sallió, salliendo,* etc. Therefore, instances with final *-l* are not demonstrative.

6 Word and syllable-final /ʃ/ (orthographic <x>), as in SEX > *sex*, FRAX(I)NU > *frexno*) may have been an exception as Torreblanca (1987) convincingly argues.

7 Other answers: 5 definitions involving different forms of the same verb *pelar*, 2 'quitar el pellejo', and 9 with unrelated words (*mondar*, etc.).

8 This implies that the tendency to group words according to their form would show great variation according to age and education. This seems to be confirmed by the results of Test 1 and 2 applied to Víctor (7 years).

References

Aronoff, Mark. 1976. *Word Formation in Generative Grammar*. Cambridge, Mass.: MIT Press.

Bosque, Ignacio and Manuel Pérez Fernández. 1987. *Diccionario Inverso de la Lengua Española*. Madrid: Gredos.

Bybee, Joan L. 1988. Morphology as lexical organization. *Theoretical Morphology*, ed. M. Hammond and M. Noonan. San Diego: Academic Press, 119-141.

Bybee, Joan L. and Mary Alexandra Brewer. 1980. Explanation in morphophonemics: changes in Provençal and Spanish preterite forms. *Lingua* 52.201-242.

Bybee, Joan L. and Carol Lynn Moder. 1983. Morphological classes as natural categories. *Language* 59.251-289.

Bybee, Joan L. and Elly Pardo. 1981. Morphological and lexical conditioning of rules: experimental evidence from Spanish. *Linguistics* 19.937-968.

Carstairs-McCarthy, Andrew. 1992. *Current Morphology*. London: Routledge.

Corominas, Juan and José Antonio Pascual. 1980/91. *Diccionario Crítico-etimológico Castellano e Hispánico*. Madrid: Gredos.

Dressler, Wolfgang U. 1985. *Morphonology. The Dynamics of Derivation*. Ann Arbor: Karoma Publishers.

Harris, James W. 1983. *Syllable Structure and Stress in Spanish: a Nonlinear Analysis*. Cambridge, Mass.: MIT Press.

Harris-Northall, Raymond. 1990. *Weakening Processes in the History of Spanish Consonants*. London: Routledge.

Kiparsky, Paul 1985. Some consequences of lexical phonology. *Phonology Yearbook* 2.85-138.

Kiparsky, Paul. 1982. From Cyclic phonology to Lexical Phonology. *The Structure of Phonological Representations* (Part I), ed. by Harry van der Hulst and Norval Smith. Dordrecht: Foris, 131-175.

Lapesa, Rafael. 1951. La apócope de la vocal en castellano antiguo. Intento de explicación histórica. *Estudios Dedicados a Ramón Menéndez Pidal II*. Madrid: CSIC, 185-226. Also in *Estudios de Historia Lingüística Española*. Madrid: Paraninfo, 1985: 167-197.

Lieber, Rochelle. 1981. *On the Organization of the Lexicon*. Bloomington: Indiana University Linguistics Club.

MacWhinney, Brian. 1994. The dinosaurs and the ring. *The Reality of Linguistic Rules*, ed. Susan D. Lima, Roberta L. Corrigan and Gregory K. Iverson. Amsterdam: Benjamins, 283-320.

Marchand, Hans. 1963. On content as a criterion of derivational relationship with backderived words. *Indogermanische Forschungen* 68.170-175.

Mascaró, Joan. 1990. Teoría de la asimilación en las lenguas románicas. *Estudios de lingüística de España y México*, ed. Violeta Demonte and Beatriz Garza Cuarón. México: UNAM and El Colegio de México, 465-487.

Menéndez Pidal, Ramón. 1944. *Manual de Gramática Histórica Española* (7th ed.). Madrid: Espasa-Calpe.

Pensado, Carmen. 1984. *Cronología Relativa del Castellano*. Salamanca: Ediciones Universidad de Salamanca.

Pensado, Carmen. 1993. Consonantes geminadas en la evolución histórica del español. *Actas del Primer Congreso Anglo-hispano*. I Lingüística, ed Ralph Penny. Madrid: Castalia, 193-204.

Pensado, Carmen. in prep. Sobre las formas *ell* del artículo.

Rainer, Franz. 1993. *Spanische Wortbildungslehre*. Tübingen: Niemeyer.

Real Academia Española. 1992. *Diccionario de la Lengua Española* (21st ed.) Madrid: Espasa-Calpe.

Rumelhart, David E. and James L. McClelland. 1986. Learning the past tenses of English verbs: Implicit rules or parallel distributed processing? *Mechanisms of Language Acquisition*, ed. Brian MacWhinney. Hillsdale, NJ: Erlbaum, 195-248.

Schede, Hildegard. 1987. *Die Morphologie des Verbes im Altspanischen*. Bern: Peter Lang.

Torreblanca, Máximo. 1987. Sobre la evolución de sibilantes implosivas en español. *JHP* 11.151-173, 223-249.

19

On the role of accent in stress systems: Spanish evidence*

I. M. Roca

0 Introduction

Generative stress theory originated in *The Sound Pattern of English* (*SPE*) in the form of a tightly knit system of rules generating the complex stress patterns of English. Subsequent developments in the theory have consistently aimed at substituting rules by metrically-based parameters. A current trend seeks to derive such parameters from general rhythmic principles.[1]

The empirical challenge faced by this program is, not surprisingly, very considerable. Two recent monographs take up this challenge from the complementary angles of universal typology (Hayes 1995) and in-depth probe of a particular language (English: Burzio 1994). The present paper tests out the rhythmic program with data from Spanish nominals (appositely compared with their Italian congeners where helpful). Spanish is particularly well-suited for the task, a wealth of previous generative studies having brought to the fore both the body of (not exceedingly complex) data and the problems they pose for the current stress theories. In addition, the predecessor system (Latin) is well known, and consistently analyzed in the literature as moraic (i.e., rhythmic and quantity sensitive). The natural assumption would be (and indeed has frequently been) that this system should in essence persist in the daughter languages. A close examination of the Spanish data, however, casts strong doubt on the empirical accuracy of this forecast, a situation readily understandable when approached from the standpoint of learnability in view of the well-known historical changes that affected the prosodic makeup of the language.

As will be shown, the Spanish evidence supports the theoretical necessity of the device 'accent', plausibly interpreted as a survivor of the *SPE* rule-based approach. The conclusion that both accent and rhythm must be simultaneously countenanced in stress theory is clearly an undesirable development for the rhythm-based program, hence its general theoretical interest. The following comment in Hayes (1995: 244) with regard to the rule of Pre-Long Strengthening in Norton Sound is revealing in this connection: "If we allow Pre-Long Strengthening directly to add a stress in syllables that precede long vowels then we are greatly weakening metrical theory by allowing rules of the form '$\sigma \rightarrow \acute{\sigma}$ / P ___ Q'. The whole point of the research program is to constrain stress rules by limiting the set of foot-parsing algorithms". The evidence presented in the present paper points to the inevitability of such weakening.

The organization of the paper is as follows. In the first section, the basic data of Spanish nominal stress are laid out and analyzed from the perspective of the standard metrical theory of Halle and Vergnaud (1987). In section 2, the new theory of Burzio (1994) is evaluated against Spanish (and some Italian) data. Particular problems concern the unmarked status of penultimate stress irrespective of syllable weight, the compatibility of proparoxytone stress with heavy penults, and the obligatoriness of penultimate stress in a subset of forms with light penults. In section 3, we turn to the analysis of vowel-ending oxytones, also problematic for Burzio's theory. Section 4 offers a principled account of Spanish (and implicitly Italian) nominal stress harmonious with Halle and Vergnaud's (1987) framework, one which is moreover strictly respectful of all the empirical idiosyncracies of the system. This account is built on a reappraisal of the role of accent, which is crucially shown to be compatible with the Spanish learner's experience. Finally, in the concluding section 5, the proposed stress algorithm is summarized, and both the role of accent in the system and the learnability plausibility of the analysis are further underlined.

1. The standard analysis of Spanish nominal stress

1.1 The data

The profusion of literature on Spanish stress[2] curiously contrasts with the apparent simplicity of the Spanish stress patterns. In a nutshell, Spanish nouns, adjectives and adverbs, the categories object of the present study,[3] may end in a vowel or in a consonant. In vowel-ending words, stress is normally penultimate, and in consonant-ending words, final.[4]

We shall now illustrate this distribution (whenever relevant to the discussion, stress will be marked directly on the stressed vowel, irrespective of orthographic conventions):

(1)	a.	mángo	'handle'	b.	mongól	'Mongol'
		aréna	'sand'		arenál	'sands'
		húmo	'smoke'		humór	'humor'
		urráca	'magpie'		huracán	'hurricane'

Deviations from this basic pattern are, however, possible:

(2)	a.	maná	'manna'	b.	mármol	'marble'
		café	'coffee'		alférez	'ensign'
		colibrí	'humming bird'		Víctor	Victor
		capó	'car hood'		Óscar	Oscar
	c.	Málaga	a city			
		pétalo	'petal'			
		pícaro	'rascal'			
		zócalo	'plinth'			

In any event, however, stress invariably falls on one of the three rightmost stress bearers (vocoids: see Roca 1991):[5]

(3)	a.	atávico	'atavistic'
		alívio	'relief'
		paralalepípedo	'parallelepiped'
	b.	atavísmo	'atavism'
		atavío	'attire'
		constantinopolitáno	'constantinoplan'
	c.	avión	'airplane'
		capó	'car hood'
		Nabucodonosór	Nebuchadnezzar

Over the past decade, the formal mechanisms responsible for this distribution have been thoroughly investigated in the frame of standard metrical theory (see Halle and Vergnaud 1987 for a complete and authoritative statement of this theory), the gap between the various positions having gradually narrowed considerably. A 'standard' analysis of Spanish stress in the categories under scrutiny can therefore be extracted without much difficulty, and will be summarized in the following subsections.

1.2 Nominal Morphology

Morphologically, nominals (an *ad hoc* common term for nouns, adjectives, and adverbs) are made up of a stem (a lexical root possibly followed by one or more derivational suffixes) and a desinence, which can be null.

There are strong grounds for the identification of the desinence as a separate constituent. Specifically, the following, completely transparent, facts are of direct relevance:

1. some word-final vowels (possibly followed by *-s*) are lost in the course of the derivation (*pasta* 'paste' → *past-oso* 'pasty-MASC'; *cosmos* 'cosmos' → *cósm-ica* 'cosmic-FEM');

2. such vowels can be subject to gender-based alternation (*hermano* 'brother' ~ *hermana* 'sister');

3. such vowels (followed by *-s* where appropriate) always occupy the word's rightmost position[6] (*past-a* 'paste' → *past-os-a* 'pasty-FEM' → *past-os-ísim-a* 'very pasty-FEM');

4. such vowels are meaningless, notwithstanding their (partial) correlation with gender (cf. *el/la belg-a* 'the-MASC/FEM Belgian', *el/la re-o* 'the-MASC/FEM accused'; compare also *cosm-os* 'cosmos' with *past-os-o* 'pasty': the first *-os* is indeed meaningless, while the second *-os*, an adjectivising suffix equivalent to English *-ous*, is roughly paraphrasable as 'full of');

5. such vowels are systematically stressless.

These facts provide strong support for a special (inflectional) suffix, made up of any of the five Spanish vowels (*i*, *e*, *a*, *o*, *u*), possibly followed by *-s*, and to which we shall conveniently refer by the label 'desinence' (see Harris 1991b for general discussion of the system).

Thus, as already hinted at in Saporta (1962) and developed in Hooper and Terrell (1976) and Harris (1980), Spanish nominals are composed of two basic constituents: a 'stem', broken down into a lexical root and any number of derivational affixes, and a desinence. Desinence gender-sensitivity is readily formalizable through lexical underspecification of the desinence's phonological substance, eventually supplied by a gender-sensitive redundancy rule.[7] The rightmost positioning of the desinence follows naturally from a construal of this constituent as an inflectional suffix. The omission of desinences word-internally following derivational suffixation is likewise accounted for straightforwardly if the derivational domain is identified with the stem, rather than with the word. Finally, and directly relevant to our present concerns, the systematic stresslessness of desinences inevitably points to weak metrical status for such a constituent.

1.3 The stem as stress domain

1.3.1 The model

The metrical weakness of Spanish desinences is formalized in Roca (1988) as direct exclusion from the stress domain. This move leads to a remarkably simple model, in which stress falls on the stem-final stress bearer, with lexical extrametricality accounting for (marked) cases of further retraction to the left. Compare for instance the derivations of *avión*, *atavío*, and *atávico* under this approach in (4) (derivational morphology plays no role in the phenomena at hand, and will therefore be systematically ignored):

```
(4)          *              *              *             line 1
          (* * *)        (* * *)        (* *)<*>         line 0
     a.   a v i ó n   b. a t a v í - o  c. a t á v i c - o
```

In keeping with Roca (1988), (4) contains line 0 unbounded constituents, but the model is equally compatible with bounded constituents, either non-iterative or eventually reduced by means of a conflation clause. As noted, the extrametricality mark in (4c) must be considered lexically-governed, given the marked condition of this pattern.

1.3.2 Problems

While the bulk of relevant data is satisfactorily accounted for by such a model, some descriptive problems remain. First, a handful of forms *with no desinence*, of which *régimen* 'regime' is the best representative,[8] have antepenultimate stress. Whatever the constituency analysis of these forms may be (a specific proposal is made directly below), their final stress bearer must obviously be extrametrical, so as to exclude it from the count:

```
(5)      *
         *  * <*>
        r é g i m e n
```

Were a desinence to be added to this representation, preantepenultimate stress would result. Thus, a (hypothetical) form *régimena* is licensed by the model as it stands, since under this account the desinence *-a* will simply be placed outside the stress domain (technically, it will not project a line 0 element):

```
(6)      *
         *  * <*>
        r é g i m e n - a
```

As has already been mentioned, however, the three-syllable window constitutes the most robust generalization available on Spanish nominal stress, and essentially admits no violation.[9] Not surprisingly, therefore, stress shift takes place when a (desinence-containing) syllable is added to *régimen* to form the plural: *regímenes*. If desinences were outside the stress domain, as they are in (6), there would be no motivation for such a shift.

A second source of potential embarrassment for the analysis under scrutiny concerns such foreign forms as *Wáshington*. Again, if desinences lay outside the stress domain, a pattern *Wáshingtona* (as, say, in a Finnish- or Icelandic-type place name) would be expected to occur in Spanish, contrary to fact, the three-syllable window being instead invariably respected.

1.4 The word as stress domain

1.4.1 Accounting for the three syllable window

While the quantitative impact of the two classes of facts just presented is relatively minor, they are, however, sufficiently real to impose the inclusion of the desinence in the stress domain. This inclusion can be made formally consistent with the observation of desinence stresslessness by simply declaring the desinence extrametrical (Roca 1990a). Given the standard constraints on extrametricality, in particular the Peripherality Condition,[10] all the relevant facts fall into place.

Thus, in *regímenes*, the desinence *-es* now contributes an (extrametrical) stress bearer, and consequently compliance with the three-syllable window will force stress to fall on the string *gime*. In the singular *régimen*, by contrast, stress on *re* is compatible with the window:

```
(7)  a. r é g i m e n          b. r e g í m e n e s
          3  2  1                   4  3  2  1
```

Formally, this result can be achieved by means of two simple additional assumptions: (i) *men* carries lexical extrametricality, and (ii) leftheaded binary feet are constructed in both forms (see Roca 1988; here and henceforth additional construction of a rightheaded unbounded word constituent followed by conflation is assumed):

```
(8)         *                        *                line 1
           (*  *)<*>             * (*   *)<*>         line 0
     a.    r é g i m e n     b.  r e g í m e n e s
```

Similarly, in a hypothetical string *Washingtona*, the three syllable window can only be implemented if *-a* is made (an extrametrical) part of the stress domain, thereby confining stress to one of the two vocoids in the string *shingto*.

1.4.2 Stem-final vs. stem-prefinal stress

We shall now see that the formal mechanism responsible for the dichotomy stem-final vs. stem-prefinal stress is awkward to accommodate within standard stress theory under the word-domain analysis just sketched.

Thus, let us suppose that contrary to our assumptions here, stem-prefinal stress (as in, e.g. sában-a 'sheet') were unmarked (cf. Otero 1986 for a defense of such interpretation). In this case, the unmarked location of Spanish stress would be derivable by means of a leftheaded binary foot on the grid's right edge (cf. the derivation of *régimen* and *regímenes* in (8) above), essentially along the lines of Macedonian (see Roca 1992a for a sum-up of the stress system of this language). In turn, marked stem-final stress, as in e.g. *saban-a* 'savannah', could be made to follow from the inclusion of the appropriate accentual mark in lexical representation, also as in Macedonian.[11] The irregularity of *régimen* (and of *Wáshington*) would now be formalizable as lexical extrametricality of the final stem syllable, as in the representation in (8) above. This extrametricality would of course be lost in the plural *regímenes*, where the lexically extrametrical syllable *-men* has ceased being peripheral, again as in (8).

It can readily be seen that, besides being in all compatible with the distributional facts of Spanish stress, this account scores high for simplicity. Were formal description to be our exclusive concern, there would thus be no reason not to stop the analysis here. As is common knowledge, however, the goal of linguistics in the Chomskyan paradigm is not merely descriptive, but also, and more particularly, cognitive. Specifically, this paradigm imposes the metatheoretical requirement that the formalization of distributional facts be representative of the speaker's mental grammar. In the case at hand, such evidence as is available strongly suggests that stem-final stress is preferred (see Roca 1990a for specific arguments). The inevitable formal consequence of this fact is seemingly the reversal of foot headedness, i.e. the rightheaded, rather than leftheaded, setting of the Spanish basic foot (i.e., *(sab$\overset{*}{a}$)<na>*, *(reg$\overset{*}{i}$)<men>*, etc.). If this step is taken, however, the formalization of (marked) stem-prefinal stress becomes problematic, since the standard theory makes available no device other than extrametricality to permit the algorithm to skip a stress bearer. In the case under scrutiny, however, extrametricality can no longer be resorted to, since it is already used up by the desinence (or by the final stem syllable in the *régimen* class).

Two reasonable strategies are available for formally overcoming this difficulty without abandoning the standard theory.[12] The first involves the postulation of two complementary types of foot for Spanish: the default foot, indeed rightheaded, and the marked foot, leftheaded (Roca 1988, 1990, 1991). A proposal along these lines can be conceptually related to Borer's (1984) and Wexler and Manzini's (1987) lexical parametrization hypothesis for syntax. Specifically, while both the head-terminalness and the boundedness parameters would be set uniformly across the Spanish lexicon (with a 'plus' value for both), the headedness parameter would be lexically marked as leftheaded in some forms, and in others (the majority) it would be left blank in the lexicon and set as rightheaded by a (language-specific) default procedure.

An alternative is offered in Halle *et al.* (1991) (see also Harris 1988/92). These authors maintain a leftheaded setting for the Spanish foot across the board, and have foot construction preceded by a rule assigning an accentual mark on the right edge of the stem, as follows (Halle *et al.* 1991: 145):

(9) "Accent (that is, mark with * on line 1) the rightmost (metrical) syllable"

Forms with stem-prefinal stress will now simply be marked as lexical exceptions to the accent rule in (9). The consequences of this formalism are obvious: in the absence of stem-final accent (following from the lexical exception mark), a leftheaded binary foot will be built, and stress will accordingly be stem-prefinal. By contrast, in the regular cases the rule-assigned accent will stump the formation of such a foot, and stem-final stress will result. The two alternatives are illustrated in (10):

```
(10)  a.  a v i ó n   a t a v í - o      b.  a t á v i c - o      Lexicon
                                             [-accent]

             *            *
          a v i o n   a t a v i - o               NA              accent


             *            *                    *                  line 1
          *  *(*)     *  * (*)<*>          * (*    *) <*>         line 0
          a v i o n   a t a v i  - o       a t a v  i c - o
```

The two accounts just sketched manifestly achieve descriptive success. This notwithstanding, they are both problematic in a more general context. Thus, the postulation of an accent rule for the *normal* pattern arguably amounts to a marked construal of this pattern, an apparent formal travesty.[13] On the other hand, the inclusion of alternative parameter settings in one and the same procedure clearly is a disfavored practice (cf. the Uniformity of Algorithm Principle of Roca 1988, related to McCarthy and Prince's 1986: 9-10 Uniformity Parameter).[14] These difficulties point to the need for a radically fresh approach to the issue.[15] One such approach, embodied in the theoretical framework of Burzio (1994), will now be presented and evaluated (sections 2 and 3).

2. A New Theory of Stress

2.1 Basic Tenets and Analysis

Burzio's (1994) theory makes available the following primitive inventory of left-headed feet (H = heavy syllable, L = light syllable, σ = syllable of either type):

(11) a. (H σ)

b. (σ L σ)

On this simple foundation, the analysis of Spanish stress will proceed as follows (cf. Burzio 199: 30-32). The domain of stress will still be the whole word. Word-final consonants will be parsed as onsets of an empty nucleus occupying the place of the desinence. Desinences (including empty desinences) will normally be metrical.

The analysis of our familiar word *atávico* 'atavistic' in the given terms will be as follows:

(12)
```
    *
  * (* * *)
  a tá v i c o
    σ  L  σ
```

Notice that, crucially, the middle syllable *vi* is light, hence the selection of the ternary foot. The stress pattern of *mármol* 'marble' will be derived along similar lines, as in (13):

(13)
```
   *
  (*   * *)
 m a r m o l V
   σ   L σ
```

By contrast, in *atavísmo* 'atavism', the heavy penult forces selection of a binary foot, hence the paroxytone contour:

(14)
```
        *
 * * (*    *)
 a t a v i s m o
       H    σ
```

So far, the theory obviously fares well for Spanish stress. We shall see in the following subsections, however, that other forms (specifically, proparoxytones with a heavy penult and polysyllabic paroxytones with a light penult) create serious difficulties for the approach.

2.2 Problems with quantity-sensitivity

As displayed in (11) above, Burzio's (1994) model incorporates syllable quantity directly into the foot shape, parallelling the strategy in Hayes (1995). In particular, the given binary foot requires the (penultimate) head to be heavy, while its ternary counterpart necessitates a light penult. We will now see both these requirements to be problematic for Spanish (also for Italian, with a closely related stress system with which comparison is fruitful, and which is also the object of Burzio's attention).

2.2.1. Unmarked penultimate stress

First, penultimate stress is unmarked in Spanish (and Italian) *regardless* of the closed or open nature of the syllable. Burzio's strategy for Italian is to analyze the vowel of stressed penultimate open syllables as long, on the grounds that such vowels are indeed long phonetically.[16] The construal of such syllables as heavy would thus account for the corresponding paroxytone stress pattern.

The formalization of the vowel in question as lexically long has however the puzzling consequence of making Italian vowel length contrastive only in (open) penults. In response to this difficulty, Burzio proposes to derive such length directly from the conditions built into template (11a), namely from the required heaviness of the head of the binary foot responsible for the penultimate stress (this strategy obviously implies a construal of the given templates as well-formedness conditions on metrical representations, in a manner germane to the Optimality Theory of McCarthy and Prince 1993 and Prince and Smolensky 1993, rather than as algorithms generating these representations).

Note however that, if the lexical representations of both *ánc*[o]*ra* 'anchor' and *anc*[ó:]*ra* 'still' are identical (/ankora/, with no vowel length marking), their surface stress patterns also ought to be the same, contrary to fact. The inevitable consequence is the representation of penultimate stress in the lexicon (cf. e.g. /ankóra/ → ankó:ra). This is at odds with the unmarked nature of this pattern, most likely in Italian[17] and most certainly in Spanish, to which language Burzio hints the analysis would carry over, as we will see below in more detail.

Moreover, this approach places final stress on a par with penultimate stress. In particular, Burzio (like Idsardi 1992; cf. note 15 above) explicitly rejects the possibility of (rhythm-generated) unary feet universally (unary feet are indeed notorious for their absence in the inventory in (11) above), and therefore final stress also needs to be formalized as fully trochaic (detailed discussion appears in section 3 below):

```
(15)           *
            *  (*  *)
          p a l t ó  V    'coat'
```

In vowel-ending oxytones, however, the weight requirements imposed by the theory on the binary foot seemingly remain unfulfilled, Italian word-final stressed vowels being consistently reported as short.[18]

The situation obviously worsens in Spanish, which lacks the special phonetic lengthening exhibited by Italian stressed open penults, the only piece of empirical evidence for the Italian analysis. Specifically, according to Navarro

Tomás (1916), Spanish stressed vowels undergo some lengthening under stress quite independently of both syllable type and position, the magnitude of such lengthening being greatest in oxytones, and this includes syllables closed by consonants other than *n* or *l*.[19] All this manifestly illustrates the phonetic nature of stressed vowel lengthening in Spanish (see Lehiste 1970 on phonetic conditioning of vowel length generally). Consequently, Spanish penultimate stress is also unmarked *on light syllables*, a situation incompatible with Burzio's (1994) theory as summarized in (11) above.

One obvious strategy to integrate the Spanish pattern in the theory involves the enrichment of the foot inventory with a third type of foot, as follows:

(16) $(\sigma\,\sigma)$

Burzio indeed uses this foot for Tiberian Hebrew, a language he manifestly approaches as quantity-insensitive.[20] This extension of the foot inventory thus captures the opposition between quantity-sensitive and quantity-insensitive systems (cf. the contrast between the moraic and the syllabic trochee in Hayes 1995). In particular, quantity-insensitive systems are now predicted to contain binary feet exclusively, whereas the feet of their quantity-sensitive counterparts are targeted as ternary, remaining binary only when their second-from-last syllable is heavy. The problem for Spanish is the inconsistency of the data, which include both ternary and binary feet, quite independently of syllable weight (cf. *sábana* 'sheet' and *sabána* 'savannah', respectively). Obviously, if the former are adopted as basic, forms with stressed open penults will have to be lexically marked, in direct opposition to the markedness scale we have been proposing. If, on the other hand, the lexical mark is carried by proparoxytones, we will in effect be replicating the standard analysis reported in section 1 above, while still failing to provide a principled account for the preference of Spanish for penultimate stress irrespective of weight.

2.2.2 Proparoxytones with heavy penults

The second problematic aspect of a Spanish analysis on Burzio's terms directly concerns ternary feet. Remember that in this theory antepenultimate stress is formalized by means of a ternary foot, as in (11b) above, rather than with a binary foot coupled with extrametricality, as in the standard theory. Crucially, the medial syllable of the ternary foot needs to be light: (σ- L σ-). Now, while Spanish patrimonial, or patrimonial-looking, forms indeed disfavor antepenultimate stress in the presence of a heavy penult (e.g. *Tubínga*, not **Túbinga*, *Lepánto* not **Lépanto*; cf. German *Tübingen*, Italian *Lépanto*, repectively), the light penult requirement is freely violated by such obviously foreign forms as *Wáshington*.

This matter has been the object of some debate in the literature. The tack adopted in Harris (1988/92) is simply to exclude the latter forms from the formal account of Spanish stress, on the grounds that, being foreign, they are stressed by mere mimicry. Clearly, if only patrimonial forms are considered, the case for treating Spanish stress as quantity sensitive will be very strong.

Some problems for such a treatment would however remain. First, it was suggested by Trubetzkoy (1939) that stress sensitivity to syllable quantity presupposes a systemic vowel length contrast.[21] Languages like Latin or Arabic, whose stress is manifestly quantity-sensitive, indeed possess such phonemic vowel length. As is well-known, however, the length contrasts of Latin vowels were lost in Spanish, where, in parallel with other Romance dialects, no new length contrasts have arisen. From a universal perspective, therefore, stress quantity-sensitivity in Spanish (or Italian) would clearly be anomalous.

Moreover, among the Spanish patrimonial forms is the place name *Frómista*, where a ternary foot coexists with a heavy penult. This form appears to be a stress isolate, and as such it is ignored in much of the literature (also on account of its being a place name). However, such an attitude is difficult to reconcile with the fact that the peculiar stress contour *Frómista* has survived intact through the centuries:[22] one would reasonably expect such an idiosyncracy to have been ironed out if Spanish were indeed quantity-sensitive, precisely as a result of its isolation. The fact that it has persisted, strongly points to an element of quantity-insensitivity in the Spanish stress system. Parallel forms exist in Italian (cf. *Lépanto*, *Ófanto*, *Táranto*, *Ótranto*, all place names, and at least two common nouns, *mándorla* 'almond', *póli*[tts]*a* 'policy'). If Italian were unconditionally quantity-sensitive, as it must be on Burzio's account, the survival of these forms would also be paradoxical.

Note that the data we are dealing with directly concern I-language, in the sense of Chomsky (1986). In particular, the natural assumption is that, in parallel with other aspects of language behavior, stress cannot simply be echoed by the (average) speaker, but, rather, it must be generated from the internalized grammar.[23] Obviously, thus, in the specific cases of Spanish and Italian, the grammar must allow for stressless heavy penults, and therefore it cannot be quantity-sensitive *strictu sensu*.

The argument applies even more forcefully to such foreign names as *Wáshington* (in both Spanish and Italian), given the open-endedness of this class. Note that a stress pattern *Wáshington* would plainly be inconceivable (and is of course counterfactual) in a French speaker *qua* French speaker in the context of present-day French. Rather than reproducing the original non-final stresses of English (or, where appropriate, Dutch, German, etc.), French speakers invariably adapt all such words to the oxytone French stress pattern, regardless of the obvious foreignness of these forms, and despite the well-known popular acceptance of 'Franglais'. The most reasonable conclusion to draw from these facts is that the French stress system is incompatible with the contour *Wáshington*, whereas the stress systems of Spanish and Italian are compatible with it. If they are compatible with it, they must at least allow for the suspension of quantity-sensitivity, and, if so, Burzio's universal requirement of a light middle syllable in the ternary foot cannot be upheld.[24]

In addition, and most revealingly, it is simply not the case that the Spanish (or Italian) speaker can reproduce *any* type of foreign stress,[25] a feat that would mysteriously place this speaker head and shoulders above his French counterpart. This claim is not difficult to verify, since the initial stress of a sufficiently long place name in Finnish, Hungarian, or Icelandic will inevitably be reinterpreted to enforce compatibility with the three-syllable window.[26] The obvious implication is that, while the proparoxytone contour of *Wáshington*, with a heavy penult, is compatible with the Spanish stress grammar, the preantepenultimate stress of, e.g. *Schéveningen* (a Dutch seaside resort) is not. If so, this grammar cannot contain an absolute ban on stressless heavy penults, although it does contain one on preantepenultimate stress.

Let us now scrutinize the reason for the usual stressing of heavy penults in Spanish (and Italian). In the first place, as we have been highlighting all along, penultimate stress is unmarked in these languages, and therefore no specific statement will be needed in their synchronic grammars to account for this pattern, whether or not the penult is heavy, a point whose full import has often been played down in the literature. Therefore, all that remains to be accounted for is the systematic absence of an exception mark under the guise of either a marked setting of the parameter or a rule-exception feature, as discussed at the end of section 1, in all (but, obviously, not only) these forms (*Frómista* mysteriously excepted in Spanish, and *mutatis mutandis* for Italian).

This narrower issue can be broken down into two subissues. The first subissue concerns the historical source of the situation. The answer is straightforward. Simply, the fact that Latin was quantity-sensitive entails that words with a heavy penult could not have been proparoxytone in this language. Moreover, as pointed out by Menéndez Pidal (1962: 36), among others, the syllabic locus of Latin stress is (overwhelmingly) preserved in Spanish (and other Romance dialects). As a consequence of both these facts, words with a heavy penult will have been historically stressed on precisely this syllable. Importantly for our purposes here, no special statement will be needed to capture this pattern in the synchronic grammar, given the noted general unmarked status of penultimate stress.[27]

The second subissue is a bit more troublesome for a quantity-insensitive position. Specifically, while a handful of paroxytones with light penults have (historically) become proparoxytones (*medúla* → *médula* 'marrow bone', *vertígo* → *vértigo* 'vertigo', *idólo* → *ídolo* 'idol', etc.; see Otero 1986), no such change is observable in words with heavy penults. Also, Núñez Cedeño (1988) reports that Dominicans who drop coda *s* do not hypercorrect (by reinserting *s*) in light penults of proparoxytones (thus e.g. *muchácho* 'boy' can become *muschácho* or *mucháscho* (also *mucháschos*), but *plátano* 'plantain' never becomes **plátasno* (although it does become *plástano* or *plátanos*)). Both these facts point to a ban on stressless heavy penults in native proparoxytones (but clearly not in proparoxytones of obvious foreign extraction, as attested by *Wáshington*, *Mánchester* etc.). The logic of Burzio's theory as presented above will however prevent the formalization of such a constraint as across-the-board quantity-sensitivity, and therefore a more specific interpretation must be sought. One such solution will be offered in section 4 below.[28]

2.2.3 Obligatory Paroxytones with Light Penults

An additional problem for Spanish quantity-sensitivity concerns cases where Burzio's ternary foot is blocked by a light medial syllable. In particular, when the word's *final onset* contains a palatal consonant or /x/, antepenultimate stress is systematically eschewed, as exemplified in (17) (hypothetical impossible forms are given in parentheses; *ñ* = [ɲ], *ll* = [ʎ], *ch* = [č], *j* = [x]; *y* spells a palatal consonant with different degrees of constriction in different dialects):

(17)	rebáño	'flock'	(**rábaño*; cf. *rábano* 'radish')
	cabállo	'horse'	(**cáballa*; cf. *cábala* 'cabal')
	caprícho	'caprice'	(**ápricho*; cf. *ínclito* 'illustrious')
	plebéya	'plebeian'	(**huébeya*; cf. *huéspeda* 'guest')
	caníjo	'wee'	(**(me)cánijo*; cf. *mecánico* 'mechanic')

A clearly desirable move would be to assimilate these cases to those with overt heavy penults, and some proposals to this effect are in existence (e.g. Carreira 1988, Dunlap 1991). In essence, in these proposals Spanish palatals are represented lexically as double segments, viz. as a non-palatal coronal (/t/ for *ch*; /n/ for *ñ*, and /l/ for *ll*) followed by what can be referred to as a 'palatal glide' (effectively the vocoid [i] syllabified in the onset that follows the coronal). The parsing of the first of the two segments in the coda of the penultimate syllable will thus render such a syllable heavy, as illustrated in (18) (in line with the pertinent literature, the 'palatal glide' is represented as *y*):

(18) a. cacho 'piece' b. caño 'pipe' c. callo 'corn'

The two heterosyllabic underlying segments must eventually be coalesced (crucially, after stress assignment) to yield the surface single palatal segment.

The analysis just given has been claimed to be justified independently of stress. Thus, Carreira (1988) enumerates the following idiosyncracies of Spanish palatals:

1. they do not occur in codas, and consequently lexical palatals depalatalize in that position (*desdén(-es)* 'disdain(s)' vs. *desdeñe-s* 'you disdain-SUBJ');

2. they cannot be followed by the front glide, and consequently a suffix-initial palatal glide is deleted after a stem-final palatal (*lam-iendo* 'licking' vs. *tañ-endo* 'ringing'; cf. however *Chiâpas*, as least in Mexican Spanish);

3. coda sonorants are disallowed before *ñ* and *ll* monomorphemically (**corño*, **conña*, **colña*, **corllo*, **conlla*, **collla*), although not before *ch* (*corcho* 'cork', *concha* 'shell', *colcha* 'bed spread').

Dunlap (1991) also points out that [y] is the only palatal capable of occurring word- or syllable-finally, and that word- final *Vy* diphthongs are invariably stressed (e.g. *convóy* 'convoy'). Such facts are however irrelevant to the issue at hand, since the segment that appears word- or syllable-finally is not a special 'palatal glide' [y], but simply the *vocoid* /i/, whose behavior parallels the behavior of its back counterpart /u/ in forms of non-Spanish origin (cf. e.g. Catalan names like *Mompóu*; the absence of such a non-syllabic /u/ in strictly patrimonial Spanish forms is an accident of history). In both cases, final stress follows from three independent facts (see Roca 1991): (i) the parsing of the high vocoids in the stem (NB. not the desinence), (ii) the stress-bearer status of *all* vocoids, and (iii) the post-stress syllabic merger of such two abutting vowels.

With regard to the palatal consonants, the double consonant analysis would account for the three facts listed above, as follows (Carreira 1988):

1. a [ny] coda cluster would incur violation of the Sonority Sequencing Generalization, and therefore [y] will remain unsyllabified word-finally, being eventually deleted by Stray Erasure (e.g. *(des)(den)y* → *desdén*);[29]

2. whatever constraint accounts for the blocking of the sequence *yiV* will automatically explain the absence of *ñiV* if *ñ* is analyzed as /ny/ (and correspondingly for the other palatals);

3. in the event of *ñ* or *ll* being preceded by another consonant, the *n* of *ny* and the *l* of *ly* would require parsing as the second element of a complex coda (e.g. /rn.y/ for *rñ*); such parsing would however violate sonority conditions (involving either minimal sonority distance or straight sonority sequencing) for the sequences *rn.y*, *rl.y*, *ln.y*, *nl.y*, but not for *rt.y*, *lt.y*, *nt.y*.

Dunlap (1991) extends this analysis to [x], the other antepenultimate stress blocker (cf. **(me)cánijo* vs. *caníjo* or *mecánico* in (17) above; *cónyu*[x]*e* 'spouse' derives from *cónyu/g/e*: cf. *conyu*[g]*al* 'conjugal'), by proposing /ky/ as its lexical source. This move automatically accounts for the stress restriction, along obvious lines. Unfortunately, however, it also carries the counterfactual implication that the segmental constraints observed for palatals extend to [x] (NB. *g* = [x] before *i*, *e*):

(19) a. reloj(-es) 'clock(-s)'
b. cog-iendo 'taking'
c. lonja 'slice', forja 'forge', aljibe 'cistern, tank'

Deprived of this support, the analysis of [x] as /ky/ obviously becomes circular.

A host of problems also beset the parallel analysis of palatals and ultimately invalidate it. In the interest of expository economy, we shall focus on the strongest, and therefore most interesting, prediction implicit in the analysis and show that it clashes strikingly with the facts (importantly, as hinted, this is by no means the only problematic aspect of the proposal).[30]

Thus, if palatals (and, if appropriate, [x]) are in effect bi-segmental, the first consonant of the proposed cluster will reamain unsyllabified word-initially (cf. e.g. *t(yo)(za)* for *choza* 'shack') to comply with Carreira's own heterosyllabicity requirement on the merger-cum-palatalization rule(s). But, if so, such a consonant ought to be disposed of by Stray Erasure, mirroring the procedure Carreira herself adopts for final position (remember: *(des)(den)y* →

desdén). The inescapable consequence is that all word-initial palatals ought to neutralize into [y], the second element of the lexical cluster (where appropriate, a surface alternation would arise: e.g. *allegar* 'to unite' ought to alternate with hypothetical [y]*egar* 'arrive'; cf. existing *llegar*). Such a prediction resoundly runs aground, palatal consonants (and [x]) appearing unrestrictedly in word-initial position (cf. *llevar* 'to carry', *charla* 'chat', *ñoño*[31] 'dotard', *yeso* 'plaster', *gente* 'people').

Carreira lays responsibility for the preservation of the unsyllabifiable coronal on extraprosodicity (e.g *<t>(yo)(za)*. All the evidence militates however against such a proposal. In particular, as is well-known, Spanish does not license extraprosodicity on a word-initial *s*- followed by a consonant (as does Romanian, a language Carreira paradoxically appeals to in support of her Spanish argument), initial epenthesis instead taking place (e.g. English *slogan* becomes Spanish [e]*slogan*). Nor can Spanish be allowed extraprosodicity word-finally if Carreira's own analysis of depalatalization, referred to above, is to go through. The obvious conclusion is that the argument for the extraprosodicity of the first element of initial palatals is entirely *ad hoc*, and consequently it cannot be accepted. In the absence of such an argument, the occurrence of full palatals word-initially obviously becomes an embarrassment. If the assumption of lexical duality of palatals is removed, however, the conundrum posed by the existence of word-initial full palatals simply vanishes.

Summarizing before drawing this section to a close, Spanish stress assignment has been seen to violate the constraint in Burzio (1994) that the medial syllable of ternary feet be light. Conversely, words with light penults are consistent with penultimate stress (indeed, the unmarked pattern). Finally, the factual prohibition of antepenultimate stress in words with [x] or a palatal consonant in their final onset remains unexplained on this account.[32]

3. Vowel-ending oxytones

So far, we have omitted explicit discussion of vowel-ending oxytones, briefly referred to in note 15, and in this section we turn our attention to this remaining set of data. Contrary to some statements in the literature (e.g. Harris 1995: 883), such forms are not in short supply, and are well entrenched in the vernacular (a word count in a standard dictionary, such as that of the Real

Academia Española, can hardly do justice to the reality of the living language).

As already mentioned, these forms raise considerable problems for Burzio's analysis. Thus, remember that this model (like Idsardi's 1992; see note 15 above) does not countenance (rhythm-generated) monosyllabic feet. If so, vowel-ending oxytones must be augmented with a final empty nucleus, which must be metrical to allow the construction of the required binary foot:

```
(20)          *
            (* *)
          m a n á V   'manna'
```

The quantity-sensitivity inherent to the system would necessitate the head of such a foot to be heavy. As in the cases mentioned above, however, there is no evidence of special length in the corresponding vowel.[33]

Burzio's framework also favors a final empty nucleus in forms like *régimen*. Here, however, such a nucleus needs to be extrametrical (cf. (21a)), since otherwise construction of a ternary foot would incorrectly result in penultimate stress (cf. (21b)):

```
(21)         *                                   *
            (*  *  *)<*>                     * (*  *  *)
     a.    r e g i m e n V              b.   r e g i m e n V
             σ  L  σ                              σ  L  σ
             régimen                            *regímen
```

The contrast between *régimen* and *colibrí* on this account is most revealing. In particular, while both forms would include a desinential empty vowel, this vowel is formalized as extrametrical only in the former form,[34] which must moreover be marked as selecting for a ternary foot, while its counterpart in *colibrí* is binary:

```
(22)         *                                        *
            (*  *  *)<*>                         * *  (* *)
     a.    r e g i m e n V              b.     c o l i b r i V
```

It is far from obvious how this result can be achieved on a principled basis, and no specific machinery to this end is proposed in Burzio (1994). By contrast, the formalization of vowel-ending oxytones is unproblematic in the standard approach, and is in fact already implicit in our discussion in section 1 above. Remember in particular that on this approach unmarked stress is stem-final. The forms under analysis here simply have no desinence (cf. e.g. the nonce formation *manaísmo* 'doctrine relating to manna', from *maná* 'manna', not *manismo*, which would be 'doctrine relating to hands', from *máno* 'hand'), and therefore stress will automatically be assigned on their rightmost vowel.[35]

One of the properties of the desinence referred to at the outset concerns the possibility of engaging in gender alternation. The postulation of empty desinences in the forms under scrutiny (e.g. /kolibriV/), carries the counterfactual implication that these forms will be alternating (cf. e.g. el/la *marroquí* 'the-MASC/FEM Moroccan', *not *la marroquía* 'the-FEM Moroccan'). Note that we cannot simply limit alternation to non-empty desinences (cf. e.g. *español-V* 'Spanish-MASC' ~ *español-a* 'Spanish-FEM'), and therefore further machinery will be needed in order to preserve the analysis. In the standard approach, however, lack of desinence accounts for lack of gender alternation in the simplest possible way, since the exponent of gender is precisely the desinence, and consequently there can be no gender exponent in the absence of a desinence.[36]

4 The reinterpretation of Latin stress in Spanish

4.1 Accent and regular stress

In the previous sections we have seen that the formulation of nominal stress in Spanish (and, by extension, Italian and other Romance languages) is problematic under a number of current theoretical approaches.[37] A reasonable question to ask at this point is thus whether Spanish stress is at all amenable to metrical analysis, or whether a radically novel approach is called for. In this section I will argue that a satisfactory formal account of this stress system can in fact be obtained on the model of Halle and Vergnaud (1987), notwithstanding present appearances.

It was pointed out in section 1 that Halle *et al.*'s (1991) analysis encapsulated in rule (9) would be impeccable for an unmarked proparoxytone pattern. Indeed, as noted in 1.4.2, one such analysis has been successfully advanced for Macedonian (see Franks 1987). The problem for Spanish is that, as mentioned at the time, its unmarked stress pattern is paroxytone.

The specific difficulty concerns the postulation of an accent rule to capture the unmarked contour (see 1.4.2 above), in the face of the fact that the canonical function of accent is the formalization of *marked*, deviant patterns (for some discussion of this point, see Roca 1992b, 1994: 219-20). As we will now see, however, there are reasons to believe that this interpretation of accent is not the only possible one, and that recourse to (rule-governed) accent in Spanish-type cases is indeed necessary to faithfully capture the essence of the system.

The paradox arises from the conflict between the identity of the stress carrier syllable in Latin and Spanish and the metrical variance of stress locus in these two languages, following independent Romance segmental changes (a result of course magnified in French, where stress invariably ends up word-final, modulo final schwas). In a nutshell, thus, if the Latin stress system had been preserved in Spanish, stress ought frequently to have shifted from the Latin carrier syllable, contrary to fact.

Consider as an illustration the form *interior* 'interior', melodically identical in both languages. The (abridged) Latin derivation is as follows:

```
(23)                                                  *
         *   * * *           *   * *<*>         *   (* *)<*>
         interi o:r    →    interi  o:r    →    interi  o:r
```

The resulting stress is antepenultimate on the vocoids, in contrast with the Spanish final stress (*interiór*). This divergence has of course a well-known historical explanation: simply, the Latin ancestor of the Spanish form is not the nominative *interiōr* of (23), but rather the accusative *interiōrem*, the metrical derivation of which is given in (24):

(24)

```
                                                        *
       *   * * *  *         *   * * *<*>        *   * * *<*>
       interio:rem    →     interio:rem    →    interio: rem  →

                *
       *   * *(*)<*>
  →    interi o:rem
```

This form exhibits stress on *or*, as does its Spanish descendant *interior*.

Let us now suppose that the Spanish stress procedure were isomorphic with that of Latin:

(25)

```
                                                  *
       *   * * *        *   * *<*>         *  (* *)<*>
       interi or   →    interi  or    →    interi  or
```

As can be seen, stress would incorrectly fall on the antepenultimate vocoid, as in the Latin nominative (cf. (23)). Clearly, this result can only be averted through a modification of the stress algorithm. What is interesting is that Spanish (in line with other Romance languages and dialects) indeed enforced algorithm modification in preference to moving stress away from the historically stressed syllable.

This outcome leads to a view of metrical algorithms as tools for the implementation of a given (non-metrical) teleology. In the case at hand, this teleology consisted in the maintenance of stress in the syllable that carried it in Latin (modulo the handful of shifts mentioned in Otero 1986). The incompatibility of this goal with the Latin algorithm inevitably led to the replacement of this algorithm. Equivalently, what the child learner hears is not algorithms, but stressed syllables. The learning task of this child therefore involves the discovery of an algorithm that will yield precisely the input stress targets (such a target-oriented perspective is of course given a more prominent role in the Optimality model of McCarthy and Prince 1993 and Prince and Smolensky 1993). This algorithm must be compatible with general metrical theory, a part of Universal Grammar, and, in the event of incompatibility, stress movement will take place (the Spanish word *regímenes* is a case in point). From this perspective, the use of accent to express regularity becomes quite orthodox, and the accentual approach in Halle *et al.* (1991) (see (9) above and (26) below) therefore quite legitimate.[38]

4.2. Quantity sensitivity in Spanish

We must at this point account for the quantity sensitivity paradoxes discussed in 2.2.2 and 2.2.3 above. A brief reminder of the relevant facts will be of help. First, while Latin was indisputably quantity-sensitive, the Spanish data have been seen to shed contradictory evidence. Second, the Latin vowel length contrast was lost in Spanish (and other Romance dialects), and therefore, following Trubetzkoy's law referred to in 2.2.2, Spanish ought not to be quantity sensitive. Quantity insensitivity will, however, leave unexplained the facts discussed above relating to the effect of stress on heavy penults and palatal onsets in the ultima.

Once more, the desired solution can be achieved through the device 'accent.' In particular, we will propose that Spanish possesses two idiosyncratic accent rules over and above the general one in (9) above, formalized here as (26). The formulation of the three accent rules is as follows (V and C are intended to represent a vocalic and a consonantal melody, respectively; the connection between the stress bearer and the rhyme material is naturally mediated by the skeleton and the appropriate feature geometry, omitted from the representation for simplicity):

(26) RIGHTMOST STEM ACCENT (= Halle *et al.* 1991; cf. Prince's 1983 *Right End Rule*):

		*		line 1
*	→	*	/ ___]$_{stem}$	line 0

(27) CLOSED SYLLABLE ACCENT:

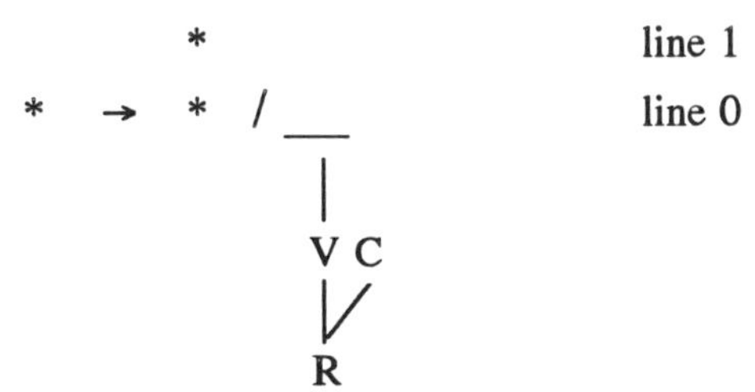

(28) PREPALATAL ACCENT:[39]

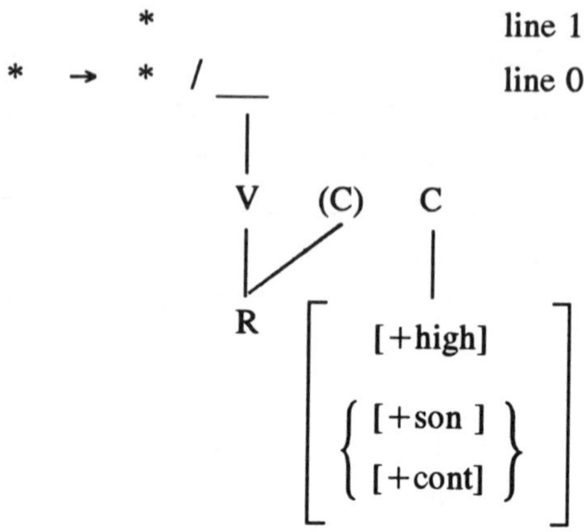

The profligacy of accent rules is imposed on us by the facts. In particular, as we have been observing, while stem-final stress (implemented by (26)) is unmarked across the board in Spanish, the robustness of this pattern is substantially strengthened when the corresponding rhyme is heavy (cf. (27)) or followed by a palatal consonant or [x] (cf. (28)). Under the present proposal, this added strength is accounted for by the fact that deviation from the predictions of each of the rules requires specific lexical exception marking. Thus, suppose that a form only meets the description of (26). A stem-penultimate pattern (e.g. *América*) presupposes an exception mark [-(26)] in the corresponding lexical entry. Consider now a form like *Aráncha*, which meets the description of (28), (27), and (26). Stem-penultimate stress would require three exception marks, one for each accenting rule. In particular, if the form is only marked as an exception to (28), it will still be accented by (27) and (26), and if marked as exceptional to both (28) and (27) it will still be accented by (26). As we now illustrate in (29), the markedness cline thus implicit in the analysis is matched well by the facts (each set in (29) contains first a sample of application of the accent rule(s), and then a sample of exceptions):[40]

(29)

a. (28) & (27) & (26)

berrínche	'tantrum'
cománche	'comanche'
rechóncho	'chubby'
Carúncho	a surname
Aráncha	a first name

[-(28), -(27), -(26)]
empty set

b.

(28) & (27)	(28) & (26)		(27) & (26)	
N/A	rebáño	'flock'	Erásmo	Erasmus
	cabállo	'horse'	comándo	'commando'
	helécho	'fern'	redóndo	'round'
	cobáya	'guinea pig'	Casílda	a first name
	conéjo	'rabbit'	Amánda	a first name

[-(28), -(27)]	[-(28), -(27)]	[-(27), -(26)]	
N/A	empty set	Frómista	a town
		Chávarri	a surname
		Wáshington	Washington
		Mánchester	Manchester
		Ámsterdam	Amsterdam

c.

[-(28)]	[-(27)]	[-(26)]	
N/A	N/A	América	America
		Rápita	a town
		rótulo	'label'
		código	'code'
		Álava	a province

As illustrated in (29a), applicability of the three rules results in across-the-board implementation, no exceptions being registered. When only (26) and one of the other two rules are applicable, as in (29b), two sets of empirical results are attested: with (28) applicability is also total, whereas with (27) there is a group of exceptions. The first result still matches well the model proposed, since suspension of application would require two lexical exception marks, a situation not unreasonably disfavored by the language. The divergence of the second result is relatable the loan nature of the source, most of the items corresponding to 'Germanic-sounding' proper names[41] (crucially, none of the source languages possesses forms which would meet (28)).[42] The remnant is exceedingly small in Spanish (the obscure place name *Frómista*, and perhaps such surnames as *Cháverri* or *Achúcarro*, if Harris' 1983 analysis of *rr* as /r.r/ is countenanced), although slightly larger in Italian *(mándorla*, *póli*[tts]*a*, and a few otherwise Romance-sounding place-names, e.g. *Lépanto*). Finally, as shown in (29c), violation of only one of the rules (inevitably (26), which each of the other two rules in effect simply bolster) corresponds with a wealth of ordinary data, precisely the bulk of cases of stem-prefinal stress.

The rules being proposed are obviously less elegant than linguistic aesthetics would favor, but this inelegance is simply a faithful reflection of the Spanish stress system, whose divergence from bona fide quantity-sensitive systems such as those of Latin (or, also, Arabic) we have been endeavoring to clarify. Therefore, it is reasonable to interpret the noted lack of elegance as a positive result, and to contend that the attainment of the same degree of formal elegance for a Spanish-like system as for Latin or Arabic would simply be spurious.[43] Crucially, while there is no formal obstacle to the idiosyncratic suspension of an accent rule through lexical exceptionality (given the well-known fact that phonological rules can and do have exceptions), there is no reason to believe that rhythm can similarly be idiosyncratically altered. Indeed, as is well-known, there is concrete evidence that rhythm violations created in the course of morphological or syntactic derivation are subject to strong pressure for regularization (cf. the widely attested rhythm-inspired stress-shifts, the Latin rhythm-inspired vowel quantity alterations discussed in Mester 1994, and so on).

5. Conclusion

The system that has emerged from the discussion can be summarized as follows:

(30) SPANISH NOMINAL STRESS ALGORITHM[44]

1) stress bearers = vocoids;

2) extrametricality = desinence;

3) accent:

i) the rightmost stress bearer
(= Rightmost Stem Accent rule (26));

ii) a stem-final closed syllable
(= Closed Syllable Accent rule (27));

iii) a stem-final syllable followed by a palatal
(= Prepalatal Accent rule (28));

4) construct leftheaded bounded feet (cf. Syllabic Trochee Construction);

5) construct a rightheaded unbounded word constituent (cf. Right End Rule)

6) delete line 1 (= Conflation)

As can be seen, the Spanish stress system preserves a metrical component from Latin, the leftheaded binary foot, indeed pervasive throughout the Spanish system (general primary stress algorithm, as in clause 4 in (30) above, stress of apocopated hypochoristics, as explained in note 44, and perhaps secondary stress, as discussed in Harris 1991a). This metrical system, however, has been augmented with a non-metrical, but still rule-governed, component, encapsulated in the accent rules (26) to (28) above. Spanish (and indeed common Romance) thus constitutes the complement class to the one observed by Steriade (cited in Halle and Vergnaud 1987: 72, fn. 9) to have undergone elimination of the lexical Indo-European line-1 asterisks. In particular, while the Indo-European accent-based 'free' stress shifted to initial stress in such languages as early Latin or West Slavic, in Spanish-like systems line 1 asterisks are by contrast being provided (as yet by rule) in positions where they are not metrically assignable. The existence of such two complementary cases of accentual/metrical historical change thus provides strong motivation for the formal independence of accent from the metrical algorithms that it sometimes idiosyncratically corrects.

As mentioned in the introduction, this independence has a direct bearing on the trend initiated by Hayes in the mid-1980s, to explicitly construe and formalize stress as a direct linguistic implementation of nonlinguistic rhythm. Specifically, in Hayes (1985, 1987, 1995), the symmetric bounded constituents generated by such a set of parameters as formulated in Halle and Vergnaud (1987) are replaced with a much-reduced inventory of foot templates grounded on general considerations of trochaic and iambic rhythm, inspired by results of (nonlinguistic) psychological perception experiments.

Hayes' (1995: 31) taxonomy of stress systems includes 'morphological' alongside 'rhythmic' types. In one such morphological variety, exemplified by English level II forms, stress is confined to a particular syllable in the stem, affixes remaining stressless (or at most bearing weak stress). In another variety, instantiated by Sanskrit, stress results from the interaction of stem and affix type (a succinct précis of this complex pattern can be found in Roca 1992a). Rhythmic stress systems are in turn divided into bounded and unbounded, along familiar lines, with Hayes' study specifically focusing on the former (Hayes 1995: 32).

Hayes also accepts the existence of mixed systems that include a bounded rhythmic component, predicted to fall within the scope of the theory he propounds. As follows from our foregoing discussion, Spanish and Italian nominals represent precisely one such mixed stress system. Hayes (1995) does not offer an explicit analysis of these languages, although both his classification of Spanish in the Latin-type group (Hayes 1995: 181) and the scattered references he makes to its stress system give a strong hint that he subscribes to the analysis in Harris (1983), which he cites approvingly, with neglect of the difficulties pointed out in Roca (1988, 1990a).

The theory in Burzio (1994), evaluated here with respect to Spanish and Italian data, is obviously related to Hayes'. Importantly, rhythmic theory, in both Hayes' and Burzio's versions, assigns an inherent role to syllable weight in the constitution of feet, and thus in the distribution of stress. The exploration we have carried out has revealed, however, that Spanish and Italian nominals at best present highly equivocal evidence for weight sensitivity, the rhythmic theory being thus ill-equipped to handle these systems.

We have seen that the ensuing challenge is best met through a compromise between the classical and the rhythmic stress theories. Accent, a remnant of the original *SPE* machinery, has been argued to play a central role in this compromise. The line we have been taking here is that the role of accent goes beyond the expression of exceptionality,[45] and that accent can also formalize regular, but non-rhythmic, patterns outside (as well as within) morphological stress systems. While an analysis of Spanish along these lines had indeed been proposed in Halle *et al.* (1991), following on from Harris (1988/92), its theoretical underpinnings remained unstated, the analysis being correspondingly at odds with the very theory implicitly espoused by the authors.

Significantly, as we have pointed out, the historical shift from strictly rhythmic stress (in Latin) to a mixed system incorporating a rule-governed accentual component (in Spanish) can readily be made sense of from the perspective of learnability. In particular, the Latin system (in Hayes' 1995 terms, moraic trochaic; see also Mester 1994) was destroyed in the course of language evolution by vowel syncope and the loss of vowel quantity. Following these changes, a strictly rhythmic grammar was no longer warranted by the data to which the learner had access. Seen in this light, therefore, the mixed stress grammar of Spanish (and arguably Italian and other Romance languages; see Roca 1996) is indeed to be expected.

Notes

* This paper is partly based on a series of talks given at the University of Girona in the summer of 1993, and I wish to thank the audience and the organizer, Pep Serra, for the stimulus they provided. Some of the material was also presented at a linguistics seminar at Oxford, and I benefited from objections raised by Paloma García-Bellido and Stephen Parkinson. For comments on previous versions, I thank Luigi Burzio, Marina Nespor, José Ignacio Hualde, and John Lipski. I especially wish to acknowledge Luigi for a lively correspondence about his stress ideas and their application to Spanish and Italian. All problems and errors that may remain are my sole responsibility.

1 The starting point of metrical phonology can of course be identified with Liberman and Prince's (1977) epoch-making paper 'On Stress and Linguistic Rhythm', where they abandon Chomsky and Halle's (1968) practice of assigning stress by rule on a par with segmental phonological processes, and replace it with a rhythmically underpinned machinery. Liberman and Prince's gestalt shift stimulated such major metrical works as Halle and Vergnaud (1978), Hayes (1980/81), Prince (1983), Hammond (1984), Halle and Vergnaud (1987), Kager (1989), and, more recently, Idsardi (1992), Burzio (1994), and Hayes (1995).

2 The following (alphabetically ordered) list of post-1980 (published) references on the topic is supplied in Harris (1995: 885, fn. 2): Den Os and Kager (1986), Farrell (1990), Halle *et al.* (1991), Harris (1983, 1987, 1988/92, 1989a, 1989b, 1991a), Núñez Cedeño (1985), Otero (1986), Roca (1986, 1988, 1990a, 1990b, 1991, 1992a), Solan (1981).

3 Roca (1992a) argues for the assignment of stress to verbs on different principles. Prepositions and other function words are either clitic or also treated like nouns metrically.

4 These markedness judgements are justified in Roca (1990), contra Otero (1986); see below for further discussion. In unpublished work by Alfonso Morales-Front, a count on a 91,000-word corpus yielded paroxytone stress in 88% of V-ending (thus effectively desinenced) forms, and oxytone stress in 97.80% of C-ending forms (I am grateful to J. I. Hualde for bringing this work to my attention).

5 There are two known classes of potential counterexamples to such a three-syllable window on the analysis of all vocoids as stress bearers. The first class is made up of the two words *alícuota* 'aliquot' and *ventrílocuo* 'ventriloquist', both including the bi-vocoid sequence *cuo* (phonetically [k^wo]). Since as early as Harris (1969), it has been commonly assumed that such a sequence can be analyzed as /kwo/ (an update of this approach appears in Carreira 1990: 120 ff.), thus making the two problematic forms compatible with a three-vocoid window. The second class includes *náufrago* 'shipwreck' and a handful of similar forms. Roca (1991) proposes to bring this class to rule through a principled separation of the stress and syllable planes. In essence, stress would first be assigned to the vocoid *u* of the diphthong *au*, in conformity with the window, and would subsequently be moved to the diphthong's nucleus following universal sonority-inspired principles of phonetic realization (see Roca 1995 for an updated analysis in the frame of Optimality Theory).

6 The domain of this statement is the simple word, and therefore the vowels in question are found word-internally in both *-mente* adverbs (cf. Suñer 1975, Roca 1986, Zagona 1990), e.g. *lentamente* 'slowly', and compounds, e.g. *casa-cuartel* (literally 'house-barracks').

7 The following redundancy rule is formulated in Roca (1989: 24) to account for cases of unmarked correlation between gender and the desinence (for F[eminine] the gender feature, [+F] thus signifying 'feminine'):

$$[\ \ ] \rightarrow \begin{bmatrix} +\text{back} \\ \langle +\text{low} \rangle \end{bmatrix} / \begin{bmatrix} \overline{\quad\quad} \\ \langle +\text{F} \rangle \end{bmatrix} \#$$

8 A certain amount of demystification will not be wasted on this word, often dismissed in the literature as 'exotic' or 'marginal. In fact, *régimen* is a very ordinary and commonly used Spanish word (in Juilland and Chang-Rodríguez's 1964 frequency dictionary, it is included in *the second topmost 500-word set*, out of a total number of 5024 counted words, with a frequency score of 66 and a usage score of 33.93). This situation is far from surprising, on account of its meaning 'slimming diet'. Also, during the Franco era Spaniards from all social strata usually referred to the political system and the people involved in it as *el régimen*. Crucially, there never was nor is there now the slightest tendency to avoid the word or to change its stress pattern, as ought to be the case if *régimen* were really marginal or exotic. The exoticity or marginality of its stress pattern in many of the extant analyses of Spanish stress, such as the one being discussed at the moment, is thus exclusively a formal artifact. From this perspective, it would obviously be nice and convenient to sweep this word under the carpet (also a handful of others, e.g. *Júpiter*, which does not feel or behave in any way bizarrely either). The exclusion of this set of legitimate and bona fide Spanish stress data would, however, be clearly unwarranted.

9 The window is never violated in nominals if syllables are counted. If vocoids are counted, such words as *alícuota*, *ventrílocuo* and *náufrago* are at first blush problematic, as commented in note 5 above.

10 The Peripherality Condition (Hayes 1980, 1982) restricts extrametricality to the element peripheral in the domain of the stress rule(s) (cf. Roca 1988, 1992b for discussion).

11 Macedonian regular stress is antepenultimate *pólkovnik* 'colonel-SG', *polkóvnikot* 'colonel-SG DEF', *polkóvnici* 'colonel- PL', *polkovnícite* 'colonel-PL DEF'. A handful of (imported) forms exhibit however penultimate stress, e.g. *konsumátor*, *romántik*, *literatúra*, etc. (a further set of irregular oxytones is irrelevant to the discussion). Note that even in these forms stress becomes antepenultimate when a sufficiently long string of syllables is suffixed: *konsumatórite* 'consumer-PL DEF'.

12 In addition, Roca (1990a: 147) accounts for the lexically marked stress retraction by means of the following asterisk deletion rule:

(i) *) → . / in specially marked forms level 0

The problem with such asterisk deletion rules (otherwise countenanced in Halle and Vergnaud 1987) concerns their apparent unrestrictiveness. In particular, repeated application of asterisk deletion (or of its essentially equivalent asterisk-parenthesis metathesis, *) →)*, favored in Roca 1991: 615, fn. 21, in preference to (i)) will move stress indefinitely away from the edge, in contravention of the window restrictions.

13 This is the stand taken in Roca (1988), where this type of analysis is explored and rejected. The reasons for the rejection are addressed directly below.

14 A further potential argument against the lexical parametrization approach concerns the headedness setting of secondary stress constituents, which would now have to be harmonized with the headedness setting of the primary stress foot, so as to preserve strict alternation (see Harris 1991a for akin discussion). It might, however, be possible to argue that, in the absence of robust empirical data, the precise nature of Spanish secondary stress remains unclear (for general discussion, see Roca 1986), in particular its phonological (as against merely phonetic) status.

15 Matters do not seem to fare better under Idsardi's (1992) modified version of Halle and Vergnaud (1987). Specifically, in Harris' (1995) application of this model to Spanish, regular penultimate stress (e.g. *sabána*) is essentially implemented by means of a leftheaded binary foot built *directly* on the word domain (NB. Idsardi's model makes no explicit provision for extrametricality):

```
                                *
(i)        *  *  *          * (*   *)
          saban-a    →     saban-a   'savannah'
```

Ordinary antepenultimate stress (*sábana*) will require the lexical presence of a right parenthesis on the left edge of the desinence's stress bearer (in effect, the rendering of extrametricality in Idsardi's theory):

```
                            *
(ii)       *  *)  *        (*  *)  *
          saban-a    →     saban-a   '(bed) sheet'
```

In *régimen*, with no desinence, such a parenthesis will instead exceptionally precede the stress bearer corresponding to the stem final syllable (cf. the extrametricality of the stem's final syllable in the standard analysis in (8) above):

```
                          *
(iii)    * *)  *       (*  *)  *
         regimen  →    regimen
```

Note that the contour of *regímenes* is unobtainable on this account, since the addition of the desinence *-es* to the unfooted material *men* creates a string capable of additional metrification (in the absence of explicit extrametricality, Idsardi's theory obviously cannot accommodate peripherality restrictions):

```
                                                          *
(iv)     * *)  *   *        (*  *)  *  *         (*  *) (*  *)
         regimen-es    →    regimenes       →    regimenes
```

The incorrect output *regiménes can be prevented only through lexical (metrical) allomorphy (a similar output is, however, correct in, e.g. *omicrónes* 'omicrons', from *ómicron*). A further, more fundamental problem is posed by oxytones (*mongól*, *capó*). In particular, Idsardi's theory disallows degenerate unary versions of the rhythmic binary foot (as generated by Iterative Constituent Construction), and consequently the targeted final leftheaded binary foot can only be built rhythmically if additional metrical material is made available in the shape of an empty desinence:

```
                                          *
(v)      *   * *        *  (* *       *  (* *)
         mongolV   →   mongolV   →   mongolV

                                 *
(vi)     *  * *       * (* *     * (* *)
         capo V   →   capo V  →  capoV
```

These representations have undesirable empirical consequences discussed in section 3 below in the context of Burzio's (1994) theory. The alternative is to mark these forms lexically in a manner parallel to *régimen*, i.e. to provide them with a parenthesis before the stress bearer corresponding to the final vowel. In the present case, however, the required parenthesis will be the left, rather than the right, one:

```
                     *
(vi)     * (*      * (*
         capo  →   capo
```

While the procedure obviously works, it is clearly unprincipled. By contrast, in the standard analysis the difference between, e.g. *capó* 'car hood' and *capa* 'cape' is naturally related to the different extension of their stems, [capo] and [cap], respectively.

16 Sluyters (1990) reports measurements by Josselyn (1900) and Parmenter and Carmen (1932) suggesting some 30% length increase in stressed vowels in open penults (Vogel 1982 narrows the difference to 25%). Interestingly, such an increase is not matched in the other positions, viz. antepenultimate and final (for measurements, see Castellani 1980, for the former, and the references in Vayra 1993, listed in note 18 below, for the latter). Vincent (1988) discusses several diachronic reflexes of vowel length that confirm the differences between the penultimate and the other positions with regard to the length of Italian stressed vowels in open syllables.

17 All standard descriptions of Italian coincide in fact in declaring penultimate stress the norm.

18 The following references (from Vayra 1993) back up this statement: Hall (1948), Fiorelli (1958), Camilli (1965), Muljacvič (1972), Vogel (1978), Korzen (1980), Lepschy and Lepschy (1981), Vogel (1982), Chierchia (1986), Vincent (1988), Basbøll (1989), Repetti (1991). Vayra (1993) discusses some interesting evidence that suggests that such syllables may in fact be closed by an abstract consonant that surfaces as a glottal stop in the appropriate environments. Note however that such an analysis metrically assimilates these forms to the Spanish *mármol* in (13) above, and therefore final stress would still not be derived:

```
 *
(*   *   *)
p a l t o C V
 σ   L   σ
```

*pálto (cf. correct *paltó* 'coat')

19 The results reported in Monroy (1980) are somewhat at variance with those of Navarro. Crucially, however, Monroy's findings add strong support to the phonetic and often idiosyncratic nature of Spanish vowel length distinctions, as encapsulated in the following statement (Monroy 1980: 43):

> "Vista, pues, la libre variación que las vocales españolas presentan en términos duracionales, tónicas al igual que átonas, no es de extrañar que el sistema se caracterice por una indistinción cuantitativa, ya apuntada por Nebrija y defendida por Pinciano." [Having thus seen the free variation with regard to length exhibited by Spanish vowels, whether stressed or stressless, it is far from surprising that the system should be characterized by a lack of length distinction, already noted by Nebrija, and defended by Pinciano].

20 The following forms are representative of Tiberian Hebrew surface stress:

(i) a. qamtém b. qá:mu: c. ka:tbú:

Underlyingly, however, the segmental structure of these forms will be as follows:

(ii) a. qamtemV b. qa:mu: c. ka:tabu:

The foot in (16) will directly yield the surface stress of the forms in (ia) and (ib), final and penultimate, respectively. The form in c. will be derived via foot-internal stress shift after deletion of the short *a* in the open syllable (see Halle and Vergnaud 1987 for justification of this analysis):

```
              *               *               *
(iii)       (*  *)          (  *)            (*)
          ka:tabu:  →   ka:t bu:  →    ka:tabu:
```

21 This statement is echoed in the following works, cited in Ohsiek (1978): Kuryłowicz (1948), Newman (1972), Greenberg and Kaschube (1976), Hyman (1977, 1985). Ohsiek (1978) mentions two languages problematic for Trubetzkoy's claim: Maung (an Australian language described in Capell and Hinch 1970) and Araucanian (Echeverría and Contreras 1965). Thus, in Maung, a closed antepenult takes stress away from the penult, the unmarked location, while in Araucanian the last syllable of a trisyllabic word will receive secondary stress if it is closed. Crucially, vowel length is not distinctive in either language. These two cases aside, Trubetzkoy's generalization seems to hold well cross-linguistically (and the facts of Maung and Araucanian may of course be open to an alternative interpretation consistent with the generalization).

22 According to the Spanish *Espasa* encyclopedia, the town in question was rebuilt by the widow of the King of Navarre Sancho the Greater in 1066.

23 In the apposite words of Kenstowicz (1990: 55), "the major factor distinguishing Generative Grammar from the dominant Structuralist school of the time was the conscious rejection of the assumption that human language is a refinement and distillation of information present in overt speech behavior."

24 The same question, of course, arises in connection with *Wáshington* in English. Burzio (1994: 58 ff.) circumvents this well-known problem (already noticed in *SPE*; see also Kiparsky 1979 and Hayes 1981, among others) by allowing syllables closed by sonorants or *s* to count as light in English. Clearly, the extension of this solution to Spanish or Italian would be entirely unprincipled (note also that a section of English data run against Burzio's strategy for this language, e.g. *agénda*, *Aláska*, etc.).

25 Note also the existence of idiosyncratic stressing in Italian in some such words, e.g. *Manchéster*. A parallel case in Spanish is represented by the traditional contour *Liverp*[ú]*l* (nowadays in apparent free variation with *Líverp*[u]*l*), which thus contrasts with *Mánchester*.

26 The consistent misplacements of pre-antepenultimate stress by Spanish-speaking learners of English constitute very strong, readily available evidence in the same direction.

27 As already mentioned, it is desirable to highlight this fact, which frequently goes unmentioned in the literature. Note that, on the most favorable interpretation of Burzio's analysis referred to above, forms with heavy penults would simply be barred from carrying a lexical mark singling them out as receptors of ternary feet.

28 A parallel proposal couched in exception features in the context of underspecification theory was made in Roca (1990a).

29 As is well-known, the Sonority Sequencing Generalization concerns the requirement that the sonority profile of the syllable must slope down outwards from the peak (see Roca 1994: 151ff. for summary discussion). Stress Erasure is a convention by which unsyllabified segments are deleted (in Itô 1986, 1989 such segments would simply fail to be prosodically licensed).

30 Carreira's account of the third idiosyncracy (**corño* vs. *corcho*), for instance, appeals to syllabification conditions: '[r], [n] or [l] are not allowed to close off a syllable followed by [ñ] or [ll] because they involve sequences of three segments that are not syllabifiable in Spanish' (Carreira 1988: 85). Indeed, it is well known that /s/ the only consonant licensed in second position in the Spanish coda (cf. Harris 1989c, Hualde 1991), as in *i*[ns]*trucción* 'instruction', *va*[ls] 'waltz', etc., a fact that underlies Harris' (1983) elegant analysis of the stem allomorphy *esculp-ir* 'to sculpt' ~ *escul-tor* 'sculptor'. If this is so, however, *corcho* 'cork', *concha* 'shell', *colcha* 'bed spread' ought *not* to be possible Spanish words (cf. *cor*/t.y/*o*, etc.), contrary to fact.

31 The shortage of *ñ*-starting words is a historical artifact orthogonal to the synchronic grammar. A few such words do however exist in the Spanish lexicon, e.g. *ñoño* 'dotard', *ñandú* 'American ostrich'.

32 It is reasonable to assume that, whatever the formalization of this prohibition may be, it must parallel the one concerning heavy syllables (cf. note 27 above). A formal proposal will be made in section 4.

33 As pointed out above, this argument applies even more forcefully in Italian, since in this language such vowels do not appear to undergo the lengthening of their

penultimate congeners. As was then mentioned, the extra length of Spanish final vowels also affects closed syllables and stressless final syllables, therefore being directly attributable to the prepausal environment.

34 In Burzio's model, extrametricality is only allowed on the (otherwise universally ill-defined) class of 'weak syllables', of which those with empty nuclei are a subset.

35 The markedness of Spanish final stress in vowel-ending forms thus follows from their deviant parsing. In particular, the final vowel of nominals is expected to constitute the desinence. If so, however, such a vowel cannot be stressed. This corollary clashes with the facts in the cases in question, hence the markedness of these words.

36 It is reasonable to assume that the same device accounts for the Italian contrast between the alternating *casa* 'house' (plural *case* 'houses') and the invariant *cittá* 'city(es)', since only the former includes a desinence (the change from singular to plural therefore simply involves a change in the desinence, parallelling gender change in gender alternating forms). Burzio (p.c.) points out that such truncated forms as *cinema[tografo]* 'cinema' or *foto[grafia]* 'photography' are also invariant for number, despite the fact that they are not oxytones. Two observations are in order here. First, it appears that all such Italian forms have initial stress (by contrast, Spanish has, e.g. *cinéma*, with *-a* clearly behaving as a desinence: cf. *cinem-ucho* 'cinema-PEJ'). Second, it is not inconceivable that Italian truncation takes place on both singular and plural full forms. If so, the truncated output will be predicted to be identical in both cases (*cinema*[*tografo*] ~ *cinema*[*tografi*]), as indeed it is.

37 In particular, analyses in the frameworks of Halle and Vergnaud (1987), Idsardi (1992), and Burzio (1994) have been discussed. There are obvious similarities of both spirit and substance between Burzio (1994) and Hayes (1995), and therefore many of the difficulties pointed out in the former can reasonably be assumed also to affect the latter.

38 This approach is very much in the spirit of Roca's (1986: 364) observation that "the fact that... secondary stress must be built on primary stressed structures... seems to point in the direction of freeing primary stress from the pressures of prosodic rhythm. Advancing further along this path, one could question the adequacy of the arboreal mould for lexical word stress, *perhaps best construed as rule-governed accent* [my emphasis]".

39 Some clarification of the formulation of this rule will be of help. First, the rule must be so designed as to accent the vowel in syllables preceding an onset with a palatal or /x/. The optional coda consonant is included in the environment in order to achieve compatibility with Hayes' (1986) 'Linking Constraint.' Second, the contextual

consonant must be [+high] and either [+sonorant] or [+continuant]. The former set defines /ʎ/ and /ɲ/, and the latter /x/ and /č/ (on the assumption of unordered subsegmental specification for affricates; cf. Hualde 1987). Notice that the strategy behind rules (27) and (28) is the complement of the strategy used by Burzio (1994) to account for the quantity insensivitity of syllables closed by sonorants or *s* in English, which he stipulates count as light (see note 23 above). What we are doing here is contrariwise to stipulate that the stress bearers defined in (27) and (28) count as metrical heads in Spanish. The accent rule in (27) obviously embodies the remnant of Latin quantity sensitivity. Importantly, the existence of rules (27) and (28) forces upon us the inclusion of a conflation clause in the algorithm, since the accents unbridledly assigned by such accent rules only surface stem-finally.

40 Note that the distribution of the exception marks can plausibly be related to lexical divisions on grounds of foreignness, Germanicness, etc.

41 This 'foreignness' could also be argued to entail lack of lexicalization for these items, a situation that would make them impervious to such obviously lexical rules as (26) and (27) (the lexical status of these rules is confirmed by the existence of exceptions). If we now were to assume that the foot-construction rule is postlexical (cf. the postlexical quantity-insensitive mode of application of the Latin algorithm discussed in Steriade 1988), all the facts would fall out, since the non-lexicalization of 'foreign' items would automatically exclude them from lexical accenting. From this perspective, the (presumably by now) native *Frómista* is appositely treated as heavily exceptional, since it must carry lexical exception marks for both (27) and (26). Note, however, that a postlexical ordering of foot-construction may create problems for the diphthongization of such forms as *huésped(a)* 'guest-FEM'.

42 In the context of the current war in Bosnia, it will be interesting to check whether Spanish-speaking reporters manage consistently to reproduce the Serbo-Croat initial stress of place names in cases where it clashes with the accent rules (26) and (27).

43 In the present connection it is most revealing to observe the alterations introduced in the stress contour of foreign place names in many Arabic dialects (I am indebted to Hussein Agali for this information): *Manchéster*, *Colchéster* (stress on heavy penult), *Liverp*[ú:]*l* (stress on superheavy ultima), *Birmingh*[á:]*m* (assimilated to the previous class by final vowel lengthening). The stress system of such dialects is identical to that of Latin except for the fact that final superheavy syllables attract stress. From this perspective, therefore, the noted alterations are readily interpretable as simple nativizations, indeed as expected on the backdrop of the cognitive reality of metrical algorithms (cf. the comments with regard to French nativisation in 2.2.2 above). The contrast with the Spanish case is striking.

44 This algorithm also provides a straightforward account of the alternation *carácter*~*caractéres*. Simply, the last syllable of the singular *carácter* is lexically marked as extrametrical, along the lines of *régimen*. Unlike *régimen*, however, *carácter* is not marked as an exception to the accenting rule (26):

```
                          *              *
(i)     * * <*>         * * <*>        * (*) <*>
       caracter   →   caracter   →   caracter
```

In the plural, the lexical extrametricality is lost as a consequence of the loss of peripherality, and (26) will place an accent on the stem-final syllable (now word-penultimate):

```
                                   *                   *
(ii)    * *   *<*>        * *   *<*>         * *   *<*>
       caracteres   →   caracteres   →   caracteres
```

Interestingly, the algorithm in (30) also contains the seeds of a solution to the problem of apocopated hypochoristic stressing, pending since Harris (1983). In particular, as Harris (1983: 95) pointed out, such forms are invariably paroxytonic: *arquitécto* 'architect' → *árqui*, *profesór* 'teacher' → *prófe*, *muñéca* 'doll' → *múñe*, *Mauricio* 'Maurice' → *Máuri*, *Lorénzo* 'Lawrence' → *Lóren*, and so on. The two relevant properties of these forms are: (i) stressless final syllable, and (ii) penultimate (equivalently, initial) stress. Notice that the final syllable is stressless regardless of weight, and therefore the construction of the binary leftheaded foot must be allowed to proceed unimpeded:

```
         *
(iii)   (* *)
        Loren
```

The stem-accenting rule (26) obviously does not apply here. This systematic situation is open to a natural interpretation in the present context: by their very nature such truncates have no internal morphological constituency, and thus no stem for stem-accenting to apply to.

45 Idiosyncratic accent is countenanced in Halle and Vergnaud (1987) alongside metrically-inspired parameters as a formal reflex of frequently attested irreducible stress irregularities.

References

Basbøll, H. 1989. Phonological weight in Italian *raddoppiamento sintattico*. *Rivista di Linguistica* 1.5-31.

Borer, H. 1984. *Parametric Syntax*. Dordrecht: Foris.

Burzio, L. 1994. *Principles of English Stress*. New York: Cambridge University Press.

Camilli, A. 1965. *Pronuncia e grafia dell'italiano*. Firenze: Sansoni.

Capell, A. and H.E. Hinch 1970. *Maung Grammar*. Janua Linguarum, Series Practica 98. The Hague: Mouton.

Carreira, M. 1988. The structure of palatal consonants in Spanish. *Chicago Linguistic Society* 24.73-87.

Carreira, M. 1990. *The Diphthongs of Spanish: Stress, Syllabification and Alternations*. Doctoral dissertation, University of Illinois at Urbana-Champaign.

Castellani, A. 1980. *Saggi di linguistica italiana e romanza 1946-1976* I. Roma: Salerno Editrice.

Chierchia, G. 1986. Length, syllabification and the phonological cycle in Italian. *Journal of Italian Linguistics* 8.5-34.

Chomsky, N. 1986. *Knowledge of Language*. New York: Praeger.

Chomsky, N. and M. Halle. 1968. *The Sound Pattern of English*. New York: Harper and Row.

Den Os, E. and R. Kager. 1986. Extrametricality and stress in Spanish and Italian. *Lingua* 69.23-48.

Dunlap, E. 1991. *Issues in the Moraic Structure of Spanish*. Doctoral dissertation, University of Massachusetts at Amherst.

Echeverría, M. and H. Contreras. 1965. Araucanian phonemics. *IJAL* 31.132-35.

Enciclopedia Universal Ilustrada. Madrid: Espasa-Calpe, 1964.

Farrell, P. 1990. Spanish stress: a cognitive analysis. *Hispanic Linguistics* 4.21-56.

Fiorelli, P. 1958. Del radoppiamento da parola a parola. *Lingua Nostra* 19.122-27.

Franks, S. 1987. Regular and irregular stress in Macedonian. *International Journal of Slavic Linguistics and Poetics* 35/36.93-142.

Greenberg, J. and D. Kaschube. 1976. Word prosodic systems: a preliminary report. *Working Papers in Language Universals* 20.1-18.

Hall, J. R. 1948. *Descriptive Italian Grammar*. Ithaca, NY: Cornell University Press.

Halle, M. and J.-R. Vergnaud. 1978. Metrical structures in phonology. Ms., MIT.

Halle, M. and J.-R. Vergnaud. 1987. *An Essay on Stress*. Cambridge, Mass.: MIT Press.

Halle, M., J.W. Harris and J.-R. Vergnaud. 1991. A reexamination of the stress erasure convention and Spanish stress. *Linguistic Inquiry* 22.141-59.

Hammond, M. 1984. *Constraining Metrical Theory: A Modular Theory of Rhythm and Destressing*. Doctoral dissertation, University of California, Los Angeles. (Distributed by Indiana University Linguistics Club.)

Harris, J. W. 1969. *Spanish Phonology*. Cambridge, Mass.: MIT Press.

Harris, J. W. 1980. Non-concatenative morphology and Spanish plurals. *Journal of Linguistic Research* 1.15-31.

Harris, J. W. 1983. *Syllable Structure and Stress in Spanish*. Cambridge, Mass.: MIT Press

Harris, J. W. 1987. The accentual patterns of verb paradigms in Spanish. *Natural Language and Linguistic Theory* 5.61-90.

Harris, J. W. 1988/92. *Spanish Stress: The Extrametricality Issue*. Indiana University Linguistics Club.

Harris, J. W. 1989a. How different is verb stress in Spanish? *Probus* 1.241-58.

Harris, J. W. 1989b. The stress erasure convention and cliticization in Spanish. *Linguistic Inquiry* 20.339-63.

Harris, J. W. 1989c. Sonority and syllabification in Spanish. *Studies in Romance Linguistics*, ed. C. Kirschner and J. De Cesaris, 139-53. Amsterdam: John Benjamins.

Harris, J. W. 1991a. With respect to accentual constituents in Spanish. *Current Studies in Spanish Linguistics*, ed. H. Campos and F. Martínez-Gil, 447-73. Washington, D. C.: Georgetown University Press.

Harris, J. W. 1991b. The form classes of Spanish substantives. *Yearbook of Morphology*, ed. G. Booij and J. van Marle, 65-88.

Harris, J. W. 1995. Projection and edge marking in the computation of stress in Spanish. *A Handbook of Phonological Theory*, ed. John Goldsmith, 867-887. Oxford: Blackwell.

Hayes, B. 1980. *A Metrical Theory of Stress Rules*. Doctoral dissertation, MIT (Distributed in 1981 by Indiana University Linguistics Club.)

Hayes, B. 1982. Extrametricality and English stress. *Linguistic Inquiry* 13.227-76.

Hayes, B. 1985. Iambic and trochaic rhythm in stress rules. *Berkeley Linguistic Society* 13.429-46.

Hayes, B. 1986. Inalterability in CV phonology. *Language* 62.321-51.

Hayes, B. 1987. A revised parametric metrical theory. *Proceedings of the North Eeastern Linguistics Society* 17.274-89.

Hayes, B. 1995. *Metrical Stress Theory: Principles and Case Studies*. Chicago: University of Chicago Press.

Hualde, J.I. 1987. On Basque affricates. *Proceedings of the West Coast Conference on Formal Linguistics* 6.77-89.

Hualde, J.I. 1991. On Spanish syllabification. *Current Studies Spanish Linguistics*, ed. by H. Campos and F. Martínez-Gil, 475-93. Washington, DC: Georgetown University Press.

Hyman, L. 1977. On the nature of linguistic stress. *Studies in Stress and Accent*, ed. L. Hyman, 37-82. Los Angeles: University of Southern California.

Hyman, L. 1985. *A Theory of Phonological Weight*. Dordrecht: Foris.

Idsardi, W. 1992. *The Computation of Prosody*. Doctoral dissertation, MIT.

Itô, J. 1986. *Syllable Theory in Prosodic Phonology*. Doctoral dissertation, University of Massachusetts, Amherst.

Itô, J. 1989. A prosodic theory of epenthesis. *Natural Language and Linguistic Theory* 7.217-59.

Josselyn, F. 1900. *Étude sur la phonétique italienne*. Paris.

Juilland, A. and E. Chang-Rodríguez. 1964 *Frequency Dictionary of Spanish Words*. The Hague: Mouton.

Kager, R. 1989. *A Metrical Theory of Stress and Destressing in English and Dutch*. Dordrecht: Foris.

Kenstowicz, M. 1990. Stress and generative phonology. *Rivista di Linguistica Generativa* 2.55-86.

Kiparsky, P. 1973. Elsewhere in phonology. *A Festschrift for Morris Halle*, ed. S. Anderson and P. Kiparsky, 93-106. New York: Holt, Rinehart and Wilson.

Kiparsky, P. 1979. Metrical structure assignment is cyclic. *Linguistic Inquiry* 10. 421-41.

Korzen, I. 1980. Il raddoppiamento sintattico e la geminata nella variante toscana dell'italiano-standard. Risultati di un'indagine sperimentale. *Studi Italiani di Linguistica Teorica e Applicata* 9.333-66.

Kuryłowicz, J. 1948. Contribution a la théorie de la sillabe. *Bulletin de la Societé Polonaise de Linguistique* 8.80-114.

Lehiste, I. 1970. *Suprasegmentals*. Cambridge, Mass.: MIT Press.

Lepschy, A.L. and G. Lepschy. 1981. *La Lingua Italiana. Storia, Varietà dell'uso, grammatica*. Milano: Bompiani.

Liberman, M. and A. Prince. 1977. On stress and linguistic rythm. *Linguistic Inquiry* 8.249-336.

McCarthy, J. and A. Prince. 1986. *Prosodic Morphology*. Ms., University of Massachusetts, Amherst, and Brandeis University.

McCarthy, J. and A. Prince. 1993. *Prosodic Morphology I. Constraint Interaction and Satisfaction*. Ms., University of Massachusetts, Amherst, and Rutgers University.

Menéndez Pidal, R. 1962. *Manual de gramática histórica española*. Madrid: Espasa-Calpe.

Mester, A. 1994. The quantitative trochee in Latin. *Natural Language and Linguistic Theory* 12.1-61.

Monroy, R. 1980. *Aspectos fonéticos de las vocales españolas*. Madrid: Sociedad General Española de Librería.

Muljacvić, Z. 1972. *Fonologia della Lingua Italiana*. Bologna: Il Mulino.

Navarro Tomás, T. 1916. Cantidad de las vocales acentuadas. *Revista de Filología Española* 3.387-408.

Newman, P. 1972. Syllable weight as a phonological variable. *Studies in African Linguistics* 3.301-24.

Núñez Cedeño, R. 1985. Stress assignment in Spanish verb forms. *Current Studies in Hispanic Phonology and Morphology*, ed. F. Nuessel, 55-76. Indiana University Linguistics Club.

Núñez Cedeño, R. 1988. Structure preserving properties of an epenthesis rule in Spanish. *Advances in Romance Linguistics*, ed. D. Birdsong and J.-P. Montreuil, 319- 335. Dordrecht: Foris.

Ohsiek, D. 1978. Heavy syllables and stress. *Syllables and Stress*, ed. A. Bell and J.B. Hooper, 35-43. North-Holland.

Otero, C. 1986. A unified metrical account of Spanish stress. *A Festschrift for Sol Saporta*, ed. M. Brame, H. Contreras and F.J. Newmeyer, 299-332. Seattle: Noit Amrofer.

Parmenter, C. and J. Carmen. 1932. Some remarks on Italian quantity. *Italica* 9.103-08.

Prince, A. 1983. Relating to the grid. *Linguistic Inquiry* 14.19-100.

Prince, A. and P. Smolensky. 1993. *Optimality Theory: Constraint Interaction in Generative Grammar*. Ms., Rutgers University and University of Colorado, Boulder.

Repetti, L. 1991. A moraic analysis of *raddoppiamento sintattico*. *Rivista di Linguistica* 3. 307-30.

Roca, I. M. 1986. Secondary stress and metrical rhythm. *Phonology Yearbook* 3. 341-70.

Roca, I. M. 1988. Theoretical implications of Spanish word stress. *Linguistic Inquiry* 19.393-423.

Roca, I. M. 1989. The organisation of grammatical gender. *Transactions of the Philological Society* 87.1-32.

Roca, I. M. 1990a. Diachrony and synchrony in Spanish stress. *Journal of Linguistics* 26.133-64.

Roca, I. M. 1990b. Morphology and verbal stress in Spanish. *Probus* 2.321-50.

Roca, I. M. 1991. Stress and syllables in Spanish. *Current Studies in Spanish Linguistics*, ed. H. Campos and F. Martínez-Gil, 599-635. Washington, D.C.: Georgetown University Press.

Roca, I. M. 1992a. On the sources of word prosody. *Phonology* 9.267- 87.

Roca, I. M. 1992b. Constraining extrametricality. *Phonologica* 1988, ed. W. U. Dressler, H. C. Luschutzky, O. E. Pfeiffer, and J. R. Rennison, 239-48. New York: Cambridge University Press.

Roca, I. M. 1994. *Generative Phonology*. London: Routledge.

Roca, I. M. 1995. There are no 'glides', at least in Spanish: an optimality account. Ms., University of Essex (forthcoming in *Probus* 9.1).

Roca, I. M. 1996. Stress in the Romance languages. Ms., University of Essex (forthcoming in H. van der Hulst, ed., *Word Prosodic Systems in the Languages of Europe*, Berlin and New York: Mouton de Gruyter).

Saporta, S. 1962. On the expression of gender in Spanish. *Romance Philology* 15. 279-284.

Sluyters, W. 1990. Length and stress revisited: a metrical account of diphthongization, vowel lengthening, consonant gemination and word-final vowel epenthesis in modern Italian. *Probus* 2.65-102.

Solan, L. 1981. A metrical analysis of Spanish stress. *Linguistic Symposium on Romance Languages* 9, ed. W. W. Cressey and D. J. Napoli, 90- 104. Washington, D.C.: Georgetown University Press.

Steriade, D. 1988. Greek accent: a case for preserving structure. *Linguistic Inquiry* 19. 271-314.

Suñer, M. 1975. Spanish adverbs: support for the phonological cycle? *Linguistic Inquiry* 6.602-05.

Trubetzkoy, N. 1939. *Principles of Phonology*. Berkeley: University of California Press.

Vayra, M. 1993. Phonetic explanations in phonology: the case for glottal stops in Italian word-final stressed syllables. Unpublished ms., revised version of a paper given at the 7th *International Phonology Meeting*, Krems.

Vincent, N. 1988. Non-linear phonology in diachronic perspective: stress and word-structure in Latin and Italian. *Certamen Phonologicum*, ed. P. M. Bertinetto and M. Loporcaro, 421-432. Turin: Rosenberg and Sellier.

Vogel, I. 1978. Raddoppiamento as a resyllabification rule. *Journal of Italian Linguistics* 3.15-28.

Vogel, I. 1982. *La sillaba come unitá fonologica*. Bologna: Zanichelli.

Wexler, K. and M.R. Manzini. 1987. Parameters and learnability in binding theory. *Parameter Setting*, ed. T. Roeper and E. Williams, 41-76. Dordrecht: Reidel.

Zagona, K. 1990. *Mente* adverbs, compound interpretation and the projection principle. *Probus* 2.1-30.

20

Stress in Spanish and Latin: where morphology meets prosody*

Mario Saltarelli

0 Introduction

This paper reflects on the familiar fact that the structure of a language is conditioned by its history, while the conceptual organization of its grammar can be fixed within a narrow set of parameters available to the learner of a linguistic system. Within this articulated diachronic and synchronic perspective it is possible, I believe, to elaborate and evaluate conceptually broader (and more coherent) grammatical hypotheses, thus enhancing their degree of descriptive adequacy.

I attempt to show, in this respect, that an explicit panchronic approach is especially useful in the study of prosodic patterns, where the interface between the two dimensions of language significantly narrows the range of hypotheses compatible with the data. If this line of investigation turns out to be fruitful in understanding prosodic conceptualization across time, we would be rescuing the legacy of comparative historical grammar, thus extending its theoretical reach beyond the constraints of real time.

The paper proceeds as follows. In section 1 the standard metrical analysis of Spanish imparisyllabic stress shift is reconsidered in view of a morphology-prosody mapping based on a principle of full phonetic interpretation (3). Comparative motivation for the proposal comes from the prosody of Latin imparisyllabicity (section 2) and the evolution of metrical parameters from early Latin (section 3) to modern Romance (section 4). Synchronic and diachronic considerations strongly support a minimalist-inspired unbounded panchronic theory (section 3.3.1-2) incorporating metrical cardinality (7") as an index of parametric variation. Developments in present-day Spanish and Italian (4.1-2) suggest (at least partial) lexicalization, an incipient tendency reminiscent of the prosodic situation which obtained in the Indo-European stress system.

1 Imparisyllabic stress alternation in Spanish

With this general linguistic program in mind, I focus on recent metrical accounts of the accentual shift which occurs in Spanish in forms such as *régimen* 'regime' versus *regímenes* 'regimes' (1).[1]

(1)	régimen (pl. regímenes)	'regime, diet, etc.'
	espécimen (pl. especímenes)	'specimen'
	hipérbaton (pl. hipérbatos,	
	hipérbatons, hiperbátones)	'hyperbaton'
	ínterin (pl. intérines)	'interim, temporary'
	ómicron (pl. omícrones)	'omicron'
	Júpiter	'Jupiter'

The familiar subset of words in (1) belongs to a stable and extensive set of consonant-stem lexical items (including those in (2)), whose members of the number paradigm (singular *régimen* versus plural *regímenes*) are imparisyllabic. Items in this set do not have the same number of syllables, in contrast with the parisyllabic number paradigm of vowel-stem lexical items in the language, such as *águila* versus *águilas*. Additionally, items in (1) differ from other imparisyllables in the language (cf. (2) in 1.2 below), in that they require primary stress on a different syllable for the two forms of the number paradigm.[2] This accentual property of the imparisyllabic set (1) has been considered 'exceptional,' in contrast with the non-alternating property of the set (2).

From a historical perspective, the lexical items in (1) constitute a quantitatively reduced subset of a larger set of imparisyllabic words exhibiting the same accentual alternation in Latin, which has filtered down to modern Spanish through the internal and external evolution of the language (see section 2 below for Latin imparisyllables).[3]

The analysis developed in this paper makes two fundamental empirical claims about Spanish imparisyllables. One, the low membership of the residual set (1) is irrelevant to their prosodic status in the language and to their conceptualization. The stress alternation which is specific to this set cannot be dismissed as an alien phenomenon; rather, it follows as a predictable prosodic pattern of the language. Two, the structural property of the set (1) which is crucial to a canonical account of imparisyllabic stress alternation is the trisyllabic constituency of the bare lexical items in the set interfacing with the antepenultimate nature of the lexical items in question.

1.1 Metrical analysis of imparisyllabic stress alternation

In prevailing metrical analyses (Harris 1983, Roca 1990a), the label 'exceptional' for the imparisyllables under discussion does not refer either to the low cardinality of the set (1) or to the near-uniqueness of the stress alternation. Rather, the items in (1), illustrated by the normative dactylic rhythmic shift *régimen* vs. *regímenes* fall outside the computational capability of the prosodic system proposed by the authors, and therefore require a special statement in the prosodic description. If such is the case (and I believe that this conclusion is implied in the metrical treatments in question), then the 'exceptional' definition of the set (1) is spurious, as theory-specific. That is, the stress alternation exhibited by the set (1) must be exceptionally accounted for in the prosodic algorithm (1') as a logical consequence of the prosodic parameter assumed, namely the bounded parameter.[4]

In this paper, I will argue that the bounded parametric option, in contrast with the above hypotheses, is too restrictive in the version proposed by the authors, thus failing to account for the stress alternations observed in (1) as a canonical antepenultimate prosodic pattern in the language. Nevertheless, the claim is made that a generalized account of imparisyllabic stress alternation is available within the current conceptualization of bounded metrical theory (Halle and Vergnaud 1987, Idsardi 1992). This paper presents independent arguments which motivate the claim and comparative evidence which supports it.

In the remainder of this section I discuss the non-canonical (exceptional) accounts of stress assignment proposed in the literature for the paradigm set (1). Briefly, the items in (1) are represented with an underlying morphological structure in admittedly arbitrary fashion (Harris 1983: 134: [[reg(i)]me(n)]; Roca 1990a, see illustration in (1')). The putative internal lexical structure of alternating imparisyllables is stipulated as a technical device that accommodates lexical extrametricality as a compounded effect of peripherality.[5]

(1') (cf. Roca 1990a: 150, (33))

[regi (men)]	[[regi (men)] (es)]	
[+rule 28]	[+rule 28]	
e i (e)	e i (e) (e)	basic stress bearers
NA	e i e	metrical stress bearers
(. *)	(. . *)	metrical structure
(*)	(. *)	rule 28 (right head erasure)
régimen	regímenes	

Specifically, Roca's derivational illustration (1') for the assignment of antepenultimate stress to *régimen*/*regímenes* assumes for (1) a lexical structure with an extrametrical root-peripheral syllable *(men)*, in addition to an extrametrical word-peripheral syllable *(es)*. It should be noted that root-peripheral extrametricality would be specific to imparisyllabic lexical items in (1), excluding imparisyllables in (2) and parisyllables. Roca's lexical characterization of the set (1) is similar to Harris' earlier analysis in its appeal to an extended (root-based) peripherality condition. In both accounts, the (non-canonical) extension of extrametricality is forced by strict adherence to a bounded (binary) theory of antepenultimate stress assignment to the set in (1). The need for this diacritical extension of extrametricality in order to account for antepenultimate stress in (1) reveals the theoretical weakness of a bounded (binary) parameter in accounting for antepenultimate stress as an effect of peripherality in quantity-insensitive languages such as Spanish.[6]

In sum, the prosodic result sought in Harris' and Roca's systems is to create an appropriate antepenultimate domain for the application of the stress algorithm which does not exceed bounded (binary) foot constituency. This goal is achieved, at least in Harris' original metrical analysis, by appealing to an extended (lexically marked) use of the inflection-peripheral morpheme in the proparoxytonic words such as *sábana*, represented as [saban(a)], in contrast with *sabana* [sabana].[7] Under this descriptive scenario, the metrical environment submitted to the prosodic algorithm is leveled to binary constituency by stem lexicalization of the inflectional morpheme. Items in the set (1), however, exceed by one syllable the domain of the bounded algorithm, which predicts an incorrect stress pattern: *[regímen( )]. This constitutes prima facie evidence that a bounded theory is too restrictive for a general account of imparisyllabic stress alternation in Spanish.

1.2 On the prosodic projection of morphological paradigms: the principle of full phonetic interpretation

In light of these considerations, we take a closer look at the structural properties of the imparisyllabic paradigm of the analytically recalcitrant set (1) and its co-set (2). For one thing, the lexical items in question all have a consonantal stem, specifically ending in a nasal, a liquid, or a spirant; and this lexical property holds no surprise, except that it has been argued to be a syllable-inspired basis for Spanish plural formation.[8]

(2) a. numen (pl. númenes) — 'deity, inspiration'
albumen (pl. albúmenes) — 'albumen'
cóndor (pl. cóndores) — 'condor'
útil (pl. útiles) — 'useful'
álbum (pl. álbumes) — 'album'
etc.

b. andén (pl. andenes) — 'walk'
sutíl (pl. sutiles) — 'fine, subtle'
color (pl. colores) — 'color'
mes (pl. meses) — 'month'

If we compare, however, (1) and (2) from the point of view of meter, a descriptive observation can be made which, to my knowledge, has not been formally submitted to linguistic inquiry; namely, imparisyllabic paradigms in Spanish can be factored out into two (and only two) rhythmic types: dactylic (´--) and trochaic (´-). While items in (1) and (2a) define a dactylic foot measure, items in (2b) define a trochaic foot. This metrical partition of Spanish imparisyllabic paradigms further distinguishes (1) from (2) in that, in the latter's singular form of the paradigm, the rhythmic measure is catalectic.[9]

From the point of view of syllabic constituency all items in (1) have tri-syllabic stems, a property which correlates with their exclusively non-catalectic dactylic rhythmic nature and their antepenultimate stress type. In correlation with these properties only items in (1) exhibit a stress shift in the plural forms, which is commensurate with a relative syllabic augment. This is an expected result under the proposed metrical classification which unifies the set (1) and (2a) as dactylic measures.

We can now confirm that the prosodically relevant property of (1) which is in correlation with stress alternation is the tri-syllabic constituency of the stem. Accordingly, the facts just discussed suggest that a prosodic mapping of the full syllabic constituency of a paradigm form must be taken into account for an appropriate characterization of stress placement in Spanish.

On the basis of these considerations, the constituency requirements on prosody assumed in this paper are stated in the provisionally defined principle (3).

(3) The computation of prosodic stress operates on a full syllabic projection of morphologically processed paradigm forms, i.e, the prosodic word.

1.3 Toward a generalized account of stress in imparisyllables

One additional remark must be made about the 'exceptional' metrical assessment (cf. 1.1) of Spanish imparisyllables within a parametric grid-driven theory of stress (Halle and Vergnaud 1987).

As reported above, the forms in (1) are assessed to be inaccessible to a bounded (binary foot constituency) parametric algorithm without appealing to lexically defined extrametricality. As a consequence, both (prosodic) word-peripheral and (lexical) root-peripheral extrametrical syllables were defined in (1'): [régi(men)], [[regí(men)](es)].

Now, if we focus on the individual forms of the paradigm, we see that it is only the singular form which the bounded algorithm is by definition not designed to process without appeal to lexical extrametricality. Hence the syllable (men) is diacritically excluded from the metrical representation, a decision forced by the fact that the stem exceeds binary foot constituency by one syllable.

In contradiction to the need for an extrametrical syllable in the singular form, we should point out that the marking of the same extrametrical syllable (men) in the plural form blocks the correct assignment of primary stress to the antepenultimate syllable. Under this scenario, the root-peripheral extrametrical syllable has the undesired countereffect of forcing the bounded algorithm to incorrectly assign stress to the pre-antepenultimate: *[[régi(men)](es)]. In fact, for the correct operation of the bounded algorithm in the plural form, the root-peripheral syllable *men* MUST be metrically computed: [regímen(es)], the word-peripheral (*es*) being the only extrametrical requirement.[10]

It is clear at this point that the postulation of (lexical) root-peripheral extrametricality for Spanish imparisyllables (1) does not correctly account for the typical stress shift phenomenon. In contrast, it is shown that (prosodic) word-peripheral extrametricality is a sufficient and necessary condition for a canonical assignment of antepenultimate imparisyllable stress within a bounded metrical theory. A uniform account of the stress alternation follows from the observable fact that, in Spanish, stress cannot recede beyond the antepenultimate syllable of a word. It is obvious in most cases, then, that the 'law of the three syllables' must be prosodically computed within the boundaries of the 'prosodic word'; namely, the precise locus of stress in Spanish is defined on a full syllabic projection of the morphologically processed paradigm form, consistent with the principle (3).

Accordingly, the forms of the morphological number paradigm (1), i.e. {[[regimen]∅], [[regimen]es]} receive full syllabic mapping onto individual prosodic domains (grid line 0), where the extrametricality parameter is strictly prosodically (word-peripherally) defined: [regi(men)], [regime(nes)]. This version of the bounded algorithm (cf. note 9) appropriately processes each form as a prosodic word and correctly parses the sequence of prosodic marks in left-headed binary foot measures (grid line 1): [ré.gi(men)], [re.gí.me(nes)].[11]

From the comparative/diachronic perspective we are also assuming that the exceptional prosodic status for imparisyllables is unexpected, given the inherited Latin conditions of the Spanish lexicon, which in general maintains an etymologically invariant locus for stress in nouns and adjectives. In the course of this paper, it will become evident that the intuitive suspicion about the so-called exceptional status of items in (1) is well-founded synchronically as well as diachronically. It will be shown, in the following sections, that a viable parametric alternative exists which uniformly accounts for imparisyllable stress in Latin as well as in Spanish.

2 Latin declension of imparisyllables: what's in a paradigm?

I will now discuss the steady-state Latin origins of the residual imparisyllabic subset (1),[12] in adherence with the linguistic program outlined in the introduction.

In the Latin grammatical tradition, the term 'imparisyllable' usually refers to the third declension paradigm of nouns and adjectives (with stems ending in a consonant or -i-). The forms of the third declension paradigms, in fact, show the highest degree of allomorphic alternation between the form of the Nominative (and Vocative) and the other cases.[13] Examples are given in (4).

(4)	SINGULAR				
	n-stem	n-stem	n-stem	r-stem	s-stem
	regimen-	*homin-*	*praedo:n-*	*soro:r-*	*arbor-*
N./V.	regimen	homo:	praedo:	soror	arbo:s
G.	regiminis	hominis	praedo:nis	soro:ris	arboris
D.	regimini:	homini:	praedoni:	soro:ri:	arbori:
A.	regimen	hominem	praedo:nem	soro:rem	arborem
	PLURAL				
N./A.	regimina	homine:s	praedo:ne:s	soro:re:s	arbore:s
G.	regiminum	hominum	praedo:num	soro:rum	arborum
D./A.	regiminibus	hominibus	praedo:nibus	soro:ribus	arboribus

2.1 On the characterization of inflectional paradigms

Following Latin grammars, the surface forms of the third declension case paradigm are subcategorized under a lexical stem type, among other nasal-stems, liquid-stems and s-stems, as in the examples given in (4) (cf. Allen and Greenough 1983: 24-37, among other sources). The paradigm stem is usually derived from the genitive plural form by omitting the desinence *-um*, with the surface alternants given as lists for the learner to memorize. The implication of a single underlying stem can be seen as an attempt to formalize the lexical integrity of the paradigm. Such a formalization has been attempted at the post-Bloomfieldian morpho-phonological interface by deriving via morpho-phonological rules of 'automatic replacement' all the alternant forms of the stem (e.g., lat. {*regimen-*, *regimin-*}) and of the desinence in the paradigm (cf. Hall 1946, Householder 1946, Saporta's University of Illinois dissertation on morpheme alternants in Spanish). Owing to the high degree of phonological indeterminacy in the Latin third declension paradigm, the morpho-phonology approach to a definition of paradigm is morphologically cumbersome and phonologically uninteresting.

One case in point, which was discussed by the eminent latinist Ernout (1954: 43-44), concerns a long/short alternation between the Nominative form and the other cases in r-stem paradigms. The Nominative *soror* 'sister' (cf. (4)) might be derived by a rule which shortens an underlying stem **soro:r*. This long form of the stem is considered necessary in order to account for the penultimate stress in non-Nominative paradigm forms as well as on the basis of comparative Italic evidence. Additional support for this hypothesis comes from the language of archaic Latin authors like Plautus, where the long *o:* before final liquid was retained. Counterevidence for the shortening hypothesis, however, are monosyllabic words like (5) for which one would need to posit the opposite (lengthening) rule in the same context.

(5) pa:r, paris
sa:l, salis
la:r, laris
ma:s, maris

A more accessible formalization of the notion paradigm is Anderson's recent morpho-syntactic/lexical definition. Accordingly, the paradigm of any lexical item will result from the interaction of the members of its stem set with the inflectional rules of the language (Anderson 1992: 134). It can be argued that this modular definition of paradigm is more closely related to the intuitive classical notion of paradigm forms as an extended word list in the familiar 'word and paradigm' view of grammar. Likewise, in a minimalist conceptualization of grammar (Chomsky 1993), morphologically processed forms, as in (4), would have independent lexical status, their paradigm coherence defined at Logical Form by the operation of feature checking.

For the purpose of a metrical hypothesis of stress, Anderson's morpho-syntactic and the minimalist conception of the notion paradigm reconfirms the lexical integrity of paradigm forms. If this assumption turns out to be correct, information about morphological and syntactic parsing of the paradigm form would not be available at the prosodic level of representation. Within this conceptual framework, grid-driven metrical representations are autosegmental projections of prosodic marks and boundaries (Goldsmith 1976, Idsardi 1992). Accordingly, each form of the paradigm is prosodically projected as a morphologically fully processed linguistic object, as informally stated in the mapping principle (3).

2.2 Imparisyllabicity and desinential augment

One more point must be made with respect to the nature of imparisyllabic paradigm forms in view of a grid line metrical representation theory consistent with (3).

In contrast with Nominative case forms, non-Nominative singular forms are projected with a syllabic augment of one at the right edge of the base prosodic grid line. Dative and Ablative forms of the plural will project a separate syllabic augment of one on the right edge of the base prosodic grid line. Thus, the bi-syllabic Nominative *ho.mo* (cf. (4)) is projected as a tri-syllabic in its singular Genitive, *ho.mi.nis*, Dative, *ho.mi.ni:*, Accusative, *ho.mi.nem*, and Ablative form, *ho.mi.ne*. As a consequence of the additive nature of the inflectional augment, the Dative/Ablative plural form, *ho.mi.ni.bus*, receives a tetra-syllabic prosodic projection, with its attendant prosodic consequences.

It will be assumed, in adherence to the full phonetic interpretation criterion (3), that syllabic augment plays a crucial role in the determination of the locus of primary stress, with consequences for a uniform definition of stress alternation in imparisyllables.

In the interest of completeness, I would like to add that what has been discussed so far about syllabic augment is restricted to desinential augment. Stem augment is, however, also observed as an extension of the range of stress alternation. For example, the bi-syllabic *i.ter* is tetra-syllabic in the Genitive form, *i.ti.ne.ris* and penta-syllabic in the Dative/Ablative plural *i.ti.ne.ri.bus*. This is an extreme occurrence in Latin, which is lexically moderated by the creation of a longer Nominative singular form, *i.ti.ner*. An equally dramatic example of stem augment is *sup.pel.lex* which also has three degrees of augmentation, namely, *sup.pel.lec.ti.lis* and technically *sup.pel.lec.ti.li.bus*.

Perhaps the self-evident example which could be adduced to clinch the argument in favor of the lexically independent status of paradigmatic forms as prosodic projections of morpho-syntactically fully processed syllabic representations is the paradigm of the lexical item *Ju.pi.ter*, *Jo.vis*, *Jo.vi:*, *Jo.vem*, *Jo.ve*. Clearly, the non-Nominative vs. the Nominative forms must be learned as lexically independent root alternants paradigmatically related by their morpho-syntactic or logical form association.

3 The parameters of Latin stress

I will now proceed with a parametric assessment of Latin stress in its historical perspective, in keeping with the comparative program advocated in the introduction.

It is well established that Latin accentuation was stress (and not pitch, as reported by the Romans themselves) on evidence such as syncope in words like *o.cu.lum* not *o.c'lum* reported in Probus' Appendix, a post-accentual 'weakening' phenomenon typical of stress languages like modern English.[14]

There is also general agreement in classical scholarship on the issue that early Latin authors, like Plautus, show evidence of a prehistoric initial accentuation (6), exemplified at least for the pre-antepenultimate syllable (see Sturtevant 1940: 177, Allen 1973: 151).

(6) (Prehistoric) Latin

a. fá.ci.lis

b. fá.ci.li.us

3.1 Prehistoric initial stress

In Halle and Vergnaud's metrical theory of stress, languages with pure initial stress, including present-day Latvian and other Indo-European and non-Indo-European languages, are characterized by a Basic Accentuation Principle (Halle and Vergnaud 1987: 84) formulated in the familiar notation of the parametric algorithm, roughly as in (7), and illustrated for (prehistoric) Latin in (7').

(7) Initial Stress

a. Line 0 parameter settings are [+HT, -BND, left]
b. Construct constituent boundaries on line 0
c. Locate the heads of line 0 constituents on line 1
etc.

```
(7')  a.                              b.
       *  .  .         line 1         *  .  .  .
      (*  *  *)        line 0        (*  *  *  *)
       3  2  1                        4  3  2  1
      fá.ci.lis                      fá.ci.li.us
```

The computation of the grid representation (7') forms unbounded, left-headed foot measures. The conventional fixing of the boundedness parameter is usually given as either [+BND] (binary constituency) or [-BND] (n-ary constituency). Accordingly, the foot-constructing algorithm (7) gathers feet which have as necessary two set conditions: arbitrary -n length and exhaustiveness of the prosodic elements in the word. One way to incorporate both conditions for initial stress systems in the notational convention is a specification of the cardinality index to -n+1. Thus, words of any length would be assigned initial stress. Under this computational system the restriction on the length of the word remains lexically open. Accordingly, an extension of the parametric algorithm (7) in the Basic Accentuation Principle would be in the form of (7").

(7") Metrical Cardinality

a. Line 0 parameter settings are [+HT, -BND_n, left]

If we adopt this convention, then, given the particular setting of the direction of foot construction on the grid line 0 and the headedness of the foot on line 1, in a 'pure' unbounded metrical system of the type (7a) the locus of stress should recede exhaustively to the left edge of the prosodic word domain. Hence, we have an operational characterization of word initial stress. One consequence of (7") is that the Exhaustivity Condition (Halle and Vergnaud 1987: 15) is derived as a property of the system, along with a definition of the categorial [±BND] metrical value.

3.2 From initial stress to pre-antepenultimate stress in Old Latin: comparative evidence

The historical evolution of the initial stress system into diachronically related linguistic systems supports the proposal (7") as a useful descriptive device, as we elaborate in the sections which follow.

3.2.1 Old Latin

Let us look first at the Old Latin reflexes (8) of the hypothesized prehistoric initial stress in Latin (6).

(8) Old Latin[15]

```
         *   .   .   .    line 1
      * (*   *   *   *    line 0
      5  4   3   2   1
         fá.ci.lis
         fá.ci.li.us
         ré.gi.men
         ré.gi.mi.nis
      re.gí.mi.ni.bus
         ó.cu.lum
      ad.sí.mi.li.ter
         uó.lup.tas
          á.va:.rus
```

Although an initial stress system is assumed for prehistoric Latin as derivative of a dismantled Indo-European lexical stress system (cf. Halle and Vergnaud 1987: 272, fn. 9, apud Idsardi 1992: 52), obviously, the stress system exemplified in (8) for Old Latin must have no longer been a 'pure' word initial type. In (8), in fact, taking the same setting as in (7"), the 'recession' index of the cardinality of the unbounded foot measure parameter appears to be regularly fixed at n=4.

3.2.2 The emergence of the n-syllable window

In this historical perspective, I would like to point out that the notational index proposed in (7"), which fixes the upper limit of an unbounded foot measure, formalizes the familiar notion of 'n-syllable window' which is itself just one incidence of the 'rule of recession' posited in comparative studies of Indo-European stress systems (cf. Allen 1973: 236, Jakobson 1937/1962). With respect to an assumed pure prehistoric initial stress, characterized as an unbounded system $[\text{-BND}]_{n+1}$, the 'rule of recession' defines the distance between the canonical position of stress from the end of the word. In general the term 'recession,' as a phenomenon restricting the unbounded foot parameter appears to be supported by comparative evidence.

Old Indian may have an initial accent seven syllables removed from the end on words like *ábubodhisamahi* 'we wanted to learn' or nine syllables removed as in *údda:lakapuspabhañjika:* 'breaking of the *udda:laka* flower.' The upper limit of recession is theoretically open and unimpeded by heavy intervening syllables. In fact, comparing Old Indian with Greek in tetrasyllabic corresponding words, the former has invariably initial stress while the latter language is limited to antepenultimate stress. Assuming common origin, the prosodic differentiation between the above languages is appropriately defined by a parametric variation in the degree of recession of the unbounded parameter on the algorithm (7), as in (9).

(9) a. Line 0 parameter settings are [+HT, -BND_n for $n=4_{OLat}$, right to left, left]

3.3 Antepenultimate and penultimate in Classical Latin: the three-syllable window

The prehistoric initial stress condition, appropriately limited in Old Latin (9), was succeeded in that language, after the archaic age of Plautus and Terence in the period down to 300 A.D., by an accent falling mostly on the antepenultimate or penultimate syllable if it was 'heavy' by nature or by position (10). As everyone knows, the characterization of this new prosodic type has been the subject of much controversy (cf. Allen 1973, Part II).

(10) Classical Latin

```
a. Antepenultimate                  b. Penultimate

           *                               (*
   *   *  (*   *   *)                  *   (*     *)
   5   4   3   2   1                   3    2     1
          fá.ci.lis                   uo.lúp.tas
      fa.cí.li.us                      a.vá:.rus
          ó.cu.lum
ad.si.mí.li.ter
          ré.gi.men
      re.gí.mi.nis
re.gi.mí.ni.bus
```

If we look at the locus of stress in the word, we notice an apparently drastic difference between Old Latin (8) and Classical Latin (10). A shift is observed, in fact, from a regular pre-antepenultimate stress type to a penultimate/antepenultimate pattern. The assignment of stress in a word strictly correlates with the rhyme quantity of the penultimate syllable. That is, primary stress falls on the penultimate if heavy, otherwise on the antepenultimate. In linear generative phonology a rule can be formulated which uniformly accounts for both (10a) and (10b) strictly on the basis of syllable structure. Given the facts in (10) therefore, the etymological antecedents of the imparisyllabic Spanish set (1) and (2) are subject to a uniform account.

3.3.1 Bounded accounts of Classical Latin stress

Contrary to the uniform analysis in the linear generative tradition (Chomsky and Halle 1968), the conceptual basis of a metrical grid driven parametric account of the distribution of the two stress patterns in (10) is disjoint. While, on one hand, penultimate stress (10b) is assigned by the familiar quantity-sensitive rule, antepenultimate stress (10a) is accounted for by the boundedness parameter set as [+BND].

The prevailing analysis of antepenultimate stress in languages like Latin and Macedonian (Halle and Vergnaud 1987: 55-56) is illustrated in abbreviated form in (11). For a full account, Latin is also subject to the quantity-sensitive penultimate rule (12a). Accordingly, the derivation of penultimate and antepenultimate stress in Latin is constructed in (13).

(11) a. Mark the final syllable extrametrical
b. Line 0 parameter settings are [+HT, +BND, right to left, left]
c. Locate the heads of line 0 constituents on line 1
etc. (Halle & Vergnaud 1987: 55, (16))

(12) a. Assign a line 1 asterisk to any metrical syllable of a word if it has a branching rhyme (Halle & Vergnaud 1987: 56, (18)).

b. Assign boundaries to a penultimate syllable with a branching rhyme.

(13) a. Antepenultimate b. Penultimate

```
       *                                              *
   *   *              1  (11c)           *            *
  (*) (*  *)  .       0  (11b)          (*    *) (*)     .
   *   *  *<*>        0  (11a)           *    *  (*)<*>
   *   *  *   *       0  (12b)           *    *  (*)  *
  reprimitur                            reprimuntur
```

It should be noted that the execution of Halle and Vergnaud's system requires an extrinsic order of application involving (12b), (11a), (11b). Moreover, it is unclear how rule (12a) should be formulated in order to properly compute penultimate stress on forms like *reprimuntur*. Perhaps (12b) is a workable, although non-conforming, alternative. One consequence of the system is the necessity for constructing metrically 'degenerate' feet, consisting of a single prosodic element.

A reformulation of the metrical grid model of Halle and Vergnaud has been recently proposed in Idsardi's dissertation (Idsardi 1992). Idsardi's bounded characterization, which is reproduced in (14-15), significantly improves the computation of Latin stress (Idsardi 1992: 24).

(14)	Line 0:	Avoid (x#			
		Project:L	Edge:RLR	ICC:R	Head:L
	Line 1:		Edge:RRR		Head:R

(15) a. Antepenultimate b. Penultimate

```
         *         Head              *
   *     *)        Line 1      *         *)
   *    (*   *) *  ICC        (*    *   (*)    *
   *     *   *) *  Edge        *    *   (*)    *
   *     *   *  *  Project     *    *   (*     *
  r e p r i m i t u r          r e p r i m u n t u r
      r e g i m e n
   r e g i m i n i s
```

A significant advantage of Idsardi's computational system over previous algorithms is the generalization of the device of extrametricality as an effect of the Edge Parameter, which defines a narrow range of possible prosodic word boundary locations. The assignment of penultimate stress (15b) is achieved by the Projection of a heavy syllable along with a metrical parenthesis, in words like *reprimuntur*.

It is important to point out that, under Idsardi's generalized extrametricality, the antecedents of the apparently 'exceptional' words in Spanish (1), like *régimen* (< Lat. *regimen* (cf. (4)), are uniformly assigned antepenultimate stress. This confirms our expectations and encourages a review of the parametric evolution of Latin prosody.

The clear descriptive advantages of Idsardi's generalized extrametricality effect in the analysis of Latin leaves unaffected the metrical grid account of the penultimate stress pattern. As one can observe in (15b), the (extrametrical) setting of Idsardi's Edge parameter cannot avoid rhythmically unfavored degenerate penultimate foot measures, robbing the theory of a grid improvement with respect to the earlier systems (cf. 13b). It can be shown, however, that a solution to this rhythmic issue is available in Idsardi's own system in conjunction with a revised setting of the Edge marking parameter in the form (14') (cf. Idsardi 1992: 4 (11)).

(14') Edge Parameter Setting: Edge:RRR

Insert a right boundary to the right of the rightmost element on the grid line 0

The appropriate setting of the right boundary, I claim, is to the right of the rightmost element on the prosodic grid line 0. In accordance with (14'), the combined application of Project and Edge parameters constructs a rhythmically perfect trochaic (binary) foot at the right edge of words with a penultimate heavy syllable. The empirical consequence of selecting (14') in Idsardi's system is the fact that in Classical Latin the final syllable does count for the correct computation of its prosodic system, contrary to prevailing metrical analyses. Furthermore, it follows from the same choice that the basic metrical parameter in this system is [-BND], the right edge bounded foot being assigned by the quantity-sensitive rule of the penultimate syllable. In the rest of the paper, I will support this hypothesis with evidence and arguments related to the evolution and acquisition of parametric systems.

3.3.2 An unbounded account: the evolution of parameters

Let us start by considering the implications of the evolution from the (prehistoric) initial stress system (7) to (9), Old Latin, in terms of changes in parameters. If the parameterization of the pure initial stress system as an [unbounded, left-headed] system is correct, as evidenced by related languages like Old Indian (see above), then the evolution into Old Latin and Ancient Greek could be accounted for in a straightforward manner by re-setting the cardinality of the unbounded parameter to n=4 for OL and n=3 for Greek (see (9)). The evolutionary variation would then be accounted for as a narrowing of the 'n-syllable window' to preantepenultimate and antepenultimate, a characterization of the 'law of recession' of classical studies. This statement of change involves no parameter resetting, rather a fixing of the cardinality of the prosodic set, a relatively minor readjustment in the acquisitional conditions for rhythm and primary stress assignment.

Assuming this historical perspective on parametric evolution, it is to be expected that an account of the difference in stress patterns observed in Old Latin and Classical Latin should involve minimal readjustments. As we see in (10), in contrast with Old Latin (8) the locus of primary stress in (10) has shifted from pre-antepenultimate to either antepenultimate (10a) or penultimate (10b). Following the lead of the parametric evolution defined in (9), the antepenultimate pattern (10a) involves minimally the further refixing of the cardinality of the unbounded parameter to n=3. As in Greek, then, in Classical Latin the incidence of primary stress falls within the familiar 'three-syllable window' counting from the right edge of the word. An account of the penultimate pattern (10b) must be by a quantity-sensitive rule, conceptually following Halle and Vergnaud's account (see (12)) as incorporated in Idsardi's reformulation (14), illustrated in (15b).

In contrast with previous contemporary metrical theories (from Hayes 1980, 1995, to Idsardi 1992), an historically and acquisitionally favored theory of Latin stress is expected to be an evolutionary variant of the same unbounded parameter of prehistoric word initial stress, subject to the quantity-sensitive 'rules of limitation' which narrows the 'n-syllable window.' Such an account is indeed characterizable in the spirit of Halle and Vergnaud's metrical grid system, as reformulated in Idsardi (1992). Such an account is proposed in (16).

(16)	Line 0:	Project:L	Edge:RRR	ICC:R,n=3	Head:L
	Line 1:		Edge:RRR		Head:R

(17) a. Antepenultimate b. Penultimate

```
        *           Head            *
  *     *)          Line 1     *        *)
  *    (*  *  *)    ICC        *   *   (*    *)
  *     *  *  *)    Edge       *   *   (*    *)
  *     *  *  *     Project    *   *   (*    *
 reprimitur                   reprimuntur
```

A discussion follows. (16) defines a metrical grid system in which the Project parameter autosegmentally projects one grid line mark (asterisk) per syllable nucleus, as well as a left boundary for the penultimate syllable if branching, for each prosodic word (cf. 3). Accordingly, in (17) *reprimuntur*, but not *reprimitur* projects a left boundary with the penultimate asterisk. Next, Idsardi's edge parameter, in its RRR selection (Idsardi 1992: 4 (11)), inserts a right boundary on the right of the rightmost element in both *reprimitur* and *reprimuntur*. Furthermore, the ICC (for which I suspend its iterative function in the context of this paper) constructs an unbounded foot measure for *reprimitur* after the third element from the right, in accordance with the defined cardinality value of the [-BND] parameter in this language. Thus, the parsing of the grid line 0 is completed without need for stipulating any order among the parameters, nor other grid-cleaning constraints. Continuing the metrical process on line 1, an asterisk is autosegmentally projected as a consequence of the left specification of the head parameter on line 0. The right specification of the edge parameter inserts the appropriate right boundary, and again as a consequence of the head parameter an asterisk is autosegmentally projected and the process is thus exhausted.

The obvious difference between the bounded hypothesis of Classical Latin stress (14-15) and the unbounded theory (16-17) is the setting of the categorial value +/- for the boundedness parameter. Historical, acquisitional, descriptive, and technical considerations favor the unbounded theory of Classical Latin.

4 From Latin to Romance prosody

In the same comparative vein, we now consider the consequences of the diachronic parametric perspective for Romance stress systems.

Remember that the locus of stress is totally shifted in the evolution from Old Latin to Classical Latin, due to two effects. One, the narrowing of the parametric syllable window from 4 to 3, which creates a new antepenultimate pattern. And two, the limitation of the same syllable window by the rhyme-sensitive metrical rule, which creates a new penultimate pattern.

In contrast, in Italian and Spanish the locus of stress is largely the same as in the system defined for Classical Latin. This state of affairs would lead one to expect, as a first approximation, that a parametric scenario like that of Latin would also account for the inherited Romance patterns, except for pattern membership of forms affected by the demise of length distinctions for which one would expect massive lexicalization.

With this in mind, let us consider how the loss of vowel length contrast in Romance would affect the prosodic computation of the specific case of Lat. *avidus* /a.vi.dus/ [ávidus] (>It. *avido* /a.vi.do/ [ávido]) 'greedy' versus *avitus* /a.vi:.tus/ [aví:tus] (>It. *avito* /a.vi.to/ [aví:to]) 'ancestral.'[16] If we assume (16), the appropriate derivation for Classical Latin would be (17').

(17') a. Antepenultimate b. Penultimate

a. Antepenultimate		b. Penultimate
*	Head	*
*)	Line 1	*)
(* * *)	ICC	* (* *)
* * *)	Edge	* (* *)
* * *	Project	* (* *
a v i d u s		a v i: t u s

Antepenultimate stress in Latin *avidus* [ávidus] (17'a) is assigned as an effect of the unbounded definition of the constituent construction parameter ICC (see (16)). In contrast, *avi:tus* [aví:tus] (17'b) receives penultimate stress by a special rule, construed as the computational result of the Project parameter which inserts a left parenthesis to the left of the penultimate heavy rhyme (cf. Idsardi 1992: 24; see also Halle and Vergnaud 1987: 56, (18), and (12) above).

In the specific case of the antepenultimate stress pattern, the prosodies of Italian and Spanish would also follow from the null parametric hypothesis (16), as illustrated in (17"a).

(17") a. Antepenultimate b. Penultimate

a. Antepenultimate		b. Penultimate
*	Head	*
*)	Line 1	*)
(* * *)	ICC	* (* *)
* * *)	Edge	* (* *)
* * *	Project	* (* *
a v i d u s		a v i t u s

As in the case of Latin *avidus* (17'a), in Italian and Spanish antepenultimate stress in *avido* [ávido] (17"a) is assigned as an effect of the unbounded definition of the constituent construction parameter ICC (see (16)). In contrast, It. *avito* [avíto] (17"b) should receive penultimate stress as the result of the Project parameter which inserts a left parenthesis to the left of the penultimate metrical element. Italian *avito*, however, as against Classical Latin *avi:tus*, can no longer compute penultimate stress on the basis of the weight of the syllable. The insertion of the left parenthesis must be computed in the corresponding Italian inherited penultimate pattern by a special (i.e. diacritic) lexically marked parenthesis. Under this theory of prosody, only lexical stress is available for the Romance reflexes of the Latin penultimate *avi:tus*, as illustrated in (17'b) and (17'b).

This state of affairs implies a systematic lexicalization of Romance penultimate stress in non-branching rhyme contexts. If the proposed account is empirically correct, then a substantial shift toward lexical stress is expected to have severe consequences for the conceptual acquisition of prosody (cf. Idsardi 1992: 52; and Dresher 1992, apud Idsardi).[17]

A uniform historical, conceptual, and descriptive perspective appears to favor the minimal algorithmic account (16) for Latin, Italian and Spanish. Any further departure from the null hypothesis would have to be argued for. In the following section, the proposal will be discussed in an expanded prosodic domain.

4.1 Between Spanish and Italian: Q-sensitivity and Cardinality

Consider (18-19) as a candidate for both the Italian and the Spanish stress system.

(18)	Line 0:	Project:L	Edge:RRR	ICC:R,n=3	Head:L
	Line 1:		Edge:RRR		Head:R

(19)

a. Antepenultimate		b. Penultimate
*	Head	*
* *)	Line 1	* *)
* (* * *)	ICC	* * (* *)
* * * *)	Edge	* * (* *)
* * * *	Project	* * (* *
5 4 3 2 1		5 4 3 2 1
reprimitur		reprimuntur
Fromista		
Lepanto		Lepanto
mandorla		
polizza		
sábana		sabana
legere		leer
leggere		
vigilant		vigilan
vigilano		vigilan
calcolano		calculan
considerano		consideran
amábamos		ama:ba:mus
		amavamo
Lancaster (Engl.)		(Burt) Lancaster
Washington		
Amsterdam		
Afganistan		
Ariston		
Metropolitan		
astracan		
Fininvest		

Under the unbounded theory (18), the parameter setting is maintained as in Classical Latin. No apparent diachronic shift in the head parameter needs to be considered. For both Spanish and Italian the Edge RRR places a right boundary to the right of the rightmost prosodic element, thus avoiding the extrametricality effect needed in prevailing bounded theories of Romance prosody with its attendant consequences discussed above. The major adjustment in contrast with the Classical Latin system concerns the projection of metrical left boundaries responsible for the typical trochaic rhythm of these languages. While in the Latin system the boundaries accounting for the penultimate stress pattern were homogeneously accounted for by the quantity-sensitive rule of the language, in Romance the demise of vowel-quantity condition requires massive lexical stress, resurrecting in a sense some properties of the reconstructed Indo-European stress system. Quantity-sensitivity effects appear to be intuitively stronger in Spanish than in Italian. In Spanish, in fact, apparently with the only exception of the place name *Frómista*, a residual penultimate branching rhyme attracts main stress. In Italian, on the other hand, the sensitivity to the branching rhyme is violated in non-inherited items. For example, place names like *Lepanto*, *Otranto*, *Ofanto*, *Taranto*, etc. have antepenultimate stress, as well as common words like *mandorla* 'almond' and *polizza* 'policy.' These items require therefore lexical stress.

Massive lexicalization is required in order to distinguish words with non-branching penultimate like *sábana/sabana* in Spanish and *Arsoli/Carsoli* in Italian, with consequences for the learning of prosody. In this respect Spanish differs from Italian in a categorial and consequential way. An historical migration from the antepenultimate pattern is well known for stem-accented verbs like Lat. [légere], [vígilat] > Sp. [leér], [vixíla] (in contrast with It. [lég:ere], [vígi:la]).

A related phenomenon which accelerates the typological differentiation between the two languages is the morphological creation in Italian of a syllabic third person plural: *-no*, as in *cantano* (Sp. *cantan*) 'they sing'. When coupled with the retention of the antepenultimate Latin pattern, this typically Italian morphological plural augment creates a regular pre-antepenultimate stress pattern in the present subjunctive and indicative: [vígilano, cálcolano, consíderano, etc.]. The consequence of this fact requires a morphologically marked pre-antepenultimate projection of metrical parenthesis on the grid line 0 in Italian for the appropriate prosodic execution.

In view of a possible theoretical tension produced by the creation of the syllabic plural augment *-no* in Italian, the canonical status of the law of the three syllables is subject to reconsideration. The steady-state nature of this pre-antepenultimate stress pattern is critical for the bounded parameter hypothesis in a metrical grid theory. In fact, assuming Hayes' peripherality condition, preantepenultimate stem-stressed verb forms like *calcolano* would be incorrectly stressed as *[cal.có.la.(no)] in a standard bounded (binary) theory, since the appropriate representational environment exceeds the constituency defined by the bounded parameter by one syllable. It is always possible, however, to posit further internal structure in order to meet the desired prosodic result [[cál.co.(la)](no)], in the spirit of Harris' and Roca's (cf. 0.2) analysis of Spanish imparisyllables. Such a bounded hypothesis cannot be accepted as an option for an account of Italian pre-antepenultimate stress for empirical and theoretical reasons similar to those adduced in 0.2 in relation to the account of Spanish imparisyllabic stress alternation.

The alternative solution is to consider the cardinality of the metrical measure a weak prosodic value admitting variations (as opposed to a parametric option) as formalized in section 2 (7"). Accordingly, adopting Idsardi's computational system, the Project parameter places a left boundary with the cardinality of n=4 at the appropriate morphological interface (cf. (3)). This option follows from an unbounded account of Latin (cf. 2.3.2), in keeping with the minimal/gradual theory of prosodic change across time and its attendant implication for a theory of conceptual acquisition across contiguous generations.

4.2 On stress lexicalization: bounded and/or unbounded?

A summary statement of the parametric theory of the stress system for Latin, Italian and Spanish is given in (20).

The view from this paper is that the prosodic system of these languages derives from an unbounded prehistoric metrical system, the variations accounted for by fixing its metrical cardinality. From a pure unbounded left-headed stress system with absolute initial stress, Old Latin narrows its unbounded parameter to pre-antepenultimate pattern. Classical Latin, as well as Spanish and Italian, reduce their canonical syllable window to the antepenultimate.

(20)

Line 0:	Project:L	Edge:RRR	ICC:R,$n=3_{\text{CLat, Sp, It,}}/4_{\text{OLat, It}}$	Head:L
Line 1:		Edge:RRR		Head:R

The stress system of these languages is further affected by the rise and fall of the quantity-sensitive rule of the penultimate syllable, with severe consequences for the acquisition of the system across generations. The steady-state quantity-sensitive conditions of Latin stress are gradually giving away to lexicalization, which might lead to a categorial unpatterned choice between the antepenultimate (unbounded) and the penultimate (bounded) type.

The tell-tale evidence of the tension between the two stress types may be inferred from signs of stress shifts which would otherwise remain unexplained. I shall speculate on some of these phenomena. The antepenultimate root-stress of Latin (including third conjugation short e-stems) verbs has shifted to penultimate in Spanish, but not in Italian. Curiously, however, the reflexes of Latin first person plural *ama:ba:mus* shows the opposite shift (from penultimate to antepenultimate) in Spanish, but not in Italian. Actually, in Spanish the phenomenon, which has been called paradigm leveling (Saltarelli 1975), generalizes the antepenultimate shift to other verb forms. Stress contrasts like antepenultimate [láncaster] as in Lancaster (England) and [lancáster] as in Burt Lancaster, would be unexpected in a steady-state quantity-sensitive system. To this set one should add the well-known cases of *Washington*, *Amsterdam*, *Afganistan*, etc., in which antepenultimate and ultimate stress are possible, but the heavy penultimate must be avoided as an impossible stress type. The equivalent set behaves exactly the same in Italian, with the added difference that final stress is also recently avoided in consonant-final words like *ariston*, *Metropolitan*, *astracan*, *nadir*, etc. The strongest inference about the empirical validity of the unbounded hypothesis as the default parameter of Italian comes from the unbounded stress pattern assigned to acronyms: *Fininvest*, *Acotral*, *Atac*, *Stefer*, etc.

Notes

* An earlier version of this paper was read at the *I Mesa Redonda de la Lengua Española*, held at the Universidad Autónoma de México, Iztapalapa, Mexico City, March 24-26, 1994.

1 The nearly exhaustive list in (1) corresponds to Roca's (1990: 149). The plural forms have been added to illustrate the syllable-shifting stress pattern. It should be pointed out that only the first two items on the list have some functional degree of usage in the language. Nevertheless, the minimal membership of the set in no way detracts from its descriptive relevance. Moreover, I found it surprising (although crucially relevant to the prosodic issue at hand) to hear that, while the accentual alternation of the exceptional words is normative, at least one speaker attested to the use of pre-antepenultimate stress in the plural form *régimenes*. This pattern, in which

primary stress is on the same syllable as that of the normative singular form exhibits no paradigmatic alternation, thus leveling the prosodic contrast in imparisyllables. We note, however, that the prosodic leveling is in violation of the 'law of the three syllables,' with its attendant typological consequences. Note, in addition, that items like *Júpiter* are paradigmatically defective. Furthermore, the anomalous *hipérbatos* is given in the *Esbozo* (Real Academia Española 1985: 182-183) along with *hipérbatons* and *hiperbátones*. Roca's list could, of course, be augmented by other words like *máximum* and *mínimum*, without any pertinent effect on the descriptive issue at hand.

2 There is another lexical item with trisyllabic stem which also exhibits stress alternation: singular *carácter* [karákter] vs. plural *caracteres* [karaktéres] 'character(s).' In contrast with the set (1), which alternates an antepenultimate stress pattern, this trisyllabic imparisyllable alternates a penultimate stress pattern.

3 It is of note that Spanish, among the Neo-Latin languages, is a diachronic link to the prosody of Latin imparisyllables, owing to the systemic potentiation of a syllabic plural augment in its consonant-stem lexicon. This residual morpho-lexical legacy (1) makes it possible for the observation and testing of the of the conceptual parameters organizing the prosodic representation of language, which are taken to be invariant across time.

4 For the standard metrical analyses of the items under consideration in this paper, the reader is referred to the argumentation and prosodic algorithm proposed in Harris (1983: 134), and Roca (1990: 150, derivation (33)). In the discussion I show that a bounded account of imparisyllabic stress alternation is indeed a theoretical option in Idsardi's (1992) computational version of Halle and Vergnaud's (1987) metrical framework, although not a favored one.

5 Cf. Roca (1994: 213) for his assessment of a debated issue in metrical theory.

6 In contrast with that of Harris, Roca's algorithm assigns antepenultimate stress not as an effect of canonical and non-canonical extrametricality but as a function of an additional diacritical mechanism (namely rule 28), a right head-erasure process which in practice shifts primary stress from a canonical penultimate to antepenultimate in lexically marked items. Under this conceptualization of prosody the classical motivation for extrametricality (Hayes 1981) is lost to the description of Spanish.

7 It should be noted that Harris' use of extrametricality in Spanish is not reconciled with the standard use made in the analysis of Latin, where the bounded parameter accounts only for proparoxytonic words. Paroxytons must, of course, be assigned stress by a separate statement in this language (cf. Halle and Vergnaud 1987: 55-56). The unification of Latin stress assignment remains a vexing descriptive problem in a parametric theory of accentuation (see Saltarelli 1994, chapter 1).

8 Cf. Saltarelli (1970) and the ensuing controversy in the literature.

9 A catalectic foot has a silent final constituent. A catalectic metrical theory of Spanish consonant final stem is developed in Saltarelli (1993) and (in prep.).

10 The line 0 parameter setting of the bounded algorithm for Spanish is assumed to be [+HT,+BND,left,right to left] (Halle and Vergnaud 1987: 99, (33)). Its operation on the metrical grid line 0 would construct binary, left-headed feet from right to left.

Roca (1990a) proposal (1') was aware of the accessibility issue with respect to imparisyllabic stress alternation. His analysis, however, appears to assess the problem not with lexical extrametricality but with the algorithm itself. This is arguably deduced from the fact that extrametricality remains unchanged in his input representation and that a right head-erasure rule is stipulated as a remedy to the accessibility of antepenultimate imparisyllables to canonical prosody.

11 The proposed principle (3) implies that paradigmatic forms are fully processed. This means that the mapping from morphology to prosody involves the allomorphic (rather than the more abstract lexical) representation of the paradigmatic form. Thus, the singular form [regimen] is prosodically mapped as [* * *] as opposed to [[regimen]es] which is mapped as [* * * *], peripherality defined as a strictly prosodic condition. Accordingly, principle (3) excludes the input line in (1') as a possible grid line representation. The empirical claim made by (3) is that prosodic principles are blind to morphological (paradigmatic) structure.

12 As far as I could determine, all of the items in the residual set (1) have been inherited from the classical languages as learned words with adjusted lexical specifications. For example, the Latin etymological ancestor of Spanish *ínterin* is not found as a noun and consequently would not be an instance of the imparisyllabic nominal paradigm in the source language. Therefore, the historical link can only be established in (1) through the prosodic properties defined by the set (as opposed to individual items in the set).

13 For neuters like *regimen* the Accusative singular form is identical to the Nominative.

14 See Allen (1973, chapter 12) for a discussion of the issue.

15 The examples in this set are mentioned in the sources (especially Allen 1973) without text citation. We must assume, therefore, that these forms are used as hypothetical exemplifications of a putative stage with a n=4 syllable window. The examples related to the paradigmatic antecedents of Spanish *régimen* are presented for specific use in this paper.

16 For the purpose of this discussion we follow the hypothesis that in Classical Latin vowel length is contrastive, whereas in Italian the length of the vowel is derived: a stressed vowel is short in a branching rhyme, long in a non-branching rhyme. The issue of vowel and consonant length in Italian is, however, descriptively more complex (see Saltarelli 1983).

17 Speakers' intuitions may also be affected by a contextually lexicalized stress system. Under this theory, the lexicon of a Romance language is prosodically conceptualized in three sectors:

Romance:	Strategy	Stress/Context
(i)	LEXICAL	penultimate/non-branching rhyme
(ii)	Q-SENSITIVE	penultimate/branching rhyme
(iii)	PARAMETRIC	antepenultimate

Assuming (16) and owing to the demise of Latin vowel quantity, the Italian learner has recourse only to special lexical information (i) in order to appropriately conceptualize penultimate stress for Italian words like *avito*. In contrast, for the Latin learner the conceptualization of *avi:tus* falls in line with (ii), a generalized quantity-sensitive conceptualization strategy:

Latin:	Strategy	Stress/Context
(i)	Q-SENSITIVE	penultimate/branching rhyme
(ii)	PARAMETRIC	antepenultimate

References

Allen, J. H. and J. B. Greenough. 1983. *New Latin Grammar*. New Rochelle, N. Y.: Caratzas.

Allen, W.S. 1973. Accent and rhythm. New York: Cambridge University Press.

Anderson, S. R. 1992. *A-Morphous Morphology*. New York: Cambridge University Press.

Chomsky, N. 1993. A minimalist program for linguistic theory. *The View from Building 20*, Ed. K. Hale and S. J. Keyser. Cambridge, Mass.: MIT Press. 1-52.

Chomsky, N. and M. Halle 1968. *The Sound Pattern of English*. New York: Harper and Row.

Dresher, B. E. 1992. Acquiring stress systems. Presentation at the *DIMACS Workshop on Human Languages*.

Ernout, A. 1953. *Morphologie historique du latin*. Paris: Klincksieck.

Goldsmith, J. 1976. *Autosegmental Phonology*. Doctoral dissertation, MIT.

Hall, R. A. Jr. 1946. Classical Latin noun inflection. *Classical Philology* XLI.4-90.

Halle, M. and J. R. Vergnaud. An essay on stress. Cambridge, Mass.: MIT Press.

Harris, J. W. 1983. *Syllable Structure and Stress in Spanish*. Cambridge, Mass.: MIT Press.

Harris, J. W. 1992. With respect to metrical constituents in Spanish. *Current Studies in Spanish Linguistics*, ed. Héctor Campos and Fernando Martínez-Gil, 447-473. Washington, D.C.: Georgetown University Press.

Harris, J. W. 1995). Projection and edge marking in the computation of stress in Spanish. *A Handbook of Phonological Theory*, ed. John Goldsmith, 867-887. Oxford: Basil Blackwell.

Hayes, B. 1980. *A Metrical Theory of Stress Rules*. Doctoral dissertation, MIT.

Hayes, B. 1995. *Metrical Stress Theory: Principles and Case Studies*. Chicago: The University of Chicago Press.

Householder, F. W. Jr. 1964. A descriptive analysis of Latin declension. *Word* 3.48-58.

Idsardi, W. J. 1992. *The Computation of Prosody*. Doctoral dissertation, MIT.

Jakobson, R. 1962. On Ancient Greek prosody. *Selected writings*. The Hague: Mouton. 262-271.

Kent, R. 1932. *The Sounds of Latin*. Language monograph number 12. Baltimore: Linguistic Society of America.

Real Academia Española. 1986. *Esbozo de una nueva gramática de la lengua española*. Madrid: Espasa-Calpe.

Roca, I. 1986. Secondary stress and metrical rhythm. *Phonology Yearbook* 3.341-370.

Roca, I. 1990. Diachrony and synchrony in Spanish stress. *Journal of Linguistics* 26. 133-164.

Roca, I. 1992. Stress and syllables in Spanish. *Current Studies in Spanish Linguistics*, ed. Héctor Campos and Fernando Martínez-Gil, 599-635. Washington, D.C.: Georgetown University Press.

Roca, I. 1994. *Generative Phonology*. London and New York: Routledge.

Saltarelli, M. 1970. Spanish plural formation: Apocope or Epenthesis. *Language* 46.1:89-96

Saltarelli, M. 1975. Leveling of paradigms in Chicano Spanish. *Proceedings of the 1974 Colloquium on Spanish and Portuguese Linguistics*, ed. W. Milan, J. Staczek, and J. Zamora. Washington, D. C.: Georgetown University Press. 123-131.

Saltarelli, M. 1983. The mora unit in Italian phonology: prosody. Special issue of *Folia Linguistica*, ed. H. Basbøll, Tomus XVII/1-2, 7-24.

Saltarelli, M. 1992. Italian rhythm and accentuation. Paper read at the *Linguistic Society of America*, 1992, ms.

Saltarelli, M. 1993. Italian rhythm and secondary stress. *Workshop on Cognitive Phonology*, University of Manchester, ms.

Saltarelli, M. (in prep.). *Rhythm and Accentuation: The Prosodies of Latin, Italian and Spanish*.

Sturtevant, E. H. 1940. *The Pronunciation of Greek and Latin*. Linguistic Society of America.